Reviews from *Sacred Places*
by Brad Olsen

T0193068

"... the ruins, mountains, sanctuaries, lost cities, and pilgrimage routes held sacred around the world." *(Book Passage* 1/2000)

"For each site, (the author) provides historical background, a description of the site and its special features, and directions for getting there." *(Theology Digest* Summer, 2000)

"(Readers) will thrill to the wonderful history and the vibrations of the world's sacred healing places." *(East & West* 2/2000)

"Sites that emanate the energy of sacred spots."
(The Sunday Times 1/2000)

"Sacred sites (to) the ruins, sanctuaries, mountains, lost cities, temples, and pilgrimage routes of ancient civilizations."
(San Francisco Chronicle 1/2000)

"Many sacred places are now bustling tourist and pilgrimage destinations. But no crowd or souvenir shop can stand in the way of a traveler with great intentions and zero expectations."
(Spirituality & Health Summer, 2000)

"Unleash your imagination by going on a mystical journey. Brad Olsen gives his take on some of the most amazing and unexplained spots on the globe —including the underwater ruins of Bimini, which seems to point the way to the Lost City of Atlantis. You can choose to take an armchair pilgrimage (the book is a fascinating read) or follow his tips on how to travel to these powerful sites yourself." *(Mode* 7/2000)

"Should you be inspired to make a pilgrimage of your own, you might want to pick up a copy of Brad Olsen's guide to the world's sacred places. Olsen's marvelous drawings and mysterious maps enhance a package that is as bizarre as it is wonderfully accessible. The historical data and metaphysical ruminations make it an intriguing read. So pick a mystical corner of the world, be it Mount Shasta, Delphi or Borobudur, and plan out a pilgrimage real or imagined among the Tungus shamans of Siberian Russia, the ghosts of Mohenjo-daro, the Muslim faithful at the Grand Mosque in Mecca, and more." *(San Francisco Examiner* 1/2000)

Reviews from *Sacred Places North America*

"An interesting book for both the armchair and the adventurous traveler, this (book) is recommended." (*Library Journal* 4/2003)

"The book is filled with fascinating archeological, geological, and historical material. These 108 sacred places in the United States, Canada, and Hawaii offer ample opportunity for questing by spiritual seekers." (*Spirituality & Health* 3/2003)

"A revealing, useful, and enthusiastically recommended guide for the vacationer seeking to fulfill their spiritual as well as their recreational yearnings." (*Midwest Book Review* 2/2003)

"World traveler Brad Olsen has compiled a book that documents 108 destination spots for 'feeling the energy' of our spiritual historical roots. Pilgrimage is one way we can find ourselves and this book will provide a guide." (*Twin Cities Wellness* 3/2003)

"The book's chapters correspond to ten regional sections of the U.S. and Canada, which are further subdivided into specific U.S. States and Canadian provinces. No less than 38 of the 50 United States are revealed to contain sacred sites — some of which are very public and easy to access, such as the House of David in Michigan, and some of which are more obscure, like Shiprock, 'the stand-alone neck of an ancient volcano core' in New Mexico. But never fear: Olsen provides lucid and detailed directions, as well as tantalizing and historically well-informed essay-portraits, for each destination. The book is also peppered with excellent maps, illustrations, and photos." (*Fearless Books* 2/2003)

"For travelers who prefer destinations with spirit ... juxtaposing local folklore and Native American legend with scientific theories to provide context." (*Orlando Sentinel* 2/2003)

"It's an odd lot, the places that have a way of touching your heart: mountains and homesteads, caves and monasteries, lakes and pathways. Author Brad Olsen has recognized that variety in this bringing together of 108 places that stir the soul. Many of the destinations mentioned come as no surprise in a collection of the hallowed: Ohio's Serpent Mound, Wyoming's Yellowstone, Colorado's Mesa Verde, for instance. But other entries serve as a delightful reminder that there is room in our hearts to expand the definition of sacred: Massachusetts' Walden Pond, Michigan's House of David, and Tennessee's (and Elvis') Graceland, for instance." (*Chicago Tribune* 4/2003)

"Olsen maps out obscure destinations brimming with intrigue and history, places where you will not have to fight thousands of tourists. You'll find lots of maps, drawings and photos. It's a travel guide for the individualist." (*Ashley Tribune* 3/2003)

SACRED PLACES

OF GODDESS

108 DESTINATIONS

Written by

KAREN TATE

CONSORTIUM OF COLLECTIVE CONSCIOUSNESS

www.cccpublishing.com   www.karentate.com

Sacred Places of Goddess:
108 Destinations

first edition

As is common in a historic and reference book such as this, much of the information included on these pages has been collected from diverse sources. When possible, the information has been checked and double-checked. Even with special effort to be accurate and thorough, the author and publisher cannot vouch for each and every reference. Because this is a book about traveling, many specifics can change overnight and without prior warning. The reader will find ample information collected from experienced adventurers, writers, academics, and travel industry experts. The author and publisher assume no responsibility or liability for any outcome, loss, arrest, or injury that occurs as a result of information or advice contained in this book. As with the purchase of goods or services, *caveat emptor* is the prevailing responsibility of the purchaser, and the same is true for the traveler.

Library of Congress Cataloging-in-Publication Data:

Tate, Karen

Sacred Places of Goddess: 108 Destinations / Karen Tate

   p. cm.

Includes index (Pbk.)

ISBN-13: 978-1-888729-11-5

ISBN-10: 1-888729-11-2

1. Spirituality—Guidebooks. 2. Goddess Travel—Guidebooks. I. Title

Library of Congress Catalog Card Number: 2005927572

Printed in the United States of America.

10 9 8 7 6 5 4 3 2 1

Front Cover Photos: © 2006 — Roy Tate   (from top to bottom) 1. Paleolithic artifact: Brassampouy, France. 2. Ladies in Blue: Knossos, Greece. 3. Isis Temple: Philae, Egypt. 4. Mother and Child: Hagia Sophia, Istanbul, Turkey. **Back Cover:** Fortuna: Louvre Museum, Paris, France.

108 Sacred Places of Goddess

Author's Karma Statement 10
Introduction – Who is Goddess? 13
Pilgrimages and Sacred Sites of Goddess. 17
108 – Language of the Universe 18
108 – Sacred Places of Goddess 19
Language of the Goddess 22
Traveling to Sacred Sites 24
Staying Safe 26
Connecting with Sacred Sites 27
Etiquette When Visiting Sacred Places 28

EUROPE AND ASIA MINOR

CYPRESS	Palaepaphos	34
ENGLAND	Glastonbury	39
FRANCE:	Chartres	41
	Goddess Focus – Legacy of Mary Magdalene.	45
GREECE:	The Acropolis	47
	Knossos	50
	Goddess Focus – Oracle of Delphi	54
	Eleusis.	55
	Gaia Alert – The Rape of the "Other" Eleusis	59
	Temple of Hera	60
	Goddess Focus – Sacred Isles of Goddess: Delos	63
IRELAND:	Clonegal Castle	64
	Kildare	66
	Newgrange	70
	Goddess Focus – Sheila-na-Gigs	73
ITALY:	Pompeii	75
	Rome	78
MALTA:	Ggantija	85
PORTUGAL:	Fátima.	89
TURKEY:	Catal Hüyük	92
	Didyma.	94
	Goddess Focus – Marija Gimbutas (1921-1994) .	97
	Hagia Sophia	98
	Ephesus	103
	Lagina.	107

AFRICA

EGYPT: Temples of Dendera 114
              Sekhmet Temple at Karnak 117
              Goddess Focus – Omm Sety 119
              Isis Temple of Philae 120
              Bubastis 123

LIBYA: Leptis Magna 126
              Goddess Focus – Queen of Sheba 129

NIGERIA: Temple of Oshun 130
              Goddess Focus – The Secret Sande Society . 133
              Gaia Alert – Gorillas in the Mist 134

TUNISIA: Dougga 135
              Goddess Focus – Human Sacrifice & Infanticide 138
              Gaia Alert – Strategies to Save the Big Cats. 139

THE MIDDLE EAST

IRAQ: Temple of Ishtar 143
              Inanna at Uruk 145
              Goddess Focus – Endheduanna 149
              Gaia Alert – On the Brink of Nevermore . . . 148

ISRAEL: Temple Mount at Jerusalem 149
              Sha'ar Hagolan 153

JORDAN: Jerash 156
              Petra 158

LEBANON: Sha'ar Hagolan 160
              Goddess Focus – Sacred Sex 161

SAUDI ARABIA: Grand Mosque at Mecca 165
              Goddess Focus – Satanic Verses 167

SYRIA: Temple of Al Lat 168

THE ASIAN SUB-CONTINENT

INDIA: Kamakhya Temple 174
              Gaia Alert – Inequality of Women: Health & Economics 176
              Dakshineswar Temple 177
              Kalighat Temple 179
              Goddess Focus – Thuggees of Kali 182
              Kanyakumari Temple 184
              Goddess Focus – Female Genital Worship . . 186
              Varnasi 186
              Gaia Alert – The Waters of Corporate Obsession . . 188
              Amritapuri Ashram 189
              Gaia Alert – Inequality of Women: Custom & Culture 191

TABLE OF CONTENTS

Naga Temple of Mannarsala 192
Goddess Focus – Female Genital Mutilation . 195
Mahalakshmi Temple 196
Gaia Alert – Saving the Lions of India 197
Chausath Yogini Temple 198
Goddess Focus – Oracles and Shaman 201

NEPAL: Kumari Temple 202
Goddess Focus – Living Life Behind the Veil . 204

PAKISTAN: Mohenjo-daro & Harappa 207

EAST ASIA

CAMBODIA: Temples of Angkor 211

CHINA: Pu Tuo Shan Sacred Island 213
Gaia Alert – The Needs of the Many 215

EURASIAN STEPPES: Kangjiashimenzi Petroglyphs 218
Burial Mounds of the Altai Mountains 219
Pokrovka Cemeteries 221

INDONESIA: Mount Batur at Lake Batur 224

JAPAN: Ise Jingu 226
Goddess Focus – Joman Earth Goddess 228
Hase Dera Kannon Temple 229
Goddess Focus – Ainu and the Fire Goddess . 231
Zenairai Benten Money Washing Shrine . . . 232
Fushima Inari Taisha Temple 233
The Ise of Kyoto 235
Goddess Focus – The Shamaness and Anime . 237
Sanju Sangendo 239
Asakusa Kannon Temple 240
Ueno Park 242
Goddess Focus – Power of the Pen 244

OCEANIA

AUSTRALIA: Mount Gulaga 247
Gaia Alert – The Black Mist Still Lingers . . 248
Arnhem Land 250
Uluru & The Olgas 252
Hindmarsh Island 254
Goddess Focus – The Putari, Miwi & Sacred Stones 256
Kapululangu Women's Center 257

HAWAII: Mauna Kea 259
Kilauea 260
Rainbow Falls 263
Ke'e Beach 264

                Ka'anapali Black Rock 268
                Hina's Cave and Sacred Heiau 269
                Pearl Harbor 271
NEW ZEALAND: Cape Reinga 274
TAHITI: Ra'iatea 277
                Gaia Alert – South Pacific 278

SOUTH AMERICA AND THE WEST INDIES

BOLIVIA: Virgin of Copacabana 282
                Goddess Focus – Fiesta del Espiritu 284

BRAZIL: Sacred Waters of the Orisha 284
                Our Lady Aparecida Basilica 286
                Goddess Focus – Mercade de Brujos 287

PERU: Machu Picchu 289
                Gaia Alert – Peruvian Grave Robbers 291
                Sacred Valley 291
                Gaia Alert – Rainforest Decimation 296
                Goddess Focus – Matrilineal Kuna Yala 297

HAITI: Saut D'Eau Waterfalls 298
                Goddess Focus – Taino Creatrix Goddess . . 299

TRINIDAD: Siparia 300
                Goddess Focus – Sacred Trance Possession . 301

MEXICO

MAINLAND: Basilica of Guadalupe 305
                Sanctuary of Coyolxauhqui 307
                Gaia Alert – Working Toward Better Health . 309
                Sanctuary of Xochiquetzal 310
                Chalcatzingo 312
                Cuicuilco 314
                Gaia Alert – Archaeopolitics 315
                Teotihuacán 316
                Goddess Focus – Women Play Ulama 318
                Tlaxcala 318
                Goddess Focus – Our Daily Bread 320

YUCATAN: Xcaret 321
                Chichén Itzá 323
                Cozumel 325
                Goddess Focus – Ix Chel Farm 327
                Isla de Mujeres 327

TABLE OF CONTENTS

NORTH AMERICA

CANADA: Sedna's Watery Domain 330

ARIZONA: Grand Canyon 333
                     Spider Rock 336
                     Goddess Focus − Kivas & Hogans: Body of Goddess 339

CALIFORNIA: Isis Oasis Sanctuary 339
                     Goddess Temple of Orange County 343
                     Kali Mandir Temple 345
                     Saint Sophia Greek Orthodox Cathedral . . . 347
                     Tien Hau Temple. 349

LOUISIANA: Vieux Carre 351

NEVADA: Temple of Sekhmet. 355
                     Gaia Alert − Activism in the Desert 357

NEW MEXICO: Huerfano Mesa 358
                     Gaia Alert − American Indian Sacred Sites at Risk. 359

NEW YORK: Lady Liberty. 360
                     Goddess Focus − Partnership vs. Dominator. 362

SOUTH CAROLINA: Brookgreen Gardens. 363

TENNESSEE: Nashville Parthenon 365

UTAH: Canyonlands. 367
                     Goddess Focus − Sacred Landscape: Yoni Stones . 369

WISCONSIN: Circle Sanctuary Nature Preserve 370

Conclusion   373
Acknowledgements 376
Glossary of Goddess 378
Author's Favorite Museums. 384
Suggested Reading List 386
Author Recommended Resources 387
                     Environmental, Social, and Animal Rights . 387
                     Publications & Education 388
                     Travel Related 391
Bibliography   393
Author Biography 406
Index   407

AUTHOR'S KARMA STATEMENT

Myths of the Great Goddess teach compassion for all living beings. There you come to
appreciate the real sanctity of the earth itself,
because it is the body of the Goddess.

—*Joseph Campbell, The Power of Myth*

In the beginning, God was a woman, and from her womb she created all that is, thus she is all things and all things are her.

Many believe she was the sun, the stars, and the moon. She was the changing seasons, the growing seasons, and the very Earth itself. Her spirit created, permeated, and transformed every living thing. She ruled over the fate of human beings, bestowing sovereignty, blessings, and justice. She was an icon of wisdom and protection. She created the cosmos and everything in it. She gave forth life, and at death it was to her one returned only to be reborn again. The face of the life force itself was that of Goddess, the Divine Feminine.

That was true 30,000 years ago and for millions it is still true today.

From the first cave paintings and carvings, humankind recognized it was the female, not the male, which conceived, gestated, gave birth, and nourished life. Hence, the Creatrix of all was woman, and it was in a female face they identified their deity. All life and everything that was necessary for sustenance came forth not from God, but Goddess. She was called by many different names in many different places, thus becoming universally known as She of Ten Thousand Names.

In parts of Asia and India her worship remained within the realm of the sacred, but in the West her devotion became unlawful or subjugated for a long time. Where her worship once thrived, she was forced to lay dormant, but she has never left us. She is with us behind the veil of Mary Magdalene, the Virgin Mary, and the Black Madonna phenomenon. Christians and Jews also know her as Sophia or the Holy Spirit, and Muslims as Al Lat and Al Uzza. She is identified as Saint Bridget of Ireland. In the far eastern reaches of Asia she lives on as Kannon, or Kwan Yin. She is Our Lady of Guadalupe in Mexico. She has remained alive in the hearts and minds of the people in India who have revered Kali for over 3,000 years. She was part of Oceanic cultures in the guise of Pele, Papa, Rainbow Snake Mother, Hina, and Haumea. To Native Americans she is Changing Woman, White Buffalo Woman, Mother Earth, and Spider Woman. To the Jewish people she is Shekinah. To the African Yoruban people she is called Oya and Oshun. Across the globe, to all these people, she is the Great Mother.

AUTHORS KARMA STATEMENT

Devotion to Goddess has been with us since the beginning of consciousness in spite of attempted suppression by those who would dethrone her. The concept of a sole male deity being the creator of the world is actually a relatively new idea, less than 3,000 years old. Many who worshipped a patriarchal or male deity attempted to destroy all reference to that which came before them and their god. They usurped her power and took it as their own. They distorted her image or made her devotion a sin. Men and women have died upholding their faith in Goddess.

Fortunately, years of work from many noted scholars, goddess advocates, and archaeologists such as Merlin Stone, Marija Gimbutas, Walter Burkett, Ian Hodder, David R. Kinsley, James Mellaart, and Keith McNeal show us that while the history books have been written by the conquerors, the truth is out there waiting to be rediscovered. The clues are in the art, pottery, textiles and manuscripts. They are in the ruins of archaeological sites, and the mythology and traditions of people the world over. There is compelling evidence to suggest that an era existed in humankind's history when matrilineal Goddess-centered societies ruled. It may come as a surprise but worship of the Goddess Isis around the globe almost surpassed that of Christianity! During the days when new political and religious zealots tried to obliterate worship of Goddess her veneration was forced underground, hidden in symbols and imagery not recognized by patriarchal authority; yet she survived. Even Joseph Campbell, the world's foremost authority and preeminent scholar on mythology, rethought some of his views regarding our collective spiritual evolution. After reflecting on the work of Gimbutas, Campbell remarked, "that primordial attempt on humanity's part to understand and live in harmony with the beauty and wonder of Creation adumbrates in archetypal symbolic terms a philosophy of human life that is in every aspect contrary to the manipulated systems that in the West have prevailed in historic times."

▲ Mermaids have long been associated with Goddess.

11

This is not a book about sacred places of a male god, past or present. That subject has been covered countless times over thousands of years. This book is about what has been lost over time — the Sacred Feminine. Because it is only when the Sacred Feminine is found, reclaimed, and embraced along with the masculine can humankind achieve balance and wholeness.

Goddess has been here since the beginning, and she will be here until the end. We invite you to be courageous and to challenge conventionally accepted beliefs. Come along for a journey long in the re-making. Please keep an open mind and open heart. Travel with me to uncover the truth and depth of Goddess as we visit Her most sacred sites around the world. From temple, church, shrine, and grove, from antiquity until today, be there as we reawaken, redefine, reclaim, and rethink all we've ever known about Goddess worship.

In closing, I would like to thank my publisher and editor, Brad Olsen, for his vision and courage. Not only has he seen the relevance of this surging interest in Goddess worldwide, but he has chosen to be a catalyst for change in the publishing industry, recognizing the need for a new usage of language and the proper names of the female face of divinity as Goddess and the Divine Feminine.

May She Embrace You in Her Golden Wings,

—Reverend Karen Tate

Mistress of Goddess Spirituality
Fellowship of Isis Adepta
The Isis Ancient Cultures Society
Iseum of Isis Navigatum
Venice, CA 2006 CE

The Dating System used in this text is based upon the modern method of using Before Current Era (BCE) instead of Before Christ (B.C.), and Current Era (CE) rather than "in the year of the Lord" *anno Domini* (A.D.). Those unfamiliar with this dating system should take note that 1 B.C. is the same as 1 BCE and everything then counts backward just the same. Similarly, 1 A.D. is 1 CE with all the years counting forward to the present, or Current Era. To assist in universal understanding, all measurements of length, distance, area, weight, and volume are listed both in the old British standard and the metric system.

INTRODUCTION TO SACRED PLACES OF GODDESS

These heretical women — how audacious they are! They have no modesty; they are bold enough to teach, to engage in argument, to enact exorcisms, to undertake cures, and, it may be, even to baptize.
—Tertullian, Christian Writer, (2nd & 3rd centuries CE)

Who is Goddess?

Answering this question warrants as much consideration as the age-old study to discern the identity and essence of God. Simply put, in the views of many, Goddess is all things and all things are Goddess, as traveling to her sacred sites will begin to reveal. Visiting her holy places around the world, peeling away the layers of her influence across continents, we begin to understand how utterly thought provoking and complex she is, yet simultaneously awe-inspiring and beautiful in her simplicity. While some of her sacred places will be obvious, others may require a bit of detective work. This is due to a vast whitewash of revisionism that has distorted society's beliefs in an attempt to obliterate Goddess from the minds and hearts of those unaware of this facet of ancient history. We suggest you open your mind and heart to prepare for the journey.

Belief in the Divine Feminine has not only continued without interruption for thousands of years through to the present, but most scholars cite evidence for worship of Goddess as far back as 30,000 years, possibly predating worship of a male deity, though some artifacts trace her beginnings as early as the Acheulian Period of 232,000 to 800,000 BCE. In a simplified and synchronized explanation of how that could be, consider that from the moment self-awareness crept into the psyches of our ancestors, they sought to explain the world around them. They noticed females both gave birth and provided sustenance to all life. They, like the creatures of the world among them, were provided the means to survive from the fruits of the Earth, consequently they deducted "all that is" was birthed and nourished from Woman. In beautiful simplicity, without knowledge of paternity, they may have reasoned the Divine Source must surely be Female. Matrilineal and matrifocal societies developed, and in rare circumstances various forms are still with us today. It is an interesting anecdote that in the ancient game of chess, known to be played by the Persians at a time when goddess temples graced Europe, Asia Minor, and the Middle East, the most powerful piece is the queen, opening the game placed on her color. Queen movements are far more dynamic than the king or any other playing piece. If the queen is captured it is the only piece that can reemerge into the game. The queen can be regenerated again and again when a pawn advances into the back row of an opponent.

Over time societies evolved and changed. Some cultures developed belief systems that incorporated a partnership view with divinity balanced between genders, while Goddess-centered worship remained strong in other cultures. As the years passed, the politics of religion and economics took their toll. Fear intervened. Sexuality was deemed corrupting. Eventually worship of Goddess was repressed, even demonized, along with the role of women in society. Goddess went from sole creatrix of the universe to a virgin or harlot. Women were reduced to the status of chattel, with prayers being recited to a patriarchal God by followers giving thanks for not being born female. Linguists can identify how ancient scriptures citing the names of the Divine were changed during translation from female to masculine pronouns and names, thus diminishing and concealing the role of Goddess. While in the early Church women were prominent in leadership, especially within the context of house churches, eventually as Christianity became socially acceptable in Greco-Roman society, such roles were discouraged among women, and, finally, forbidden altogether. Today the results of this shift reverberate profoundly as we live in our patriarchal world. We are left to contend with the results of having removed the female from the sacred equation. Today in India women have acid thrown in their face for threatening male authority, and in places within the Middle East women must wear slippers so that even their footsteps are not heard. The Chinese, with their "one child only" law, routinely

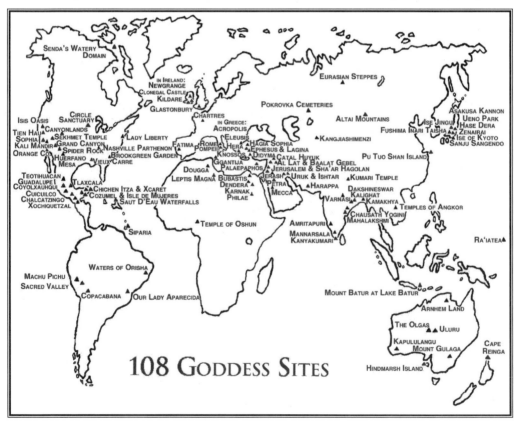

108 GODDESS SITES

abort girls for want of a boy. We can only imagine what a different place the world might be if there was not such a concerted effort to obliterate Goddess from the hearts and minds of the people.

The details of how and why vary from location to location, age to age, and culture to culture. From meteorites and red ochre markings on cave walls, to Gothic cathedrals, the chapters that follow will provide a mere glimpse into this long and interesting history as it relates to the 108 sacred sites we will visit. Excavating sacred sites and the spirituality associated with the worship of Goddess will prove provocative and enlightening. Uncovering long buried truths, like precious ancient artifacts, may tug at your heart strings, pique your curiosity, or could provoke anger. Lifting the veil to expose the motivation, ideas and politics behind long established religious and cultural beliefs may even cause an eyebrow to rise or jaw to drop open. All this is awaiting discovery and can be gleaned from visiting the sacred sites of Goddess across the globe. Yet this is hardly the alpha and omega of the story. Readers are encouraged to follow the clues and continue the journey beyond this book, perhaps using the extensive bibliography as a springboard for more discoveries.

As readers travel the world with *Sacred Places of Goddess: 108 Destinations*, these snapshots of herstory (the past from a matristic perspective) as viewed through the lens of sacred sites will no doubt raise questions and emotions. Answers are provided as the scope of this book allows by noted authors, scholars, researchers, anthropologists, and archaeologists, as well as worshippers and advocates of the Feminine Creatrix. Their views concerning the essence of Goddess will often agree, though sometimes not, thus giving readers a wide perspective of both the scholar and practitioner. Discourse on Goddess herstory will also vary with the diversity of personal perspective, places, peoples and politics, yet the overwhelming evidence of sacred sites and the disclosure of the associated herstory will overwhelmingly prove the prevailing existence of Goddess for over ten thousand years. Readers will have a clear sense of her worship throughout the long history of humankind which cut a large swath across continents, spiritualities, and cultures. These chapters will no doubt raise questions, inspire more in-depth research, challenge long held beliefs, and introduce new ideas and knowledge perhaps unknown to readers until now. Ideas and beliefs will inevitably continue to be debated as long as humans draw breath, scrolls are uncovered, and archaeologists revise dates. What is certain is the sites within this book will reveal quite plainly that the age-old inquiries about where life began and who is the Divine Source must not only be examined within a masculine framework, but also within a context that includes a female face, namely the Divine Feminine.

Today we see a resurgent interest in reviving, redefining, and reclaiming the Divine Feminine in our world. Statistics prove it. Social forecasters have predicted it. Traditional religious scholars understand the need for it. To some, Goddess is an omnipotent being, the very essence of nature, or energy within the universe. To others she is a psychological phenomena or archetype, representing the possible patterns within our psyches. Goddess aids women in reclaiming their personal power, beauty, and sexuality. But Goddess spirituality is not just embraced by women; it is also important to men as they process what it means to come into wholeness, accepting attributes within themselves identified as feminine or female. Goddess spirituality is important to the environmentalist who fears the rape and plunder of the resources of Gaia, or Mother Earth, and the lover of nature who feels the Divine within the redwoods, oceans and heavens. She is essential to

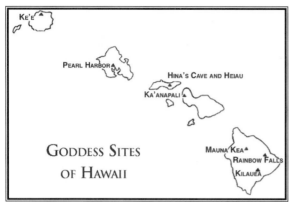

GODDESS SITES
OF HAWAII

Ke'e
Pearl Harbor
Hina's Cave and Heiau
Ka'anapali
Mauna Kea
Rainbow Falls
Kilauea

the political and social activist fighting for what is best for all of humanity. As said, Goddess can be all things, and all things can be Goddess.

This is not a feminist fantasy or a New Age creation. The long herstory of Goddess worship is gaining wider acceptance as the established history of the patriarchal status quo is reexamined. We see the impact of Goddess spirituality on the rise in all phases of life. The Vatican publicly began taking notice at a summit in the summer of 2004 discussing how they would combat "alternative religions" which were enticing away members of their congregations. Sexist language is being removed from liturgy. The Vatican issued an apology for the Inquisition and has corrected misinformation about Mary Magdalene. Women continue to challenge for their rightful place within the leadership of the Church. Books about women's roles in early Christianity remain on top of the New York Times best-seller list for months on end. Millions sit in the presence of Ammachi, the Living Goddess of Kerala, India. Eminent scholars such as the late Joseph Campbell, and Dominican-turned-Episcopal priest, ecologist and international lecturer Matthew Fox, are just two of the well-known and respected individuals who attest the importance of Goddess Spirituality. Cambridge University archaeologist Ian Hodder, recognized for his involvement in excavations at Catal Hüyük in Turkey, has taken a somewhat cutting-edge position professing that interpretation of the past cannot just be controlled by the academy. This opens dialogue and provides a forum for more varied views toward interpreting the past. The importance of gendered archaeology, which looks at the contributions that men and women make to the archaeological record and cultural development, is finally being recognized in the field. An interpretation of the language of the Goddess in Neolithic artifacts as presented by the late archaeologist Marija Gimbutas now enriches the scope of archaeology and anthropology. The political Goddess, namely the Statue of Liberty, was out in full force wearing a pink slip in the 2004 presidential election as her effigy was used by women concerned for the future of humanity, freedom, and the environment in the years ahead.

Goddess is in temples, churches, polling booths, archaeological sites, homes, museums, libraries, and on best-seller lists! She saturates the Internet. Her image is used in advertising campaigns and inspires jewelry and clothing design. She is the subject of theatre and upcoming Hollywood film releases! In her name practitioners help the oppressed: mainly the homeless and those refugees of animal and women's shelters. Her ritual processions are seen on public beaches and streets. Her importance to her practitioners is expressed in public displays of art. Her sacred sexuality is being restored on stage and screen. Altars to her are erected at events that attract multitudes. She is or has been part of most of the religions of the world, including Christianity, Judaism, Hinduism, Gnosticism, and Islam, something our travels to sacred sites will reveal. The jig is up! The cat is out of the bag! The Divine Feminine is lowering her veil and becoming a vital part of mainstream life.

Pilgrimages and Sacred Goddess Sites

A survey of sacred Goddess locations around the world is extremely varied as this book will attest. Highlighted will be sacred areas which occur naturally within nature, sites which have been built with the toil of human hands, and places which embody the essence of the Mother. Naturally occurring contours, sometimes called the sacred landscape of Goddess, include caves and yoni stones as symbols or metaphors for her womb, mountain peaks which might be her breasts, and rivers which are her life-giving milk. These sites might be as simple as sacred trees on which are tied prayers made of cloth strips, or as massive as Mount Fuji in Japan. The site might be a rock face or overhang that has artistic renderings venerating or invoking Goddess. Wells, waterfalls, streams, and rivers have always been closely associated with Goddess as it was believed the water carried the power of healing, purification, and rebirth. Choice locations have always been groves of trees, mesas, grottoes, valleys and certain islands. Oftentimes these natural places were chosen for their extreme beauty and prominence within the landscape. Sanctuaries built by humankind might be passage graves, temples, cathedrals, and stone monuments. Forgotten stone circles in a farmer's field may have long ago been a sacred place, as are natural locations featuring carvings or statuary. Scholar and lecturer Kathryn Rountree cites Morinis who describes a sacred site as one "where the divine issues forth into the human realm. The shrine is a rupture in the ordinary domain" through which the divine penetrates. Rountree describes this rupture as a "breach between the sacred and mundane realms, between the pilgrim's human body and the earth's body, and between past and present worlds." Rountree quotes Jean Shinoda Bolen, a Jungian psychotherapist, who believes sacred sites are where "worlds overlap or interpenetrate and life is imbued with depth and meaning." Bolen states sacred landscapes affect us like dreams or poems or music, moving us from the mundane into archetypal realms.

However travelers choose to view or experience these sacred sites, all these places have one thing in common. They are thought to be an axis mundi, where Earth and Divine meet, or where one might commune with their Creatrix. Usually these are places where people have gathered together for worship over a long period of time in awareness or reverence of Goddess. Often these temple structures are reused by different people and cultures over time, continually enhancing the potent energy that builds there by practitioners who have conducted ritual, made offerings, and prayed on that spot. These are sites in which pilgrimages are made and miracles have been known to occur. The site can represent the home or place of worship of the deity, the deity itself, or a place where one feels more closely aligned with the sacred essence of the deity. Ancient architects have been known to build sacred structures on ley lines, or pathways of electromagnetic energy. Like in days of old, visitors today in sync with these subtle energies claim an intensified intuitive awareness in these places charged by the amplified energy residing there. Structures have also been built to specifically align with celestial movements which were associated with agriculture and life.

Sometimes the natural landform or physical structure changed over time, becoming more sophisticated, as trees were replaced by stone circles, stone circles gave way to temples, and cathedrals or mosques were built atop the demolished pagan temples. People returned to the site to worship the deity of the place, perhaps under a new name. All the while, the site is believed to take on a collective energy from the emotional and spiritual intent focused there by the devoted, coupled with the natural energy of the site.

Pilgrimages, whether made as a solitary worshipper or with a group, have occurred for thousands of years as participants hope to gain enlightenment, curry favor, or receive guidance from the Divine. History is full of accounts of pilgrimages undertaken as a means of showing devotion, commitment, and sacrifice to their deity. These sacred journeys were thought to provide a means of healing the physical, emotional, spiritual and mental well-being. These sacred places provide the devoted a connection to their spiritual community and the Divine, their family lineage or spirituality, a perceived past life, or a need to commune with something greater than themselves.

Modern pilgrimages are undertaken for all the same reasons as in times of antiquity, but to contemporary Goddess worshippers, there is the added element of connecting with ancient traditions of this re-emerging spirituality and dawning awareness of the Female Creatrix. When standing in the Holy of Holies within the Temple of Isis in Philae, Egypt, feeling the essence of the Divine Feminine in the valley at Aphrodiasis, Turkey, or dipping one's hands into the waters of the sacred spring at Delphi, one is immediately plugged in and the distance of time becomes irrelevant. Sharing sacred space with like-minded devotees today or experiencing where ancestors have done so in the past, envelopes the worshipper in the collective consciousness of the sacred.

The following is an account of this author's past group pilgrimage to the Castalian Spring at Delphi, Greece. After the crowds of tourists had gone for the day, devotees were able to rethink the legends of the first Pythia, called Sybil, and try to become "one with the place." One pilgrim remembered her experience as thus: "The water flowing down is cold and clear and we kneel at the flow and cover our face and arms and hair with the sacred waters. As we do so, even in our t-shirts and tennis shoes, we awaken the feeling we are sharing in an ancient ritual and revel in the special energy our gestures create. We are giddy with delight and our eyes swell with tears because we are so thankful to have perpetuated the acts of our ancestors. Somehow, there is a knowing, a remembering, perhaps on a cellular level; this place of Athena and the Pythia conjures special meaning even in this lifetime."

108 — Language of the Universe

In keeping with the Consortium of Collective Consciousness' sacred places series honoring the significance of numbers as a divine language of the universe, and in particular the number 108, the following is contributed to illustrate the significance of this potent number. There are 108 aspects of the Goddess Tara, and 108 energy lines converge to form the heart chakra, considered the chakra of the goddess Kali. Bells are rung 108 times to mark the Buddhist New Year, and there are 108 wooden struts in the temple of Nyatapola Mandir which represent 108 aspects of the Goddess Siddi Lakshmi. It is sometimes said there are 108 *shakti pithas* or seats of Goddess where her sacred body parts fell to Earth. There are 108 beads in a *mala* necklace. There are 108 forms of sacred dance in the Indian traditions. In astrology, there are 12 constellations and 9 arc segments called *chandrakalas*. Nine times twelve equals 108. In Nepal there are 108 sacred lakes of Gosaikunda, and Lord Shiva is known to have 108 *gopis*, or female consorts. There are known to be 108 names for Ganga Ma, or Mother Ganges, and pilgrimages made around Varnasi, India and the Ganges River sometimes number 108. Goddess is known to be aligned with sacred geometry and specific sacred numbers. The sri yantra, symbol of the masculine and feminine, but often used as a symbol for the all encompassing Mother of the Universe, has within it 108 points. As the above examples imply, it would seem the number 108 also fits comfortably within the spirituality of the Feminine.

108 — Sacred Places of Goddess

Choosing the 108 sites to include within this book was difficult indeed! So many magnificent sites dot the globe with each a reflection of the multi-layered meaning that Goddess embodies. Sites chosen in this text represent the most significant cultural, historical, and religious locations in the pantheon of Goddess worship. This will enable travelers visiting these sites, or armchair travelers, to have a background for the locale as well as understand how the location relates within Goddess spirituality. Some of these sites were locations where God was also worshipped, such as Mecca. Other places some may say are imbued with male energetics, like Mesoamerica and Peru. Obviously sacred locales of both deity genders are not mutually exclusive and certainly energy work is very subjective and within the eye of the beholder. It should be remembered the focus of this book is the Divine Feminine and in doing so, there is little opportunity to also cover male deities. Energy grids may run through many sacred sites but their locations have not influenced the 108 selections. Herstory, tradition, and heart knowledge were more important considerations. When various Goddess-oriented subjects might have been relevant at a location, the author used personal discretion in choosing subject matter, opting to introduce new information which would add further elements to this odyssey of discovery. As an example, certain places in Greece were chosen because they bring to the forefront some ideas why and how Goddess began to be perceived differently in the world. Some sites in India were selected because they establish a living tradition alive today, provide insight into how these living traditions manifest, or give readers a window into the world of the priestess of long ago. A few sites were chosen to introduce the work of controversial archaeologist Marija Gimbutas. Whether one agrees with her findings or not a goddess-oriented book should include her important theories. Also included are sites that establish a long timeline of Goddess worship. Sacred places were also chosen which embody the essence of the Divine Feminine today.

Besides historical, spiritual, and cultural significance being criteria for choosing the sites, the physical richness of the site was also considered. Places that were in good physical condition were chosen so that travelers would be steered toward places with exciting visual elements. There is nothing more exhilarating than to walk onto a sacred landscape and be able to visualize what this place once looked like in the time Goddess was worshipped there. That being said, if an archaeological site represented an important ideological shift of a major Goddess it was not necessarily eliminated

▲ The ubiquitous "108" reveals itself in everyday life.

because the site has not yet been fully restored. As previously stated, some of these sacred sites have been so for thousands of years and the accumulated energy there, as well as the history of the site, made inclusion necessary. Sites that have particular importance in our current culture also made the list, such as places where ancient and modern worship or different faiths honoring Goddess are housed under one roof. Sites where Goddess manifests in a non-traditional framework were also included in an effort to show the broad diversity and exclusivity of Goddess spirituality across continents. And as an added bonus, a bit of *lagniappe*, or a little something extra has been thrown in. Sprinkled within these official 108 sacred places are clues to other Goddess sites located within their general vicinity.

The sites generally fell into five general categories, which occasionally overlapped:

Goddess Remembered. This category includes archaeological sites where Goddess was formerly alive and worshipped in ancient times.

Living Goddess. Here are sites where traditional Goddesses are still actively worshipped today, including Mary, the mother of Christ, Mary Magdalene, and the Black Madonnas.

Goddess Redefined. These are sites that have traditional and non-traditional Goddess worship being reinvented or redefined in a modern context. It also includes places that embody the essence of the Goddess.

Goddess as Nature. Whether built by human hands or a naturally occurring landform, these are Goddess sites within nature.

Goddess in Art. These are museums where Goddess is prominently represented. It also includes Goddess as she is characterized within the context of ancient or modern art work. This category often overlaps with other categories.

▲ The Venus of Willendorf is over 22,000 years old.

It should not be forgotten that worship of Goddess survived around the world with varying success. In most instances Christian or Muslim missionaries obliterated the existing cultures they found leaving little physical or cultural trace of the indigenous worship practices honoring Goddess. Scholarship, research, and excavations have also been more focused in certain parts of the world than others. As an example, much more information can be provided on the influence of Goddess in Europe than in Oceania. Another difficulty is what we know of a culture may not come directly from the indigenous people themselves, therefore the view we have might be a bit slanted as is the case of some of our information of Goddess in India. Much of the historical information and context for the Goddess in India comes to us from the Greeks, whose ideas of Goddess and the female began to shift from authenticity, as is explained within the Europe chapter. Added to this sometimes lopsided or slanted availability of data is the issue of privacy of living cultures which must be honored. Case in point is the Aboriginal people of Australia. They retain a unique aspect of Goddess worship within their culture and this author feels a responsibility to uphold their rights to keep their locations of "woman's business" private, therefore the sites indicated are only those which have already been made public in various domains. There is also less research pertaining to Goddess in South and Central America. Obviously funding is needed by scholars to expand gender archaeology in these regions.

It must be remembered this is foremost a travel guide written to introduce readers to a multitude of places throughout the world which are sacred to the Divine Feminine. An attempt has been made to give an explanation about the Goddess and her cultural aspects of each site to enrich travel to these special locations. Occasionally material presented may seem to conflict. The reason is because scholars and authors do not always agree. Competing views at some sites can be very controversial. And as this book points out, new information is being discovered everyday. An attempt has also been made to include various viewpoints and interpretations not only of scholars, but Goddess advocates, and cultural diffusionists. It is not within the scope of this book to discuss detailed or definitive theories on religion, archaeology, or anthropology. Some of these subjects are open to personal interpretation. It is up to the reader if they wish to delve deeper into any of the subjects introduced. What the author has attempted to do is open a window onto a beautiful garden where Goddess grows for the enjoyment of readers. Tantalizing seeds have been planted and many varieties of flowers have taken root and are ready to bloom. It is up to readers if they choose to cultivate the garden and become an expert on any plant that grows there. A great place to start would be the work of the incredible scholars and authors found in the extensive bibliography at the back of the book. An anonymous writer once said, "A wise person never thinks he has all the answers, instead he hopes he knows the right questions."

What About God? Countless books have been written over thousands of years extolling the characteristics and story of God, in all His many names. Sites designated sacred to Goddess may also be sacred to God. Both the female and male face of divinity may have peacefully (or not) coexisted in any number of these sites at different times of history. Many books tell about these places in the context of patriarchal divinity, but few tell readers about what has been lost — the sacred feminine. That is the scope of this book and it is in no way meant to diminish belief in God. In fact, many goddess advocates perpetuate the belief in the need for a Mother and Father to restore balance in the world. Many cultures have retained the female face of god over humankinds long history, alongside and equal to their male face of god. One beautiful quote which reflects this philosophy comes from Abdul-Baha (1912), "The world of humanity is possessed of two wings: the male and the female. So long as these two wings are not equivalent in strength, the bird will not fly."

Gaia Alerts. Most chapters will include Gaia Alerts which are notices of ongoing or impending ecological or cultural devastation. These alerts are sprinkled throughout each chapter to raise awareness of environmental concerns or the need for action to protect sacred sites within that particular part of the world. As Goddess is synonymous with Mother Earth, readers are challenged to become more knowledgeable about forces which endanger the planet. Gaia Alerts encourage the reader to reconnect with nature and not take for granted the air

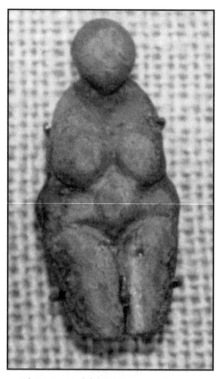

▲ The Grimaldi statue portrays an ample-figured totem ...

we breathe, the water we drink, and all life Mother Earth sustains. If priorities do not change, life as we know it may cease to exist on this planet. Animals that once thrived might only be seen in zoos or books. Every day species disappear and cultures begin to fade. Every day we lose precious natural resources that cannot be replaced. We are all the stewards of the planet and protectors of the creatures that inhabit it. This is not an issue that can continue to be put on the backburner of life. Everyone must take more seriously their personal role in society as it relates to honoring nature and those creatures which fly, walk, slither, and swim.

Goddess Focus. These are side panels to enrich the sacred site entries within each chapter, often dispelling myths and explaining concepts and the contexts for life in earlier times which might be difficult to put into perspective using contemporary mores. Modern themes are also explored which have an impact on the female gender within society as these issues directly or indirectly are the result of the subjugation of the Feminine Divine within today's culture. Scholars of Goddess themes are also highlighted.

Language of the Goddess

As with any emerging concept or belief, there might not be existing language which supports the new ideas, thoughts, or context, and Goddess Spirituality is no exception. That being said, a few new words or word usages are being introduced. To begin with, Goddess is capitalized and considered a proper noun just as God is. The history and worship of Goddess in earlier times until today will be loosely referred to as Goddess Spirituality. Within the ranks of the Goddess Spirituality movement certain names are recognized as proper names for Goddess. These include many epithets including Divine Feminine, Feminine Divine, Creatrix, Divine Female, Mother, Mother Earth, Magna Mater, Sacred Feminine and many more. Goddess has literally been called She of Ten Thousand Names, so a bit of latitude is being employed throughout the book when referring to Goddess by name. Of course, when appropriate, she will be called by the name she was known in various times and by various cultures.

Through the lens of travel to sacred sites many will be introduced to the perspective of Goddess Spirituality for perhaps the first time. Terminology sometimes must change as a result. Therefore the use of newly created feminine versions of words known within Goddess Spirituality will be introduced to replace masculine versions. These words more fully convey the feminine or female essence, rather than using masculine terms for a female concept. These words might sometimes include "herstory" for history, "patroness" for patron, "creatrix" for creator, "ashe" for amen, "womyn" for woman, while the word "shaman" is genderless. Words which are not inclusive of the female are seldom used, therefore the word human-kind often replaces mankind. Sometimes these words vary from region to region and country to country just as slang and colloquialisms develop. These new words, or variations on the spellings of the words will be kept to a minimum considering the scope of this book.

The name Feminine Divine has been used within this book as being interchangeable with Goddess. This choice has been made because these terms have long been established, accepted, and recognized as a name for Goddess within the spirituality movement. This is not meant to be politically incorrect, nor is it meant to infer all women are or must be feminine. This choice is not intended to perpetuate inaccurate stereotypes or diminish the role of women within society. It is not chosen to add distress or discomfort for those who would prefer to see the term for Goddess changed to Divine Female. The author is aware of the discourse on this subject and honors those feminist theorists who write and teach on the subject in an effort to make positive change and raise awareness within our culture. Feminine and female certainly do have two vastly different meanings, however readers will surely recognize this author's intention is to enhance, not diminish all that being female or the sacred feminine embodies. That being said the author has made a subjective decision to use the established term Divine Feminine or Feminine Divine for the sake of simplicity and ease, not politics.

▲ ... while the Monpazier figurine is slender. Both represent a life-sustaining Paleolithic goddess.

Finally, do not let the terms "cult" and "pagan" fool you. The term cult is used in this book only in the scholarly sense of the term. Cult referred simply to a sect or group of people with a particular religious preference and implies no unusual or bizarre behavior on their part. Cults of Goddess are nothing like some groups which have been labeled cults in modern history with charismatic leaders who convinced them to drink poisoned Kool-Aid or ready themselves for a ride on an incoming comet. The term cult within a goddess-oriented context carries no negative connotations that have come to be associated with the word in contemporary times. The term "pagan" or "paganism" is rarely used within the context of the book because this umbrella term is too vague and limits understanding of the vast array of beliefs and practices of the ancient and modern world. Particularly problematic are belief systems that originate in the Middle East and Greco-Roman antiquity. Paganism originally began as a term to distinguish early Christians from non-Christians. As a consequence it linked many people with many varying beliefs, from many different countries and cultures under one label. The term allowed no distinction between unique belief systems, rendering the term meaningless except for the distinction that these people were other than Christian. Because the term is nonspecific, and often derogatory within contemporary culture, it is seldom used within this book. This situation is being addressed somewhat within contemporary living traditions that venerate Goddess as evidenced in the worshippers of the Egyptian Goddess Isis calling themselves Isians and their groups, Iseums.

▲ The Dordogne Valley in France produced a rich array of prehistoric Goddess artifacts.

Those who venerate the deities of the British Isles or northwestern Europe may choose to call themselves Celtic. Many people who adhere to a Goddess-centered spirituality in a universal sense have begun to call themselves a Daughter or Son of Goddess, or a Goddess Advocate rather than the vague term "pagan" or "neopagan." Spiritual leaders can be referred to as Reverend, Priest/ess, or simply Clergy of Goddess.

Traveling to Sacred Sites

Whether readers have traveled to these sacred places or not, it warrants mentioning that to return with goddess-colored glasses adds a fuller, richer experience of a place. It is the opinion of this author and many travel companions that such a focus on a return trip opens new horizons at old destinations. Therefore readers are encouraged to look at old sites with new eyes and see what may have been hidden from the surface, as whole new layers of history and thought emerge. Egypt transcends the pharaohs, pyramids, and mosques. Greece had a rich history before Classical times, and Mecca was not only the domain of Allah. Take these new ideas and incorporate them with a "purposeful travel," a trend which has dramatically increased in recent years. Many people are no longer satisfied at poolside lounges sipping mai tais as they bask in the sun. People are seeking personal fulfillment, spiritual exploration, new and extraordinary experiences, along with meaningful journeys for their precious time away from work. Travel can enrich lives, broaden horizons and help us define our personal identity. Many travelers are quenching these desires with travel to spiritual destinations they find have the capacity to energize, heal, and transform their psyches. According to Dr. Kathryn Rountree, a Senior Lecturer in Social Anthropology at Massey University in Auckland, New Zealand, "Goddess pilgrims avidly seek both spiritual rapture and bodily pleasure. Asceticism and austerity are not ideals which have a place in pagan religious philosophy where the spirit/body split is meaningless and earthly pleasures are heartily celebrated." She cites travelers to these sacred sites are seeking both the spiritual power and pleasures unique to the particular environment of the destination. Not only do visitors want a spiritual experience, but they also want to taste modern local traditions, learn about ancient culture, and take in all the activities an area has to offer.

Depending on where you live, visiting sacred sites might be as easy as taking a bus across town or hopping on a plane to a nearby city and renting a car. For more exotic destinations, travel becomes more detailed and the type of transportation one chooses can be important to the overall enjoyment of the vacation. Good planning, flexibility, and practical expectations are imperatives of a successful journey.

First decide the intent of your trip. This will help determine the destination options. Once you have decided where you want to go, the next important decision is how and when you want to travel. Do you want to save money and travel on shoulder (mid-season), or off-season? Consider that this tact may risk less desirable weather. Do you want to take an escorted tour with like-minded people or will you save money and travel independently? Consider your budget, time constraints, and your goals. Will people at your destination speak your language? Do you have experience traveling abroad, going through customs, taking local transportation, and maneuvering through subway or train schedules? Choose what best suits your personality and capabilities. Your first journey abroad is not the time to push your physical and emotional limits.

Escorted tours to sacred sites of Goddess are available, and are usually comprised of fewer people than some more traditional tours. Sometimes the tours are for women only and other times both genders are welcome. With escorted tours the stress of getting from point A to point B is handled by your tour leader and tour operator who have made all transportation, tour, transfer, site, and hotel arrangements in advance of your arriving. You sit back and enjoy the chauffeured ride. They have pre-planned the little details like the best places to shop or stop for meals, when museums are open, and have locked down an efficient itinerary. No need to closely study a guide book before or during each destination. You have a tour guide along, well-versed in the history of the place, and subject matter of the tour. Most expenses of the tour are included in the trip, with the exceptions of some meals and incidentals, so there are usually no monetary surprises. You have minimal chance for blunder on the escorted tour, and you make an efficient use of your time. Have anxiety about your roommate for the duration of the trip? No worries. Just pay for a single supplement and have a room to yourself. Don't speak the language? No problem. Escorted tours, while more expensive than going alone, usually pay for themselves in convenience and relaxation, taking the stress from a new environment out of the equation.

Some precautions when signing on for an escorted tour would be to insure you know what you are paying for. Do not be afraid of asking a lot of questions. You might not want to get to Ephesus and find out the only glimpse you are getting of the Temple of Artemis is from the bus window, 200 yards away, as you careen down the highway doing 50 miles an hour. Does the tour stop at all the places listed on the itinerary and for how long? Inquire about the background and "puppy papers" of the tour guide or organizer. Will the group perform rituals, or reverent ceremonies on the journey? How? Where? Usually Goddess-oriented tours have planned activities besides the sightseeing on the agenda. These activities might be dream interpretation, divination, sounding, dancing, and various forms of ritual, conducted at the discretion of the tour leader. Sometimes these activities take place at the sacred site, or they may be held at your hotel or in a conference room. These activities help the members of the group develop a collective and cohesive energy as well as encourage connection with the sites being visited. Often times it serves to validate experiences tour members might be having. According to Dr. Kathryn Rountree, "women's sacred journeys and performances at sacred sites potentially contribute to a radical re-inscription of the female body by exposing women to alternative representations of the feminine and by providing contexts in which the feminine can be re-imagined, re-experienced and performed differently through symbolic activity and ritual." She believes the places are "reciprocally re-inscribed" through ritual acts performed at the sacred sites, and this relationship or "mutual impact" between the sacred place and visitor alters the "morphic field" of the place.

Other questions might be: do you need to provide anything besides your passport, or are special visas required for the country you are visiting? If the latter is appropriate, who is in charge of obtaining it? Nothing worse than getting to the airport unprepared. Are any inoculations suggested? What does the U.S. State Department say about travel to that country? Do you want to obtain travel insurance, and what does it cover? What is not covered by travel insurance? Is your money refundable and under what circumstances? What is the exchange rate in the country you are visiting? Will you have time on your own? Assume nothing. Be sure.

Do not be afraid to ask about the other people signed on for the tour, particularly if the group is small. Can the tour leader speak in general terms about the age, interest, and background of those who will share this journey with you? Will there be a pre- or post-trip meeting? If you have any special medical needs, be sure to discuss that with the tour organizer before you sign up for the trip. Some operators can even make recommendations about what clothes to bring, or how to pack light. Do your homework. Check with people who have traveled with the tour organizer before and with those who have experience traveling to your anticipated destination. Set reasonable goals and have practical expectations about the outcome of your trip. It is the norm to be asked to sign terms and conditions and waivers of liabilities for circumstances beyond the control of the tour organizer. Just read the fine print and ask anything that seems appropriate or questionable.

A drawback of escorted tours is you might get to travel faster and see more if you are not accompanied with a bus load of other people. You do not have to listen to fellow travelers, Sally and Sam, yammer on about their recent souvenir negotiations, but on the flipside, you might miss meeting some very interesting people who always add flavor to a trip. Alone you can make your own time schedule, and if you want to change plans or take an impromptu side trip, you can. You eat, shop, and snooze when you choose. Just remember you will be responsible for figuring out the train schedule that might be written in a foreign language, and if you miss the boat, you have the responsibility of choosing a back-up plan. Independent tours are for heartier, more courageous adventurers who do not mind preparing each evening studying the road or subway map for tomorrow's journey. To the intrepid traveler, this is all part of the fun. You enjoy rubbing shoulders with the locals, communicating with your English-foreign language dictionary strapped to your backpack. You have already studied up on the sites you plan to visit before you arrived, so you do not need a tour guide. You are happy as a clam because if you want to spend an extra day at the Louvre, you can!

Staying Safe

It is important to do your homework. Even if you are taking an escorted tour be sure the areas you wish to travel within are safe. Call the Foreign Embassy for the country you are traveling to and check if there are any travel advisories or warnings. Embassies are located in major cities and their telephone number might be in your phone directory. Check with the U.S. State Department. They are located on the internet and list travel restrictions for any destination that might be an area for concern. Many of these sacred sites, particularly those in the Middle East, are in political hot spots and travel there can be precarious. Some places Western tourists are not welcome, however they have been listed in this book because it is important for readers to know they exist and what relevance these sites have in Divine Feminine herstory. Besides, travel conditions can change quickly and areas once closed become open, and vice versa.

Connecting with Sacred Sites

You have arrived. Now what? Connecting with sacred sites is a personal experience whether you are traveling alone or with kindred spirits. Even on escorted journeys where your tour leader will probably have activities planned to enhance your spiritual experience, you will want to find time alone at sacred sites. Here are some suggestions for getting the most of being in these sacred places of Goddess.

Foremost, as already mentioned, do not pressure yourself with unreasonable expectations. Do not have a predetermined outcome in mind on which you base the success of the trip. Be open to what comes or does not come. Surrender to the experience. Going on a trip with the desire of having a vision of the Divine is a sure recipe for disappointment.

Try to get as much rest as possible. For those who practice a form of Goddess spirituality or a tradition involving energy play, go to bed early the night before. Abstain from heavy eating and alcohol, perhaps take a ritual cleansing bath before bed, and end the evening with a prayer to Goddess to be with you and share any guidance she may wish to impart. Try to remember your dreams, if any, that night. Keep a journal near

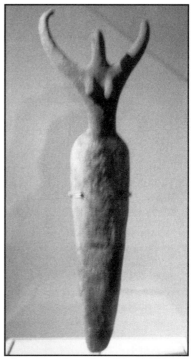

▲ This "River Goddess" depicts another artistic style of prehistory.

the bed just in case. In fact, it is a good idea to take the journal with you during the day to jot down insights that might come to you to avoid forgetting them in the excitement of the journey.

The next morning, stay focused and grounded. Avoid getting caught up in any excitement, stress, or distractions. You might want to arrive early to avoid crowds. Once there, if you cannot have private time in the cella, or holy of holies of a sacred site, try to find a quiet place where you are least likely to be disturbed. Trust your intuitive senses as you look for the place to sit or lay. If no strong impressions come, do not let that discourage you. Ideas might suggest to place your body against a particular stone, under a tree, or near a water source. If you already have a preferred method of meditation or means of connecting with the Divine, by all means use what you are comfortable with. If you do not have your own method of meditation or trance here are some brief suggestions, but remember, there is no right or wrong way to do this. Do not get bogged down with details. You want to be in your body, feeling, listening, and being aware, not worrying about the details of your every move.

After you make yourself comfortable, close your eyes if you can, or keep them barely open. Connect with the beating of your heart or your steady breathing. Do that for a few minutes as you settle in at the place. Take your time and go within. Then slowly open yourself to the surroundings. If the sacred site is on or in proximity to an energy grid or ley line, perhaps you may be able to sense the subtle frequencies of the place. Some people prefer to say a prayer for protection and guidance at this point, or surround themselves with white light. Raise your awareness to embrace the elements of the location; sun, water, air, and earth. Are any of these particularly dominant here? Be with the feelings, thoughts, or visions the place evokes.

State your intention in words out loud or with quiet thoughts. You might want to keep your mind and body open to thoughts, messages, sounds, or sensations. How do your hands feel? Your crown chakra or third eye? Be patient and remember, put no pressure on the outcome. Ignore any chatter that might come and go through your mind or the occasional noises from tourists nearby.

Another method to connect with Goddess at the sacred sites is to focus on what you know about the Goddess. How does she appear? What are her attributes and history? Why are you drawn to this Goddess? Vision yourself in her embrace or within the sacred site. Let your mind be guided.

Follow your intuition. Does your body want to move? Are sounds aching to leave your throat? Do you prefer to be in stillness? Try not to be self-conscious. That is easier if you are there alone in early morning or late evening when tourists generally are snuggled away in their hotel for the night. Just be careful and do not take any chances being alone in unsafe or unknown surroundings. Trust in the guidance you are feeling. Do not question your emotions. There is no judgment. They are just guideposts of the journey. Just go with it, feel it, experience it, remember it.

When you feel the experience is coming to a close, remember to give thanks for the experience, even if it might not have been quite what you hoped for or expected. Trust that your experience was perfect for you at this moment in time. Consider leaving an offering of a single flower, tobacco or corn meal. Do not leave anything that is not biodegradable. Do not pick flowers from the area. If you have come without an offering, a well-intentioned prayer of thanks is always perfect.

Before you get up to leave, be sure you have all your mental faculties together. Shake off any residual meditative moods or trance states of consciousness. Take a bite of that apple you have in your backpack as you savor the beauty of the place and drink in the essence of the sacred. Again, remember, the connection you made at the site may not manifest itself in any recognizable way until you dream or reflect in the following weeks. If you are traveling with others and they seem to have had a more profound experience, trust that everything is perfect and you have received what you need. Added knowledge of the site and the Goddess who resides there is equally valuable as magical or experiential revelations. Continue to journal any thoughts, feelings, or sensations to process later.

Etiquette When Visiting Sacred Places

It is important to conduct yourself properly when traveling to sacred places whether you are there as a pilgrim or detached visitor. Always keep in mind that even if these sites do not look like the holy sites contemporary travelers are used to visiting, such as temples and churches, these are places that may be sacred to ancestors, herstory, and many devotees today. Never behave disrespectfully even if you might not recognize the place as sacred. At best, be an ambassador for your culture and spirituality and conduct yourself with the utmost tolerance and dignity. At the very least be a respectful observer.

When visiting a shrine of any type one must adhere to a certain conduct of sanctity and respectability. Offerings specific to the deity of the shrine are most welcome in these wonderful settings. Flowers brought from home or your hotel is usually a safe choice. Never climb on the rocks or any of the structures. Furthermore, it is recommended to never move any rocks from the site or remove any objects as a souvenir. Though some may suggest it in places such as the Polynesian Islands, it really is not recommended to wrap a rock in a leaf as a traditional offering. Do not leave offerings of money, crystals, candles, incense, or foreign objects that are not readily biodegradable or natural to the area. Take away any trash or food brought in. Never put out cigarette butts in sacred places, even if they are located outside in natural settings. Do not disturb any creatures living in these places. It is best not to scream and shout or allow children to run around unattended. Always obey posted signs.

If you are collecting water to bring home from a sacred place, do not ingest it in anyway. Some water, such as Nile River water, may contain harmful bacteria. Exceptions might be water from sacred shrines in existing and functioning churches, but travelers would have to check with authorities on-site to be sure. Travelers that collect water from sacred places may keep it on their home altars or use it in sacred ceremonies. Often "waters of the world" are combined and used this way. Be sure your container closes securely to avoid any accidents in your travel gear. The best rule of thumb is to leave only footprints, and return home with only photographs, good thoughts, and lasting memories.

Always be aware of where you are, including the contemporary social, political, and religious climate. Locals may not understand your interest or devotion. It is always best to smile, be polite, and honor local customs. You may have to take your shoes off when visiting a mosque. You may have to cover your head or bare shoulders, so carry some type of scarf along in your day pack. Women might not be allowed in the same places as men. If you get some curious or hostile stares, just keep smiling and send out kind and compassionate vibes. People in some places you visit might not have seen or met anyone like you. Women might want to take along in their backpack or purse one of those crinkle skirts that look good even if they have been rolled into a ball forever. Pulling it over short pants at your holy destination shows respect for local spiritualities as well as those places other travelers consider sacred.

When engaging the locals you might find some to be very curious about you, often hoping to practice their English. Be polite and oblige them if you can. This can lead to some of your most cherished memories as discoveries are made about cultures living across the globe. In the process you might also leave a lasting good impression of your own! Be generous and patient, remembering what you put forth in the world leaves important ripples. That being said, try to avoid giving hand-outs to children you may encounter. While this may seem heartless, usually it is the best course of action as sometimes local adults feel this encourages the children to solicit. Some see this behavior as insulting and demeaning. When in doubt, check with your tour guide about local custom.

A final word about language barriers. On escorted tours the visitor may be somewhat buffered from having to directly communicate with locals who might not speak any foreign languages. However, if you are traveling independently, you are on your own. Making an attempt to speak another language may seem tedious and awkward, but from experience this author can tell you the effort goes a long way toward goodwill in most cases. Failing that, sounds and hand gestures also work. You may look silly, but it may assist in getting those much needed directions, with the smiles and laughs exchanged a priceless memory.

BOOK DEDICATION

A prayer heard and answered ...

This book is dedicated to Isis, She of Ten Thousand Names and Thoth, Scribe of the Gods.

▲ Egyptian Goddess Isis protects the deceased on a sarcophagus.

EUROPE

AND ASIA MINOR

**The Goddess in all her manifestations was a symbol of the
unity of all life in Nature. Her power was in water and in
stone, in tomb and cave, in animals and birds, snakes and
fish, hill, trees, and flowers. —*Marija Gimbutas***

EUROPE AND TURKEY PROVIDE THE PERFECT TABLEAU from
which to view the impact of the Feminine Divine as she evolved
in the lives of people from the Ice Age to contemporary times.
The abundance of sacred sites of Goddess from the many vital cultures
and traditions of our European and Turkish neighbors provide the traveler
with options for a lifetime of travel, pilgrimage, and discovery! This region
alone might have easily garnered our 108 destinations had the intent of
this book not been to introduce travelers to the sacred places of Goddess
throughout the world. Visitors who experience this rich cultural and
spiritual heritage soon realize the incredible magnitude of Goddess from
the moment self-awareness crept into the collective spirit of our earliest
ancestors, to the living traditions of Goddess practitioners today. What
follows is a mere glimpse into the copious assemblage of sites within this
region which stand in declaration to the widespread veneration of the
Divine Feminine over tens of thousands of years.

SACRED PLACES OF GODDESS

Both in Europe and Asia Minor, Goddess is represented in temples, archaeological sites, carvings, and ancestral groves. Areas around and within the Mediterranean Sea are particularly replete with monuments standing in honor of Goddess, and each season archaeological digs uncover new information that shapes and informs herstory, or the record of the Divine Feminine. In the British Isles, for example, carvings of Sheila-na-Gigs (see: Goddess Focus, Ireland, page 73), spirals, and mermaids symbolize aspects of the Mother, while in other areas of Europe and around the Mediterranean, she is represented in the forms of lunar crescents, fish, horns of consecration, vulvas, swastikas, and serpents. Worship of Goddess is thriving within contemporary traditions rooted in older practices associated with trees. Groves house her shrines in natural settings, and single trees, called clootie trees, are tied with strips of prayer cloth to invoke her blessings.

Goddess was alive for many peoples across the continent of Europe and Anatolia, or Turkey, since the Ice Age over 30,000 years ago! Finds such as the Earth Mother of Willendorf stand as evidence of her early relationship with humankind. In the oldest megalithic structures on Earth, located in Malta, ancient builders toiled for unknown periods of time creating her likeness in female shaped temples. Though not universally accepted, some see these "Fat Ladies" as images of Goddess. Moving forward in time, other artifacts of Goddess reveal her as the Mistress of Animals (Catal Hüyük, Turkey), and as Fish Mother (Lepinski Vir, Yugoslavia, 6000 BCE), as identified by the controversial and beloved archaeologist Marija Gimbutas. Figurines from Neolithic Europe establish Goddess as a continuing influence for the next 3,000 years, to about 3500 BCE. She lived on during the Iron and Bronze Ages and through the introduction of monotheism. Many scholars and goddess advocates alike

32

speculate that women-centered matrifocal societies thrived such as on the island of Minoan Crete in Greece until about 1600 BCE. At the time of the birth of Jesus Christ, Goddess was still a dominant force in society and the rising power of patriarchal belief systems had to contend with the formidable cults of Demeter, Isis, and Artemis. In fact, the Apostle Paul was run out of Ephesus by an angry mob when they believed he insulted their Goddess by calling her a mere idol fashioned by the hands of man. We will delve into these accounts in greater detail when the individual sacred sites of the Goddess are explored.

What aspects of Goddess the patriarchy could not obliterate they absorbed and incorporated into a new spin. One obvious example is the imagery of Mary holding Jesus which was co-opted from the Goddess Isis on the throne, holding her son Horus. Another instance may be found in Classical Greece as goddesses are suddenly born from male gods, taking on personas with less dignity, independence, and sophistication under the thumb of patriarchy. A case in point is the Goddess Hera. Once stately and self-possessed, she became subordinate to the patriarch Zeus of the Olympian pantheon with her character described as jealous and petulant. Some scholars believe the incessant squabbling of Zeus and Hera reflects the disharmony of the emerging patriarchal paradigm.

In the fourth century, the current accumulated volumes now included in the Bible were codified and circulated throughout the Mediterranean world. Churches were built directly upon pagan temples and shrines of gods and goddesses after the reign of Constantine the Great, a habit greatly increased during the reign of Theodosius I (379-395 CE), an emperor famous for ordering all pagan temples closed in the year 391 CE. With the rise of patriarchy came new ideas about Goddess, women, and the subjugation of sexuality. The Feminine Principle was a growing threat to the incoming male-dominated leadership and had to be dealt with. Sexuality and the female body, synonymous with Goddess, became taboo, a temptation to man, and a polluting influence on thought and behavior. Over time, "the feminine" was toppled by the encroaching male-dominated regime. Once beloved, Goddess, who sustained life from womb to tomb, was suddenly being cast as a demon by the new religious status quo. Isis' temples lasted in the ancient world until the time of Justinian's reign (527-565 CE). According to scholar Elinor Gadon, the closing of the last temple of Isis in Gaul likely marked the official end of Goddess worship in the West.

The Goddess has been with humans since the earliest days of our beginning and devotees believe she will remain with them until the end of time. Just looking at some of the monuments built in her honor, some created by seemingly unfathomable means for their time, speak volumes toward understanding the magnitude of devotion which Goddess inspired. There is probably no better time than the present to seek out the ancient people — too numerous to name — who venerated her, many of whom are our ancestors. There is probably no better time to seek the contemporary people who venerate her, many of whom are our neighbors, friends, and travel companions. There is no better way to make this journey to seek herstory than through the lens of her sacred sites. And so the journey begins ...

CYPRESS

Evidence for a settlement near Old Paphos, Cypress extends back at least 5,000 years. Excavations have revealed thousands of terra-cotta female figurines of the Archaic and Classical periods. Archaeologists believe the Goddess was worshipped here before the Chalcolithic period (3800-2300 BCE), though by what name she was venerated is not completely certain. Many possible names for this ancient goddess are extant from dedications uncovered at the archaeological site, including Wanassa, Paphia, or Golgia. Some of the female figurines depicted women with uplifted arms while others portrayed pregnant females with uplifted arms in the process of giving birth. By the time of the arrival of the Greeks, Paphos was in full swing as an established religious center. That is not to say the Greeks did not make their mark in Paphos since archaeological evidence seems to suggest both the Arcadian King, Tegea, known for his exploits in the Trojan War, and the indigenous King Kinyras, both contributed to the herstory of Aphrodite's temple. Homer records both a sacred grove and a great altar located at Paphos. The holy site continued to retain its prominent position in the ancient world largely due to the temple of Aphrodite, until of course Theodosius I outlawed pagan religion in 391 CE.

Palaepaphos

Aphrodite, mistaken too long as simply the "Boudoir Babe," reveals her true identity at her temple near Old Paphos, or Palaepaphos, renowned throughout antiquity for its fabulous wealth and reputation as a great religious center. Like the Goddess, her temple displayed a blend of Aegean and Oriental flavor. This was considered her most important shrine — for here she was believed to have been birthed from the sea foam, a metaphor for the semen of her father. Aphrodite is very, very old, and many believed she was around at the beginning of creation. In actuality, she was a universal Mother Goddess of prehistory, probably hailing from the Near East, and is likely of a non-Indo European origin. Ancient records place one of her earliest temples in Syria. Older than the Olympians, she appears on the scene long before her relationship as the daughter of Zeus in Classical Greece literature, the role usually cast for her by popular culture today. The close proximity of her temple in Cypress to Anatolia, Crete, and Mesopotamia greatly influenced the blend of traditions making up the Cypriac Goddess worshipped here for over 1,500 years. Without a doubt, she is more than just a beautiful woman rising from the sea foam, the beguiler of Paris, or the adulterous wife of Hephaistos. In fact, her persona certainly warrants a reintroduction to contemporary travelers and readers due to stereotypical misinformation that seems so pervasive — such as her portrayal in the much loved television series, *Xena, Warrior Princess!* This much is certain, from her sanctuary on Cypress a clearer image of Aphrodite is allowed to emerge.

Aphrodite, whose name in Greek (aphros) means foam, reflects her unusual birth. According to the ancient poet Hesiod, in the beginning there was Chaos, but soon the Great Mother Earth, or Gaia, and her consort, Ouranos, the Heavens, bore numerous sons and daughters. Yet, the youngest, Kronos, hated their father. One night Kronos took a sickle from Gaia, cut off Ourano's genitals, and threw them into the sea. In this headstrong act, Kronos severed Earth from Heaven, thereby revealing light between his parents. From where the genitals of Ouranos were discarded in the waters there suddenly emerged foam, and moments later, Aphrodite emerged from the deep. Thus, her birth was a central part of early creation myths. Not far from her temple in Paphos is *Petra tou Remiou*, or "Aphrodite's Rock," where she is said to have first emerged from the foam of the sea and made her first steps onto land. As her feet touched the soil, grass was said to have sprouted to life, invigorated by the fertile touch of Goddess. Visitors can see these three large rocks that emerge from the bay.

An artistic rendering of this birth is the famous painting, The Birth of Venus, created by the artist Botticelli, depicting Aphrodite rising from a large scallop shell, a motif of female genitals. It reflects a version of her birth story, where, after Aphrodite arrived via her shell on the shores of Cypress, she was greeted by the Hours. They proceeded to assist her from the water, clothing her in heavenly garments. This tale of her birth was essential to her worshippers at the temple at Paphos, shedding light on some of the rituals occurring here and exposing a far deeper meaning. Her emergence from the waters at birth became synonymous with the cycle of the seasons, namely the renewal of the Earth, symbolized by the renewal of Aphrodite's virginity. Obviously it was not impossible to regain virginity once lost if you were a Goddess! (Of course, virginity of a Goddess held a different meaning than for mere mortals.) The Hours were actually the seasons, who assisted by the Graces, would take part in welcoming the birth of Aphrodite as the Maiden, or a metaphor for spring. This was probably enacted by ritually bathing and clothing a statue of Aphrodite or Aphrodite's priestess, as her earthly incarnation. A terra-cotta bath tub was found in a sanctuary building during excavations.

With the strong possibility of Oriental origins, Aphrodite logically shares traits with Babylonian Inanna/Ishtar, Philistine Atargatis, Phoenician Astarte, and the Semitic Ashtoreth. Aphrodite, Isis, and Inanna/Ishtar, were all considered the embodiment of the heavenly planet Venus, the name by which Aphrodite was called in Rome. The story of Aphrodite's son-lover Adonis mirrors that of Dumuzi and Tammuz, the consorts of Inanna and Astarte respectively, as well as Attis, the consort of Cybele. With her close proximity to the Middle East, it is no surprise that she shares several titles. Being the daughter of Heaven and Sea, she is again associated with Astarte (Virgin of the Sea), and Asherah (Lady of the Sea). Like life itself originating from water, so was Aphrodite a creatrix. The rites of Aphrodite established here were celebrated under the sign of Pisces, the fish. Naturally, other than the fish, Aphrodite's other nautical symbol became the net, typically tied around her waist or

▲ Similar to Cybele and Artemis of Anatolia, Aphrodite takes on many appearances and attributes.

▲ Aphrodite's Temple at Aphrodisias in Turkey sits in a lush valley of red poppies.

worn over her robes. Her priestesses, in turn, often dressed in the same manner — although some had been known to wear the nets over their heads. In her "The Language of the Goddess," Doctor. Marija Gimbutas believes the net imagery dates back to Neolithic times, possibly linked with the vulva of the Sea Goddess. Hence, she becomes viewed in connection with "Living Water," the sacred primordial liquid from which all life arises in the beginning. Many of her temples and shrines were covered with seashells, especially those along the shores of the eastern Mediterranean Sea.

She is further identified with the Egyptian Isis in title and trait. Her son Eros is sometimes compared with Isis' son, Horus, as is her consort Adonis with Isis' husband/brother, Osiris, both of them dying and rising vegetation gods sometimes depicted as bulls. It should be noted that Eros (Cupid), most commonly recognized as the agent of Aphrodite who pierces his victims with magical arrows and wounds them with the gifts of desire and love, actually has earlier origins than Classical Greece. Some stories tell of Eros not as the child of Aphrodite, but appearing on the scene soon after the beginning of creation making him a much older deity and his true nature a bit elusive. Scholars have sometimes speculated he too may have portrayed the role of the son-lover, though the truth has been shrouded in the mists of time. The veneration of these deities by their people and the sacred union or marriage between these Goddesses and their consorts, or Lords, came to represent a covenant between man and the Divine in order to secure continued fertility of life and the land. Another interesting parallel is proposed by scholar Miriam Robbins Dexter who shows the similarities between Aphrodite and Eros with the Indian Goddess, Shri Lakshmi and her son, the "love god," Kamadeva, both having foamy births according to ancient myth and literature. The more one studies, the more one realizes the similarities of belief across continents and centuries.

Aphrodite has many aspects, but came to embody two separate aspects by the fourth century BCE. In her Aphrodite *Ourania* aspect, we find her associated with higher ideals, celestial love, and inspiration for the soul. As Aphrodite *Pandemos*, she is concerned with desires of the flesh, and mundane matters related to the existence of her people, much like Ishtar. It might be said she reigns over the realm of the lower chakras, making her a Goddess whose priestesses offer the service of sacred prostitution. It should be noted Paphos was renowned as such a temple of sacred prostitution, of which the contextual meaning bears little resemblance to what it implies today. No mere brothel, the sacred marriage act (whether literally performed or in metaphor) in temple prostitution carried with it true religious meaning, to insure fertility, achieving enlightenment, or perhaps a closer communion with the Divine.

Her image has varied over time and place. She shares possible bisexual attributes with Astarte as both reveal iconography depicting themselves with beards. In one case of Aphrodite, the image is emerging from a scrotal sac and may relate to her title of philom-medes, meaning "to her belong male genitals," and her aforementioned origins. She was once worshipped as a conical stone at Paphos which scholar Merlin Stone notes was anointed during annual Cyprian celebrations. Her iconography often shows her naked with long flowing tresses or her hair in a bun, semi-naked, or clothed in fine robes with generous amounts of jewelry. She seemed particularly fond of necklaces.

Her image from Aphrodisias, Turkey depicts her with a *polos*, or tower, on her head and her body replete with registers of animals, much like Artemis and Cybele, Mistress of the Animals. Aphrodite shares that title as it has been said that she soothes the savage beast, and encour-ages acts of procreation between them rather than acts of predation. Animals are said to love her and follow her across the natural places.

Her animals are the dolphin, swan, goose, goat, and dove. She is often depicted riding upon the back of a large bird or seated on a swan, or some-times holding a box of her gifts she bestows upon the world. In her relationship with the dove, long an animal linked to Goddess, she becomes related with the Virgin Mary and the Holy Spirit.

She is said to have a magical embroidered girdle, or *kestos imas*, that inspires "beguilement, fond discourse, yearning and love," bringing readers full circle toward understanding the gifts and charms of a more authentic Aphrodite. She is the Goddess of Love, but love in its most sacred, ecstatic, and divine sense, the concept of which might be lost in a contemporary context. Quoting Anne Baring and Jules Cashford, she represents, "humanity's longing for reunion with the whole," and "playful affection and exhilarat-

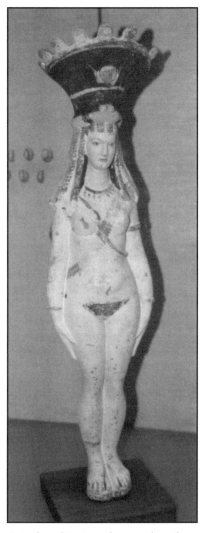

▲ Aphrodite-Isis depicted with an elaborate headdress.

ing joy, mixed with awe and respect." They cite Erich Neumann who states the divinity of Aphrodite has been sacrificed to the patriarchal sexualization of the feminine causing us to forget who she really is. Aphrodite is a zest for love and sex without fear or shame. She is the sweet smelling gardenia wrapped in wis-dom. She makes things beautiful and life worth living. She showers humankind with her golden laughter. According to the poems of Sappho, she prevents life from being overtaken by cares and weariness. She is the blissful element, the Sacred Feminine, that got filtered out with the coming of Judeo-Christian ideol-ogy. Humanity was left with a nurturing mother, void of sexuality, disconnecting humankind from the sensual and sexual pleasures of life and nature itself, which is a vital part of Goddess, particularly that of Aphrodite.

Excavation began at Palaepaphos in 1888 and unearthed the first shrine which was erected in 1200 BCE. According to archaeologists like Franz George Maier who has written several books about the site, the Late Bronze Age complex greatly deteriorated over time but they can detect that it once consisted of a large open temenos with a smaller, covered inner sanctum. Tombs contemporary to the first hall and temenos have revealed a fair share of Mycenaean pottery, further dating the complex to around the 12th century BCE. Since this earliest Aphrodite was of an unmistakable Oriental flavor, the sacred compound displays these influences, comprising a court sanctuary and featuring such architectural elements as horns of consecration, stepped capitals, and ashlar masonry. One outstanding feature at Paphos was its megalithic temenos wall and the pillared hall adjoining it to the north. It is thought the conical stone which embodied the Goddess was likely kept within that area. With the coming of the Romans, the sanctuary was rebuilt when it suffered during the earthquakes of 76-77 CE. Only a part of the Late Bronze Age Sanctuary was incorporated into the Roman building. The Roman Sanctuary of Aphrodite covered an area of 86 x 73 yards (79 x 67 m) and was erected approximately toward the end of the first century CE. Originally composed of a complex group of buildings from different periods, it included a hall and a component of the temenos from the Late Bronze Age sanctuary. The Romans added banqueting halls with mosaic floors surrounded by raised platforms. The temple contained many altars and statues but the shrine did not contain a statue of Aphrodite in human form, instead her conical symbol was thought to have stood in the Roman Court or in the temenos of the old sanctuary. Today it lives in the village museum in Kouklia. Aphrodite never had a classic Greco-Roman temple on Cypress. The large monolith which stands at the temple site today is part of the Bronze Age temple, though it is no longer in its original location. Though the temple is in ruins, it is nonetheless sacred and worthy of making our select list of 108 sites due to Aphrodite's importance both then and now.

Getting to Palaepaphos

Cypress is the third largest island in the Mediterranean, located 51 miles (74 km) south of Turkey and easily accessible by plane or boat. The Temple of Aphrodite is located on the western side of the island, adjacent to the modern village of Kouklia, which is 14 miles (21 km) southeast of the modern city of Paphos. Two museums are located at the excavation site. At the time of this writing, there was no public bus service directly to Kouklia so visitors must arrive by taxi or private tour. Be sure to visit Aphrodite's Rock on the road between Paphos and Limassol, her baths which are located 8 miles (13 km) west of the city of Polis, and a temple of Astarte just within the city of Larnaca.

ENGLAND

One potent reflection of Goddess in Great Britain is symbolized in the sacred landscape and the contours of the land, sky, and sea, which are considered her body. Seekers find her sacred abodes within natural and human-made stone circles, passage graves, mounds, megaliths, and maze-like labyrinths. Goddess practitioners who visit these sites associate mounds and megaliths to the recurring themes of birth, death, and rebirth that often embody Goddess. They believe these huge stones were tools to mark celestial events such as solstices and equinoxes within the heavenly domain of the Divine Feminine. Travelers can discover the meditative qualities of the labyrinth which takes the seeker on a sacred inner journey toward connection with the Divine both within and outside themselves. In the case of the labyrinth in Knossos of Minoan Crete, scholars speculate this maze-like palace may have had the dual purpose of providing space for ritual processions, while simultaneously reflecting the regenerative body of the Mother. Another controversial idea is Stonehenge, with its lunar and solar orientations, may well have been identified with the "sacred marriage," even the body of the Goddess, while the Irish passage graves of Newgrange, Knowth, and Dowth are thought by some to identify more with the life passages of birth and death. Many look at the great Neolithic monuments with fresh eyes, and as they do the language and religion of Goddess become more apparent to her advocates.

Glastonbury

With traditional eyes Glastonbury embodies the myths of King Arthur, the Knights of the Round Table and the cup of Christ. Through the lens of Goddess Spirituality, Glastonbury is seen in a new light. Visitors to Glastonbury can experience herstorical sacred places where the Goddess has been worshipped by our ancestors for over 5,000 years, but as of Imbolc (February) 2002, they can now participate in the newest living tradition of worship of the Feminine Divine at the Goddess Temple in Glastonbury. This first Goddess Temple of our modern age in the British Isles is dedicated primarily to the Lady of Avalon and secondarily to the Goddess of Ten Thousand Names, so that anyone working with Goddess in any of her guises, including Goddess as the one primal Goddess, will find a place of welcome. It has been recognized as a registered Place of Worship since June, 2003. According to Kathy Jones, who is associated with the temple, this is a herstoric event since this is the first time a sacred space has been recognized as a place of worship which does not rest within the patriarchal religious belief systems, but instead within the arms of the Goddess. In a private communication, Jones described the temple as a large violet room which is redecorated every six weeks according to the time of the year. The background vibration is violet because this is the energy color which radiates forth from the Lady of Avalon.

The temple congregation believes in the Great Goddess, who is the One and Many, who is immanent and transcendent, personal and impersonal, constant and changing, local and universal, within and without all of creation, manifesting herself through the cycle of the seasons and the Wheel of the Year. They believe the Divine Feminine reveals herself and communicates through the whole of Nature and the sacred landscape, through visions and dreams, senses and experiences, imagination, ceremony and prayer. They believe that no form of words can ever encompass Goddess. As Goddess People of Avalon, they believe in the Goddess, who is the Lady of Avalon as she expresses herself through the landscape, mythology, and culture of Glastonbury.

▲ Glastonbury Tor is the rumored home of King Author and Camelot.

Temple priestesses called "melissas" are in attendance to look

39

▲ The Brigid Shrine is a location of peace and worship.

after the space, perform ceremonies, and offer healing to the congregation. As funds and volunteers become available, the temple will be open longer hours. Larger ceremonies are held during the annual Glastonbury Goddess Conference, often attended by as many as 400 people. The temple is used by the people of Avalon and the surrounding area for all life passage ceremonies, as well as for healings and classes. Visitors to the temple find not only the Goddess, but other like-minded Goddess-loving people. The temple is supported entirely by donations from the public.

While in Glastonbury, it would be a shame not to stop at a few other Goddess related landmarks. First is the Labyrinth of Glastonbury Tor, a mound rising high above the flat landscape of the surrounding area and upon which sits Saint Michael's Tower. Liz Fisher in *Goddessing Regenerated News Journal* quotes Kathy Jones describing the site as follows: "The hollow hill on Glastonbury Tor is where (the Goddess) Rhiannon rides her white mare between the worlds. The terraces visible on the inside of the Tor mark the pathway of the seven circuit Goddess Labyrinth." The winding labyrinth-like terraces of the Tor have become a popular meditative tool for Neo-Pagans to walk on their inward journey to commune with the Goddess within and outside themselves. Seven circuit labyrinths are found throughout the ancient world and dedicated to Goddess. (See Chartres, France page 41)

Here in Avalon, which means the place of apples, the contours of the landscape are reminiscent of the shape of the swan. Fisher cites Jones who describes the Goddess, "Brigit (who) is known as the White Swan and the First Ancestor of the Swan Clan. As the White Swan, Brigit is the ancient Bird and Snake Goddess in one form, with the body of a bird and a snakelike neck ... The outline of a swan in flight can be seen marked out by the contours of the hills which make up the Isle of Avalon at Glastonbury as it rises out of the surrounding Summerland meadows."

Fisher further associates Brigid, or Brigit, with healing waters of the Chalice Well in Glastonbury, adding that Jones believes Brigid's bag of healing herbs and her bell are hidden in the ground near the well. A more conventional myth claims the cup of the Holy Grail from the Last Supper of Christ might have been buried here by Joseph of Arimathea. Another association for the Grail involves the Druids who recognized the cup as the Cauldron of Cerridwin, the womb of the Mother, from which her devoted might be reborn. A design motif of the well, the vesica piscis, is an ancient pre-Christian symbol associated with the Goddess, which later became a Christian fish. It is known to represent the blending of feminine and masculine, the yin and yang, or the meeting place of the conscious and unconscious. It is related to the almond shaped *mandorla*, sometimes called the yoni. Glastonbury Abbey is believed to have been built on an early sacred site of Goddess and it is said that the monks of the abbey may have uncovered the gravesite of King Arthur and Guinevere on abbey grounds. The Goddess Temple is currently open to the public for prayer, ceremony, meditation, and worship on Tuesdays and Saturdays from 11 am to 5 PM and on Friday afternoons. Ceremonies in praise of Goddess take place on these days. Tours are available that introduce a goddess herstory of the sites around town.

Getting to Glastonbury

From London by car, take the M3 out of London, then take the A303 west-bound. Follow the directional signs to Glastonbury. Going directly from Heathrow Airport takes about 2 hours, and from Gatwick airport takes about 3 hours. If within central London, take the train from Paddington to Bath, Bristol or Taunton. Then take a coach to Glastonbury. Another option is to take the train to Castle Cary and hire a taxi the rest of the way to Glastonbury. National Express coaches are available from Victoria Station to Glastonbury twice a day. The temple can easily be contacted at www.goddesstemple.co.uk, or write: The Goddess Temple, The Courtyard, 2-4 High Street, Glastonbury, Somerset BA6 9DU England. Visitors should contact the temple in advance of visiting and exact directions to the temple will be provided.

FRANCE

Despite the pressures of the patriarchy and the infliction of the Inquisition, which decimated many of those women and men who lived close to Goddess and her gifts of the land, animals, and the seasons, Goddess has survived in quiet confidence, even if she was sometimes shrouded. The essence of the Divine Feminine is incorporated within the sacred geometry of architecture and stained glass created by the sweat and determination of humankind who venerated her. Gothic architecture and symbolism within the plethora of cathedrals that sprung up in the Middle Ages are dedicated to Goddess in the form of "Our Lady," the Virgin Mary, hence *Notre Dame* (both Isis and Artemis of the Ephesians were called by the epithet "Our Lady"). Some believe the very features within represent female anatomy, namely the almond shaped lancet windows and arches of Gothic cathedrals that reflect female genitalia. Roses, bees, and wheat are common imagery on stained glass windows which have their symbolism rooted in Goddess worship. The Church itself was referred to in feminine terms, and the congregation oftentimes viewed as the Bride of Christ. The Jesus of Gnostic texts, an advocate of the feminine and viewed by many as being within a lineage of consorts of Goddess, might hardly recognize most of what has been written about him and the Kingdom he preached. The patriarchal religions could not obliterate the people's love and desire for the natural feminine principle or the love and stability that Goddess provided, so she endured in the metaphoric underground, behind the veil of the Black Madonna, and in the guise of the Virgin Mary. She is also found in sites associated with Mary Magdalene which dot the countryside in France. Through the lens of our travel to sacred sites, reawakened herstory becomes quite clear.

Chartres

Encapsulated within Chartres Cathedral are a plethora of features and concepts personifying the Feminine Divine like no other single structure. The very site on which this current cathedral stands, dedicated to the Virgin Mary, has for millennia been a sacred place of the Earth Mother. First called Carnute, Druids were believed to have worshiped here in the sacred grove, practicing

their skills of divination
at the holy well, in close
is said the local tribes wor-
image depicted her giv-
case with so many sacred
chosen as the location for
A Romanesque cathedral
1020, but was subsequently
Of this structure, only
tower, and crypt survived.
treasures stored within this
piece to survive was the
cathedral soon rose upon
church, completed in just

▲ Black Madonnas are viewed by many of the Christian faith as a Goddess.

and related esoteric powers
communion with nature. It
shipped the Goddess whose
ing birth. Later, as was the
pagan sites, the area was
a grand Christian structure.
was first begun here in
destroyed by fire in 1194.
the west front, the south
Curiously, of all the sacred
wealthy church, the only
Veil of the Virgin. A Gothic
the ashes of the previous
25 years, in 1250 CE.

Those venerating Goddess at Chartres simply began to call her by a different name, the Virgin Mary, recognizing her as one and the same. According to
authors Anneli Rufus and Kristan Lawson, Catholic officials devised a term for
images of Mary previous to Mary's birth called "prefigurations of the Virgin."
This shows another method by which assimilation of the Goddess and Mary
occurs. Called by many as the greatest of the French Gothic cathedrals, Chartres'
powerful allure speaks to the faithful who have always been drawn here. Beloved
scholar and mythologist Joseph Campbell is noted to have commented on the
huge impact this sacred site rendered on his psyche. Besides its hallowed location, the vast collection of Goddess imagery within includes a Black Virgin, the
tunic of the Virgin Mary, the aforementioned sacred well, the labyrinth upon the
floor, sacred geometry, feminine architecture, and the famous rose stained glass
windows.

Beginning below the structure and working up, the large underground crypt
is part of the original pagan shrine that was on the site from earliest times. The
largest crypt in France includes two galleries running side by side and Saint
Lubin's vault, dating to the ninth century. One finds the sacred well, named
Saints-Forts, directly beneath the church nave, and where the original statue of
the Mother Goddess giving birth, renamed Our Lady Underground, or Notre
Dame de Sous-terre was kept. It is believed the original statue was destroyed
during the French Revolution, and a replica replaces it in the crypt today. It was
carved of dark brown wood in Romanesque style which classifies her as a Black
Madonna. She is placed upon the altar of the Chapel of our Lady of the Crypt,
another of her epithets. Tours are given of the crypt, but like in Malta, do not
expect the guides to focus on the pagan history of the well or statue.

Moving inside the church one finds the other Black Virgin, Notre Dame de
Pilier, referring to the 10-foot (3-m) *pilier*, or pillar, on which she stands, or perhaps it is a reference to the pillar that once stood in the Temple of Solomon in
Jerusalem. She is just one of the many Black Madonnas, or Black Virgins, which
are found throughout Europe. (Other important Black Madonnas are found
in LePuy, France and Montserrat, Spain). These images are important within
Goddess Spirituality, because these figures of Madonna and Child show continuity between the pagan Goddess with the Virgin Mary and through Mary, the
Goddess remained in the spiritual and public lives of the people. Just as with
the aforementioned early tribes, to many Goddess advocates, there is no difference between Mary and Goddess. In fact, many even embrace Jesus as the son

of the Goddess, adding another layer of assimilation between the iconography of the enthroned Egyptian Goddess Isis who holds her son Horus upon her lap exactly like Mary holds the baby Christ. Jesus is easily assimilated in the figure of Horus, just as Jesus has been called the son of Sophia. Some of these Black Virgins have been found to retain beneath their surface layer of paint, the name of Isis. Readers should remember that Mary, Cybele, and Isis, were all called "Queen of Heaven," and conceived their sons by other than natural means.

When church officials are asked about the dark skin of the Black Madonna, they sometimes make the absurd reference to the statues being dark due to the soot from candle smoke, never admitting association with Goddess. As other site entries within this book will show, some of these statues just miraculously "appeared" to fishermen and farmers. Others say these dark skinned statues came back with soldiers who had been on the Crusades. Theories proliferate regarding the darkness of her skin, with some scholars citing the Black and Brown Madonnas as originating from Africa, or with the darker skinned Isis and Artemis. Practitioners of Goddess Spirituality often identify her darkness as a metaphor for the identity of the Goddess being "veiled" behind the guise of Mary. Some see her darkness as representative of the Gnosticism and alchemy she embodied, or the dark unfathomable depths of "knowing" which is Wisdom or Sophia. Scholar Margaret Starbird, when speaking of Chartres, notes it became a "center of enlightenment, the seat of a cult of Maria-Sophia, a goddess of wisdom." Her darkness might even be synonymous with her chthonic powers of regeneration. Her darkness is also related to Mary Magdalene and the Grail lore which has taken hold in popular culture. Whatever the specific source of her darkness, and there were no doubt many, there was a resurgence of interest and devotion in the Feminine which accounts for all the Madonnas and Cathedrals established during the medieval period. Pilgrimages to these images of the Divine Feminine became all the rage, and cathedrals built in her name became the focus of master craftsmen such as the Templars and Freemasons who employed elements of sacred geometry within the architecture of these sacred structures.

One of these elements is the spire which has been associated with the sun and moon and combines the masculine and feminine in balance. This cosmological connection was often positioned within sacred geometry, ascribing a delicate balance and harmony, not to mention order of heavenly bodies. Starbird believes the Knights of the Temple, or Knights Templar, were behind the design and construction of Chartres as

▲ The Gothic cathedral of Chartres is a treasure trove of Goddess imagery.

they attempted to restore the feminine principle in medieval society. She states the Templars, "had access to the exoteric wisdom of the classical world, perhaps preserved in Islamic sources that members of the order encountered in the Middle East. Their knowledge of mathematics and engineering gave birth to the Gothic style of architecture, which spread almost overnight, as if by prior plan, across the face of Europe during the period from 1130 to 1250." She states the guild who built Chartres were named the Children of Solomon, a direct reference to the King of Jerusalem thought to have written the Song of Solomon, a metaphor for the "sacred marriage." Interestingly, she tells of medieval gypsies who believed the Notre Dame cathedrals of northern France were situated to form a mirror image of the constellation Virgo. Until the time of the Inquisition, the ancient arts and sciences of astrology, alchemy, mysticism, and psychology flourished within cathedral architecture and popular culture.

Imagery in which the Feminine lives within Chartres are the depictions of the Virgin in stained glass, including the rose windows associated with Mary Magdalene and the Grail myths. The lancet windows of Chartres are sometimes believed to be representative of the female vulva, the womb of birth and regeneration. The tunic and girdle thought to be that of the Virgin Mary are kept here and were objects of veneration for thousands of medieval pilgrims. According to Elinor Gadon, Mary was wearing the tunic when Gabriel told her she would bear God's child, and the girdle was believed to have dropped to Earth from her body as she ascended to heaven at the Assumption.

While sculptures around the church are replete with imagery related to Mary, the final aspect of Chartres to be covered is the 11-circuit labyrinth inlaid on the floor of the church. It measures 42 feet (13 m) wide and is said to be the same dimension as the aforementioned rose window. While labyrinths were a common element of medieval churches, this particular one is said to have at the center a brass plaque depicting a rose with figures of Theseus, the Minotaur and Ariadne, all associated with Goddess herstory from Minoan Crete (some interpret Ariadne leading Theseus from the labyrinth as a metaphor for rebirth). The word labyrinth, which means "House of the Double Ax," comes directly from the word labrys, which is the sacred double-sided ax of the Minoans in Crete. It also contains four seven-circuit labyrinths making the meditative journey within even longer. According to the Church, this labyrinth either represented a pilgrim's journey to Jerusalem and back again, or the Way of the Cross. Often used for penance, each respective pilgrim was expected to follow this path on their knees. Labyrinths, which are similar in form to swastikas, have pre-Christian roots and may symbolize an inner journey, or a return to rebirth. It might be likened to the symbolic meaning of the kiva of the Native Americans. Unlike a maze, one cannot get lost in a labyrinth as there is only one way in and out. It also symbolizes one's journey into the otherworld where one might commune with the Divine. It is a meditative tool, helping one to become centered. The symbol of the labyrinth is spiral-like and as such is reminiscent of the spirals on the Neolithic sites of Newgrange and Malta, indicative of the concepts of death and rebirth. The "in-and-out" movement one experiences while walking a labyrinth have been adopted into spiral dances which practitioners of Goddess Spirituality often incorporate into rituals and celebrations (See Glastonbury, page 39). Interestingly, the labyrinth is said to have marked the gate of the Sybil of Cumae, an oracle similar to those of Delphi and Didyma. In pagan tradition this was an entry to the underworld, but in Christian context, it became the door to Hell.

Getting to Chartres

The city of Chartres is about 60 miles (97 km) southwest of Paris, and 20 miles (35 km) from the famous Palace of Versailles. Apart from the Cathedral, Chartres is a small and charming town and the author recommends walking around after visiting the Cathedral if one has not yet experienced such a quaint locale. Most travelers who come to Chartres arrive from Paris, which is about an hour away by train or bus. The cathedral dominates the oldest center of town and is easy to find. It is easily located within walking distance from the train station.

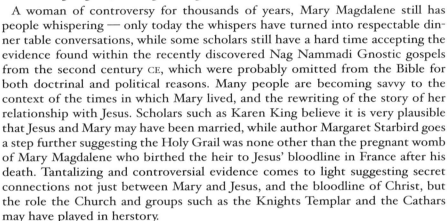

Goddess Focus
The Legacy of Mary Magdalene

A woman of controversy for thousands of years, Mary Magdalene still has people whispering — only today the whispers have turned into respectable dinner table conversations, while some scholars still have a hard time accepting the evidence found within the recently discovered Nag Nammadi Gnostic gospels from the second century CE, which were probably omitted from the Bible for both doctrinal and political reasons. Many people are becoming savvy to the context of the times in which Mary lived, and the rewriting of the story of her relationship with Jesus. Scholars such as Karen King believe it is very plausible that Jesus and Mary may have been married, while author Margaret Starbird goes a step further suggesting the Holy Grail was none other than the pregnant womb of Mary Magdalene who birthed the heir to Jesus' bloodline in France after his death. Tantalizing and controversial evidence comes to light suggesting secret connections not just between Mary and Jesus, and the bloodline of Christ, but the role the Church and groups such as the Knights Templar and the Cathars may have played in herstory.

Sites within France, where the pregnant Mary is believed to have fled after the crucifixion of Jesus, are becoming contemporary pilgrimage sites of veneration to Mary Magdalene by those accepting these non-traditional views. She is looked upon by Goddess advocates not just as the wife of Jesus, but the missing element of sacred sexuality so yearned for in the patriarchal Judeo-Christian world. These sites include Saint Maximin and Saint Vezelay in Provence, near Aix-en-Provence. According to French tradition, Mary and Lazarus arrived at Marseilles and began to convert southern Gaul. During this period, some believe she gave birth to a daughter. When she died, she was said to have been carried by angels to Aix and to the oratory of Saint Maximinus established there. These relics are first mentioned by the chronicler Sigebert in 745, when he states that they were removed to Vezelay in order to protect them from Muslim invaders. In 1279, Charles II, King of Naples erected a convent at the site of old Saint Maximinus, calling this Dominican establishment "Saint Baum," and in the process of construction discovered this shrine consecrated to Mary Magdalene, along with an inscription relating why this martyrium was kept secret. The church was destroyed during the French Revolution and restored in 1814. The former Saint Maximin (now officially called "Saint Maximin-la-ste-Baume") is believed to posses the "true relic" of Magdalene, including her skull which is carried through the streets in procession on her Feast Day of July 22. Her skull is encased in a bronze gilt reliquary dating to around 1860. Located amongst rolling hills and vineyards, Saint Baum includes a fine basilica with a 14th century Gothic apse and a sprawling monastery surrounding a central garden. The

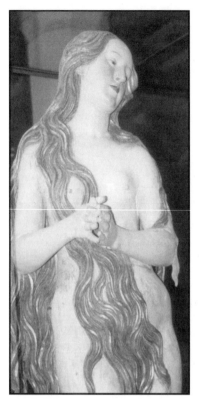

▲ Mary Magdalene represents the lost sacred feminine.

basilica rests upon an ancient crypt that was once the burial vault for a Roman Villa previously standing at the site. Today, this is the cave where many believe Mary spent her last days and where she was later buried with Saint Maximin, the first bishop of Aix. The large cathedral in Vezelay, located between Paris and Lyons, is dedicated to the Magdalene and was the keeper of her true relics before they were moved to Saint Maximin. The Church of La Madeleine in Paris with its magnificent painting of Mary being taken up to heaven by angels is on the pilgrimage site, as are the elusive sites of Rennes le Chateau and Saintes Maries de la Mer in southern France. According to the Eastern Church, Mary Magdalene accompanied the Apostle John and Mary, the mother of Jesus, to Ephesus and died there, her bones were later brought to Constantinople in 889 by Leo the Wise. The famous historian of the Franks, Gregory of Tours (538-94 CE) concurs that Mary Magdalene died at Ephesus.

In 591 CE, Pope Gregory the Great deliberately linked the Bible story of Mary Magdalene with an unknown prostitute, possibly as a political device to thwart female leadership within the Church which saw sexual intimacy as corrupting. It took the Vatican 1,378 years to correct the mistake, which it finally did in 1969. In the meantime, important information, including the role of Mary and other women leaders of the early Church had been eclipsed. Mary Magdalene has been called the greatest of saints, a key Apostle to whom Jesus appeared first upon his resurrection, and quite possibly his wife. Though some scholars will not admit Mary Magdalene existed and others doubt the evidence for this theory of Mary being the wife of Christ, it is important to consider the following two quotes as food for thought. Author Karen King, scholar from both Harvard and Claremont Graduate University, reminds readers of an important truth when she states, "Sometimes religion is presented as being fixed or stable and we must accept or reject it, but the fact is, religious traditions and certainly Christianity among them, is very diverse and filled with possibilities. Religion is fluid and we must take responsibility for the kind of religion we make." May we all keep our hearts and minds open.

GREECE

W hile the Divine Feminine is the mountain itself, she also reclines in the cool darkness of caves, which to practitioners can been seen as her sacred vulva. Here within, women once went to give birth and to perform rituals that celebrate the life passages of birth and menarche. Like Eileithyia on the isle of Crete, or Plouton at Eleusis, the cave was both womb and tomb, and well as places of birth, death, and rebirth, where women were embraced within the darkness of Goddess' body. Those who have sounded and drummed within these mountain caverns have reportedly made sacred connections. Ritually decorated with art and red ochre pigments that symbolize the life giving blood of Goddess, these sacred caves are where practitioners were transported ever closer toward communion with the Chthonic Mother. One can imagine being embraced within her dark red recesses, almost as an embryo within her living womb!

The Acropolis

The Acropolis, a prominent hill rising above the busy Greek capital Athens, was a sacred site of Goddess long before it became the home to Athena, protectress of the city, Goddess of Wisdom, and symbol of victory in war. Athena's ancient origins are believed to be rooted in Minoan or Mycenaean cultures, both of whom scholars know exchanged trade and concepts. Nilsson associates her with the Snake Goddess of Minoan Crete because of her connection to Neolithic snake symbols of regeneration seems undeniable. Yet there is evidence for her roots in sanctuaries of Mycenae, the place where descendants of the Indo-Europeans once called home. Yet it is the Classical Greek Athena that is most well known within mainstream culture. Birthed from the head of Zeus, Athena became the perfect example of a Goddess assimilated by a patriarchal culture. Here on the Acropolis, she represented the epitome of that shift from Goddess centered in the body to Goddess centered primarily within the mind. Mircea Eliade describes Athena as representing the "sacrality of technical invention and the myth of intelligence." From her place atop the Acropolis, Athena can cast her eyes down upon the city that birthed Western philosophy and thought, a society valuing the victory of the mind over the forces and rhythms of nature, a society that began to see the male as superior to the female.

Athena began her association with Athens as she vied for patronage of the city with Poseidon, each deity making proposals and counter-proposals to the people. The men voted for Poseidon, the women for Athena. Athena won by one vote when the people finally accepted Athena's gift of the olive tree and thus chose the Goddess as their protectress. This offering of the olive tree was one of

the rare examples of Athena acting as an earth or vegetation goddess. Unfortunately, this decision came with a price. Poseidon decided to flood all of Attica, a territory ruled over by Athens. In an attempt to appease his divine wrath, the Attican men subjected women to three punishments. First, they would have no rights to vote. Second, their offspring would not bear their mother's names. Third and finally, they would not be called Athenian women. Effectively, the patriarchy

▲ No building in ancient Greece matches the grandeur of the Parthenon — sanctuary to the Goddess Athena.

▲ Classical Athena represents a shift from goddess centered in the body to goddess centered in the mind. The shift also represents male authority overwhelming the matriarchal order.

had an excuse to subordinate women, and female citizens lost their status in society. But choosing Athena was not without its rewards. In her three aspects of Hygieia, Polias, and Nike, she provided health, protection, and victory, respectively. She also taught the women spinning and weaving, and they in turn invoked Athena during childbirth. She was also the hero's Goddess, providing courage, advice, and assistance. She came to the aid of Achilles when he faced Hector, as well as Agamemnon, the Spartans, Heracles, Odysseus, and Perseus when they faced adversity. She also provided prudence and self control in the heat of battle.

But Athena is a shift away from the aspects that have come to be associated with the Divine Feminine. She is so far removed from her sexuality and woman-hood, she even denies the role of her mother, Metis, Goddess of Wisdom, in her birth. In patriarchal Greek mythol-ogy, Athena fails (or refuses?) to acknowl-edge her mother, who was pregnant with her at the time she was swallowed by Zeus. The mighty king of all the gods, in turn, gave birth to Athena from his head several months later. Athena thus sprung forth from the patriarch's head in full battle regalia. But Athena is not only a warrioress, she is the Goddess of Wisdom, an attribute she received from her mother. Scholar Miriam Robbins Dexter describes Athena as lacking the "power within," that comes from a con-nectedness to the life force. Instead Athena serves the philosophy of the patriar-chy which dominates in a "power over" modality of society. Athena was rendered autonomous in her celibacy, yet in this form of virgin she is a "storehouse" of energy who provides nurturing for society and may impart that power to man. As a virgin goddess (a term that had nothing to do with chastity, but instead with inner-stored power or energy), Athena could store untapped power and transmit it to heroes of Classical Greek mythology as indicated above.

In a sense, it might be said Athena assisted as a taming force of civilization. Scholar Walter Burkert speaks of Athena giving Athenians the cultivated olive tree, not a wild one. Her response to Poseidon's gift of the horse was the bridle and chariot so that humankind might utilize the beast. Poseidon whips up the seas and Athena provides a ship to traverse the chaotic waters. Hermes multi-plies the flocks and Athena introduces spinning and weaving to utilize the wool. Athena is mentor to her heroes and appears in their time of need. Burkert cites a proverb that describes Athena's capacity to assist which states "In league with

Athena set your own hand to work," and Walter F. Otto describes Athena as the "Goddess of Nearness," making the impossible become possible. She is a symbol of intelligence and achievement, yet she is disconnected from the rhythms and wisdom of Earth.

Athena was venerated at the Acropolis in her annual celebration called the Panathenais Festival held in the month of Hecatombion (July-August). During this time, women would weave the sacred garment of Athena, called the *peplos,* which was embroidered with battle scenes. Oil from her sacred olive trees would be given to victors of competitions held during the ceremony. Ancient writers tell of a saffron robe being draped upon the 40-foot (12-m) statue of Athena, made of gold and ivory by Pheidias, which dominated the center of the Parthenon. Today the whereabouts of the statue is unknown, but we know the design was one with Athena bearing helmet and shield, a snake wrapped around her wrist, with an aegis on her breastplate. She holds Nike, Goddess of Victory, an aspect of herself, in her right hand. The rim of her sandals depicted the battle scene between the Greeks and centaurs. The east frieze of the building depicted the sacred procession and the presentation of the peolos to Athena, while the west showed the procession departing. One pediment that honored Athena's birth bore the inscription, "She who was never fostered in the dark of the womb."

The Acropolis consists of four primary buildings. The Parthenon, housed the 40-foot (12-m) statue of Athena, where she is worshipped as Parthenos, or the Virgin. It was known as the largest cella, or holy of holies, on the Greek mainland. It was the largest Doric temple and was made entirely of marble from nearby quarries. Over time it underwent various uses including a storehouse for ammunition, a barracks for soldiers, and a bank. The Erechthion, on the site of an ancient temple to Poseidon, is where the olive tree given to Athens by Athena is thought to have grown. This is a small and ancient building believed to be where Athena invited the Chthonic Furies to stay in consolation for their loss of a court trial. There they sought justice for the murder of Clytemnestra at the hands of her son Orestes. Interestingly, this court case can be viewed as a metaphor of the battle for supremacy between the traditions of the archaic Chthonic forces of Goddess and the usurping patriarchy of the Olympians — and it is Athena who settled the case in favor of Apollo and the Olympians over the Furies here at the Erechthion.

Through Apollo's defense of Orestes during this trial, the full power of Goddess diminishes as the sexuality of the male replaces the female role as the generative power for reproduction. To set the stage, Agamemnon had sacrificed his daughter with Clytemnestra prior to the start of the Trojan War. In retribution, Clytemnestra killed Agamemnon. Orestes then killed Clytemnestra in retribution for the life of his father. Apollo submitted that Agamemnon's death was the more serious of the two crimes because by his seed, Agamemnon, not Clytemnestra, was the true parent of their dead daughter, thus the female womb was no more than an incubator for the male seed. Athena tipped the scales of justice in Apollo's favor saying in *The Eumenides,* "I am always for the male. With all my heart, and strongly on my father's sides." In fact, the very victory of Athena over Poseidon for patronage of the city is recognized by some as another defeat over the Chthonic powers by the Olympians, as Poseidon was considered the husband of Earth, or Gaia. The feature most easily identified with the Erechthion is the Porch of the Maidens, where female figures called Karyatides are displayed.

▲ The Lion's Gate of Mycenae, which harkens back to the times of Homer, features felines associated with Goddess.

Those seen by visitors today, however, are mere copies. Some reports suggest snakes were once kept in this building — no leap in logic, considering Athena's serpent connections to the Neolithic times.

The third building on the Acropolis, once crowded with monuments and shrines, is the white marble temple of Athena Nike, now off limits to visitors. Standing at the entrance to the site is the Propylaia, where worshippers crossed the threshold from the mundane into the sacred world of the deities. According to Harrison Eiteljorg, just east of the Propylaia stood the most venerated of Athena's statues on the Acropolis, a mound used from at least the Neolithic period onward. In this guise as Athena Promachos, or Defender of the City, the common people honored Goddess, reserving the inner sanctums of the temple for use by priests. According to Pausanias, this thirty-foot (9-m) bronze statue with silver detail shone so brightly in the sunlight, sailors at the port of Piraeus (6 miles or 10 km away) were said to be able to see her. Another important monument on the Acropolis was Athena's altar, which lay to the east of the Erechtheum, where burnt offerings were ritually offered to Goddess. There is a nice museum on the site. There has been talk of replacing the missing statue of Athena with a replica, though to date, that has not happened.

Getting to the Acropolis

The Acropolis, or High Place, is located in the middle of the older section of the city of Athens. The site is open daily, though museum hours are a bit more limited. This is the most important site in Greece's capital which bustles with tourists all year round. It is visible on its lofty perch for miles around in all directions. A General Admission ticket is valid for all the archaeological sites of Athens: the Acropolis site and museum, Ancient Agora, Theatre of Dionysos Kerameikos, Olympieion, and the Roman Agora. For a real treat, take in a play at the open air theatre at night. Simply magnificent!

Knossos

The reconstructed palace of Knossos on the island of Crete represents to Goddess advocates the last and possibly best example of what is possible within a matrifocal society where the central deity is female. Knossos is a unique glimpse at an evolved Neolithic Greek culture free from invasion and Bronze Age interruption. It is believed that at its zenith, Knossos, and other settlements on the island of Crete enjoyed a sophisticated and flourishing civilization, living in harmony with nature and each other, with gender equality, abundance in food, material prosperity, and a thriving interest in the arts. This seeming magical epoch sometimes serves as a testament to what *might be* possible in a partnership rather than dominator model of society where genders are in-sync with the natural rhythms of Goddess.

In 1900 Sir Arthur Evans, a British archaeologist, bought the site on which stands the Palace of Knossos. He uncovered the remains of a vast complex., and during the next 25 years he restored the palace using modern materials, amid much controversy. Thanks to his efforts, important buildings were saved from collapse and travelers today enjoy a potent glimpse of what life in Minoan Crete might have been like until it was destroyed in a cataclysmic event between 1450 and 1400 BCE. There is still much debate as to whether the eruption on neighboring Thera Island actually contributed to the destruction of Minoan civilization. Findings from excavations on Crete over the last decades remain largely unpublished, and difficult questions may necessitate a rethinking of the chronology of the Late Bronze Age and the accepted scholarship related to the eastern Mediterranean. Evans named the civilization he discovered Minoan for the legendary King Minos, though the origins of the inhabitants of the people of Crete are not completely clear. It is generally believed around 6000 BCE settlers from Anatolia inhabited Crete, a large island conveniently surrounded by three major continents: Asia, Africa, and Europe. For several thousand years the civilization of Crete thrived. The people raised livestock, hunted, and farmed. Their society developed in sophistication over time, but the pervasive constant was worship of Goddess and their connection to nature, including an acceptance of the cycle of life and death.

According to scholars, worship was solitary and personal within the Early Minoan period when Goddess was venerated as Regeneratrix in caves, utilizing female figurines, amulets, and talismans that often depicted incised pubic triangles, symbols of the Earth Mother. Later, worship became communal within the Middle Minoan period of 2200 BCE and peak sanctuaries atop mountains were established. Artifacts found in these places tell archaeologists that ancient devotees once tucked meaningful figurines into rock crevices — as if placing it within the Mother herself. One ancient seal discovered at Knossos reveals the epiphany of the Great Goddess upon a mountain peak, surrounded by lions ascending the slope on either side of her, and set before her worshipper, with arms raised to the eyes, indicating this devotee's ability to see the awesome deity in full splendor. Ritual and worship became increasingly complicated as it evolved from the Early to Middle and into the Late Minoan periods, with the latter time frame associated with libations, sacrifice, music, dance, processions, and bull jumping. Frescos from Knossos depicting bull leaping are thought by some to represent men and women's acceptance, understanding, and communion with the laws of nature. Peg Streep believes as dancers face the danger of bull jumping they symbolically face the potential of life and death meted out by Goddess. Other scholars cite bull leaping as initiation rituals of priests and priestesses. Despite the evolution and sophistication in their worship, the Minoans remained closely connected to the earth, ancient values, and their Minoan Goddess, whose ancient name is unknown. Streep quotes Gertrude Levy who describes the religion as "unusually detached from formal bonds, but emotionally binding in its constant effort to establish communion with the elemental powers." Clergy of the Minoan religion were thought to invoke the Goddess by blowing a triton or through the use of sacred dance which might encourage trance. Artifacts of faience models of ritual garb found in the Sanctuary of Knossos are suggestive of votive offerings, leading scholars to believe priestesses might have utilized sacred clothing

that when worn indicate they embody the deity in human form. This is similar to the menat collar of Hathor priestesses or the collar of the Kumari. It is interesting to note that the sacred knot representative of the Goddess on Crete bears a remarkable resemblance to the reed bundle knot of Inanna and the knot of Isis, perhaps suggestive of the collective unconscious of humankind.

▲ The Snake Goddess figurines of Knossos display imagery representing life, death, and lunar events.

Temples dedicated to a deity were not known to be built within Minoan culture, instead, according to scholar Walter Burkert, cult chambers were found in palaces and houses. Worship also continued in caves and peak sanctuaries atop mountains dotting the landscape. The Palace of Knossos had an underground labyrinth-like design composed of many pillars, prompting Sir Arthur Evans to conclude that the Minoans may have been a "Pillar Cult." This was believed the underground domain of the famous Minotaur of Greek myth which some scholars believe was a metaphor for the sacred marriage which took place at Knossos. The palace had flushing lavatories and bathrooms suggestive of purification rites. The well-known Snake Goddesses were found within the Central Palace Sanctuary of Knossos and are dated at 1600 BCE.

The two best known Snake Goddesses are shown bare breasted, with tiny waists, in flounced skirts, and exude a confident sexuality and certainty of fertility. They both represent an image of Goddess as regeneratrix with the coiled serpents, symbols of life and death, in both of their outstretched hands and arms. One image of the Snake Goddess wears a cat or lioness atop her headdress, while the other has more snakes at her waist. On the skirt of one Snake Goddess is a net-like design suggestive of her connection to or power over the web of life. The seven layers of her skirt are thought to be associated with lunar events. Scholars Evans and Nilsson believe the Snake Goddess may have been a house or domestic guardian as local customs survive today wherein some people put out bowls of milk for serpents in exchange for their care and protection. Much of what we know of Knossos and Minoan Crete has been derived from art and imagery heavily sourced from Neolithic times. Minoan writing has never been deciphered. Yet many interesting associations reveal themselves in seals, frescos, and pottery, such as the origins for the myth of Demeter and Persephone being rooted in Crete.

The Minoan Goddess was embodied within a multitude of symbols, from the pillar and tree, to stalactites and stalagmites of caves, to birds, snakes, poppies, seashells, doves, butterflies, and most ubiquitous, the labrys, or double ax. It was from this Minoan symbol we derive the term labyrinth, rather than from the maze association commonly understood today. The world referred to the House of the Double Ax in Knossos, or the sanctuary of the Goddess. Marija Gimbutas makes the connection between the butterfly, the ax, and Goddess citing the butterfly represented aspects of transformation, and the labrys reflected the "hourglass-shaped Goddess of Death and Regeneration." It is thought the double ax was a ritual object, possibly used in ritual sacrifice of bulls, but never utilized by men. It is also important to understand that while the bull was representative of masculine strength in Indo-European cultures, here, the horns of the bull were associated with the female powers of regeneration, (as in Catal Hüyük, Turkey), with some suggesting their shape even reminiscent of the female reproductive organs. The importance of the bull horns were further represented in the iconography of the horns of consecration found around Crete and Knossos. Sir Arthur Evans, understanding their significance, reconstructed these horns on the western wall of the Palace of Knossos. They make a great photo opportunity! The ax was also thought to be utilized in the ritual cutting of sacred trees, another symbol of Goddess.

Bees were another important symbol of the Goddess on Crete. It is known the Minoans were bee keepers and the honey harvested used to embalm and preserve bodies, as well as in rituals. Bees or melissae were priestesses of Demeter, as well as Artemis Ephesia, who, as previously mentioned, might have had her origins in Crete. The humming sound of bees was associated with the voice of the Goddess.

Knossos has been excavated for decades, with most findings going unpublished, however in 1979, Peter Warren of Bristol University, who worked at the site for more than thirty years, discovered bones of children suggesting human sacrifice. He speculated their flesh was stripped from the bones and cooked with snails in a ceremony to ward off pending disaster. To no avail, the end of Minoan Crete probably coincided with the volcanic eruption on the island of Santorini (Thera) located north of Crete in the Mediterranean Sea. All the other palaces on Crete ceased to exist at this time, most likely destroyed by tidal waves created by the world's greatest recorded volcanic explosion. While Knossos alone survived, this magnificent palace subsequently entered into a swift decline and was never rebuilt or inhabited again. While the original frescos

▲ The Palace of Knossos contains many secrets of the ancient Minoans.

from Knossos reside in the Athens museum, and the original Snake Goddesses can be found in the Archaeological Museum of Heraklion in Crete, visitors to the site will enjoy many reconstructed portions of the central palace at Knossos. Columns and walls are beautifully painted in the vivid colors of the Minoans in shades of gold, black, red, blue, and green. Copies of the actual frescos from this time can be seen on walls that show devotees in procession, as well as the more famous murals usually recognized in association with Knossos such as the "three sister priestesses," "bull leaping," and the "plumed prince." Walking around the site travelers can glimpse the Throne Room and other interesting areas, including the Queen's Megaron, thought to house the first flushing toilet. Clay pipes are still evident as proof of the Minoan's knowledge of drainage systems. When Evans unearthed the multi-storied complex it revealed more than a thousand rooms.

Getting to Knossos

Knossos is located on the northern coast of Crete, approximately 4 miles (6.4 km) southeast of Heraklion. Private tour companies can be utilized to visit Knossos which provides a guide on site. Individuals on their own may take public bus transportation which runs frequently from Liberty Square and El Greco Park in Heraklion. Come prepared with a map and guidebook, or plan to hire a guide who can be acquired at the entrance, though it will be difficult to ascertain who is knowledgeable and few may focus on the significance of Goddess. The site is open daily, but it is best to come early in the morning or late in the afternoon once the main thrust of tourists have departed. Visitors to Knossos enjoy the best shopping for Snake Goddess statuary in stores along the street leading up to the site. Get what you need here. Don't wait until Athens because choices are more limited.

Goddess Focus
Oracle of Delphi

Delphi is perched along the side of breathtaking Mount Parnassus in Greece, only a few hours drive from Athens. One of the most famous oracle site of the ancient world, Delphi is a popular sacred destination for both tourists and pilgrims today. According to scholar James Rietveld, citing *The Eumenides*, the author of prophecy was herself the Earth, or Gaia. Gaia gifted her daughter Themis, an older chthonic deity (closely associated with the Earth and death from pre-Olympic times) with the renowned Oracle of Delphi long before it fell into the possession of the god Apollo. As such, Delphi, with its landscape bound in symbols of the Goddess became known as the site of struggle between the old order of the chthonic Goddess and the incoming Olympian gods. The Pythia, or oracle priestess of Delphi, was consulted by leaders throughout the Mediterranean world in matters of life, death, and war. Dressed in white with a gold headdress, she sat over the omphalos, thought to be the navel of the world, inhaling vapors that rose from a deep chasm below her stool which had a live serpent coiled around its base. According to geologist Jelle Zeilinga De Boer and archaeologist John R. Hale doing research at Delphi, ancient sources state the Pythia went into two different types of trance: The usual was "a benign semi-consciousness" that allowed her to answer questions in "a strangely altered voice" or less often, a "frenzied delirium characterized by wild movements of the limbs, harsh groaning and inarticulate cries." They cite Plutarch who stated after the benign trance, the Pythia was restored to a relaxed state, but after the frenzied trance, the Pythia often died and was replaced. The advice or prophecy given by the Pythia has been the subject of much debate and speculation, as the divination was said to be incoherent, vague, or inconclusive. The replies were also suspected to have been influenced by the priests who helped interpret her prophecies. In spite of

▲ The Tholos rotunda, sacred to Athena, was located in the Sacred Precincts of Delphi.

this, monuments at the entrance of the sanctuary are inscribed with thanks for battles fought and won, presumably on the advice of the Pythia.

According to De Boer and Hale, despite testimonies of ancient writers such as Strabo and Plutarch (who was a priest of Apollo at Delphi) about the inhalation of gases which induced the trance states, contemporary scholars did not believe the prophecies were connected with gaseous emissions. However, after a geological survey of the site in 1996 and with the assistance of toxicologist Henry Spiller, De Boer and Hale believe the trance states of the Pythia were indicative of exposure to the hydrocarbon gas ethylene. Down from the sanctuary is the Castalian Spring, believed to have been used by the Pythia to ritually bathe before offering pronouncements, though other sources say it is the place pilgrims purified themselves before their audience with the oracle. Not to be missed is the circular Temple of Pronaia Athena located across the road and 600 feet (180 m) down from the spring. Athena was said to be the protector of this sacred site, and a helper in restoring the power of the Goddess snatched away by the Olympians. A wonderful museum is on-site as well as other temples and structures situated on terraces along the mountainside of the archaeological site.

Eleusis

The Sanctuary of Demeter at Eleusis was famous for the *mystai*, or initiates of the elusive Eleusian Mysteries who took an oath of secrecy never to reveal the secrets of their religion. And remain silent they did, leaving today's scholars and practitioners with little more than scant evidence for much of what transpired within their ancient esoteric mysteries. Yet the myths and mysteries of Demeter and Persephone are some of the most important metaphors for the Goddess as Earth Mother, the cyclical vegetation cycles she embodies, as well as the life cycle represented within a single being. At Eleusis, mysteries were taught and celebrated, and pilgrims from around the Mediterranean world traveled to take part in these secret rites, suspected of enlightening the practitioners on the wonder of the true meaning of life and death. Eleusis and the Sanctuary of Demeter was the final stop of a 14 mile (22.4 km) journey that began in Athens, as hundreds

▲ The famous Eleusian Well at the Sanctuary of Demeter.

— maybe thousands — of devotees followed the clergy, including a virgin priestess, who carried the basket, or *cista mystica*, that held holy objects, or *hiera*, that would be used in the Greater Mysteries of Demeter once they reached their destination.

One short version of the story of Demeter and Persephone goes something like this: Persephone is picking flowers with Athena and Artemis when all of a sudden, up from a chasm in the earth comes Hades, Lord of the Underworld on his chariot. For sometime Hades had his eye on the Virgin Goddess and deciding he desired her for himself, snatched Persephone up and taking her away with him. Demeter, Persephone's mother, searched the world for her daughter for nine days in her guise as the crone. During this time, (like Isis in Byblos), she became employed by a king. She attempts to grant the gift of immortality to the king's son by dipping him nightly into fire. One night the queen saw this ritual and without knowing the generous intention of Demeter, naturally bursts out in anger as any good mother would. Then Demeter revealed her identity to the royal couple and their subjects, requesting that a temple be constructed for her in Eleusis. They agreed. Still without her daughter Persephone, Demeter mourns. With her sadness, the earth goes fallow, vegetation ceases to grow, and the people are near starvation. In time Zeus insists that Hades return Persephone to Demeter — for whom else would be left on Earth to serve the immortals? Hades reluctantly complies, but trickster that he is, he tempts Persephone to eat a pomegranate seed before she leaves the Netherworld, an act that forces her to return to him for one third of every year. When Persephone is in Tartarus, or the underworld regions, Demeter annually mourns, thus the crops do not grow. When Persephone returns to the surface Demeter is joyous and the seedlings sprout forth and multiply, feeding the people and everyone lives happily for another year.

In another version of the story, the Goddess Baubo performs a bawdy dance during which she exposes her yoni to Demeter while she is in mourning. Baubo's silly antic causes Demeter to laugh and her divine light is revealed. Soon after the return of light to the world, the crops began to flourish, and life goes on as usual. Seeing Baubo's yoni was a reminder to Demeter of the power of fertility and creation associated with the cycles of birth, life, death, and rebirth. Similarly, Persephone's return from the Underworld into the loving arms of her awaiting mother was also a metaphor for these themes. Persephone, the Virgin Goddess of potential is synonymous with the seedling which will sprout forth new life. As the cycle of life (and vegetation) evolves, they will mature, die, and be reborn, thus the myths offer knowledge and understanding of the cycles of life. Demeter and Persephone (or Kore) viewed as two elements of a single entity can then be seen as maiden, mother and crone, three stages of a woman's life, exhibiting the life cycle within a single person. Scholars believe it was these mysteries in the form of dramas, festivals, and enactments that might have taken place during various Eleusian Mysteries. This is the same theme of the dying and rising king mentioned in the sites of the Middle East and Africa associated with Inanna and Dumuzzi, Isis and Osiris, Aphrodite and Adonis, and though a controversial thought, Mary and Jesus.

According to religion scholar James Rietveld the religion of the cult of Demeter was always held in high esteem. He quotes Everett Ferguson who explains the rites at Eleusis originally belonged to one family, and then became open to the town's citizens, eventually being adopted by the people of Attica at large. Eventually, the cult at Eleusis became a universal belief system, open to all regardless of race or place of origin and later spread when the cult became avail-

▲ The Eleusian temple sat before the Ploutonium, or Cave to the Underworld.

able to those considered "Barbarians," specifically the citizens of the Roman Empire. Walter Burkert stated, "women, slaves, and foreigners were admitted" into the Eleusian Mysteries, while another noted scholar, Simon Price, states dedicates must meet only one standard, namely, "the candidate for initiation should be pure and not of unintelligible speech." That requirement being met, an initiate only had to get past the hurdle of the travel expense of the undertaking. Traveling to Eleusis was expensive, as was procuring a sacrificial animal, not to mention the initiation fee. But when there is a will, there is a way. One particularly public ritual of the Greater Mysteries of Demeter took place on the 16th of Bocdromion, (the month of September), when initiates, or *mystes*, purified themselves in the sea with their piglet, which later would be offered to Demeter in sacrifice. Some scholars suggest the blood of the pig was actually the sanctifying agent for the initiates' purifica-tion. Rietveld compares this dip in the ocean to "Christian baptism where the community observed these outer acts as representing an internal transformation."

In her book, *"Mysteries of Demeter, Rebirth of the Pagan Way,"* author Jennifer Reif discusses the festivals and celebrations of Demeter and Persephone which cor-responded to the life cycles of the grain and the agricultural season. Mother and Maiden, Demeter and Persephone were honored during the Spring Festival of Chloaia sometime between February and March, depending on the location of the region. Thargelia was the harvest festival, and Kalamaia, the threshing festi-val. Reif interprets the first part of the Skira Festival as having been Persephone's descent into the underworld, with the conclusion of the festival, associated with the underground storage of the seed grain. The Proerosia Festival concerned preplowing rites, and the Stenia Festival was an enactment of Baubo's erotic humor causing Demeter to release her dark aspect and become the fertile mother again. In Reif's interpretation of the Arkichronia Festival, gifts of the immortals are commingled with the seed to create fertility talismans before any planting takes place. The final three festivals are Nestia, when Persephone leaves Hades, Kalligenia, as Persephone (as Kore) ascends to Earth where the planting may begin, and finally Haloa, as mother and daughter delight in the beginning of the growing period.

According to authors Rufus and Lawson, the initiated Eleusian clergy, called *"epoptai,"* along with initiates, gathered in the telesterion to witness the mysteries. Next they uttered the "formula of the Eleusian Mysteries," as mentioned by Clement of Alexandria, where they declared: "I fasted; I drank the draught; I took from the chest; having done my task, I placed in the basket, and from the basket into the chest" (Exhortations to the Greeks, II.18). Some believe a vision of Persephone's return might have been enacted or actually seen as a "Great Light." Concerning the mysteries at Eleusis, one papyrus fragment from the time of the Emperor Hardian (117-138 CE) states: "I have beheld the fire ... I have seen the Kore." Others suggest an ear of corn, embodying many layers of meaning, was presented to those gathered. Still a few believe part of the mysteries may have included some type of sexual rites. No doubt the hierophant showed the holy objects, or *heira*. Suggestions for these items are offered by scholar Walter Burkert: mortar and pestle, assorted cakes, balls of salt, a serpent, pomegranates, fig branches, fennel stalks, ivy leaves, poppies, marjoram, a lamp, a sword, a woman's comb and symbols of Ge Themis. These sacred objects would be in keeping with the suspected meaning of the mysteries being concerned with teaching initiates the meaning of life and death as the poppies and serpent were symbols of death, while the pomegranate, stalks, and leaves were symbols of rebirth. Professor Marvin Meyer believes part of the mysteries may have included initiates beholding a great light within the inner sanctum, which Plutarch compares with initiation into philosophy.

Another important and interesting aspect associated with this myth is the controversy over whether Persephone was actually raped. Reif does not agree with this patriarchal device of domination of Persephone. Even the pomegranate was a means to control the Goddess. She believes Persephone might have descended into the Underworld, a place of the unknown with some trepidation, but no fear of rape. (And let us remember, she has Hekate to aid her and light her way). She contends that the mysteries were matristic in focus, surviving within a patriarchal Greek period and reminds us that most of the initiates were women. Readers should keep in mind that Demeter harkens back to the time of the older order of the Goddess, before the time of the patriarchy when female deities were subjugated by the Olympians. Reif is firm in her belief that, "women would not use this model of a relationship based on violence as the foundation of their theology." Increasingly other scholars are coming to rethink the accuracy of this rape version of the myth. Reif cites author Clarissa Pinkola Estes who states, "During the time of the matriarchies, women were guided to the Underworld by deep feminine powers," and Charleen Spretnak who finds evidence that the original myth did not contain rape until the emergence of patriarchy within society.

Today visitors can see the Eschara, a pit where sacrifices were made, sections of the Sacred Way, the Callichoros Well where it is believed women danced and prayed, and the Ploutonium, the sacred cave believed to be where Persephone entered and exited the Underworld in order to live with Hades/Pluto. Like at Delphi, the omphalos, the sacred navel at the bridging the gap between heaven and earth, was situated within the cave. Here the participants met a young lad designated through casting lots as the "boy of the hearth" representing the king's son, Demophoon, destined for immortality by Demeter until his purification into pure spirit was interrupted by his worried mother. Beyond is what remains of the Telesterion where the initiations took place. This structure once measured

177 feet (54 m) by 170 feet (52 m) with 22 columns supporting the roof, surrounded by tiers of stone steps for seating around the walls. The Telesterion once featured a peaked roof that opened up to form a chimney during ritual occasions, allowing grand displays of fire and smoke to burst forth from the mysterious building. An interesting side note about the Priestess of Demeter is she was the only married woman permitted to watch the Olympics. While maidens might watch the Olympics, perhaps allowing them to look over potential mates, married women were barred from the games under penalty of death. Professor Thomas Scanlon suggests the priestess of Demeter might have enjoyed this privilege because an ancient altar and sanctuary to Demeter was located in the middle of the stadium seating area.

Getting to Eleusis

Like many locations chosen in ancient times as sacred domains of Goddess, the landscape of Eleusis reflects the contours commonly recognized as ideal holy sites that embody the Feminine. Once lush and fertile, it still enjoys a close proximity to mountains and water, however today Eleusis is located within an unattractive industrial area of Attica called Elefsina. Still the importance of the site begs overlooking the modern developments which sometimes render the atmosphere polluted and noxious. It can be reached by public bus # 853 or #862 from Eleftherios Square in Athens, which is about an hours drive away. Once off the bus, walk toward the water for about three blocks, following the well-marked signs along the route. There is a museum on site.

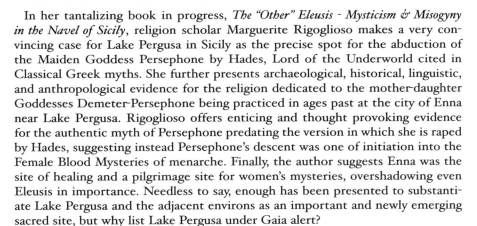

GAIA ALERT

THE RAPE OF THE "OTHER" ELEUSIS

In her tantalizing book in progress, *The "Other" Eleusis - Mysticism & Misogyny in the Navel of Sicily*, religion scholar Marguerite Rigoglioso makes a very convincing case for Lake Pergusa in Sicily as the precise spot for the abduction of the Maiden Goddess Persephone by Hades, Lord of the Underworld cited in Classical Greek myths. She further presents archaeological, historical, linguistic, and anthropological evidence for the religion dedicated to the mother-daughter Goddesses Demeter-Persephone being practiced in ages past at the city of Enna near Lake Pergusa. Rigoglioso offers enticing and thought provoking evidence for the authentic myth of Persephone predating the version in which she is raped by Hades, suggesting instead Persephone's descent was one of initiation into the Female Blood Mysteries of menarche. Finally, the author suggests Enna was the site of healing and a pilgrimage site for women's mysteries, overshadowing even Eleusis in importance. Needless to say, enough has been presented to substantiate Lake Pergusa and the adjacent environs as an important and newly emerging sacred site, but why list Lake Pergusa under Gaia alert?

Today Lake Pergusa looks more like a swamp than the sacred lake described as an Eden by historian Enrico Sinicropi as recently as 1958. About the same time Sinicropi was enjoying the splendors of the region, construction began on a four-mile autodrome or race track around the perimeter of the lake. Over the years, the lake has become filled with sediment, vegetative residue, and polluting runoff from the autodrome. Every year Lake Pergusa continues to dry up. Once 21 feet (6.4 m) deep, when last measured, the lake was only a depth of three feet (0.9 m).

▲ The Temple of Demeter commanded a clifftop position overlooking Lake Pergusa.

Its perimeter has shrunk from 5 miles (8 km) in diameter to 3 miles (4.8 km) as the lake disappears. Activists in the area have continually met resistance from local politicians and "underworld figures" more concerned with loss of revenue should the racetrack be demolished rather than the environmental impact of the race track on the lake and nearby wildlife. As Nature is the Goddess, even the Feminine incarnate, Rigoglioso compares this abuse, neglect and misuse of Lake Pergusa, the womb of the Mother, to the rape of Persephone as the Divine Feminine. Local environmentalists need a boost of morale, funding, and international pressure to keep up their work. If you wish to help in any way, go to www.lakepergusa.org to find contact information for activists who speak English or Italian who would appreciate your help.

Temple of Hera

Located on a Greek island two miles from the Turkish mainland, the Temple of Hera on Samos, has been a sacred site of Goddess since Neolithic times. Eight layers of prehistoric remains from 2500 BCE were unearthed here in the Heraeum, which along with Argos, makes this site one of the most important temples of Hera in the Mediterranean region. Many temples of Goddess have come and gone here over hundreds of years, the victims of fire and flood, but at its zenith the first century CE writer Strabo describes the site visitors would have seen as they approached the island. Travelers would have been awed at the Temple of Poseidon on a promontory of Mount Mycale. Casting their eyes left would reveal the Heraeum, the shrine and Temple of Hera. The shrine was said to have been a repository of many votive tablets, with the small chapels of the temple precinct full of art, some of which were open to the sky where many statues were kept. Some of the more prominent statues within the sacred complex were those of Athena, Heracles and Zeus.

Hera's Temple was located near the Imbrasus River, where legend describes Hera annually bathing to renew her virginity, thus renewing the eternal cycle of life. In this aspect, she is very much like Aphrodite who was annually bathed at her temple on the island of Cypress. It was understood that their emergence or rebirth from the waters, their virginity restored, was synonymous with the birth of spring and all its flowering potential. Hera, the daughter of Thea and Cronos, is said to have been born on the Imbrasus riverbank under a sacred willow tree associated with her cult. Here she was also thought to have married the patriarchal Olympian Zeus though as tales tell, it was never a happy union. Hera is a very old Goddess, with origins long before the Olympians come onto the scene in Greece. According to Patricia Monaghan, her name might actually have been something else as Hera roughly translates to "Our Lady." Prior to her image becoming petulant and jealous at the hands of the Greeks, she was a woman of independence and dignity. Hera's new personae during classical times is a reflection of a shift in religion and culture from worship of the ancient chthonic Goddess to Goddess with a new image that was more in keeping with patriarchal norms. Goddesses became subordinate to male deities, often relinquishing their powers to them, even being birthed from male gods.

Monaghan reports that Hera, the Goddess of women and sexuality, passed through three phases of life: maiden, mother, and crone. Each of those might be described as youth, prime, and old age, also reflecting mortal females. With the temple's close proximity to Turkey, it is no wonder that Hera's devotees participated in competitive games much like female devotees of Artemis and Hekate. Monaghan cites women honored Hera by celebrating these games held every four years, (possibly annually) which predates the Olympics commonly known to have taken place in Greece strictly among men. The games were called the Heraea and the women who participated were the prime examples of strength, independence, and empowerment. Their short dress, an "off the shoulder chiton" revealed their right breast and shoulder as indicated by a bronze statuette of a girl runner dated 560 BCE. In describing their clothing, Professor Thomas Scanlon explains this garment was an adaptation of a hot weather garment worn by men of the time rather than a garment of Amazon warrior women. Monaghan states there were three age groups participating in the Heraea to coincide with the three phases of a woman's life. One of the games known to have been played in Argos was the 160 yard dash. Monaghan states there were three winners who received an olive branch crown and a share in the cow which was sacrificed at the festival. The cow was sacrificed in honor of Hera who was worshipped by the people as their "cow-eyed sky queen." Winning competitors also won the right to leave a statue of themselves in Hera's shrine. Scanlon reports a slightly different version of the games with participants ranging in age from six to 18 years. Citing the ancient writer Pausanias,

Scanlon states there was one event, a footrace for maidens, whose course was shortened by one-sixth the size of the men's track, to compensate for the shorter stride of the female gender. Winners received an olive wreath crown, their share of a slaughtered ox, and their portraits were hung in niches within Hera's Temple.

According to Monaghan, Hera embodied the following three Goddesses during the three different phases of her life. As the virgin maid, which had no relevance to chastity, she was Hebe or Parthenia. She was also the "flowering one," called Antheia.

▲ Hera with Zeus may represent the struggle between matriarchy and patriarchy.

▲ The statue of Hera inside the Heraeum on Samos Island may have looked something like this.

During her prime of life, she was called Nymphenomene or Teleia. The former meant "seeking a mate" and the latter, "the perfect one." In her final crone age she was Theira, beyond maternity, with her life reverting as her own once again, wise in her years, her sacred bloods kept within her womb. In the afore-mentioned ritual of renewing her virginity on the riverbank, Hebe or Parthenia was her emerging essence as clergy bathed her statue in ritual at the river. Probably twice more during the year, as the season waned, her statue would be carried by her clergy down to the waters and it was understood Hera would emerge in the respective mature or death/crone aspect of Teleia or Theira to coincide with the cycle of year currently being celebrated.

Monaghan describes Hera's worship as strong, and the Goddess as having no consort before the patriarchal tribes infiltrated Greece. She uses parthenogenesis, having conceived and birthed her son Hephaestos of herself. Eventually a marriage of sorts was arranged between the patriarch of Olympia, Zeus and the reluctant Hera, beginning an uneasy alliance between Goddess and God. Monaghan aptly describes her as "making a mythic nuisance of herself to the father symbol of the patriarchy."

Hera's temple precinct on Samos was destroyed and rebuilt several times, but at its zenith, the sacred compound was described as a forest of columns that contained colossal statues, shrines and temples to other deities. The Sacred Way leading toward the entrance of the Heraeum was an impressive 15,750 feet (4,800 m) long. It was such a profound temple that it became the inspiration for the Artemis Temple of Ephesus, one of the Seven Wonders of the Ancient World. Today all that remains of Hera's monumental temple is a lone column and shorter pillar stumps which in no way represents the great Ancient Mother she once was. To the east of the Great Temple are foundation remains of a 5th century CE church dedicated to the Virgin Mary thus combining once again, as happens so many times over, the essence of Goddess in pre-Christian times with that of her Christian descendant.

Getting to the Temple of Hera

Samos is located within the northeast Aegean island group, closest to Turkey, where little tourism is carried on as indicated by the somewhat limited plane and boat schedules to the island. Excursion boats, steamers and hydrofoils make the trip from neighboring islands periodically, sometimes daily. Flights from Athens are an option, as are daily departures by boat, but the latter takes 13 hours. If arriving by plane, take an airline shuttle or taxi from the airport into Samostown where a taxi can be hired to reach the main city of Pythagorian. Bikes or taxis are options to reach Hera's temple from town. One daily public bus makes the route or walking may take a little more than an hour. Try to see the museum in Samostown with its artifacts dedicated to Hera, as well as the Eupalinus Tunnel, an engineering marvel from ancient days that brought water into town. This 383-foot (105-m) underground tunnel is considered a "must see."

Goddess Focus
Delos — Sacred Archaeological Isle of Goddess

As one travels over the blue-green sea from Mykonos toward Delos, the gentle rocking of the boat and the island ahead growing ever closer becomes a trance-like journey taking visitors from the mundane world into the sacred. In ancient times Delos was mentioned in Homer's *The Odyssey* as a well-known religious center. Inhabited today only by French archaeologists and island caretakers working on the island, Delos with all its temples, mosaics, structures, and superb museum is a treasure trove of sacred sites dedicated to a multitude of goddesses.

This isle is one site thought to be where the pregnant Leto, paramour of Zeus, took refuge from the jealous Hera. The other was in Ephesus. Here under a palm tree it is said Leto gave birth to her twins, Apollo and Artemis. It was purified twice during its history to purge the island of the profane. The dead were disinterred and reburied elsewhere, and the dying and pregnant were banned from the isle. Over time many cultures including the Egyptians, Syrians, Phoenicians, Palestinians, Jews, Greeks and Romans all settled close to the harbor. With all those cultures in one place, it is no wonder there are temples dedicated to Athena, Artemis, Atargatis, Aphrodite, Hera, Demeter, Leto, and Tanit. One of the best restored temples has two Doric style columns and is dedicated to the Egyptian Goddess, Isis. It is situated upon a high place and her headless statue is within her sanctuary, which is adjacent to an unrestored temple of

▲ The headless statue of Isis still stands in her temple on Delos Island in the Aegean Sea.

the God Serapis, her consort. Another restoration is the Artemision, the temple of Artemis, once considered one of the focal points of worship on the island. Scholar Walter Burkert states as an important place of sacrifice, "the Horn Altar of Artemis on Delos which was made from goat horns and famed as one of the wonders of the world." Both temples have wonderful panoramic views of the island and the blue waters of the Mediterranean beyond.

IRELAND

As a country completely surrounded by the ocean, Ireland has a long association with Goddess and water. The nourishing milk that is Goddess runs swift in springs, wells, lakes, and rivers and it is no coincidence that civilizations discovered her and thrived near these life-giving bodies of water. From the sacred wells of Brigid in Ireland, the Seine River of Sequana in France, and Persephone's Lake Pergusa in Sicily, to live near water was synonymous with living near the Giver of Life where her mysteries were close at hand. Devotees continue to collect the healing waters that spring forth from the sacred places where Goddess has appeared in her many guises. The apparition of the Mother Mary at Lourdes and Knock, or the epiphanies of Artemis at Ephesus are two examples. Sulis Minerva's spring in Bath, England, and Chalice Well in Glastonbury, both run a shade of red reminiscent of the sacred life-giving blood of the Mother. In some of these holy sites Goddess as water is personified with many villages in England still choosing to venerate the sacred waters with celebrations called "well dressings" that harkens back to their ancestral pagan roots.

Clonegal Castle

The Temple of Isis at the 17th century castle in Clonegal, Ireland is no museum, relic, or ruin. It is a working temple atop a sacred well beneath the castle in a multi-room, labyrinth-like womb-space of the Mother. It is home to the international organization, The Fellowship of Isis, and rituals and ceremonies are still carried out in Clonegal Castle. They honor the Goddess in her many forms under the guidance of one of the organization's founders, the 90-year-old Lady Olivia Robertson. Lady Olivia, her brother, Lawrence Durdin-Robertson, and his wife Pamela Robertson founded the temple and organization in the mid 1970s. At this time other leaders raising the consciousness of Goddess Spirituality were also making their presence known in other parts of the world.

Lady O, as some of the members of the Fellowship of Isis call her, has always been a liberal and open-minded thinker, even when it was not fashionable for a woman to be a rebel. While a successful novelist in the 1950s, she began exploring esoteric sciences in order to put into practice psychic gifts gained as a child. She saw spirits and angels all her life, but was shocked and puzzled when she received a vision of the Goddess Isis in 1976. Furthermore, she could resonate with the practices of psychics, healers, magicians and the likes of her cousin, Robert Graves (author of *The White Goddess*), despite the fact he was not highly thought of in the family or "proper society" of the time. Lady Olivia and Lawrence believe they can trace their family tree back to an Egyptian Priestess of Isis named Scota, "the dark one," daughter of the Pharaoh Cincris, and hereditary Daughter of Isis. It was after Olivia's vision from the Goddess Isis in the mid-seventies that Olivia,

Lawrence and Pamela decided to turn their ancestral home of Clonegal Castle into the home of the Fellowship of Isis.

Although Lawrence and Pamela are now deceased the Fellowship is thriving — with more than 20,000 members across the world at the time of this writing. In 1990, the Fellowship of Isis, or FOI, formed an order of chivalry called the Noble Order of Tara, comprised of members dedicated to working for the environment. They have been instrumental in helping save Mount Leinster from strip-mining, and have other ecology-minded activities underway. In 1992 the Druid Clan of Dana, named for the Irish Mother Goddess, was formed and dedicated to the Druidic mysteries. Their magazine, *Aisling*, is active in the Council of British Druid Orders and they organized the 1993 Druid Convention in London. Also in 1993, the Fellowship of Isis was one of two Goddess oriented religions to be represented at the World Parliament of Religions held in Chicago.

Though the Fellowship honors all Goddesses, why does Lady Olivia primarily resonate with Isis? In her own words, "Isis is the universal Goddess — the Isis of Ten Thousand Names. She includes them all ... Demeter, Lakshmi, Kwan Yin, Dana, Ngame, Mary." To Lady Olivia, as most Neo-Pagans might agree, Mary of the Christian religion was Isis. Christ was both Osiris and then Horus after Osiris' resurrection. Lady O believes the Goddess Isis is manifesting physically and spiritually during this time of global transition and emergence of the Feminine Divine. Millions everywhere claim to hear the Goddess call as they turn back to the "old ways." These devotees believe that unless we again honor females and the

Divine Feminine, the devastating effects inflicted by a patriarchal society on the Earth and its peoples, ecologically, spiritually, and technologically, will ultimately lead to catastrophe. Goddess spiritualists believe the plan of Mother Nature is to restore harmony, a love for each other so that healthy, abundant life can be nurtured and enjoyed by all.

The castle temple consists of 26 shrines, including the main sanctuary, naive, Chapel of Brigid, and shrines dedicated to the twelve signs of the Zodiac. The shrines change occasionally, but this is an example of what one might see upon entering. At the sound of a gong, devotees enter in procession through ornately carved doors, and immediately before them is the Egyptian god, Thoth, guardian of the mysteries. Stone steps lead down to a landing. Everywhere symbols of the Goddess shine

▲ The healing well in Clonegal Castle.

forth. There is a plaque depicting Jesus, surrounded by more iconography depicting the Divine Feminine. To the left would be the main temple area with statues of Goddesses around the perimeter of the room. Ahead is an iron gate leading to the ancient castle well. To the left of the gate is a huge Tibetan bell used to announce entrance into the Temple. The interior of the temple is 79 by 40 feet (24 m by 12 m) and built of granite. There is a large sanctuary and naive with a row of nine stone pillars. Two brick pillars stand before the High Altar with a low brick wall creating the sanctuary. On a low raised stone dais before the High Altar, the clergy make invocations.

The High Altar of Isis is the central focus of ceremonial activity within the temple. Its central image is of Isis of 10,000 Names, carved for the Fellowship of Isis by the talented woodworker, David Robertson, son of Lawrence and nephew of Olivia. There are five main chapels featuring elemental attributes. The Chapel of Brigid contains the ancient Druidic well which is 17 feet (5 m) deep with noted healing properties. From Brigid's chapel, carved doors lead to the Holy of Holies, also known as the Chapel of Ishtar, dedicated to the fifth element, Spirit. The temple is used daily for meditation and ritual as Lady Olivia helps heal and attune with members worldwide. The castle sits on the beautiful and lush landscape of Ireland, adjacent to a sacred grove of trees. Work continues to evolve at the Fellowship of Isis headquarters whose mission is bringing back the Goddess into the world through whatever means the Divine Feminine deems appropriate. Rituals often consist of theatrical performances that teach universal mysteries. The vision and dream of these dedicated people within the FOI has grown from a group of three to a vehicle for thousands to know and honor Goddess.

Getting to Clonegal Castle

Clonegal Castle is located in the small village of Clonegal in southeastern Ireland. Rituals are by invitation only. Drop-in visits are not considered proper etiquette, therefore specific directions for visiting the castle will not be provided here. For information about visiting Clonegal Castle, please write: Lady Olivia Robertson, Fellowship of Isis, Clonegal Castle, Enniscorthy, Ireland. The FOI has iseums and lyceums in the United States and throughout the world. One can find information about the nearest FOI group by going to the Fellowship of Isis on the internet. The FOI offers correspondence courses, a newsletter, and Lady Olivia has published books and rituals in print and on tape which can be purchased.

Kildare

While it is very difficult to visit conservative and Christian Ireland and not literally trip over aspects of Goddess, Kildare offers pilgrims, in one general locale, the opportunity of experiencing at least four varied aspects of the Divine Feminine. Seekers of Goddess will find a Sheila-na-Gig, a sacred well of Brigid, a fire sanctuary of Brigid, and the Sisters of the Solas Bride (pronounced breed), the Brigidine Sisters who keep the flame of Brigid alive.

Celtic Brigid falls into the category of Virgin Goddess similar to Athena and the Vestal Virgins of Rome (See Rome and Athens). Considered a triple Goddess, she is the patroness of poets, healing, and smiths. Brigid is also a generative force of energy in her aspects of flowing water and burning fire as indicated by her sacred well and fire sanctuary in Kildare. Interestingly, when water and fire meet, steam is produced, certainly another form of perpetual power and energy. Her fire melts the metal of the smith, then the water cools it to create useful tools for humankind. Through her association with the beneficent female serpent called "the queen" she demonstrates discernible links with her Neolithic ancestry. Later she was assimilated into Celtic Christianity and canonized as Brigid the virgin nun. It is through this connection the Solas Bride or Brigidine Sisters of Ireland honor both Brigid the Goddess and Brigid the Saint as one. Keeping the ancient tradition alive, the modern day nuns keep the flame of Brigid burning and in their holy place visitors may see the flame and take it back home with them. This is done by lighting a candle from the perpetual flame of the Solas Bride, then passing the metaphoric flame to other candles, wick to wick.

According to Miriam Robbins Dexter, the river Brigid in Ireland, Braint in Wales, and Brent in England were all named for the Goddess Brigid or Bride and she quotes Geraldus Cambrensis regarding the perpetual flame of the Goddess. "At the time of Brigid twenty nuns here served a master as would a soldier, she herself being the twentieth ... when indeed every night through every succession they cared for the fire ... on the twentieth night the last nun said: 'Brigid, I have cared for your fire ... and thus, the fire having been left ... it was found again, unextinguished.'" Scholar Barbara Walker cites Archbishop Cormac Mac Cullenan's Cormac's Glossary (908 CE) describing Brigid as "the female sage ... Brigit the goddess, whom poets adored, because her protecting care over them was very great and very famous." Scottish scholar J. A. Mac Cullock in 1911 said that Brigid, "originated in a period when the Celts worshipped goddesses rather than gods, and when knowledge — leechcraft, agriculture, inspiration — were women's rather than men's." Brigid had female clergy and men were thought to be excluded from her cult, as the tabooed shrine at Kildare suggests.

Barbara Walker and Robert Graves believe that like other aspects that the Catholic Church failed to eradicate, they assimilated, and so Brigid became a nun who founded a convent in Kildare, celebrated for its fertility and abundance. They say the village cows never went dry, flowers and shamrocks sprang up in Brigit's footprints, eternal spring reigned in her bower. Writers and poets insisted Brigid was no mere saint, but the Queen of Heaven, thus identifying her with Mary. Graves says Brigid was called "Mother of my Sovereign, Mary of the Goidels, Queen of the South, Prophetess of Christ, Mother of Jesus." Marija Gimbutas stated Brigid, like Artemis and Diana, was associated with childbirth and was the "midwife to the Blessed Virgin and thus the foster mother of Christ." Others associated Brigid with June Regina, and Tanit, the Heavenly Goddess. Gimbutas states Brigid, like the Greek Artemis Eileithyia, Thracian Bendis, Roman Diana, and the Fate Goddess of the Baltic, were all prehistoric descendants of the life-giving Goddesses who survived Indo-Europeanization in the form of Nature, the bestower of health, and in the guise of birds and animals. Like her European sisters, Brigid was linked with weaving, spinning, twisting and sewing and it is said this women's work must be suspended on Friday, the holy day of Goddess.

Interestingly, she was linked with Saint Patrick, said to have been a pagan before being converted to Christianity, and sometimes thought to be a Christianized version of Brigid's early Pagan consort, Dagda, or "father." According to Irish lore, Saint Patrick is responsible for there being no snakes native to Ireland. These associations along with Brigid being connected with the Neolithic snake imagery, begs speculation that perhaps the story of Saint Patrick driving out the snakes from Ireland is a metaphor for the patriarchy subjugating Goddess spirituality. Gimbutas states that on the day of Imbolc, Brigid's holy day, the "serpents are supposed to emerge from the hills," and local customs include making effigies of snakes. Walker states the nineteen priestesses of Brigid (herself making twenty) at Kildare represented the nineteen year cycle of the Celtic "Great Year." She further discusses how the Greeks told of Apollo who would visit the "temple of the moon goddess" (Brigid) every nineteen years, alluding to the solar and lunar calendars. These Great Years were marked with posts around the circle at Stonehenge. Scholar Patricia Monaghan connects Brigid linguistically to Bridestones, or sarsens, the massive sandstones used in the construction of Stonehenge, suggesting awareness of Brigid in early Neolithic, pre-Celtic times.

Walker cites another aspect of Brigid associated with the martial arts and her soldiers known as brigands, a further example of devotees of Goddess being demonized, as were the Thuggees of Kali and the "Assassins" who worshipped the Arabian Moon Goddess. Scholar Patricia Monaghan offers a slightly different version of Brigid, who is known as Brigantia in England, Bride in Scotland, and Brigandu in Celtic France. In this mythic cycle, Brigid is the human daughter of a Druid baptized by Saint Patrick and later canonized. It was said the abbess had unusual authority to appoint bishops, who were required to be goldsmiths, and the Christian Brigid had many of the same qualities and powers of the Goddess Brigid. Brigid's feast day is February 1, called Imbolc or Candlemas, and Gimbutas states it was a festival which celebrated the "lactation of the ewes, symbolic of new life and the coming of spring." She says a libation of milk was poured onto the Earth and links the life-giving substance to the dandelion, Brigid's flower, which produced milky juice when pressed thus providing food for the young ewes. This festival is also a celebration of the return of the light when the world is re-emerging from the darkness of winter, and anyone who has spent time in the darkness of Ireland's winters knows what a psychological boost it is to begin to see the light again, the symbolic fire of Brigid. This was a happy time of ritual baking, processions, dancing, and singing. According to Gimbutas, "Paying homage to Bride, the presentation of gifts, making dolls, baking of special cakes, welcoming of the Saint in every house, and expectation of her visit as a blessing must have roots deeper than the last centuries of paganism; much of it carries on Neolithic traditions."

Rufus and Lawson describe Brigid's fire sanctuary in Kildare as a "low stone wall, rectangular and not circular as in ancient times. Neat, tidy, and understated ... the reconstructed shrine speaks little of its life as a spiritual magnet for Irish women, both in the Goddess' time and for centuries afterward." Brigid's Fire House is located in the churchyard of the Cathedral Church of Saint Brigid in the center of Kildare. Before leaving the cathedral, check inside for the Sheela on the 16th century tomb of Bishop Wellesley, set below the left-hand corner of the top slab and neatly juxtaposed above a crucifixion panel. The Sheela has her legs parted and her pubic hair showing.

Brigid's Well, called Tobar Bride, is about a mile away from the fire sanctuary. The site would indicate it is dedicated equally to the Saint and the Goddess with both a statue of Saint Brigid in her nun's regalia and the natural well of healing waters at the holy site. The pagan symbol of Brigid, the Cross of Brigid, is painted on the brick arch that spans the sacred stream-like well.

▲ Brigid's Well is an integral part of Kildare's sacred landscape. While overtly Christian in appearance, its roots are clearly pagan.

Remember to bring a container to take home the healing waters of Bride. Votive offerings are regularly left at the site including rags or strips of cloth tied to trees, sometimes called *clootie* trees. Gimbutas citing Wood-Martin, "The rag or ribbon, taken from the clothing, is considered to be the depository of the spiritual or bodily ailments of the suppliant. Rags are not merely offerings, or votive, they are riddances." (In another form of riddance ritual, the *brat Brighide,* or Saint Brigit's mantle, a strip of cloth placed on a tree or bush several days prior to Saint Brigit's Eve, was distributed among family members by the matriarch of the house to protect the family from misfortune or illness during the coming year.) Since Neolithic times, Brigid's waters are also known for their ability to heal and this explains why many wells beneath churches dedicated to the Virgin Mary and temples (Clonegal, Chartres, Lourdes) may have continued to have this miraculous reputation. Certain sacred wells of goddesses were thought to help women become fertile. On the first day of spring, devotees would ritually visit the wells and perform acts of purification, washing their hands, face, and feet, tearing strips of cloth from their clothing, circumambulating the stone, praying, chanting, bowing, and drinking from the sacred waters. Gimbutas again citing Wood-Martin states they might then visit "a river stone which has footprints" where they would continue to pray. Here at Tobar Bride, footprints can be seen inscribed in the stone at the sacred waters.

The Sisters of the Solas Bride, nuns of the Church, eagerly embrace Brigid the Goddess and those who venerate her. It is possible to visit their sanctuary, but not without making arrangements prior to coming. Interested parties will be required to make personal contact to arrange a visit. The Sisters welcome individuals and groups and have eagerly accommodated and shared ritual space with small groups of dedicated practitioners of Goddess Spirituality.

Getting to Kildare

Kildare is located 32 miles (51 km) southwest of Dublin and easily accessible by train, bus and private car. If driving, take the N7 Dublin-Limerick Road to the center of the town of Kildare where the Cathedral is located. The well is located one mile south of Kildare. Take the signs out of town toward the Japanese Gardens and about 300 yards (270 m) before you reach the Gardens there will be a sign to direct motorists toward the Tobar Bride down a small road to the right. About 100 yards (90 m) further will be another sign that points left down the lane, bringing visitors to the well. For meeting the Sisters of the Solas Bride, see contact information in Resource List at the back of this book.

Newgrange

Pick up a guidebook, just any old guidebook, and it will say the great megalithic tomb of Newgrange ranks alongside the temple of Ggantija in Malta as one of the most impressive prehistoric monuments in Europe, but mainstream scholars still do not agree on how to interpret the meaning for this magnificent site of Goddess built over 5,000 years ago. Some experts say the imagery found on megalithic art in Western Europe is related to altered states of consciousness. Sometimes the altered states are the result of taking hallucinogens, other times it might be from shaman trance dances. Many goddess advocates break the mold of traditional thought when they find the work of controversial archaeologist Marija Gimbutas compelling. Thanks to decades of study by Gimbutas, specializing in Neolithic archaeology and the meaning of art and artifacts in a cultural and religious context, passage graves such as Newgrange take on a fuller and richer meaning, though even Marija could not say *exactly* what happened at Newgrange. Based on the pictorial language she developed, folk literature, and a bit of intuition, advocates believe that Newgrange was a site sacred to Goddess, and its imagery reflects ideas of birth, death, and rebirth, with the passage grave being both "womb and tomb." Author Peg Streep calls Newgrange, "The heart of the religion of the Goddess in the British Isles." Without a doubt it is certainly a place of ritual, procession, and important gatherings that are suggestive of the religion of the early Neolithic builders!

Many state Newgrange is the finest example in Western Europe of a passage grave. Carbon dating points to 3200 BCE as being the approximate time period it was erected. The people who built Newgrange were farmers who raised livestock. They worked with stone rather than metal, observed and studied celestial movements, and managed the incredible feat of building this sophisticated structure that demanded not only incredible effort, but an understanding of architecture and engineering. It is 45 feet (14 m) high and 265 feet (81 m) in diameter and was once circled by 35 standing stones or menhirs, of which only 12 exist today. Streep suggests this circle might have separated the sacred precinct of the womb of the mother from profane space. Today the mound is covered with grass, but is thought by several scholars to once was covered with white quartz. This stone was not readily available and had to be procured from some distance away, thus the quartz would have significant rather than just cosmetic meaning. Gimbutas likens the mound to the cosmic egg or womb of the world and the white covering was meant to suggest the surface of an egg. It is estimated 180,000 tons (163,080,000 kg) of stone were required to build Newgrange.

The passageway into the mound is oriented toward the midwinter sunrise. The long 62-foot (19-m) passage leads to a central chamber, branching off to three side chambers. A roof box lintel at the entrance allows sunlight to stream into the chamber on the midwinter solstice. When one is inside during the solstice, the sun can be seen slowly filling the inner passage until it reaches the back chamber and illuminates a triple-spiral carving believed by some to represent the Goddess. Perhaps this creates the effect of awakening her powers and a symbolic (or literal?) rebirth and regeneration of the dead. The light fills the cavern for a time before retreating back down the entrance passageway, leaving the mound in darkness once more. It has been suggested this dramatic effect might have been enacted at other important times during the year using a polished mirror, but that is only speculation.

Gimbutas believed the Goddess was invoked using sacred imagery and patterns that repeat across the continent of Neolithic Old Europe. Streep quotes Gimbutas as stating that, "ritual action" was "for communication with the divine, an evocation of the Goddess' regenerative powers hidden in stone." The iconography of the art encompasses the concepts of life, death, and regeneration, all realms of the Goddess. These concepts were represented in the imagery of the owl and snake, symbols of death and regeneration. The structure itself and orientation of the mound on a commanding location near the bend of the Boyne River (named after the Goddess Boand) are also suggestive of these ideas.

Some of the images are more abstract, but when studying them across the European continent a language and a consistent iconography begin to emerge. Triple snake coils that represent a triple life source are clearly carved on the stone at the main entrance at Newgrange. Just like at Neolithic Catal Hüyük, imagery begins to appear in groupings of threes. At Newgrange side cells, stone basins, engravings of triple snake spirals, coils, cartouches, and the brow ridge of the Owl Goddess are all revealed in triplicate. Gimbutas recognizes large snake coils engraved on orthostats associated with V's, M's, chevrons, and zigzag bands. She theorized that arcs, wavy lines, bands of zigzags and serpent forms were indicative of the belief in generative potential of water and the connection between the snake and the power of stone.

On the walls and curbstones at Newgrange imagery of triangles can be seen. Sometimes they are alone, other times encircled by arcs or in rows and pairs joined at the tip or at their base. Gimbutas explains these images are of the Goddess of

▲ The entrance to Newgrange is surrounded by giant boulders containing the spiral motif, a symbol of Goddess.

71

▲ Newgrange is womb and tomb of birth, death, and rebirth.

Death and Regeneration. Most interesting is her interpretation of the "serpent ship" imagery that is associated with the cult of the dead. At Newgrange the combination of zigzags or winding serpents (symbols of renewed life) joined to triangle or lozenge (both special signs of the Goddess of Regeneration) form abstract images of "serpent ships" literally interpreted as ceremonial ships associated with rituals of death, carrying the dead toward renewal. Time and lunar movements also seemed to be marked in stone carvings at Newgrange as Gimbutas describes sphere and snake coils representing a full moon, opposed crescents alone or with a snake coil in the middle depicting a moon cycle, and wavy lines of winding serpents measuring time. She states that serpentine forms with fourteen to seventeen turns represented the number of days the moon waxes, while up to thirty winding snake turns referred to a close approximation of the lunar month. With imagery representative of both sunlight and water, and the structure associated with death and rebirth, it might be conjectured that Neolithic practitioners incorporated both of these elements in their death ritual. Which brings theories back around to folk literature intermixed with a bit of whimsy.

What is known about ancient Ireland comes from the study of inscriptions, figurines and writings of the Romans. For the most part, Celtic literature was not common until the second millennium CE, so what came before is largely uncertain. It is accepted that Brigid embodied both aspects of water and fire (or light), and associations with the snake, whose origins trace to Neolithic times. Perhaps we should consider for a moment that she might be connected with Newgrange, with her imagery and her essence beginning to be understood and venerated within the rites practiced at this very mound. In addition, we should note that folk literature says the god Dagna, sometimes considered Brigid's consort, built Newgrange for himself and his sons. What if this is merely a patriarchal slant on the tale? It is fun to imagine if Dagna did in fact build Newgrange as a dramatic symbol of love for his consort, much in the same vein as Ramses who built the small Temple of Hathor at Abu Simbel for his great love Nefertari, or that other monument to love, the Taj Mahal.

Another version of folklore says the Gaelic name for the landscape around Newgrange, *Bru na Boinne*, is translated as, "the home of the Goddess of the River Boann." It states the River Boyne, (also Boinn or Board) very near Newgrange, is named for the Goddess Board (she of the white cows). Considered a primary Earth Goddess of ancient Ireland, Board is the personification of the bounty and life within water, or the equivalent of nourishing milk flowing from a sacred cow. Buvinda is a transliteration of Boyne, its contemporary Celtic name, which has been translated as "illuminated cow." The Celtic word also means brightness, white, and wisdom. In the River Boyne lives the wise salmon, like many fish associated with the Goddess. Similar to Eleusis, perhaps the priestesses and priests of the Goddess imparted the wisdom of life and death to their people during ritual at Newgrange. Legend says Boann and her consort Elemar were the first inhabitants of Newgrange until Elemar was replaced by Dagna, which brings us back again to Brigid. Might Boann have been an early aspect of Brigid? We already know Brigid had rivers named after her. The River Boyne was also noted for its healing powers, and Brigid is a Goddess of Healing. Certainly no definitive answers are possible, but many connections raise the eyebrow and elicit a thoughtful "ah-ha" from cultural diffusionists.

Getting to Newgrange

Newgrange is in the Boyne Valley which lies to the south of the N51 Drogheda-Navan Road, about 6 miles (10 km) west of Drogheda. Train or buses are options to Newgrange from Drogheda. The Knowth and Dowth mounds are found on the nearby road to Slane. There is also a human-made ritual pond called Monknewtown dating from prehistoric times within the Bru na Boinne complex which might warrant a look. If driving, consider a day trip from Dublin located 28 miles (45 km) south of the site. It is recommended calling ahead as there was discussion about limiting access to Newgrange's interior, however, there is a Visitor's Center on site. Walking around the grounds will reveal much of the imagery discussed. It is practically impossible to be within the mound on the solstice since people are wait-listed for years to experience the privilege, however, the powerful experience of the sun entering the chamber is reenacted by guides using a flashlight to give visitors some sense of the experience. Travelers might want to have a small container with them to collect waters from the River Boyne.

Goddess Focus
Sheila-na-Gigs

Sheila-na-Gigs, or Sheelas, are stone carvings of female genitalia found on the walls and doorways of primarily Celtic churches and monasteries of Western Europe and the British Isles, though similar imagery appears in Indonesia, South America, Australia, Oceania, and India. The actual purpose of Sheelas is not precisely known, though most contend they were icons or symbols of protection, much like the guardian gargoyles on Gothic cathedrals or the gorgon on Athena's shield. This author agrees with that premise suggesting that the symbol might have represented the concept that to be within the structure on which the Sheela is carved is tantamount to entering the sacred vulva, a gateway toward the safety of the womb of the Mother Goddess. It is has been argued that the figures might be symbols of exhibitionism due to their posture of squatting, reclining, or standing with legs akimbo with fully exposed yonis, but that hardly seems likely as they were found carved on sacred places. Rufus Camphausen has suggested possible connections to Baubo

▲ Sheila-na-Gigs uniformly feature the same theme ...

73

▲ ... a naked woman exposing her sacred yoni.

and Ama-no-Uzume, and raises another interesting theory that Sheelas are linked to Celtic or pre-Celtic versions of Oriental and Mediterranean sacred prostitutes. He offers the term nu-gag, meaning "the pure and immaculate ones" which referred to the sacred temple prostitutes of Mesopotamia as a possible linguistic clue to the origins of Sheila-na-Gigs.

Sheelas are often seen with the carved area of the yoni worn from the touch of many hands making contact with the image presumably in reverence or prayer. It calls to mind fertility symbols which certain cultures believe can bestow the gifts of abundance and children if touched. Author Shahrukh Husain puts forth the idea that the Sheela is associated with the Celtic Goddess Brigid and believes she may have been a symbol of the "split-off of the sexual aspect of a virginal goddess." Archaeologist Marija Gimbutas associated Sheelas with similar imagery of the spread-legged prehistoric Frog Goddess, the frog-headed Egyptian Goddess Haquit (Heket), and Hekate of ancient Greece who was called "Baubo," i.e. toad. Gimbutas claims names given for toad in European languages mean "witch" or "prophetess," and states the "toad was incarnated with the powers of the Goddess of Death and Regeneration, her functions were both to bring death and to restore life." At an archaeomythology conference in Madouri, Greece, Professor Joan Cichon reports scholars Miriam Robbins Dexter and Starr Goode believe the iconography of the Sheelas reflect the "Sovereignty Goddess" of the ancient Irish. Some contemporary females have begun turning up their noses at cultural taboos and adopting the brazen imagery of the Sheela to signify their empowerment, sexual liberation, and awareness of their connection to the Goddess.

ITALY

Sometimes Goddess can be found in a museum behind glass or in a busy city square, yet the essence and inspiration of the Divine Female pervades the entire fabric of Italy. In Rome, her obelisks sit in the Vatican's Saint Peter's Square and marks the location of ancient lyceums, or schools for learning Goddess mysteries. Just south of Sicily her statuary still resides in the megalithic temple structures of Malta. Walk into the Louvre in Paris or museums in Turin,

London, Naples, or Ankara and find statues, artifacts, and textiles depicting her from Paleolithic through contemporary times. She is shown in wondrous cave paintings from Lascaux, France, dating back to 15,000 BCE. She is also found in intimately touching palm-size artifacts such as the Venus of Willendorf (25,000 BCE) found in Austria. Tapestries such as the La Dame a la Licorne, The Lady and the Unicorn, found in the Cluny Museum of France, continue to inspire and suggest the profound beauty and essence of Goddess. All this awaits the intrepid pilgrim on their journey across Europe to sacred sites.

Pompeii

The city of Pompeii, partially unearthed from the fallout of the eruption of Mount Vesuvius in 79 CE provides a unique glimpse to a past frozen in time. When walking down the streets of Pompeii travelers can still read graffiti and advertisements on walls, admire mosaic tile floors, and take heed not to trip on the ruts in the stone streets left by carriage wheels. With a little imagination, one can hear and smell the activities of ages past. There are villas to explore, as well as stadiums, brothels, temples, and private homes. Even the remains of some poor individuals who did not escape the volcanic eruption are preserved for the curious to view.

The Temple of Isis is one of the best preserved structures in this vast city and stands out as a perfect example of Isis worship as it spread beyond Egypt to places in the Greco-Roman world. Immigrants, sailors, soldiers, merchants, and her priesthood of men and women all sang the praises of Isis throughout the Mediterranean region and Asia Minor. In these other countries she became intermingled with local deities. In fact Isis was so beloved throughout the known world that her worship for a time was in serious competition with other mystery religions, including the cult of Mithras and infant Christianity. According to R.

▲ The Isis Temple occupied "prime" real estate in Pompeii.

75

E. Witt in *Isis in the Ancient World*, "If Western civilization could have somehow developed on a matriarchal basis, Isis might have been too stubborn a mistress to dethrone."

When worship of Isis left the shores of Egypt, some aspects of her worship did change. Isis' consort was now the Ptolemaic hybrid god Serapis rather than the green-hued and exotic Osiris. Serapis was a Hellenized aspect of Osiris-Apis avoiding the Egyptian animal head depictions the Greeks and Romans misunderstood They did not understand these deities embodied the powers of the animals they reflected. Horus followed Isis out of Egypt as Harpocrates, and Anubis also made the journey. (There is an interesting statue of a Hellenized Anubis in the Vatican Museum which reminds visitors of the cartoon character Scooby Do.) While many other ancient Egyptian deities were fading in many countries, Isis sometimes had her own temple, or often shared a temple with a local goddess. Her temple was sometimes relegated to the outskirts of town in an area designated for foreign deities rather than being centrally located, such as her shrine at Delos. This however was not the case in Pompeii, a major Roman city adjacent to the port of Ostia where grain from Egypt arrived regularly to feed the country of Rome. Here the Isis temple sat on prime real estate!

Isis was very popular with many of the Roman elite and her temple in Pompeii was a focal point in the city and in the lives of many of its inhabitants. Worship of Isis in Pompeii included processions, a ritual practice which might have been an Egyptian creation. We know ritual processions were also practiced in Mesopotamia, making it hard to know where the practice developed first. But gone, even in Pompeii, are the vast temple estates built in the style of Egypt. On foreign soil, Isis temples called iseums, were more modest but still adhered to many Egyptian traditions. They consisted of an underground crypt below the above-ground temple structure. The crypt was for storage, ceremony, and ritual. The Nilometer was important in Egyptian temples because it measured the life-giving water level of the Nile upon which life, fertility, and prosperity depended. In Pompeii, it was still in use but was modified as a more symbolic device. Evidence points to some iseums and homes of Isian priesthood, such as the one belonging to Loreius Tiburtinus, which actually were designed with permanent water channels which could symbolically reenact the overflowing of the Nile flood waters. Though followers of the religion outside Egypt gradually became distanced from the original significance of Nile water, frescoes of processions and scenes on temple walls depict sacred ritual pitchers and situlas, or sacred pails, in use. Presumably these contained symbolic or actual Nile water which was carried or used in ritual — a more practical manner to incorporate the traditional importance of the Nile during Egyptian worship while away from the actual source.

In Pompeii, travelers can visit the Temple of Isis prominently located near a theater, the Forum, and the temple of Asclepius and Neptune in the public quarter, though Isis' temple was small by the standards of a typical modern Christian church. At the center of the sacred quadrangle compound was the temple. In front of the temple at ground level were several round columns. As one walked up the seven steps to the temple itself, there were three more round columns to the left and right before entering the pronaos, or front hall, which was a little less than 98 square feet (30 sq. m) in size. Beyond the pronaos was the inner chapel or cella which housed two pedestals for statues of Isis and Serapis. The building was decorated throughout with frescoes and depicted scenes of Isis and Io, practitioners in ritual, priests, flowery trellises, the mummy of Osiris, Anubis, Isis with an ankh, Perseus liberating Andromeda, Mars, and Venus. There were also several altars and niches.

On ground level a few meters from the temple was the Purgatorium where the Nile water was stored. Below this was an underground crypt or Megaron, presumably for initiations. To the rear of the temple were rooms for the Isian priesthood and meeting rooms for the initiates. From fresco scenes, it appears that men and women shared equal prominence in the priesthood of Isis. Priests were shown holding the caduceus alongside the priestess holding a baton, and both holding the sistrum, or ancient rattle. Priests and priestesses are both shown performing sacred duties. Engraved on a goblet is a priestess crowned with a serpent carrying a tray on which there is a cake, while the priest is depicted carrying a censer. Another goblet shows the priestess again with a serpent, carrying a sistrum and situla. The priest is carrying the hydeion, a long spouted pitcher usually used to carry Nile water.

As the worship of Isis grew outside Egypt, stories of other gods and goddesses stayed in Egypt and were not carried abroad. The myth of Isis and Osiris survived outside Egypt and the Egyptian traditions were taught to the masses via Isian festivals which became more public. One such public festival was the Ploiaphesia, or Sailing of the Ship of Isis, also called the Isidis Navigium, held every March 5th. This festival began in Egypt, but was also held in places such as Pompeii. It marked the beginning of the sailing season. The priesthood of Isis and large sections of the community participated in the ritual procession. Isis, who presides over the water, was invoked to bless the merchants and sailors so they might safely navigate the seas, trade with neighboring countries, and return home with the necessary items required for daily life. In Pompeii, as in most places honoring this holiday, the ritual ship, called the Ship of Isis, was launched out to sea as an offering to the Goddess after being loaded with gifts and prayers. Worship of Isis was at its height at the beginning of the third century CE. The mysteries

of the cult included secret rites, daily services, and many festivals in which all could participate. She was considered a wisdom Goddess with magical powers and insights into the mysteries of life and death. She became viewed as the *one* Goddess by many, expanding the more original Egyptian conception of a transcendent monotheism as indicated in the following inscription from Capua, *Una quae es omnia, dea Isis* or "Thou who, being one, art all, Goddess Isis."

While the cult of Isis grew in Pompeii among the slaves and families of freed men employed by the great houses of the wealthy, the worship of Isis in Pompeii gradually and firmly took hold of the aristocracy until it became the city's semi-official religion. Roman emperors had statues commissioned depicting them in Egyptian regalia in honor of Isis. Daughters of commoners and high

▲ Female imagery from a private residence in Pompeii may resemble Nike.

77

ranking government officials devoted their lives to Isis in the capacity of priestess. The wealthy had shrines in their gardens to honor her. We know this because the eruption of Mount Vesuvius on August 24, 79 CE left Pompeii remarkably well preserved for over 1,700 years. Modern archaeologists digging into the rubble discovered an almost perfectly captured glimpse into a moment of history.

The vast city of Pompeii was home to many Goddesses and temples of the Divine Feminine. Other fine restorations are the Villa of Mysteries, Temple of Venus, and Temple of Fortuna. Many frescoes are vibrant and give a glimpse into the artistry and color of these ancient days. The bordellos are also interesting, yet sad little cubicles and phallus symbols invoking fertility are found in abundance.

Getting to Pompeii

The ancient city of Pompeii is adjacent to the modern and friendly city of Pompei and is reached most easily by an organized tour, but can be reached by public train if one is up to the hassle of the Italian railroad system. Take the Circumvesuviana to the Pompeii-Villa dei Misteri stop, which is about a 30 minute ride from Naples. It leaves you outside the western entrance to the site. Another option is the Circumvesuviana to Pompei-Santuario station which is at the sites' eastern entrance. Tours and trains also leave from Rome for Pompei daily, and an entire day should be given to the site. There is a nice restaurant on the site to grab lunch or a cool drink and the restrooms are kept clean. Come prepared with hat, sunscreen and guidebook.

Rome

To choose only one site sacred to Goddess in the entire city of Rome is as impossible as eating only one potato chip! How can you stop at only one? One simply cannot. So many places cry out "Goddess," readers will benefit from this author's zeal for all the sites about to be mentioned. So, as they say in New Orleans, get ready to receive a bit of *lagniappe*, or a little something extra, as travelers discover more than 10 sites in one! Jump onboard as the bus pulls out for a city tour of the sacred sites of Goddess in Rome!

First Stop — **Palatine Hill.** Adjacent to the Colosseum, the Palatine Hill was once the site of elite residences in ancient Rome. From the word *palatine* the word "palace" in the English language is derived. The Palatine Hill has seen a lot of history. For instance, according to Roman historians, the Emperor Caligula was stabbed here. The Temple of Cybele, dedicated in 191 BCE, was built here by the edicts of the Sibyls who insisted Rome would not defeat Hannibal unless the meteorite of Cybele traveled to the city. She came to Palatine Hill, Hannibal lost, and the people of Rome reveled in the experience of wild and weird festivities in honor of Cybele. In ensuing years conservatives of Rome frowned upon the chaotic celebrations which venerated both Cybele and Attis. Some ancient writers speculate the Sibylline Books of prophecy were housed on the hill but destroyed in a fire. During the annual theatrical games, the famous playwrights, Terence and Plautus premiered many of their most popular comedies on a wooden stage erected directly in front of Temple of Cybele. The tufa podium of this temple dedicated to the Great Mother still survives, located south of the Farnese Gardens and just west of House of "Livia." The foundation of temple stones dedicated to Victory and Victoria Virgo ("Maiden Victory") also grace the hill. Once featuring tall slender Corinthian columns, the shrine was decked with fabulous

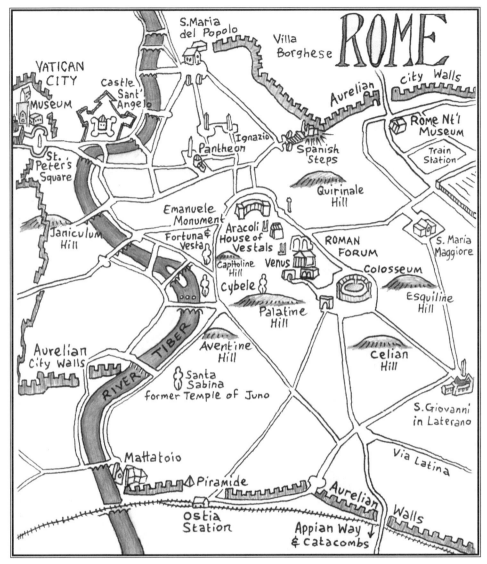

floors of red and white breccia rosa, pink-grey Chian marble and black slate. The pediment, in turn, was decorated with a throne at the center, reclining figures holding tympana and felines on each corner of the triangle. Among the discoveries at the site was an enthroned goddess, once flanked by lions and now headless. The ancient Street of Victory passed through a tunnel below the substructure of this temple complex. According to Tertullian (160-225 CE), a shrine dedicated to the Magna Mater was also positioned directly in the middle of the famous Circus Maximus directly below the southern brow of Palatine Hill. Ancient coins reveal a giant statue of her on the spina of this circus, wearing a mural crown, riding sidesaddle, and surrounded by lions. The Palatine Hill is a labyrinth of ruins dedicated to many gods and goddesses. Also on Palatine Hill are the Basilica or Aula of Isis and a Temple dedicated to Venus. Just bring a map because the site is not well marked and the on-site staff is less than helpful.

▲ This obelisk marks the location of the former Iseum of Rome.

Across the street from Palatine Hill is the **Roman Forum** with many fragments of Goddess temples, such as the Temples of Venus, Vesta, and the House of the Vestals, though none are totally intact. Vesta can be described as the living feminine flame of Rome, or its divine essence. Votive offerings to Vesta, Goddess of the Hearth date back to 575 BCE. The once circular structure is believed to be symbolic of an ancient Latin hut wherein princesses of ancient tribes kept the fire of the tribe lit. In ancient Rome, it was believed that the fires of the Roman Temple of Vesta were lit from the embers of Her temple in Troy. Temple vestal priestesses were charged with keeping the fires of Rome aglow, and they did this service for 1,100 years. The vestal priestesses also kept the Seven Holy of Holies of Rome protected and preserved. These sacred relics included the Palladium, a wooden statue of Pallas Athena which was supposed to have fallen from heaven then brought to Rome from Troy; a terra-cotta chariot from Veii; the ashes of Orestes; a needle used by the Mother of Gods; the shields of Salii; the 12 Leaping Priests of Mars; the scepter of Priam; and the veil of Ilione. Failure to keep the fires burning or to protect these relics would result in calamity for the city, or so the Romans believed. Punishment for failing these tasks could result in flogging, banishment, or even death.

While the term "virgin" goddess usually does not refer to being of a chaste state, but rather an unmarried female, independent and unto herself, virginity was a literal requirement for Vestal Virgins. Punishment for a Vestal Virgin who lost her virginity was inhumation according to the ancient writer Ovid, "Nor will it be said that under (the emperor's) leadership any priestess violated her sacred fillets, and none shall be buried alive in the ground. It is thus that an unchaste (Vesta) perishes because that (Earth) which she violated, in that earth she is interred; and indeed Earth and Vesta are the same deity." Scholar Miriam Robbins Dexter gives context for chastity being so important in Roman society. Chastity was considered irrevocable, though they left a little wiggle-room for parthenogenesis, or birth through a mother without male participation. Chaste Vestal Virgins were a storehouse of untapped energy, like a charged battery, and it was their job to impart their sacred energy for the good of Rome. Dexter continues, "if a woman was neither virgin nor married, she became a threat to the patriarchal, patrilinear establishment, because she became autonomous. Any woman who took control of her own sexuality, in Rome as in other male-centered societies, was both condemned and feared by those societies."

Moving away from the Forum toward the Tiber River, off the beaten path, are two fully intact houses of worship of the Feminine Divine, namely, the **Temples**

▲ The temples of the Vestal Virgins and Fortuna reside not far from the Roman Forum.

of Vesta and **Fortuna**. The Temple of Vesta is a circular building, and a few yards away, the Temple of Fortuna, Goddess of Destiny, who is often commingled with Isis, is venerated in a temple which resembles a mini-Parthenon. These are two of the best preserved Goddess temples in Rome. Encircled by Corinthian columns, the round temple was spared only because it was converted into a church first referred to as "Saint Stephen of the Carriages" in 1132 CE. Across the street is the **Church of Santa Maria in Cosmedin**, the basilica where nuns used to hand out bread to the poor. The church has been associated with the Greek community here in Rome since the 8th century and the title "Cosmedin" may refer to the city "Constantinople." In ancient times, this structure was dedicated to the Roman Goddess Ceres, from where we derive our word "cereal." The church, reported to have an underground tunnel leading to the Temple of Vesta across the street, emits a discernible "Goddess energy" within according to Goddess advocates, described as a evokes a warm, welcoming, and safe feeling, almost like walking within a literal Sheila-na-Gig, or womb. Lacking the gold gilding and busy facades usually cluttering many Christian churches in Europe, the clean and simple architectural lines of this basilica evokes a mysterious, "out-of-the-way" atmosphere, almost as if this place was a neglected step-child of the Church. The walls are nearly barren, punctuated by a few fading floral murals, and large chandeliers suspend from the ceiling with candle holders. Entering the cool, dark, stillness of this church, the sounds and chaotic energy of the city disappear and the presence of the Goddess is said to be palpable. On the floor of the church are symbols suggestive of sacred geometry and some see the four elements and spirit within the design. Behind the main altar is an image of what appears to be wheat, symbolic of the goddess Ceres. She was worshipped in Rome during her festival, the Cerealia on April 19th, and also celebrated in the Circus Maximus near Palatine Hill. It seems, according to Rufus and Lawson, a part of the original temple of Ceres still remains in the church, though locked away from public view. If visitors have the time it is well worth visiting San Nicola in Carcere, located just northwest of Santa Maria in Cosmedin and directly across from Tiber Island. This 11th century church stands on the site of the temple dedicated to Juno Sospita (the Savior). Seven of the columns from the first century BCE temple are still extent on the south side including part of the entablature above them. The ancient podium is in excellent condition where Juno Sospita was praised as a warrior Goddess.

Roughly occupying where **Santa Sabina** stands today (as verified by two dedicatory inscriptions discovered nearby), the Temple of Juno Regina was the most famous shrine dedicated to Goddess in Rome. Following the destruction of the last Etruscan stronghold of Veii in 396 BCE, the Roman dictator Furius Camillus removed their patron goddess and brought the ancient wooden figure to this site on Aventine Hill. Later, in 207 BCE, two statues of Juno Regina fashioned out of cypress wood were set up in the temple. On coins, Juno Regina is often depicted beside Jupiter holding a long scepter and patera. She is usually veiled as a queen, wearing a diadem and accompanied by a peacock. Most of the offerings to her were given by women, including a bronze statue (in 218 BCE) and a golden basin (in 207 BCE). Peculiar to Juno Regina on the Aventine hill was her direct association with Diana, the Goddess of the Moon and Hunt, an identity no doubt influenced by her Etruscan roots. As a result, Diana became Juno's hostess as the deity presiding over asylum (a characteristic foreign to the Latin Diana, but not the Diana/Artemis of Asia Minor). Meanwhile, via this association, Juno herself becoming both savior and protectress. The simple Church of Santa Sabina was founded on the site in 422 CE, but most of this basilica dates from the 9th century, having fine white Corinthian columns lining the nave. The Dominicans inherited the church in the 13th century.

No trip to Rome is complete without visiting **Santa Maria Maggiore**, the grand Roman basilica dedicated to Mary as "Mother of God." According to legend, the Virgin Mary appeared to Pope Liberius and instructed him to build a church precisely where he saw a patch of snow the next day. Since Rome was currently experiencing one of their typical hot summers, the fact that he found snow at the summit of the Esquiline Hill the next morning (on August 5th) was thought a miracle indeed! In commemoration of this event, every year thousands of white petals are released from the ceiling of the church to "snow" upon the awaiting congregation below. While in the past these were rose petals, they are now usually petals from dahlias. After the church Council at Ephesus in 431, when Mary was declared as giving birth to God (theotokos), Pope Sixtus III (from 432-440 CE) dedicated a new basilica on the spot. The triple nave is part of this original 5th century basilica. Most of the mosaics in the apse are devoted to the Virgin Mary and made by Jacopo Toritti around 1295. What is curious is his preoccupation with natural themes, scenes of birds nesting, flowers blooming, animals crawling and everywhere a splendor of vegetation. At the center of this cornucopia of natural splendor is a medallion depicting the Coronation of Mary by Christ amongst a canopy of golden stars. Just to the north of Santa Maria Maggiore on the Esquiline Hill, stood the Temple of Juno Lucina upon the minor Cispian Hill. At first a sacred grove, the precinct finally received a temple dedicated in 375 BCE. Pliny the Elder states that two ancient lotus trees, pre-dating the temple, were venerated within the gardens. Every March 1st, the Feast of the Matronalia was celebrated here. All wives were expected to receive presents on this day from their husbands. Juno Lucina was closely associated with a birth cult, but not much else is known of her. And some think Hallmark created Mother's Day!

The **Church of Santa Maria in Aracoli**, on an ancient site formerly a temple of Cybele and Juno Moneta, has within the church a multitude of Goddess symbols. A bull (associated with Osiris and Adonis) crowned with a star on the marble floor, and high atop the entrance wall of the church is a stained glass depiction of three bees. The number three was sacred and bees were associated with Persephone, Demeter, and Artemis, as well as Cybele. The priestesses of Demeter were also called *melissae*, or bees. The Temple of Juno Moneta was originally vowed to be built in honor of this goddess by the Roman dictator Furius Camillus during the war with Aurunci in 345 BCE and dedicated the next year on June 1st. A mint was established within the temple in 273 BCE, hence the epithet, "Moneta." According to Anneli Rufus and Kristan Lawson, another story states the future Roman Emperor Octavian, later known as Augustus, is believed to have seen an apparition of a "beautiful lady" here who asked him to build her a shrine. He did and the rest is history. Augustus went on to enjoy unrivaled success and power. Later on the Church claimed the lady he saw was the Virgin Mary, even though the vision happened before the birth of Jesus. Within the church is a chapel for the Bambino, the Christ child. Cards and letters can be seen on the altar from the devoted who are asking that their petitions be granted. Goddess advocates visiting the church see the Christ as representing Horus, the son of Isis, or a young Attis, the son of Cybele who had a temple on this hallowed spot. The church facade was completely rebuilt in the late 13th century, while the grand steps before the basilica were made in thanksgiving for deliverance from a devastating plague in 1348. Twenty-two of the columns on either side of the nave date from ancient times, some of them sculpted from Aswan granite. Just to the south of the steps leading to the Church of Santa Maria in Aracoli is the famous graded ramp leading up to the Piazza del Campidoglio, situated at

▲ Diana the huntress played a prominent role among Roman Goddesses.

the crown of the ancient Capitoline Hill, once dominated by a massive temple dedicated to Jupiter. Of particular interest along this 16th century ramp are two black granite crouching lions standing proudly at the base. Originally from Egypt (perhaps dating to the 4th or 3rd century BCE), the emperor Domitian (81-96 CE) brought the two lions to Rome in order to decorate the Temple of Isis on the Field of Mars.

The Egyptian Goddess Isis had a strong following among the common folk and elite in Rome. She was so revered that it was speculated for a time whether the Isian faith or Christianity would spread as the world religion. Isis' popularity stemmed from several facts. Her Egyptian mysteries promised immortality after death, but also key to her popularity was her accessibility. Far from the image of a vengeful and unapproachable male God, her aspects as an all powerful mother and wife familiar with affliction in her life similar to her devotees, caused devotees to believe she would understand their needs and answer their prayers. One important devotee of Isis was the Emperor Domitian, who built Isis temples and shrines in and around Rome. Domitian was obsessed with his own disposition after death and built an Iseum of Isis roughly where the **Piazza del Collegio Romano** is today. Three obelisks, one in front of the Pantheon in the Piazza della Rotunda, another in the Piazza Navona, and the third atop the back of an elephant in the Piazza della Minerva are from the Iseum Campestre, which was at a time as important as Saint Peter's Basilica. The obelisk riding aboard the elephant in the Piazza della Minerva dates to the year 6 BCE. Interestingly, atop all the obelisks, including the one in Saint Peter's Square in Vatican City, sits a Christian cross. Absent any official explanation for the positioning of these crosses, some have conjectured their position shows an attempt of symbolic domination of Christianity over paganism.

▲ Sandaled foot of Serapis from the temple of Isis or Serapis.

The **Iseum Campestre** of Isis still lies beneath the churches of Santa Maria Sopra Minerva and Saint Ignazio, with a Temple of Minerva beneath the Iseum. Ironically, this church dedicated to Mary retained the epithet of the goddess formerly worshipped at the site. The Temple of Isis, once occupying the site where the Jesuit Saint Ignazio now stands, was rebuilt by Domitian after the fire of 80 CE and was said to have been handsomely embellished with statues by Alexander Severus (222-235 CE). A flight of stairs leading up the front entrance was comprised of a facade of four Corinthian columns surmounted by a deep lunate pediment containing a statue of Isis Sothis seated on a dog running to the right. Within the inner shrine was a standing statue of Isis. The Iseum was in close proximity to the Serapeum, or Temple of Serapis, her consort, positioned just beyond a broad doorway divided into bays by three columns. The Serapeum was a separate building, rectangular in shape, with monumental entrances situated along the square that once contained the Temple of Minerva. The sacred precinct of Serapis was known as the hangout of the libertines. To the right of the church, if one takes a slight detour up the Via del Pie' di Marmo one will find a colossal marble foot at the corner of Via S. Stefano del Cacco. This sandaled foot is thought to have belonged to the Iseum or Serapeum which stood nearby, and quite possibly could have been that of Serapis. By the time of Caligula the Isis cult was firmly entrenched within Rome, however prior leaders such as Augustus, Agrippa, and Tiberius tried to repress the cult. Tiberius was rumored to have taken an image of Isis and thrown it into the Tiber River, though the authenticity of that tale is hard to substantiate. Isis became a universal Goddess considered a savior to the people who adored their Mistress of Magic and Wisdom. One graffito from an Isian sanctuary in Rome declared: *Te Isis, te salus ad tuos* or "Thou Isis, thou art salvation to thy followers." Today devotees of Isis who walk the narrow stone streets as ancient devotees have done centuries earlier, discover the foundations on which the Isis temples once stood, report a sense of her red cord of life connecting them to the web of life and her worship, past and present, near and far.

Last Stop — **Vatican Museum**, with all the rumor and innuendo about what might be housed in the vaults, it is not to be missed. Artifacts of goddesses are so varied and numerous, it is almost as delicious as a visit to the Louvre in Paris. Hundreds of Greek, Roman, and Asian goddess statues await the traveler, as do paintings in the Borgia Apartments associated with the Goddess Isis. The Egyptian section is particularly wonderful with unique statuary not found in other museums. Seated Sekhmet statues can be found in outdoor gardens and casually placed outside gift shops.

Getting to Rome's City Tour of Goddess Sites

Getting around Rome is easy. Travelers who are not on organized tours can ride the subway which has stops at key locations and tourist sites, many of which are described above. For instance, the stop at the Coliseum will easily give one access to Palatine Hill and the Roman Forum. Armed with a good map and walking shoes, pilgrims can easily make their way around the city on foot. Just watch for pickpockets. It is recommended visitors allow a day for the Forum, Palatine Hill, and nearby Temples of Vesta, Fortuna and the Church of Santa Maria in Cosmedin, which are within walking distance of each other. The Vatican Museum can easily require a full day as well. If time will allow for another day in the area, a few easy and recommended excursions outside Rome are the archaeological city of Ostia Antica, Tivoli Gardens, and the Villa of Hadrian — all with Goddess connections.

MALTA

Dutch scholar Veronica Veen, with theories that break away from traditional thought, indicates Malta was one of the most marked centers of the cult of the Great Goddess and claims the megalithic temples as a kind of "multifunctional cultural center." While present day Malta is very conservative and Roman Catholicism is the state religion, with almost as many churches on the islands as days of the year, it seems to be quite a paradox that Veen finds the culture, visual arts, crafts, and stories imbued with the feminine. One tasty example is a local delicacy that would certainly catch the eye of Goddess advocates — the vulva-shaped savory ricotta cheese cakes called "pastizzi." Another is the baking of special loaves of bread for holidays. Making lace is another local craft particularly associated with roles of women in Malta. These and other of Veen's findings might indicate a connection between Goddess cultures of the Neolithic Age and the contemporary lives of women on Malta. The ancient Goddess energy is manifested today in the deep devotion to Mary of the Maltese. Her image is found throughout both Malta and Gozo, with two feast days of the Madonna (August 15th and September 8th) recognized as national holidays. In fact, the healing shrine of Our Lady of Mellieha in the town of the same name, complete with *milagros,* or votive offerings, prayers, x-rays, and crutches, shows the tremendous veneration and gratitude for petitions answered. Once a matriarchy, (in this context defined as a society in which women dominated, not ruled), changing priorities and economic necessity have diluted these traditions here in Malta.

Ggantija

To goddess advocates, there is probably no better literal representation of Goddess within the landscape than the monuments which venerate her on the small islands of Malta, located just south of Sicily. The temple structure of Ggantija, situated on a prominent plateau on the island of Gozo, is dated to 3000-3600 BCE making this one of the oldest free-standing stone structures on Earth. With Newgrange, it ranks as one of the two most impressive prehistoric monuments in Europe. Unique to Maltese temples such as the double-temple of Ggantija, (pronounced GEE gan tee ya), is its particular form, which contemporary Goddess advocates intuitively recognize as a silhouette of two female bodies — some say mother and daughter, or dual aspects of Goddess. Advocates

▲ A "Fat Lady" of Malta.

identify a larger body, presumably the mother, and a smaller one, possibly the daughter, each with head, breasts, hips, and vulva. The fullness of the "bodies" is very much in keeping with the voluptuous female artifacts found on Malta, lovingly referred to at times as the Fat Ladies.

The human occupation of Malta began 7,000-8,000 years ago with inhabitants from what we know today as Sicily. Very little is known about the ancient temple builders, even though excavations have been going on since the late 1800s. One reason for the uncertainty is Maltese sites were excavated or emptied without using proper archaeological techniques that would reveal clues to the history of early inhabitants. Curiously, local legends tell of a female builder (some say giantess) who — with a baby at her breast — single-handedly built Ggantija stone by stone in one day, leaving the stone wall to finish that night. Now that's a powerful Goddess! Stories such as these instilled pride and esteem among the people. What devotees of Goddess believe about the temples is based on intuition, artifacts, folklore, and the imagery on the monuments deciphered by archaeologists such as Marija Gimbutas. Symbols such as spirals and animal imagery, repeated throughout Europe, are among the repertoire that many have come to recognize as the *language of the Goddess*, a theory explained in her book of the same title, which is somewhat of a controversy within academic circles. Many archaeologists do not agree with Gimbutas' conclusion and believe scholars should refrain from inferring religious or cultural meaning to artifacts, and should instead only catalog them. Nor do some agree with the theories similar to veronica Veen.

The megalithic stones which are assembled to form temples such as Ggantija weigh many tons. These Neolithic temples are thought to have begun as smaller one-room cellas, or chapels, and eventually expanded into connecting rooms until the rounder shape of the "female" was achieved. If one accepts these feminist theories just looking at some of the monuments built in her honor, created by seeming unfathomable means for their time, and by people using only stone tools, speak volumes toward understanding the magnitude of devotion which Goddess inspired. It is thought the stones were rolled into place using stone balls beneath the megaliths. In fact, some stone balls have been found at Maltese archaeological sites. In actuality, it probably took the inhabitants of the island hundreds of years to complete the temples. Goddess practitioners believe the pale off-white colored megalithic stone temples have been built to reflect the body of the Mother Goddess and were, in their opinion, probably considered sacred places where the natural processes of life were venerated. Life, death, and rebirth,

▲ Hagar Qim, like Ggantija, is a megalithic temple featuring rounded corners and womb-like enclosures.

themes associated with Goddess, were in all likelihood the major focal points in the lives of these ancient people.

What we know about the people who lived on Malta during the time these magnificent structures were built is that they sometimes buried their dead in the fetal position and used red ochre in burial sites. These agricultural people lived in caves and huts, used no metal, and had no weapons. Scholars believe their religious life was their inspiration and focus. Near Ggantija is the Xaghara (shara) stone circle, a prehistoric underground burial temple where beautiful stylized votive grave goods and Goddess figurines were found, including a double goddess statue covered in red ochre. Peg Streep, quoting other scholars, speculates that these temples may have been an oracular center. Gimbutas theorized the double image of the female, or Goddess, represented mother and daughter in their aspects of death and regeneration. We are reminded of Demeter and Persephone who together represent two aspects of a woman's life, namely, maiden and mother. This is further substantiated from the snake design incised on the temple walls which Gimbutas has deciphered to represent regeneration.

The series of temples at Ggantija were first excavated in 1827 and many of them date back as early as 2800 BCE. The Ggantija temple type is characterized by slightly concave facades, flanked by two upright stones (called "orthostats"), a large slab and, finally, a special stone featuring a bowl-shaped indention intended as a foot-washing basin. Some of the coralline limestone facades can rise as high as 20 feet (7 m). Upon entering the vulva-like opening of the "mother" temple at Ggantija, looking left and right one sees rounded rooms or apses which form the hips of the female form. As at the other temples, the interior walls are made of globigerina limestone, much softer than coralline. Continuing forward through her narrow waist area, one comes to a central space with rounded rooms to the front, left, and right which form her breasts and head. Throughout are altars, niches, stone slabs, a hearth, and basin. The main altar has two holes that were likely for draining an animal's blood after sacrifice. The two apse-like rooms located at the very rear of this temple may have been a kind of sacred quarter or "holy of holies." The "daughter" temple is very similar, though smaller in size. Unfortunately, much of the central hall and altar are reduced to rubble. Both are totally encircled by a stone wall. It does not take a lot of imagination to intuit the initiation or rites of

▲ The Sleeping Lady statue was found buried in a ceremonial pit at the Hypogeum.

passage ceremonies which might have taken place within these temples. Many of the temples were equipped with libation and oracle holes.

Recent excavations at Brochtoroff Circle, which was integrated by the builders with Ggantija Temple only 990 feet (300 m) away, is revealing tantalizing clues about the lives of the early island inhabitants. New competing evidence suggests to archaeologists Malone, Bonanno, Goulder, Stoddart and Trump, the early culture of Malta evolved over time into an elaborate cult of the dead. Beginning first with small single family graves and burials, in time the inhabitants seemed to develop elaborate rituals of death and hundred of bodies were now being buried together at one site. Eventually burials were replaced by cremation. These scholars hypothesize that the religion of the people included a Mother Goddess, but may have gone beyond that idea as indicated by the number of animal and male motifs also present. Other working theories suggest the demise of these people was related to economic and environmental pressures, as well as their isolation thought to be imposed by their religious leaders. Evidence seems to suggest obsession with temple cults may have distracted them from farming, trade or other activities that might have helped stabilize their society. Obviously much work remains to be done and there is much discussion and controversy about the interpretation of archaeological findings.

It should be noted that when traveling to Malta, this author found out first hand that visitors cannot generally expect to learn of the female herstory, so do your homework. Some tour guides nowadays tell unsuspecting visitors the large headless "fat ladies" who were once found in the temples, now housed in the National Archaeological Museum in Valletta, are like sumo wrestlers! Okay, the lady is corpulent, but she is wearing a skirt! It also might be interesting to note some scholars cite evidence for the worship of the Goddess Astarte and Tanit in some sacred sanctuaries within Malta.

Getting to Ggantija

The island of Malta is rather small, only 25 miles (40 km) long. The Ggantija temple is found on the smaller island of Gozo, accessible from Malta by ferry or helicopter. Driving around the islands is not easy and confusing at best. The Maltese drive on the left side of the road and have the highest number of traffic accidents in Europe! There are regular flights to Malta from London, as well as other European cities. When on Malta, be sure to visit the newly renovated UNESCO World Heritage site, the Hal Saflieni Hypogeum, a three-story underground "womb" of the Mother decorated with red ochre spirals. Visitors can also check out www.heritagemalta.org for more information. The Hypogeum can be reached by buses departing from the main terminal in Valletta. It is here the famous Sleeping Lady artifact was found suggesting one ancient practice was dream incubation. The Lady is now safely sleeping in the National Archaeological Museum on Republic Street in Valletta.

PORTUGAL

As much as the Church would have liked the Goddess to wither away, She only became more potent in Her many guises. Her essence lived in the writings of courtly love mingled with metaphysical expressions of union with God written by female Christian mystics such as Hildegard of Bingen or Mechthild of Magdeburg, known as the Beguines of Holland and Belgium (1100-1300 CE). Her mysteries were kept alive in the symbology of the Holy Grail chalice, the Lady and the Unicorn, and in tarot decks. Her memory fueled the inspiration of the dedicated: so-called heretic artists, troubadours, the Order of the Knights Templar, the Cathars, and Merovingians. Pilgrimages to Goddess' "veiled" holy sites became all the rage across France, Germany, and Spain. The popularity of "Goddess" in Fátima, Portugal is still readily apparent. The Feminine Divine was recognized as Sophia, or Wisdom, within Christianity, a concept still very much in vogue today, within Gnosticism, Orthodox Christianity, Kabala and Neo-Pagan groups who have kept alive or rekindled her rituals and provided a container for her further reemergence.

Fátima

On May 13th, 1917 a female apparition, presumed by most to be the Virgin Mary appeared to three illiterate shepherd children, ages ten to thirteen, who simultaneously saw her image standing within the branches of an oak tree in Cova da Iria, near Fátima. She reappeared in the same oak tree on the 13th of the month for several consecutive months. During these visits, only the children could see or hear her, and in each visitation she communicated with them, sometimes asking them to pray for world peace and for the end of World War I that was raging in Europe. At the July apparition the Virgin Mary shared three secrets with the children, and although versions of the story differ their prophecies are believed to have come true. One foretold the death of two of the three children, the second warned of the

▲ The religious city of Fátima hosts five million visitors per year.

coming of World War II, and the third secret is believed to have been a warning of the attempted assassination of Pope John Paul II in 1981. Mary also declared herself to be "Our Lady of the Rosary," instructing the children to recite the rosary on a daily basis.

Between the time of the first and sixth apparition, the authorities heard of the events and put pressure on the children to recant their stories, though none of the children would, even under threat of bodily harm. Finally, months later, on October 13th, 1917, the Divine appeared for the last time. It is said there were 70,000 pilgrims in attendance, all anxiously standing there in the rain, awaiting a sign. Unlike previous appearances, in this apparition, known as the "Miracle of the Sun," all who gathered witnessed her presence and the mysterious phenomena that accompanied the Lady. At high noon, the downpour suddenly stopped, and the sun began to swirl in the sky sending bright rays of light dancing in all directions until witnesses swear the ball of light darted off toward the eastern skies. Some say the ground shook beneath them. Others claim the swirling ball of light dried the wet clothes on their back. The Divine Feminine was said to have identified herself as Mary, and asked that a church be built in her honor. Some believe this miracle at Fátima helped the Church stem the tide toward secularization that was rising in Portugal, and others have suggested the event worked against the rise of communism. Politics aside, the apparition site continued to draw pilgrims for years. A bridge was built on the site, followed by a chapel, until in 1921 the existing basilica was erected which has been described as a 7-ton (6,350-kg) bronze crown supporting a huge crystal cross. Goddess devotees often embrace the symbols of the Goddess embodied within the apparitions. The lady giving prophecies, called the Virgin Mary by Christians, is believed by many to be the Goddess herself. Trees have long been sacred to Goddess going back to the time of Asherah, Inanna, and Isis in the Middle East, continuing with Artemis, Diana and the Druid clans. The Goddess is also associated with the sun, reflected in her guise as Japan's Amaterasu, Egypt's Isis, Sekhmet, Bast and Hathor, as well goddesses in the Celtic pantheon.

Even more important than iconography, the Shrine of Fátima has come to represent to Goddess devotees the power of the Feminine Divine to open her arms and encourage all people of all faiths to come together under one roof. This was proven possible at Fátima on November 1st, 2003 when the Portuguese News reported on the common vision for Fátima shared by delegates attending the Vatican and United National Annual Interfaith Congress entitled, "The Future of God." Monsignor Luciano Guerra, rector of Fátima, addressed people of non-Christian faiths stating, "The future of Fátima, or the adoration of God and his Mother at this holy shrine must pass through the creation of a shrine where different religions can mingle. The inter-religious dialogue in Portugal, and the Catholic Church, is still in an embryonic phase, but the Shrine of Fátima is not indifferent to this fact and is already open to being a universalist place of vocation." The article stated Guerra reached out to Muslims as he illustrated the obvious fact that Fátima was also the name of Mohammed's daughter, an indication the shrine must be open to all faiths. Guerra closed by saying, "Therefore we must assume that it was the will of the Blessed Virgin Mary that this comes about this way." Considering Goddess devotees often recognize the Holy Spirit as Sophia, Goddess of Wisdom, it is particularly interesting to note the comments of another theologian quoted as saying, "The other religious traditions in the world are part of God's plan for humanity, and the Holy Spirit is operating and present in Buddhist, Hindu, and other sacred writings of Christian and non-Christian faiths as well."

Though the comments from the delegation drew a fire storm of protest from traditional Catholics causing some back-peddling from Vatican spokespeople, the Shrine of Fátima continues to win the hearts and minds of people drawn there, no matter their faith. Veneration at the shrine is reminiscent of that at many Black Madonna and Guadalupe shrines where the predominant pilgrim is female. Women can be seen crawling to the shrine, giving thanks for prayers answered, praying for boons yet to be granted. The atmosphere is one of folk tradition closely connected with the Earth. Located on the site beside the basilica and plaza is the

▲ The tradition of Black Madonna worship spans the European continent.

Chapel of the Apparition, and another shrine where Mary had appeared for the fourth time. The famous oak tree is believed to be in front of the basilica. If readers are wondering what became of the three children, two died as predicted by the Lady during the 1918-1920 flu epidemic, and Lucia Santos left Fátima in 1926 to become a Carmelite nun at Coimbra. Lucia wrote two accounts of her visions between 1936 and 1942, declaring within what she believed was the "Threefold Message of Fátima," specifically Penance, reciting the rosary, and the full "Devotion to the Immaculate Heart of Mary." The Vatican authenticated the miracle of the visitations in 1930, however, it was not until 1960 that they permitted Lucia's "full secret" to be revealed and published. It should be noted for the sake of accuracy, some aspects of the story have Lucia seeing an apparition of a male spirit prior to that of the Lady of Fátima. And not all goddess advocates, especially those who call themselves "recovering Catholics," embrace Mary as the Divine Feminine or the veiled icon which kept the Sacred Feminine alive during the time when belief in goddess could result in one's death.

Getting to Fátima

Fátima is located in west-central Portugal, in the region of Leiria, approximately 87 miles (140 km) north-northeast of Lisbon. Buses run frequently between Lisbon and Fátima, a rural village, home to one of the most visited shrines dedicated to the Virgin Mary. Another option to reach Fátima is the train. From Lisbon, take the train to Chao de Macas located 12.5 miles (20 km) outside Fátima. From here, a 20-minute bus ride will drop visitors off in Fátima.

TURKEY

Sacred sites seem to have been chosen for their locations. Bounded by mountains, perhaps within energy grids, near fertile plains or close to water, earth energy seems to radiate out from these places and feed the human soul. Ephesus, a holy place of the Great Mother Goddess resides adjacent to Mount Pion, near a river, and the sea. Even today, one can appreciate how the magical and protective powers of Artemis reached out like a cord from her temple on the outskirts of Ephesus, connecting to the city and her people along the Via Sacra, or Sacred Way. Certainly in Aphrodiasis, Turkey, it is difficult to stand in the fertile valley sacred to Aphrodite as it blooms with the lush growth of red poppies and surrounded by the adjacent snow-capped mountains and not feel within the embrace of the Earth Mother. Is it any surprise that the ruins of her temple are beside a natural spring? Visitors who venerate the Feminine Divine have been heard to come home sharing the discovery of a powerful nurturing energy from this site radiating like a beacon. This author knows travelers who have discovered the power of the Mother after meditating before sacred trees, taking a dip in sacred ponds, or awakening from a nap at a power site. Goddess, as the Mistress of Animals, has even been thought to manifest peculiar behavior in animals — particularly in birds and cats that are encountered on these pilgrimages and tours.

Catal Hüyük

Never have so few physical remains at a site spoken such volumes! And these remains say different things to various scholars. According to some, this 32-acre (13-ha) archaeological site dates back to an ancient Goddess-centered civilization that illuminates the potential of what a great society can be. Rather than look to Classical Greece, social anthropologists and archaeologists also point to earlier Catal Hüyük for alternatives to structuring society. Here is one of the best examples of one of the world's first urban cultures of the Neolithic period (6500-3500 BCE). Scholar Marija Gimbutas and archaeologist James Mellaart unearthed the remains of this peaceful agricultural civilization absent of military dominance and class hierarchies. Inhabitants appear to have been a sophisticated people with specialized skills of carving, weaving, spinning, cultivation of crops, building, pottery, cloth dyeing, and basket weaving.

Within the burial sites, which reveal so much about the social organization of a culture, were found no weapons of war, though we know they did smelt copper and lead by 6400 BCE. Burial sites of many different people contained similar artifacts. Mellaart's excavations revealed little evidence of social stratification and determined that society was organized around a religion focused on the Goddess who represented all aspects of life. He believed Goddess was worshipped in numerous shrines rather than at a central temple. These shrines accounted for one-third of the total number of structures. Both shrines and houses were about 82 square feet (25 sq. m) in size. Shrines can be distinguished from residences by ornate decorations, particularly with depictions of the horns of a bull or bucranium. This imagery directly links Catal Hüyük with contemporary civilizations of Old Europe and the Minoan-Mycenaean cultures (see Knossos, page 50).

Within the shrines, the Goddess is sometimes represented by a pillar and the bull's horns reflect her regenerative powers. She is also drawn on some walls, with her son represented by a bull. In the corners of the central room of the residence / shrine were sleeping platforms which served a dual purpose for the family, since the area beneath the platform was also utilized for burials of their loved ones. The matriarch of the home had as her sleeping platform the largest and most central location, usually placed on the east side of the house or shrine. It is believed the men and women of the household performed both secular and non-secular duties. Symbols of the clergy seemed to be obsidian mirrors for the priestess and belt fasteners of polished bone for the priest.

It has been suggested no animal sacrifice was made here to the Goddess, instead she was venerated with offerings of grain burned in clay ovens which were located within each house. This suggests grain, bread, and its preparation were sacred to Goddess. This is further implied by statuettes of Goddess being found in grain bins, such as the famous 8,000 year old terra-cotta figure of the Mother Goddess giving birth on her throne between two leopards, which were sacred at Catal Hüyük. These felines appear later with Bronze Age goddesses, some scholars even theorize women may have learned to domesticate these big cats. The Mother Goddess in her act of giving birth, a rare image within Old Europe, was synonymous with her ability to give birth to abundant crops to fill the bellies of her people. Four times as many female figurines were found in comparison to males (33 to 8). Mellaart believes the absence of sexual imagery suggests the people were more focused on Goddess' gifts of birth and sustenance. Plants and flowers are also painted on imagery of the Goddess within the site suggestive of her role as this vegetation deity.

The Goddess in her triple aspect of maiden-mother-crone was known at Catal Hüyük with figurines sometimes showing these aspects conjoined. One such figurine had one body with one set of arms topped by two heads and two sets of breasts which is suggestive of the maiden and mother aspects of Goddess, the forerunner of perhaps Demeter and Persephone. Mellaart discovered a unique shrine, perhaps a birthing room, he named the Red Shrine because of the life-giving color so prevalent. Goddess is displayed here as a sculpture high upon the wall, shown legs akimbo, as if giving birth to the three bulls which are shown beneath her. What might be a muzzle of a fourth bull peaks out from the area of her vulva. In other shrines, her crone aspect, Goddess of Death and Regeneration, is shown as vultures painted on the walls in red as they hover over headless human beings who await their rebirth in the embrace of her wings. The few figurines of a male depict him as either husband or son. He is shown with the felines, or as a hunter wearing a leopard skin hat, with spear, seated on a bull. Imagery shows the close connection between mother and daughter, the son and consort, which might reflect what later became the myth of the son-lover, who is sacrificed for the promise of life regeneration. Other images on the walls include insects and flowers, as well as patterns that might have been used in weaving kilims.

There is no clear reason for the end of civilization at Catal Hüyük, but with only one-twentieth of the site excavated, perhaps scholars might one day know the whole story of the largest Neolithic city in the Near East, what Mellaart called,

▲ Aerial view of Catal Hüyük.

▲ Possible early depiction of Cybele found during excavations.

"a supernova among the rather dim galaxy of contemporary peasant cultures."

Excavation continues at the site which has a small museum, but the best artifacts unearthed can be found at the nearby Ankara museum, a sure favorite of the author! Goddess advocates travel to Catal Hüyük in pilgrimage and once there honor the Divine Feminine in ritual. Some of the more learned share ideas with the archaeologists at the site, which may have caused archaeologist Ian Hodder to comment that history cannot just be informed by the Academy. Hodder, who has worked on the site in recent years has his own opinions and contends that with such a small percentage of the site excavated and most of the study placed primarily on the middle and early levels of the existing 18 levels of habitation, much is still yet to be discovered. Hodder's current theories are the roles of women and men were quite complex and his working theory is gender did not necessarily determine ones role in society. Both sexes served important key functions in Neolithic life, perhaps just in different realms, i.e., men hunted and women were more involved in agriculture. Responsibilities may have overlapped or have been shared. He believes the next five years of research into the upper levels of habitation (where fat lady artifacts were found) may reveal a clearer picture of Catal Hüyük society, but at this time there is no evidence for either a patriarchy or matriarchy.

Note that there is not much to see at the archaeological site itself, though the importance of this site as mentioned above catapults it to the top of any list of important sacred sites of Goddess. It should also be stressed that those visiting here should do so in a respectful manner, being aware that locals may or may not agree with this herstorical perspective of the site, nor appreciate the attention this site has brought their neighborhood. This author is reminded of the curious and sometimes hostile glances travel companions have received from women behind their veils toward Westerners, and it is important for visitors to be tolerant and patient of the local culture and religion.

Getting to Catal Hüyük

Catal Hüyük is located on the Plain of Konya, near the town of Cumra, 62 miles (50 km) south of the city of Konya (home of Rumi, the Sufi mystic). The author highly recommends going on an organized tour rather than independently. The intrepid solitary traveler can get a bus from Eski Garaj, the Old Garage, in Konya for the 45 minute ride to Cumra. A taxi will be needed to make the last leg of the journey, or consider a taxi for the entire trip. While in Konya, try to visit the Tekke and Museum of the Whirling Dervishes and the impressive mosque which houses the grave of Mevlana Celaleddin Rumi, the famous mystic. Note that this rural part of Turkey does not see Westerners on a regular basis, so be prepared for lots of stares. When in doubt, just be courteous and smile! And just a heads up — expect squat toilets.

Didyma

Little was certain about the Turkish oracle site of Didyma, meaning "temple of the twins," until the last decade when it was proven to be associated with Artemis, as well as her twin brother, Apollo. The origins of the name Didyma and

Didymaion were the subject of much debate with only speculation as to how the sacred site might be related to both siblings. Now this new assertion can be made official thanks to excavations along the Sacred Road between Miletus and Didyma which revealed the presence of the cult of Artemis as well as shops, votive fountains, tombs, and baths. This finding comes as no surprise to scholars because Dindymene, (of Mount Dindymus), one of the Anatolian Goddess Cybele's ancient names, was so closely related to the word Didyma. Cybele, also called Magna Mater, Isis, Hepat, and Kubaba, has always been closely associated with Artemis and Apollo. This being said, it is now understood the Artemision and Didymaion, temples of Apollo and Artemis, were the origins for the word Didyma.

In keeping with sacred Goddess sites, the oracle site is believed to have been located near a sacred spring, and visited by kings such as Necho of Egypt, and Croesus of Lydia, in the 7th and 6th centuries BCE respectively. Pliny the Younger ranked the Artemis Temple the second of all Greek shrines in splendor, only exceeded by Artemis' temple at Ephesus, one of the Seven Wonders of the Ancient World. The largest surviving Greek temple in the world, this predominantly roofless enclosure built by the Milesian people included a village settlement, oracles, shrines, and a sacred grove within its confines. Expense was not spared as it was known to house some of the most costly art of the known world. According to Pausanias in the 2nd century CE the oracle and temple of Apollo were much older than the settlement, with Artemis' temple dating farther back than the sanctuary of Apollo. In keeping with Anatolian motif, the Temple of Artemis was known to be decorated with lions and considered Phoenician in style. Richard Chandler explored the site in 1760 and wrote "The columns are so exquisitely fine, the marble mass so vast and noble, that it is impossible perhaps to conceive greater beauty and majesty of ruin." What remains today of the temple are from Greco-Roman times. Theodosius II turned the temple into a church in the 5th century CE and by the 10th century CE much of it had again been destroyed by fire.

At its zenith, the temple was described as measuring 129 x 66 yards (118 x 60 m) at the krepdoma or base platform. The double ionic colonnade contained 108 columns with 12 more in the forecourt, or pronaos. The wall toward the west forecourt had a 26 feet (8 m) entrance raised 5 feet (1.5 m) above the floor of the forecourt. The roofed chamber of the cella, or inner sanctum, contained two Ionic round columns to support the roof which opened to the north and south sides into smaller chambers which contained staircases leading toward a terrace at roof level. The western end of the cella had three doors that led to a grand staircase which is where the unroofed inner-most sanctuary was located. Here in the naiskos, or innermost sacred chapel is where the sacred spring was located and where the priestess gave her pronouncements.

The priestly caste of Branchids once administered to the temple where priestesses gave divinations every few days or months from within the *naiskos*, or chapel, usually after fasting for three days and purifying themselves in ritual baths. The oracle priestess sat suspended over the sacred spring where she answered questions posed to her. She would dip her foot or the hem of her dress into the spring before giving a reply in the form of prose that was then turned into verse by the priests. Certainly it is doubtful if the common man would have the funds to access the oracle at shrines such as Didyma. For the less wealthy another form of divination was known, called the dice oracles. According to scholar James

▲ The ruins of Didyma allow the visitor an interesting glimpse into an ancient city.

Rietveld the dice oracles were in use in Asia Minor and were possibly introduced to the area from Egyptian influences, such as the Ptolemy's who owned a strip of land along the coastline for some time. The dice oracles, or *astragali,* were made of the neck bones of sheep. They were four sided and each side represented the numbers 1,3,4,6 which corresponded to a fixed set of prophecies for every possible throw of the dice. Rietveld deciphered a particular Greek inscription found on a temple wall in the nearby city of Termessus which told of the dice oracle divination process. In Termessus, seven astragali were thrown at a time to answer a query. This number of dice resulted in 120 possible prophetic replies. One would make the roll of the dice, then look up the list of possible interpretations. Each roll had an accompanying deity and provided three verses of advice. If one rolled the seven dice and the numbers 4,4,4,6,6,2,4 came up, the deity associated with the throw was Cronos the Child Eater and the course of action said "Stay home and do not go elsewhere lest the destructive beast and avenging fury come upon you, for I see that the business is neither safe nor secure."

Located on the Aegean Coast south of Kusadasi, half of the ancient temple from the 2nd and 1st centuries BCE still stands making an impressive site at this seldom visited sacred place of Goddess. It was dwarfed in size only by the Temple of Artemis at Ephesus and the Temple of Hera on the island of Samos. Work continued on the temple until the 2nd century CE. Local legend says that when Alexander the Great arrived from Macedonia, the sacred spring flowed once more. Alexander had great plans to rebuild the temple but they were never completed. Pilgrims the world over visited the oracles and shrines until the practice was outlawed by Emperor Theodosius I. The statues that once graced the temple have been sent off to the British Museum but there is yet much worth seeing. The sacred spring used by the priestesses for prophecy still trickles water on the site, so bring your water bottles! Visitors can still climb the stairway to an upper level facade of the temple which is only a small fraction of what remains of this magnificent temple. The bases and lower sections of many of the columns are still intact. One source says the Greeks were able to move these colossal marble pieces with the aid of lubrication in the form of soap. It seems the Greeks constructed long shafts of stone leading to a building site. These shafts were lubricated with soap so the large pieces of marble were able to slide to the position where they were needed. Visitors once waited in the Hall of Twelve Columns, (probably the aforementioned forecourt) for prophecies of the priestesses, though only two columns are visible today. There are still traces of the sacred fountain and the inner sanctuary where the oracle received her prophecies.

Getting to Didyma

Located near Selcuk, Didyma lies just south of Kusadasi. Escorted tours are available from Kusadasi or Bodrum and include the nearby ruins of Priene and Miletus, which are certainly worth a look. Priene has been a noted oracle site and features a Temple of Athena nearby. Miletus is a larger archaeological site which includes a museum. All three can be visited in one day, though for maximum enjoyment and study of the sites, it might be worthwhile to consider breaking the visit into two days. Some tours can be obtained out of Selcuk. If traveling by public bus, use Soke as a hub. Inexpensive pensions can be obtained in the city of Didyma, also called Didim, which overlooks the temple.

Goddess Focus
Marija Gimbutas — (1921 - 1994)

On February 7, 1994 the Associated Press issued a notice of the passing of Marija Gimbutas, an archaeologist challenging conventional views by concluding that women were worshipped in Neolithic Old Europe, and held high status alongside men in an egalitarian and peaceful society. Gimbutas, considered a pioneer in gender archaeology, beloved by her colleagues, scholars, and advocates of the Women's Spirituality Movement, died at age 73 of cancer. Part of her lifetime achievements included authoring 20 books, receiving a doctorate in archaeology in 1946 from Tubingen University in Germany, becoming a professor emeritus of European archaeology at the University of California in Los Angeles, and raising three daughters. She was a Peabody Fellow at Harvard throughout the 1950s, and director of five major archaeological excavations in Eastern Europe. In the film commemorating her life's work, *Signs Out of Time*, by Belili Productions, noted scholars such as mythologist Joseph Campbell praised her work which had in turn influenced their own. Campbell stated, "Gimbutas has not only prepared a fundamental glossary of pictorial keys to the mythology of the otherwise undocumented era of European prehistory, but has established the main themes of a religion in veneration both of the universe as a living body of goddess-mother creatrix and of all the living things within it as partaking in her divinity."

Whether called social anthropologist, archeomythologist, or feminist archaeologist, Marija is known as one of the most influential and controversial scholars of this century. She confidently withstood the criticism she received when she introduced her findings about the peaceful, goddess-centered cultures of early Europe. She fearlessly believed in her work and challenged findings and criteria favored by the "establishment" of her time. She wanted scholars to look behind Greek culture, to the Neolithic period of 6500-3500 BCE for new political, social and religious traditions that might better serve humanity. She believed the academy should not just catalog data, but also try to understand the meaning and religious context of artifacts. Since her passing, gender archaeology is becoming a special niche within academia, and scholars such as Ian Hodder are coming around to say history cannot just be informed by the Academy. Joan Marler, writing for the Pacifica Graduate Institute website states: "During the last few years of his life, Joseph Campbell spoke frequently of Marija Gimbutas, profoundly regretting that her research

▲ Marija Gimbutas revolutionized new realms of archaeology.

on the Neolithic cultures of Europe was not available during the 1960s when he was writing *The Masks of God*. Otherwise he would have "revised everything." Campbell compared the importance Marija's work to Champollion's decipherment of Egyptian hieroglyphics."

Marija is buried in her hometown, near her mother, in the Petrasiunai Cemetery in the town of Kaunas, the second largest city of Lithuania, a region known for preserving its ancient traditions and beliefs. According to her daughter, Marija's grave can be found along the path, about 100 feet (30 m) beyond the entrance to the cemetery, toward the right-hand side. Her resting place is surrounded by a low white fence, identified by the tall pillar-like headstones topped by a statuette holding a child. There was a time in history it was considered heresy to believe in certain ideas which we know today are proven scientific facts. Humankind is often slow to embrace new ideas, especially if these concepts upset the apple-cart of accepted "wisdom," yet we live with the reality that the next archaeological find may potentially blow the lid off history as we know it. Controversy aside, this author honors Marija for her daring propositions, dedication, and discoveries, and submits her resting place as a sacred site of pilgrimage in honor of this foremother of Goddess herstory.

Hagia Sophia

This sacred site of the Divine Feminine suggests a delicious irony. On or very near the location that once was a Temple of Aphrodite, stands the Hagia Sophia, or Aya Sophia, intended as a fantastic monument for a patriarchal monotheistic religion. Commissioned by the famous Emperor Justinian (reigning 527-565 CE) and built by Athemius of Trallas and Isidorus of Miletus, the greatest mathematicians trained in the sciences of Classical Greece, Hagia Sophia was dedicated on December 26, 537 CE. Concerning the size of the massive edifice of the church, Justinian was known to boast: "Oh, King Solomon, I have outdone thee!" This church turned mosque and then turned museum, with its design literally defying gravity, was dedicated to the Holy Wisdom, Sophia, the Divine Feminine, which both Greece and later Western Christianity sought to diminish. Encompassed within the walls are eight green columns of porphyry from the Temple of Artemis in Ephesus, along with some dark purple columns from Thebes in Egypt. The purple columns are visible from the center of the upstairs gallery at the far end of the church where women were relegated to worship when the structure was a church or mosque. Two Hellenistic alabaster urns stand near the entrance, looted from nearby Pergamum. Also of special interest is the so-called "sweating" pillar of Saint Gregory Thaumaturgus (213-270 CE). Known for his miracles, legend tells how he appeared soon after the construction of Hagia Sophia and touched this pillar, giving the stone unusual powers of healing. Today, pilgrims from all around still insert their fingers into a certain hole within the pillar in order to be cured. Gregory was from the northern part of what is today Turkey and he is most famous as the very first recorded Christian saint to receive a vision of Mary.

Images of the Virgin Mary are seen prominently in mosaics that fill the museum, including one situated over the southwestern entrance where she is handed the city of Istanbul (then called Constantinople, capital of Christendom) on her right hand, and the Hagia Sophia, the shrine of Holy Wisdom, on her left. This Byzantine Mary is clad in a robe of lapis lazuli with her feet resting upon a pedestal. On either side of her head are medallions bearing the Greek monograms "MP" and "OY," standing for "Mater" (Mother) and "Theou" (of God). This same monogram combination surrounds the Mary standing between Emperor John II Comnenus and his wife Irene on the eastern wall of the southern gallery, dating to 1122 CE. Perhaps one of the most impressive mosaics of Mary is situated within the interior of the half dome within the apse, where the Virgin sits upon a majestic throne, wearing the purple robes of royalty and surrounded by a golden backdrop. Originally created in the 6th century, it was destroyed during the iconoclasm movement (a group advocating that all representations of God were idolatry), only to be restored in the 9th century. Through Wisdom, many advocates believe, common ground might be realized and a bridge between paganism and Christianity rebuilt.

In pre-Christian Constantinople, named Byzantium by its Roman founders, the goddesses Io, Hekate, and Isis were all venerated in the city. The famous festival of Isis, the Isidis Navigium, was also known to be conducted on the nearby waters today known as the Sea of Marmara. Incidentally, according to one ancient commentary, Plato the Scholiast, the word "Bosporus," the name of the straits dividing the European side of Istanbul from the Asian shoreline was actually a corruption of the word *Phosphoros*, or "light bringer," and named after the Goddess Hecate. That Isis and Inanna have even been known to be early aspects of Sophia is particularly well known — for even Isis was known as a Goddess of Wisdom. The Goddess was even identified as Sophia by many in the well known Christian Gnostic text *The Thunder, Perfect Mind*. Perhaps no more than pure coincidence, but it is curious that two of the architects of the Hagia Sophia bore the name "Isidorus," when translated means "beloved of Isis." Scholar R. E. Witt cites an entry of *Wisdom Literature* that declares of wisdom, "She is the artificer of all things." Lady Wisdom has instructed mankind in the natures of living things as well as in the diversities of plants and the virtues of roots. Witt associates this wisdom, or Sophia, with an aspect of Isis called Isis Medica, well known for her knowledge of pharmacology. The Valentinian Gnostics were known to have developed a doctrine that identified Isis as Sophia and her son Horus with that of Logos or Christ.

Sophia was not only viewed as a Wisdom Goddess, but a Creatrix and Redeemer. Knowledge of her has survived and kept alive within Jewish and

▲ The Hagia Sophia dome is the largest in the world.

Christian theology and Gnosticism, the latter growing out of the esoteric teachings of Egyptian, Hebrew, and Greek religions. According to Proverbs, Sophia was at God's side before the birth of the cosmos and delighted in the newly created human race. Jesus, who was once an emissary of God, became the incarnate of Sophia, occasionally even considered her son. Some scholars theorize that within some of the writings of the Gospels of Matthew and John as well as the letters of Paul, the name Jesus was substituted where Sophia's name was originally, as when Paul stated Jesus was the one from whom all things are, through whom all things were created in heaven and on earth, and through whom all things continue to exist. Sophia, or the Holy Spirit, also lived in the guise of the Shekinah of the Kabala, a Jewish mystical tradition.

Many today might think it odd to hear divinity spoken of in the feminine voice, or to even consider the possibility that the Supreme Being was often perceived as female at first by many cultures around the world, continuing to be seen in this manner for tens of thousands of years. When not recognized as the Mother Goddess, the Feminine Divine lived as Wisdom, or the Holy Spirit, until Wisdom later became associated as Logos or Jesus, a gender shift that occurs in part as a result of language. Languages such as Hebrew, Greek, and Latin have gender distinctions, but English does not. Wisdom started out as feminine in the Hebrew word *hokhma*, the Greek word *sophia*, and the Latin word *sapientia*. Wisdom then became known as a neuter gender to the Greeks called Pneuma, though Pneuma was personified as a dove, an image long known to be associated with the Goddess. Wisdom later became assimilated as Logos, or Jesus, and again in Latin as the masculine Spiritus Sanctus, with English having no gender distinction for names. In English God might have been male or female.

Besides linguistically, how did this battle of the sexes come about in the Western world? Why were males considered superior to females? At the time of the Greek poet Hesiod's writing Theogony in the 8th century BCE, Earth was a vibrant, robust, and active creatrix who gave birth to the world, sometimes in partnership with her consort, who she probably created. By the time of Plato, 400 years later, the feminine was suddenly this passive receptacle in the act of creation, a literal incubator for the male seed. Plato refers to the feminine saying,

"She is the natural recipient of all impressions, and is stirred and informed by them." According to scholar Karen Jo Torjesen, "It is the cosmic Father who is the cause of all things, specifically of the Forms, which enter into and go out of her and are the likeness of eternal realities. The male principle produces the eternal, unchanging patterns for all things in the cosmos; these Forms have in themselves the power to order and shape uninformed matter." She continues, "Plato's use of reproduction as a primary metaphor for cosmological processes, the value of male honor, expressed in male agency, and female shame, as a correlate of female passivity, became a part of the very structure of the cosmos." These ideas filtered down and affected social and religious structure. Men were viewed as active and ruled, women became passive and subordinate. Sexuality was corrupting and the rational mind the norm. Nature was inferior to spirit. Consequently, any woman who was independent and audacious enough to defy this paradigm was considered improper and immodest and cast as a harlot. It was these ideas of gender and their assigned characteristics which formed the basis for our civilization. Gone was the natural order of things from the Neolithic times when the female was generatrix, and society was thought to be egalitarian, without gender hierarchy and shame of sexuality. It was replaced by a warrior class composed of political and social hierarchies with the generative power replaced by the verbal and rational creativity of the male, such as when God commanded, "Let the earth bring forth living creatures." This social and religious context might have been the reason why Mary Magdalene was reputed to have been a fallen woman. Finally, 1,378 years later, in 1969, Mary was vindicated when the Vatican apologized for Gregory the Great's misdeed in the intended conjoining of the personage of Mary with an unknown prostitute. It has been theorized that in the early years the Church's purpose of besmearing Mary was to help the efforts to curtail or prohibit leadership by women. The Church believed that priests could only be those made in God's image, and women, without a penis and associated with sexuality rather than rationality, were therefore considered inferior.

Fortunately Sophia, the embodiment of Wisdom, remained alive within Gnostic Christianity where her role was recognized as the "Great Mother" and consort of God — that is until Gnosticism was repressed in 326 and 333 CE by Constantine, who built the first version of the church of Hagia Sophia. The Goddess as Sophia was forced to retreat from the psyches of humankind until she rose again a few hundred years later in the Middle Ages. Her resurrection came in the guise of the Virgin Mary, whose image is prolific at this beautiful church in Istanbul. Sophia, or Sapientia as Wisdom, was also revered in the Black Virgins or Madonnas which were the inspiration for pilgrimage in Europe. Under the top layer of paint of some of these Madonna statues have been found names such as Isis, clearly indicating that Goddess was not lost, but became veiled within other imagery. The secrecy guaranteed that those who venerated her would not be killed by the reigning patriarchal authorities. Gnostic Sophia reemerges in the 12th century CE and credit is given to the Order of the Knights Templar, the Cathar Church of the Holy Spirit (also known as the Church of the Grail), Jewish Kabbalism, and various Alchemical orders. Gnostic ideas of Wisdom were based less on Goddess and more on Wisdom, or Sophia, as the image to which the soul aspires on its journey back to its source. In Gnosticism, the "sacred marriage" is not between Goddess and God, but it is a union of soul and spirit.

The mosque/church of Hagia Sophia, once the center of Eastern Orthodox Christianity, for over a thousand years, was turned into a museum in 1933 when

▲ The exterior of Hagia Sophia is world famous, but the interior is equally spectacular.

the beloved leader of Turkey, Ataturk, had all the golden mosaics restored. Just behind the Hagia Sophia is a smaller church called Hagia Irene (Divine Peace) once sharing a sanctuary with Sophia. Both the Hagia Sophia and the Hagia Irene seen today are not the original structures, both having burned down and subsequently rebuilt since their construction by Theodosius. Hagia Sophia is in its third incarnation as it was originally built by Constantine, before Theodosius, then rebuilt by Justinian with completion in 537 CE. Saint Sophia is awe-inspiring both beneath her domes and on the exterior as her adjacent minarets create the most magnificent sight against the horizon! Within the church/mosque, alongside mosaics of Mary and the many different hues of marble, are medallions which bear the names of Mohammed, Allah, and other leaders of the Islamic faith as the Church was captured by the Ottoman Turks in 1453. It might be said that within these hallowed halls dedicated to Holy Wisdom, the Goddess embraces both the influence of Christianity and Islam under her wing.

Getting to Hagia Sophia

The church turned mosque turned museum of Hagia Sophia, or Aya Sophia, is located in the center of the old city of Istanbul very near the Bosporus waterway where the continents of Asia Minor and Europe come face to face. The city has an international airport with modern and efficient public transportation. Justinian's great church is visible from all over Istanbul, which makes it very easy to locate. The majestic Hagia Sophia towers near the Topkapi Palace in the Sultanahmet section of the city.

Ephesus

In the middle of the 2nd century CE, Pausanias declared: "All cities worship Artemis of Ephesus and individuals hold her in honor above all the gods," succinctly summing up the importance and splendor of Artemis at her sacred temple, one of the Seven Wonders of the Ancient World. Here, the famous meteorite fell to the earth, the stone soon associated with Cybele and, in turn, Artemis of Ephesus. With special thanks to scholar James Rietveld, one of the foremost American experts on Artemis of Ephesus, many new and some as yet unpublished discoveries associated with the Goddess and her worship excavated by the Austrian archaeologists currently working at this site are reaching the general public. Vital to understanding the religion of Artemis is her cult image. Unless scholarship follows the development of the cult images of Artemis, the diversity of this Goddess is truly lost. As this site information will show, Artemis was integral to the lives of the Ephesians and far from being primarily a civic or political Goddess who solicited good moral behavior from the citizens.

Some myths establish that Ephesus was founded by both indigenous female Amazon warriors and Ionian Greeks, a theory supported by the two shrines excavated at the site where Artemis' first temple would later stand. Other stories tell that it was the Carians who first designated a shrine at the spot. Whatever the foundation story, these two populations worshipped the Phrygian Mother Goddess, called Magna Mater, or Cybele of nearby Mount Pion, and the Greek Artemis, respectively. The image of Artemis began as a wooden statue, probably associated with trees, if not a tree itself, considered to be made of holy material. Her image

evolved into the early rigid looking statues, thought to be a blended image of Artemis from these two aforementioned cultures living in the area. Artifacts uncovered here reveal the fact that some of her earliest cult-figures in the naos of the temple of Artemis were elaborately clothed and made of gold. Soon her image transformed into the one most recognized worldwide with the many protuberances which have been the cause of so much debate among scholars.

Many ideas circulated concerning the nature of her protuberances, running the gamut from hanging fruit to bull's testicles, the latter theory considered very weak by most scholars today and reflective of antiquated 20th century Western gender biases suggesting masculine power and virility. Other interesting and little known ideas suggested the protuberances represented a mantle of movable pieces of clothing, a cornucopia-like sheep skin bag, called a *kursa*, which contained fat, grain, wine, maturation,

▲ The Temple of Artemis is on the outskirts of Ephesus.

longevity, and progeny, or finally, even the severed breasts of the Amazonians. Rietveld believes the most likely explanation for the protuberances are that they "once represented hanging fruit, but, with the advent of a more individualistic age, these objects became anthropomorphized into the more intimate breasts; a sign of a mother's nurturing care rather than a more remote fertility deity." He further quotes scholar LiDonnici who professes her belief that the imagery of Artemis reflects, "an Ephesian society in a constant state of transformation, with each period containing its very own set of expectations and demands." In short, the statue of Artemis reflects the changing needs of the people and thus continued to remain in a state of flux.

Not surprisingly, due to the close association of Ephesus and Egypt (both were ruled by Ptolemy), Artemis' magical life-preserving breasts and powers over fate connect her with the Egyptian Goddess Isis, from whom some of her potent magical abilities may have originated. Artemis has even been depicted with Serapis, normally the consort of Isis in the Greco-Roman world. Statues were found in Ephesus bearing both the names of Isis and Artemis, with imagery showing them sharing attributes, such as Isis carrying Artemis' quiver. All Artemis iconography combined reflects her multiple magical powers over fate, fertility, protection, preservation, nurturance, and magic. She was an overall stabilizing force for the benefit of the inhabitants of Ephesus. She develops from merely a fertility or civic deity protecting the city and its economy to a personal Goddess, even called upon during childbirth. It is important for the sake of continuity of the worship of Goddess to understand that the composite Artemis-Isis was assimilated into a third figure, the Virgin Mary, acquiring the characteristics of both goddesses by the Council of Ephesus in 431 CE.

In the phenomenon cited by Professor David Frankfurter as, "stereotype appropriation" the Ephesians begin to view their religious rituals as magical, another similarity with popular attitudes in Egypt. In fact, the local population utilized special magical words called "Ephesian Letters," which, according to some ancient authors, were depicted on the image of Artemis at her feet, on her scepter, girdle, headband, and polos, effectively making the statue a magical amulet of protection when carried through the city of Ephesus in various weekly processions, thereby radiating her magical powers along the Via Sacra. It is through Artemis's association with magical powers that she becomes increasingly linked with her darker alter ego, Hekate, Goddess of the Underworld, moon, and the hunt. According to Rietveld, the Ephesians believed Artemis' magical image was viewed as a stabilizing force, without which the city would cease to thrive. These Ephesian Letters, spoken as magical spells and inscribed on talismans, acted as a liturgical formula for protection, salvation, initiation, fertility, good luck, and overpowering an adversary, creating a culture where magic and religion were inextricably intertwined. It is believed these Ephesian Letters were invented by the Idaean Dactyls, magicians and metalworkers (alchemists?) of the Great Mother Goddess on Mount Pion with whom Artemis becomes conflated. The Dactyls have been associated with the priesthood of the Ephesian Artemis, called the Curetes, thought to have protected Leto when she was giving birth to Artemis and Apollo under an olive tree in the holy Grove of Ortygia on the outskirts of Ephesus. They are believed to be an extension of the Goddess' magical powers, becoming both her agents and attendants. The image of Artemis was perceived as so powerful that she was found held as a magical implement on many statuettes of the gods themselves, including Zeus, the Great Mother Goddess of Mount

Pion, and even Fate herself, indicating their increased power with Artemis as an ally. The magical implications of Artemis can no longer be ignored!

Once Artemis Ephesia is understood within her religio-magical context, she must be examined related to the sacred geography of Ephesus. To begin with, the nature of Asia Minor, where Ephesus is located, was more exotic, emotional, and ecstatic, rather than rational Greece. People of Ephesus were passionate about Artemis and joyously took part in her weekly processions, a hallmark of her worship. The boundaries between the Olympian and Chthonic deities were virtually non-existent here. The Artemision, or Temple of Artemis, the focal point of the cult, dedicated to Artemis, Cybele, and Hekate was located on the outskirts of town. It is believed an early sacred tree, and also a sacred well, was once located within what would later become the sacred precinct of the Artemisium. It was linked to the city of Ephesus via the Sacred Road, or Via Sacra, which was divided into two streets. When it reached holy Mount Pion from the direction of the Temple of Artemis, one branch proceeded northwest and the other southwest. Both roads, two parts of one sacred circular processional route, joined at the other side of the mound at the Triodos Gate, a square near the Library of Celsus and another at the Altar of Artemis, the most photographed site in Ephesus. Visitors who would like to walk the Via Sacra should allow about two hours to complete the entire walk. Altars of Artemis used in the ancient processionals can be spotted intermittently along the way.

Mount Pion was dedicated to the Mother Goddess since prehistoric times, and an ancient cemetery at the base of the mountain was the realm of Hekate. The portion of Via Sacra southwest along the lower skirt of Mount Pion, once called the Prytaneion, was dedicated to Artemis and Hestia. The stadium along the northwest route is famous for the Artemisium games and the theatre was the assembly place for festivals of the Goddess, notable for the gathering of a mob that ran the Apostle Paul out of town for insulting their patron goddess. The two roads met at the monumental Altar of Artemis next to the statues of Artemis and Hekate near the New Triodos Gate (called the "Gate of Hadrian"), dedicated to Hekate in her triple aspect. The Old Triodos Gate is the current Mazeus-Mithridates Gate directly next to the Library of Celsus. A faded relief of Hekate in triple guise still survives on the north side of the gate by the eastern passageway. The New Triodos Gate connects to the road that leads to the Ortygia Grove, where Leto bore Artemis and Apollo and where many of the mysteries of the cult

▲ The Temple of Artemis at Ephesus is one of the Seven Wonders of the Ancient World.

were performed. The House of the Virgin Mary overlooks the area that once was this legendary grove. During the many weekly processionals, the Via Sacra became a vital artery linking the people with their primary goddesses Artemis, Cybele, and Hekate.

The last known Temple of Artemis built at the site was three times larger than the Parthenon in Athens and according to the ancient writer Strabo, was painted in abundant and flashy gold tones and prominently featured the color red, considered the color of ancient wisdom. While the two previous temples had been built and burned to the ground, the temple that survived the longest contained 117 Ionic columns, each 58 feet (17.7 m) tall. A U-shaped altar in the courtyard in front of the temple sheltered a cult statue of Artemis. Rows of colonnades and stalls for oxen effectively making it a slaughterhouse where Rietveld quotes Romer and Romer asserting that, "all the city's meat was slaughtered" here "under the watchful eye of the Goddess."

The image of Artemis on the sacrificial pedestal, central to the magic of the Artemisium, was perfectly aligned with an "epiphany window" that created the illusion of the Goddess peering down onto her congregation in golden splendor whenever the sunlight shone through the window opening in just the right fashion. This certainly created a feeling of magic and awe among those gathered. This epiphany window, clearly an explanation for her epithet of Epiphanes, (referring to her as a divinity that appears), links Artemis Ephesia to Cybele and Mary, two other deities known to "appear." On the interior of the temple housed commanding images of Artemis and Apollo, and on the other side of the shrine behind the temple was the little known statue of Hekate, upon which visitors were warned not to gaze upon too long, providing further evidence for a cult of Hekate at the temple. Rietveld states, "As a Goddess of protection, the temple of Artemis was a place of asylum for those in need of refuge, a bank for those wishing to secure their financial wealth, and a shrine for virgins desiring to protect their chastity."

Many of the famous landmarks in Ephesus now bear new names as a result of new discoveries. The famous Syrian-arched Temple of Hadrian is now known to be a shrine dedicated to Artemis, and the Gate of Hadrian, is now called the New Triodos Gate. And while the massive U-shaped structure (once called the Altar of Lucius) has become the Altar of Artemis, the often photographed Mazeus Mithridates Gate is now the Old Triodos Gate of Hekate, revealing structures thought to be civic in nature are actually identified as religious and dedicated to Artemis-Hekate. Evidence for Hekate is everywhere, including in the district called the Embolos and the Temple of the Flavia Sebastoi, as well as all the unidentified figurines found at the site. The scope of this entry does not allow for further description of the sites along the Via Sacra, or description of the rituals or clergy of Artemis, however, suffice it to say, much has been discovered and awaits publication! The entire processional route was sacred to Artemis and believed to embody her magical powers. It should be noted, the cults of Demeter and Isis also had a considerable presence at Ephesus.

Getting to Ephesus

The archaeological park of Ephesus, or Efes as the Turks call it, is located 50 miles (80 km) southeast from Izmir, a major port city located on the Aegean Sea. Izmir is serviced by ferries from Greece and bus routes extending all over Turkey. Izmir is close enough to Ephesus that it can be visited on a day trip, but it is more practical to stay in the town of Selcuk near the ruins. Several days are necessary to fully explore Ephesus and its surrounding sites. From Selcuk it is a hot 40-minute walk to Ephesus. Taxis and most dolmus minibuses leave from the bus station upon demand. It would not be prudent to think it would be possible to see much of Ephesus on a 1/2 day tour available off a cruise ship, which is the way many visitors glimpse Ephesus. It should be noted the magnificent Temple of Artemis is in a sad state of disrepair with barely a single column standing intact, however, the magical essence of the place is tangible and certainly worth a look. It is a great place for a picnic.

Lagina

Little known, yet historically very relevant, the Hekateion at Lagina was the only temple known to be solely dedicated to the Goddess Hekate (or Hecate). Her temple itself reveals extant foundations, measuring 490 by 440 feet (149 by 134 m) set within a monumental stoa. Situated among vegetation and near a sacred spring still visible today, the age of the temple is questionable, but by the 2nd century BCE Lagina was already associated with Hekate as inscriptions can attest. Artifacts reveal after 81 BCE, two celebrations were held here. One was the Hecatesia-Romaea celebration which was enacted every four years. The other was an annual festival which alluded to Hekate as keeper of the keys to Hades in her role as an underworld Goddess which was called "The Bearing of the Key." It consisted of games proceeding for several days, with the festival culminating in a procession by devotees from the city to the Temple of Hekate. Inscriptions in the nearby city of Stratoniceia declare miracles performed by the grace of Hekate. A prominent position for clergy of Hekate was that of "Key Bearer," usually a young woman related to a priest with the responsibility of opening and closing the temple on a daily basis. Eunuchs were known to serve the temple by tending the vegetation of the sacred precincts. After the 3rd century CE priestesses joined priests in leadership of the cult of Hekate, which included special "mysteries."

During the Bronze Age, Hekate is sometimes known as Bendis, an Earth Goddess from Thrace. According to scholar Miriam Robbins Dexter, Hekate is a Goddess of Regeneration, concerned with life and death, whose story begins when she is a Titaness, a Greek deity on the scene before the Olympian gods. The ancient writer, Hesiod, maintains Hekate was not punished by the infiltrating Olympian deities as were the other Titans, and she was able to retain her "honor on earth, and in the sky, and in the sea." Thus Hekate was a Goddess of the heavens, but she had her lunar aspects as well. He

▲ Hekate's Temple is prominent among the ruins of Lagina.

▲ This triple image of Hekate was found at Lagina.

further identified her as being a powerful force who sits in the Assembly of Judgment, with the power to withhold or grant humankind their wishes and needs. Like Athena, she was a warrioress, though she had her nurturing aspects as well, mainly overseeing the realms of midwifery. Hekate is sometimes linked linguistically with the Egyptian Goddess Heket, also associated with fertility and parturition, whose name seems so closely tied to the Egyptian word Heka, known to mean magical words of power. There is certainly a basis for comparison between Hekate and Heket, the former a sorceress, the latter an Egyptian deity with a talent for powerful incantations.

Later Hekate's more powerful and multi-faceted nature began to diminish, as she became more associated with the underworld, death, night, ghosts, and witches. According to Dr. Dexter, this was often the case as the Indo-Europeans relegated the Goddess of Regeneration to places associated with the Underworld. Hekate begins to be considered the Goddess of the Crossroads with her three faces (atop one body) that look in three directions at once, her image sometimes represented as a female, other times with the head of a serpent, a horse, or a dog. In her Hekate Triformis aspect, she appears as three full bodied but conjoined women with six arms, each facing a different direction. Also called Queen of the Night, scholar Patricia Monaghan identifies Hekate with the dark of the moon, and informs the Goddess is inclined toward nocturnal ramblings as she walks the dark roads accompanied by her sacred dogs, carrying a torch to light the way. Herself the dark and waning moon, Hekate is also associated with Artemis in her new moon aspect, and Selene or Demeter in their full moon phase thus forming a trinity which personifies the life passages of woman, from virgin, to mother and finally crone. Then again, Selene or Persephone is sometimes regarded as New Moon, Artemis Full Moon, and Hekate the Waning Moon. Lunar association aside, Hekate is associated with Artemis in her darker, more edgy aspect.

Monaghan tells of worshippers who "gathered inside to eat Hekate suppers in her honor, gatherings at which magickal knowledge was shared, the secrets of sorcery whispered, and dogs, honey, and black female lambs sacrificed." Leftovers from supper were placed outside for Hekate and her sacred dogs. Author Lori Nyx reveals Hekate was not always associated with darkness since Greek poets have described her as, "the golden one," "tender hearted," and "bright haired." Nyx states Hekate was shown in ancient art not as a crone, but as a young woman carrying two torches, and cites Robert Von Rudloff who described her early role as that of a protector and guardian, with her triple image utilized to ward off evil. Hekate, Demeter, and Persephone, all three chthonic Goddesses associated with underworld aspects, become inextricably intertwined. Hekate, her epithet as

Phosphoros, or "light bringer," leads Demeter and Persephone back and forth from the Underworld. Hekate is known to have witnessed the rape of Persephone by Hades. The Goddess later became Persephone's companion in the Netherworld as she awaited her return to Mother Demeter on earth in the spring. These three are also viewed as the maiden, mother, crone trinity, depicted respectively as Persephone, Demeter, and Hekate. Scholar Walter Burkert states Hekate was known to be able to send one into a frenzy or madness, the latter sometimes believed to be a form of epilepsy, called the sacred disease, which was treated with rituals or purification. He reveals her triple form Goddess of the Pathways as being related to the three masks that were traditionally hung at the meeting of three pathways during nocturnal meanderings.

Pagans today venerate Hekate as the wise crone who offers guidance. She no longer menstruates, withholding the power and magic of her sacred bloods. Sometimes associated with death, her womb space is now seen as a metaphoric tomb, a place for regeneration and rebirth, rather than as a vessel for childbearing. One can see her at the Hekateion as she stands at the crossroads, holding her lantern, helping the traveler choose which path will decide their fate. Devotees pray to Hekate when a difficult decision must be made. She is believed by her followers to be with them at the moment of birth and death, encouraging that next step into a new and unknown realm. As midwife, she can bring forth new life, and cares for the dead. She is a vessel of sacred knowledge and an instrument of the mysteries. In Turkey, Hekate is often associated as the crone aspect of Artemis as indicated at Ephesus where she contributes to Artemis' role as a powerful Goddess of magic. Her most ancient roots find her origins among the Carians of Asia Minor.

Getting to Lagina

Lagina is located in the Carian Heartland of southwestern Turkey between Lake Bafa and Bodrum, and south of Ephesus and Selcuk where travelers will find a plethora of sacred sites. Lagina is situated a bit north of Stratonikya near the village of Turgut, which can be found between the larger towns of Milas and Labranda. Unless visitors are on a specially designed tour with an itinerary that includes Lagina, the only way to reach the site is by private transportation. Lagina is a great place for a quiet picnic lunch, just remember to take only photographs, and leave only footprints.

AFRICA

I am all that has been, that is and that will be.
No mortal has yet been able to lift the veil which covers me.
—Neith, Egyptian Mother of the Gods.
Inscription from temple sanctuary in Sais as reported by
Plutarch, Greek biographer

AFRICA IS TO GODDESS WORSHIP as the hothouse is to horticulture. The variations and cross-pollination of species cultivated over time and place compose an arboretum of delights enabling the traveler to pick and choose which sacred sites will fill his or her tour bouquet. Short of having the luxury of a time machine to witness the past as it happened, travelers have the next best thing. This is due in large to exciting advances in both technology and gender perspective within archaeology which can play a pivotal role in unearthing and analyzing new discoveries. This progress, coupled with the foresight of past scholars and scribes who preserved truth and clarity of the past for future generations, provides historical markers and scholarship which laid dormant and, in some cases, had been lost until recently. The Nag Hammadi Scrolls found in the Egyptian desert in 1945 are one such discovery. Travelers learn how cultures merge — yesterday's indigenous culture became intertwined with that of the invading Phoenicians, and today African traditions mix and mingle with Christianity and Islam. A current phenomenon is that of Goddess spiritualists who, recognizing the Feminine Divine as the Christian Virgin Mary, have begun to make pilgrimages in the last several decades to Kibeho, Rwanda, Zeitoun, Egypt and Ngome in South Africa to pay homage to the Divine Feminine at sites of famous Marian apparitions. Those present at the Zeitoun apparition stated the Divine had an inclusive and universal flavor,

▲ Hathor is featured prominently at Abu Simbel.

appearing to the devoted as they expected to see her. Christians saw Mary; Muslims saw Fatima; and pagans saw Isis.

Can our knowledge and impressions of this part of the world be balanced and complete if the whole story has not been told? Are travelers willing to look at discoveries which may be unsettling, especially when they unravel existing schools of thought or inaccurate cultural beliefs? Just as African-Americans who travel to Africa learn that their ancestors played a large part in the success of the insidious slave trade, other truths come to light as knowledge is shared. History, at times unpleasant, can even be revolting when it reveals barbaric and political truths. Slavery, infanticide, genocide, and human sacrifice are part of humanity's collective past, and the true seeker must bravely follow the evidence wherever it may lead. That can be by land, air, and water. On camel, ship, or four-wheel drive, travelers caravan the vast sand dunes, spelunk deep caves, cruise backward-flowing rivers, renew themselves at life-giving oases, and safari the savannah and bush lands in search of Goddess in her multitude of manifestations found across the continent of Africa.

Moving the clock forward, the Yoruban people of Africa continue to worship the Divine Feminine in association with sacred waters. The popular Oshun and Oba are Goddesses of the rivers named for them. Oshun is known by devotees to be healer of the sick and mid-wife of pregnant women. Oya, Goddess of the Niger River, and Olosa the Goddess of lagoons, join with Yemaya, Goddess of the Ogun River to embody the life-giving attributes of water which sustain and support the local people. One can conclude throughout Africa, bodies of water are considered realms of the Divine, and as such are treated with reverence and attended by priestesses and priests. Today many tribes revere the Earth Mother, who is known across the continent by a variety of names. The Dahomey, Zulu, Ibo, Akan, Ashanti, and Shona all have their own tribal goddesses, and some still believe in the authority of matrilineal lineages, or family descent through the female line. The water Goddess still oversees the realms of wisdom and justice, care and fertility of the land, as well as being creatrixes of the world and rulers of the underworld. Teacher Ashphodel Long cites expert Judith Gleason who identifies Oya as a patron of feminine leadership. Long explains how African Goddesses are closely connected with nature and the morality of their people. Devotees of the Goddess Dugbo of the Kono people believe their social behavior affects the earth, and moral codes have as their basis a right relationship with the land. They equate social justice to appreciation and care for the earth with people's behavior and choices affecting humanity's future. She compares that to patriarchal faiths which believe they have dominion over Mother Nature, and the concern of soul salvation. The result is our misogynistic personal and societal attitudes exploiting nature which might possibly lead to global environmental disaster.

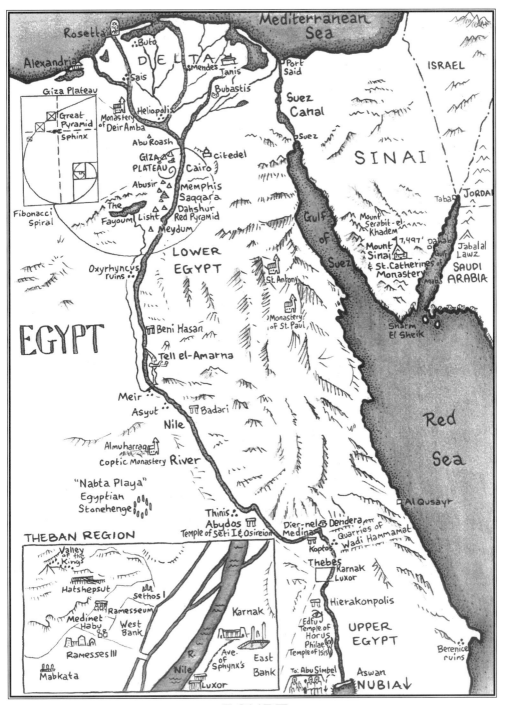

EGYPT

Though not always readily recognized as such, Egypt is part of Africa, a land that has produced many queens and female pharaohs who venerated the "Goddess of Ten Thousand Names." This is the kingdom of Cleopatra VII, famous priestess of the Egyptian Goddess Isis, a queen who ruled one of the mightiest kingdoms in the world, and but for a different outcome in a naval battle with Rome, might very well have ruled the known world, changing the course of history, religion, and the rise of patriarchy, and monotheism. Even though Cleopatra lost to the Roman Empire, veneration of Isis spread beyond Egypt, Greece, and Rome, to the Middle East, the Black Sea region, and throughout Europe, moving as far north as Britain. Temples and chapels at sacred sites dedicated to many other female deities of the Egyptians were venerated all along the length of the Nile River, and within the interior of Egypt, as far south as Nubia. An early representation of the Divine Feminine was embodied within the bird headed snake goddess (4000 BCE) of pre-dynastic Egypt. Other divine names ring out through herstory as devotees worshipped the Goddesses Bast, Hathor, Maat, and Neith. Rumors persist today that women perform nocturnal rituals at the feet of the Goddess Sekhmet at Karnak, as they pray for healing and liberation in current times.

Egypt can claim several of the Seven Wonders of the Ancient World; the Pyramids of Giza, as well as the Lighthouse of Alexandria, now lost. The great Library of Alexandria, once a pinnacle of learning and knowledge in centuries past, is on its way to being restored today. Besides the lineage of Cleopatra, power and influence were held by other goddess worshipping women such as Hatshepsut and Sheba whose baths are visited by tourists at Axum, Ethiopia. According to Dr. Miri Hunter Haruach of Project Sheba, the subjects of the Queen of Sheba, the Sabeans, whose kingdom is thought to have stretched from India to Arabia and Zimbabwe to Chad/West Africa, worshipped Venus, the Star Goddess, or Astarte.

Temples of Dendera

The sacred complex of Dendera, temple of the Egyptian Goddess Hathor, or Het Her in Hieroglyphic language (meaning House of Heru, or Horus) stands as a hallmark to her complex celestial, mortuary, and regenerative roles. Thought to date back to archaic times in Egypt, Dendera was known as a healing temple, where those in need would come and partake of the blessed waters of the sacred lake believed to cure any disease. The famous Egyptian zodiac on the ceiling of an upstairs chapel is one example of the temple being home to astronomer priests who tracked celestial phenomena. Carvings on the walls, underground chambers, and chapels in the many buildings within the complex attest to the diverse nature of Hathor's cult within Egyptian mythology, and her close association with sacred astronomy, healing, and funerary observances. Her close relationship to the pharaoh, the gods Horus and Ra, as well as cultic practices, and sacred objects can all be found inscribed here.

Hathor was often seen in her guise as a woman with a human face and cow ears. Author Fekri Hassan reminds us cow associations to Goddess date back to Neolithic times when cattle, long held sacred, were seen as a source of nourishment and regeneration. Caring for cows, often women's work, was a hedge against drought and famine. Cows and women became linked together for their abilities to give milk, and together with water were considered the foundations for birth, death, and resurrection — the three main elements that shaped Egyptian religion. When seen as a woman with cow horns embracing a solar disc, her imagery was reflective of her nature as a sky goddess, called The Golden One, and related to the sun god Ra, who is associated with gold, eternity, and immortality. One of her favorite votive offerings was believed to be a golden mirror, a symbol of the sun.

Hathor was not identified with attributes of a domesticated cow, but rather the wild cow of the marshlands which was a symbol of fertility and abundance.

Hassan maintains that tree symbols have long been associated with certain goddesses, and Hathor is within this select group. Called Lady of the Sycamore, Hathor was depicted in relief carvings offering food and water from the tree to the deceased. Because of its mortuary significance, this tree, also sacred to Isis and Nut, was often planted near cemeteries and used to make coffins. It was believed when one was buried in a wood coffin that person, in essence, returned to the mother's womb where they could be reborn. As a funerary Goddess, she was called Lady or Guardian of the West, the location of the necropolis of the dead in Thebes. The golden cliffs bathed in sunlight have been referred to as her very body, and the tombs within the mountainside metaphorically embodied within her regenerative womb. Dead were often shown sitting under her tree where they yearned for Hathor's sustenance, renewal, and to become part of her retinue within the nether regions.

Hathor was also seen as the Mother of the Pharaoh. She protected him and suckled him with her divine milk. She could be depicted in totally bovine form, as well as atop pillars which were carved into the likeness of a human face with a Hathor wig and cow ears as seen in Dendera. She could be depicted wearing a cap in the shape of a vulture. The more usual wig and cow ears imagery was often surmounted atop the handle of a sistrum, or sesheshet, her sacred musical instrument, given as votive offerings. When shaken, it was thought to warn away negative forces and awaken cosmic forces of the universe.

Other realms of Hathor were sexual love, music, and dance. One story speaks of Hathor releasing Ra from his depression with her naked, sensual dancing, and as such, it has been suggested the Dance of the Seven Veils, which originated in Egypt, might be connected to Hathor. Her sacred number seven also relates to her association with the seven stars of the Pleiades, and her seven cow aspects associated with determining the destiny of a child at birth. According to author Naomi Ozaniec, another cult object specific and sacred to Hathor is the menat collar or necklace shaken by her priestesses, and believed to emanate the power of healing. When worn, it signifies the wearer as the embodiment of the Goddess on earth. Both the sistrum and menat are shaken to awaken the deity in ritual.

▲ The head of Hathor graces the top of many pillars at the
Temples of Dendera.

Hathor has been closely associated with Aphrodite and Astarte. Within Egypt, some of her primary cult centers were Dendera, Memphis, the necropolis at Thebes, and many chapels within the temples of other deities and royalty. Her veneration spread to the Levant, Byblos, Nubia, and the Sinai region, where in the 1980s Israeli archaeologists found a temple and cave believed to possibly be the biblical Mount Sinai. Within the cave were Sinaitic carvings from the time of Moses which were deciphered to read El, or God. Temple and cave were located in what is thought to be a sacred precinct of Hathor, and along with all the female Goddess figures found in the Levant, corroborates worship of the "golden calf" by the Israelites. Called Mistress of the Vulva, she was closely associated with conception, childbirth, and healing. Her image, as well as images of other Egyptian goddesses who assisted women in labor was often found on small enclosures in some Egyptian houses, recently identified by archaeologists as birthing rooms. So beloved was she by her devotees that they often took her name as part of their own. While some in the ancient world (or even today) with little understanding of Egyptian Mysteries might have viewed Hathor's rituals as depraved, scholar Rosemary Clark believes Hathor represented vital metaphysical principles within the practitioner's life cycle from conception to sexual awakening, and on to death. She cites the calendar and astronomical elements preserved at the lunar temple of Dendera demonstrate the importance of sacred astronomy to the cult of Hathor. The Temple of Horus at Edfu is important to Dendera, both liturgically and calendrically, which explains why clergy traveled the 100 miles (160 km) between temples for sacred festivals, including the "sacred marriage" of Hathor and Horus.

Today's devotees of Isis and Hathor are dedicated to these Mother Goddesses just as ancient people were long ago. They save their money for years to make pilgrimages from their homes across the globe, descending upon these ancient Egyptian temples, where they venerate the Goddess in her earliest abodes. Here they dance, sing, make offerings, and do ritual to honor the Divine Feminine. They create altars in their homes; re-create ancient rituals with a modern flair and intention complete with ornate garb reminiscent of the Egyptian culture. They recreate sacred objects such as scepters, crowns and sistra, instruments used for music and magic. They gather for classes, conventions, and fairs in veneration of Goddess. Many are ordained ministers with the authority to marry, bury, and conduct other rites of passage ceremonies. Worshippers call upon these deities today as in ancient times during situations in which the aid of a higher power might be deemed necessary.

Within the main temple of Hathor are many chapels, chambers, underground crypts, the stellar twenty-four Hathor-head pillars within the hypostyle hall, and a reproduction of the famous circular zodiac inscriptions on the ceiling of one of the rooftop chapels. Outside the main temple, and within the complex are a small iseum, or temple of Isis, (who eventually assimilated Hathor's attributes), the sacred lake and sanatorium where the sick came to stay during their healing, a small Roman era mamissi, or birth house, honoring Hathor in childbirth, and the remains of a Coptic church.

Getting to the Temples of Dendera

The easiest way to reach Dendera is by a one-day tour or private taxi from Luxor 35 miles (56 km) to the south. Dendera is just 3 miles (5 km) west of the small agricultural city of Qena. If time allows, it is recommended to make a side trip to Abydos, one of the oldest temples in Egypt, provided the political climate is peaceful. Merchants sell their wares outside the temple and refreshment stands enable the weary traveler to get a cold drink. Oftentimes children from the nearby village will crowd around curiously but it is not recommended they be given any handouts of money or gifts. While this might seem harsh, some tour guides will explain this encourages behavior which their elders find demeaning.

Sekhmet Temple at Karnak

Sekhmet, the lion-headed female Goddess, one of the oldest, most powerful deities known to the human race, resides within a small temple enclosure she shares with her consort Ptah on the periphery of the Karnak Temple complex. She has been called: Lady of the Place of the Beginning of Time; Mother of all the Gods; Mother of Mystery; Great Harlot; Flaming One; Destroyer of Rebellions; Empowerer; and the Great One of Healing are just some of her 4,000 epithets which give clues to her nature and abilities. It is said Amenhotep III had 572 statues of Sekhmet commissioned for the Karnak compound, perhaps as a hedge against plague or pestilence. Each statue received due homage and sacrifice by Sekhmet's magician-priests, known throughout the kingdom as the most skilled physicians and exorcists. It was believed the deity might reside within the statue, and from the deity/statue, practitioners might receive healing and teachings. According to scholar Robert Masters, certain of these statues were "essential statues," kept in the holy of holies, only brought out for public display for special festivals, as these statues manifested the most powerful of magical abilities.

Sekhmet's black granite statues are noted for actually moving, a phenomena called Hanu, according to the Masters. Both in ancient times and now, rumor has it, the leonine Goddess might "choose" a devotee for a particular teaching or to do her bidding, and the chosen would be privy to seeing or sensing this movement. Of particular interest is the statue within the Karnak enclosure, believed by superstitious locals to have been responsible for the murder of some local boys employed by archaeologists. Locals were said to have taken retribution against Sekhmet, by breaking her statue into three pieces, though fortunately the statue has since been repaired. Her devotees countered by saying that this senseless killing was not the way of the lioness Goddess, but if her hand was involved, these boys must surely have committed some heinous crime and were beyond redemption! Rumor also speaks of women who secretly attend the statue during nocturnal rituals, though proof of this veneration within the Karnak temple is difficult to substantiate. This author has interviewed Western women who have performed rituals within the confines of this temple and report they have come away with knowledge of healing, feelings of empowerment, and stories of mystical experiences.

▲ Statues of Sekhmet used to line the corridors at her temple at Karnak.

▲ Lion-headed Sekhmet at Karnak is revered by women today who embrace their personal power.

Sekhmet is most notable for the myth in which Ra directs her to punish mankind. She goes on a killing spree, hence obtaining a reputation for being a wanton, blood-thirsty killer, which does not serve her authentic demeanor. Sekhmet is very much a protector of good against evil. She protects those whom she loves, and can retaliate with savagery toward the wicked that might damage her kin. She very much reflects the lioness, capable of doing great harm if provoked or if her young ones are threatened, however she is not prone to savagery for the sake of pleasure or sport. She personifies righteous anger, justice, and power. In ancient days she was believed to respond to provocation with plague and drought. Sekhmet is the patroness of many women today as they seek personal empowerment, and struggle to obtain their proper rights within society and culture. Devotees utilize statues of Sekhmet as icons for healing, passing them among those within the community, requesting the power of the Goddess to aid them in their illness in a kind of sympathetic magic or prayer. Likewise, men and women carry pictures or pocket-size representations of Sekhmet as amulets of power when they must go into situations in which they require justice to be meted out fairly, or when they anticipate their limits might be challenged. Worshippers of Sekhmet often have a particular affinity with felines of all sizes and shapes, often honoring Sekhmet by dedicating time to animal shelters, money to wildlife conservation, and being active in animal rights.

Sekhmet is associated with the creative force of the kundalini, and ecstasies of love. Her name, according to Wallis Budge, is derived from the root *sekhem*, meaning strong, mighty, and violent. She personifies the heat of the sun's rays, thus is associated with purification. She is said to reside in the sun god Ra's brow from where she can spit flames at his enemies. A feisty and formidable foe, pharaohs called upon Sekhmet's power and grace before battle. Usually associated with the edgier side of Hathor and opposite the more benign cat Goddess Bastet, all three Goddesses share the designation of "Eyes of Ra," with Bast and Sekhmet sometimes called his daughters. Mother of Nefertem, god of doctors, consort of

Ptah, the builder and creator god, Sekhmet is usually depicted in a red dress with rosettes over her nipples, an ankh in hand, a sun disc and uraeus on her head. She carries the flint knife of the embalmer, her animals are the lioness and cat, her scent is civet, and her tree, the juniper with medicinal properties.

Sekhmet is one good example of Dutch historian, G. van der Leeuw's contention that Egyptian goddesses have different natures than their neighbors to the north in Greece. Paraphrasing scholar C. J. Bleeker on van der Leeuw, the historian states while goddesses of the Greeks embodied the Great Mother Goddess with connections to Earthly realms, the Egyptian goddesses originally possessed their own separate characters that often times eclipsed that of their Greek sisters and they kept these personas over centuries. Generally their roles might not have been viewed as quite so motherly nor were their domains linked primarily to the chthonic. One might say Egyptian goddesses were multi-faceted and had more diverse interests. Further, while Greek mythology chokes with male supremacy, even having goddesses birthed from the male deities, Egyptian history does not so degrade or humiliate the Feminine Divine, giving female deities their full authority and proper and equal place within the Egyptian pantheon. This equality among the Egyptian male and female deities may well have influenced the relationships between genders and suggests a reason why women in Egypt enjoyed such high status as opposed to women of other cultures during the same period of time. Wives and mothers were respected and seen as equals to men. They could own their own property and had many rights unknown to their sisters in neighboring lands.

Getting to the Sekhmet Temple at Karnak

Discovering the sacred sites of the Upper Nile is one of the most profound pilgrimages on Earth. All one has to do is take a convenient flight into Cairo, and then take a train or domestic flight into Luxor. Taxis, horse drawn carriages, and tours all converge on the Karnak temple compound, the site of wonderful nightly light shows that tell the history of the temple. Once in Karnak, when standing at the first pylon entrance near the Avenue of the Rams, veer toward your left in the area that looks less excavated, and probably will be less visited by tourists. Look for the Temple of Ptah. It's a small enclosed three room temple, with a headless Ptah in the central cell, and Sekhmet off to the right. Temple caretakers can usually be spotted outside and can be persuaded with a minimal gratuity to give devoted tourists a few minutes of uninterrupted meditation time with Sekhmet.

Goddess Focus
Omm Sety — 20th Century Priestess of the Mysteries

Was she a mythomaniac, schizophrenic, or Priestess? Many who knew Dorothy Eady as Omm Sety were not quite sure which more accurately described this British woman (1904-1981 CE) who believed herself to be the reincarnation of Bentreshyt, a priestess of the Egyptian Goddess Isis, who became a great love of the Pharaoh Sety I (1306-1290 BCE). At the age of three, Dorothy had an accident and hit her head, which she believed lifted the "veil of forgetfulness" to past lives, thus enabling her to remember her previous life in the royal court of Sety, the father of the great Ramses II. While the tale is quite a stretch for most to swallow, after reading Jonathan Cott's account of Omm Sety's life, the impossible seems not just possible, but probable. Dorothy moved from Britain to Abydos,

▲ These four coins of Isis can be found in the Museum of Alexandria.

the site of Sety's court during their past life together, and there she spent most of her life in service to the old deities, and in communication with Sety I through the means of astral projection. Local villagers named her Omm Sety, Arabic for "Mother of Sety." (She named her son, Sety, after her beloved king.) She was able to carry on her life at Abydos for decades, employed by the Egyptian Antiquities Department, for whom she cataloged artifacts, translated inscriptions, and gave lectures to visitors. Here in what she considered her true home, Omm Sety worked shoulder to shoulder with the best minds in archaeology and Egyptology, many of whom had the utmost respect for her abilities and insights.

Though very discreet about her religious and esoteric beliefs most of her life, in her final years Omm Sety was the subject of a BBC documentary shown in 1981 entitled *Omm Sety and Her Egypt,* as well as a National Geographic film. While specialists offered possible explanations for Omm Sety's psychic abilities, none could of course disprove reincarnation for her compelling story. She has been described as knowing what she could not know, and being able to do things she should not have been able to do. Cott cites noted scholar of Egyptology and parapsychologist Dr. Bob Brier who after meeting Dorothy stated "Omm Sety had the best feeling of anybody I've ever met for what ancient Egypt was really like. When you conversed with her you felt that there was no distance between her and life as it was lived in the olden days." Lady Olivia Robertson, co-founder of the Fellowship of Isis, enrolled Omm Sety as member #2089 back in 1981. When interviewed by Jonathan Cott, Lady Olivia stated she believed Omm Sety's psychic discovery of her 3,000 year old lover, and recognized Omm Sety as a "latter day Isis, enacting in everyday life the time-honored Mystery of the search for and finding of the dead Osiris and his awakening by a loyal wife."

Isis Temple of Philae

The Isis Temple on the island of Agilkia, referred to today as Philae, was the last stronghold of Egyptian pagan worship in a world being converted to Christianity. Located on the remote southern-most frontier of the Roman Empire, Philae stood as a bastion of Isian worship until the middle of the 6th century CE. In this small jewel of a temple, Isis, perhaps the mightiest and most beloved Goddess for three thousand years, made her last stand against patriarchal monotheism in the ancient world. All the more interesting is the fact that Isis, in her warrioress aspect, is depicted here at the boundary of what was considered the civilized world. According to scholar David Frankfurter, her worship lasted so long here in large part due to the devotion of the strong civilization of the Nubian Blemmyes who staffed and maintained the site, and with whom Greco-Roman authorities wanted to maintain peace.

Auset, more commonly known by her Greek name Isis, was not only the greatest Goddess in Egypt, but her worship was spread by Roman legions, merchants, sailors, and missionary priesthood from the continent of Africa, to Greece, throughout the Roman empire, as far north as Britain, west toward France and Germany, and northeast into Turkey, and the Middle East. She is believed to have made her way into India with Alexander's soldiers, and some believe she traveled the Silk Road into the Far East where her aspects can be seen in the beloved Buddhist Goddess Kwan Yin. More than any other Goddess, Isis was a challenge to the emerging patriarchal religions, her worship coming close to superseding that of Christianity. If seekers look closely, they will see within Christianity much imagery, philosophy, and ritual assimilated from the religion of Egypt. Just a quick glimpse and one can immediately see the similarity between the *Egyptian Book of the Dead* and the Ten Commandments. The Egyptian ankh, symbol of immortality and eternal life, and the djed pillar of Osiris may have influenced Egyptian interpretations of the Christian cross. Furthermore, by the second and early third century CE, the head of the ankh-cross became elongated into a form of a circle, making the symbol in total appear as the Greek Letters "chi" and "rho," the well known monogram of Christ as demonstrated by some of the grave shrouds discovered in Antinoopolis. The image of Isis sitting on her throne with son Horus, beloved and familiar imagery in the pagan world, was without a doubt co-opted by the Church in hope that devotion might be transferred to the infant Christ as he sits atop Mother Mary's lap.

So what made Isis so beloved for thousands of years? She is the quintessential mother, sister, and wife. It did not hurt her image that she was known to be a powerful warrioress, mediator, healer, and savior. Isis embodied the power of nature, and she manifests in the growing things and animals, thus she can insure fertility and prosperity. Alongside her husband/brother Osiris, they made a powerful duo, the two naturally seen as the embodiment of yin and yang, female and male, the androgynous Divine One. Isis was beloved by kings and queens, soldiers and mid-wives, men and women. No matter one's culture, social standing or gender, she loved all her children and all loved her. She searched the world for her murdered husband, lamenting the loss of him. Using her powers of magic, she breathed the breath of life into his lifeless body, resurrecting him long enough to be impregnated. Later she brought their son Horus back from death by drowning. Humankind recognized Isis as an approachable Goddess who had experienced the pain and trials that mortals must endure during life. They saw her suffering, and knew she would understand theirs. They saw her joy, and knew she could bestow grace and happiness upon them. They saw her power to overcome obstacles, and prayed to her for successful outcomes of their own. They saw her standing beside her husband Osiris, Ruler of the Underworld, and knew it was the Divine Couple, their Mother and Father, whom they will meet upon their death, and who will give them eternal life.

Isis' symbol is the throne, and according to Baring and Cashford, it represents the primal order of the beginning, whose shape embodies the mound of creation. Mound symbology, associated with the mountain, even the ziggurat, has been identified as a symbol of the Mother, both as womb, and the place closest to the heavens. With her symbol of the throne, Isis bestowed kingship to pharaohs with proprietary and responsibility with all that entails, just as many other god/kings

▲ The Isis Temple was relocated to Agilka Island to protect it from the rising waters of the Aswan Dam.

received their sovereignty from queens and goddesses. In Egypt, the pharaoh is seen as sitting on the lap of Isis, his mother, who suckles him with her divine milk, instilling within him the right and ability to rule the land and the people. It is through her and the power of her throne that her son/lover, the king, is made.

Oldest of the old, Isis, also called Auset, has been with humankind since the beginning of recorded time. She is depicted in Neolithic form as the bird goddess, and serpent goddess of the Upper and Lower waters of Egypt. In Neolithic times, she was both the pig and vulture goddess. Another of Isis' abilities that promoted her popularity was her absorption of attributes belonging to other deities. She merges with Bast, Nut, Hathor, Sekhmet, Maat, and deities of Greece, Rome, and the Middle East. She shares attributes and temples with Aphrodite, Demeter, Astarte, Artemis, and Hera. Her imagery moves forward in iconography embodied within the Black Madonna, the Virgin Mary, and Sophia — collectively Isis' persona becomes one of her most famous titles, She of Ten Thousand Names. As Mother Nature, she holds reverence for the flora and fauna of Earth, as depicted in the zoomorphic imagery of Egyptology. She has the capability to manifest the attributes of creatures within her queendom. Thus, Isis came to personify a multitude of creatures as her sacred animals. A mini-list includes the cat, serpent, hawk, scorpion, beetle, peacock, and cow. As a universal deity, Isis is a primary creative force, even surpassing that of her beloved Osiris. Then and now, her devotees honor her ability to embody all as they sing her epithet, "Isis is All Things, and All Things are Isis."

The sistrum, sacred to Isis, Bast, and Hathor, was a musical instrument used to keep the energies of the universe flowing and to ward off evil spirits. A symbol of regeneration, it had a phallus-like handle, and a womb-like upper loop. The knot or buckle of Isis, also called "thet," was created by folding Greco-Roman women's over-garments into a knot-like configuration at the breast. This is a sure way to recognize Isis or her clergy in statuary and paintings. The thet is a symbol of Auset's womb, or sacred blood, and a metaphor for her creative forces. Often made of red carnelian, a thet amulet was worn for protection, and thought to confer the power of the life-giving menstrual blood of Isis upon her devotees. Associated with the star, Sirius, the sun and moon, the Tree of Life, Isis is also called Mother of the Universe. A role model for females everywhere, Isis has become the Goddess embraced by mothers, wives, and feminists alike as women recognize within Auset their rights and personal power. Isis' temples thrived in the ancient world until the time of Justinian's reign, 527-565 CE, when pagan shrines were closed and churches were built upon the sites of earlier deities. Philae, a healing temple in ancient times, did not escape desecration, and wall relief carvings today still show signs of defacing at the hands of Christians who converted the site for their worship.

Once actually located on the island of Philae, Isis, or Auset's Temple, had been moved stone by stone to the adjacent Agilka Island. There it was rebuilt in 1964 to escape the rising waters created by the Aswan Dam. Truly a magnificent sight to behold, visitors are usually awed as they approach the island by motor-launch. Once on land, visitors will see elaborately carved columns, as well as temples dedicated to Hathor and Horus, the Birth House, the Kiosk of Trajan, and most importantly, the Holy of Holies within the inner sanctum of Isis' temple. The neighboring island of Bigga is sacred to Osiris, and is one of the places devotees believe Isis' beloved consort was buried.

Getting to the Isis Temple near Aswan

Flights arrive into Aswan from Cairo and Luxor. Buses also travel regularly from Luxor to Aswan. Once in Aswan, hire a taxi down to the boat dock where tourists can join an organized tour, or hire a private motor-launch to Agilka Island. It is best to go very early in the morning or later in the afternoon. This is one of the major sites in Aswan, a jewel in the crown of Egypt, and crowds by the hundreds gather during prime time hours.

Bubastis

During ancient times, multitudes converged on Bubastis to celebrate at the festival of the Goddess Bast in a style similar to modern Spring Break or Mardi Gras. Herodotus reported worshippers traveling there by boat down the river Nile, making merry, drinking, singing, playing music, with women lifting their skirts in joy all along the journey. As many as 700,000 were said to make the pilgrimage to Bubastis each year, and during this festival more alcohol was consumed than throughout the rest of the year! Women shook their sistra, the sacred rattle of Bast, Isis, and Hathor. Sacrifices were made at the temple of the cat-headed Goddess which Herodotus described as being on a sort of island, with two canals that did not meet surrounding the temple mound.

Instead, a paved processional way intersected the shaded 100-foot (30-m) wide canals which led to the 60-foot (18-m) tall gates to the temple. Within the temple grounds was a sacred grove where the statue of Bast resided, a configuration unique to Egyptian temple designs. This standard design usually had groves growing adjacent to the temples rather than being inside the holy of holies, or cella, of the temple. Herodotus, who had traveled far and wide, and seen many a temple in his day, described this one as "a greater pleasure to look at." Red granite walls were carved with typical Egyptian scenes, and one can just imagine the grove being inhabited by a multitude of temple cats.

Information on Bast, or Bastet, is fragmented, but it is clear from the popularity of her festivals and the multitude of cat cemeteries, and feline statues unearthed from archaeological sites throughout Egypt, she was as beloved in ancient times as she is today. People even took her name as part of theirs, such as in the name Senobastis, meaning Son of Bastet. An older deity mentioned in the *Book of the Dead*, Bast was originally a Sun Goddess in lioness form, called the Eye

▲ The goddess Bast was depicted as a cat or a cat-headed woman.

of Ra, and described as the sun god's avenger, with her earliest aspects not totally benevolent. She was capable of stealth and ferocity when she defeated Ra's enemy, Apophis (Apep), the serpent of the nether regions. Called Lady of the East, her cult lasted over 3,000 years being venerated in other Egyptian cities such as Memphis, Heliopolis, Herakleopolis, Esna, and Denderah. At first depicted as lion-headed and later cat-headed, she was often seen holding a basket, perfume jar, was scepter, ankh, or papyrus wand, and could have a pectoral or aegis bearing a lion or cat's head. Later, as Bast merged with the Greek Artemis, she was recognized as a lunar deity.

Though her own mother is unknown, Bast is mother to the lion-headed god, Mihos. She is sometimes considered the wet nurse, or older than Isis (who eventually absorbed Bastet), and called the "soul of Isis" and sister of Horus, which obviously is a bit conflicting as that would make her the daughter of Osiris and Isis. Conflicting facts are common when there are multiple myths surrounding goddesses, gods, heroines or heroes. Unusual statues of Bast that have come to be called "housewife Basts" have been found having the head of a cat and wearing long flowing robes which include an Isis knot. She is associated with Hathor, Neith, Tefnut, and Mut, and is often described as the opposite of the fierce Sekhmet. Scholar R. E. Witt concludes the assimilation of Isis and Artemis could not have taken place without Bast as an intermediary and states, "the irony of the pagan figure of the Virgin Mother is the result of the fusion of Artemis with Isis which owes its beginning to the mediation of a goddess with the features of a cat."

She is recognized today primarily as a Mother Goddess, and her attributes are involved with fertility, music, dancing, joy, domestic tranquility, protection, happiness, prosperity, and playful sexuality. She is also associated with nurturing and childbirth. The Goddess Bast was believed to have the nature or attributes of a lioness and a cat. Today women recognize her aspects to echo their own domestic cats. Cousin to the mysterious, powerful, and ferocious leopard and lioness, the felines who share our homes are approachable, patient, dignified, sensitive, and loving, even if they have their occasional aloof, cantankerous, wily,

▲ Barley restored, the ruins at Bubastis include a well, museum and cat cemetery.

and independent moments as well. Bast is considered by many devoted to her as the Goddess protector of their beloved feline familiars, pets, and family. Her aid is invoked if a pet goes missing, becomes ill, or is about to give birth. An important point to make is while cats were sacred to Bast, she was not considered a cat herself, and cats were not worshipped, though they were revered.

The Egyptians domesticated the cat about 4,000 years ago and so beloved were they, Herodotus states upon the death of a cat, the owner would shave their eyebrows in mourning. Witt tells of a Roman in Ancient Egypt who killed a cat and faced an angry mob. The Egyptians referred to the cat as *miw*, and they served spiritual as well as practical purposes. Cat fat was thought to ward off rats if it was smeared on walls. The fat was mixed with other substances for medicinal purposes such as to aid the pain of arthritis. Female cat hair was mixed with milk and resin and applied to burns. To satisfy the demand for this beloved creature, catteries that bred cats were a part of sacred temple precincts where the devoted might obtain a cat that might be used as a votive offering to Bastet. Bubastis is mentioned in Ezekiel in the Bible where it is called Pibeseth. When a cat passed away, it was taken to Bubastis, embalmed and buried, though their organs were not preserved in canopic jars as was done during the human mummification process. So many mummified cats were buried at Bubastis, perhaps in excess of 180,000, it is said thousands were shipped from Bubastis to England and used in making fertilizer.

Bubastis was once a city of great importance along the routes to Memphis, Mount Sinai, and Asia. Today the site is not on most tourist itineraries though it has been included in the 108 chosen sacred sites because of Bast's prominence within Goddess spirituality, and the general popularity of felines in general. Not yet fully restored, there is currently no standing temple of Bast, though it does have some scattered ruins from her red granite temple and other temples. A well, a museum, and ruins of mud brick cat cemeteries can be found here. Rosemary Clark reports there is a black granite altar of Sekhmet at the site. When E. Naville excavated the area in the late 1880s, he found "heaps of white cat bones," bronze cat statues, and cat masks. Since Naville's discovery there has been much looting of artifacts.

125

Getting to Bubastis

Located on the southeastern edge of the city limits of El Zagazig (Lower Egypt) between the railway line and town center, the city is approximately 50 miles (80 km) northeast of Cairo via Bilbeis. There are no structured tours to this region, so one would have to hire a private car or drive to the site. The site is also known as Tell Basta.

LIBYA

The North Africa countries of Libya, Tunisia, Ethiopia, and Morocco are host to a plethora of holy sites dedicated to Goddess. In Libyan Cyrene stands a temple dedicated to Demeter and Persephone as well as another to Isis. At the World Heritage site of Sabratha stands another temple of Isis which looks out across the sea. In Volubilis, Morocco, once a part of Roman Mauritania, there stands a temple to Venus, which harkens back to the worship of Astarte. History notes this is the city of Cleopatra Selene, daughter of Cleopatra VII and Marc Anthony, a queen noted to have carried on the legacy of her mother as a priestess of Isis. Certainly temples dedicated to the Egyptian Goddess Isis or Au Set, in ancient Egyptian, once stood in Volubilis, as do temples dedicated to Minerva and Juno. At one point before the rise of male centered religions such as Mithraism and Christianity, there was a movement toward a uniformity or monotheism of these feminine deities.

Leptis Magna

The ancient city of Leptis Magna, while not only a World Heritage site and possibly the world's best preserved Roman-era city, is also a sacred site to the goddesses Cybele and Artemis with their temples still standing intact today. These two aspects of the Divine Feminine found throughout Europe, Turkey, and the Mediterranean share mutual characteristics. At one time both were venerated in the form of a black stone, just like the goddesses of the Kaaba stone at Mecca. They were also both high profile goddesses in Asia Minor, or Phrygia, each holding sway over animals and the wild things of the earth with Cybele earning the title, "Mother of all gods and men." Scholar Savina Teubal suggests Cybele may represent the transition toward domestication of animals as she was usually depicted with leopards. Teubal states the "taming of wild animals, such as leopards (for protection or sympathetic magic for healing) or sheep, goats, and cattle (as livestock), would more likely have initially been in the hands of the women who bore and reared their own young."

Cybele or Kybele, the Phrygian Mother, was also called Mother of the Mountain, Magna Mater, meaning Great Mother or Mater Kubile by the Romans. Cybele has been associated with Rhea and Demeter, and equated to Aphrodite. According to scholar James Rietveld, Cybele was a Near Eastern Goddess from Pessinus in Phrygia, "the heartland of ecstatic religions of all kinds" and her worship, described as "hierarchical, exclusive, and exotic, with very strange rituals and a troop of adherents who performed acts of self-flagellation" spread into Greece, Rome, and neighboring countries. While in Anatolia, (the region roughly occupied by Turkey today), devotees saw her as a grain Goddess and carried her image in a cart which they pulled across a field in hopes for a bountiful harvest. They also washed her image in a river to symbolize the irrigation of the fields. Scholar Walter Burkert reports her figure was often carved in rock facades or niches made for her image which was often depicted standing between two lions. Some images show her crowned with a high headdress, or *polos,* between lyre and flute players. Her more benign rituals were often accompanied by the wild and chaotic music of flutes, drums, and cymbals hypnotically leading her practitioners into a kind of trance possession of ecstatic bliss.

When Hannibal of Carthage was threatening Rome, the Cumaean Sybil prophesied the only avenue to victory for the Romans was veneration of the powerful Goddess in the guise of her meteorite stone. This would require her stone to travel from Anatolia to Rome, though the Phrygian king was not too willing to let Cybele's image leave his kingdom until Cybele herself appeared to him in a dream and expressed her desire to go. King Attalusat could not deny the Goddess this request, so her image traveled to Rome and the Romans eventually defeated Hannibal.

Cybele's cult was celebrated by the Phrygians, Greeks, and Romans and known throughout the regions for the galloi, or self-castrated male clergy, honoring Cybele by mimicking her lover Attis thought to have torn off his penis in anguish for having betrayed Cybele. Attis is said to have bled to death from this act, though it is understood his death is a metaphor for the growing seasons and his sacrifice gives life to the land. Despite this macabre castration element that sometimes did take place according to ancient reporters like Ovid, scholar Burkert states this mutilation was "far from always part and parcel" of the cult. Romans were more tolerant of the rites of Cybele due to the aforementioned prophecy found within the Sibylline Books that stated no army could invade Rome as long as Cybele resided in the city, yet the galloi were restricted to the

temple precinct on Palatine Hill in Rome. Scholar Renee Salzman cites the galloi of Rome were allowed outside the precinct only during special April celebrations, and their feminine appearance and dress was a curiosity to the conservative Romans. Greeks, on the other hand, were reported to have thrown clergy of Cybele into a ravine where criminals were hurled, according to scholar Robert Turcan. Rietveld, quoting Arthur Darby Nock, states that "we must not be surprised that the eunuch priest, in spite of his special holiness, often failed to receive public respect" since they enacted "an un-Greek custom."

Author Henri Schindler describes the Roman rituals embracing Cybele and Attis in 204 BCE as celebrations of debauchery that culminated in some of the priests of Attis emasculating themselves with their severed organs reverentially placed upon the altar of the deities. The castrated priests were given the reward of a phallus image to wear around their neck as a token of their sacrifice, which Schindler says was used to entertain other male members of their group. Soon cross-dressing and wearing masks became the rage and men dressed as women offered themselves to other men in their congregation. In a private conversation with Mr. Schindler, he made associations between these ancient rituals with traditions still

▲ Statue of the many-breasted Black Artemis.

alive in the Roman Catholic Church. Interestingly, he noted that the hand gesture used by priests today in blessings with the index and second finger pointing up, while the other two digits and thumb are down, is called the "hand of Attis." Today priests still wear elaborate dress-like vestments and practice celibacy, both according to Schindler, are remnants of these ancient rituals. Some scholars referred to this cross-dressing and the relinquishing of the masculinity through ritual castration as a means to connect more closely with the feminine aspects of nature or Goddess. And not to be overlooked, circumcision, a lesser form of genital mutilation widely practiced in today's society, is well documented as having its origins as a requisite ritual in which humans made a covenant with God.

Here in Leptis Magna it was probable that ancient ceremonies included the procession of the images of Cybele carried on carts and wagons, pulled by garlanded oxen. The images were taken down to the nearest stream and ritually bathed before being returned to the temple. The ox was usually sacrificed and its blood used to anoint the celebrants in order to wash away their sins. According to Schindler, in France, Druid priests celebrated their spring rite called *fete du soleil* in which they led a young bull through the street, festooned with flowers, before sacrificing it to the Druid deities. Reflections of these ancient rituals are alive today as the carnival floats in the Mardi Gras parades in New Orleans often depicting imagery of ancient gods and goddesses, along with the fourth float of the Rex parade always being the *Boef Gras*, or fatted ox. Until 1960 when the Boef Gras became made of paper mache, an actual ox was used in the parade, which was slaughtered afterwards.

Scholar Patricia Monaghan tells of a renewal baptism performed by Cybele worshippers once in their lifetime, or every few decades, where a devotee would stand in a pit and allow himself to be thoroughly covered in the blood of a slaughtered ox to enact his rebirth and emergence from the womb revitalized in this love for Magna Mater. Worship of Cybele was far and wide. Interesting associations include the heretic second century Christian sect called Montanists who venerated Cybele and associated Attis with Jesus, as well as the Roman Emperor Augustus who believed his wife Livia was Cybele's earthly incarnation.

The city of Leptis Magna began as a Phoenician port of call around 900 BCE and later flourished under the Roman rule of Septimus Severnus in 193-211 CE. Many of the major buildings are from the reign of Severnus and include a multitude of monuments which would take all day to visit. There is a Roman forum, temples, nymphaeum, basilica, the standing market called the Macellium, and an amphitheater which was adjacent to the temple of Artemis. The shrine of Magma Mater (Great Mother) was built during the reign of the Roman Emperor Vespasian in 72 CE by a certain Iddibal, son of Balsillec, a native of the city. It is said Hannibal arranged to buy elephants at Leptis Magna for his crusades against the Romans, who later procured elephants here for their warped amusement in the Roman Coliseum.

Getting to Leptis Magna

Leptis Magna is located 123 miles (198 km) east of Tripoli. Travel to Libya is no longer restricted. Major airlines fly into Tripoli, though travel is restricted to organized tours and tour operators who are responsible for requiring the necessary visas. Ground travel by way of Tunis is another option. There is a check point at the Tunisia-Libya border. At Matmatma, in Tunisia, Libyans meet tourists and escort them into the country. Once past the checkpoint, with papers in order, it's smooth sailing. With the ever-changing political climate in our modern world, it is always important to double check travel restrictions, and recommendations of the U.S. State Department before traveling to places that might possibly have become unsafe for tourists. Organized tours will probably include the ancient cities of Sabratah and Cyrene, both of which have standing temples dedicated to goddesses.

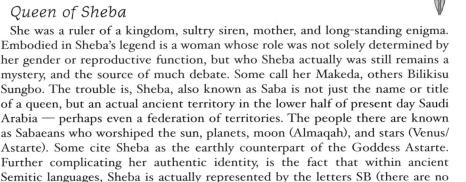

Goddess Focus
Queen of Sheba

She was a ruler of a kingdom, sultry siren, mother, and long-standing enigma. Embodied in Sheba's legend is a woman whose role was not solely determined by her gender or reproductive function, but who Sheba actually was still remains a mystery, and the source of much debate. Some call her Makeda, others Bilikisu Sungbo. The trouble is, Sheba, also known as Saba is not just the name or title of a queen, but an actual ancient territory in the lower half of present day Saudi Arabia — perhaps even a federation of territories. The people there are known as Sabaeans who worshiped the sun, planets, moon (Almaqah), and stars (Venus/ Astarte). Some cite Sheba as the earthly counterpart of the Goddess Astarte. Further complicating her authentic identity, is the fact that within ancient Semitic languages, Sheba is actually represented by the letters SB (there are no vowels) so Sheba may be Saba, Seba, Sabe, Sheba, etc. According to Dr. Miri Hunter Haruach of Project Sheba, linguistically, the root of the name can be connected to interesting associations; sabbath or shabat (Jewish Ethiopian for daughter of god), Ni-Saba, the Sumerian goddess of grain, writing, and wisdom literally translates to Lady or Queen (Ni) of Sheba (Saba). Haruach begins to see a pattern for a queen giving her wisdom to kings, which brings us to Sheba's visit to King Solomon in Jerusalem.

There is little archaeological evidence to support contact between the Levant and Southern Arabia, and consequently for the meeting of Solomon and Sheba. Scholars believe the story was designed to enhance the importance of Solomon and Yahweh. Yet, the legends hold on with the tenacity of a vise grip. The son of Sheba and Solomon is believed by some to have become the first in a line of kings who were keepers of the Ark of the Covenant, and with him the matrilineal practice of the Sabeans was believed to have ended. These advocates contend the Ark is located in Ethiopia. Many scholars disagree, with some believing the Ark was more likely sent to Babylon where it was destroyed, while others believe it may still lay buried within the Temple Mount in Jerusalem.

Uncovering the identity of Sheba or the location of the lost Ark will not happen in this book, but sacred sites which are identified with Sheba are certainly worth a look! In June 1999, archaeologist Dr. Patrick Darling working in conjunction with Bournemouth

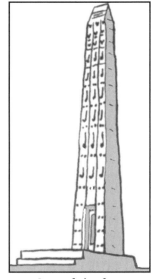

▲ One of the famous Axum obelisks.

University uncovered the site of Eredo, a few hours from Lagos in Nigeria. While inconclusive, they are tentatively making connections to Sheba, particularly as hundreds of thousands of pilgrims visit a grave here in honor of Bilikisu Sungbo, also known as Sheba to some. Eredo has been described as a magical grove and shrine under tall trees. Next is the Temple of the Moon God uncovered in Marib, located within the southern Arabian desert in northern Yemen, where, incidentally, women had developed a female dialect unintelligible to outsiders, though it is dying out under the influence of television and modern education. Called Mahram Bilqis, this impressive site was sacred to pilgrims from 1200 BCE to 550 CE. Originally excavated in 1951, continuing excavations are planned by the University of Calgary. Our final stop is Axum, Ethiopia, where tourists can visit Sheba's bath, the ruins of her palace, and gaze upon the church which is noted to house the Ark, though no one is allowed inside.

Sheba's legacy, a kingdom that spanned from India to Arabia, and Zimbabwe to Chad/West Africa, is a role model for women, and perhaps knowing exactly who she represents is not as important as what she means to women. In the words of Haruach, "The Consciousness of the Queen of Sheba is emerging ... because our consciousness as a planet is turning or re-turning to values that exemplify the concepts of respect and honor for the feminine, for nature and for our planet. She is calling us to become outrageous, audacious and courageous ... to embrace a more active definition of the word woman ... to make a commitment to become eco-spiritualists who work for justice ... to remember we are capable ... and lastly, she is calling us to accept and love ourselves. This is a formula for spiritual, cultural and social transformation. This is the work of the womanist."

NIGERIA

From the Sahara region of Africa hail the astonishing Dogon tribe, at first blush primitive and unsophisticated, yet long knowledgeable of stars in our sky only recently discovered with powerful telescopes. Dogons revere the star Sirius, associated with Isis, whose worship thrived over 3,000 years ago, and whose temples are numerous throughout northern Africa, Egypt, and Europe. Sacred sites left by the Phoenicians, Carthaginians, and Romans in northern Africa along the Mediterranean are a testament to the worship of not only Isis, but Astarte, Minerva, Ceres, Tanit, Cybele, and Aphrodite. Vicki Noble cites Gorgon tribes of warrior women from northern Africa as the predecessors of the three Gorgon sisters of classical Greece, which includes Medusa. They had snakes for hair representing the female fighting spirit, carried double axes, and were proficient as oracles. These Amazon-like warrior women are thought to have roots in Libya, which to the Greeks referred to the entire continent of Africa rather than the country now known as Libya. Noble quoting Barbara Walker and others cites the North African Berbers still call themselves "Amazigh," and recalls the Amazon-like Dahomey women warriors of Benin West Africa. Amazon-like women were known to traditionally venerate Goddesses such as Artemis, Mother of the Animals, and Diana the Huntress.

Temple of Oshun

Oshun, one of the most beloved of the Yoruban Goddesses is venerated by devotees at her temple within the confines of the 400 year-old Sacred Forest of

Oshogbo, situated near the river of the same name. The shrine, a centerpiece of Yoruban cultural pride, was built by artist Suzanne Wenger and devotees of the Goddess in the 1950s. It is surrounded by a wall made of mud, steel, and cement in an earthy style that befits the natural landscape, and captures the fertile essence of the Goddess it was built to honor. A depiction of Oshun herself in a welcoming open-armed posture is visible beside the river. She stands on a sacred fish, the symbol of her son, who became the first *Ataoja*, or of regal lineage. The rocks near her image are associated with her legends of indigo dyeing. The Goddesses Oya and Iya Moopo, as well as Yoruban male deities are all depicted in the grove. Located on the outskirts of the town of Oshogbo, the Sacred Forest is replete with unique Yoruban shrines, but none match in size or wonder as the Temple of Oshun, the River Goddess.

According to Professor Emeritus E. O. James from the University of London, Oshun, an *orisha* or divine spirit of the Yoruban tradition, is believed to be able to affect the fortune of her devotees thus creating an interdependent relationship wherein devotees adopt the principle of *do ut des,* described as, "I give that you may give." Like other orishas, which have also been described as archetypes and patterns of energy, Oshun is closely connected to her devotees. Practitioners provide nourishment for the Goddess and according to James quoting Robert Farris Thompson, Historian of African Art, she in turn activates the *ashe,* or "power to

bring to pass," which lies dormant within the universe in order to affect change as necessary. Through the intimacy of ritual trance or possession, where the orisha inhabits the body of the devotee, the Goddess is able to assist the practitioner toward spiritual growth. The orisha is called by specific drumming rhythms, and will only inhabit the devoted during ritual ceremonies, thus the devotee does not have to worry about being possessed at inappropriate or unwelcome times.

Devotees and clergy are quick to recognize the different orisha when they appear during ceremonies as they each have distinct personalities and mannerisms, and they show up in response to being called by the practitioners who invoke them with rhythms, likened to dialing their phone number. Trance possession has been described as the orisha descending down upon the devotee and during this "joined" state, the orisha can partake of the dancing, festivities, and feasting through the human vessel she or he inhabits. As the trance and spiritual abilities of the devoted is enhanced during these exposures, the gap between the human and divine diminishes, allowing the person to see and absorb aspects of deity within himself.

▲ The riverside Temple of Oshun is a mysterious place.

The following paraphrases Professor James quoting Fernando Ortiz, expert in Afro-American studies, who describes Oshun's personality as she appears during ceremonies in which she has been called. When she first inhabits a devotee or clergy her swaying movements are like her birth upon the river waterways. Next she brings her arms up over her head, shaking her bracelets like bubbling springs, and then lowers her arms. Next stage she may be seen combing her hair and looking upon her image in the reflective waters of her river. Finally, she begins to take on the mannerisms of a flirt, her body swaying and strutting while she laughs, kisses, and hugs those around her. These mannerisms or the drama acted out is called *caminos*, meaning path, or road. What is important to realize is during this trance possession the deity and human are able to communicate and the Goddess can assist the practitioner in matters of prophecy, health, and spiritual development. This is considered a sacred gift. According to Mircea Eliade, religious historian, this process of making the mythic world of the gods present belongs to the nature of all religious ceremony.

The Goddess or orisha, Oshun, has been described as vivacious, sensuous, and is associated with the life-giving waters of the Oshun River, as well as the Goddess Aphrodite/Venus. The swaying of her hips is compared to the flowing waters, and she embodies a beautiful and erotic woman, confident in her erotic sexuality. She loves fine gifts and is a connoisseur of good food and drink. Her experience in the arts of lovemaking have earned her the name La Puta Santa, or whore-saint, as well as Puta Madre, mother-whore, similar to that of Mary Magdalene and the Virgin Mary within sacred feminine realms. Oshun has also been called our Lady of Charity. It is important to understand while at first blush Oshun may seem cast in the light of a prostitute, she is more accurately the sexually liberated woman who gives pleasure to herself and of herself when she so desires, reflecting the true meaning of the virgin Goddess who is powerful within herself. While monogamy might not be Oshun's forte, she is considered loyal, refusing to have her behavior defined by social mores. She is the independent woman that sometimes sends shivers through the hearts of men. A multifaceted Goddess, Oshun is also known to be Yeye Kari, or mother of sweetness, and Iyalode, or mother of fishes, and mother of birds, the latter connecting her with magical powers of air. She is the patroness of women who venerate her and ask her blessings for matters uniquely female: fertility and reproductive problems, childbirth, and problem pregnancies. Her devotees are not put off by her healthy appetite for pleasure because she is loved for her good counsel and care of them.

Patricia Monaghan elaborates on Oshun, known for her beauty, charm, and characteristic brass bracelets, and white stones from a riverbed. Altars to her usually include beautiful ritual items such as fans, brass objects, jewels, yellow copper, mirrors, and more bracelets, which she loves. Food offerings can include onions, beans, and salt, a dish called *omuluku*. Her annual ceremony, known as Ibo-Osun, consists of the offerings of yams, dancing, and women taking on names which include that of the Goddess to honor her. Held the last week of August, it is a great time to visit the temple. The local celebration continues for about nine days, culminating in offerings being made to Oshun in her inner sanctuary by the priesthood, followed by a ceremony on the river where offerings are made to the River Goddess in her fluid form, while devotees pray for their petitions to be granted. It should be noted, tourists are usually only allowed in the anterooms of shrines. This is viewed as important to protect both the shrine from spiritual defilement, (as well as tourists from taboos), and the powerful forces that might unsettle the uninitiated. Pilgrims are reminded this is a sacred precinct and proper respect is required around the shrines, river, and sacred forest. The shrine has had problems in the past with intolerant religious extremists who have attempted to desecrate the shrines, therefore those who visit here are asked to do so with only good intentions.

Getting to the Temple of Oshun

The city of Oshogbo is located in Nigeria, 142 miles (228 km) north of Lagos, the capital. Oshogbo can be reached by bush taxis, or share taxis from the capital. From Oshogbo, the Sacred Forest and shrine can be reached on foot. It is about a 30-minute walk from Oba's Palace on Oshun Shrine Road, and located by the sacred river near the Lya Mapa grove. Huge sculptures show the way. The Oja Oba market across from Oba's Palace has stalls selling items related to the Yoruban deities where one might purchase an offering for the deity before visiting the temple. Travelers are advised to check on the current political climate of the area before making a pilgrimage.

Goddess Focus
The Secret Sande Society — For Women Only

The Sande Society is the training ground for young West African women, particularly within Sierra Leone and Liberia. Membership insures young women will learn all they need to know in order to prosper in their society. They are taught about politics, sex, beauty, arts, healing, parenting, and herbal recipes to make all manner of potions. They learn to sing and dance, how to earn a living, and behave within marriage where husbands are shared with other co-wives called *mbaa*. The time spent with the Sande Society is considered a time of initiation, and when they return home young women will have taken a new name to signify their rebirth, and are then considered ready for marriage. Sande governs educational, moral, social, and political aspects of women's lives, protecting them, and giving them access to ancestor spirits and sacred knowledge. While the society exists within patriarchal culture where women are subordinate to men, the Sande Society is central to communities and exerts considerable power. Girls who do not go through Sande Society initiation are considered to have fewer good prospects for the future, have little connection to their culture, and might be considered outcasts.

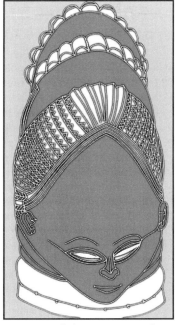

Another interesting aspect of Sande Society is a masked dance which celebrates Sande ideals. Initiates direct male wood carvers to create interpretive masks called *sowei,* which might be more accurately described as helmets. These masks are used by the girls in Society functions, festivals, and special events. In simplest terms, the masks are

▲ One of the many Sande Society masks.

believed to characterize Sowo, a female water goddess, or mermaid, called *Tingoi,* who embodies attributes of truth, beauty, and wisdom representative of the ideals of womanhood and female culture. It is believed when the woman's head is within the divine sowei mask, a transformation occurs bringing the mind and awareness of mortal woman and the sacred spirit together into a universal spirit. Masks can be carved into any design that represents female beauty and virtue, sometimes even stylized female labias or penis imagery are used.

For the obvious benefit to women, there is a tragic side to initiation into the Society, and the reason for secrecy. At a designated time, girls are called into the *kpanguima,* or sacred compound, which is strictly off limits to men, and everyone but female Sande elders and initiates. To the sounds of shouting, drumming, and continuous music, the cries of pain and terror are muffled while a clitoridectomy is performed on the new initiate. The female excision complete, a girl has now "died into Sande," or *ha hale ma*. It is believed the young initiate is reborn a *nyaha,* a finer, better person. The rite of passage from childhood to womanhood complete, the young woman will now be assured a better place in society, despite the pain and complicated medical problems she will continue to endure for the rest of her life. When confronted by international organizations interested in obliterating the custom, the late president of Kenya, Jomo Kenyatta, stated these rites were so essential to the fabric of societies, the abolition would destroy the tribal system. Clitoridectomy, obviously not viewed as an abuse or a health hazard within these tribes, is so deeply entrenched within these societies, it will take decades of education to eradicate.

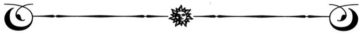

GAIA ALERT
GORILLAS IN THE MIST

Dian Fossey's heart-wrenching 1988 film *Gorillas in the Mist* brought attention to the decimation of the mountain gorillas in the Virunga Forest of Rwanda, Uganda, and the DRC, the Democratic Republic of the Congo. Poaching, loss of habitat, and civil unrest were the proverbial "nails in the coffin" for this species, and their future looked bleak. Extinction, however, was not to be the case. There is new cause for celebration as census figures show the mountain gorilla is holding on and has even grown 17% in numbers since 1989. Peace, the promise of tourist dollars, and anti-poaching efforts were key components in the rise of their population. Tourists are charged $250 to get up close and personal to get that perfect photo! Fortunately, some locals realize the benefit of long-term planning that the tourist revenue can generate for the future. Others must still be educated against poaching them to extinction for their perceived medicinal value, or for their paws which become souvenir ashtrays or trophies. Their numbers are still low, with a census of only about 700 animals on the face of the earth. Conservation groups continue to work with governments and locals to insure potential disease, civil unrest, or diminishing economic conditions do not adversely affect the remaining gorillas.

Mountain gorillas are usually 10 year-old before they have their first baby, and they only become pregnant every 3-4 years. This makes insuring the survival of the species and increasing the population a very slow process. On May 19, 2004, a young gorilla mother named Nyabitondore, who lives in Volcanoes National

Park of the Virunga Heartland, created a sensation as she delivered rare gorilla twins. Taking care of two babies is challenging for any mother, and Nyabitondore is no different. Everyone is saying a prayer for Nyabitondore, her new offspring, and for the park rangers who defend the animals. Recently five park rangers were killed in their homes when renegade militia looted and burned one of the Congo's national parks. Conservationists have begun to build a wall around part of Virunga, one of Africa's oldest national parks, to prevent settlers from destroying habitats, the biggest threat to the species. The commandments of conservation are worth repeating: "Think Globally, Act Locally. Donate and Volunteer. Never buy souvenirs made from the bodies of any animal. Humans are stewards and keepers of Mother Earth, and her creatures are not inexhaustible commodities. Mankind has no right of dominion over wildlife."

▲ The magnificent creatures could disappear from the Earth.

TUNISIA

Moving from the deep recesses of our earliest past through recent history, Goddess has been with all of humankind in a variety of forms as she appeals to different people across time and place. In the desert regions of Tunisia and North Africa are some of the oldest rock carvings ever discovered. According to cultural historian Lucia Chiavola Birnbaum, worship of the Dark Mother Goddess, began where there were the first sparks of life, on the continent of Africa, once called the Dark Continent. She theorizes that "everyone's genetic 'beautiful mother' is African and dark, and that she is the oldest divinity we know." Eventually worship of the Dark Mother radiated out as people of the region migrated throughout Asia, into Sinai, and beyond. Birnbaum says to look for the red ochre (signifying blood of life, childbirth and menstruation), and the pubic "V" symbol in caves and rock cliffs, and one can learn where the Divine Feminine's earliest worship occurred. Lucia's theory is supported by Italian archaeologist Emmanuel Anati who believes the Garden of Eden was located in the valley of the Rift in central and south Africa where humans appeared 100,000 years ago. Of course competing theories cite the Garden of Eden as being located elsewhere. Anati concludes the oldest religion we know was centered on a woman, and believes before the invention of writing, our "greatest and most significant historical archive" is rock art painted or incised on caves and cliffs. Ochre red, sign of the dark mother in rock art may, states Anati, "be the most ancient evidence of artistic creation in the world." Symbols of the Goddess are: spirals, straight or wavy lines, petals, concentric circles, and the pubic 'V,' also recognized by feminist scholars such as Marija Gimbutas. There is still much to learn about the ancient and complicated renderings in caves and on cliffs, and there are divergent views. Many sites throughout Africa, such as Tassili N'Ajjer in southern Algeria of the Sahara, is comprised of rock images by the thousands, suggest examples to some scholars of an association of worship with the Ancient Mother.

Dougga

The internationally obscure, and sometimes controversial Goddess called Tanit, was known to be venerated in this small city of Dougga, boasting social, cultural, and religious grandeur rivaling larger, richer cities like Carthage (modern Tunis). Dougga, known once as Thugga, was the place to see and be seen in ancient times. Rituals, processions, and performances dedicated to local deities were described as elaborate and on-going affairs. Enticing still today as a sacred destination, Dougga is the mother lode of pilgrimage sites. Enthusiasts of Goddess spirituality can visit holy places dedicated not just to Tanit, but also Minerva, Ceres, Juno, Cybele (as Tellus Mater), and Venus — all here in one place! But it is Tanit who is unique to the area. Called Mother Goddess of the Heavens by her devotees, associated with Astarte and Ugaritic Anat, she is thought to have been a deity of the indigenous Berbers. Others connect her linguistically to the Phoenicians, making her the by-product of cultural assimilation, specifically the Africanization of a Phoenician divinity. Situated in a natural bowl-like valley surrounded by hillside temples and olive groves, this North African city has

▲ Women participating in a shamanist trance dance.

been described today as striking and evocative, pleasing to even the most jaded traveler, and a "must see" destination among Mediterranean cities.

Tanit, also called Dea Caelestis, or Caelestis, which means Heavenly Goddess, was the sky Goddess of the Punic people. Patricia Monaghan describes Tanit as "the winged goddess with a zodiac around her head and the sun and moon in either hand." Tanit was sometimes relegated to the status of moon goddess but Monaghan believes Tanit ruled the sun and stars as well. Barbara Walker says Tanit's priestesses were noted astrologers and diviners, often as sought after as the Cumaean Sybils. She cites the story of Aeneas who came from Carthage to found Rome and tells of Queen Tanaquil who bestowed sovereignty on the early Roman Tarquin kings as being none other than the Libyan Goddess Tanit. This power of the Goddess to bestow sovereignty repeats itself in many cultures and in many lands. Susan Ackerman citing R. A. Oden proposes the caduceus imagery of Tanit originated from the sacred date palm iconography representing the Canaanite Asherah. Other names for Tanit, according to Monaghan, were Astroarche, Queen of the Stars, and Libera, Goddess of Libya, whose annual festival was celebrated in Rome during the Ides of March.

Tanit (who was worshipped in Malta, Sardinia, and Spain) arrived on the scene in North Africa around the fifth century BCE, and was thought to represent aspects of motherhood and fertility much like the Greek Hera or Roman Juno. Goddess scholar Monica Sjoo reveals Tanit as further associated with death, rebirth, resurrection, shamanist rites, healing, and the otherworld. Astarte eventually became Tanit and was often accompanied by her consort Baal Hammon. It is believed her veneration surpassed his as her name appeared on texts thousands of times over several centuries. As the Phoenicians of the fifth century became more interested in agriculture and landownership, the celestial deities of Baal and Tanit, representing the sun and moon, became primary deities of veneration — their powers believed to bring fertility to the land and cities, thereby bringing prosperity to the people. Thus Baal was transformed from a sky and solar deity to a god of earth, and families made sacrifices to this duo of their infant children, which were later replaced by animals. Archaeologists have found many of the bones of these sacrifices at archaeological sites.

Another interesting aspect of this Goddess is her symbol, the Sign of Tanit, which still leaves scholars pondering its exact meaning and use. Found on multitudes of figurines, amulets, mosaic floors, pottery fragments, and stele it is generally depicted as a triangle on the tip of which rests a horizontal bar (sometimes with ends lifted), itself surmounted by a circle or disc. Interpretations of the symbol include the frontal view of a feminine figure with arms extended, a variation of the Egyptian ankh, the portrayal of an image of a nude goddess, a praying man or woman, a deity receiving prayer, or even a hierodule. Considering the parts separately, the lower half could be an altar, the upper part a possible a crescent moon and solar disc. Everything considered, the symbol is sometimes looked upon as what we would recognize as a modern logo — one symbol that encompasses and conveys a variety of religious ideas, meanings, and thoughts.

Tanit, Goddess of fertility and the moon, eventually became the Roman Goddess Juno Caelestis. Around 225 CE, a special temple was dedicated to Juno Caelestis, situated within a larger semicircular colonnade of 24 columns. This portico layout referred directly to the celestial vault, each column representing an hour within the 24-hour daily astral cycle. The Corinthian style temple within the hemicycle possessed six columns along the porch and ten along each side. Another temple not to be missed is the magnificent temple of the Capitoline gods, still standing at its original height and complete with the crown of her fine pediment featuring the apotheosis of the Emperor Antoninus Pius (by way of an eagle carrying him to the heavens no less). Built in 166 CE, this temple was dedicated to Jupiter, Juno, and

▲ Symbols of Tanit.

Minerva. Even the inner cella survives! Without doubt, this is the perfect place for recapturing the sacred atmosphere once created by these ancient temples.

Dougga is a glorious site which would take an entire day to properly visit. There are brothels, chapels, an underground hypogeum, fountains, a market, fort, mosque, and temples galore, just to name some of the larger structures worth visiting. Nearby are the cities of Bulla Regia with its Temple of Isis, Sbeitla, featuring a well-preserved complex of temples dedicated to the Capitoline triad, and Mactaris with its temple dedicated to Hathor. In the Mustis/LeKef (ancient Sicca Veneria) region there are temples of Ceres and Astarte, the latter of which was known for ritual prostitution, a practice which will be demystified in a Goddess Focus entry this chapter. Famous Carthage, also a sacred site of Tanit and many of the aforementioned goddesses, should not be missed, though the site is not thought to be as spectacular as Dougga.

Getting to Dougga

The town of Dougga is located in the interior of Tunisia, and is not the most easily reached or convenient destination for the regular tourist trade. It is located 4 miles (6 km) from Teboursouk, which can be reached by bus from Tunis, however travelers will find there is no regular transportation between Teboursouk and Dougga. Consequently the most avid traveler will have to walk the rather short distance of 4 miles (6 km), or hire private transportation. Tours of the area are available and would probably be the most convenient way to see the vast amount of archaeological ruins in the surrounding area.

Goddess Focus
Adult and Infant Sacrifice

While the idea of such brutality is unthinkable today, it is important to understand that, within its time and context, child sacrifice and blood letting was an element of many ancient religions. The substance of blood was thought to transmit life, and as such, these acts were the norm in ancient times. In some cases those making the ultimate sacrifice of their child did so with the best of intentions, and may have even considered it an honor or necessity of life. Readers might recall within early Judaism, Abraham unquestionably went to sacrifice his son Isaac at God's request as worshippers of Yahweh often practiced immolation. Scholar Charles Francis Potter cites Sir James Frazer, author of *The Golden Bough,* who connects the origins of Hebrew Passover to the sacrifice of newborn infants which he considered to have been an article of ancient Semitic religion and notes passages in Exodus, Micah, and Numbers as evidence.

▲ Child, animal, slave or virgin could be the object of a sacrifice.

Recent archaeological finds in Abydos, Egypt suggest artisans and servants were killed at the time of King Aha's death assuring they would accompany him into the afterworld and see to his every need. According to religion scholar James Rietveld, "the Greeks employed human sacrifice in their early history, as did the peoples of Mesoamerica. Some might even consider the Inquisition, carried out in the name of Christianity, in a similar category, even if the lives lost were not given freely or sacrificed before an altar during a sacred ritual. There has been brutality, sacrifice and injustice associated with religion throughout history. Goddess religion, like many others, is no exception."

Infanticide and adult sacrifice were not just spiritual, but often economic decisions. Daughters were victims of infanticide more often than boys since males were seen as potential heirs and caregivers for parents in later life, while girls often necessitated a costly dowry upon marriage. Arab fathers killed daughters until Mohammed attempted his reforms. Romans subjected babies to abandonment or exposure when they were born deformed, and Greeks killed later born children to insure the quality of life of previous children. Rietvelt quotes scholar Sege Lancel on the manner of these sacrifices. "Before the statues of Baal Hammon and Tanit was a great pit. To the accompaniment of flute and tambourine players, the father and mother came forward and handed the baby to the priest. He cuts the infant's throat in a *mystikos,* or mysterious fashion and then places the baby on the outstretched hands of one of the divine statues (probably Baal), from where it slips into the furnace."

GAIA ALERT

A TOOLBOX OF STRATEGIES MIGHT SAVE THE BIG CATS

According to reporters for *National Geographic*, Terry McCarthy and Andrea Dorfman, who quote naturalist David Quammen's recent book *Monster of God*, "The last wild, viable, free-ranging populations of big flesh eaters will disappear sometime around the middle of the next century." Future generations may only know the few remaining lions, tigers, cheetahs, snow leopards, cougars, jaguars, and lynx in zoos or breeding programs unless conservationists can get innovative, and use what scientist Allan Rabinowitz of the New York Wildlife Conservation Society calls an a "toolbox of strategies" to save our Big Cats.

The Mugie Ranch, a livestock operation in the Laikipia District of Kenya, six hours north of Nairobi, has taken a shiny new tool from the box and is testing a new strategy. As part of the Laikipia Predator Project, run by wildlife biologist Laurence Frank of the University of California, Berkeley, techniques suggested by the indigenous Masai tribesman have been expanded. Animal pens are built larger and stronger, and livestock are guarded. This is proving economically prudent since fewer animals are lost to predator cats, and the lions on the ranch generate income by their presence from tourists seeking a view of the beloved felines. Other ideas in the toolbox are linking habitat preserves which create corridors so big cats have enough protected land to roam and hunt rather than facing decimation of habitats. This sometimes includes restoration of habitats, such as the Terai Arc Landscape Program, where forests and grasslands are replanted to provide natural

▲ Nearly all big cat habitats are threatened worldwide.

cover for the roaming animals moving within the habitats, as well the re-emergence of their natural prey so that the cats have food. People of the region reap the benefit of new timber growth to cut and sell, so the people and the cats can co-exist. Variations of these methods are being tried in India and Nepal. Rabinowitz has proposed a similar linking of habitats from Mexico through Central America to northern Argentina to aid the declining jaguar population.

Another useful tool to African ranchers are the 160-pound (60-kg) trained Anatolian guard dogs imported from Turkey who can protect herds from predator cheetahs. Through this ingenious effort of Laurie Marker with the Cheetah Conservation Fund, the remaining 3,000 cheetahs of Namibia have a fighting chance to survive. Another idea helping the cheetahs is ranchers who raise their cattle without harming the cats can export "cheetah friendly" beef to the European Union, an idea borrowed from "dolphin friendly" tuna campaigns. The International Snow Leopard Trust of Kyrgyzstan, within the former Soviet Union, is helping the dwindling snow leopard population where only 6-10 known animals remain. Wives of park rangers make crafts which are sold in the United States and in gift stores at the entrance to the reserve with the Tien Shan mountains. This supplements their income, making poaching less tempting, and if no leopards are killed during the year, they receive another monetary bonus. Innovation, cooperation, monetary support, and patient determination must all coalesce to save the big cats in their natural habitats.

THE MIDDLE EAST

Inanna, your breast is your field.
Your broad field pours out plants.
Your broad field pours out grain.
Water flows from on high for your servant.
Pour it out for me, Inanna.
I will drink all you offer.
—Dumuzi-Tammuz to Inanna, The Sacred Marriage

ONE HAS TO DIG DEEP, LITERALLY AND FIGURATIVELY, to find the holy precincts of Goddess in the Middle East. In this modern age her worship and affiliated temples are not highly esteemed due to the domination of patriarchal faiths. Yet this region is filled with remnants of Divine Feminine worship, practiced for thousands of years in pre-Islamic and early Judeo-Christian times. Herein contains much of what has been left on the cutting room floor when the usual account of religious history is retold, not because this aspect of history failed, but because this account of the past did not advance the version of history the conquerors wanted told. Knowledge of these sacred sites is derived from hard evidence: surviving inscriptions on temple walls, artifacts salvaged from ancient sites, and texts recently discovered in libraries or from burials unearthed beneath the sands of long ago.

Each new discovery might challenge long held beliefs, not only of academia, but of firmly entrenched religious thought. In this land, where Orthodox Jews believe buried remains should not be disinterred, workers at dig sites will have stones cast upon them if they disturb ancestor bones. Sometimes archaeologists are assaulted to thwart controversial scholarship. Different ideas about religion and politics can rally men to acts of violence in the name of God. This is an area where people are passionate to "prove" or protect the underpinnings of their faith, (such as in the cases of the Shroud of Turin, the True Cross, the James Ossuary Inscriptions, and most recently, the cave in Israel touted as the site where John the Baptist and Jesus may have done ritual). Fakes, forgeries, and shoddy scholarship have been known to ruin careers. Therefore, within this hotbed of controversy, the literal "womb" of the three major patriarchal religions — Judaism, Christianity, and Islam — pilgrimage to Goddess must be undertaken with a degree of caution. Within this Middle Eastern powder keg history has previously disclosed that upsetting the patriarchy usually carries a price. Just turn on the nightly news. Here Goddess devotees are often an outright thorn in the side of Muslim, Jewish, and Christian leaders fighting hard to suppress the Divine Feminine. In our culture where trained experts are sometimes biased in terms of gender perspective, or their own personal spirituality, it is important to give certain discoveries a second look.

Whether myth, legend, archetype, or the Divine, words and deeds shape our culture, traditions, and psyches. Priestesses, queens, mothers, and goddesses were as integral to various cultures as prophets, kings, fathers, and gods. The thespians of this life epic are legion, and include Canaanites, Phoenicians, Nabateans, Egyptians, Sea Peoples, Hyksos, Sumarians, Assyrians, Israelites, Muslims, Babylonians, Christians, Gnostics, Romans, Greeks, Hittites, and Sabaeans — to name just a few! Some might recognize the creators and creatrixes as the producers of the drama: Asherah, Al Lat, Astarte, Al Uzza, Venus, Inanna, Cybele, Artemis, Isis, Ceres, Aphrodite, Tanit, Tyche, Sophia, Shekinah, Atargatis, and Lillith. On the other side of the aisle are Allah, Yahweh, Almaqah, Jehovah, and Baal.

▲ Lillith was an important deity in Sumeria.

The rich landscape of this region is a traveler's dream. The ziggurat, minaret, and mosque rise up against the horizon alongside the Bedouin tent, stone temple, and beehive house. Here is where law, writing, and the wheel were born (although recent Indus Valley discoveries challenge the origins of the earliest writing claim). Camel caravans laden with exotic spices, incense, and purple dyes traveled across these ancient trade routes. It is a land of scorpions, nomads, and architectural marvels, interspersed with unending sand dunes, life-saving oases, and rivers. The rivers in particular provided fertile soil for crop growing and the capacity for early civilization to flourish. Also the birthplace of religion, it is a land where devotees once worshipped stone idols. Sacred prostitution, crucifixion, animal sacrifice, and infanticide were accepted ways of life. Readers must be open to new ideas to properly understand the context of ancient customs, and refrain from comparing them to modern morality.

This is a part of history (or some say *herstory*) that must be reported and remembered, lest it be forgotten. It is a part of the past some believe important for the future. Within this dense account of times past, interwoven in empires, politics, and religions, lie the sacred sites of the Middle East. Therefore, this controversial drama warrants its rating of "OMN" for "Open Mind Necessary." To uncover and understand the buried truths of this land, a breeding ground of diversity and adversity, with its host of conundrums and conflicts, the audience must be fearless. All inclinations toward political correctness, prejudice, current mores, and personal or spiritual preferences must be momentarily set aside. Now sit back. Grab the popcorn. The story begins as the caravan pulls out for the region ironically known as The Holy Land!

IRAQ

Depending on which scholar you speak to, possible sites for the Garden of Eden could be either near Qurna, Iraq, or the Rift Valley of Africa. That independent grand dame, the Goddess Lillith, was banished from the Garden in Iraq for daring to exercise her right of equality with Adam. Many continue to believe the she-demon stories about Lillith, and embrace her more obedient replacement, Eve, who became Adam's second wife. Nisaba (also Nidaba) was the ancient Goddess of the Reeds in Babylon, or modern Iraq. Gimbutas cites deposits of large bird bones in northern Iraq that she describes as symbols of death within Goddess culture.

Temple of Ishtar

The Tower of Babel, the Temple of Ishtar, and the Hanging Gardens of Babylon are three places veiled in the mists of wonder such as the world has rarely seen. Herodotus is said to have described Babylon as surpassing in splendor any city in the known world. Ancient Babylon, the center of the world centuries before the birth of Christ, was home to Inanna/Ishtar, considered the Virgin Queen of Heaven and Earth and one of the three great Bronze Age goddesses. Much later, she was misrepresented, misunderstood, and disgraced when called the "Mother of Harlots" and "Whore of Babylon" in biblical scripture.

Inanna, divinity of southern Sumeria, and Ishtar her Semitic Akkadian counterpart as she was called in Babylon to the north, are difficult to differentiate and eventually fused, so they will be discussed here in syncretized fashion. Inanna/Ishtar was one of the most popular and revered deities in Mesopotamia, contemporary to Isis of Egypt, and Cybele of Anatolia. According to Anne Baring and Jules Cashford, Inanna/Ishtar "relates the Neolithic Great Mother (such as Nammu/Tiamat and Ki/Ninhursag) to biblical Eve, Mary, and Sophia. Her imagery is the foundation of Sophia (Hebrew Wisdom), the Great Gnostic Mother, and the medieval Shekhinah of the Jewish Kabbalah." Once a fertility and storm goddess who came to be known as overseer into all realms, Inanna/Ishtar was powerful and omnipotent, with her hand in all phases of life, including human fecundity, love, sexuality, life, and death. A goddess

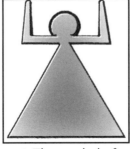

▲ The symbol of Tanit / Astarte.

▲ Ishtar, Great
Mother of
Mesopotamia.

of beauty and wisdom, related to Anath, Asherah, and Astarte, she had been worshipped at least since 3500 BCE as the Great Mother.

An early cylinder seal shows her image as a staff atop a rooftop alluding to the first temples of Inanna/Ishtar. In later imagery, she has wings, a horned crown, and is shown with lions, birds, and sacred trees. She can be depicted as gateposts, or rosettes as seen at the Eye Temple of Tell Brak. She has been depicted naked, with conical hat, pronounced pubic triangle, and alongside fish, turtles, and goats. In other early depictions she could be recognized as a staff at the entrance of sacred buildings, evolving later to the evening and morning star associated with the star Sirius (as was Isis), and planet Venus (or the crescent moon and evening star) which inspired her title "Queen of Heaven." Both title and symbols were later associated with Mary, the mother of Jesus.

Baring and Cashford suggest other similarities between Inanna/Ishtar and Mary. Rare cylinder seals show Inanna holding her son above her lap under the eight-rayed star and lunar crescent as if presenting him to two men who look upon the Mother Goddess and child. This is certainly reminiscent of the nativity story when Jesus is presented to the Magi who followed a star to find the child in Bethlehem. Inanna/Ishtar and Mary share similar stories of their dying and resurrected sons, both dubbed "The Lamb" after mutual sacrificial deaths. Inanna claims as her titles, "Holy Shepherdess" and "Keeper of the Cow-byre," and her son Dumuzi-Tammuz had been called "Shepherd" and portrayed as a fish god. Baring and Cashford present the idea this early Babylonian story of Inanna/Ishtar and her son-lover Dumuzi-Tammuz may be the precursor to the story of Mary and Jesus. It would seem Hebrew and Christian culture may have inherited much from the Sumerians right down to the story of the Great Flood. Archaeologists have uncovered artifacts which show their culture was derived from among three younger civilizations — Assyrian, Canaanite, and Semitic Akkadian — which came to be collectively known as Babylonian.

During the height of Babylon's splendor, under the reign of Nebuchandnezzar II, the Temple of Ishtar and the Ishtar Gate were constructed of glazed bricks. Bulls, the symbol of the god Marduk, and horned dragons, the symbols of Ishtar, were shown in relief on the walls. The Esaglia complex in Babylon was said to have a seven-story ziggurat called Etememanki, meaning, "the house that is the foundation of heaven" which is thought to perhaps be the Tower of Babel. Contemporaries of the time describe Babylon as having outer walls 56 miles (87 km) in length, though they were probably closer to 10 miles (16 km) long, 80 feet (24 m) thick, and 320 feet (96 m) tall. Within the enclosure were fortresses, temples, and statues of gold. In modern times, the site underwent reconstruction using new brick and mortar replacements per the direction of Saddam Hussein who inscribed his name in the walls alongside that of Nebuchandnezzar. At the time of this writing, it has been reported that Babylon has survived the war between Iraq and the United States without being blown to bits, but looting is a major problem. Nearby heavy equipment is threatening fragile sites. The site also begs further excavation and restoration as pottery fragments litter the site awaiting scholarly scrutiny. Excavations have yet to definitively determine the site of the Hanging Gardens of Babylon.

Getting to the Temple of Ishtar

The ruins of Babylon lie along the banks of the Euphrates river 7.5 miles (10 km) north of the modern town of Al-Hillah. The site is 55 miles (90 km) south of the Iraqi capital, Baghdad. People of most countries, including citizens of the United States, are restricted from travel in Iraq. Independent travel is not possible in Iraq and if or ever travel does open up, do not expect average package tours to be available via mass marketing. At this time it is completely uncertain as to when tourism may open, but those "in the know" seem to think the first types of groups allowed in will be small, exclusive groups dubbed "archeotourists" who will visit the site with expert guides.

Inanna at Uruk

Uruk, the city of Inanna, dates back 6,000 years and could very well be the first city in the world. When inhabitants of the British Isles were living in huts, the Sumerian civilization in southern Iraq enjoyed a thriving and sophisticated urban culture where cuneiform writing, the wheel, engineering, agriculture, poetry, pottery, art, mathematics, astrology, and astronomy flourished. Here in Uruk, her primary cult center, Inanna's main temple was called the Eanna. At the zenith of this civilization the temples were said to have been embellished with gold, silver, lapis lazuli, and red limestone. One temple built by King Karaindash to honor Inanna in 1415 BCE is said to have a frieze of molded baked bricks that depicted gods and goddesses carrying vases of overflowing water, which was a common Mesopotamian motif of the times. Inanna, said to have bestowed civilization upon humankind and handed down sovereignty to kings, could certainly be proud of her work in Uruk!

Uruk was conquered by King Sargon, an Akkadian monarch from northern Mesopotamia, and his daughter, Enheduanna, became the first in a long line of "En Priestesses" serving in the temple of the Nanna, the Moon God. In this capacity, Enheduanna was seen as the highest ranking religious official in all of Mesopotamia, possibly even higher in importance than the king, because it was she who was the intermediary between the deities. King Sargon was credited with encouraging the fusion of Inanna of the north and Ishtar of the south, and his daughter was seen as the earthly counterpart of Ningal, the Moon God's wife. Legend says that Sargon himself was the son of a high priestess, and while it cannot be fully substantiated, some scholars suppose this relationship may suggest a tradition for the kings of Sumeria being a consort or relative to the resident temple priestesses. Sargon's childhood legend is sometimes viewed as the predecessor for that of the biblical Moses, as Sargon was also found floating down the river in a basket before being rescued. Like Moses, Sargon grew to adulthood and became an important leader of his people. In the case of Sargon, he ruled a vast empire and was responsible for forging an alliance between the Sumerians and Akkadians. Statuary of clergy of the time have a unique style and show both genders in long tiered garments, often rigidly seated, with extremities and facial features suggesting an intensity in their purpose. Sometimes their wide-eyed look was made of blue lapis but outlined in black, reminiscent of Egyptian reliefs showing the use of kohl. Clergy lived in the temple compound, and people believed the deities inhabited the temples. The compound was a center of spirituality, law, and healing where worshippers of Inanna might come to remedy solutions in any of these matters.

▲ The seal of Innana as seen on a cylinder, likely used as a stamp.

Temples to the deities were designed in the form of a ziggurat, a symbolic cosmic mountain that spiraled upward toward the heavens. Baring and Cashford offer the theory that this structure is symbolic of the body of Goddess, and offer an explanation for its relationship to the sacred feminine. While it represented a symbolic connection between earth and heaven and encompassed the three dimensions of heaven, earth, and the underworld, it also reflected the Divine Feminine's womb and tomb. This is in keeping with the Neolithic mound, or Bronze Age beehive chamber, omphalos, and sacred enclosure imagery also recognized as the womb of Goddess. While we cannot know for sure, the hollow sacred space beneath the temple, the womb, was perhaps where the sacred mysteries of birth were played out, as one entered through a special gate that was her vulva. It has been speculated the summit of the ziggurat is where the deity descended to meet the priest or priestess who made their ascent to the chapel of the high place where the sacred marriage took place. The high priestess, known as the En or Entu, took the role of the goddess, and the king took the role of the bridegroom. Offspring from such a union may have been seen as both human and divine.

Inanna/Ishtar was the keeper of the *me*, or Divine Law. Like the Egyptian Goddess Ma'at, she dispenses justice and keeps the natural order in balance. In this capacity her sacred symbols are the caduceus and the double-headed ax. Professor Miriam Robbins Dexter elaborates on Inanna and her relationship with the chthonic Goddess Ereshkigal, and their primary functions as identified by their animal associations. Inanna, Goddess of life and death, and Ereshkigal, Goddess of birth and death, the former associated with snake, the latter with birds, when combined, constitute a whole, and were descendants of the ancient Neolithic goddesses of regeneration, depicted as both bird and snake.

In her aspect as "Queen of Heaven," Inanna/Ishtar embodies the Virgin, not as a reflection of chastity but holding her powers of creation, or manifestation, within herself. Animal imagery for her life-giving aspects are the dove and swallow, while her life-taking imagery is the scorpion or viper. Cylinder seals depict her standing on lions, symbols of life and death, while holding a caduceus in her hand. Baring and Cashford elaborate on Inanna as the goddess of the grain and the vine. "Cakes of the goddess Inanna" were baked on her temple altars as an offering of herself to feed her children. This may have been the beginnings of baking "cakes for the Queen of Heaven" which sounds oddly familiar to receiving the body of Christ in the sacrament of communion during Catholic mass.

Inanna's warrior/goddess aspect was depicted as riding on the back of a lion, reminiscent of the Indian Goddess Durga. Baring and Cashford report the mighty defensive walls of Uruk being 8 miles (13 km) long, 20 feet (6 m) high, 15 feet (4.5 m) thick, with 900 turrets placed at intervals of 39 feet (12 m). Here at Uruk, she bestowed kingship and was protectress of the city. Her temple, the Sacred House of Heaven, or Eanna, is described by Elinor Gadon as follows, "the oldest preserved temple at Uruk. An enormous mud-brick construction, more than 30 x 30 meters in size, the main temple is set on a limestone base, an unusual feature in a region where stone is so rare. The temple has a three-part plan composed of two aisles flanking a nave, and at the end of the nave, a rectangle central shrine, the "holy of holies." The main temple is connected to a smaller shrine by an astonishing portico that is supported on colossal circular columns of mud brick. The portico faces a broad open court whose walls are covered with bold and colorful geometric mosaics in red, black and yellow. A statue of the Goddess stood in a niche in the shrine." Another site within the area that has a great temple to Inanna/Ishtar is Ur, where Sir Leonard Woolley uncovered from the Great Death Pit 68 richly attired and bejeweled women guarded by six armored men. This was incidentally the home of the famous priestess/poet Enheduanna. The ancient city of Nineveh also contained an important Mesopotamian shrine of Goddess.

Getting to the Inanna Temple at Uruk

The Sumerian city of Uruk survives near the Iraqi town of Warka, also called Erech in the Bible. Most nationalities are restricted from travel inside Iraq, but if entry were possible it would be by bus from the southern Iraqi city of Basra. A train from Basra to Baghdad also stops at a town near the ruins.

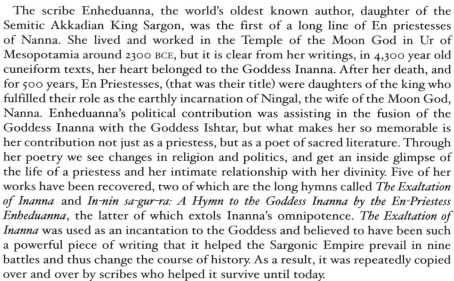

Goddess Focus
Enheduanna, Priestess of Nanna

The scribe Enheduanna, the world's oldest known author, daughter of the Semitic Akkadian King Sargon, was the first of a long line of En priestesses of Nanna. She lived and worked in the Temple of the Moon God in Ur of Mesopotamia around 2300 BCE, but it is clear from her writings, in 4,300 year old cuneiform texts, her heart belonged to the Goddess Inanna. After her death, and for 500 years, En Priestesses, (that was their title) were daughters of the king who fulfilled their role as the earthly incarnation of Ningal, the wife of the Moon God, Nanna. Enheduanna's political contribution was assisting in the fusion of the Goddess Inanna with the Goddess Ishtar, but what makes her so memorable is her contribution not just as a priestess, but as a poet of sacred literature. Through her poetry we see changes in religion and politics, and get an inside glimpse of the life of a priestess and her intimate relationship with her divinity. Five of her works have been recovered, two of which are the long hymns called *The Exaltation of Inanna* and *In-nin sa-gur-ra: A Hymn to the Goddess Inanna by the En-Priestess Enheduanna*, the latter of which extols Inanna's omnipotence. *The Exaltation of Inanna* was used as an incantation to the Goddess and believed to have been such a powerful piece of writing that it helped the Sargonic Empire prevail in nine battles and thus change the course of history. As a result, it was repeatedly copied over and over by scribes who helped it survive until today.

In her role as Sumerian High Priestess and En Priestess of Nanna, Enheduanna held a powerful and influential position, perhaps even exceeding the importance of the king. Betty De Shong Meador, an expert on Enheduanna, suggests, "Unlike

▲ Enheduanna at her throne.

her predecessors, she could use the effective tool of the written word to spread her influence and beliefs." Besides being a voice of authority in the realms of religion, her other duties included administration of the temple, along with overseeing the management of the land to which the term "en" refers. Crops, livestock, fisheries, and the employees who worked within these industries were all under her control. Within the spiritual realm, she had to organize and oversee rituals, temple personnel, interpret dreams, and embody Ningal, the female moon and consort of Nanna, the Moon God in the sacred marriage. Enheduanna insured Ningal (who was probably venerated as a statue) was well cared for with proper food and offerings. Ningal's menstrual cycle was charted suggesting the Goddess was a prototype for mortal women. Her living quarters within the temple compound was called the *gipar*, which in Sumerian means "storehouse," a clue to the fact that Enheduanna was perceived as the representation of abundance and preservation of the harvest for which her people depended. A portrait of this magnificent individual survives from a limestone plaque, showing her as high priestess performing a libation before a stepped altar, now on display at the University Museum in Philadelphia.

GAIA ALERT
ON THE BRINK OF NEVERMORE

The Middle East has its share of environmental disasters, not the least of which is caused by war, burning oil, and bombs. Salt blowing from the Dead Sea encrusts on delicate sandstone, weakening buildings, and damaging inscriptions on many ancient sites around the Levant, the coastal region of the eastern Mediterranean from Syria to Egypt. Short-sighted government policies in Lebanon favored development at the expense of archaeology resulting in seven million cubic feet of ancient Beirut being dumped into the Mediterranean Sea. Other threats in the region are numerous, without easy solutions, or an immediate rescue. These include the disappearance of Iraq's legendary marshlands thought by some to be the location of the Garden of Eden and the Great Flood. Marsh Arabs, or the

Madan, have always occupied the marshy areas. They found themselves and their habitat under assault from Saddam Hussein in the 1990s as water was diverted to drain the marsh, leaving 93% of the area a salt-encrusted wasteland. Iraq is also plagued by the destruction and neglect of valuable and irreplaceable archaeological sites, as well as theft of artifacts.

▲ The Great Pyramids and Sphinx in Egypt are also at risk of over-exploitation.

Hussein's order to drain the Madan marshland was tantamount to genocide of one of the oldest cultures in the world. While the current political situation in Iraq remains uncertain, a coalition of international scientists, engineers, anthropologists, and hydrologists are working together to try to restore the marsh habitat. But heroes and heroines of preservation and restoration are not always available. According to National Geographic News, of the 6,000 languages known today, half are no longer taught to children, and each day ancient practices, skills, and wisdom fades from the landscape of human imagination. That could potentially be the fate in Iraq as ancient cities such as Nimrud, Nineveh, and Tell Billa are showing signs of distress. Organizations such as the World Cultures Fund are working to preserve sites where the history of civilization is at risk and on the brink of nevermore so that humankind may never again lose ancient knowledge which can never be restored.

ISRAEL

A prolonged period of Goddess worship is substantiated by artifacts discovered throughout Israel. The Canaanite city of Megiddo, which once fell to the Egyptians, revealed the veneration of Hathor and Astarte. Devotees of Isis and Astarte left behind their sacred objects in Ashkelon, a city in Israel on the coast of the Mediterranean where coins were minted depicting the head of Athena. Double divine female images were discovered at Peqi' Cave, and archaeologists uncovered goddess portraits in many houses in Jericho, while in a nearby settlement, a stone carved with breasts was found in the remains of a temple. As many as 1,000 figurines were found at Byblos, along with molds for a naked and horned female statue, probably Astarte, since the likeness matches known cylinder seals. Jewelry from the Bronze Age Levant features gold sheet pendants engraved with a fertility goddess displaying only her head and female organs.

Temple Mount at Jerusalem

Jerusalem is regarded as a holy city to three major faiths — Christianity, Judaism, and Islam. The city has seen its share of struggles for 3,000 years, not the least of which occurred between the adherents of Goddess and the people of Yahweh — often one in the same! In the beginning the Temple Mount, or Mount Moriah, was the nexus where the underworld met the heavens. Some say it was here the Semitic Babylonian Goddess Tiamat (called Tehom by the Hebrews), the serpent-dragon Mother of the Gods, was slain by her grandson Marduk in a mythological incident marking the early struggle between the sky gods over the older earth-based goddess religions.

Jerusalem was sacked many times by diverse peoples professing different religions. Until the destruction of the first temple in 586 BCE, Shekhinah, the feminine aspect of the mystical Jewish tradition of the Kabbalah, known as the Holy Spirit, resided on the mount. In the time of Rome's conquest, Hadrian renamed the city Aelia Capitolina for the family of the emperor and the Capitolina gods. This resulted in the construction of a temple dedicated to Jupiter, and the goddesses Juno and Minerva on the temple mount itself. According to scholar Ephraim Stern, half of all the female figurines found in Judah were excavated very near the Temple Mount despite the best efforts by some of the kings of Judah to stamp out worship of Goddess. Today, modern scholars are finally starting to see beyond their theological conservatism, recognizing that Yaweh was often accompanied by a female consort and so demonstrating archaeological proof for pagan Yahwism.

Layered in politics, his-tations, Temple Mount have sacrificed Isaac, the thought to have ascended up his tent and housed Within the Temples of royal worshippers of ers were probably consid-of the Mother Goddess speculated that Solomon Asherah, citing all of the lions and trees used in not forget the Song of temple mount, a corpus Solomon's alliance with

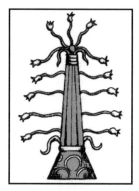

▲ The symbol of Asherah.

tory, and religious conno-is where Abraham would prophet Mohammed was into heaven, and Moses set the Ark of the Covenant. Solomon and David, both Goddess, their queen moth-ered the earthly incarnations Asherah! Some have even really built the temple for goddess-related imagery of the temple motif. One can-Songs originated from this of poetry inspired from the Queen of Sheba, herself

a worshipper of Venus-Astarte, and their sacred marriage arranged by Bath Sheba. Even Solomon's Seal, the Star of David, the hexagram of two triangles, one inverted and one not, may have been recognized here, although many believe they originated elsewhere. Solomon's Seal bears an uncanny resemblance to the sri yantra, a symbol of the female yoni and male lingam from the Tantric sages of the Far East. One might say that within this symbol, representative of perpetual creativity or intercourse of male and female energy, are Shiva and Shakti, Jehovah and Sophia, Goddess and God.

Susan Ackerman, Professor of Religion, makes a strong case for queen mothers of the Israelite and Judaean monarchies as not only associated with counseling their son's court, but involving themselves in matters of royal succession. After all, it was usually through Goddess a king received sovereignty. The theory is that if Yahweh is the divine father of the king and Asherah is his consort, then Asherah is the divine mother of the king. Taking that a bit farther, then the biological mother of the king would be Asherah's earthly counterpart. This does not mean that the queen was unfaithful to the religion of the state, namely Yahweh, it means in all likelihood, through the queen mother, Yahweh and Asherah were worshipped side by side. Perhaps as teacher Savina Teubal surmises, women had separate rituals, possibly having to do with matters of reproduction. As a matter of fact, cult objects for Asherah, namely her golden serpent or tree symbol called *asheras* are noted to have been within the Temple of Jerusalem. Ackerman cites queen mothers as having both economic and political power and suggests the women who wove the royal garments for Asherah at the temple were probably under the queen mother's direct authority and employment, noting that these cult functionaries would have also taken part in making sacrifices to Asherah. A number of queen mothers in the Old Testament are cited, from Bath Sheba, right down to Mary, the mother of Jesus, who was believed to have possibly been in service to the temple and her tribe one of which who made cakes for the Queen of Heaven.

The Canaanite Goddess Asherah was said to have been the mother of over 70 gods. She was recognized by her Hathor style headdress, and stood upon the back of a lion, holding a lotus plant in her right hand, and a serpent in her left. Her sacred symbol was the tree which was spoken of many times in scripture, usually in the context of Yaweh's devotees trying to destroy it. Her symbology certainly calls into question the real nature or role of the Tree of Life or Tree of Knowledge in the Garden of Eden, as well as the tree associations with the Jewish menorah, itself a stylized tree. Sacred prostitution and the Sacred Marriage were known sacred rites within the Temple of Solomon administered by the priestesses of Asherah, sometimes called Astarte or Anat, who would have been involved in this rite to insure the fertility of the land. Ackerman points out that there is no hard evidence for the ritual prostitution of the *qedasim,* or cult personnel, to have actually involved sexual intercourse, and scholars are beginning to rethink the reliability of Herodotus on this subject.

Ackerman cites within the Christology of the Gospels of Matthew, the apostle introduces the genealogy of Jesus within the line of David which actually makes him King of the Jews. This positions Mary, the mother of the Redeemer and Messiah, as the queen mother within the lineage of queen mothers and ancestors of David's line, namely Tamar, Rahab, Ruth, and Bath Sheba. This also makes for interesting associations with Jesus following in the footsteps of Osiris, Tammuz, and Adonis within the dying/rising vegetation god/king paradigm of pagan mythology, or within the Gnostic rites wherein death and resurrection are metaphors of spiritual initiation and enlightenment or the sacred marriage of soul and spirit. Coming full circle, Mary, as queen mother would have been perceived as the earthly representative of the Mother Goddess. A foundation for this is the second century *Infancy Gospel of James* in which Mary is said to have been dedicated to a life of service in the temple, and had been chosen as one of the seven virgins to weave new curtains for the sanctuary. Ackerman concludes that this certainly echoes the service within the temple for the cult of Asherah mentioned earlier, and she follows up with gospels of Phillip and Thomas to bring the point home. Within the Gnostic meditations of the Gospel of Philip, Mary is interpreted as a "female heavenly power, the Holy Spirit" and within Thomas she is said to "correspond to a figure in the heavens, a mother figure who in an earlier period was the Goddess Asherah."

Taking things one step farther into a dawning popular cultural belief, the role of Mary Magdalene, seen by many as a Jesus' partner or wife and a priestess of the Goddess, is being more closely examined as evidenced by the controversial furor around the best-selling fiction book, *The DaVinci Code* (Dan Brown). Non-fiction works such as *Woman With the Alabaster Jar* (Margaret Starbird), *The Gospels*

▲ The author at Temple Mount, Jerusalem.

of Mary (Marvin Meyer), *When Women Were Priests* (Karen Jo Torjensen), and *Holy Blood, Holy Grail* (Baigent, Leigh and Lincoln) investigate different aspects of Mary Magdalene's life. All things considered, we have hardly scratched the surface, so it is no wonder many believe much of the basis for Christianity has its roots firmly planted in paganism and worship of the Mother Goddess.

The Temple Mount area of King Solomon's temple stands as both an ancient and current symbolic bastion for the worship of Asherah-Astarte-Venus, Juno, and Minerva. No doubt it was a struggle by patriarchal kings to take away Goddess, particularly from women who clung to their rituals of making cakes for the Queen of Heaven, a female divinity who met their spiritual needs as women. As we know, female figurines of Mother Goddesses have been found throughout Israel and the Middle East, greatly outnumbering figurines of males or animals, which ties into teacher Savina Teubal's suggestion that female iconography "supports the concept of a separate religious practice for women that may or may not have included men, but in which males were not central." She believes the "prohibition of graven images helped erase female links with the divine and opened the way for literary characterization to absorb all former female traits into Yahwism." When these women lost their Goddess, they not only lost their place in religious society, they lost their spiritual identity, and their control over their reproductive life, among other things.

Reflective of the importance of Asherah-Astarte-Venus in Jerusalem, the emperor Hadrian constructed a massive temple dedicated solely to the Goddess Aphrodite on the very site where the Church of the Holy Sepulcher stands today. Originally the site of a quarry, Hadrian leveled out the area in order to build a great retaining wall intended to support this temple, the remains of which can still be viewed at the Russian Hospice, one of the many hospices located within the Church of the Holy Sepulcher complex. The same kind of large dressed Herodian stones incorporated in the famous Wailing Wall were used to build this retaining wall. In addition, this hospice contains the remains of part of an embellished arched gateway, stylized like a Roman triumph arch, once providing access from the Roman marketplace into the temple precinct. Some of the columns of this temple are situated directly beneath the rotunda of the current church. On good authority, Eusebius from the nearby coastal Palestinian city of Caesarea asserts that this temple was indeed dedicated to Aphrodite. Of course, Christian gossip circulated about how Hadrian reputedly tried to obliterate the tomb of Jesus by building this monument honoring Aphrodite.

Getting to Temple Mount at Jerusalem

As the capital of Israel, Jerusalem is a major city, and is easily reached by train or bus from all parts of the country. Most international visitors arrive via the Ben Gurion Airport in Tel Aviv, less than a two-hour drive from Jerusalem. Highway No. 1 connects Tel Aviv with Jerusalem. The New City of Jerusalem is a crossroads for the Egged and Arab bus networks, making the city a convenient base for exploring the rest of Israel. Once in the city, be sure to stop at the Church of the Holy Sepulcher which is known to have been built over a temple to the Goddess Aphrodite-Venus. There are also a multitude of sites sacred to Mary, mother of Jesus, who some believe was a devotee of the Queen of Heaven!

Sha'ar Hagolan

Three is a charm and that number describes the attributes of Sha'ar Hagolan. First, it is an important Pottery Neolithic archaeological site whose ancient residents were known Goddess worshippers. This site was once home to 3,000 inhabitants, and their advanced lifestyle has "completely altered the traditional picture of a primitive culture and society," according to Dr. Yosef Garfinkel, from the Institute of Archaeology at the Hebrew University of Jerusalem, who has been excavating at the site since 1989. Now a *kibbutz* it represents a style of "partnership" for communal living, an ideal live/work situation to those who perpetuate non-dominator models for society. The kibbutz, meaning a Jewish settlement or collective farm, is adjacent to the 8,000-year-old archaeological excavation site of Sha'ar Hagolan.

The Yarmukian culture is believed to have venerated Goddess, a theory supported by the hundreds of female figurines found at this 74-acre (30-h) settlement. After eight seasons, excavation revealed a well-planned village containing the oldest streets in Israel, and one of the three oldest wells ever uncovered. The site consists of many courtyard houses surrounded by a number of smaller rooms suggesting occupation by an extended family with a few nuclear families. These courtyard houses are huge for their time varying from 2,688 to 8,065 square feet (250 to 750 sq. m). The social organization, size of living quarters, and sophistication of the Yarmukian lifestyle suggests a rethinking of the academy's understanding of the Neolithic period. Their art, in the form of the hundreds of aforementioned female figurines, represents the richest collection from prehistoric times uncovered in Israel and throughout the world. As many as 70 figurines have been found in one building alone!

Dr. Garfinkel states, "The rich iconographic representation of the female figure at Sha'ar Hagolan opens new horizons for understanding and interpreting female figures in one of the most crucial stages of human evolution: the transition to village life and the beginning of farming 8,000 years ago." It is rare to find human figures in prehistoric sites, with the norm only one or two, but Sha'ar Hagolan has become a case study with its assemblage of hundreds of these goddess artifacts. These figurines fall into several categories, the largest being "coffee bean eye" clay figurines, pebble figurines, and eye figurines. Interestingly, very few male images have been found while other types of pottery containers unearthed depicted zoomorphic figurines such as dogs.

While it is true that some scholars view these female statues as mere fertility objects or prehistoric Barbie dolls, more of academia is coming around to accept this imagery as worship of the great Dr. Beth Nakhai and Child Images Claremont University nent school of religion explained that deci- be a complex problem. the statues represent in domestic and pub- our Western gender have to be careful not tions with Western a time when men and roles, motherhood of authority. We are knowledge of the Goddess. There is gender from a linguis- And there are so many from the Middle East! ring depictions include

▲ An abstract female stone figure found at Sh'ar Hagolan.

being suggestive of the Earth Mother. Recently lectured on Mother in the Middle East at in California, the preemi- in the country, where she phering the figurines can Ultimately she believes relational partnerships lic spaces that transcend expectations. Thus, we to color our interpreta- cultural norms. This was women took on many itself was seen as a role severely limited in our social context of ancient also confusion about tic standpoint as well. varied images of females Some regularly occur- women holding babies,

pregnant women, naked women holding their breasts, images with holes in their pregnant stomachs, and others with exaggerated pubic triangles. Thousands of pillar-based figurines of women with large breasts have been unearthed in Israel. Some had a head with a pinched face and were called "bird's head" figurines. Sometimes the Goddess is holding a dove or playing a drum or tambourine. Judahite figurines were often painted in bold colors of white, black, and red with prominent eyes and an occasional necklace. Female images were even found flanking entrance portals on miniature models of shrines.

Do these figures represent actual mortal women or goddesses? According to scholar James Rietveld reporting on Dr. Nakhai, these figures were more often than not made by the best craftsmen using the finest materials of the day. They were found as votive offerings inside sanctuaries and temples, and served special ritual purposes. When polled, some of the best scholars in the field could not imagine these female figures were mere humans or substitutes for mortals. More scholars are coming around to thinking these images were clearly being vener- ated by the people who made them, thus concluding that they are images of Goddess, or *bastu*, namely divinity personified.

Taking understanding and recognition of Goddess a step farther beyond Neolithic times, despite some theological sensitivity, more scholars are becom- ing accustomed to the idea that Yahweh had a consort in Israel and Judah in pre-exilic times in spite of protests and efforts of reforming kings and religious leaders. Some researchers and scholars even believe Goddess pre-dates Yahweh. The art of the time tells the story. Her image of Asherah is often depicted as a tree-like icon. At the center of Kabbalah, or Jewish Mysticism, is the Tree of Life and associated with it is Shekinah, the Divine Female. Some scholars such as the late Asphodel Long, have recognized this Tree of Life and the tree from the Garden of Eden as the tree imagery associated with Goddess Asherah. Taking

this concept to the next logi-
Cook who relates the Jewish
tree and states the menorah
in Exodus 25: 31-40 as part of
of the Covenant (which also
dess imagery). As such, the
the menorah is seen by many
Goddess which lives quietly
altars in Jewish temples and
homes.

cal level, Long cites Roger
menorah to the cosmic
as being first mentioned
the furnishings of the Ark
consisted of other god-
stylized tree imagery of
as a long lost symbol of
hidden in plain sight on
in most Jewish family

Sha'ar Hagolan has proven
standing a time of true cul-
Levant. It is forcing academia
ideas, just as other areas of
reassessed with each new
Similar to pilgrimages to Catal
Hagolan is now becoming a
worshippers. Because sacred
Goddess and her devotees,

▲ A Goddess
with pronounced
hips from Sh'ar
Hagolan.

to be pivotal in under-
tural evolution in the
to rethink established
religious study are being
archaeological discovery.
Hüyük in Turkey, Sha'ar
site visited by Goddess
dance is so important to
at least once a year an

international festival for oriental and belly dancing is held at the kibbutz where
dancers and worshippers respectfully dance among the ruins of the ancient settlement. Prayers are recited to Goddess thanking her for life, fertility, and peace.
The kibbutz has 42 rooms and 14 suites, all with air conditioning, and other
amenities. There is an open air cinema, mini-zoo, swimming pool, barbecue area,
and playground on site. Reservations can be made on-line for the kibbutz. While
there is an on-site museum, other objects from Sha'ar Hagolan can be viewed
at the Metropolitan Museum of Art in New York and the Musee du Louvre in
Paris.

Getting to Sha'ar Hagolan

The kibbutz and archaeological site is located very near the Yarmuk River,
about a mile south of the Sea of Galilee, at the foot of the Golan Heights, near
the Jordanian border. The closest large city is Tiberias to the northwest. Sha'ar
Hagolan is due north of Masada and the Dead Sea. If driving it is located west of
Highway 98. It is not recommended to arrive at the kibbutz without reservations
since this is the home of those who occupy the kibbutz. Nearby places of interest
include the Roman ruins of Capernaum and associated biblical sites around the
Sea of Galilee.

JORDAN

The desert regions of Jordan and its immediate surroundings have long inspired
Goddess researchers. The ornately carved Nabataean Treasury in Petra, made
famous in Hollywood by an Indiana Jones film, is actually a sacred precinct of
Isis and Al Lat. Some believe the Tower of Babel, thought to be ziggurat, might
have been a temple devoted to Ishtar. Sacred Mount Sinai, known as *Har Karkom*,
where Moses is believed to have received the Ten Commandments is believed by
Goddess advocates to have first been a site of Goddess worship where she was
worshipped in the form of a stone. And the Red Sea, parted by Moses, was known
as the blood of the Goddess Tiamat, also called *Tehom*, or the Deep.

Jerash

The highly esteemed Artemis, Goddess of Asia Minor, revered throughout Turkey, the Middle East, and the Mediterranean region was the primary patroness of Jerash. Today one can still feel the splendor and charm of this remote city influenced by the Moses-era Nabataeans. The city later flourished under the Romans who build shrines in Jerash to many goddesses including Isis and Diana. But it is to Artemis, with her close associations to Cybele, Isis, Hekate, Demeter, and Mary the mother of Jesus, which will be discussed in this entry.

Born on the Greek island of Delos according to some versions of the myth, Artemis was sister of Apollo and daughter to Zeus and Leto. Her sanctuary was supposedly the most beautiful and important temple within Jerash, once containing fine marble paneling and a richly adorned cult statue within the inner chamber. The Corinthian columns of her temple, built between 138-174 CE, soar impressively from its commanding hilltop site, with 11 of the 12 pillars still standing. A stunning 300-yard-long (270-m) processional way once provided devotees entrance to the central gate of the Artemis Temple which now begins at the Propylaecum built over the spring running through the city with walnut and poplar trees prospering along its banks. One proceeds toward the Artemis Temple along this processional way, across the river Chrysorhoas, flanked by columns and ornately carved porticos en route. The temple's perimeter walls were 46.6 feet (14 m) high and 40 feet (12 m) wide. Flanking both sides of the gate were two-story shops. An open air altar stood immediately in front of the Temple of Artemis. In most cases, the grand processions were concluded at this outside altar with an elaborate sacrifice, better suited to accommodate festival crowds. The temple walls had three entrances decorated with Corinthian pilasters. Inside several steps divided by seven platforms led one to the front courtyard tenemos enclosed by a colonnade. The inner courtyard and altar were positioned several steps beyond the tenemos. The famous Jerash archaeologist, C. S. Fisher, excavating the temple in the 1930s, proclaimed that this temple was "in all probability the finest single structure ever erected at ancient Jerash." Archaeologists have discovered pottery shards around this site dating no earlier than the Roman period, indicating the temple is "new" by ancient standards. A series of kilns dating to the 7th and 8th century CE were also unearthed here, used to reduce the temple's fine marble into lime. The Temple's terrace later supported a 6th century Byzantine church. At one time a small fort was located within the temple but it was destroyed by Baldwin I.

Earlier statues were often made of wood decorated with fruits, beads, and precious jewels. Yet another depiction of Artemis has a columned torso, stiff outstretched arms bent rigidly at the elbows, braided

▲ The Temple of Artemis at Jerash is remarkably well-preserved.

long hair, and an ornate crown. The image more commonly known is the poly-mastic, or many breasted Artemis of Ephesia found in Anatolia and throughout the Roman Empire. Theories abound regarding the protuberances on her upper torso ranging from palm-dates, acorns, eggplant, ostrich-eggs, bags to hold amulets, bee eggs, zodiacal signs, bunches of grapes, magical flames of a virgin's cloak, bulls testicles, or breasts. James Rietveld, one of the preeminent scholars of Artemis Ephesia, theorizes that the protuberances represented fruit and other offerings symbolizing fertility, but by the first century, as Artemis became a more personal Goddess, they became breasts. Evidence found on nipples carved on the later statues and accounts of Minucius Felix and Jerome also say they were breasts. Smaller statuettes copied the cult statues and were sold locally to be used for protective amulets which transitions Artemis from the realm of a public deity to a very personal divine being of individuals.

Artemis is one of the oldest and most individual aspects of the Divine Feminine, yet she shares many attributes with other powerful goddesses wor-shipped throughout the ancient world. She is considered one of the most power-ful mistresses of magic, and as such is closely related to Isis with her magical and life-preserving breasts, both revered as beloved deities, saviors who hold the fate of humankind in their hands. So powerful was Artemis that other deities were depicted on coins holding an image of Artemis as a representation of power over fate. Artemis is closely associated with Hekate in their shared underworld aspect, and their protective powers over death. Many of the attributes of Artemis were passed to Mary the Virgin Mother by the 4th and 5th centuries. She is associated with Cybele or Magna Mater; both have been venerated as stones, sometimes sharing a temple, and both called Mistress of Animals. She is the Goddess of hunters and hunting with related customs going back to the Paleolithic. She is also associated with Anahita of Iran, mother of the waters who bestowed wisdom and strength.

Processions were a particular form of worship of Artemis, and the grand pro-cessional way here at Jerash made a splendid locale for such an elaborate spec-tacle. The citizens of Jerash and elsewhere expressed their devotion to Artemis by acclamations, sacred hymns, and sacrifices by her altars accompanied by the burning of incense. Scholar Walter Burkert states that offerings to Artemis included items signifying rites of passage, or "turning points in life, such as a girl would dedicate the playthings of her childhood in a sanctuary and present her girdle to Artemis before marriage ... The bride in particular must not forget to show reverence to the virgin Artemis." In Asia Minor at least, May 6th was considered the birthday of Artemis with the entire month set aside as sacred to her. *Curetes*, or the male and female clergy of Artemis, each had their own specific duties in veneration of the Goddess. Offerings to her included bulls, fish, fruit, and incense. Paeans were always sung with the offerings enacted as often as 365 days a year. Artemis is thought to have Gorgon aspects and as such, young girls typically placed in service to Artemis, participated in rituals wearing Gorgon masks assuming the attributes of this Goddeas as Gorgon. A goddess revered by females, she is called upon by a woman before she is wed, on the birthing bed, and to ward off dangers at crucial life passages.

Visitors to Jerash in July will enjoy the Jerash Festival, an international cultural event instituted by Queen Noor in 1981. Jerash is in an excellent state of preser-vation and considered the most complete city of the Decapolis, a confederation of Ten Roman Cities dating from the 1st century BCE. Touring the city can easily take a day as there are many other sites to be seen within the archaeological site, including a museum. Downtown Amman has a nice museum, and more archaeological sites worthy of visiting.

Getting to Jerash

Considered the "Pompeii of the East," JETT (Jordan Express Travel and Tourism) offers a regular service in air conditioned coaches between Jerash and Jordan's capital city of Amman. By car or taxi, from the Sport City interchange in Amman, head northwest past Jordan University and Jerash is 82 miles (51 km) north, or about a one hour drive from Amman. Ladies, just be prepared for squat toilets! They are the norm in many cities within the Middle East.

Petra

The Treasury building, built in 131 CE to commemorate Hadrian's visit to Petra, was and still is the most notable of the sites within the city, often recognized as a site holy to the Egyptian divinity Isis, the protectress and patroness of the city. Petra, with its splendid otherworldly red and pink hued rock sanctuaries, home of the Nabataeans, was also the holy place of many other goddesses and gods. Located at the nexus of trade routes connecting the region, the inhabitants were in contact with many peoples and thus adopted a syncretic approach toward veneration of deity. Besides Isis, Al Uzza, Aphrodite, Tyche, Atargatis, and Ishtar were all worshipped here, with Al Lat worshipped in outlying areas around Petra. In the book of Zacharias 8.5, King Mundhir is said to have sacrificed 400 virgins to Al Uzza, and Procopius depicts Mundhir sacrificing a son of Harith to Aphrodite, the Greek name for Al Uzza. Ninus 6 referring to Al Uzza states, "They prostrate themselves to the morning star and sacrifice the best of their spoils to it." Sprinkled throughout the site, visitors find hundreds of niches, sanctuaries, reliefs, and high places where this assortment of the Feminine Divine in varying aspects and cultures were revered, often in the guise of sacred anthropomorphic stones, called betyls, in the open air, as was the tradition. They were honored with sacrifices of animals, fruit, incense, and perfume during pilgrimages, processions, public confessions, and religious banquets. In these "canyons of the divine," with hundreds of shrines to all manner of gods and goddesses, the Nabataeans obviously saw their religion as a major part of everyday life.

Egyptian papyri describe Petra as a major cult site of Isis, with several shrines dedicated to her within the canyons. Without a doubt, the easiest site for the untrained eye to locate a spot reserved for the veneration of Isis within Petra is the Treasury, the salmon-colored temple-like structure seen when one emerges from the narrow canyon corridors, or the *siq*. Also referred to as Khaznet al-Faroun, the site was once thought to be a tomb or mausoleum where Isis was revered in several of her aspects, including guardian of the dead, grieving widow, and creatrix of life and fertility. The Treasury is a two story building about 130 feet (40 m) high and 90 feet (27 m) wide, carved out of the rough sandstone in lovely detail using Corinthian columns, a rounded template with conical top called a *tholos*, and engravings of foliage, griffins, gorgons, scroll decorations, lions, and reliefs of female figures. Upon closer examination, you can see that the female reliefs are Amazon-like, wearing tunics and holding axes. The figure in the tholos is that of syncretized Isis/Tyche/Al Uzza. Her figure holds a cornucopia in one hand and a patera, or shallow libation dish used in ritual, in the other. Below her are a solar disc, ears of wheat, and two more cornucopias. The interior of the Treasury is nothing like it is depicted in the famous *Indiana Jones and the Last Crusade* movie. Like most of the rock carved sanctuaries within Petra, it consists of plain walls without any paintings or carvings. Within the Treasury interior is a vestibule with side rooms off to the left and right. Behind the vestibule is a great hall with niches carved into each of the three walls to the back and on either side. In the middle of the walkway between the vestibule and great hall was a purifying basin.

Another sacred spot of Isis within Petra, which means "rock" in Greek, is a carved niche where her statue once stood on the outskirts of the city. The now decapitated image is in profile, with Isis on a throne atop a podium. Visitors can easily identify the Isis knot upon her clothing. Another shrine of Isis dated to around 25 BCE is composed of several badly decomposed niches, with inscriptions indicating reverence of Isis and one can still make out where she once sat on a stool. There are also several betyls within Petra which were probably revered as the syncretized Isis/Al Uzza. One has been described with a crowned headband depicting a solar disc with horns and ears of wheat, suggesting fertility aspects. The Lion Griffin Temple was another site believed reserved for the worship of Isis since clay statuettes were found here showing her in mourning, presumably for her deceased husband Osiris. In a private communication with author de Traci Regula, an expert on Isis and her sites, Regula believes Sidd Al-Ma'jjin once possessed a shrine dedicated to Isis. Still located within the Petra metropolis, this

spot is known for violent flooding during the winter season. Here, Regula believes Isis held a "position of importance" and might have been venerated as a river Goddess. This would be in keeping with the Nabataean water engineering, expertise in capturing, conserving, and controlling water in this dry region that receives about 6 inches (15.24 cm) annually. The citizens of Petra venerated Allah and Al Lat for the life-giving spring waters. Al Uzza, considered the deity of the people, was also often symbolized as a lion.

Nabataeans preferred open air sanctuaries in the highest of places to honor their deities. On the ridge of Zibb Attuf, the God Dushara and Goddess Al Uzza are represented by obelisk-like stones, thought by some to be an influence of the Egyptians on Nabataean culture. It is believed these obelisks are also representative of fertility as modern

▲ The siq leads to the fantastic Treasury Building, now known to be a Temple of Isis.

Bedouins call the site *Zibb Attuf*, which translates to "The Place of the Merciful Phallus." Arab historian Hisham Ibn al-Kalbi states that rather than having a temple or statue, Arabs simply used a stone to venerate their deities.

Other interesting associations with Petra are the aforementioned Queen Zenobia, who once ruled this area, and a former king of Petra, Malichus I, who was instrumental in Cleopatra VII and Marc Anthony's battle against Rome. It seems Malichus I sent troops to support Marc Anthony's forces against Octavian at the famous battle of Actium, a turning point in the war between Egypt and Rome, yet in a gesture of playing for both sides and fearing Octavian's wrath, Malichus I ordered Cleopatra's ships, anchored off the Gulf of Suez to be set afire. This sealed the fate of Cleopatra, famous Queen of Egypt and Priestess of Isis, preventing her escape and bringing an end to her empire. Queen Zenobia was a priestess of Isis and descendant of Cleopatra VII (see Syria, page 168).

Getting to Petra

Located in southern Jordan, 319 miles (255 km) south from Amman, Petra covers approximately 400 square miles (320 sq. km), and has 800 known buildings and temples, 75% of which remain unexcavated. People intending to spend more than a day at the ruins usually stay in the village of Wadi Musa, two miles (3 km) uphill from the site entrance. Bus tours and service taxis frequently travel the route from the Jordan capital of Amman to Wadi Musa. Most of the tours are round-trip, returning tourists to their hotels in Amman on the same day. Tour groups also leave from Israel and return back the same day. Fun options to travel through the canyon passages of Petra are on camel, horseback, or by carriage, all of which are available for rental at the site entrance.

LEBANON

Byblos, or Jbail, one of the oldest continually occupied settlements in the world, dates back at least 7,000 years. Once called Gebal, and Giblet, it was finally named Byblos by the Greeks for the scrolls of papyrus imported from Egypt through this ancient port city. Interestingly, it is from the Greek name *byblos*, for papyrus, we derive the words books, biblia, and bible. In exchange for papyrus and gold, Byblos sent numerous pharaohs and the famous King Solomon the much desired cedarwood with which they built their temples. Like Jerash, Byblos also possessed a fine monumental colonnaded street terminating at a grand square featuring a large nymphaeum. This ornamental fountain was adorned with statues of Hygeia, Orpheus, Achilles and Penthesilea. Esteemed as the daughter of Asclepius, Hygeia, literally "health" personified as Goddess, her name was proclaimed immediately after her father's name in the Hippocratic Oath. Penthesilea was the daughter of Ares, god of war, and the Amazon queen Otrere. She was famous for leading an army of Amazons in defense of Troy, fighting bravely until finally being killed by Achilles who, in turn, mourned her death. According to the *Iliad*, Thersites, the ugliest man at Troy, laughed at Achilles' great love for Penthesilea. In response, Achilles killed him.

Temple of Baalat Gebal

Byblos is a holy site of Goddess with all the elements of a steamy drama — love, sex, murder, ritual prostitution, magic, and betrayal — all coming together in the shared Phoenician-Egyptian mythology of the female deities Isis-Baalat-Astarte-Aphrodite, and the male deities, Adonis-Osiris. Both Byblos and neighboring

Sidon worshipped a triad of gods designated as supreme god, a mother-goddess and a young god of regeneration respectively. Byblos will forever be inextricably intertwined with the stories of fertility and love, of sister and brother, of goddesses and gods. As the lamenting wife-queen, Isis searched for the sarcophagus of her husband-king Osiris, which was set adrift by his murderous brother Set. The sarcophagus came to rest here at Byblos, and was erected as a pillar at the king's temple. With the finding of the sarcophagus, comes a melancholy end to a sad journey of the Mysteries seeking a loved one who had been lost and had died. Similarly, with Aphrodite and Adonis, love, death, and fertility of the land are themes of the drama that unfold for these ill-fated divine sibling lovers. Annual lamenting rituals known throughout the ancient world to commemorate the suffering of Adonis and Osiris occurred here in Byblos as mourners, men and women alike, shaved their heads and beat their breasts, in honor of the fallen gods.

In the ancient city, still visible today, lies a deep spring near the obelisk temple. This is thought to perhaps be the spring where Isis drew water while in the employment of the king during her search for Osiris. About 333 feet (100 m) from the spring is the Great Residence built about 2500 BCE, generally thought to be the king's palace where Isis was the mid-wife to the king's son, and where the sarcophagus of Osiris may have once been located. Considering Osiris' role as the Green God of vegetation, and ancient Lebanon's famous timber trade, it seems logical that his sarcophagus became intertwined with a tree such as the ones used to support the Great Residence and other structures in Byblos.

Various myths and rituals developed around the composite figure Osiris/Adonis, one of the most popular of which regarded the so-called sojourn of his head to the shores of Lebanon from Egypt. Lucian notes in the second century CE: "Each year a head comes from Egypt to Byblos, making a sea journey of seven days, and the winds drive it, by guidance of the gods, and it does not turn aside in any direction, but comes only to Byblos. And this is wholly marvelous. It befalls every year, and happened the time that I was in Byblos, and I saw the head that is of Byblos." The head was probably of papyrus, making it buoyant enough to follow the natural current from the Nile delta to the Phoenician shore. In Cyril of Alexandria's commentary on Isaiah 18, it is not a head but an earthen pot containing a letter from the women of Alexandria that reaches Byblos. As for the contents of the letter, it simply proclaimed, that "Aphrodite had found Adonis."

About 333 feet (100 m) north of the Great Residence is the Baalat Gebal temple where the Lady of Byblos was worshipped in syncretized veneration with Hathor and Aphrodite-Astarte. Coins of Baalat of Byblos were embossed with her name, but her form was depicted in the guise of Isis-Hathor, namely with a sun disk between cow horns. Her temple was described as having wooden pillars supporting a roof of grass or reed, with stone bases at the foundation.

▲ Headless Aphrodite.

Coins dating to the short-lived reign of Macrinus (217-18 CE) reveal that this spectacular temple dedicated to Aphrodite-Astarte had an adjoining porticoed courtyard and a *baetyl*, or conical stone, on top of a balustrade altar inside. Historian Fergus Millar suggests the fluidity of the divine identities as indicated above and noted Phoenician Baalat was depicted in typical Egyptian dress and style. Scholar Patricia Monaghan embellishes on Baalat, chief deity of the Phoenicians, and female equivalent to the god Baal, called "wise old lady of the trees by the Sumerians," describing her naked images as being sculpted in a well-endowed fashion as she holds her life-giving breasts in her hands. When clothed, she appears a "stylish matron in a shoulder-strapped tight robe and elaborate Egyptian hairstyle." It seems within the Byblos sanctuary compound it is difficult to determine just which temple belongs to whom, but clearly scholars believe Aphrodite and Adonis were venerated here along with a strong flavor of Isis and Osiris.

Byblos was a major center of ritual prostitution. According to Lucian of Samosata, a second century CE writer, it was customary for men and women to shave their heads during the lamenting rituals of Adonis. Any woman who refused to shave her head was penalized and required to spend a day of "work" offering her beauty for sale in a marketplace of foreigners. What payments she earned were then offered up at the Temple of Aphrodite. Byblos, along with Tyre and Sidon, situated on the Phoenician coast, were known as places of ritual prostitution and some were closed down by the Christian Roman Emperor Constantine because he viewed the sacred sexual acts, whether literal or symbolic, as morally depraved. The description Whore of Babylon is derived from Tyre, right down to her Tyrian purple attire!

Getting to the Temple of Baalat Gebal

Located 25 miles (40 km) north of Beirut, Byblos is a great base from which to visit the sites of Lebanon which avoids the traffic crunch of Lebanon's capital city. Taxis run along the Beirut-Tripoli highway and can drop travelers at Byblos while taxis for return trips into Beirut are easily obtained from hotels or any of the main streets that run through town. Until political tensions ease, it is best to check with the U.S. State Department or Lebanese Embassy about travel recommendations. Once travelers get the green light, two nearby sites on the "not to miss" list in Lebanon are Ba'albek and Afqa. No one knows the history of Ba'albek's founding, though older ruins, maybe Phoenician, lay below existing Roman temples presumably dedicated to divinities such as Venus, the Muses, and Jupiter. The small natural setting of Afqa, or Aphaca, is directly linked to the death of Adonis, with a grotto and spring, both sacred landscapes traditional to Goddess. There is also a temple of Aphrodite on the sacred site. This holy place is still actively venerated today as pilgrims tie prayer strips to fig trees that grow among the ruins in hope the Goddess will answer their prayers.

Goddess Focus
Sacred Sex

To understand the true nature of the sacred marriage, or sacred prostitution as it has been incorrectly described, and the role of the *hierodule*, or sacred prostitute, one must be willing to set aside today's sexual morality as well as the negative connotations these words imply. Their authentic meaning is not easily understood in modern culture which has been heavily influenced by Judeo-Christian moral expectations. Herodotus painted a rather seedy picture of ancient mores, along with other writers who suggested the sexual activity was designed to mellow men's lust, yet scholars today are reexamining their opinions. Another explanation is that during many times and places, sexual roles and acts were honorable and conducted with pure sacred intention. The unions were a means to attain enlightenment. It was believed a man needed a woman to attain apotheosis, or be elevated toward a divine state. Even the Tao of Islam teaches the sexual act provides the occasion to experience God's "greatest self-disclosure," according to Muslim scholar, Ibn al-Arabi. Ancient sex, whether literal or symbolic, was not performed as lewd or licentious acts, perversion, or for personal sexual gratification. This was not sex for money, or sex

▲ The Sacred Marriage insured the fertility of the land and people.

performed to dominate another, and it must be remembered this was during a time when there was no shame about sexuality and our bodies. The pleasure or bliss derived from such acts was not unclean, dishonorable, taboo, and neither did it elicit feelings of guilt. During intercourse and birth, divine and generative energy was palpable! Imagine a mind-set where one could share such intimacy with the Divine!

Girls who lost their virginity in this context did so within a sacred construct, in a sense offering their sexuality to the Goddess. This offering of sexuality was mimicked when men castrated themselves as a sacrifice in service to the Goddess, an act which was the predecessor of the Roman Catholic clergy's vow of celibacy. The Greek *heterae* (or Mesopotamian hierodule) was no prostitute in the modern sense of the word. She was a sanctified dedicate who worked within the temple and servant of a chosen deity. These were the best educated and artistically refined women and men who dedicated themselves in service to Goddess and their community. Barbara Walker likens their gifts to Hindu Karuna, which can be described as providing comfort, love, tenderness, mystical knowledge, and sex. When the hierodule (or heterae) engaged in the sacred marriage or intercourse, she was considered the sacred embodiment of Goddess, aiding an individual in

▲ The ancient Greeks depicted sacred sex on their pottery designs.

need of healing, or in attaining spiritual transcendence. She was a mediator between the mortal and divine. She understandably played a powerful female role, whom the upcoming male dominated culture wanted decimated and cut from the spiritual equation, not unlike the role of Mary Magdalene and Inanna who were both branded a harlot.

As the embodiment of Goddess the hierodule, or temple priestess, conjoined in the sacred marriage with the king or priest (the incarnation of the dying/rising god), and this sacrosanct ritual became intertwined with the fecundity of nature. This served to insure the citizen's livelihood, often based on animal husbandry and agriculture. Their coming together to procreate was synonymous with the land being planted and harvested. Their fruitfulness was symbolically the same as husband and wife coming together to be fruitful and multiply with children. Sharing the pleasure of the act was also seen as a means of honoring the Goddess upon whom the people depended for favorable weather, crops, and matters of life and death. Remember, these were times when war, drought, and famine could destroy a civilization, and there was no corner market to pick up dinner! People still recognized the sacred interconnection between deity, people, animals, and things. They were not detached from nature as we are today, and as such, they believed sexual union between mortals, or mortals and deity, effected the world in which they lived. People wanted deities who loved and cared for them, and these unions helped insure the deity would smile down upon them so their land, family, and business would prosper.

Rather than just a sexual tryst between a man and woman, the sacred marriage was a veiled story within the *Hymn to Inanna*. King Dumuzi had the play performed so that their people would prosper. The same sacred marriage is believed by most to be depicted between Sheba and Solomon, not the king and the community, in the *Song of Songs*. Priests, kings, and consorts represent the Greenman/vegetation and dying/rising god-kings, associated with the annual marriage and sacrifice of the consort of the Goddess, so that the land will flower with new crops as the earth may renew itself. The hierodule was known throughout the ancient world and survived until the dawning of the powerful patriarchy. In India they are called the *shaktis*. This form of Tantric spirituality is the closest example of this tradition that exists today. It should be noted that within Kabbalism, mystic Christianity, Islam and Gnosticism, the sacred marriage is considered the union of the soul with the Holy Spirit.

SAUDI ARABIA

Worshipping a deity within the form of a plain rock, or a stone with peculiar properties, was not only common in Arabia, but throughout the Mediterranean region and the world. Outside Saudi Arabia, Aphrodite was worshipped as a stone in her Cypress temple. Cybele was worshipped as a stone by Greeks and Romans, Baal and Baalat were worshipped as stones in Byblos, and Al Lat was worshipped in the form of Athena on a stone stele complete with a coat of mail, a shield, and spear. In neighboring Petra, deities were represented by *betyls*, sacred stones venerated as the seat of the deity, which often had some facial features carved upon the stone. Meteorites were particularly seen as gifts from heaven, and the Ka'ba stone was said to have come down from Paradise with the Holy Ghost on the breath of Allah.

The Grand Mosque at Mecca

It might come as a surprise, but Al Uzza, the Mighty One, was tutelary Goddess of the Ka'ba (Kaaba) stone alongside Hubal, in her holy city of pre-Islamic Mecca. Al Uzza was the most prominent deity of Mecca during Mohammed's time, followed by Al Lat, then Manat. These Goddesses were at the crux of the controversy surrounding *The Satanic Verses*, both the title of a novel written by Salman Rushdie and the sacred verses within the Qu'ran (Koran) considered the direct word of God. Today, in Islamic Saudi Arabia, when Muslims make their prescribed pilgrimage to Mecca in honor of Allah during the Hajj, they circumambulate seven times about the Ka'ba stone in the ritual called *tawaf*, repeating the very same ritual practiced by their ancestors. Rufus Camphausen cites historical evidence that seven priestesses of Al Uzza and her worshipers circumambulated the black stone of the Ka'ba seven times in veneration of the Goddess and the seven ancient planets.

Al Uzza is thought to originate from the region of Mount Sinai, and was brought to Mecca by the Quraysh, Mohammed's tribe, keepers of the Ka'ba, who venerated both her and Al Lat. Al Uzza was often represented as a stone larger

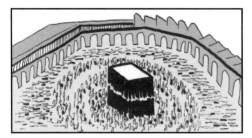

▲ The Grand Mosque at Mecca is the focus of Muslim prayers worldwide.

than the god Dushara, in which she was seen as three-fold, representing not just herself but Al Lat and Manat. Scholar Alfred Guillaume cites sources such as the Christian writer Nilus to demonstrate that evidence for her worship was prevalent as late as the 4th century CE. Tradition states that in his youth Mohammed sacrificed a white sheep to her. The Arabs offered human sacrifices to Al Uzza, and furthermore, "the blood of the victim was smeared or poured on them while the tribe danced around the stone ... The devotees licked the blood, or dipped their hands in it, and thus a reciprocal bond held them to one another and the deity to whom the stone belonged." Ibn Ishaq states Al Uzza had a slaughter place, and the scholar Andrae named the place as Mount Hira where Mohammed worshipped Allah and Al Uzza. This was before Mohammed later began to preach his message which controversially omitted goddesses, dispelled paganism, and according to Camphausen, "focused on Allah and male dominion over nature and women." Mohammed preached his creed to his tribe for 12 years, and they eventually cast him out, but he returned with an army to destroy the false idols. The Meccans who opposed Mohammed carried Al Uzza's banner into battle against the prophet. Mohammed ultimately won victory and had all of Al Uzza's temples destroyed. Mohammed died in 632 CE, two years after he rededicated the Ka'ba sanctuary as a purely Islamic pilgrimage site. Pilgrimage to Mecca for the Muslim faithful emphasizes the idea of unity of faith despite differences of culture or race.

Camphausen elaborates on the Ka'ba stating it was a place of power where men and women worshipped the Goddess in the form of her yoni. The black meteorite stone, 7 or 12 inches (18 or 31 cm) in diameter (reports vary on size), is inlaid at the southeastern corner of the Ka'ba. Not far away from the Ka'ba stone is the Zam Zam well with its life-giving waters. Some believed the well attracted Abraham and Sarah who had for years been unable to conceive a child, and by these fertile waters, representative of the Mother Goddess's powers of fecundity, did Abraham lay with Hagar to conceive a son. Some say the stone at Mecca is that of Al Uzza, others Al Lat, though it has been shown that the two goddesses are often conjoined. According to Ikbal Ali Shah, the Ka'ba stone radiated a greenish hue in the early times when it was worshipped as Goddess, and only later did it turn black from those gazing upon it with all their imperfections.

Al Uzza's worshippers also made pilgrimages to her in her guise as a stone pillar at her valley sanctuary, complete with harem and sacrificial altar at Hurad or Nakhla, located on the road from Mecca to Iraq. Associated with the celestial Venus, Al Uzza is thought by some, including Muslims, to represent the other symbol on the star and crescent Islamic flag. Although Muslims generally reject veneration of pictorial representations and symbols it is hard to forget that Al Lat was represented by the full moon or crescent moon. Over time as many as 360 deities were worshipped in this area now predominately sacred to Allah.

Getting to Mecca

Tourist visas are not available for travel in Saudi Arabia, and visas of other sorts are very difficult to obtain. Pilgrims wishing to visit Saudi Arabia's holy cities must arrange a visitor's visa from someone already in the country who can verify the visitor's faith. Mecca is off limits to non-Muslims. Steep fines are imposed for just turning up at the checkpoints to the sacred city. Use the special road exits for non-Muslims approaching the holy cities or else you'll be in big trouble! All pilgrims coming to the Kingdom have special visas that declare their religious status in Arabic.

Goddess Focus
Satanic Verses

Whether divine utterance or a literary device designed to encourage reconciliation among splintered Arab tribes, the Satanic Verses have been a major point of Islamic controversy that helped obliterate the stature of Goddess. The two verses of Mohammed that were taken out of the Quran (within Sura 53:19-20), are "Have ye thought upon Al Lat and Al Uzza and Manat, the third, the other?" Now many believe based on very good evidence that these verses were originally followed by: "These are the exalted cranes (intermediaries) whose intercession is to be hoped for." The cranes whose intercession was recognized were, of course, the three Goddesses. The same accounts tell us that after this revelation was completed, Mohammed, his followers, and the pagan Arabs all fell in prostration. In fact as a result, tensions eased, reconciliation seemed possible, and all were delighted. But Mohammed soon retracted the overture of compromise, though how soon afterward is not clear. The account continues that Jibril, or Gabriel, the angel of revelation, informed Mohammed that Satan had used Mohammed's desire for reconciliation with the pagan leaders to insert into the revelation of God the verses about the interceding cranes, otherwise called "the satanic verses." The verses which follow, not the satanic verses, serve as the proper sequence to sutra (53:19-20): "Are yours the males and His the females? That indeed were an unfair division!" (53:21-22) In other words, saying the pagan Arabs preferred their sons to daughters then it was unfair to say that God has daughters.

Undoubtedly, this was a conscious effort of a patriarchal worldview stepping in with the very explicit intention of gradually eradicating the presence of the Divine Feminine over time. Inherent in this course of action is the prejudice against women in general, in that daughters and not sons, were attributed to Allah. This new position was also denying an intermediary position (helping cranes) between man and Allah, although evidence for the Satanic Verses mentioning this inter-cessory role played by the three goddesses is overwhelming, regardless of what many Muslims wish to believe. In addition, the esteemed reputation of the three goddesses cannot be denied since they are mentioned throughout the Quran. There was even a recall by Caliph Uthman of editions of the Quran that held the verses and other problematic texts. Today, most scholars of Islam realize that not all of these scriptures were turned in, some even survive in places like the libraries at Cairo. In fact, four different early Muslim scholars and biographers of Mohammed

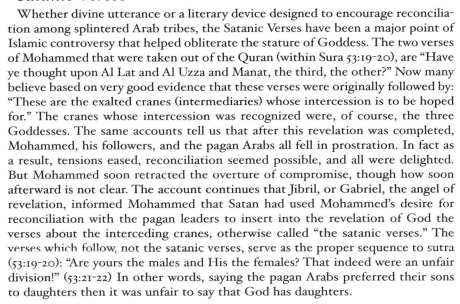

▲ The crescent moon and star, symbols of Islamic goddesses, can be found on national flags of Islamic countries.

(Ibn Jarir al-Tabari, Al-Wakidi, Ibn Sa'd/Sa'ad and Ibn Isaq/Ishaq) wrote about the satanic verses, and inferences to the verses still remain in the Quran. As to the role of the female, some say there is no evidence of women, or goddesses playing a superior role in pre-Islamic Arabia, but Rufus Camphausen cites Omar, a faithful disciple of the prophet Mohammed, who stated, "When we came among the Helpers (Medina tribe), they proved to be a people whose women dominated them, and our wives have come to copy the habits of the women of the Ansar." Interestingly, he adds that the priests who serve the shrine today are still known as the Beni Shaybah, or "sons of the Old Woman." That being said, in the larger context of his influence, separate from putting down worship of the Divine Feminine, Mohammed was a genius who accomplished what no other had been able to do in the region, uniting the splintered Arab tribes, and introducing more progressive ideas, including improving the status of women and stopping the abhorrent practice of child sacrifice. As a point of clarity, the "cranes" were literal helpers and should not be mistaken for "birds."

SYRIA

In Syria, Goddess was reigning quite nicely through the 2nd century CE. The Great Mosque of Damascus in Syria was once a sacred site venerating the female divinity Atargatis, and a throne of Astarte still stands at Eshoun in Lebanon. Recent discoveries in Umm el-Marra, 200 miles (320 km) northeast of Damascus revealed several richly ornamented tombs for women of high status. In one of these graves archaeologists uncovered one female corpse wearing a small lump of iron (perhaps a meteorite) on a pendant around her neck, tempting some to conclude that she was once a priestesses of Goddess. In Iran, the Goddesses Ninhursag, Annhita, and Jaki were venerated, the latter associated with menstruation, until the subject became taboo, and Jaki was then reduced to a demoness. Professor Marija Gimbutas cites *bucrania*, or bull head horns, associating them with regenerative symbols of Goddess worship also found in Iran. Some Iranian cities where goddess figurines have been unearthed are Susa, Nahavand, and Eslam-abad Gharb, while another region called Gorgan revealed 5,000-year-old female statuettes. With the Muslim invasion, worship of Goddess went underground in Iran, but still existed in some secret creeds, including within sophist poetry.

Temple of Al Lat

Isolated at the edge of the Roman Empire is the city Palmyra, or Place of the Palms, a municipality that was a major center of trade and pilgrimage for centuries. Palmyra was home to the ancient Arabian Goddesses Al Lat and Manat, the Sumerian Mother Goddess Belili, and the Semitic Queen Zenobia. Camel caravans once took four days to reach Palmyra from Damascus, or an additional day by horse. Today, after merely three hours by car or bus, visitors will find themselves gazing upon one of the most ethereal archaeological ruins in the Middle East. Practitioners of Al Lat worshipped here. The dynamic Queen Zenobia, who claimed descent from Cleopatra VII herself, ruled from this city, aspiring to reign over the East. She was able to expand her Syrian kingdom as far as eastern Asia Minor and Egypt before she was eventually defeated by the Roman Emperor

Aurelia in 272 CE. Aurelia was quite taken by her heroic ability and seemed to have counted himself lucky as he complimented her to his contemporaries, "If you only knew what a woman I have been fighting! And what would history say if I had been defeated?" The Near East was a place where roles of women and goddesses were not always defined by gender or biology. Here they challenged patriarchy and threatened gender ideologies. Of course they were mothers and creatrixes, but they were also powerful and determined warriors and queens who bestowed kingship, and protected cities by divine law.

Al Lat, a complex divinity with varying associations, is sometimes considered a feminine version of the Arabic Allah, and one of the three principle Arabian Goddesses. Her name meaning "The Goddess" implies a universal flavor, and she is usually believed to be associated with the sun. It is thought she was introduced into Arabia from Syria, the former where she may have been the moon goddess of North Arabia. Sometimes called "Lady of the Temple" in the pantheon at Palmyra, scholar Javier Teixidor states one finds "different names for the same deity such as Al Lat ... (Atargatis) ... Astarte ... all conceal one sole goddess, the female deity of heaven in whose cult Arab as well as members of the western tribes were united." She was worshipped all over the world as the Great Mother under various names. She is mentioned by Herodotus, in old Arabian inscriptions, and by pre-Islamic poets. We know of an interesting divination technique associated with Al Lat and other Arab deities, typically involving casting lots using inscribed arrows.

Al Lat's moon symbol is believed by some, including certain Muslims, to be on the flag of Islam, though Islamic ideology officially rejects any reverence of images and idols. She is also considered a chthonic, or underworld deity, sometimes associated with Al Latu, another name for Erishkigal, and Kore/Persephone. As such, some make further associations between Al Lat and the seven gates of Inanna/Ishtar's journey to the underworld with the seven priestesses, circumambulations, and planets linked to the Ka'ba stone. Linguistically, in the vowel-less ancient Semitic language, (through word variations of SB, Saba, or Sheba), the black Ka'ba stone is associated with the imams who attend the Ka'ba, namely the Beni Shaybah, known as the Sons of the Old Woman (possibly Al Lat), Sons of the Seven (Beer-Sheba or well of seven), and the Sons of the Oath, as Al Lat is associated with covenants.

Al Lat's chief place of worship was Ta'if, near Mecca, where she was represented by a square stone called Al Rabba, or sovereign, a title that also belonged to Ishtar (Belit) and Astarte (Baalat). Mohammed's tribe, the Quraish, as well as many other Arabs used to name their children after her as in the name Zayd al-Lat. Other specific tribes known to venerate Al Lat were the Hijaz, the Hisma, and the Nabataeans. Al Lat's priesthood was often from a long hereditary line as evidenced by the following inscription: "It is known in 56 CE that Rawah, son of Malik, son of Aklab, son of Rawah, son of Qasily rebuilt the temple of Al Lat which he claimed was first constructed by Rawah, son of

▲ This statue of a guardian lion was found at the Temple of Al Lat, Syria.

Qasily." According to Robert Hoyland, Al Lat was asked to extend solicitude, display mercy, provide safe travel, good weather, prosperity, overall well being, and is particularly invoked to protect against enemies, vengeance, blindness, and lameness. Scholar Javier Teixidor states her guardians or priests were of the Bene Maazin tribe. Fidelity and contracts were also areas of her concern. One of the two other Arab goddesses Al Lat is linked to is Al Uzza, the Mighty One, tutelary Goddess of the Ka'ba stone in her holy city of Mecca. She is associated with Venus, and as such is thought by some to represent the star on the Islamic flag alongside Al Lat's moon. It is possible both were worshipped alongside each other at Palmyra.

The third, oldest, and possibly original of the three Arabian Goddess was Manat, thought to be associated with fortune and fate, based on her name which means "to mete out" and in this guise, pre-Islamic Arabs believed Manat controlled their destiny. In some of her early representations, she was a wooden image covered with the blood of sacrifices made during worship. The Aus and Khazzraj tribes were known to venerate Manat. She was thought to watch over graves as indicated by a tomb inscription that reads, "And may Dushara and Manat and Qaysha curse anyone who sells this tomb or buys it or gives it in pledge or makes a gift of it or leases it or draws up for himself any document concerning it or buries in it anyone apart from the inscribed above." Manat was worshipped at Palmyra alongside Baal before venturing into Arabia. Her worship was recorded and traced from the territories of Mecca to Mleiha, known today as the Arab Emirates.

Palmyra, with its monumental Corinthian colonnades, sanctuaries, porticoes, public buildings, and temples is often called a "pearl in the desert." Al Lat's temple at Palmyra had as its cult statue a marble figure of Athena with whom Al Lat was equated. Today that statue is located on-site in the Palmyran Museum. The 11.5-foot (3.45-m) limestone relief that had stood within her sanctuary depicting a lion holding a crouching gazelle in its paws is now located in the museum garden. Al Lat was also venerated in conjunction with Artemis in Palmyra as evidenced by an inscription on her temple which read "Al Lat who is also Artemis." And just in case readers want to know Queen Zenobia's fate, it is generally believed following her procession in golden chains through the streets of Rome during Aurelian's victory celebration, she finished out her life in the Villa at Tivoli outside Rome. Not a shabby end!

Getting to Temple of Al Lat

Palmyra, or *Tadmor* in Arabic, is located three hours drive west from Damascus, or the city Deir ez Zor. Palmyra is easily reached by tour coach, public bus, or private taxi from Damascus, or Dumeir, and possibly Deir ez Zor. Taxis are usually waiting near major hotels. Once at Palmyra accommodations are available, such as the Zenobia Hotel, where Agatha Christie and husband Max Mallowan stayed. Private cars can be obtained for one-way or round-trip journeys.

THE ASIAN

SUB-CONTINENT

By you this universe is borne.
By you this world is created.
O Devi, by you it is protected.
—Devi Mahatmya

THOUGHTS OF THIS REGION conjure in the mind a rich mosaic of people, religions, and customs. One imagines men in turbans riding atop elephants, musicians wearing loinclothes enticing cobras from baskets with exotic melodies, and dark-eyed women bedecked in silken saris with bindis on their foreheads. As is usually the case, reality lives somewhere between romantic fantasy and popular assertion. Yet this is certainly a land of sights, sounds, and smells all sprinkled into a melting pot of rich sensations. Visions of sacred landscapes of lingams and yonis are juxtaposed with skyscrapers and Gothic architecture. Delectable edibles such as curry, maas, dal, and khata tempt the palate. Holy men in caves, temple rats, riverside funeral pyres, and cows roaming busy streets startle the Western mind, while the art, music, and religious festivals entice visitors into a symphony of sensory overload. This is a land where mythology, tantras, and epic poems have created a recipe for spiritual potency and those who sit at the table to partake of this exotic dish, with its multitude of unique ingredients, are certain to fill themselves from the delicious buffet. From the Taj Mahal, the ultimate monument of love, to yogini temples, archaeological sites, floating palaces, forts, sacred caves, and mud thatch homes, here one finds it all.

The Who's Who list of notable personages from the Sub-Continent could fill books. We have all heard of the famous Indira Gandhi and Mother Theresa but we may yet still discover the lesser-known Kalpana Chawla, the first Indian woman astronaut, and Lakshmi Bai, the "Rebel Queen" who fought British domination. They have all left their mark on the hearts and minds of the Asian Sub-Continent. While many have heard of the Kama Sutra, others like Sai Baba, Amma, and Sri Ramakrishna are hardly household names. What the average person knows of the region comes from neighborhood Indian restaurants or what filters to the mainstream Western audience by pop culture from the likes of the Beatles, Indiana Jones, and Bollywood. Few realize this land is the home of our foremothers and forefathers, and where Goddess worship has gone uninterrupted for thousands of years. Since the earliest of times, when a sophisticated civilization flourished in the Indus Valley, the Oldest of the Old was the Divine Mother.

In the interest of world harmony, it must be stated that from this region a cultural and spiritual heritage is shared amongst ancient Egyptians, Persians, Greeks, Romans, and even Germanic peoples. There are direct parallels between Hindu, Middle Eastern/African and European deities ranging from Lakshmi to Ceres. Furthermore, there even exits an "Indian Isis," who while appearing as Kali or Parvati, resembles in an uncanny way, the Greek goddesses Hera, and Hecate as well as the penultimate Egyptian deity. Scholars have often argued that the stories behind the Judeo-Christian book of Genesis share several roots of the Hindu myths, including the story of Manu and the flood. The Indo-Europeans or Aryans, the ancestors of Vedic India, intermarried with indigenous Indians and swept from the Caucus/Black Sea area to the east into India, and to the west into Europe and are related to many peoples of European heritage through a common history in language, blood, and religion. Vedic traditions are Indo-European! The West is closer to India than many might realize!

This region is bordered to the north by the Himalayan Mountains, the "Rooftop of the World," the mountain range considered by some as an emerging feminine vortex, the Goddess herself. To the east, west and south are the waters of the Bay of Bengal, Arabian Sea and Indian Ocean. This is a region where religion is so palatable and imbued within everyday routine, one can almost taste it! Particular trees, rivers, stones, mountains and caves, such as the grandiose Ellora Caves replete with Goddess imagery, are all sacred. Even the monsoon season is seen as a magical transformation of the landscape and a time for renewal and hope. Families cremate their dead along the banks of the life-giving anionic river Goddess, the Ganga, generally known as the Ganges River. Immersing themselves in the Ganges, home of river dolphins, practitioners and pilgrims purify themselves, many arriving from all over the world to collect Ganga's sacred waters for healing and ritual. This is the land of Shakti, the female force of the universe, catalyst of the life-force itself, sacred for thousands of years into the modern age.

▲ The Taj Mahal is a funerary monument devoted to a beloved wife.

Thousands of various goddesses reside in India where Hindus believe all are one with Devi. Reflections of her many aspects range from the obscure Nirriti, to the well known Lakshmi, Tara, Durga, Uma, Sarasvati, Parvati,

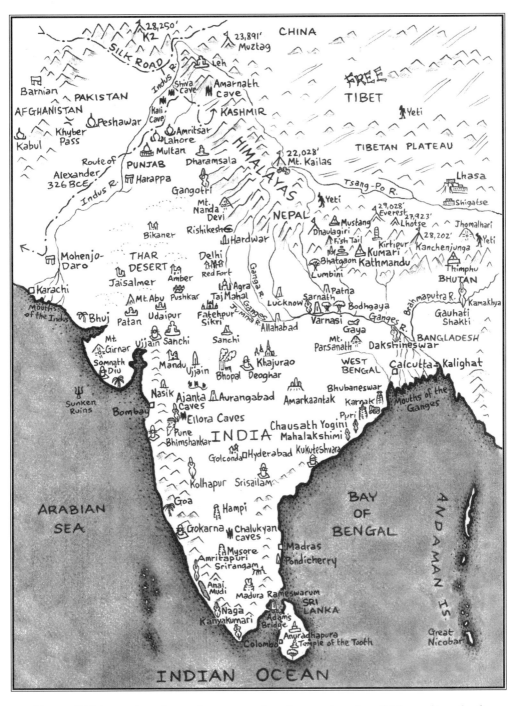

Ganga, Taleju, and perhaps the most misunderstood and unfairly maligned of all, Kali. Here Goddess is worshipped in sacred rituals or pujas, processions and prayer throughout the year. Here her temples, shrines and natural sites for veneration are abundant. We see her image embraced in contemporary Indian cultural movements in order to elevate the status of women as well as in ancient folk rituals to ensure abundant crops. This is a part of the world where Goddess is a living tradition in the most literal sense, her continued and ongoing reverence is undeniable as we see her embodied in the young girl considered the Living Goddess Kumari of Kathmandu and in Ammachi of Kerala, beloved the world over. No place better serves to show the resurgence of Goddess worship or the all-embracing Goddess becoming one supreme Divine Feminine than within the Asian Sub-Continent.

INDIA

Through its very long and complex history India has been influenced by the indigenous Puranic peoples, nomadic invading Indo-European Aryans, Jains, Christians, Zoroastrians, Muslims, Bon and Buddhists — to name just a few! Alexander the Great entered northwest India on his conquest to extend Hellenistic culture far and wide. The apostle Thomas, while spreading Christianity, encountered Kali here. The face of the country was changed by the Mughals, the British Raj, Queen Victoria and Mahatma Gandhi. The vast majority of people in India are Hindus, the Sanskrit word originally a geographic designation for an area defined by the Indus River. It later became the name of the faith we know today with its earliest roots in prehistory. Today practitioners of Hinduism, Buddhism, Bon, Parsis (ancient Zoroastrianism), Jainism, Christianity, Tantra, Shamanism, Islam, and Sikhism live side by side, often blending traditions into a unique tapestry of faiths which weave this part of the world into one of the premier spiritual centers of civilization. It is a region with unique traditions including arranged marriages, sacred cows, castes, gurus, genital worship, and purdah. Unfortunately, in this patriarchal society, the phenomena of sati, also known as "bride burning" or "dowry murders" are still common travesties in certain regions of India.

Kamakhya Temple

Nilachala, or blue mountain, is not only home of the beloved beehive-shaped Kamakhya Temple, undoubtedly one of the most sacred sites in all of India, but it is also home of the Ten Wisdom Goddesses or Dasamahavidhyas in their prehistoric shrines that dot the landscape of the mountain. Commanding an impressive view of the world below, the faithful believe Kamakhya's shakti pitha shrine is where the yoni of the Goddess once fell to earth. The "yoni" is the "holder," "receptacle," or "vagina" of Goddess, often shown in conjunction with the linga of a male deity, together representing the divine generative energy that helped spark all of creation. This longtime center of Tantric Hinduism became home to the literal symbol of the shakti, the yoni mandala, located in the labyrinth-like cave sanctuary of the shrine. Author Rufus Camphausen, in his book *The Yoni*, quoting S. C. Banerjee and sacred texts tells us that a cave well "reaches down into the netherworld" and the actual opening of the so-called yoni "measures twelve fingers all around."

Pilgrims come from miles around in celebration of the symbolic menstrual blood of Goddess. From mid-July to mid-August reddish waters (containing iron oxide and red arsenic) naturally flow from a spring over the moist cleft of the yoni stone at Kamakhya. The spring reveals Goddess in this aspect as appreciating the full splendor of sexuality as well as representing the axis mundi, or center

▲ The Kamakhya Assam Temple is renowned in India as a Shakti Pitha site.

of the universe. Many believe Kamakhya resides here in the shakti pitha where the sacred stone conforms to the shape of a yoni, though it is often difficult to see as it is covered in sacred cloths and all manner of ritual items. The most important seasonal celebration takes place during the Ambubachi festival, between mid-July and mid-August, the Indian month of Assar. During this celebration, pilgrims can eagerly anticipate beholding the goddess Devi covered with a red cloth in candlelight. Following proscribed tradition, this festival culminates in the sacrifice of a buffalo. At another annual celebration, women arrive from all over the world and cook porridge for the Goddess.

The legend of the shakti pithas is first recorded in the Daksa Yaina chapter of the Kalika Purana. When King Daksha, father of Sati neglected to invite his daughter and her husband Shiva to his grand celebration, Sati decided they should attend anyway, uninvited. Upon arrival she discovered her father was very upset they had come because, apparently, he did not especially like his son-in-law, the god Shiva. Deeply insulted, Sati killed herself. Shiva went mad, picking up the dead body of his wife Sati and wandered the world with her body upon his shoulders. Finally Vishnu came upon Shiva and cut Sati's body into 51 pieces and tossed the parts from heaven down to the earth below. Thus, wherever her various body parts fell became the shakti pithas or shrines/seats of the Goddess. The numbers of shakti pitha sites vary. Some say only four: Odra in the west, Jala Saila in the north, Purnasaila in the south, and Kamarupa in the east. Other sacred texts say there are as many as 108 shakti pithas. Of course Shiva did not remain single for very long, eventually marrying Parvati, daughter of Himalaya, who was a mixture of two Goddesses, the heavenly Vedic Aditi and the indigenous Earth Goddess Nirrti. Because Parvati was originally a Mountain Goddess, she was eventually related to the great Mountain Goddess Durga, another consort of Shiva and, in fact, the two eventually became one and the same in later traditions. By the time of the Vamana Purana, the Goddess even assumes the name "Parvati-Kali."

The Goddess Kamakhya at Guwahati is made of eight metal alloys and seated on a throne with five jewels. To reach her statue pilgrims must go down a dimly lit flight of steps. Further within the cave shrine is the well and yoni mandala clearly indicating worship began with the spring and cave long before the temple was built. Goddess is also worshipped here in the aspects of Durga, Kali, Tara, Kamala, Uma, Chamunda and Shakti. The temple dates to the 17th century and follows the Assamese style in overall design. The exterior of the oval-shaped temple is accented with seven spires topped with golden pitcher-like forms on lotus blossoms. Atop the flowers are golden tridents. Pilgrims coming to the temple believe the residing Goddess may help barren women become fertile and drinking the sacred waters of the Mother will cure ills or prevent rebirth, important to Hindus who view life on Earth as suffering. The Tantric priesthood that ministers to the temple and the community are usually friendly and welcoming of all non-Hindus interested in the shrine and the rituals performed here.

Getting to Kamakhya Temple

Located on Nilachal Hill (also called Mount Nila or Nilchla) the temple is located about 5 miles (8 km) from the town Guwahati, (Guahati) in the Kamrup District of Assam. On a map, Assam is the easternmost province of India. The temple can be reached by tours from Guwahati or busses that leave every 10-15 minutes from Guwahati to the foot of Nilachal Hill. Travelers can reach the hilltop by taxi drivers who await passengers getting off the bus. The closest airport is Borjhar from where bus or taxi can be obtained for the 16-mile (25-km) jaunt to Guwahati. It should be noted, access to the inner holy of holies is sometimes forbidden to outsiders and cameras are not allowed in the shrine.

GAIA ALERT

INEQUALITY OF WOMEN: HEALTH & ECONOMICS

Because of economic factors an important natural resource is currently at great risk. No, we are not discussing the effects of erratic weather conditions upon food production nor the results of raw sewage upon rivers and lakes, we are talking

▲ Women are mostly malnourished and illiterate in rural India.

about a resource even closer to ourselves — in fact, it may very well be ourselves! These special resources are women and girls, residing in various economically disadvantaged parts of the world, those who are the foundations and life-givers of families. They are disadvantaged from childhood, receiving inadequate health care and education in Nepal, India, and much of Africa. Kati Marton, reporter for *Newsweek,* noted that among the health issues threatening many of these women are the inaccessibility to effective contraception which leads to unwanted pregnancies which are often terminated under unsafe circumstances. Genital mutilation affects two million women worldwide, which can cause infertility, long-term health problems and sexual dysfunction. In India, 90% of female AIDS infections occur within marriage as the disease is spread from husband to wife, often resulting in women being shunned by their families. Most women in Zambia did not feel they even had the right to ask their husband to wear a condom. Marton cites some sobering statistics. Women make up two-thirds of the world's 880 million illiterate adults and up to 70% of its poorest citizens. Children and pregnant women account for 90% of the one million malaria deaths each year in Africa which often results in the contraction of tuberculosis after immune systems are weakened. In Nepal, women have abnormally high mortality rates and low literacy averages. The United Nations estimates one in three girls will be a victim of domestic violence as sexual coercion, rape and battery all put underprivileged young women at risk.

Dakshineswar Temple

Many famous stories circulate about various appearances of Indian Goddesses, including one manifestation before the Apostle Thomas on July 3, 72 CE, as well as a visit to Rani Rasmani, a pious and wealthy woman in the mid-1800s. In Thomas' account, he was on a mission to spread Christianity across India when he passed a Kali temple and was invited inside by her priests. In his writings of that experience Thomas reports he actually saw an apparition of Kali. When Kali visited Rani Rasmani, her apparition became the guiding light for the building of the Dakshineswar Temple in Calcutta. History states that Rasmani was going on pilgrimage to Varnasi to worship Goddess. Her convoy of 24 boats was set to depart, but on the eve of the journey Kali appeared to Rani and instructed her to instead build a temple in Calcutta on the banks of a Ganges tributary. The rest is history. During 1847 to 1855 the building project progressed resulting in a temple complex of Goddess visited by thousands daily.

The resident sage, Ramakrishna Paramhansa, lived and worked over three decades at Dakshineswar while bringing the temple fame with his philosophy on the oneness of all faiths. According to devotees, he became a channel or conduit for the Divine, famous for embodying Shiva, Kali, Krishna, Christ, and Mohammed. His fame as an avatar grew, bringing thousands of pilgrims from all over the world to the temple as they learned of his ecstatic trances that brought him the ultimate bliss derived from his connection to the Divine.

Speaking to a type of trance experience, many Indians from Calcutta who immigrated to other places around the world brought with them varying forms of this practice of trance associated with shakti puja or ritual worship to experience God/Goddess. Discussing a form of this trance worship or possession, scholar Keith McNeal elaborates on this practice that activates the *shakti*, a conceptualization of cosmic power or energy within Hinduism that is associated with the Mother Goddess. The temporary animation of shakti by way of a human medium constitutes the practice of *jharaying*, or spiritual purification and blessing. This spiritual state is typically accompanied with the practice of chewing leaves from the sacred neem tree, believed to possess magical properties. In fact, many

Indians hang neem leaves above the door lintels of their homes as a protection against evil spirits. McNeal notes that possession mediums often place flaming cubes of camphor into their mouths as a sign that an authentic spirit manifestation is taking place. Many pilgrims will attest that even lay members and visitors to the temples on puja days can also be possessed by shakti energy on a temporary, ritualized basis, but these manifestations are typically considered to be generalized episodes of shakti and are not necessarily identified with a specific possessing divinity. McNeal states that shakti, or divine power, has the capacity for inter-identification of devis within an abstracted and encompassing concept of ultimate feminine power making shakti puja traditions highly dynamic, contextually resourceful, and potentially adaptable.

McNeal further describes shakti as being "a refracted-like prism or a plethora of differentiated goddesses with their own individuated personalities and mythic shakti powers positioned by gradations along a single continuum. What is important is the Goddess' astonishing ability to unite, however paradoxically, the opposite yet intimate poles of life and death, good and evil, order and chaos." Kali's detractors have selectively focused on her negative or ferocious characteristics without the clarity of a deeper understanding of her ability to unite polar opposites.

▲ The Dakshineswar Temple is a powerful place of worship for the misunderstood deity Kali.

Taking the concept a bit deeper, in the words of Elizabeth Usha Harding, foundress of the Kali Mandir Temple in Southern California, they have yet to understand "Kali the Benign and Kali the Terrible who creates and nourishes, kills and destroys. By Her magic we see good and bad, but in reality there is neither. This whole world and all we see is the play of Maya, (illusion) the veiling power of the Divine Mother. God is neither good nor bad, nor both. God is beyond the pair of opposites which constitute this relative existence. Kali is the full Universal Power." And it is when this basic concept is truly understood and taken within, and fear no longer rules, the practitioner believes one is truly liberated. Western women identify with Kali in her Creatrix aspect in their youth when their bodies flow with life-giving sacred menstrual blood. Later in life, when mortality is more tangible and bodies are receptacles for sacred wisdom rather than the life-giving sacred fluids, they relate to Kali as the Destroyer and the taker of life.

Ever since the first millennium BCE, the conception that all Goddesses are one has been a recurring theme, later greatly substantiated by the beloved sage Ramakrishna Paramhansa. In fact these Goddesses were perceived as embodying both the male aspect of the Divine in conjunction with the female, as in Shiva and Shakti, soul and nature, yin and yang, and principals of opposites. Furthermore, Sri Ramakrishna came to believe in One Supreme Being. The importance of this concept should not be overlooked in a world ravished by a long and bloody history of murder and destruction in the name of religion as followers of opposing faiths wage war in the belief theirs is the only true religion and theirs the only true god. Speaking about the inclusive nature of Goddess, religious scholar James Rietveld sums up that the fostering of a collective identity, especially when this commonality is literally unknown, may be beneficial toward eroding the false perception and stereotypes in the minds of most Western audiences. For them, India is an exotic land, but, in truth, it is very closely linked to Western culture.

Approaching the Dakshineshwar complex, a truly beautiful sight from the river, one walks through an arched main gate decorated with swastika-shaped designs (no relation to the Nazi symbol) before reaching the main structure dedicated to Kali, a white-washed temple sitting on a high plinth. The roof sports nine cupolas and rounded cornices creating an impressive architectural marvel against the backdrop of the daylight sky. Within the inner sanctum stands an image of an incarnation of Kali as Bhavatarini or Mother who is Savior of the World. The temple retains the room of sage Ramakrishna Paramhansa in its original state. There are 12 smaller subsidiary temples dedicated to Shiva and Krishna around the compound. Remember shoes are not allowed inside most temples and it is customary to purify oneself by washing ones' hands with Ganges water before entering the temple. And for devotees, do not forget an offering for Ma which can be purchased from the vendors near the temple.

Getting to Dakshineswar Temple

The temple, which is open daily, is located 8 miles (12 km) north of Calcutta (also referred to as Kolkata on some newer maps) at 24 Parganas district and can be reached by bus, boat, rickshaw or motor taxi from Calcutta. By car, the ride to the temple is about 30 minutes from central Calcutta.

Kalighat Temple

Kalighat is a shakti pitha site in Calcutta where four toes of the right foot of Sati are believed to have fallen to Earth from the heavens. It is also a sacred site of a living goddess tradition that has been maligned and misunderstood, thus warranting a closer look. This cosmopolitan city of bazaars, museums, and Victorian mansions was once the capital of Britain's Indian empire, recently re-named Kolkata in 2001 to reflect the Bengali pronunciation of the city name. Missionaries such as William Ward wrote in 1802 that even officials from the British East India Company made offerings to Kali, much to the disapproval of European missionaries working in India. These missionaries and British officials have done much to misrepresent Kali and her worshippers. These unfortunate stereotypes persist today as evidenced by accounts that yet sensationalize Kali and her association with thieves and human sacrifice.

Today, Kalighat remains one of the most famous pilgrimage sites in India, with thousands of the devoted coming to pay homage to the Mother daily. Fortunately travelers today are better educated, more sophisticated, and often understand the agenda of those providing earlier fear-based accounts of Kali and her worshippers, so it is important to repeat a fair and balanced herstory of this place and the Goddess associated with it.

Calcutta also hosts the late Mother Theresa's Mother House and her *Nirmal Hridaya*, or "pure heart," home for the destitute. Nuns there wear blue and white saris as they care for the sick and dying who have come to Calcutta to attain *moksha,* or final spiritual liberation, before they die. Down the street is the Kalighat Temple, home of Kali, Mother Goddess of death and regeneration, to whom many people pray and believe they return at the time of their death. In the inner sanctum or holy of holies, one can find the image of Kali at Kalighat. According to scholar Sanjukta Gupta, Kali is worshipped not just as the reaper, but savior, cosmic mother, sovereign, and divine power controlling the universe. Kali punishes wrong-doers, but is forgiving and helps them in their misery. Gupta describes the image of Kali as dark and beautiful with serene eyes and wavy black hair. Her body is adorned with flowers, ear and nose jewelry and a lovely sari. She has four silver arms — one holds a sword, one a severed head, and two form sacred *mudras,* or gestures, granting safety and fulfilling wishes of the devoted. Kali is petitioned by pilgrims for all manner of difficulties. Representations of ailing or cured body parts are often left at the altar to petition assistance or thank the goddess for a body healed. As this is a shakti pitha where the toe of Sati was believed to have fallen, pilgrims often come here and touch the feet of the image of Kali, worshipped here as Mother Kalika.

Many believe all the other Goddesses of India are but aspects of Kali. Gupta tells of watching a priest lead followers here in mantras calling the name of another Goddess, Sarasvati, using mantras for a non-vegetarian Tantric Goddess with mantras intended for a vegetarian Goddess. This account exemplifies the Hindu belief that all Goddesses are but the One Devi, while it serves to note the shift in the embodiment of Kali over the centuries. During the 11th — 12th centuries Kali was the necessary ferocious aspect of Parvati who joins with Ambika to fight and defeat demons threatening the world. Ambika/Parvati/Kali conflated are one divine power into which other Goddesses such as Radhika (cowherd woman beloved of Krsna or Krishna), Sasthi (protectress of children), Sitala (Goddess of epidemics) and Manasa (snake Goddess) all merge by the 15th century. Through the 15th century, Kali's ferocious aspect was further tempered by the influence of the Puranas and Krsna Vaisnava traditions. Thus by the 18th century, Kali becomes described as a benign and youthful mother. At Kalighat, Kali is revered for her Mother aspects, though her image exudes the youth, charm and femininity of the Maid, her aspect more revered in the West.

Another important aspect of Kali worshipped here is her Feminine Savior aspect, not unlike the savior aspects of Egyptian Isis, Artemis of Ephesus, or Hekate. She forgives, rescues, preserves and bestows grace. It is to Kali one prays to be liberated, thus she has become a patroness for women and men the world over seeking refuge from the shackles of political, cultural or economic oppression.

Here her function is parallel to a Christian savior god and explains why Kali can be so easily embraced the world over, including such far away places as Trinidad where immigrants from India found themselves indentured servants of the British, as discussed in the South America/West Indies chapter.

Gupta further explains that in West Bengal, where some of the sacred centers or shakti pithas are located, religious devotion

▲ Ritual bathers in the Hooghly River in Calcutta. The Kalighat Temple is nearby.

has a regional essence, being more relaxed as evidenced by those who worship at Kalighat and how they practice their faith. Here one finds two types of Hinduism under one roof — the priests who consider the temple deity to belong to their family tradition, in this case the relatives and kin of the Haldar priestly lineage, and those who worship under the tradition of the Puranas and Tantras. In Kalighat there has also been a blending of the non-vegetarian Sakti/Tantric traditions with the vegetarian Vaisnava/Krsnaite traditions. This attitude of tolerance and ignoring sectarian boundaries speaks volumes about the inclusive power of Goddess to overcome obstacles and embrace all her children with love.

Mentioned in Bengali religious texts from the 16th century, Kalighat is located in southern Calcutta on the River Hooghly, once the old course of the sacred Ganga River. The rectangle-shaped temple consists of one large room, the inner sanctum surrounded by an elevated, circumambulatory, open balcony. Two doors open from the balcony, one in front of the image for a full view of Goddess as one walks around her and one at the side, opening onto a flight of steps leading down to the inner sanctum. Goddess sits on a rock-like pedestal in the center of the room.

Worship begins at 4 AM when Haldar priests enter and clean away offerings from the previous day and wash the feet of Kali. New flowers then refresh the Goddess and the temple is opened for public services which begin at 6 AM and lasts for about two hours. About 2 PM various cooked foods are offered to Kali. Later in the day an additional ceremony, or puja transpires and concludes with Kali being made ready for sleep at about 11 PM when she is freshly clothed and decorated with more flower garlands. This is when Vaisnava's mark made of sandalwood paste is restored to her forehead between her eyes, having been wiped off earlier in the day when Kali was served cooked fish and meat — thus reflecting the dual vegetarian/non-vegetarian practice occurring simultaneously under one roof. Devotees entering the temple call Kali "Mother," and per ritual traditions harkening back to days of old, goats are sacrificed to the Goddess daily by pilgrims hoping to have a petition granted. It is certainly not a sight for the faint of heart, but it's important to understand that animal sacrifice is not considered an absolute requirement of Goddess and many Kali temples in the West forego this type of practice. In fact, many of her devotees are vegetarians and animal rights advocates.

Getting to the Kalighat Temple

Located in greater Kolkata/Calcutta on Ashutosh Mukherjee Road, the temple is open daily, but most busy on Tuesday and Saturdays. The Kalighat is located just outside the southern part of Calcutta's Old City. It is possible to walk to the temple, yet taking a taxi, bus, or rickshaw may be a better transportation option in the congested streets of Calcutta.

Goddess Focus
The Thuggees of Kali

While Kali has become one of the most misunderstood and maligned of all the Goddesses, some of her devotees, called "Thuggees," were cast in the worst possible light. Kali's true nature will be revealed in more detail at her sacred sites, however, taken at face value, her dark skin, red tongue and necklace of skulls certainly might give the uninformed a moment of pause. Yet with clarity, one begins to understand her dark skin represents the limitless void, her wild hair is liberation, her red tongue can be viewed as activity and sound, and the skulls represent alphabets that correspond to creation itself. Her third eye is wisdom and the severed hands at her belt are for creating. She is the power of time that swallows up the universe yet is the sound that created it as well. She is the ultimate Creatrix and the Destroyer of Evil. By association, the Thuggees, worshippers of Kali, who rebelled against English oppression during the time of the British Raj, were cast as maniacs and "thugs" — from where the English language derives the term. Kali and her worshippers have been unfairly minimized, and demonized through sensational and inaccurate accounts. Scholar Cynthia Humes reports "by mid-century, the Thuggee Goddess and her minions had been re-imagined as direct threats to the British themselves and the tone was suffused with sexual and ethnic overtones." Researcher Hugh Urban reports the rituals of Kali were described as being a kind of "black mass" or inverted communion with a vampire-like Goddess. It is time we discard moralistic polarities, set the record straight, and allow the truth to be shed upon these misconceptions!

While Thuggees may have been rebel bandits, their reputation was greatly exaggerated by their British oppressors. The prejudiced British misunderstood the outlandish Thuggee culture, and European missionaries were certainly at odds with their peculiar religion. The racial stereotypes and fears projected by the British live on. Anyone who saw *Indiana Jones and The Temple of Doom* remembers how the Thuggees and Kali were portrayed as lunatic Indians worshipping a blood-thirsty demoness. Scholar Jeffrey Kripal reminds us how in this 1984 movie,

▲ The Kali Yantra.

Hollywood cast the Thuggees and Kali as possessed priests who would tear out the hearts of their innocent victims before lowering them into the steaming bowels of a molten pit as an offering to their demon Goddess. Kripal notes "this unfortunate 'split' between popular and scholarly understandings of goddess figures has resulted in gross distortions and even demoralizing representations ... which hardly advance the cause of cross-cultural understanding and could easily be avoided, or at least partially remedied, by a more active dialogue between the popular and scholarly levels of Western culture."

Kanyakumari Temple

At a seaside temple on the southern tip of India pilgrims flock in huge numbers to revere the Virgin Goddess Kumari. Her temple is considered especially holy because it is located at the natural convergence of the Indian Ocean, Arabian Sea, and the Bay of Bengal which all meet directly at the cape. In this very special place the Goddess is revered in her youthful or virgin form of Shakti, as well as Durga, a conquering aspect of Goddess. Kumari is located in the inner sanctum and described as being made of black stone. She wears a gold nose ring and is usually adorned with fresh and scented garlands. The temple has a beautifully painted panel of the Mahishasuramardini, (Durga killing the demon Mahisha) depicted on one wall. The shrine within the temple also exhibits what practitioners believe to be the very footprints of the Goddess as she came down from the heavens. A very auspicious time to visit is under the full moon of the April Chaitra Purnima festival when the natural phenomena of both sun and moon are simultaneously visible on the horizon.

At this site herstory revolves around a trick played upon the god Shiva by Baanaasuran, a demon. Shiva was supposed to arrive here at midnight to marry Kumari/Shakti, the Goddess who came to Earth as part of a plan to defeat Baanaasuran and save the world. Shiva departed before marrying Kumari, duped by the crowing of a cock that made him think the hour of the wedding had past. His withdrawal left Kumari distraught, and she chose to spend her remaining days as a virgin, though it is believed in this unmarried state she became a much more powerful Goddess. Legend further identifies the wasted food from the wedding feast as the colored sand now seen on the seashore. Needless to say, Kumari was not happy with Baanaasuran. When he later attempted to force her into marriage, she slew him. It should be noted this belief reflects a social norm in which women must be married and under the control of their husband in order to subdue their dangerous sexuality. Thus, in many Hindu legends the Goddess becomes a consort to a God who uses their relationship to subdue her power. That concept is juxtaposed with the idea that virgin Goddesses, without a consort, are wholly powerful and sufficient unto themselves.

Camphausen explains the Virgin Goddess Kumari is related to the loss of physical virginity. By that association the Kumari puja ritual, in which Kumari is venerated, sometimes may involve the defloration of selected virgins in patriarchal societies. Anita Diamant's novel, *The Red Tent*, which became a bestseller, cites defloration within women's societies as described in the Old Testament. Camphausen continues, "Chapter 15 of the Kaulavali Tantra states that rituals performed without carrying out the kumari puja or virgin worship are to be compared to a body without a soul ... and the ritual defloration of selected virgins, was held among other places, at Kanyakumari, a temple whose name translates as "Young Virgin." He continues that Kumari puja is said to be indispensable to Tantric ritual and these *kula* rites may have been accompanied by more sexual rites with the young girls being paid

▲ Kumari is the embodiment of the Virgin Goddess.

very well for the loss of their virginity. This all smacks of ritual prostitution and the reader may ask, why? Camphausen further elaborates. It seems to Tantrics, the defloration ritual, an important rite of passage, warrants more care and attention than a casual romp. The opening of the hymen then becomes a sacred act of reverence and is usually done to the young girl by a mother, priest, shaman, or midwife. The ritual has its roots in the "magical blood," similar to menstruation blood. Sometimes the defloration occurs as proof of chastity, other times it involves "diverting the feared energy of her blood." It is believed the potency of the energy surrounding a virgin's "first blood" might even be harnessed to serve the community.

Getting to Kanyakumari Temple

The temple is located beachside near the town Nagercoil at the southernmost tip of the Indian subcontinent. The region of Kanniyakumari is also known as Cape Comorin. National highways 7 and 47 converge here so the city is accessible by car or bus. The closest domestic airport is Tiruma-Nagalam and the major city of Madurai is 146 miles (235 km) to the north. It should be noted that the inner sanctum is sometimes inaccessible to non-Hindus.

Goddess Focus
Female Genital Worship

Archaeologists find evidence dating back to 35,000 BCE for reverence of the *yoni*, or female genitalia, a symbol of the Divine Female through her life-giving abilities. Yoni worship preceded worship of the phallus. The yoni image appears across the globe in the form of triangles and circles carved on stones or drawn in caves. Sheila-na-Gigs, the holed dolmen stones of Europe, revered rocks that naturally occur in the shape of a yoni or lingam (penis), such as the Grandmother and Grandfather stones of Hinta Hinyaii on the island of Koh Samui in Thailand,

▲ Female genital worship has been a common practice for thousands of years.

184

▲ Sculptures depicting sexual poses grace temple facades all across India.

are all various examples. One such yoni stone in a shakti pitha temple of Assam, India (see site this chapter) is used during the year in ritual since the seasonal reddish colored water flows through the stone symbolically representing the menstrual blood of Goddess. India and Nepal have erotic imagery and *yonilinga*, symbolic representations of the creative genitals of the Goddess and God, Shakti and Shiva. This stands in direct contrast to other customs and traditions where women are not looked upon with such reverence or respect.

Worldwide yoni worship combines various ritual acts of different religious and cultural groups. A common theme is to identify the yoni as the womb of Goddess, or universal womb, including the worship of the yoni as an organ of creation. All manner of yoni puja, or vagina ritual, is practiced including visualization, touch, meditation with sacred imagery objects resembling the yoni, or with actual women. The intent with live women is to create the "lotus nectar," or *yonitattva,* secreted by the yoni. The lotus nectar, and sometimes menstrual fluids are utilized in sacred rituals including the mix of fluids with wine before drinking, or using the mix to anoint sacred objects such as a talisman of protection or power. Cloth anointed with menstrual fluid or lotus nectar is greatly sought after. Yoni power or magic has been recognized across the world and held in high esteem for millennia. Rock paintings from Tassili in the Sahara of Africa dating to 7000 BCE show the Goddess transmitting power from her yoni to man and beast. Women in southern India believe they can subdue storms by exposing their genitals. Women hoping to become pregnant or cure female-related medical problems touch, anoint, or lick images with exposed female genitals. This volume has documented the transformative powers of female genitals from the Greek Baubo to Uzume of Japan. In ancient times the yoni has been a source of protection, healing, magic, and life-giving power. It is a symbol of the shakti, the Goddess herself, a sacred portal of life, from which cosmic change, communion with the Divine and enlightenment may come forth.

Some cross-cultural names for the yoni veiled behind flowery language include: Chalice or Mystic Rose (Western); Dark Gate, Jade Gate, Doorway of Life, or Red Pearl (Chinese); Secret Cavern (Taoist); Ghanta (Sanskrit); Hor (Hebrew); Lotus of Her Wisdom (Sanskrit/Tantric); Quiff (Celtic); Konnos (Greek); Guhe (Nepali); Qitbus (Gothic); Cwithe or Queynthe (Old English); Navel (Old Testament/Song of Songs); and Ka-t (Egyptian).

Varnasi

Both Sarasvati and Ganga are goddesses associated with the flowing, purifying, regenerative, life-giving waters of the rivers they personify, believed by millions to originate in heaven. Scholar David Kinsley describes them as "divinity in liquid form" providing tangible blessings, comfort, redemption and acceptance. They connect Earth with heaven, effectively creating a "watery axis mundi." Since the time of the Vedas until today, age-old Hindu rituals have been enacted on riverbanks with the faithful immersed in purification practices associated with water. The Vedas are the oldest sacred writings of Hinduism that include many references of ritual cleansing. In the mind of a devotee, these flowing rivers washed clean both physical and spiritual pollution, brought enlightenment to the mind, and, at the same time, cleansed the Earth and the body from disease. They were both associated with fertility of the land, with Ganga in human form depicted holding an overflowing plate or food pot. Her waters provided her children with water as a mother provides her child with nourishment from her breast. Kinsley states Ganga's image was also at the entrance of temples, as a threshold or transition deity, connecting people with god and the Earth with celestial realms. Obviously the entire length of the Ganga is sacred and there are doubtless hundreds, if not thousands, of sacred places along its banks where people gather to commune with Ganga Ma. One such place is near her source in the Himalayas. According to Vandana Shiva, a temple dedicated to Mother Ganga, the Gangotri, stands at an elevation of 10,500 feet (3,200 m) at the source of the Ganges where Ganga is worshipped as both river and Goddess. Mother Ganges flows approximately 1,600 miles (2,575 km) from its source in the Himalayas into the Bay of Bengal.

One of the best places to experience the power of the River Goddess is at the sacred city of Varnasi, or Benares, a shakti pitha site, which is also home to temples dedicated to the goddesses Durga and Chinnamasta. The temple of Durga has been described as having a multi-tiered golden spire, or sikhara, which can be seen from beyond the compound walls. From here Durga protects the city and her sacred water tank within the precinct of her temple where she is shown adorned in her red sari, riding a tiger, holding her instruments of protection — a mace, trident, and sword — while inside she is embodied within a silver mask fringed with red cloth. On the banks of Ganga Ma at Varnasi the concept of death and life are tangible, visual, and inextricably intertwined. Here Goddess is not only Ganga Ma, but in spring she is also the Goddess Annapurna, the goddess of food and sustenance who makes offerings to the god Shiva. (Readers might recall Annapurna is often depicted as a Rice Goddess). From her life-giving waters, the devoted purify themselves, make offerings to her, and return to her at the time of their death, once again bringing together the themes associated with Goddess: life, death, and rebirth. Everyday thousands of people converge upon the river at Varnasi. They believe drinking the water will purify them for a lifetime of sins and to bathe in the water means they will be ritually cleansed. Pilgrims often begin their pilgrimage with a bath in the Ganges at daybreak then proceed along specified routes, sometimes stopping at 108 shrines before the circuit is complete. To die near the water is fortuitous for it will surely free them from the cycle of birth, death, and rebirth called *samsara*.

Funeral pyres can be seen in designated places along the four miles (6 km) of riverside ghats, or banks of steps that lead down into the waters. To the Western sensibility, it is a surreal experience to see corpses wrapped in white or red cloth being cremated along the river. In a conversation with a special friend, she revealed to this author that she was standing at one such ghat, witnessing a funeral for the departed, when suddenly she looked down and a very skinny dog was staring up at her with a human spine bone in his mouth. Needless to say, the experience is not one she will soon forget.

Pilgrims come from across the globe to collect the sacred waters and bring it back to their communities. They do this because the devoted believe this water from heaven surely contains special powers. This author experienced the dedication of one such a pilgrim who sat within the confines of an economy class airline seat, denying himself food or drink, with the five gallon water jug beneath his feet for the 12-hour flight. Special attributes Mother Ganga certainly must possess, not only in inspiration and faith, but in her purifying capabilities as well. It has been said that despite the tons of sewage and rotting corpses that daily descend into the waters, the Hindus apparently are no worse off for ingesting the waters where it is said river dolphins dwell. At night the scene on Ganga Ma is particularly enchanting as she is illuminated with hundred of floating lamps.

Sarasvati too is associated with purification and renewal. Her attributes include being a bestower of bounty and fertility with a function of creating the world. She is further believed to represent transcendence of physical limitations, and as such her symbols are the swan and lotus. Though the Sarasvati River has all but disappeared today at Hakra in Rajputana, Sarasvati retained her significance beyond the time of the Vedas who considered her a wisdom Goddess called "Mother of the Vedas." She is certainly associated with the aforementioned Ganga-like attributes, and as ancient rivers personified as divine, it is interesting to think these may have been among the earliest examples of humankind's recognition of the contours in the world landscape as being the body of a life-giving deity. Sarasvati was also the matron of inspiration, speech, wisdom, the arts (particularly music), thought, intellect, science, and learning, with devotees praying for boons to

▲ The bathing ghats at Varnasi are full of activity from sunrise until the evening.

acquire these cultural aspirations. The original Sarasvati River, frequently mentioned in the Vedas, was most likely a stream once flowing through the very heart of Brahmanical/Aryan territory, a region acclaimed for its great wisdom — hence this reputation for learning fell upon the Goddess of the river. Sarasvati is declared as the one who is *manasakanya*, or born of thought, arising from the head of her consort/husband/father/brother Brahman in much the same manner as Athena was born from the head of Zeus, who was also, incidentally, a Goddess of Wisdom. By the time of the Yajur Veda (1400 BCE), Sarasvati was equated with Vac, Goddess of speech. Vac was literally the "Word" coming out of the mind of God. The sacred speech of Vac was believed imbibed with universal creative powers. In Rig Veda 10.125, Vac declares: "I am queen, gatherer of riches, knowing, the First among those worthy of being honored. I am she of many stations and much bestowing, whom the gods have distributed in many places. Through me, he who discerns, who breathes, who indeed hears what is said, eats his food. Though ignorant of this, they dwell in me. Hear that you are heard? What I tell you is to be believed. I myself, say this welcome news to gods and men. He whom I love, I make him powerful, I make him Brahmin, I make him seer, I make him wise ... I have entered into heaven and earth. I bring forth the father at the summit of creation. My Yoni is within the waters, in the ocean. Thence I extend over all worlds, and I touch heaven with my uppermost part. I also blow forth like the wind, reaching all the worlds. Beyond heaven, beyond earth, so great have I become through my grandeur." Vac is undeniably immanent, as well as transcendent in creation, moving within the primordial waters and sustaining the natural world. Vac's attributes soon become Sarasvati characteristics. Sarasvati is often seen depicted as a four armed woman holding rosary-like prayer beads, water pot, lute, and book.

Getting to Varnasi

Varnasi, also known as Benares, one of the oldest and most sacred cities in India, is located 178 miles (286 km) southeast from Lucknow. Flights arrive daily at the airport 14 miles (22 km) northwest of the city. Bus and train service arrive daily from neighboring towns and cities in northern India. River tours and boat rides are available along the Ganges.

GAIA ALERT

THE WATERS OF CORPORATE OBSESSION

Some might remember the movies starring Mel Gibson who plays Mad Max, a character who tries to survive in a post apocalyptic world where the most precious commodity was not money, gold, or other trappings of wealth, but water. Most probably thought that scenario was far from ever becoming reality. Well, think again. Vandana Shiva, physicist-turned environmental, human rights and anti-globalization activist brings attention to the politics of water. Shiva cites the dangerous trend toward corporate globalization and monocultural thinking that bring mono-crop agriculture, biotechnology and biopiracy that thwart or destroy sustainable agriculture and long proven effective indigenous farming and conservation techniques throughout the world. One recent trend is the control of water, a natural resource imbued with spiritual significance as in the Goddess Ganga, the personification of the Ganges River.

Some today are beginning to view water as a commodity to be plundered for corporate greed while others maintain water as a sacred gift to the world and owned by no one. Shiva believes communities, not global corporations, should control their resources and she promotes water democracy and sovereignty over community biodiversity. She warns of the connection between corporate globalization and the erosion of social and political democracy. In her book, *Water Wars: Privatization, Pollution and Profit,* she cites centralized economic systems that take away community involvement to create a culture of insecurity. Losing democratic control of natural resources, economy, and the means of production undermines cultural identity which can be replaced with adversarial identities born from scarcity. Centralized economic systems such as the World Bank, the International Monetary Fund and the World Trade Organization take away economic democracy. Politicians are left with issues of race, religion and ethnicity to manipulate, giving rise to fundamentalism and violence. Shiva contends we cannot have a sustainable future for all as long as we allow nations and corporations to declare war on the planet and do nothing about economic insecurity, cultural subordination and ecological dispossession. The feminine principle must be considered in environmental and social choices we make for the future.

▲ Free fresh water is quickly becoming a scarce resource in many parts of the world.

Amritapuri Ashram

The sacred site of the Amritapuri Ashram is headquarters and home of Sri Mata Amritanandamayi Devi, lovingly known as Mother, or Amma, to the millions who have been touched by her. Considered a true, tangible and living embodiment of Goddess, she is a Mother of unconditional, ever-embracing love on this Earth. The ashram, described as a model of a silent spiritual revolution, is located where Amma grew up in the backwaters of a small fishing village called Amritapuri. Amma relates the meaning of the ashram by saying, "Children, this ashram exists for the world; it belongs to you, to all the people who come here." This reflects the Indian ideal of *vasudhaiva kutumbakam* or "the whole world is one family." Followers of Amma arrive from all over the world to bask in the glow of her love where they live together under one roof as they search for peace, harmony, and the meaning of life.

Born here in 1953, Amma may not always be in residence as her work takes her on worldwide travels spreading her message of love, hope, and acceptance. Mother has become renowned the world over as thousands flock to hear her speak and receive her healing hug, or accept a personal mantra. Devotees stand in line for hours waiting for a mere moment at the feet of Devi and receive her darshan.

▲ Millions of Amma's faithful adherents feel she is a living saint.

Millions who have experienced such an audience and blessing come away feeling that something truly genuine and remarkable is moving through this living, breathing woman called a saint, Goddess, or Mother. Many have reported feeling overwhelming feelings of deep emotion or charges of electricity from her touch. Amma has been known to sit for as long as 20 hours and give as many as 18,000 hugs a day to those who come seeking her message of love!

At birth Amma was named Sudhamani, meaning Ambrosia Jewel, and she describes entering the world with knowingness, or "an old soul" as some say. She said she had "no feelings of strangeness upon entering the world." She explains everything was so utterly familiar to her. "When one knows everything about the world one can only smile. When one beholds the entire universe as a play of Consciousness, what else can one do but smile?" Amma was born to a fisherman father and mother who remember Amma smiling rather than crying as she was born. She walked and talked before a year old, and at three years old she loved to sing. By five, she composed hymns to Krishna. As she got older she spent her time meditating, singing, and indulging in ecstatic dance by the seashore, all of which annoyed her family who felt she should be using her time for work and more practical pursuits. At nine she had to leave school to care for her ill mother and seven siblings. During this difficult time she became acutely aware of the suffering of village neighbors and the world through her own struggle and pain. Her heart poured out to those in need, sometimes at the expense of her own family. Some cite this as the beginning of her ministry. She helped the elderly, the starving, or anyone in need of kindness and love. She says she endured that time of hardship by meditating, praying and singing to Lord Krishna (described by Barbara Walker as an erotic incarnation of Shiva, born of the Goddess Devaki) whose photo she carried in her pocket. She imagined her toil and hard labor to be performed solely for the Divine.

Amma's teachings are described as universal and her religion is "Love," not unlike the teachings of Jesus Christ. Contemporary theologian Joseph Campbell describes a similarity to Native American belief, who addressed all of life as "thou" rather than "it." This fundamental concept is reflected in Amma's belief that the Divine exists in every living thing — whether it be a person, plant, or animal. Further, Amma views this unity and oneness as the essence of spirituality, the way to end suffering with the power to transform the world. She asks no one to believe in God, nor give up their own faith, but only learn their true nature and believe in themselves. Amma is described as an untiring servant of the people and feels "in this world of luxury and comfort there are many who live in dire poverty." She proclaims, "Compassion to the poor is our duty to God."

The ashram which sits on the property of Amma's childhood home is the headquarters of her worldwide mission which annually helps millions around the world in direct and indirect ways. Direct aid builds homes for the poor, women's shelters, orphanages, hos-

▲ Taking the lagoon ferries to Amritapuri Ashram is a fun way to make a pilgrimage.

pices, hospitals, and community aid centers. She assists by disbursing pensions to over 50,000 widows. Educational facilities are sprouting up all over India as a result of her work. She strongly encourages Western devotees to serve selflessly in their own communities. This sacred site of her beginnings as well as her current work, the ashram, is also the spiritual home of Amma's monastic disciples and householder devotees who dedicate their lives toward realizing the Divine and being in service to the world.

In 2000, Amma represented a select delegation of "preeminent religious leaders" at the Millennium Summit for Religious and Spiritual Leaders at the invitation of United Nations Secretary General Kofi Annan. In 2002, she was presented with the Gandhi-King Award for Nonviolence at the United Nations General Assembly Hall in Geneva, Switzerland. This honored her lifelong work and her views of the perpetuation of nonviolence. Only the fourth person to receive this award, she is in good company with the three previous award winners being Kofi Annan, Nelson Mandela, and Jane Goodall.

Getting to the Amritapuri Ashram

Flights arrive from either the airport at Trivandrum (68 miles (110 km) south of Amritapuri), or Cochin (87 miles (140 km) north of Amritapuri). Travelers are recommended to go to the Airport Taxi Service counter, and ask for a prepaid taxi to Mata Amritanandamayi Ashram at Amritapuri in Vallickavu (pronounced Vallickow). From Trivandrum the ride to the ashram is about 3 hours, or from Cochin the ride is about 4 hours. The route is via a beach road from Karu-Nagappally. This road crosses the backwaters by a bridge bringing pilgrims to the ashram premises. If dropped off in Vallickavu, take a boat across the backwater. It is also possible to take a boat from many of the towns in the vicinity of the ashram.

GAIA ALERT

INEQUALITY OF WOMEN: CUSTOM & CULTURE

Tradition and culture have often put women at great risk. Though there are some exceptions where matrilineal rules apply, most of India is a patriarchal society where there is the dichotomy of women being both revered and abused

▲ Many women, young and old, are caught in cycles of cultural, social, and spiritual oppression.

in "dowry deaths" or "bride burning." Unfortunately these atrocious acts still occur in certain parts of the country. Even though the custom of demanding a dowry is against the law, it is still part of tradition. When a woman is married, her family is expected to pay the husband large sums of money, jewelry, animals, or assets. If the family cannot meet the demands of the dowry, often the woman is harassed to the point she will light herself on fire rather than suffer the physical and psychological abuses. Sometimes the in-laws murder the women and the death is made to look like a "kitchen accident." Young girls are frequently forced into marriage as young as 12 without their consent, then without proper education, they can find themselves later in life forced to sell sex for food, clothing, or other necessities of life. In the case of India's child widows, they can become isolated and shunned by society. Lower caste ritual prostitutes of southern India, called Devadasis or Jogathi of Ellamma are the untouchables of society, and sometimes no more than sex slaves.

Another problem confronting some women in India and Nepal is selective abortions. Like in China boys are preferred by husbands and their families. Sometimes Indian women are encouraged to abandon their female offspring. Customs vary but often when certain Indian and Nepali women marry, they are no longer considered a part of their own family, and often do not inherit family assets which are instead passed down to sons. In some Nepali cultures, a girl reaching menarche is confined to a shed for one to three weeks for the "sitting in the cave" ritual. While this is a time for the young woman to contemplate her new role as a reflection of Goddess or a giver of life, it is also designed to isolate her during this so called unclean or untouchable time and thus perpetuates unhealthy attitudes in men towards female sexuality. Fortunately most Buddhist, Hindu and mountain tribe women of Nepal enjoy more freedom. It is obvious the subjugation of women and their contribution to society, their families, and relationship to men needs a serious reevaluation.

Naga Temple of Mannarsala

Nagas, holders of mystic knowledge and protectors of the source of life, are a more unusual form of Goddess in the guise of the serpent. These divine stewards of precious minerals buried deep within the bosom of the Earth are especially revered at Mannarsala, the best known of the four Naga Temples of India. While accounts differ, the mythical Nagas are commonly believed to protect families. According to scholar Miriam Levering they are sometimes considered

Bodhisattvas, with power over mundane forces and gifted with great insight and trance ability called *samadhi*. Nagas, or sarpas, are from a time before Buddhism and have been described as handsome serpent-like beings with human faces or heads crowned with up to seven fully expanded cobra hoods. Those resembling beautiful women are adorned with heavy jewelry (but with a snake's lower body) are sometimes called Yahski and they are believed to embody the power of the shakti as well as being bringers of food and water. The role of the celibate priestess oracle, or *amma* (not to be confused with Amma of Amritapuri) residing here is much like a female shaman, in service to the Naga, and assisting the followers of the temple, many of whom are Buddhists who consider the Naga their principal deity. The current priestess at Mannarsala has been in service for decades and is known far and wide for her charity and healing powers. Obviously within this setting the serpent is transformed into a powerful icon of divinity rather than conforming to the demonized, maligned creature, often associated with the devil in other cultures and faiths. Much as the snake was a symbol of power, protection and regeneration, recognized as a symbol of divine kingship in ancient Egypt, here too the snake is revered by various people of the region for its many potent abilities to aid them.

▲ Serpent goddess Nukua with consort Fuxi are powerful Nagas.

Barbara Walker cites that here in Kerala, where matrilineal communities still exist, the Naga is associated with the Vedic Goddess Kadru and relates the Nagas of southern India with "tribes who retained matriarchal customs, practiced matrilineal inheritance and laid no sexual or marital restrictions on women." In return for proper reverence, the snake Goddess bestowed long life upon the devoted. This seems to be supported by Levering who says Naga princesses were female ancestors of some South Indian dynasties. Called marumakkathayam, Kerala has a matrilineal family system where inheritance is passed through the family line of the mother. The Nairs of Kerala are known for this practice which some believe began in the 10th century although anthropologists believe it has more ancient roots to the early Goddess cultures of India. In this system, after men and women marry, she stays in the family home, and he lives with his family and visits his wife. Men have responsibility for the children in their maternal home where they are a father figure. This enables women and children to be guaranteed a home and support regardless of their economic or marital situation.

Paraphrasing Levering quoting Diana Paul she explains the Nagas were believed to inhabit aquatic paradises of rivers, lakes, oceans and all manner of splendid water palaces and inaccessible mountain caverns. They guarded the treasures of the sea and the source of life which was symbolized by the waters in which they resided and by their self-rejuvenation, illustrated by the shedding and replacement of skin. Their attribute of "holders of mystic knowledge" coincides with one account within Mahayana tradition where Nagas are entrusted with the Prajnaparamita, a teaching of Buddha, and with the greatest Mahayana philosopher's name, Nagarjuna, a derivative of the name Naga. Stories about mermaid or water-sprite-like Naga maidens coupled with human heroes are common in folklore and Buddhist literature. Sarasvati/Benzaiten with Uga Jin, and the Chinese Nu Kua with Fu Xi come to mind. Buffie Johnson states "the serpent was a factor in the religions of India and Indonesia and within the Buddhist faith the Aitareya, a Brahman chant, quotes hymns to the Queen of Serpents who presides over all that moves. Attributes of serpents have long been symbolic of female deities until usurped by patriarchal traditions." That is perhaps why popular culture has the Nagas often represented by male gods, who in the form of Yaksha, became the God of Wealth. The serpent is also associated with the kundalini energy that resides in the spinal column like a coiled snake until aroused when it then ascends toward the brain. It this point it is believed to bring wisdom, enlightenment and paranormal powers.

According to Hindu mythology, the Nagas are descendants of Kashyapa, known as the "tortoise" and often associated with the sun, and Kadru, one of the daughters of Daksha who bears her husband a thousand children in the form of these serpent-like beautiful creatures. One of the most prominent of all the serpents born from Kashyapa and Kadru was Manasa, Goddess of fertility and marriage rites. While her special veneration probably originated as a folk cult amongst the jungle tribes, by the 14th century she began to be assimilated into Shiva's entourage. Soon, Manasa was viewed as the Goddess responsible for removing poison from Shiva's throat following the great Churning of the Ocean (Samudramanthana), one of India's most popular creation myths. In this regard, Manasa becomes the "remover of poisons" and a shape-shifter, able to perform any number of miracles when called upon. Her popularity grew quickly in southern India and even began to rival the cult centered around Shiva. In reaction, another contesting tale arose with Manasa beginning her existence as a result of Shiva's semen falling upon a lotus flower which, in turn, descended down to the netherworld of Patala, the realm of snakes, where she was turned into a beautiful woman by the mother of Vasuki, king of the Nagas. Thus the Brahmanical form of Shivaism was able to successfully co-opt this indigenous deity. Scholar, Anna Dallapiccola states that "it has been suggested that the name Naga may refer to a non-Aryan tribe opposed to the Aryan culture."

Here at Mannarsala, the temple is located in a thick grove of trees among thousands of serpent shrines of varying styles and sizes. Ancestral homes of the Nair and Namboothiri people often have protective snake groves where a serpent stone honoring the snake is maintained as sacred. Real snakes are kept here, often cobras, and they typically receive milk offerings. In lieu of their own special snake grove, usually located at the corner of their garden, those devoted to the Nagas are expected to provide a serpent stone to the temple as an offering to the Naga. Sometimes individual sacred trees are homes of a particular Naga family and can be recognized by the manner of decorations and the kind of offerings laid at the base of the tree. Temples of the area also have niches set aside for the Naga Snake Goddess. During September and October, the Malayalam months of Kanni and Thulam, the festival of Ayilliam occurs where the serpents of the grove are processed to the *illam* or temple and offerings of *nurum palum* (rice flower and milk) and *kuruthi* (a red liquid made of turmeric and lime) are made to the deity.

Getting to the Naga Temple of Mannarsala

Located in the city Harippad in the Alappuzha district of Kerala in south India, the Naga Temple is 82 miles (132 km) northwest of Thiruvananthapuram, Kerala's capital city where the nearest airport is located. The Naga Temple is accessible via boat tours of the Kuttanadu Backwaters. Bus transportation is also available to the temple which is located between the larger cities of Kollam and Alappuzha.

Goddess Focus
Female Genital Mutilation

Practitioners of Tantra and Shakta are among the few religious systems in which women's blood and genitals are not viewed as unclean, dangerous, or something to be hidden. These practitioners are in the minority. Consider the patriarchal countries with traditions still engaging in the more barbaric and insidious circumcision, excision, or clitoridectomy practices in modern times: Egypt, Niger, Ethiopia, Kenya, Ghana, Ivory Coast, Yemen, Zaire, Tanzania, Sierra Leone, Sri Lanka, Malaysia, Oman, United Arab Emirates, and pockets of Central and South America. The practice operates in Arabia, certain castes of India, the Australian Arunta tribe, some tribes in the Amazon, along with Skoptsi sects of Romania and Russia. East Africa traces its roots to early Copts and the pre-Talmudic Jews of Ethiopia. Some tribes in Africa still practice infibulations, an even more drastic procedure. Amnesty International cites an estimated 135 million of the world's young women have undergone genital mutilation, and two million girls a year are at risk of mutilation — approximately 6,000 per day! Industrialized countries with large immigrant populations are also seeing a rise in FGM, or Female Genital Mutilation.

Individuals and organizations such as Amnesty International, the World Health Organization, and the United National Children's Fund are working toward obliterating these deeply entrenched circumcision customs only found within highly patriarchal cultures, where cultural norms render these young women emotionally dysfunctional, physically scarred, and inhibited from enjoying the pleasures of their natural sexual state. Brilliant and resolute women from within these very cultures are determined to stem the tide of the ritual mutilation of young girls, to champion the cause of their silent sisters, and to weed out the very roots of this injustice in the form of demonizing cultural stereotypes and archaic misogynist laws. With the long ago demise of Goddess Spirituality, many believe women's sexuality became an object of fear, causing the widespread subjugation of female rights across the globe. Hopefully with continued education, compassion and fearlessness, these perversions may soon become actively outlawed in these male dominated societies. Some countries are working toward offering asylum to females in fear of FGM and others are working toward making the tradition a criminal offense. Women should no longer remain victims of their culture or the possession of their husbands because of their sexuality.

▲ Only education can wipe out ignorance.

Mahalakshmi Temple

The Shri Mahalakshmi Temple is a shakti pitha where Goddess is represented in an ancient form of a monolith encrusted with semi-precious stones. Built in the 7th century, this naturally occurring 3-foot (.90-m) tall black monolith or *swayambhu* is venerated as Lakshmi, the lotus Goddess, a symbol of spiritual enlightenment. It was upon these lotus petals that she floated at the time of creation. Believed by some to be a pre-Vedic Goddess, Lakshmi does not have many temples in India, but her image is everywhere, associated with wealth, prosperity, good fortune, and rice. Banks and businesses are named for Lakshmi, and even cows, sacred in India, since by her own name these gentle creatures are a source of life which provides sustenance with their five gifts of milk, yogurt, ghee, dung, and urine. Cow urine is used for medicinal purposes and the dung for fertilizer or fuel. Her altars in temple and field receive sumptuous offerings of oil, milk, and flowers. Practitioners who honor Ma Lakshmi with songs, chants, and meditation believe she is generous in her boons.

Lakshmi's association with rice is not known from any sacred text, but rather by observing daily routines of the people of India. Images of Lakshmi as a beautiful woman with black wavy hair and golden skin holding rice in her hand, and an owl (a sign of money) at her feet are found in average homes on calendars and rice pot lids called *sara* paintings. Lakshmi is worshipped weekly, quarterly and annually, at the autumn full moon rite of Kojagari where these sara paintings are a major component of ritual, or *lakshmipuja*, usually initiated by the woman of the house. In both Bengal and Orissa, Lakshmi is the Rice Goddess who provides sustenance and prosperity through good harvests. She is closely associated with Dewi Sri of Indonesia, both goddesses having Vishnu as their consort. (The Indian Rice Goddess is also worshipped as the Goddess Ponniyamman in Tamil Nadu and as Annapurna, a manifestation of Parvati, in Varnasi and Nellore, which when translated means "town of rice.") In rural fields, makeshift altars are erected to the Rice Goddess, often with a flat altar stone and trident. This three-pronged implement of Goddess is often seen at shakti pithas.

▲ Lakshmi is the Lotus Goddess of Prosperity.

Like the Egyptian Goddess Isis who fed the pharaoh a soma-like nectar called "sa" bestowing divinity and the right to rule, Lakshmi is also the bestower of sovereignty as in the myth of Indra becoming king of the gods ordained through her feminine power. In the case of Lakshmi and Indra, he received the soma or "wise blood" from Lakshmi's body, giving him wisdom and enabling him to appear to give birth and be fruitful. According to scholar Roy Hamilton ancient texts cite Indra as a rice god and from his body the grain emerged. This seems to ignore that his gift originated from the Mother and her potent blood. Lakshmi's nature supersedes the taboos of hierarchical caste systems. Because of Lakshmi, all Hindus, regardless of caste, may share *prasad* or eat from the same blessed rice pot at the Jagannath Temple in Puri, Orissa.

Author Linda Johnson explains that while most pray to Lakshmi for wealth and money, yoginis petition Lakshmi for divine knowledge because Ma Lakshmi is seen as a vast intelligence dwelling in the *Devi Loka*, or Goddess World. She can remove barriers to deeper realities and realms of consciousness that allow devotees to know the Divine. Lakshmi was once called Sri and was considered an aspect of the Devi Shakti or the sexual principle. Her passion for Krishna, an avatar of Vishnu, her husband, inspired erotic poetry. Sometimes she is said to have arisen from a sea of milk churned up by the gods, and she has been called the source of life. Vedic gods who desired her many gifts are said to have taken from her kingly influence, imperial authority, martial energy, priestly glory, dominion, force, splendor, and nourishment. Another of her aspects is Sita, the faithful wife of Vishnu, together forming a couple of perfect compliment.

The Diwali Festival celebrating the Hindu New Year is another time of her veneration during which devotees light lamps of oil or ghee in hopes of attracting Lakshmi, who is synonymous with prosperity. Clearly, practitioners devoted to Lakshmi, Goddess of the Lotus and the Corn, believe through her boons they may receive both gifts from the Earth as well as the joy of her divine grace thereby receiving sustenance for both their spiritual and physical needs. The temple here at Kolhapur is designed so that the rays of the sun fall upon Mother Lakshmi's face within her inner sanctum for three days during the months of Pisces and Leo. Worship here begins at 5 AM when the deity is awakened with singing. About three hours later a puja is performed wherein Lakshmi is offered 16 different foods, followed by three more services during the afternoon and evening hours.

Getting to the Mahalakshmi Temple

The Mahalakshmi Temple, also called the Amba Bai Temple, is located in Kolhapur on the banks of the Panchganga River. This important pilgrimage site can be found 140 miles (225 km) south of Pune, the city with the nearest domestic airport. The temple is easily accessible by car, train, or bus via National Highway 4 between the cities of Pune and Bangalore. While there, do not miss the Old Palace, located behind the temple, where the maharaja's family lives.

GAIA ALERT

SAVING THE LION OF INDIA

Mattias Klum thoughtfully stated in *National Geographic* that in ancient India one of the greatest tests of leadership was to fight a lion, while in modern India, it may be to save one. Klum was reflecting on the plight of the diminishing species in India where only about 300 Asiatic lions remain. These noble beasts had been hunted and poached to near extinction during the early 1900s. Today the few

▲ Asiatic lions are on the brink of extinction.

remaining lions live in the Gir Forest of Gujarat, India, just one of the 400 wildlife sanctuaries throughout the country. India is currently trying to create a second lion sanctuary to reduce the chance of diseases, natural disasters, and problems related to a limited gene pool that might kill off these magnificent felines in one potential disaster. Some are being moved 500 miles (806 km) away to the Kuno Wildlife Sanctuary in central India, but with land in short supply, finding a habitat for a pride of lions is difficult.

The Asiatic lions, smaller than their African cousins, have shorter manes and a long fold of skin on their underbelly which helps discern them from their African relatives. Breeding is difficult because statistics show lions may couple as many as 500 times before producing a viable pregnancy, and within the limited gene pool of Asiatic lions, about 75% of sperm are deformed resulting in spontaneous abortion or virtual infertility. Fortunately European zoos and American facilities are attempting to rescue the species and increase the population with strict breeding programs.

Since as early as 7100 BCE lions have been associated with Goddess, divinity, strength, and solar energy. The powerful healer and warrior Goddess of Egypt is Sekhmet, usually depicted with the body of a woman and the head of a lioness. Lions are at the side of the Mistress of the Animals in artifact and relief as her guardian and mount. They have been thought to protect the dead, and images from Italy (500 BCE) show a lioness assisting Medusa while giving birth. They are associated with Inanna as her symbol of life and death while Lillith stands upon a lion. Lionesses are the hunters of their prides providing nourishment for their families, not unlike the Goddess herself.

Chausath Yogini Temple

To many faithful the Chausath Temple represents the embodiment of an all-powerful Divine Female figure, as yogini statues employ the creative force of Shakti to work her will. Her yellow-beige sandstone circular structure, 25 feet (8 m) in diameter, resides atop a hill and is open to the sky in keeping with the traditional style of yogini temples. It houses 64 manifestations of the Goddess Shakti within the inner niches of this womb-like abode. Ranging in size from very small to two feet in height, the images of Devi, the catalyst of creation, are carved of black chlorite stone. Each is within their own niche, standing upon their celestial mount, or *vahanas*, depicted as inanimate objects or animals such as a camel, crow, crab, corpse, elephant, flower, human head, snake, tortoise, or wheel. Scholar Elinor Gadon believes the vahanas helped votaries identify the yoginis. The central yogini of the temple is described as having ten arms and resides in the 31st niche. Four male images of various forms of Bhairava, a fierce aspect of Shiva, are in the middle of the enclosure. On the outer walls of the temple are nine niches, each containing a female figure. The temple entrance has skeletal males on either side wearing garlands of skulls and snake anklets. One holds a severed human head. Also depicted are jackals and hounds of the cremation grounds. Gadon describes the enshrined yoginis as being carved in classical medieval Orissan style with full breasts, narrow waists, ample hips and the epitome of grace and sensual beauty.

Places such as Chausath were temples of the Yogini Cult, an esoteric tradition in Hinduism and Buddhism within medieval India between the 8th and 12th centuries. Interestingly, according to Gadon, this was also the time of the Bhauma-Kara, a dynasty of six queens that ruled along the Orissan coast and whose lineage passed from mother-queen to daughter-queen. According to legend, eight yoginis (later expanded to 64) emanated from the protectress Goddess Durga to become her special helpers. Anna Dallapiccola relates that the Yoginis "represent the forces of fertility, vegetation, illness, death, magic and yoga" — all forces or states in which Shakti holds sway.

One of the simplest anecdotes that perfectly conveys the definition of Shakti comes from Joseph Campbell. The eminent mythologist compared the interaction between male and female desert Bushmen during the living tradition of a ritual they performed together. He said the women sat in the center, around which the men danced. The women controlled the dance by keeping the rhythm with singing and the beating of their thighs. Effectively and symbolically, the woman represented life, and the man is viewed as the servant of life. Similarly, Shakti is the life-giving cosmic power in the universe. Without her and her creative force human and god are rendered powerless and passive unless activated by Her. Shakti has been defined as Great Wisdom or Mahavidya. One Tantra states, "women are divinity; women are vital breath." The Lalita Sahasranamam, a tantric text in praise of the Goddess Kali-Shakti described her by saying, "The series of universes appear and disappear with the opening and shutting of Her eyes." These concepts closely represent the power of the Goddess as Creatrix, a powerful yogini, worshipped and invoked at temples such as Chausath, built around the 9th century. Chausath was a sacred ritual ground not just for Goddess as yogini in her 64 manifestations of Shakti, but for her mortal esoteric practitioners, the shaman-like female Yoginis, or Kapalikas, who invoked her and knew how to harness her energy.

The 64 yoginis first appear in the *Agni Purana*, an orthodox Hindu text, within Chapter 52 entitled "Attributes of the Goddess." Gadon quoting Vidya Dehejia cites the origin of the yoginis probably can be found in the worship of local village goddesses, or *grama-devis*, who are thought to preside over the welfare

▲ The round Chausath Yogini Temple housed 64 manifestations of Shakti.

of the villages including the occult practices of agricultural and tribal peoples. Vicki Noble quotes Dehejia who credits these shaman-like women with "extraordinary powers which are often of a magical and yogic nature." Some of their powers included "complete control over breathing and other bodily functions, levitation ... and control over living creatures." They were believed to demonstrate the "eight magical *siddhis*" or shape-shifting abilities in round outdoor temples dedicated to "The Mothers" as early as the 3rd century BCE. Noble describes these women as versed in weather working with control over natural elements. She quotes Miranda Shaw who reports the Indian yoginis "could become invisible, had mastered the ritual gazes, and had the power of fleet footedness, the ability to traverse vast distances in a matter of minutes." Gadon cites their secret practices were thought to include blood sacrifice and yogic ritual sexual union to gain control over ones' mind and body. They were also believed to have the ability to raise the dead. Their tantric rites (more accurately defined as affirming female energy and spiritual capacities) were related to Goddess and her power to stimulate nature and channel the energy of the universe.

Yogini were skilled in the preparation of soma, their secret and sacred mind-altering plant. The Rig Veda, sacred Hindu literature, tells how the soma plant was gathered by moonlight and taken to the ritual place to be prepared. Paraphrasing Noble quoting David Spess, he describes the secret soma and the essence of the Vedas as the "honey doctrine" which is reflected as the Indian yoginis' favorite drink, a honey-brewed beverage made with ginger, lemon, and black peppercorns that was fermented for 12 days. Noble theorizes "these oracular shaman priestesses are embedded in the ritual preparation of the soma (or haoma) before it was taken over by male priests. Their ingestion facilitated a communal religious experience wherein people were liberated through direct (primordial) experiences of the divine."

Without doubt, the sources suggest that these yogini had become skilled in working with energies comprising the very dance of life from birth to death. So what happened? Noble believes that with the shift from female-centered sacred sexuality to a male-dominated rational one, the yoginis lost ground and were eventually replaced by priests. "The direct, Earth-based, body-based intuitive practices developed and facilitated by the magical shaman women over thousands of years of communal ecstatic rituals gradually gave way to more formalized, abstract and internalized visualizations and energetic transactions of the men." Thus the deep connection and skill of these yogini priestesses became less potent, less practiced and often lost over time. As for the term "yogini" itself, it became applied to any woman believed to possess supernatural powers and was later directly associated with the words "sorceress and demoness." Now the term is usually used to describe the wonderful Goddess statuary of India. Chausath Temple was rediscovered in 1953 when the Archaeological Survey of India was completed. Shrines such as Chausath were in use until the early 16th century.

Getting to the Chausath Yogini Temple

The temple is located at the far side of the quaint village of Hirapur, which is 9 miles (15 km) southeast of Bhubaneswar, a major city of Orissa state with the service of a domestic airport. Bhubaneswar is also about a one-hour drive or train ride from Calcutta. When in Hirapur it is advisable to hire a taxi to reach the Chausath Yogini Temple.

Goddess Focus
Oracles and Shaman

Author Naomi Ozaniec quotes noted scholar Joseph Campbell on the significance of the shaman: "when properly fostered, (the shaman) yields an adult not only of superior intelligence and refinement, but also of greater physical stamina and vitality of spirit that is normal to members of the group." Shaman are the cousin to psychics in popular culture who often have received their "power of sight" from some traumatic experience or ecstatic state that leaves them connected to another realm of power or consciousness. Often the credibility of authentic psychics is proven as they offer aid in police investigations when normal leads have gone cold. Shaman, sometimes called oracles or deity dancers, are prevalent today in Kali worship. These can be men or women of high or low caste who have had a profound physical or psychological experience that leaves them transformed, reborn, and awakened to the world beyond our five senses. These shaman then serve the community with their "gift" by helping others with healing, prophecy, and advice.

Scholar Patricia Lawrence tells of propitiatory Hindu rituals where the shaman goes into a trance, has dissolution of self, and begins to identify with the female energy of the cosmos. She describes these chosen people as having touched death in some way through the loss of a loved one, or perhaps themselves having survived a near-death experience. Sometimes their ability is hereditary. Oracles are also known to advise oppressed people experiencing the fear and hardship of military occupations, or on the fate of their loved ones who have disappeared or have been arrested. Using body and voice, the oracles becomes one with the "disappeared," an instrument of their voice, experiencing and enacting the physical sensations of the victim in order to give speech to those

▲ The oracle served as a vessel for divination and divine interaction for many cultures over many centuries.

who have been silenced, tortured, murdered, or spiritually disconnected, so that families have someway to know what has occurred to their loved one. Lawrence concludes that oracles serve Indian communities as agents of Kali, allowing families to express their suffering, overcome political silencing, embody memory and reconstitute a diminished world. To sum up Kali's power in the words of a author Lori Nyx, the Goddess of time and darkness is born out of righteous anger in response to ignorance, arrogance, and overweening ego. One calls on Kali when all else fails. She's the "mother of all bad-asses" who can defeat insurmountable odds to fight evil and set the universe toward righteousness.

NEPAL

Kathmandu Valley, also known as the "Nepal Mandala," has long been considered a far-away place steeped in mystery and mysticism. It is little wonder the very name embodies both exoteric and esoteric meaning to millions of people. The exoteric term mandala was an administrative term in the ancient Indian language that designated an area or country, such as Nepal, while the esoteric term mandala refers to a mystic circle to focus the consciousness on cosmic or individual energies. In the case of the sacred or esoteric geography of Kathmandu Valley, the mandala is composed of three concentric circles which encompass the valley representing body, speech, and mind, the three components of Tantric Buddhism. Situated adjacent to the soaring Himalayan mountains, long considered home of the deities such as Shiva and Parvati, Nepali practitioners of old and today worship at many altars, from those closely associated with animism and shamanism, to orthodox and tantric Buddhist and Hindu shrines. The three cities that dominate the valley are Kathmandu city, Patan, and Bhaktapur. Each city is replete with holy places where pilgrims and locals, comprised of many castes, ethnic groups, and tribal associations thought to once be matriarchal, venerate many aspects of Goddess.

▲ Parvati and Shiva are highly revered in Nepal.

In Nepal people revere the Nagas, serpent-like beings protecting the Earth and ruling the domain of rivers and rain. Folk religion of the shaman produce the region's healers. Hinduism and Buddhism combine to embrace aspects of Goddess resulting in Devi being recognized in a multitude of aspects such as Durga, virginal Kumari, maternal Lakshmi, and Mahakali as the crone. Scholar Keith Dowman describes Goddess as the primordial collective anima of the valley where the Tantra shakta cults conceived the Divine Feminine as a non-dual matrix of the universe. Shiva in his form of Pashupati, Lord of Animals, dwells in the valley in his lingam form sharing veneration with his consorts the Goddesses Durga and Parvati. Avalokiteshvara, a Buddhist deity known here as Krunamaya, Bodhisattva of Compassion (also know as Kwan Yin in female form), is also very popular with the Nepalese. Regional Goddess Taleju, a lineage deity of Malla kings is a royal Tantric Goddess associated with Durga, Bhagavati, and Maheshasuramardini. Another beloved Goddess that figures into the religious tapestry of Nepal is Tara, a Tibetan Buddhist Goddess, worshipped by the Nepali people in many of her colorful incarnations. Tara is regarded as a Savior Goddess who grants longevity, and assists the devoted in their quest to cheat death as she saves them from suffering and imminent danger.

Kumari Temple

The young Kumari, also called "The Living Goddess," is a supreme Tantric divinity worshipped by the Hindus as Durga and by the Buddhists as Vajradevi. A Virgin Goddess whose powers are considered potent and unlimited also performs the duty of validating the kingship of Nepal. She is Goddess of the Kathmandu Valley and considered an emanation of both Vajravarahi (the esoteric or secret Yogini aspect of Tantric Newar Buddhist practice) and Vasundhara (the exoteric or public face of secret deities of Tantric Newar Buddhism). This exoteric/esoteric dualism is fundamental as the inner agam shrines of Vajravarahi are not available to the uninitiated Tantric practitioner. The lay person instead bonds with the abundance-giving Vasundhara aspect of her divinity.

Kumari as Vasundhara, the "Bearer of Treasure," is associated with wealth, abundance, and prosperity. She is cousin to Lakshmi in attributes, thus Kumari is regarded as one of the most popular deities of Nepal. In art she is depicted with six arms, one face, and yellowish skin. Her first right hand makes a bountiful mudra hand gesture, the second holds jewels, the third makes a mudra gesture paying homage to Buddha while dangling mantra beads. The first left hand holds a jar, the second a stalk of grain, the third carries a book entitled *Perfection of Wisdom*. She sits in a posture of ease. Her head is adorned with a crown and various ornaments. Her attributes associate Vasundhara with bliss, fecundity, and wisdom. She is considered the mother of all Buddha's. Esoteric interpretations of Vasundhara have her depicted with three faces representing the three aspects of Tantric Buddhist yoginis. Her left face is radiant orange-red in color and symbolizes creation and generation. Her central face is yellow and represents her role as sustainer. Her right face is vermilion and is associated with the yogini Vajravarahi. At certain *pujas,* or esoteric rituals, Vajravarahi is represented in the guise of red powder placed in an auspicious jar. Vasundhara can be present in the form of a pot of yogurt. Annual rituals celebrate Kumari as the living manifestation of the Goddess Vajravarahi invoked at her investiture. Kumari also wears yellow ritual garments that indicates her identity as Vasundhara at important pujas.

Just as when a priestess of the Egyptian Goddess Isis wears a menat collar signifying her embodiment of the Divine Goddess, this is also true with Kumari when wearing the *tayo* necklace. It is understood when this jewel is upon her person, she is the Goddess manifested in the human realm. She is bliss-body of Vajravarahi; the fully-enlightened Buddha; the powerful esoteric and mature yogini. The tayo is designed with many symbols of the Goddess including a peacock, Kumari's vehicle or *vehana*, and the Nagas representing divine kingship. Kumari wearing her bride symbols then transforms into an archetype of Vajravarahi as the newlywed. In this aspect only married Newar practitioners, male and female, may seek her empowerment or apotheosis.

When the Buddhist Kumari is worshipped in Kathmandu as the emanation of the Hindu Goddess Durga, she may also be accompanied by the male deities Ganesha and Kumara. She is associated with the Goddess Kali and the regional Goddess Taleju of the Malla kings who were accepted as incarnations of Vishnu. While there are informal Kumari-types around the countryside of Nepal, only the Royal or State Kumari is

▲ The Kumari Temple near Durbar Square is one of Kathmandu's biggest attractions.

▲ Stupas, temples, and shrines greet the visitor around every corner in the Kathmandu Valley.

recognized as the authentic Kumari. She is housed elaborately in the Kumari Bahal on Durbar Square of Kathmandu. She will live out her life here until she reaches menarche or sheds her first blood. This child Goddess is usually invested at the tender age of two to four years old.

Candidates are chosen from girls of the Shakya caste who meet specific criteria and pass certain tests. Her horoscope must not conflict with that of the king. The young girl chosen to be Kumari must leave her family home and reside in the Kumari Bahal where attendants see to her every need. Here she holds public audiences and those who attend the Kumari Puja are said to receive good fortune. She must be present at auspicious rituals and official functions. Every few days she makes an appearance to the people from a window of her house on Durbar Square. Once Kumari reaches puberty, it is believed the Goddess no longer inhabits her body and a new Kumari must be chosen. This leaves the former girl attempting to lead a normal life after having been cared for as a divine manifestation whose feet never once touched the ground! The government provides former Kumari goddesses a small salary, but taboos discourage men from taking a previous Kumari as their bride because superstition has it these men will die young.

Getting to the Kumari Temple

The Kumari Temple is located in Kathmandu's Durbar Square's outer principal courtyard, just west of the Basantapur Tower in the red-bricked Basantapur Square. The Kumari's home is next to the Vishnu Temple on the western edge of Basantapur Square, which is adjacent to Freak Street to the east. Here one finds a multitude of vendors and low-cost accommodations. Check Durbar Square for the Durga, Parvati, and Taleju temples. Be aware the sister cities Patan and Bhaktapur also have Durbar Squares. While in Nepal, try to stop at the Vajra Yogini Temple on the outskirts of Sankhu where the "supreme Dakini of all Buddhas" is revered as the Blue Tara.

Goddess Focus
Living Life Behind the Veil

Purdah, a Persian word for curtain, is where women are secluded and must be completely veiled in public, forcing women to live their lives behind a veil. While some areas are more progressive, the custom of purdah still survives in northern and central India where it is practiced by Hindus and Muslims to different degrees within different families and faiths. Anthropologist Doranne Wilson Jacobson, Ph.D., lived in an Indian village for three years, witnessing the effect of purdah on the lives of rural women. She saw young brides coming to the home of their new husbands, living almost a shadow existence, and having to defer to mother-in-laws who could live more openly. The status of young brides did not improve until they matured or until the senior woman of the family died. Jacobson observed Hindu women forced to veil themselves before certain men, all older people and in-laws, and before their husbands when they are in the presence of other people, however veiling is not always required in the home of their parents. Women are careful not to hand anything directly to men. Men must be careful not to enter the areas where unveiled women may reside. While men have more freedom and privilege, they too have few rights in selecting their mates, deferring to decisions made by their parents who often select their wives from neighboring villages and comparable castes.

While purdah requires a full-length sari to be worn, including ankle ornaments and a veil that can be pulled over the face, the more extreme *burka*, worn over clothes so that not an inch of skin is visible, is worn by conservative Muslim women in India and other Muslim countries. The burka is sometimes shortened and gloves and stockings are no longer a requirement in most Muslim societies, but it is usually still the traditional garb of both single and married women. Though more rigidly attired, in some cases Muslim women in India have more inheritance rights than their female Hindu counterparts and can unveil themselves in the presence of their husbands and his close relatives. According to Jacobson, veiled Muslim queens called *begams* were known to wield religious and political power in regions of India such as Bhopal state until 1926. While terribly restrictive by Western standards, Dr. Jacobson surmised the women and men living behind the veil of purdah and burka believe the custom strengthens and aids family function by providing security, defining duties and roles within families, and "permits enforced togetherness to operate without too much friction." But times are changing. Even in remote villages, as education spreads, purdah and the burka are being challenged and sometimes set aside.

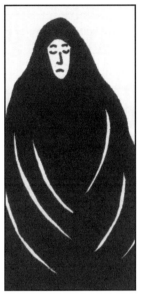

▲ The "curtain" is beginning to open.

PAKISTAN

In the locale where civilization originated it seems appropriate to discuss Goddess in her oldest form. In what is today Pakistan the earliest lineage of the Divine Feminine can be traced through her evolution as the Puranic Goddess of fertility worship of non-Aryan indigenous people, to one of her earliest incarnations as Nirriti ancestor of Kali, to Uma (who some believe is as old as Nirriti), then to Parvati. (Here too, around 1500 BCE, Vedic hymns of the Aryans started to mention the Sarasvati River near Mohenjo-daro, named for the Goddess of the same name, as being associated to this day with holy bodies of water.) Nirriti is first mentioned in the Rig Veda, the most sacred literature of the Hindus.

According to scholar Sukumari Bhattacharji, Nirriti is from a very old tradition dating to before the first millennium BCE, and originating from beyond the territories of India. The depiction of her (naked with snakes and periodically with a dove) resembles Earth Goddess imagery from western Asia, Mesopotamia and the Mediterranean providing evidence for an earlier tradition with a common background that is inclusive of Indian and Syro-Aegean culture. Bhattacharji continues on to compare Nirriti with Greek Persephone in light of the fact that her sacrifices of black sheep included a peculiar ritual element whereby the facilitator of the offering was proscribed to turn away his face. This action is reminiscent of the Indian ritual to the ancestors where, once again, the sacrificer is required to turn away his face, and must avoid any contact by touch. Nirriti is also compared to Isis in the context of Apuleius' Golden Ass, where she identifies herself before the protagonist Lucius as Nature, the Universal Mother, and Queen of the Dead, since this ancient Indian Goddess is likewise associated with decay and death. Discussing the pre-Vedic period Bhattacharji quotes Dr. Mackay who believes Nirriti might have been associated with the pre-Aryan Goddess Jara described as both youthful, of divine appearance, and a monstress who resides in every mortal dwelling. The discrepancy of her attributes is resolved as we realize her pre-Aryan existence was partially reconciled within Vedic tradition. So what we have is Jara, an Earth Goddess of the indigenous Indus Valley Complex (IVC), probably of Austric pre-Aryan origin, combining with the Vedic Nirriti, who later becomes Kali. Bhattacharji cites both Nirriti and Yami (and Kali by association) in their earliest forms as the Earth itself, the oldest of the old, though some literary references challenge this and name Uma as the older Goddess. Scholar Anna Dallapiccola defines Uma, whose name means "light," as a pre-Vedic Goddess, considered the nourisher and sustainer of the world who later assimilated the characteristics of Ambika (the mother), Durga (the inaccessible), Gauri (the golden), who later blends with Parvati and became Shiva's wife. Curiously, Nirriti is also associated with the Goddess Yami, whose consort was her brother Yama. Possibly as the result of cross-cultural diffusion, Yami and Yama resemble the Egyptian Goddess/God, sister/brother, wife/husband duo of Isis and Osiris.

To understand the syncretisation of Nirrti, Uma, and Parvati, and her associations with other female divinities it is necessary to expand a bit further. Around the world holy family cults began to develop, first comprised of mothers and sons and later to include fathers as the role of men in procreation was realized. Bhattacharji notes that Parvati becomes associated with one of the first "holy families" in the trinity of Shiva, herself, and Karttikeya. In Egypt the trinity was Isis, Osiris, and Horus. In Christianity, the earthly trinity is Joseph, Jesus and Mary, with the divine trinity being Father, Son and Holy Spirit, the latter being represented by a dove, a longtime symbol of Goddess the world over. (Even Jung believed "In Christian uncanonical phantasies ... the Holy Ghost has feminine significance.") So here we have Holy Family parallels that spread from Pakistan to Egypt and back again to Palestine. But there is more. Parvati, by her association with the heavenly/solar mother Aditi and the Earth Mother Nirrti, takes on benign and malign aspects, resulting in the syncretized Uma/Parvati, retaining dual chthonic and regenerative/procreative aspects as corn goddess, reflective of Olympian/Chthonic duality in Greek tradition, thus bringing the Greek Goddess Demeter to mind. Additionally, the late Prof. David Kinsley, one of the foremost scholars of Hinduism, describes Uma (also called Usas) of the Rig Veda as the dawn and a maiden, also called the breath of life (generally associated with the female Holy Spirit) of all living creatures, associated with cosmic, social, and moral order, the mother of cows (Egyptian Hathor perhaps?), and the marker of time, a constant reminder of people's limited time on Earth. As such,

Uma certainly embodies the triple Maiden, Mother, and Crone trinity of early Western tradition. As was stated in the opening, the West is closer to India than we sometimes think since language, myths, peoples, and traditions originated in the east and moved west!

Mohenjo-daro & Harappa

Within the confines of Mohenjo-daro and Harappa, two of the more famous of the many ancient archaeological sites from the Indus Valley Civilization (IVC), we find evidence of the oldest forms of Goddess worship. Nirriti has been discussed previously. Other sources suggest cave paintings in the region dating to 28,000 BCE depict perhaps the earliest images of God and Goddess, much later known as Shiva and Shakti. Here we find rudimentary images of the indigenous agricultural pre-Aryan civilization. Evidence for the Earth Mother is in the clay images of females unearthed in the ruins excavated during the 1920s. In a private communication with the well-noted anthropology professor and author, J. Mark Kenoyer, expert on the Indus Valley sites because of his direct work there, he addressed a question about the female figurines found in the IVC stating: "We assume that fertility had some role to play in their symbolism and that some of them may have represented Mother Goddesses. They can be correlated to the general types of figures that Marija Gimbutas discusses in her various books." Very true, but it should be noted that Marija Gimbutas referred to them as depicting life, death, and regeneration cycles, not limiting the figurines to only fertility.

The Indus Valley prehistoric sites date back to 250,000 BCE, with agricultural settlements appearing about 7000 BCE. Archaeological evidence reveals layers of flourishing civilizations, the oldest being the most advanced, with well-developed agricultural practices, brick structures measuring two levels high, streets planned in a north-south-east-west grid pattern, and clay pipe drainage systems emerging by 2500 BCE, all suggesting a well-organized central authority or government. Homes had flush toilets, underground sewers, central courtyards, and were supplied with water from brick-lined wells. This society traded ideas, goods, and languages with surrounding regions such as Sumeria and Mesopotamia, and employed uniform weights and measures. They had their own script of 419 symbols and though it remains undecipherable, Vicki Noble cites in an *India News* article reporting recent work decoding the script may indicate the Goddess Durga was central to Harappan civilization around 4000 BCE. Very recently, pottery uncovered in Harappa dated to be about 6,000 years old challenges established beliefs about the age of the civilization, along with a new timeframe when writing originated, only proving what we know about prehistory is always subject to the next potential archaeological find!

▲ The Indus seals are so old they sometimes depict long-extinct animals.

At their zenith these twin cities were some of the richest in the world. The prominence and size of the city baths suggest a purification or religious tradition which might have been the roots of modern Hindu cleansing rituals. Absence of temples suggest religious worship centered in the home, perhaps without a priesthood. Artifacts in the Metropolitan Museum of Art show pipal, or fig trees, found on seals and pottery that seem to be associated with deity, and may have contributed to the later worship of sacred trees in India. The earliest civilizations around the Indus began with indigenous people, followed by the Dravidians, and later by invading Indo-Europeans or Aryans, all influencing in succession the developing Hindu faith. Potentially, the cities of Mohenjo-daro and Harappa may have been populated by as many as 35,000 people.

Getting to Mohenjo-daro & Harappa

Over many centuries the Indus River has shifted its course several times and today the ruins of Mohenjo-daro are 2 miles (3.5 km) away from the current riverbank. Trains from either Karachi or Lahore access this remote location. Departing from Larkana train station, hire a taxi or auto-rickshaw to take you to the site. Private tour buses also travel direct to Mohenjo-daro from major Pakistani cities, but are more expensive. There is a small museum at the site with a good collection of the various finds. Harappa is located 400 miles (645 km) upriver from Mohenjo-daro. It is southeast of Sahiwal, the interior city of Punjab, and accessible by train or by car.

EAST ASIA

No worldly or celestial beings can know
The features of your appearance and form,
Even if they were to observe you for endless eons —
So limitless is your form and hard to imagine.
—Sudhanas's Praise of the Night Goddess
Prasantarutasagaravati

THE FEMININE DIVINE SATURATES THE LANDSCAPE of East Asia, from the northern steppes of Mongolia to the archipelago of Indonesia. Goddess in these remote locations demonstrates to her devotees a continued resilience, wide diversity, and prominence from ancient times until today. Currently Goddess is at the heart of Shinto celebrations as millions fill the streets of Japan in the footsteps of their ancestors. Her image is carried on palanquins through road and field. Her temples reside near lakes, within grottoes, and she towers atop mountain shrines. The tourist and devoted wash money in her holy sites as they pray for prosperity, bring egg offerings to her sacred messengers, and effigies of babies lost and hoped for to her temples. She rivals all the deities of the Buddhist pantheon, and her wedding is still celebrated annually in ritual. Her essence and power is further welcomed in young people's lives through the pop culture phenomena of anime, and sacred pilgrimage is not just an act of monks and holy men. With perhaps the exception of India, there is probably nowhere in the world where Goddess is currently so publicly out front and central to people's lives and entrenched within their culture. Here in East Asia, the Divine Feminine is visited by businessmen on their way to work as they pray for her ear in corporate negotiations. She has the nod of some governments who pay her homage with offerings, and fly her symbol as their national flag for the entire world to see!

Goddess thrived in East Asian matrilineal societies and survived patriarchal culture. She is personified in nature and symbol, the barriers of time and place eradicated, as she dominates the hearts and minds of women and men who walk her sacred pilgrimage routes. Devotees call out to her in childbirth and death, during times of peace and war, in shamanic trance, and agricultural ritual. Her practitioners believe she answers with miracles, sustenance, inspiration, and hope. While "Goddess Past" survives in the imagery of textiles, archaeological artifacts, spirituality, and art, "Goddess Today" is renewed daily with every sacrifice, prayer and chore performed in thousands of temples, shrines, and homes. She inspires followers who honor her with their faith and embrace her through their creativity expressed in the strokes of brush and pen, written word, stitching of cloth, weaving of straw, clanging of bells, pilgrimage to sacred sites, and digging with sticks. Her worship is carried forth atop shoulders on golden palanquins, beasts of burden, wooden ships, and the very breath of worshippers. It is evident in so many ways and places, by so many people, how Goddess nourishes the lives of devotees of the Far East, not just yesterday and today, but certainly for all time to come.

CAMBODIA

When most of us think of Cambodia our minds are filled with memories of the Vietnam conflict, the "Killing Fields" and the ruthless Khmer Rouge, but flip the pages of history back to European medieval times and Cambodia was emerging as a major power in Southeast Asia, with evidence of Goddess worship prominent among the people. The once-mighty Angkor empire, which 800 years ago stretched into what is now Vietnam, Laos, Thailand and the Malay Peninsula, was ruled by a succession of strong-armed kings, with some historians comparing its greatness to Rome. Before the Angkor kings, the first Cambodian civilization was the 3rd century CE kingdom of Funan, which began as a successful trading post called Chenla southeast of the present-day capital Phnom Penh. Funan acted as a buffer between India and China, two mighty empires that influenced the religious beliefs of the Cambodians, introducing to them the rich tapestry of Hindu and Buddhist mythology. The early Nak Ta, or ancestor people, who built the temples of Angkor, spoke a language called Khmer and are sometimes said to have been named for the Goddess Mera. These simple and indigenous Khmer people who toiled in the fields and depended on rice for their sustenance called upon the rice goddess Po Ino Nogar for daily nourishment. As time went on, Po Ino Nogar and her many sons and daughters inspired the hearts and minds of the people along with the Thevadas, Apsaras, and other female deities borrowed from the Hindu and Buddhist pantheon.

▲ The slightly smiling faces of Bayon number over 200 in the Angkor Thom temple complex.

Temples of Angkor

Meaning "Capital City," or "Holy City," the temples of Angkor are collectively regarded as the world's largest temple compound. This 135 square mile (220 sq. km) complex is a patchwork of sandstone temples, chapels, causeways, terraces, and reservoirs. Adorning the temple walls are thousands of carvings depicting battles between deities, sensual dancing women, royal processions with kings riding elephants, and many scenes from classical Hindu mythology. Surrounding Angkor within the natural landscape are the rice fields, the domain of the Rice Goddess Po Ino Nogar, called the "Great One," who rules over agriculture and fertility among its people. Like Aphrodite, she is born of sea foam (or the clouds), and has in her entourage 97 husbands and 38 daughters. One of these daughters is Po Yan Dari, known as the Destroyer of Life, who also oversees healing from disease. She is infused within the landscape of caves and grottoes, alongside Prah Thorni, considered the Earth Goddess.

Other aspects of the Divine Feminine at Angkor are the Thevadas, which can be compared to the Devatas of the Indian subcontinent who are earth deities of natural and wild places. They rule over the different classes and spheres of the physical world. The curvaceous and sensual dancing girls, sometimes described as celestial water nymphs, called Apsaras, are thought to possibly harken back to the more ancient river goddesses of the pre-Vedic Indus Valley civilization. Cambodia was not without its darker aspects of the Feminine Divine, such as Po Bya Tikuh, another daughter of Po Ino Nogar, called the Mouse Queen, (perhaps because the rodent threatened the rice crop?) or Khmoc Pray, mother or guardian spirits who are associated with women who have died in childbirth. And the Nagas, serpent-like aspects of Goddess who hold mystic knowledge and protect the source of life, are carved throughout the temples of Angkor.

▲ Angkor Wat is one of the most spectacular stone temples in the world.

211

Hindu Goddesses, which adorn the walls at various places within the Angkor complex, are Durga, Lakshmi (sometimes referred to Devi Sri in this part of the world), Sarasvati, Saptamatrikas or the Seven Mother Goddesses, Uma, Sita and Parvati. With the Buddhist influence, particularly the influx of Mahayana Buddhism, the very popular Prajnaparamita, the Goddess of Transcendent Wisdom and Mother of the Buddhas entered the scene, as well as the Bodhisattva Avalokiteshvara, also known as Kwan Yin. In fact, Jayavarman VII saw his royal divinity as being bestowed to him by Avalokiteshvara, when previous rulers perceived their sovereignty as being sponsored by Shiva or sometimes Vishnu.

Obviously there are many legends of the history of Angkor Wat. Other accounts say the magnificent Angkor Wat is a sacred site dedicated to Shiva and Vishnu, or a composite of the two Hindu gods called Hari-Hari. Still earlier, in the pre-history of Angkor, it is said five goddesses, or Devis, came down from Heaven and one remained at Angkor Wat, where she married a farmer and made him rich from her great skill at making beautiful cloth. They had a son, Visvakhrman, (later considered an aspect of Vishnu,) who trained in the Heavens where he became the most skilled of all mortal architects and is credited with having built this sacred site. Therefore, in Vedic myth, it is from the loins of Goddess the architect of Angkor Wat was born!

Other celebrated temples in the Angkor complex are Angkor Thom, and most recently Ta Prohm, made famous by the scenes filmed there for the Hollywood movie *Tomb Raider*. However, a little-known jewel in the crown of Angkor is

Banteay Srei, which has come to be called the Citadel of Women in modern times by local Cambodians. Though officially consecrated to Shiva, this small pink-colored sandstone temple is filled with female imagery and has an air of feminine energy. The light filigree of rosettes, delicately carved ladies holding lotus flowers and wearing traditional skirts, gods and goddesses filling every niche the eye can see, is a miniature temple of exquisite and meticulous detail. There are mythical beasts, monkey heads, geometric patterns, and guardian beings on every surface leaving no space without adornment. Banteay Srei is of rectangle design, surrounded on three sides by a moat, with a processional way leading toward the inner sanctuary. Relief carvings depict images of Indra with Vishnu in his man-lion incarnation, Sita (the incarnation of Lakshmi) being abducted by Ravana, Kama and Siva, Shiva with Parvati, and Krishna, Vishnu's earthly incarnation.

▲ An Apsara sculpture at Banteay Srei.

Getting to the Temples of Angkor

The many temples of Angkor are located in northwestern Cambodia, situated just north of the town Siem Reap. It isn't the intrepid traveler who ventures to these fascinating temples anymore, but now large tour groups are streaming in and transforming Siem Reap into a booming tourism town. Only in 1995 Khmer Rouge terrorists targeted foreign tourists, but today the region is completely safe for travel. From Phnom Penh, there are buses, trains, flights and a boat route over Tonlé Sap lake to Siem Reap. Banteay Srei is located 13 miles (21 km) northeast of the Angkor Thom temple complex.

CHINA

Long ago, Goddess traversed the Silk Road on camel back, leaving her mark on textiles, cliff walls and caravansaries along the way. The Silk Road was the main artery of culture from China in the east to the Mediterranean in the west. She traveled with many nomadic peoples like the Sauromatians, Saka, Samarians, Scythians, and proto-Celts as they migrated east. She rode on horseback with warrior queens and priestesses of the 13th century Golden Horde and along with descendants from Genghis Kahn, as the Mongols acquired one of the largest known empires in history. A recent archaeological discovery of the Kurgan burial mounds has revealed many of these early nomads who traversed the Eurasian steppes in far western China worshipped the Earth Mother. Researchers believe these nomads were descendants and contemporaries of the women who inspired tales of the Amazons while cultural diffusionists make the case that these women warriors *actually were* the Amazons referred to by Herodotus.

Pu Tuo Shan Sacred Island

Kwan Yin (Guanyin), called Holy Mother of Compassion and Savioress, has one of her most sacred sites on Pu Tuo Shan, a small island in the East China Sea. At first glance it might not seem that Buddhist and Goddess spirituality combine in a harmonious blend, yet Chinese history reflects a people who have had their trials and tribulations and through their suffering, it was the female bodhisattva Kwan Yin in whom people put their faith. It was Kwan Yin that women turned to more often than men. She was believed by the devoted to understand their struggle and pain, and lent strength, love, and compassion. Kwan Yin would be their protectress at the birthing bed, or in their struggle for freedom and recognition. It was she who would bring their husbands back from war or the sea. Kwan Yin, who originally came to China as the androgynous male bodhisattva Avalokitesvara (Tibetans regard the Dalai Lama as this bodhisattva's incarnation), was said to have been born of a ray of light shining from the right eye of Amitabha, the Buddha of Infinite Light. In time, Kwan Yin was later recognized as a female bodhisattva or Goddess. Chinese society and culture are overwhelmingly patriarchal and women are usually only considered useful or whole after they have given birth. Kwan Yin offered women solace. Her popularity grew exponentially and it is said that by the 9th century there was a Kwan Yin statue in every monastery in China. Pu Tuo Shan, meaning "beautiful white flower" is one of the four sacred Buddhist mountains, located on the island of the same name, and sacred to Kwan Yin. Here she is called the Goddess of the Southern Sea and patroness of fishermen. Images of her associated with Pu Tuo Shan show Kwan Yin crossing the sea seated on a lotus, or with her feet on the head of a dragon.

An island of beautiful beaches, caves, valleys, monasteries, and temples, it is an idyllic getaway for those on the Chinese mainland. People come here from all parts of Asia on pilgrimage to honor and pray to Kwan Yin. Many Buddhist temples are located on Mount Pu Tuo, but the three most important are Puji Temple, the main temple for Kwan Yin worship, Fau Temple, famous for its architecture and wood carvings, and Huiji Temple on the peak of Foding Hill which exhibits a large collection of ancient carvings of Kwan Yin. The peak of Pu Tuo Shan is reached by climbing 1,060 stone steps, or by taking a cable car. A new temple to Kwan Yin, called Nan Hai Guan Yin, or South Sea Guan Yin, proudly honors the Goddess with a giant statue, exquisite stone carvings, and murals that explain the history of Kwan Yin.

Guanyin is regarded by some as having pre-Buddhist roots in the more archaic Chinese deity Nu Kwa or Nugua who created the Chinese people and the natural order of the universe. She was sometimes depicted as half snake and half woman, creating her brother/consort Fu Xi from her own body, thus when shown intertwined they resemble the kundalini symbol or caduceus. According to Merlin Stone, images of Kwan Yin riding upon a dolphin may be related to the fish-tailed images of Nu Kwa. Both Kannon and Kwan Yin have been associated with carp or salmon, and other fish images, which are seen as fertility symbols. In the Chinese cosmology myths, mountains are sacred pillars that separate heaven from earth and in the "Reparation of Heaven" myth, Nu Kwa repaired the broken sky and used the four feet of a large turtle to keep the heavens from falling onto the earth. The feet of the turtle became the four sacred Buddhist mountains, of which one is Pu Tuo Shan, thus she effectively restored harmony to all natural life. Kwan Yin is also associated with the young Miao Shan, a devout Buddhist who was killed by her father in a fit of rage because she did not want to marry, wishing instead to join a nunnery. After death her soul was returned to earth where she attained enlightenment, and spent her days relieving the suffering of those in distress. Miao Shan was believed to live on Pu Tuo Shan Island for nine years (as was Kwan Yin) where she healed and saved sailors from shipwrecks.

Kwan Yin is believed to have 33 manifestations; some aspects have 11 heads or 1,000 hands and eyes, enabling her to hear and see the cries of the needy and answer their prayers. Devotees of Kwan Yin believe effective prayer to her consists of repeatedly chanting her name or the Avalokitesvara mantra of "Om Mani Padme Hum" which translates to "Hail to the jewel in the lotus." Images of Kwan Yin show her in various postures, most of which have her tall and slender, barefooted, in flowing robes, holding a vase containing *amitra,* or the dew of compassion, which she pours forth upon humankind. The amitra is said to have the power to extend life, cure, and purify body, mind, and speech. Sometimes she is

sitting on a lotus flower, fish, elephant, or upon a lion-like beast. She can be nursing a baby or holding a child. Sometimes her male and female assistants Lung Nu and Shan Ts'ai are at her feet on either side of her. Some of her symbols are a scroll of truth, a jar of healing water, a spray of willows, the holy jewel of aspirations, and she also has a nude form. Kwan Yin has been compared most often to Mary, the Virgin Mother of Jesus, or the Egyptian Goddess, Isis.

Rebecca Love, a teacher in China, comments that the vast majority of Chinese do not practice or have little interest in religion though

▲ The Sacred Precinct of Pu Tuo Shan Island where Kwan Yin presides over all.

some worship nature, meditate and pray to the Goddess of Mercy. Female statues everywhere in China are identified as The Motherland. Statues of Kwan Yin are often found on quiet hillsides near villages that have a willow branch (classic symbol of womanhood), and water from a sacred spring for self-blessing at the sacred site. The water blessing is believed to have the power to save lives and bring good fortune.

Getting to Pu Tuo Shan Island

When in Shanghai, from the Shanghai Shiliepu Harbor near the Bund, the main passenger harbor of Shanghai, there are morning buses that take visitors to Luchaogang Harbor. Daily shuttle boats from Luchaogang Harbor access Pu Tuo Shan Island, located approximately 155 miles (250 km) to the east of Shanghai, across Hangzhou Bay in the East China Sea. This trip takes about 3.5 hours. There is also a night boat that takes about 12 hours to reach the island departing from Shiliepu Harbor. Once on this small island of only 5 square miles (12 sq. km), located in the Zhoushan Archipelago of Zhejiang Province, several bus routes take visitors to the main sites. Hotels are available on Pu Tuo, as are accommodations in private homes, which can be arranged upon arrival at the island.

GAIA ALERT
THE NEEDS OF THE MANY

Sumatran tigers are on the brink of extinction. Indonesian orangutans could disappear within two decades due to loss of habitat. In Myanmar (Burma), poachers kill bears for $8, their paws considered a delicacy. Leopards are hunted for body parts used in traditional medicines. Gold miners inadvertently poison ponds with cyanide and mercury runoff. The Japanese red crowned crane, a national treasure that has long inspired art and tourists alike, is fighting for survival, struggling for breeding territory as it competes for valuable open space. The eagle owl, the world's largest and most endangered owl, is dwindling in numbers as their nesting sites in old growth trees are cut down. In Tokyo Bay, sardine supplies diminish as the wetlands that serve as natural pollution filters are slowly disappearing. Though industry strives for zero-emissions, air and water are foul, and landfills inhibit water flow needed to help cleanse the bay. In the China Sea, toxic runoff destroys once abundant fisheries, and coral reefs are endangered by blast and cyanide fishing, pollution, and development. China's giant pandas are on the verge of extinction due to loss of habitat. Jakarta's rivers are choked with refuse, while logging, palm oil plantations, and forest fires destroy habitats in Irian Jaya. The environmental impact of a road and gas pipeline proposed for the Altai region from southern Siberia to China would be significant, and could have the Ukok Plateau, a World Heritage Site, in environmental distress. Complicating the matter, a nuclear power plant and storage facility for foreign nuclear waste is being proposed within Altai.

▲ Asian bears are suffering from over-hunting and loss of habitat ...

▲ ... while human populations are at an all-time high throughout Asia.

The needs of the environment along with that of our feathered and furred creatures continue to be sacrificed for economic development and corporate greed. Other times they fall prey to short-sighted schemes or internal political, religious, and ethnic strife. However, there are some glimmers of hope. In Indonesia, where two tiger subspecies have already become extinct, The World Wildlife Fund, working to fund anti-poaching patrols, has helped prosecute poachers, and invests in habitat conservation. Japan is working on global warming issues as evidenced by their adoption of the Kyoto Protocol, and subsequent efforts toward prevention. Their conservationists are committed to finding ways of saving and protecting remaining wildlife habitats while ecologists search for solutions to clean up Tokyo Bay. Myanmar Forest Department is working to triple the size of wildlife sanctuaries. Other organizations look to work with regimes in power to help them understand the importance of co-existing with wildlife and finding alternatives to farming methods that destroy habitats. Educational research and awareness campaigns draw attention to the plight of the dwindling orangutans of Borneo, and reintroduction projects help relocate some of the primates. UNESCO and the United Nations are getting involved in the development plans for the Altai region so that discussion, study, and agreement might take place among all involved. In all these issues, for the sake of human and wildlife alike, we must think globally, act locally, and pray sanity and wisdom will prevail. Be an aware consumer and conscientious volunteer, both important steps to help Mother Earth.

EURASIAN STEPPES

Within the Eurasian Steppes and Silk Road, cross-cultural images unearthed in frozen graves, cemeteries, and cult sites continue to yield proof of Mother Goddess devotion across this vast region spanning thousands of years. All along the Silk Road, west of Kazakhstan, through Siberia, Mongolia, and China, this central Asian region connected various people, cultures, traditions, and spiritualities of East and West for over 4,000 years. Some scholars believe one of the contributing factors to the migration of diverse peoples may have been due to catastrophic flooding in the Black Sea region. Littered with burial sites and petroglyphs that scatter across the landscape, these steppes hold clues to priestesses, warrior-queens, and the possible origins of Amazon-like females, daughters of Artemis and Cybele, regaled by Herodotus, yet thought to be only myth. Images recognized in Greece, Italy and Thrace have been found as far to the east as the Altai Mountains which Dr. Davis-Kimball believes is evidence of a "priestess cult." Out Of Place Artifacts, or "OOPAS," found in Kurgan burial graves have challenged traditional archaeological theory about the people and culture of the region. (To avoid confusion, it should be noted that Dr. Davis-Kimball has communicated to the author that she does not believe the nomads which are the subject of portions of this chapter are related genetically or culturally to the famous Kurgan wave invader theories of Marija Gimbutas. While the scope of this travel book does not allow for in-depth discussion of this and the many diverse spiritual, historical, or scientific concepts touched upon within these chapters, readers are encouraged to refer to the extensive bibliography for further discovery.) Thanks to the dedicated field work of researchers such as Jeannine Davis-Kimball, Natalya Polosmak, Sergei Rudenko, and Mikhail Gryaznov, this region is beginning to reveal evidence that requires a rethinking of history, particularly relating to the role of women during the Iron and Bronze Ages. A recent example is the Issyk Gold Man from Almaty, Kazakhstan which has been re-identified as the Gold Warrior Priestess. What gave it away was a conical headdress traditionally worn by Kazak brides, and the whip bound with strips of hammered gold found in her grave, similar to artifacts found in other warrior priestess graves. Such has been the case in gravesite after gravesite. Art, textiles, and grave goods help archaeologists and researchers rethink conventional theories, connect the dots, and articulate a clearer picture emerging from the Eurasian steppes. Much of what we know about this region comes from Dr. Jeannine Davis-Kimball. She spent four years excavating more than 150 mounds of nomads near Pokrovka, Russia. Her book, *Warrior Women*, clearly presents the vast area of the Eurasian Steppes, littered with sacred places used for ritual and burial. She cites how this land was filled with many people who worshipped many Goddesses. The Amazon-like Sauromatians and Sarmations tribes probably worshipped an Earth Mother deity. Scythians revered Tabiti, Goddess of the hearth and family, Api, an Earth Goddess, and Argimpasa, patroness of fertility and marriage. Phrygian Matar, mother of the gods, humans and animals, associated with mountains and fertility, morphed into the Goddess Cybele. A perfect example of this synchronization was uncovered in a mound at Tillya Tepe in Afghanistan (ancient Bactria) which revealed layers of ruins of successive peoples.

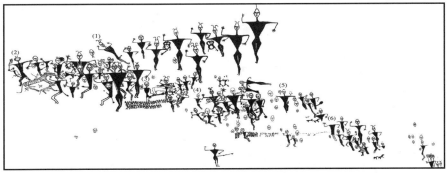

▲ Ancient petroglyph of a fertility scene from Xinjiang, China.

Kangjiashimenzi Petroglyphs

A grotto of cave art called the Kangjiashimenzi Petroglyphs, depicting fertility scenes on a sandstone cliff, suggests the spirituality of these shamanic nomads had reached Xinjiang (pronounced shin-jun), China thousands of years ago. Dr. Davis-Kimball first saw the images in 1991 in an area then closed to foreigners because of the proximity to military installations and political prisons. Located outside the city of Hutubei, in the most northern part of the old Silk Road where raiders, traders, caravans, herders, and travelers went to and fro. The professor described it as a huge dark red sandstone rock wall visible across several valleys reminding her of a Gothic cathedral, yet more fortress-like in presence. After walking up a steep hill from the base of the hill, a grotto revealed the petroglyphs.

The tableau consists of more than 60 bas-relief petroglyph carvings ranging in size from very small to larger-than-life. Composed of animals and humans, the images depict felines, goats, hermaphrodites, women with conical headdresses carved larger (6 feet (1.8 m) tall) than the men (3 feet (0.9 m) tall) who are portrayed with erect and huge phalluses. The women have inverted triangle torsos with prominent hips and thighs forming a second smaller triangle, the pubic triangle being a symbol of female fertility. Dr. Davis-Kimball further described the images as expressive, well realized, and representing their own fecundity, rather than the "animal style" usually employed by ancient Iron Age or Neolithic peoples. This

▲ The Kangjiashimenzi Petroglyphs depict symbols of female fertility.

29.5-foot (9-m) high and 45.93-foot (13.5-m) long tableau required technology and leadership to create, therefore she surmised it was created during the Bronze Age, and represented the Caucasoid migrating to the Tarim Basin. Females dominate the scene in shamanic dance and trance poses, with legs akimbo, receptive to their male partners. Felines and goats also have erections in this obvious fertility ritual scene which Dr. Kimball believes was incorporated into vital regenerative rites actually held by priests and priestesses at this remote site.

Even more important, the women wear tall headdresses denoting their exalted status — perhaps priestesses responsible for fecundity of the people they served. Dr. Kimball was able to satisfy her theory that these Europid images were created by the migrants from Eastern Europe and were connected to the Proto-Celtic Caucasoid mummies that arrived in the Tarim Basin area, peoples that traced their roots back to the Goddess known as Cybele.

Getting to the Kangjiashimenzi Petroglyphs

The Kangjiashimenzi Petroglyphs are located in the Tien Shan Mountains of Xinjiang Uygur, in the far northwest of China. This remote and rugged region is located outside the city of Hutubei, about 60 miles (97 km) southwest of Urumqi. The grotto is located in an intermountain valley of the Tien Shan, the northern most part of the old Silk Road. Government procured documents must be obtained to visit and informed guides are a must. Both can be arranged in Urumqi.

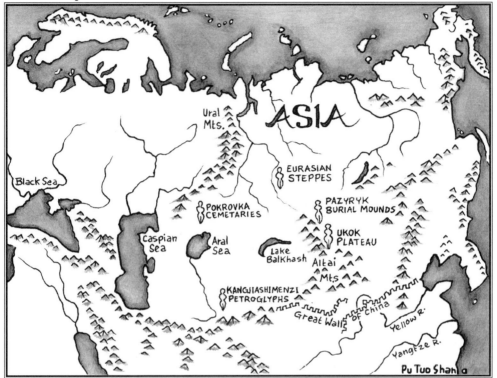

Burial Mounds of the Altai Mountains

Thousands of sacred burial mounds and ritual sites lay within the Altai Mountains, home of the famous Ice Maiden, a warrior priestess discovered by Natalya Polosmak on the Ukok Plateau in 1993. The Ice Maiden was part of the Pazyryk/Saka culture believed to revere the Earth Mother. Her mummy sported a blue tattoo in the design of a griffin-like creature in Scythian style, was only the second tattooed Pazyryk body ever found. Dr. Davis-Kimball explains the iconography of these fantastic animals such as a griffin (combination of eagle and lion) were reserved for those of elevated status who would be more likely to call upon the powers of such a potent beast that embodied the powers of these two powerful animals. It was typical to find such hybrid zoomorphic images in priestess burials. Other burials had unearthed images of winged snow leopards, and deer with a griffin head at the end of antlers found on the Ice Maiden's left arm.

The Lady, or Ledi as her excavators called the Ice Maiden, wore silk and wool clothes, with a hair and felt headdress that required a coffin nearly eight feet (2.4 m) long to accommodate her 5' 6" frame and tall pointed hat. On her hat was "animal style" iconography reflective of steppe art in the motifs of eight gold covered and carved felines (probably Tien Shan snow leopards), birds on the branches of a tree, and a pair of wooden swans. Her coffin was carved from a solid log of larch wood with a leather appliqué for decoration, and placed in the Kurgan burial mound with her head facing east.

Buried with her were gilded ornaments and a hand mirror with a deer carved on its wooden back, carefully wrapped in red cloth. She wore beaded bracelets on her wrist and more tattoos on her wrist and thumb. In the grave were six horses elaborately harnessed that had been sacrificed to travel with her in the afterlife. Her last meal of mutton was beside her on a table with a bronze knife, as were coriander seeds, perhaps to help with the smell of the decomposing body. Her body had been prepared in the way of her people. She was gutted and her skull split with her brain removed, and muscles scraped away. Her remains were embalmed with aromatic herbs, and her skin was stitched back together. Ledi was only about 25 years of age when she died.

Many of the graves still wait to be uncovered, yet those excavated have produced startling results! It is the artistic clues that tell researchers the deceased warrior-queens and priestesses buried within the Kurgan mounds likely worshipped some aspect of the Earth Goddess. These clues are spiral tattoos that remain on their bodies, grave goods with motifs depicting a eunuch or transvestite, snow leopards and deer (which may have served as helpers of the priestess), elk, rams, goats, and birds on a tree of life. Personnel items in the grave often included a single or double conical hat, (which ironically conform to the stereotypical guise for witches in the imagination of Western society centuries later), mirrors, and special cups and spoons used for *koumiss,* or mare's milk. Fertility rites and mystical animals depicted in petroglyphs at the cultic site of Tamgaly in southern Kazakhstan, 100 miles (161 km) northwest of Almaty, at Kangjaishimezi in Xinjiang (pronounced shin-jun), China, also hold clues to the shaman, priestess, and Earth Goddess. The now famous Urumqi mummies of Proto-Celtic origin with Caucasoid characteristics are certainly considered OOPAS, with light to red hair, round eyes, towering 6 feet (1.8 m) in height, wearing textiles and sporting tattoos. The Urumqi mummies also suggest connections to our theme, as does the Chowhougou archaeological site, both in the Xinjiang province of western China.

Today, the inhabitants of the land still consider the shamaness a woman of exalted status, and the people of the land consider the landscape sacred. Max Dashu, teacher and historian, tells of the revered white-manned crone Goddess, Ayyyhyt, who lives atop World Mountain at the center of the Earth. She sits

▲ Both warrior women and warrior priestess grave goods were found in the Altai Mountains.

beneath a blessed Tree, and inscribes the fate of all living beings on its leaves, a creatrix who provides the peoples of the region with life and a "ceaseless breathing." Mount Bekukah, a sacred peak within the Altai mountain range, is still home to those who refer to Goddess as Mother of the World, and Mongols are still careful to pay tribute to Khoito teebi, or Northern Granny.

Getting to the Burial Mounds of the Altai Mountains

In this extremely vast region within the Altai Mountain range, covering the Eurasian four corner region of Mongolia, China, Russia and Kazakhstan, many such places are often off limits to all but scholars and official government personnel. Depending on the political climate and special circumstances, sometimes access is granted, however the casual visitor must inquire with each country for the region they hope to visit because the Altai Mountains are not yet considered a tourist destination. Besides, the Ukok Plateau has inhospitable weather most months of the year with few traveler amenities.

Pokrovka Cemeteries

More than fifty ancient Kurgan burial mounds have been unearthed near the town of Pokrovka, Russia yielding skeletons of women who worshipped the Earth Mother, with one priestess found as recently as 2003. Dr. Davis-Kimball believes some of these Sauromatian (Sarmation) women might have inspired the Amazon legend made famous by Herodotus, while cultural diffusionists make a case for these women warriors being the descendants or contemporaries of the Amazonians.

Called Oiropata, or "killers of men," by the Scythians, these women may have produced progeny with some of these Scythians who became the nomadic Sauromatian tribe. Her analysis of the Pokrovka burials seemed to suggest three categories for women within the nomadic culture. The first and largest category, "femininity and the hearth" yielded burial goods with functional clay spindle whorls, bronze spiral earrings covered with gold foil and luxury items such as colored glass and stone beads. Those found in the "warrior" category were buried with weapons and armor with some skeletons bow-legged from riding horseback. One such skeleton wore an arrowhead amulet in a leather pouch around her neck, and buried beside her was an iron dagger, and a quiver with more than 40 arrows tipped with bronze. Next, those identified with the "priestess" category of the shamaness were often distinguished by carved stone altars, intact bronze mirrors for healing and divination, fossilized seashells, and other items used for spiritual purposes. Finally, the smallest sub-category of women overlapped both the warrior and priestess categories, perhaps suggesting the highest of all status, the warrior-priestess, buried with spiritual tools and weapons.

While it is not crystal clear what the distinction or inter-connection was between hearth women, shamaness/priestess, and warrior women, certainly multi-tasking for women is not a modern phenomenon. Dr. Davis-Kimball believes religious leaders of the ancient nomads were almost always women and were considered among the elite. Women had babies, watched over the herds, defended their property, and had a voice in politics. The shamaness/priestess was the one who also communicated with the ancestors, animals, and spirits of the Earth. She spoke the sacred words, foretold what was to be, healed the sick, and buried the dead, probably as early as Neolithic times. She was acutely

▲ Pokrovka Cemetery burial of a warrior woman.

aware of the web of life and the fragile balance that must be maintained, and by association, she was therefore connected to Goddess, Mistress of the Animals, Mother Earth.

The Pazyryk burials, unearthed in the 1950s by Sergei Rudenko in southern Siberia, revealed startling grave goods including a large 15-foot (4.5-m) by 20-foot (6-m) felt wall hanging with six panels depicting a woman giving audience to a man. This has been interpreted by scholars as the Goddess and a king. In this image, the female is larger than the male, establishing her higher status, and iconography of the tree of life point to fecundity, a typical Earth Mother domain. The man appears to be a Saka chief with Iranian-like features, and by their postures it is believed the Goddess is either granting this king his right to sovereignty, as was the tradition in some Goddess cultures, or he is seeking approval or divination for some portentous campaign. This wall hanging, along with other accouterments associated with the priestess class, were found in a double walled log house buried within this early Iron Age nomadic kurgan, and belonged to the Saka priestess entombed here. Another priestess artifact found here was a pointed hat, a mark of high status, which originated in Anatolia, where Goddesses such as Artemis and Aphrodite were depicted with likewise tall and brimless square headdresses called polos.

The conical style of headdress was later assimilated by the Scythians, and was similarly found in the graves of a 5th century BCE priestess in western China. According to Davis-Kimball, this pointed hat would become the hallmark of the witch centuries later in Western culture. Vicki Noble observes the similarity between the peaked black hats worn by Eruopoid immigrant priestesses in China and those worn by one of each pair of chariot-driving "Amazon" Queens depicted on either end of the famous sarcophagus of Aghia Triada found in Bronze Age Crete. She further quotes Mallory and Mair who see the similarity between the "witch hats" and the pointed hat of a Russian "baba" on display in the Tanais museum.

Today the shaman is still employed by the people in this region for assistance with sickness, guidance, and spiritual matters. In India, Korea, and Japan women tend to dominate the profession. Vicki Noble quoting Dr. Davis-Kimball informs us that "the lineage of Medea of Colchis, a shaman woman or 'sorceress' known for her regenerative magic, may continue even today in a group of mostly women and girls living in the Caucasus (areas around the Black Sea) who are "called messulethe and described as sorceresses." They live in tribes considered to be descendants of Scythians and Sarmatians and they "fulfill a role very similar to that of Altaic shamans, falling into trances, escorting the dead to the underworld, or reincarnating them."

Getting to the Pokrovka Cemeteries

The Kurgan burial mounds in the Pokrovka Cemeteries are just inside the Russian border within the Kazak Steppes of Kazakhstan. Empty now, leaving only an empty hole in the ground, there is not much to see as their artifacts have been safely spirited away to museums in Orenburg, Novosibirsk, Gorney Altai or The Hermitage in Saint Petersburg. To find these grave sites a guide familiar with the excavations would have to be located and employed. The knowledge of these sites is important as these relatively new discoveries call for a rethinking and rewriting of herstory of the women and their roles which dominated the landscape, as well as their association to Mother Earth, also called Mistress of the Animals.

Specialized tours are available to the Altai Mountains and to places along the Silk Road, like the famous stop to see the Mummies of Urumchi. One can reach the Altai Mountains by plane from Moscow to Barnaul, and then by bus to Gorno-Altaisk, a site rich in archaeological finds, located 186 miles (300 km) north of the mountains. Tour operators are based in Barnaul. Novosibirsk, about 373 miles (600 km) north of Altay, Mongolia — a stop on the Trans-Siberian railway. Some operators even arrange tours where travelers can visit local shamans, healers, and psychics. To visit sacred Mount Belukha where ceremonies are conducted for healing Mother Earth, it is highly recommended before leaving for such remote destinations that you plan carefully, and diligently check out the reputation of prospective tour providers. Be sure to make calls to the consulates of the countries you are considering visiting, particularly if you wish to inquire if the excavations might be accessible to the public.

INDONESIA

As in other times and places, the Feminine Divine has acquired many names. In Bali, she is Ida Ratu, who provides water to irrigate rice fields insuring the sustenance of life. She is Guan Yin, or Kwan Yin in China (called Kannon in Japan), who pours forth her mercy and compassion for the world. In Japan, she is also Benten, Goddess of good fortune, Amaterasu, the Sun Goddess, and Inari when in the guise of the Rice Goddess who nourishes her people. She is Tien Hau or Ma Zhu throughout Asia and Indonesia. Whether her worship evolved from Cybele, Artemis, Athena, Aphrodite or other female deities who traveled the Silk Road eastward, the Earth Mother was part of everyday life of many in the Altai and Tien Shan mountain regions touched by the great trade routes. In the sacred Tianshan Mountains of eastern China, she is Dou Mu, Lady of the Emerald Clouds or Tai Granny. As Xi Wang Mu, she is the Taoist Queen Mother of the West, who holds the peach (a fruit associated with the yoni) of immortality in her garden in mythical Kun Lun Mountains. In mysterious Angkor Wat, female divinity is recognized in the images of the Apsaras and Devatas from the Khmer civilization thought to be named for the Goddess Mera. For the Hindu devotee she is Lakshmi, Kali, Sarasvati, and Durga. The Ainu of the Hokkaido region of Japan called their fire goddess Fuchi. Her history, though sometimes suppressed, continues to reveal itself in newly discovered frozen grave sites which forces us to revision and rethink what really transpired through the ages.

Lake Batur at Mount Batur

Batari Sri Dewi, the Rice Goddess, is one of the most beloved deities on the beautiful island of Bali with her annual wedding performed in the Pura Besakih Temple. Dewi Danu, Goddess of Lake Batur at Mount Batur, provides water for the cultivation of rice, the most important product of the island. Together these complementary Goddesses are revered by the people of Bali to whom they are their providers of the sustenance, good fortune, and life itself.

Pura Ulun Danu Batur, temple of the north, is one of the nine directional temples, or *kayangan jagat,* believed by the Balinese to protect them and their island. These public temples are composed of an inner, middle, and outer courtyard, with the entrance marked by a *candi bentar,* or split gate that gives the appearance of a temple split down the middle from top to bottom. Features of the temples usually include a tower with wooden bells used to signal certain groups or events, courtyards where offerings are prepared and participants gather, and musicians and dancers perform. The inner courtyard, the most sacred, has pavilions for offerings to the gods, which may or may not appear in the form of a relic. Other features of the temple compounds include *merus,* or many-tiered pagoda-like structures with roofs thatched in sacred palm fibers. Sometimes there is a place set aside for the oracle of the temple, the *Taksu,* or a lotus throne, a raised stone seat, where the deity is invited to sit during ceremonies. Roy Hamilton quoting Lansing explains Dewi Danu, Goddess of Lake Batur is worshipped at the public temple, Pura Ulun Danu Batur, on Mount Batur, overlooking Lake Batur, which serves as a central reservoir for the irrigation system covering a large part of the island. Lansing sums up the importance of Dewi Danu. "Because the Goddess makes the waters flow, those who do not follow her laws may not possess her rice terraces."

▲ A mask of Batari Sri Dewi — beloved Rice Goddess.

Rice is the single most important crop in Bali, and each rice field has its own shrine to Batari Sri Dewi. The planting and harvesting of the agricultural cycle are marked by ceremonial offerings, reflecting the physical life cycle of the Rice Goddess herself. Sri Dewi images called *cili* are placed in the fields. The cili, fertility symbols predating Balinese Hinduism, are made of folded coconut palm leaves depicted in hermaphrodite effigy of the Rice Goddess having female breasts and male genitalia. These cili are forms of Balinese art with religious function. Used not just for fertility of the rice fields, the cili are also used for prosperity and abundance in other areas of life, such as business success, or for protection, even company logos.

Pura Besakih, Bali's "Mother Temple" is a huge complex of Hindu temples on Mount Agung, and the most sacred group of temples in all of Bali. It is considered the center of the nine directional

Photo courtesy Metro Government of Nashville / Gary Layda

▲ The Nashville Parthenon rivals the
Greek Parthenon in Athens.

Photo by Roy Tate

▲ An ethereal golden glow surrounds Mary
and Jesus in the Hagia Sophia, Istanbul.

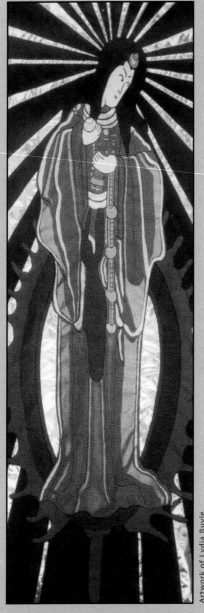

Artwork of Lydia Ruyle

▲ Amaterasu is the Sun Goddess of Japan.

Photo by Roy Tate

▲ The fox at the Fushima Inari Taisha Temple in Kyoto is popular with photographers.

Photo by Roy Tate

▲ The Asakusa Kannon is a colorful temple in downtown Tokyo.

Photo by Carol Nowlan

▲ One of many chalice wells in
Glastonbury, England.

Photo by Carol Nowlan

▲ Sacred waters permeate the lush landscape of
England, such as the Vesica Piscus Well here in
Glastonbury.

▲ Temple ruins from the sacred precinct at Didyma, Turkey.

▲ Cave to the underworld at Eleusis, Greece.

▲ Mermaids are celebrated worldwide, even in landlocked Prague, Czech Republic.

Photo by Roy Tate

▲ Hathor head columns depict her bovine attributes.

Photo by Roy Tate

▲ A colored relief sculpture of Isis from Abydos, Egypt.

Photo by Roy Tate

▲ Philae Island in the Nile River is dominated by the spectacular Isis Temple.

Photo by Roy Tate

▲ Miniature reproduction of the disc of Coyolxauhqui found in Templo Mayor, Mexico.

Photo by Marlene Ehrenberg

▲ This relief of the "Goddess of Living Waters" is from Chalcatzingo.

Photo by Roy Tate

▲ Ixchel was a major female deity to the Maya people of the Yucatan.

Photo by Brad Olsen

▲ Statuary of Hindu female deities
grace Indonesia's tropical island of Bali.

Photo by Lydia Ruyle

▲ Machu Picchu in Peru is the domain
of Pacha Mama.

Photo by Roy Tate

▲ The Ggantija Temple on the Mediterranean island of Gozo is one of oldest in the world.

Photo by Roy Tate

▲ Early Mother Goddess statue found in the granaries of Catal Hüyük.

temples. Before the coming of Hinduism, Mount Agung was probably worshipped as a sacred mountain, and it too is one of the nine directional temples believed by the Balinese to protect the island. According to scholar David J. Stuart-Fox, here the divine couple, Goddess Bhatari Sri and God Bhatara Sedana, Goddess and God of Rice, is annually wedded in a ritual called Usaba Ngeed which takes place on the day of a full moon. It is the last major ceremony in the cycle of agricultural rituals although its significance goes beyond being purely agricultural. Pura Banua is the temple within the Besakih complex dedicated to Bhatari Sri, Goddess of Rice. While numerous and elaborate rituals and processions are performed surrounding the "wedding," including the *panurun* (meaning "go down") where the deity is brought down into his or her god-symbol or statue by a *pemangku,* or priest, rituals done at the temple are always aimed at securing fertility of crops, which in turn means abundance and wealth for the people. Hence, the Goddess provides rice and good fortune, while her consort offers up wealth and prosperity.

It should be noted that Pura Besakih is not listed as a sacred site by the Balinese because they do not consider the temples sacred unless the deity is in residence for a particular ceremony. During the normal course of the year, the deities reside on the mountain, at the lake, and in the rice fields, the primary sacred sites of the deities. According to David Stuart-Fox, when in residence (or in natural settings), offerings to deities at Balinese temples can include large cones of rice called *tumpeng,* considered models of the cosmic mountain, the axis mundi, linking the upper world, human world, and underworld. Roasted chicken is one of the common offerings as it represents the meat element. Other customary offerings include different kinds of rice cakes, fruits, flowers, and palm-leaf decorations. But without doubt, rice is the primary ingredient for offerings in all manners of color, configuration, complexity, and consistency. The sacred vocation of creating these many types of offerings fall primarily within roles reserved for women. After the deity has consumed the essence of the food, it is usually taken home and eaten by the family. There is a temple to Dewi Danu, designated as Goddess of the Sea, high atop Pura Luhur Ula Watu, a 660 feet (200 m) cliff overlooking the ocean in the Badung Regency. The cliff itself is thought to represent the "Ship of Stone." This is another of the nine directional temples protecting Bali.

Getting to Lake Batur at Mount Batur

Located in the Bangli Regency, or northeast corner of Bali, Mount Batur is a double volcano near the village of Kintamani. From Kintamani, drive to the rim of the volcano where you can view Lake Batur. On the western rim of the crater near the town of Kintamani, the new temple to the Pura Ulun Danu Batur, the Goddess of the Lake, was built in 1920 after a volcanic eruption threatened the original temple down near the lake. (It should not be confused with the old temple of the same name situated on the lake).

A paved road follows the crater rim and the first stop is Penelokan. North from Penelokan toward Kintamani you find the meru complex or nine temples of Pura Ulun Danu Batur. The 11-tiered temple is specifically for the Lake Goddess, also called Ida Ratu Ayu Dalem Pingit, who is the provider of irrigation water for the crops on Mount Batur. Best recommendation is an organized day trip from a tourist center such as Candi Dasa, Ubud, Sanur, Kuta, Nusa Dua, or Lovina. If driving, take the road north from Rendang and turn about 1.8 miles (3 km) down the road on your right. Surface of the road is reported to be good. The walk up from the parking area is steep, but motorcyclists can be hired to take you up.

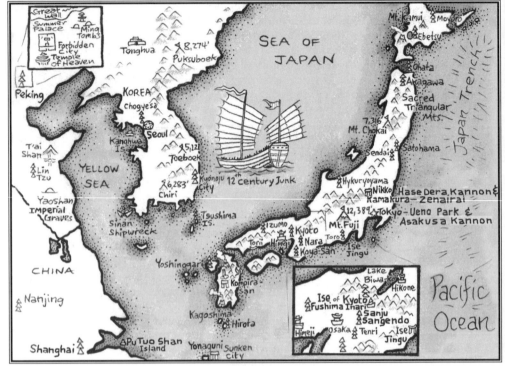

JAPAN

Goddess continued moving and shaping as she traveled across the seas with sailors and laid claim to the sacred pillars, trees, lakes, mountains, islands, and forests of Japan. Much later her worship began thriving in temples, hearths, and shrines. Her essence captured the psyche and influenced the spiritual practice of the shamaness of the nature-oriented Shinto, Taoist, Buddhist, Hindu, and the indigenous Ainu. She is indispensable, shaping cultures such as Japan's mystical origins of creation, through the pre-history of the Joman Period dating back 12,500 to 14,500 BCE. Today her symbol, the rising sun of Amaterasu, is proudly displayed on Japan's national flag! As a testament to her diversity and all embracing love, she is believed to have miraculously appeared in her aspect of Mary, the Mother of Jesus, in non-Christian Akita, Japan. During this Marian apparition she was known to provide devotees with messages and prophecies, while a statue at the site was believed to have wondrously shed tears, and oozed a reddish-brown, blood-like fluid.

Ise Jingu

On par with the Saudi Arabian holy city of Mecca, millions of Japanese believe strongly that it is their duty to make a pilgrimage to Ise, at least once in their lifetime. The most sacred of all Shinto shrines, Ise Jingu is sacred to both Amaterasu, the Sun Goddess, and Toyouke, the Rice Goddess. Although it is Amaterasu who is the primary deity, or *kami,* within the Shinto faith, Ise Jingu represents the indigenous nature of Japanese spirituality. Amaterasu, also called Amaterasu-omikami, has had an earthly abode in the inner shrine at the Ise Jingu shrine for

2,000 years. While her celestial home in the heavens represents the life and light of the world, and the highest manifestation of *kunitokotachi*, she is worshipped as the unseen spirit of the universe, and it is through her guidance that they have developed their civilization, and created a way of life.

There are two main sanctuaries at Ise Jingu that comprise the inner and outer shrines, the *naiku* and *geku*. Also called Kotaijingu and Tououkedaijingu, respectively, each is comprised of three sections separated by a fence, the most interior shrine open only to Shinto clergy and reminiscent of ancient Egyptian temples in design and practice. This innermost building of the naiku is believed to house Amaterasu's earthly representation, a mirror. In fact, the mirror is believed to be the very one Amaterasu gave her grandson. It is rarely seen, available only to high-ranking clergy and the Emperor. To the left of the main sanctuary of the naiku is a small building in which at least one priest remains at all times as a guardian to protect the august mirror of Amaterasu.

Statues or imagery of Amaterasu are rare and only come into use much later with Buddhist influence. Today, as in ancient times, Amaterasu is traditionally depicted on *kami-dana,* or altars*,* by the Japanese kanji character for her name, or by the symbol of the mirror, considered a *goshintai,* or object into which she can descend. The mirror is also the symbol for the imperial sovereignty of the royal family, who claimed to have descended from Amaterasu. According to Victor Harris, ancient stone circles within shrine grounds at Ise confirm the continuation of religious customs going back to the Joman Period. In her earliest veneration, Amaterasu was sanctified in the form of a sacred pillar.

The outer shrine at Ise, was founded 1,500 years ago, and is dedicated to the Rice Goddess. Called Toyouke Omikami, she is charged with the task of providing food for Amaterasu. Considered an agricultural goddess, she oversees food, clothing, and shelter. The outer shrine was built by the Emperor Yuryaki. He believed Amaterasu spoke to him in a dream saying she could not properly secure her meals, and asked that Toyouke be brought to Ise to oversee her nourishment. The emperor obeyed the ancestor deity and built the Geku. The rest is history.

Set adjacent to the sacred Isuzu River, among a thick and towering ancient cypress forest, the shrine feels perfectly located for a faith whose essence lies in nature worship, or gratitude toward nature. Ceremonies are performed daily, with the sacred rice and vegetables grown on the sacred grounds, which have been watered from the sacred Isuzu River, utilized as offerings to the Divine Goddess, Amaterasu. Here the oldest traditions, rituals, and architecture are preserved. Within and around the sanctuary are several auxiliary shrines dedicated to many Shinto deities. Adjacent the naiku is the shrine of Aramatsuri-no-miya which enshrines a separate (some say more aggressive) aspect of Amaterasu. Nearby are shrines for her parents, Izanagi and Izanami, her sibling, Tsukiyomi-no-kami,

▲ Approaching the Amaterasu Temple at Ise Jingu.

the Moon Goddess (sometimes depicted as male) who presides over the world of night, and shrines for the deities of the wind. The sacred stables for Amaterasu's beloved white horses and the architecture of her own temple bring to mind interesting associations with the Divine Feminine farther to the West. Curiously, Marija Gimbutas cites patriarchal Indo-European mythology wherein the prime role of the horse, particularly the white horse, is a sacred and sacrificial animal, and the incarnation of divine power of the shining sky god. Here it would seem a gender reversal occurred in early matriarchally-oriented Japan, as this sacred white horse imagery is instead associated with the divine female of the heavens. Another example is Amaterasu, provider of sustenance, has her temple built in the configuration of the early rice granaries, coincidently (or is it?) reflective of Sumerian Inanna, whose symbol was sometimes seen as the storehouse.

Amaterasu is the daughter of the kamis, Izanami-no-mikoto (She Who Invites), and her male partner Izanagi-no-mikoto (He Who Invites), cocreators of the Japanese islands, other deities, and humankind. Izanagi is believed to have birthed Amaterasu from his left eye, though other myths have her birthed from Izanami's menstrual blood. The divine couple is represented on earth as sacred rocks called Meoto Iwa, or Wedded Rocks, connected together by a sacred rope made of rice straw called a *shimenawa*. They can be found just off the beach of Futami, a small town near Ise.

Finally, Ise is a marker for cultural diffusionists, the belief that at times something cannot be absolutely proven, yet circumstances require some supposition, conjecture and analogy. At Ise we find a curious "OOPA," or Out Of Place Artifact. The Kagome Crest at the Ise Shrine looks like a Star of David. It is just one of the many symbols and associations some researchers have used to make a case for the ancient Japanese being a lost tribe of Israel. Some have drawn comparison between Amaterasu and the Israelite goddess Ashtaroath. Other startling similarities between ancient Japanese and ancient Israelites involve language, names, laws, folk songs, ancient stories, and customs, according to some, too numerous to be a coincidence. In any event, this curious theory makes for interesting research!

Getting to Ise Jingu

Take the "Mie" rapid train from the city of Nagoya to Ise Jingu with trains departing often throughout the day. There are also options from Osaka and Kyoto, but less frequently. Once at Ise, walk out the front door of the train station, cross the street and follow the signs to the Grand Shrine of Amaterasu. A three block walk will take you to the geku, or outer shrine. After visiting there, come back outside the sanctuary, cross the street and take bus #52 or #55 for a 15-minute ride to the inner shrine or naiku.

Goddess Focus
Joman Earth Goddess

Joman culture, a peaceful, hunter-gatherer society which made clay images of the Earth Mother, derives its name from the cord-marked patterns found on dated pottery shards. Much of the pottery has a distinctive style and complex patterning, some made with protuberances reminiscent of flames called *umataka*.

Other clay images were that of women called *dogu*, shown pregnant or depicted in the act of giving birth. Female images were designed with a left hand on their abdomen as if protecting the fetus, while the right hand soothingly stroked the back under the strain of impending motherhood. Interesting large-eyed female figures called *jiboshin* are believed to be representations of the Earth Mother. Snakes were another sacred theme recurring on Joman pottery, often shown coiled in the hair, possibly depicting an overlap with worship of the Earth Mother and her snake cult giving assistance with childbirth.

Like the matriarchal families living in the Yongning Region of Yunnan Province today, or the 6,000 year-old matriarchal Yangshao culture excavated from Banpo Village, outside Xian, in the Shaanxi Province of China, the even older Joman Period of Japanese history (dating from 14,500 — 12,500 BCE) may also have been inclined toward matriarchy. At a time when there was still a land bridge connecting Japan with the continent of Asia, it is believed the Joman, ancestors of the later indigenous Ainu, might have been related to immigrants from Polynesia, Korea, and Siberia.

Scholars believe the Joman worshipped the sun and moon and held fire to be sacred. This supports the belief that their descendants, the Ainu, later worshipped the fire Goddess Fuchi, and may have been the first to worship the Sun Goddess Amaterasu. A culture that learned by oral tradition and memory, they celebrated rituals that marked life passages such as birth, marriage, and death, as well as roles within society, including the community's

▲ A statue of the Joman Earth Goddess.

relationship with nature. This latter element, along with ancestor worship and particular attention to funerary ritual may have been the precursors to establishing Shinto beliefs. Village configurations suggest communities were oriented to worship a mountain, such as Mount Fuji, where the fire Goddess Fuchi was venerated. Archaeological remains also suggest to anthropologists the Joman had parturition and menstruation houses to isolate women during what was perceived as a mystical and powerful time. This isolation also protected others within the village, namely the men, who were perhaps seen as less magically endowed. The Joman Period lasted at least 10,000 years, disappearing about 300 BCE with the coming of the Yayoi agricultural society.

Hase Dera Kannon Temple

Kannon is honored by legions at Hase Dera in Kamakura where her essence is venerated in the largest wooden statue in Japan (28-foot, 9-m) which has only recently been shown to the public. Gazing upon her towering gold leaf image, feeling the energy of the temple, soaking in the ambiance of this sacred place, even the most detached visitor might be moved to emotion. This temple complex is set on a high hill with a view of the town below and the ocean beyond, in keeping with Japanese tradition of placing sacred sites in natural splendor, particularly on mountains, which are believed to have a sacred character. Kannon's history at this temple dates back to the year 721. A monk carved two images from a camphor tree. One was placed in a shrine in Nara, the other set adrift in the ocean to find the place it was most needed. It is said the image of Kannon appeared here in Kamakura 16 years later, and in Hase Dera she sits. This statue is unique in that it is the only one which holds a lotus in her left hand and the cane of the Buddha Jizo in her right. Kannon may bestow upon practitioners a double scoop of both Buddha Jizo's mercy (deity of compassion) as well as her own.

Inside the Kannon Hall resides the statue of the eleven-faced Hase Kannon, displaying different expressions said to represent the eleven different aspects of a bodhisattva, a being striving for the enlightenment of Buddha. The many faces also symbolize her capability to hear and answer the multitude of prayers of humankind. Alongside the main Kannon Hall is the Benzaiten Hall and Grotto, dedicated to the Goddess Benzaiten (Benten), the only female of the Seven Gods of Happiness and Good Luck. She is the goddess of love, beauty, wealth, and creative endeavors. She is often depicted playing a musical instrument. Within the cave-like grotto of Benzaiten are carved images of herself and her sixteen children, described as her servants and minor gods. Within one small room of her grotto are many small carved wooden images of Benten, or Benzaiten, on which devotees write their name and their wish, leaving it behind in the grotto, trusting in the Goddess to answer their prayers. An eight-armed image of Benten resides in her hall beside the Hosho Pond.

▲ The 28-foot gold leaf Kannon statue residing within the Hase Dera Temple astounds visitors.

Another area of the temple complex is the Treasury to the left of Kannon Hall where 33 different aspects of Kannon can be visited. The Jizo Hall, named for the aforementioned deity Jizo, is where women place small images of Jizo which represent their miscarried, stillborn, or aborted babies. On the grounds are additional temples to other deities including the Rice Goddess Inari, a beautiful koi pond, numerous statuary, and the always present ema station where petitioners write their desires on wooden plates and leave them at the temple in hopes their prayers will be answered. On the 18th of every month a special Kannon ceremony is held here.

Hase Dera is the fourth stop on the Bando route of 33 pilgrimage shrines of Kannon in Kamakura, located in the Kanto area of Japan. Here as with most Buddhist temples, the customary manner of prayer is to approach the temple and to purify oneself with the smoke of the incense usually just outside the main sanctuary. Next, the devotee rings the bell or gong that is usually present to announce one's presence. At this point, worshippers make their prayers and bow, then leaving their offerings before departing. Visitors can also buy talismans for good health, business success, academic excellence, love, or traffic safety. They can avail themselves of the tradition of drawing fortune sticks from a special container. The person seeking divination shakes a can of numbered sticks until one falls from a small hole. The number on the stick corresponds to a written fortune handed out by the temple attendant.

Getting to the Hase Dera Kannon Temple

The city of Kamakura where the Hase Dera Kannon Temple is located is a quick ride from Tokyo on the JR Railway. Once arriving in Kamakura, transfer to the Enoden line with its streetcar-like trains. Get off at the Hase station. From there, the temple is a five minute walk, but you might need a Japanese/English map. Other options are taking bus #2 to the Hase Kannon stop, or hiring a taxi.

Goddess Focus
Ainu & the Fire Goddess

The Ainu, descendants of the matriarchal Joman Period, are indigenous Japanese who live in northern Hokkaido. They worshipped the sun, moon, bears, and the Fire Goddess, Fuchi, also called Huchi or Apermeru-ko-yan-mat, who was a goddess of the hearth. She was venerated atop Mount Fuji as Sengen-sama, an intermediary between deities and humans. An animistic people, their culture, like many other ancient people across Europe, Asia, and North America, was centered on a bear cult even as recently as the 20th century. The bear was considered a gift from the gods, providing meat and fur for warmth, and bear cubs were thought to be children of the gods. Ainu folk tales relate the bear as being half-human because a village chief's son married the bear-goddess. In ancient times, an *iyo-mante* ritual of rebirth, started with a prayer to Fuchi, then a female bear would be sacrificed to send her spirit back to the mountain gods. Fortunately, today, bears are no longer ritually sacrificed but are instead exhibited in places such as the Noboribetsu Bear Park.

Each Ainu's home had a fireplace, the home of Fuchi. People made shaved sticks, or *inaws*, in the shape of birds that might carry their prayers to the gods. These inaw were dedicated to Fuchi and placed in the northeast corner of the hearth

▲ This 19th century photo shows an Ainu family in the far north of Japan.

box. According to scholar E. Ohnuki-Tierney, a female shaman, or *tusu-kur*, would go into a trance during nighttime rituals within a house which is considered a miniature universe and abode of Fuchi, or Grandmother Hearth, the most powerful deity in the Ainu pantheon. The female principal of the Ainu is evident in the rites being held within the home, the domain of the women, near the hearth where Fuchi, the female counterpart of the bear deity resides and where the woman cooks. Cooking is considered a shamanistic act of healing, i.e., the same symbolic purpose as the bear ceremony — using deities and nature for human spiritual and physical nourishment.

Ohnuki-Tierney explains that although women are lower in status than men and the smell of women's menstrual or parturient blood was considered repulsive, during times of epidemic, the blood was considered an extraordinarily powerful antidote. Hunters have been known to carry undergarments of their mother or sister to ward off demons or dangerous deities. Women past the age of menstruation are elevated in status, and are the sacred caretakers of bear cubs. That being said, generosity is important among the Ainu and the roles of men and women are complementary. Men cannot start a healing process or make important decisions without first consulting a female shaman for her diagnosis or prognosis. Expert Kyosuke Kindaichi states "almost all females were mediums in the Ainu society until recently, without even asking the elders ... The females were considered chosen to cook sacred food for the gods, as well as be possessed and give revelations." The belt of a shamaness served practical and esoteric purposes and was buried with her. Ainu women handed down to descendants in their matrilineal line their work tools, clothing patterns and styles of embroidery, as well as a ritual menstruation belt worn beneath their clothes. Sacred sites of the Ainu were mountains such as Fuji and Daisetsu, the highest peak in Hokkaido, as well as altar-like places of offerings called *nusa*.

Zenairai Benten Money Washing Shrine

Benten, whose messenger is a white serpent, is honored at this folk shrine where visitors come to literally wash their money in the shrine's sacred spring so abundance might come to them two-fold. Here at the Zenairai Benten temple (*zenairai* translates to "coin washing") rumor has it, the magic works! Benten or Benzaiten is a blend of Shinto kami and Buddhist deity, one of the *shichifukujin*, or Seven Lucky Gods, and a derivative of the Hindu river goddess Sarasvati. She is often depicted with a *biwa*, or musical lute, or a snake. The shrine is dedicated to Benten who is associated with snakes because the temple founder had a divinely inspired dream in the year of the snake, in the month of the snake and on the day of the snake, in which he was instructed to build a temple to help bring peace to the country. Offerings here are made not only to Benten but also to her snake as visitors leave eggs, the snake's favorite food. One of the merchants adjacent to the shrine has a live albino snake as part of his *kamidana,* or altar, in his shop. Author Buffie Johnson names Benten's serpent deity Uga, of the Uga-Jin serpent cult, and says his image decorates the chignon of the Goddess,

▲ A rock-cut tunnel leads to the Zenairai Benten Money Washing Shrine.

sometimes revered as the Japanese Goddess of Love. His altars were allowed to fall into ruin with the rise of Buddhism which found the serpent god barbaric. According to Martha Ann and Dorothy Myers Imel, Benten was believed to take the form of a dragon woman and swam under the islands of Japan, mating with the white snakes that lived there. She did this to prevent earthquakes that could injure her followers.

When visitors come upon the temple, they first see a red torii gate marking the entrance into a tunnel carved through a mountain. After a short walk into the tunnel visitors see some of the more unusual accouterments of a sacred place where Shinto and Buddhism are both practiced in one place: incense, purification font, talisman merchants, and a Buddhist temple complete with Shinto *gohei,* the zigzag straw or hemp ornaments with the appearance of thunderbolts, which signifies that the space is sacred, or the presence of the kami is within. Farther back is the sacred spring where the money washing takes place in a small grotto-like cavern within the mountain. Bamboo baskets and ladles are provided for people to rinse their currency. Colorful straw and hemp talismans hang from the ceiling of the grotto which is also filled with candles. Visible across the sacred spring are statues of Kwan Yin / Kannon and serpents. Just to the right of the money washing grotto is an altar with a mirror as its central object. Within walking distance of the shrine along the path beyond the vendor booths is a path that leads to an Inari shrine of the Rice Goddess, and farther along, a hiking path is available that connects the shrine with the Great Buddha.

Getting to Zenairai Benten

While some say it is a 25-minute walk from the Kamakura station, signage is not easily found and is not always in English. Taxi is the best recommendation to reach the shrine located in a residential area of Kamakura. The annual event of the shrine is Benten Matsuri, or festival, on the first Serpent Day of February.

Fushimi Inari Taisha Shrine

Inari, the Rice Goddess of Japan, is celebrated by 10 million Shinto and Buddhist visitors praying for abundance and prosperity as they follow in the footsteps of their ancestors who visited this 8th century shrine south of Kyoto.

Thousands of Inari shrines such as this are found throughout Japan and are easily recognizable by the presence of the guardian foxes, messengers of the kami, or to some the actual rice deity. Toward understanding the significance between crop and deity scholar Roy Hamilton explains, "across a broad spectrum of Southeast Asian cultures with diverse religious traditions, rice is held to have originated through the activities of a goddess. Secondly, the Rice Goddess herself is sacrificed and the rice produced from her body. Thirdly, due to its origin directly from the body of the Rice Goddess, rice itself is sacred and divine. Finally, the life cycle and fertility of the rice plants are equated with the life cycle and fertility of the Rice Goddess."

Rice was introduced to the Japanese islands 3,000 years ago. Besides being food rice is made into straw and used to make many sacred objects including gohei rope that marks off sacred boundaries where negativity may not enter, called gohei. According to Toshiyuki Sano, it is not surprising this cultural symbol and its appurtenances appear as motifs in the decoration of cloth and clothing, one of the most important of Japanese art forms. It became the custom to wrap the body with rice-related images, but as these images were almost exclusively on women's garments, it seems to have connected female fertility with the rice cycle. Hamilton believes Inari to have both male and female forms, and is represented in both Shinto and Buddhist traditions in Japan. Originally Inari did not have a specific gender — female gender rose later in relationship to rice and fertility customs while male aspects were more closely linked with the spread of Buddhism. Depictions of Inari can be of an old man holding rice panicles, a young goddess, or an androgynous bodhisattva astride a white fox. Hamilton explains that many devout Inari worshippers are led by charismatic women reminiscent of shamanic traditions, and these groups, though marginalized by the male dominated Shinto establishment, make pilgrimages to Inari shrines, particularly Fushimi Inari.

Scholar Patricia Monaghan reports interesting anecdotes about Inari the rice goddess. She was said to enjoy wrapping herself in a fox's body, or in the form of a human woman so she could pleasure herself with men, who were then rewarded with great rice crops. One such man was awarded for his discretion concerning their affair when Inari caused his crop to grow upside-down thus enabling him to avoid the rice tax. Another fun story has Inari as a living woman who had the ability to turn herself into a flying fox, but the story ends badly when an enemy thwarted her magic causing her to lose her powers and some say her life.

Just outside of the Kyoto city center, this Inari shrine is famous for the thousands of red tori gates that follow the path up the mountainside. Devotees practice a specific form of worship by offering to the shrine a tori gate or a sacred stone called an *otsuka*. At last count there

▲ The Fushima Inari Taisha is one of the most popular temples to visit near Kyoto.

were about 10,000 tori gates and 20,000 otsuka within the shrine precincts. The vermilion color of the tori gates represents peace and good harvest while the bushy tails of the many foxes within the grounds symbolize fruitful years of rice. Two large foxes are found at the temple entrance. The stone in mouth of the one fox represents the spirit of the deities while the key between the jaws of another fox secured the rice granary. Along the sloping mountain paths are scattered shrines and statuary, including sacred spots dedicated to the Goddess Kannon, a Buddhist bodhisattva or bosatsu.

Shinto ceremonies such as the ones here at Fushimi Inari Taisha generally consist of four basic elements: purification, offerings, prayer, and a symbolic feast with devotees and the kami, which are practiced during traditional ceremonies throughout the year. More than 1,500,000 people come in prayer on New Year's Day for happiness and protection during the coming year. On January 5th, rituals are held offering sake on the sacred stones. January 12th is Hosha-sai, an archery ceremony that drives evil away, and May 3rd is Inari Sai, when those congregated express thanks for their prosperity, and five divine palanquins are carried in procession. June 10th is a rice planting festival for abundant harvests, and November 8th is the fire-burning festival in order to give thanks for an abundant harvest.

Getting to the Fushima Inari Taisha Temple

From Kyoto station, take the JR Nara line to the JR Inari Station, five minutes south of the Kyoto station. Exit the station, walk across the street and visitors will see before them the entrance to the shrine. Follow the cavern-like torii gates uphill to the shrine. It is also possible to ride a bike to the shrine, but a good map of Kyoto should be acquired first.

The Ise of Kyoto

The 1,500 year old Ise shrine of Amaterasu, Goddess of the Sun, divine child of the primordial gods, was built before the city of Kyoto, when the region was called *Yamashiro no Kuni*, or "Land of Mountain Castles." Here at what is often also called the Hyuga or Himukai shrine, Amaterasu is also evoked as Hino Omikami. Myths depict her as having supernatural powers, and she is said to have ruled the otherworld of over eight million Japanese gods. Later she gave the art of silk-farming and the five basic grains to man to nourish the earth and feed humanity. Martha and Dorothy Myers Imel describe Amaterasu as overseeing areas of education and knowledge, families, and tribes, and is considered to have both mother and guardian aspects. It is said the Sun Goddess sent her grandson to earth with the three holy talismans of Shinto, the mirror, the jewel, and the sword, to rule over men and civilize them.

Situated in a valley surrounded by holy mountains, the shrine is thick with groves of cypress, cedar, and pine trees. Smaller than the Grand Shrine of Ise Jingu, this "Jewel of the Sun" was once a major stop on the road that connected Kyoto and Edo (Tokyo). Today it has the feel of an unspoiled jewel tucked away in an intimate mountain hideout. The Shinto priest and caretaker of the shrine explained the outer shrine, or *geku,* was dedicated to Amaterasu's granddaughter, the inner shrine, or *naiku,* to Amaterasu herself. Unlike Ise Jingu, which is vast and spread out to accommodate the millions that visit here on pilgrimage annually, these shrines are smaller, within close proximity to one another, evoking a feeling of sacredness and intimacy.

SACRED PLACES OF GODDESS

Upon entering the Ise of Kyoto torii gates, the traditional approach to a shrine, is the area of ablution where visitors purify themselves by rinsing their mouths and hands with water. Once entering through the gate, which separates the mundane from holy precincts, visitors find larger shrines with altars not only to the Sun Goddess and her granddaughter, but smaller altars to the gods of sea travelers, prosperity, family safety, good luck, matchmaking, ease in child-bearing, artistic inspiration, and literary pursuits. A sacred spring separates the geku from naiku where some have said they have seen an apparition of a Shinto priest who still roams the grounds, caring for Amaterasu's sacred place. Even more special, secluded away off to the side, and up about 50 steps from the main shrine, is the *Iwato*, or sacred cave, evoking the myth of Amaterasu. (It should be noted there is also an Iwato near the Ise Jingu Grand Shrine, but it is not so easily found and visited.) Worship at a Shinto shrine is simple. One approaches the altar or shrine, bows twice deeply, claps twice, bows deeply again, then states their prayer. Following this, the worshipper places their offerings in the box provided. Shrine visitors write wishes on wooden plates called *ema* and leave them at the temple in hopes their wishes will come true. Paper fortune telling strips called *omikuji* are visible at most shrines. Visitors believe they can rid themselves of bad luck or bring themselves good fortune with this custom of tying the paper fortune strip to a tree, similar to the tradition of tying prayers to clooty trees in Ireland.

As in all Shinto shrines, talismans, or *mamori,* are available to the visitors to insure traffic safety, good health, business success, safe deliveries, and scholastic achievement. The holy shrine structures here are built according to ancient religious proscriptions in the architectural style called *shinmeitsukuri* Shinto, meaning "way of the gods." It is a faith without a founder or dogma so ceremonies are the people's highest expression of their faith in the kami. Some festivals or rituals performed here are the Wakamizu-sai, or New Year's First Water, commemorating the miracle during the reign of Emperor Seiwa when it was believed the waters from the shrine cured an epidemic. This spring is only one of three miracle founts in Kyoto. February celebrates Setsubun, Lunar New Year, when warding off evil, and seeking good fortune are prayed for in earnest. During this ceremony people enter the sacred cave and bow. With that bow, all ills of mind and body are purified, and the good graces of heaven pass through those in the cave. October 17th is the Feast of the Inner Shrine, or Kanname-sai. This ritual originates from the Ise Jingu Grand Shrine, and is the time when new offerings of sacred food are made to Amaterasu. Kagura dance dramas and Bugaku ancient court dances are also performed during these rites.

The stories of Amaterasu were written in the *Kojiki,* a sacred text known as the Record of Ancient Matters and in the *Nihongi,* the Chronicles of Japan. Contemporary Shinto is an outgrowth of these original myths of the kami just as the bible provides direction for Judeo-Christians, and the *Koran* for Muslims. In one myth similar to the Greek Goddess Demeter and the powerful but unrestrained Baubo, Amaterasu withdrew from the world causing the earth to become barren and bleak, only to reappear and restore fertility to the land in response to a raucous performance. According to the Kojiki, the Sun Goddess secluded herself in a cave to avoid her brother Susano-o-no-mikoto because his behavior had so distressed her. In some stories he sexually assaulted Amaterasu, and in other stories he tormented her and defecated beneath her seat in the palace. Retreating to the cave, she rolled a stone across the entrance, and by doing so, the light of world vanished. Numerous deities tried to convince Amaterasu to exit the cave as they enticed her with jewels, paper streamers, and mirrors they hung on a sacred tree near the cave entrance. Nothing worked until the bawdy dance antics of an unashamed Ama-no-Uzume finally lured the Sun Goddess from her seclusion. Amaterasu peeked out from behind the stone, her curiosity piqued by the laughter and clapping inspired from Uzume's performance, particularly when she lifted her skirt to show her yoni. As her face slowly was seen emerging from the cave, the Sun Goddess caught sight of her own image in a bronze mirror, and

▲ The Ise of Kyoto is devoted to Amaterasu.

dazzled by her own radiance, restored light and fecundity to the world. This myth reflects an aspect of Amaterasu's association with a mirror and offers a glimpse at the power and awe inspired by the yoni across cultures as a catalyst for creation, change, healing, or protection. In later stories, Amaterasu gave a mirror to her grandson to enable him to remember her divine form. (This is in contrast to Zen Buddhism where a mirror reveals the nature of the object it reflects). It is said the very mirror Amaterasu gave her grandson is the one preserved at the inner shrine, or holy of holies at Ise. The aforementioned dance of Uzume was the predecessor of today's sacred dance drama called the Kagura ritual, of which there are 35 types. One type, which has been enacted yearly since the earliest of times, has a priestess play the part of Uzume, exposing her yoni to assembled temple followers. This heavily veiled custom, originally intended to worship female sexuality, and the regenerative and magical power of the female genitals to orchestrate change, has unfortunately also inspired the more profane *tokudashi*, coarsely called "cunt stunts," performed in men's clubs of Japan's "red-light districts," where female performers expose their yoni from the stage to curious clientele sometimes equipped with tiny flashlights.

Getting to the Ise of Kyoto

Located off the Tozai Subway Line, the shrine is walking distance from the Keage subway stop. After exiting the Keage station, walk across the street and go right. Follow the sidewalk until you reach a sign for the temple that leads uphill and through a residential area. The shrine will be to your left, and the entrance marked by the tori gate and purification fount. Bring your walking shoes!

Goddess Focus
The Shamaness and Anime

Has girl power come full circle? During Japan's early history society was comfortable with female rule. Empress Himiko, a priestess-shamaness, closely associated with the Sun Goddess Amaterasu, and a descendant of the matriarchally inclined Joman culture, united Japan in the second century. Other ruling queens such as Empress Jingu followed in her footsteps with great success, some embracing both the Buddhist and Shinto faiths. Within Ainu culture, the pattern continues with the female shaman, considered the more powerful gender, endowed with the natural gift of prophecy.

With the coming of Buddhism centuries ago, women's place in society took a bad turn when female authority began to be suppressed. Many Buddhists at that time believed women were not to be trusted and were deemed beyond salvation. Matriarchal societies and the role of women diminished, though folk religions and worship of Amaterasu, the Great Sun Goddess Shining in Heaven, central figure of the Shinto pantheon, prevailed. Currently Japan is frequently viewed as a nation dominated by patriarchy and many in Japan and abroad believe roles of women have not achieved a level of status equal to that of men in spite of the obvious devotion to the many Shinto, Tao, Ainu, and Buddhist bosatsu, bodhisattvas and goddesses, perhaps suggesting the continued desire for a feminine face of God. Yet within this male dominated culture, the possible yearning for female influence may be on the rise.

Today the female shaman, also called *itako* woman or *miko*, dominates in India, Korea, and Japan. In Okinawa, the shaman-priestesses, referred to as *yuta* or *kaminchu*, retain their mystical and spiritual power as they practice a synchronized blend of ancestor worship, and a reverence for Mother Nature, or Goddess, while sometimes still influenced by Buddhism and Shinto. Kaminchu

officiated at religious rites while yuta offer spiritual guidance gleaned from the spirit world. According to Naomi Ozaniec, one such shamaness, Kitamura Sayo, called Ogamisama, or great goddess by her followers, established Tensho Kotai Jingukyo, the Dancing Religion. She was renowned for her miracles and is today worshipped as a living goddess even after her death in 1967. Kyoko Motomochi Nakamura tells us Sayo was closely associated with Amaterasu and the shrine of Ise, believing herself heir of the Sun Goddess, and her body the temple where Amaterasu resided.

▲ An illustrated shaman in a ritual dance.

Reflecting on this elevated status of female power to guide and protect, it is interesting to note that the younger generation of Japanese men and women are being drawn to anime characters that depict female power saving the world. Perhaps harkening back to Japan's ancient past, it is an intriguing phenomenology that a country whose ancient roots began with female divinity and rule, yet became patriarchal over time, would now see a selective resurgence of female power in film, the vehicle of modern mythology. Girl power has been on the rise with characters in such series as "Oh My Goddess," "Sailor Moon," "Princess Mononoke," "Devil Hunter Yohko," "Vampire Princess," and "Shrine Maidens of the Morning Mist" where young women wielding magic and weapons save the world in each episode. While certainly a reflection of Japan's shamanistic heritage, might this also be an unconscious (or conscious?) manifestation of this society's desire for a return to a time of equality and elevated status for women?

Sanju Sangendo

Kannon, mother of the human race, the Goddess of Mercy and Compassion, the "Mary of the Orient," is represented at Sanju Sangendo where she is depicted 1001 times in 1001 cypress-wood statues covered in gold leaf. Her statues, standing 10 rows deep, 50 statues per row on either side of one gigantic seated *joroku,* or double life-sized thousand-armed Kannon as a central image. These impressive statues were made in the 12th and 13th centuries. When looked upon closely, subtle differences begin to reveal themselves in each statue. Kannon, or Kwan Yin as she is called in China, is represented here in her aspect as Juichimen Senju Kannon, the 11-headed, 1,000-armed Goddess. Around the crown of her head 11 small faces are depicted. She is said to be able to save 1,000 worlds and has the hands to do it! She has 42 arms, two of which are regular arms. The remaining 40 arms represent the 25 Buddhist worlds (40 x 25 = 1000) with every hand having the power to save 25 worlds. In the grip of these many hands are found objects which might fight off all manner of misfortune that may befall humanity: a rosary, trident, sword, lotus, bow and arrow, ax, mirror, wheel, bell, and statues of Amida.

Sanju Sangendo translates into Hall of 33 Bays or spaces between the pillars in front of the main altar. This number is also significant to Kannon who can manifest into 33 different aspects, certainly a Goddess for any occasion, who hears the prayers of the world. It is believed she grants the wishes of those who repeatedly chant her name. The temple brochure boasts with 1001 Kannons, each capable of 33 aspects, result in 33,033 manifestations of the Bodhisattva virtually residing at Sanju Sangendo. These many images are intended to create for the visitor a

▲ Exactly 1001 statues of Kannon grace the inside of the Sanju Sangendo Temple.

sense of intimacy with Kannon. Perhaps one can even find a face of a loved one among her many faces. All kidding aside, this is quite an awesome place worthy of a much loved and honored Goddess! In addition to the 1001 Kannons here, there are 28 statues of her attendant deities, who protect believers from many obstacles and save them from danger.

Kannon, like the Virgin Mary, is worshipped by all classes and genders, monastic and lay people, rich and poor. She is the most beloved of the Asian deities, a universal savior who has brought a kinder and gentler feminine face to Buddhism and Confucianism. The 1001 statues of Kannon are housed here in the longest wooden building in Japan, measuring almost 400 feet (120 m) long. The length of the building has inspired annual archery contests since the 1600s when young women celebrating Coming of Age Day would arrive attired in beautiful traditional dresses and competed against each other with bow and arrow.

This temple is located in eastern Kyoto with the Kyoto National Museum just across the street and certainly worthy of a visit. Within walking distance of Sanju Sangendo are the Ryozen Kannon and the Rokuharamitsuji temples. The Ryozen temple, set against the backdrop of an evergreen-covered mountain range, is a spectacular 500 ton (4,530 kg), 80 foot (24 m) tall image of Kannon seated atop the building housing her shrine. The temple was built to commemorate the sacrifice of Japanese unknown soldiers of World War II. The Rokuharamitsuji temple is number 17 of 33 on the pilgrimage, or *junrei* route of 33 Kannon temples in the Kansai region of Japan. Devotees believe making the circuit of shrines in the proper order will bring the worshipper everlasting life. Rokuharamitsuji is known as a temple for the repose of the souls of those people who have no living relatives. Inside the main hall are numerous images of the 11-faced Kannon along with a larger-than-life statue of the Goddess in the outer courtyard.

Getting to Sanju Sangendo

Taking a bus in Kyoto is easier than one might think. Signs are easily discernible at bus stops, and many of the shrines are easily reached by walking a few blocks from the bus stop. To reach Sanjusangendo, take either bus 206 or 208 which will stop either alongside the temple or across the street from the Kyoto National Museum. Kyoto is also a great city to ride a bike. Bicycle rental shops can be found in many locations downtown.

Asakusa Kannon Temple

Millions of faithful annually visit Asakusa Kannon, also called Sensoji, making it the most famous center of Kannon worship in Japan. The Tokyo temple saw its beginning around 628 CE when fishermen found a small gold statue in their nets. The statue was later enshrined in the first of several sanctuaries built over the years in this general area. Surviving fires and war, the Buddhist goddess Kannon has continually been worshipped here since the temple's inception. One sutra is known to say "as soon as peoples' cries of agony reach Kannon, the bodhisattva takes pity on them and saves them from the tortures of Hell. Devotees believe with sincere prayers offered to Kannon, fire cannot burn them, and water cannot drown them." She is believed to be the spiritual child of Amida, sometimes appearing as male, more often female, androgynous, even with a small mustache. The Buddhist nun, Chujo Hime, is said to be an incarnation of Kannon. Here is another example of the Buddhist and Shinto faiths existing alongside each other for the benefit of the faithful who most times easily assimilate both in their lifestyle.

On the grounds are also found a temple to the Rice Goddess Inari, and to the Shinto Goddess Benten. Inari's name symbolizes her importance (*ina* means rice, *naru* means to grow) and role to her people. Under Buddhist influence Inari is also recognized as Dakiniten (as in Tibetan Dakini) a feminine guardian

▲ The Asakusa Kannon Temple is one of the top religious attractions in Tokyo.

of Buddhist wisdom and initiation. The Hikan Inari shrine, established in 1854 CE by a local fireman, contains numerous clay images of foxes, and messengers of the deity.

Bentendo Hall enshrines an image of Benten, goddess of music, creativity, and riches who is associated with the Hindu Goddess Sarasvati. She is the patroness of geishas and oversees speech, learning, and eloquence. She is believed to be able to assume the form of a snake which represents eternal life to the Japanese. It is thought the shedding of the snake skin is representative of this immortality, and having a shed skin in one's possession is considered a talisman of good luck and prosperity.

At the Kaminarimon, or thunder gate, visitors first approach Asakusa. Within the gate they see a central giant red lantern. To the left is Raijin, god of thunder, and to the right Fujin, god of wind. Behind these statues are statues of the dragon gods. Proceeding through this front gate, visitors are distracted by dozens of stalls for souvenirs — actually the best tourist shopping in Tokyo! After that obstacle course is mastered, one naturally approaches the Hozomon Gate containing rare sutras printed in 14th century China. Beyond is the Gokuden, or main sanctuary, where it is believed the riverside statue of Kannon found in 628 is enshrined. Monks chant sutras three times a day. Visitors purify themselves in the incense smoke before entering the temple then throw coins in the offertory box after making a petition to the Goddess that their prayers be answered. Talismans and candles can be purchased. The Yogodo Hall is another building on the compound dedicated to Kannon and eight other deities. Throughout the temple precinct are many pagodas, shrines, halls, and a lovely pond.

Asakusa, a main pilgrimage center since the 7th century, has a circus-like atmosphere and is number 13 of 33 on the contemporary Bando pilgrimage route. Outside the main gates are stalls of merchants with souvenir shoppers bursting out of their tiny shops. With millions visiting each month, no wonder the Buddhist monks appear tired of the parade of faces constantly entering, taking pictures, making purchases, praying, buying fortunes and asking silly questions. The temple feels more like a tourist attraction than a holy place, though devotees would probably feel that Kannon, in her divine wisdom, is a patient mother, and embraces even her most unruly children with kindness and mercy.

Getting to the Asakusa Kannon Temple

Located in the northeastern part of Tokyo in the area called Asakusa, the shrine is easily reached by many subway and train lines such as the Ginza or Toei Asakusa lines. Just get off at the Asakusa station and signs in the subway or train station lead you toward the temple which is a very short walk from the station. If time is not a problem, there is water taxi that runs between Asakusa, Hinode pier, and Odaiba on the Sumida River. It takes about 40 minutes, but the ride is an interesting alternative to subway and bus. Finally, every 30 minutes there is a double-decker bus that runs between Asakusa and Ueno stations that stops close to the Thunder Gate of Asakusa/Senso-ji.

Ueno Park

As Japan's largest urban park, this 300-acre (122-ha) complex consists of one main temple and 36 subsidiary temples right in the heart of Tokyo. Ueno Park is home to several temples and shrines dedicated to both Buddhist and Shinto goddesses: Kannon, Benten, and Inari. Kiyomizu Kannon-do Temple, a miniature of the Kiyomizu Temple in Kyoto, is one of the oldest temples in Tokyo. Established in 1631, it overlooks Shinobazu Pond and enshrines Kosodate Kannon, in her aspect as protectress of women and children. Women hoping to become pregnant come to this shrine and pray to Kannon for fertility and safe deliveries. Those whose prayers have been answered return bringing dolls which are placed in the temple to the right of the main altar and can be seen by visitors when they enter to pray. The dolls are symbols of their children or children they hope to someday have.

▲ Within Tokyo's Ueno Park are several shrines dedicated to Asian Goddesses.

On September 25th a service is held for all the dolls which are then cremated. Kannon, who is associated with the Chinese Kwan Yin, though usually depicted as pious and proper, has been shown in some paintings and statues of certain Japanese sects to raise her hem a la Baubo and Uzume, perhaps suggesting she too is a link in the chain of Divine Females, a Creatrix, with the power of the female genitals as a catalyst for change. Her mantra, or *shingon,* "Om Aro Rykya Sowaka Kannon" is believed to ward off danger, and lend assistance to her devoted. Her statues are depicted here in several aspects including one with a thousand arms and eyes, many faces, or the version venerated by farmers, and herders where Kannon is depicted with a horse atop her head.

Outside the temple is the ablution font for individual purification in front of the shrine. Using the provided ladle, devotees thoroughly rinse out the inside of their mouths, discarding the water on the white rocks alongside the water basin. After rinsing their hands, they habitually allow the water flow back over the ladle where it has been held. As one approaches the temple, it is customary, devotee or tourist alike, to sound the gong. Worshippers believe the gong announces their presence before the deity. Again, regardless of religious persuasion, it is a matter of respect to take off your shoes before entering the shrine. An interesting symbol to note at the highest peak of the exterior of the temple and noticeable from the ablution font is the ancient swastika with its roots originating in early Earth

Mother culture. Scholar Barbara Walker states that this ancient religious symbol has been in use since 10,000 BCE. In Sanskrit the swastika represents "amen" or "so be it." The swastika has been on images of Buddha, coinage in India, and Roman figures of Goddesses. It has been on artifacts from the 13th century BCE onward in Asia Minor, Greece, China, Persia, Libya, Scandinavia, Britain, and Iceland long before a version of the symbol was co-opted by the Nazi party of Germany who used it to instill fear in the hearts and minds of millions.

A short walk from the Kannon temple toward the Shinobazu Pond one finds a small Inari shrine dedicated to the Rice Goddess. It's unmistakable because of the foxes wearing red bibs who are messengers of the deity, and the torii gate. Adelle Getty makes an interesting, and perhaps Western association with Goddess and the oft seen torii arch, which delineates sacred space from the mundane, seeing it as a symbol for the Great Mother. On the feast day of the dead, Japanese fill thousands of little boats with food and messages intended for departed souls. The spirits of the departed are invited to enter the boats which are gently set free upon the regenerating water and sail through the gateway of a torii arch (when it spans water). In this context, the torii arch is an exit and entrance, leading only back to the Mother of Life, making it a perfect sanctuary for wandering souls. It is also considered by some as a symbol of the yoni, a gateway of life and death. As for Inari, who is sometimes seen as a male deity, authors Martha Ann and Dorothy Myers Imel see her as female, and a Goddess of commerce, travel, wealth, and life. They say she is invoked for prosperity and long life, sometimes characterized as a Shinto vixen goddess associated with rice and smith craft who is prayed to for successful love relationships.

Ueno Park (pronounced way-no) provides the perfect setting for a Benten shrines being adjacent to or over water. A bit further toward the entrance to the Shinobazu Pond is the walkway leading to the Benten-jima Temple flanked on either side by concrete lanterns commonly seen on the approach to temples. Martha Ann and Dorothy Myers Imel tell another story of Benten. It is believed on New Year's Day, as one of the Seven Deities of Luck, she rides on the Takara-bune, or treasure ship, as it sails into port. A Santa of sorts, Benten on the treasure ship has magical gifts for people such as a hat of invisibility, a lucky raincoat, a sacred key, and an inexhaustible coin purse. Furthermore, it is believed that by putting a picture of the takara-bune under your pillow, lucky dreams will follow. Benten, or Benzaiten, is known to be prayed to in matters of luck, wealth, and creativity. She is associated with serpents and water and also looked upon as having mother-guardian aspects. Outside her temple, which is actually on the Shinobazu Pond, stands an ablution font to purify oneself, and a life-size lute, the symbol of Benten in her aspect as patroness of the arts. Another myth tells that the island of Enoshima (near Kamakura) rose up to receive her footsteps. Visitors should remember to remove their shoes before entering the temple, and be sure to look up at the ceiling to see the temple's famous golden dragon.

Getting to Ueno Park

Ueno Park in Tokyo could not be easier to find. Take any of several subway lines that pass the Ueno Station. Exit the station, walk across the street, and there is the entrance to the park. It is best to go with an English language map because most of the signage in the park is in Japanese. A short walk across Ueno Park, past the zoo is the not-to-be-missed Tokyo National Museum. On exhibit here are early Joman Earth Mother artifacts, Buddhist Goddess images, and Middle Eastern Goddesses too!

Goddess Focus
Power of the Pen

▲ Woman's secret script, or Nushu.

Despite what many per- / ceive as a prevalent tendency
in Japanese culture toward / restricting women's ability to
express themselves, a move- / ment beginning most notably
with the advent of Buddhism / to the island and proceeding
on through most of Japanese / literary history, the feminine
collections of poetry and sto- / ries of the Heian period were
considered the great literature / of Japan. Through these self-
fashioned literary works we have / provide a glimpse into female
life, spirituality, and women's / communities. Women's *nikki*,
or literary diaries similar to / autobiographies, were written
with the intent of distribu- / tion. From the Gossamer Years,
exploring a woman's relation- / ship with her husband, to the
romance tales of The Sarashina / Diary, the greatest works of
all were by Murasaki Shikibu, / author of *The Tale of Genji*, and
Sei Shonagon's Pillow Book.

Women were not taught to write Chinese in the early days so Chinese women of Hunan were busy creating their own secret language! Called *nushu* or women's script, it is a single-sex writing system composed of about 1,500 characters. Chinese scholars scrambling to preserve this exclusive language before those fluent have passed on believe it is the only one of its kind. Some believe origins of the language may date to the 3rd century. The wispy, elongated letters of *nushu*, read from right to left, represent sounds rather than ideas. "Sworn sisters" within villages poured their hopes, dreams, and sorrows into their diaries written in nushu, which their husbands could not decipher. According to Cathy Silber, they exchanged nushu texts at sewing circles and temple fairs such as the eighth day of the fourth lunar month known for its women-only potlucks. This language was a way for women to share their spirituality, fight illiteracy, empower themselves, and express their deepest feelings and thoughts.

Barbara Niederer raises our awareness of traditional Chinese script, which originated from pictograms and depicts elements of the language with characters. She explains, as with most cultures, the language reflects the attitude of the culture. Chinese script has been described as suggesting associations and analyses, regardless of accuracy. Many pictograms come under the key for "woman" and come with a variety of misogynist connotations such as to follow, slave, to quarrel, accuse, dumb, to fornicate, bad, egoistic, shameless, perverse, sneaky, disorderly, and thou shalt not. Another group of "women characters" represent behavior such as modest, gentle, obedient, smiling, ugly, coarse, underhanded, and slanderous. Chinese women believed negative associations were being put forth using "women characters" and the inequality between the genders was perpetuated through this usage of language. In 1949, appeals to change derogatory characters were made to the Committee for Character Reform and the editorial board of the journal, Languages in China. The appeals fell on deaf ears.

OCEANIA

Dear Kunapipi, Great Kunapipi, I do not forget you as I climb back into your holy womb to make contact with my spirit soul, crawling into the crescent vessel of your protection dug deep into the soil of your body, carved into the precious earth beneath me.

—Hymn to Kunapipi, First Mother of the Aboriginal Tribes of Australia

AUSTRALIA, NEW ZEALAND, HAWAII, and the islands of Polynesia, comprising part of Oceania, are lands where life was once strongly influenced by *kapu* or *tapu* and *mana*, all meaning taboo and spiritual power. Goddess and the sacred work of "women's business," and "ancestral womanhood" still effect everyday life. Here oral traditions have been passed from mother to daughter, father to son, grandparent to grandchild since the first days. Tales of the ancestors and creation mythology are expressed in story, dance, movement, chant, and song. Oceania is home to an assortment of indigenous people such as the Maori, Hawaiians, Tahitians, and Aboriginal tribes who take very seriously their responsibility as stewards of the land. Though some belong to mainstream faiths, many Hawaiians and Tahitians still cling to their cultural and spiritual heritage revering the Goddess as Mahuea, Hi'iaka, Hina, Laka, and Pele. The Aboriginal and Maori peoples are deeply connected to Mother Earth, sometimes calling her Papa, Papatuanuku or Yhi, who informs them of their spiritual and mundane perspectives, their identity, and their way of life. It is in the land, their *taonga* or treasure, that they are united and sustained.

Oceania in its myriad of manifestations reflect the many faces of Mother Nature. Boasting volcanoes both dormant and spewing forth molten, fiery lava, isolated atolls, gigantic monoliths, vast sandy deserts, serpentine cave systems, cascading waterfalls and lush rainforests, this paradise is where the landscape dominates the psyche and often charts one's path. The coral reefs and blue-green waters of Oceania are an undersea kaleidoscopic realm of sea life. This is also home of many unique land creatures — the platypus, kangaroo, koala, and various feathered friends too many to name. Earthy, evocative tones of the Aboriginal didgeridoo and joyful, uplifting Polynesian *mele oli* chants fill the air already heavy with the scent of a vast array of tropical and exotic flora. In Oceania one has the rare and blessed choice to stand among heavenly clouds on a mountain top, wander through a fern grotto, survey the horizon at the "Red Center," or view the continuing formation of new land expanding beneath turquoise depths.

These islands are alive with ancestral myths and legends that have been passed down from those who came before. Here the hula and canoe are containers that carry forth integral pieces of Oceanic identity and culture. Remains of ancient *marae,* or sacred meeting places, tiki, petroglyphs, pictographs, and *heiau,* or sacred altars, dot the lush and fertile landscape. Here also is a repository for the powerful and resourceful female ancestors and the rich heritage of Aboriginal "Dreaming." Encompassed within these cultures we see both the tangible and intangible heritage of the Creatrix as she lives in the voices and movement of her people, in the sacred landscape they call home and in the essence of women's business which permeates their lives and is embodied in the land.

AUSTRALIA

The Aboriginal people do not view Goddess in the same form or sense that is recognized by dedicates in Western culture. These are a people whose identity, culture, and heritage are connected to the land. Encapsulated within the Dreaming are stories of their ancestors, passed down from generation to generation, for tens of thousands of years. These stories are part of a rich multi-layered oral tradition that explains everything to the Aboriginal people from first consciousness to the afterlife. Like a handbook for living, the stories of the Dreaming explain how the world was created, where and how they can hunt and gather, and what foods they can or cannot eat. Dreaming may prohibit them from swimming in a certain stream that might be off-limits, and can assist in choosing a mate or weaving a basket. The ancestors come in a variety of forms from elemental spirits, to land formations, male, female or androgynous and anthropomorphic beings. These entities teach and inform the Aboriginal people about every manner of physical, emotional, and spiritual life. Readers will see comparisons with the "active reality" of Changing Woman from Native American mythology.

It is through their collective Dreaming that Aboriginal people are deeply connected to the land, creatures, and elements, in an almost animistic kind of cosmology. One's Dreaming encompasses laws of nature, duties of the individual, information on one's tribe, rite of passage behavior, inspiration for creativity, and their instinctively acute awareness of the land. Knowledge will vary from tribe to tribe, region to region, gender to gender, and dissemination of the knowledge is through storytelling, story boards, music, and dance. These concepts and the connection to sacred places might be referred to as "gender-embodied land."

Without Dreaming, the Aboriginal person would be hollow within and stripped bare. Sacred sites are usually a significant feature in the landscape, although sometimes they may be very nondescript. Therefore giant monoliths, trees, creek beds, or even a crevice in a rock may be considered sacred. These locations will usually have a myth or legend associated with actions of an ancestor connected to the site.

Access to places of women's business has become restricted due to outsiders and observers who have set a tone of repression and control rather than celebration, joy, respect, or reverence for sacred traditions. Christian missionaries have further driven these ceremonies and rites of passage underground. In respect for these people, their land and age-old beliefs, some sites included in this chapter will only be listed if they are publicly known, and even then the exact location may not be revealed simply to deter vandalism or intrusion. While some sites have no restrictions, many of the Aboriginal lands can be visited only with permission of the local tribes. In some places there are laws against trespassing and tourists should not venture out before checking local regulations for each site. Some tour companies have made arrangements with tribes to bring visitors on their lands. When visiting these sites or the surrounding areas, always be aware this is a sacred space and personal actions should be in proper accordance. It is recommended each visitor establish a dialogue with the leaders of these communities before visiting in order to state the intention of a future visit.

New South Wales

Mount Gulaga

From the Australian Heritage Commission (AHC) we know of Gulaga, sometimes called The Mother, a sacred mountain of the Yuin Aboriginal People. Mount Gulaga has long been considered instrumental in women's Dreaming. Men and women have their own separate knowledge of this mountain, replete with legends and songs pertaining to their gender. The famous peak is located near Tilba, New South Wales. It was first sighted and named Mount Dromedary by Captain Cook in 1770.

▲ Mount Gulaga is a prominent fixture on the horizon for many miles in all directions.

247

▲ The landscape of Mount Gulaga contains many aspects of the Divine Feminine.

To explain the deep interconnection of these gendered places with the life of an Aboriginal person, the AHC quotes a Barroloola woman who said this about women's daily life and ceremonial law: "We are Aboriginal women. We talk for our hunting business, ceremony business. We used to go hunting, we can't wait for the men. We are ladies, we go hunting and feed the men too. Men never used to boss over the women. We are bosses ourselves, women ourselves. Sometime man used to work for woman too when we come back from hunting, tired and everything, and husband to work for us. We still have ceremonies these days for young boys. Women dance with the old people only, but then everybody see us too. And we have other ceremony our own with the woman herself, that important, nobody see, only *djunkai* can stay there to watch, old man. He look, and he off again. When we have the big ceremony business and we can't see men. (sic)"

According to award-winning author Seph Scorzazie, Gulaga is a great woman whose umbilical cord reaches out under the water to her son, Montague Island, off the coast. Dolphins are said to swim in the tunnel of the cord. This is believed a sacred mountain where the world began and where sacred creator beings engage humans. The Sacred Tors atop Gulaga are stone repositories of information thought to be "Caretakers." Women come to Mount Gulaga to center themselves and seek guidance. They share sacred ceremony. Together Gulaga and women connect. Within the landscape of Gulaga are three types of rainforests and a eucalyptus forest currently under threat of logging. May wisdom prevail over greed!

Getting to Mount Gulaga

Air New South Wales flies to Bega from Sydney, the main town in the South Coast area. From Bega, go north toward Tilba the town nearly in the shadow of Mount Dromedary. Tilba is located between the towns of Narooma and Bermagui. Tilba is 11 miles (18 km) south of Narooma, the latter being 214 miles (345 km) south of Sydney. Bus and train are available. On Montague Island is a lighthouse and a colony of seals and penguins. A four-wheel drive vehicle and sturdy shoes are needed to climb Mount Dromedary.

GAIA ALERT

THE BLACK MIST STILL LINGERS

The media release of the Aboriginal website *Irati Wanti* reads "50 Years Later: The Black Mist Still Lingers." This is in reference to the atomic bomb, Totem One, detonated in 1953 at Emu Junction in the South Australia desert. According to the locals, no one was warned and the fallout was responsible for massive increases in radiation-related illness and genetic birth defects in the outback communities. Today the government plans to build a national nuclear waste dump in the far north of South Australia. The Kingka Tjuta who were not given a voice after the atomic bomb devastation are campaigning against the waste dump proposal. Their six decade-long fight continues.

▲ From strip mining to nuclear testing, Aboriginal lands have been seriously disrespected.

Aboriginal people across the continent have endured colonization of their lands and government sponsored "assimilation" to try and turn them to the White Man's way. They have been evicted from their lands and have seen their lands sold. They have faced racism, intolerance, and ignorant officials who turn a blind eye to their rich heritage and think little more of them than cannibals. Yet they persevere, holding on to their heritage and culture as best they can. While some lands have been restored to native tribes, places like Kakadu National Park were leased to outside companies before the establishment of either the park or Aboriginal land rights, resulting in ongoing struggles to resist development and depletion of resources. From diamond and uranium mines, to nuclear waste dumps and atomic detonations, the indigenous people of Australia are better prepared today than a century ago to stand up and "fight the good fight" to preserve their sacred lands and way of life.

Northern Territory
Arnhem Land

Arnhem land is a vast area at the northernmost tip of the Northern Territory where much is going on related to "women's business" and what scholar Selena Fox calls "ancestral womanhood." Both are connected to the aforementioned paradigm of "gender-embodied land," and the Divine Feminine takes a different form than those deities and archetypes traditionally recognized. In cultures where there are no deities per se, the force we call the Divine Feminine can manifest through social and cultural practices. This belief system harkens back to the most ancient times before deity had a specific form. When doing their women's business the women of a tribe are creating an experience we know as Goddess. She is alive in ritual and ceremony, and she dwells within the women. She is a force within the landscape and she is most potent in places associated with women's business. Besides being a place of rich cultural activity, these areas within the Northern Territory are a natural wonderland of six topographical regions that include forests, rock formations, savannahs, floodplains, waterfalls, caves, lagoons, and abundant wildlife. It also has many rock shelters used for habitation dating 20,000 years ago, and as many as 5,000 rock art images. Some images date back 20,000 to 50,000 years. The land and the rock art is sacred and integral to Dreaming.

▲ Rainbow Snake, a bisexual creator deity of Arnhem Land.

At the Nourlangie art site is the image of Barrginj, wife of Namarrongon, the Lightning Man and Creator ancestor. Barrginj is depicted with legs akimbo, which seems to be a popular stance in Aboriginal art. Her grasshopper children are thought to have given the Aboriginal people their language, beliefs, values, and the structure of society, with grasshoppers and praying mantises generally being associated with fertility. Professor Margaret Grove documented the correlation between these female grasshoppers and praying mantis as being sacred beings in mortuary myths involving rebirth. These arthropodal female figures are on the ceiling near a burial location, thus accenting the desire of these people for rebirth. There are also family groups shown in rock art, some of the women have dashes painted on their breasts, a sign of breast feeding. Some of the images of copulating men and women have been associated with fertility or sex magic.

Grove's research suggests these sexual images reflect men and women's healthy enjoyment of their sexual natures which, though controlled during the normal course of a day, loosen up during ritual time when they might engage in sexual relations with one another more freely and with less taboo. These images are perhaps actual representations of ritual activity. Why does Grove believe the paintings show ritual interaction? Body painting on each other was a major step in preparing for ritual. The women painted the women in seclusion from the men and vice versa. The youngest painted the oldest, always in order of age, with the eldest or highest ranking women being painted last. Sometimes the highest ranking would be the woman who initiated the ritual or who had the lead in teaching the ritual dances. Songs were sung while the body painting took place. In most of the rock art, the bodies are highly decorated and painted with extreme care and thus in her learned opinion, Grove believes the images reflect ritual enactment or the desire for that interaction. Further, these body paintings offered a plethora of information and were not just decorative, often also noting the participant's identity. Some Arnhem Land paintings show young maidens painted just before or after their puberty rituals, which were generally not sexual in nature, with the exception being the act of breaking the hymen, which was enacted more sexually in some clans.

The lagoon area of Arnhem Land belongs to the Gummulkban and Ulunji/Bunji clans. It is an area where many rock art images of females are found. Located just past the Alligator River from Kakadu National Park, it is private land and off-limits without permission to enter. Some images are thought to be Warramurrungdji, a female Creatrix who Grove explains carries dilly bags (woven palm bags), around her head. In these bags she carried food stuffs (such as yams), languages, and children to populate the land. She placed each on a portion of land from which the different clans were to arise. The dilly bag thus becomes a metaphor for the uterus of the female and in some puberty rituals an empty dilly bag is placed around the neck of the young maiden to indicate her potential to become fruitful and multiply.

Near Katherine, south of Arnhem Land and Kakadu, is another rock image of a female with legs akimbo in a small curved rock shelter where it is said that birth takes place. Nearby is a painting interpreted by the clan to be that of a grasshopper, which ties the symbology to fertility. According to Professor Grove, women are also believed to give birth here and throughout Australia under trees so that the baby might have an individual identity.

Rainbow Snake, an androgynous or bisexual creator deity is associated with the sacred waterholes of Kakadu National Park, where the deity personifies a source of live-giving water. Within the area of the Northern Territory we see ritual further commingled with the sacred landscape as the Yarralin people, who recognize trees as symbols of fertility, incorporate them into men and women's business. The Yarralin believe trees around the Lingara area sprang forth from seven *karu*, or non-initiated males who stopped in this area during their dream tracking. Contemporary males use the bark from the trees in a potion to help attract females and enhance their virility, while females believe similar trees insure their fertility.

Nearby in the Jabiluka area of Kakadu National Park, women have been taking care of business as they fight to keep a uranium mine from operating in the area. The struggle is summed up in the words of one of the elders, "We hunt on the floodplain and we rely on the animals and plants. That mine will interfere with a sacred site ... it will spiritually poison the area. It can have a catastrophic affect on us."

Getting to Arnhem Land

Arnhem Land is strictly an Aboriginal reserve and travel to outside persons is restricted. As with other Aboriginal reserves, visitors must obtain an entry permit. No paved roads exist in Arnhem Land and getting around is very difficult. Swampy marshes, unmarked trails, and estuary crocodiles — some growing to 26 feet (8 m) — make overland travel a hazardous proposition. Most travelers opt to visit only neighboring Kakadu National Park, which is far more accessible, open to tourism, and just outside the city of Darwin.

Uluru & the Olgas

Ayers Rock, called Uluru by the Aboriginal people, is one of the most famous tourist destinations in Australia. Aboriginals call Uluru's "sister" mountain Kata Tjuta, or the Olgas. The two are located in almost the exact middle of the continent, referred to as the Red Center, because of the red sand that goes on endlessly for many miles in all directions. Stepping out of the Aboriginal paradigm for a moment, this seems a rather accurate, though unintentional metaphor for a sacred site of the Divine Female with her association of red ochre and life-giving sacred blood. Together, these two primordial landscapes which formed during a geologic event 500 million years ago, might be seen as grand monuments to a balance of yin and yang energies. Uluru is a giant monolith rising out of the desert like a phallic. Kata Tjuta is often said to resemble a giant female body, or yoni. This duo is a repository of Aboriginal and psychic knowledge, representing earth mysteries dating back to 40,000 BCE when the first Aboriginal arrived in Australia from Southeast Asia.

Putting this male and female association in an Aboriginal context, Rainbow Snake, one of the oldest and universal Aboriginal deities is thought to embody characteristics of both genders and the duality of water as a life giving and destructive force. One Dreamtime story shows how this balance of the genders is kept in check. It is said the male aspect of Rainbow Snake is called Yulunggur, while the female is sometimes called Kunapipi, or Old Woman. Yulunggur is said to swallow the female eggs of Kunapipi, thereby making man the keeper of tribal lore and law. However, power cannot be unbalanced which Yulunggur soon learns. Without the female, he is barely fertile and alone cannot withstand the powerful monsoon rains. He is forced to eject the eggs from his stomach, thereby

▲ An outback journey to the interior of Australia is hot, dry, and arduous, but not without occasional surprises alongside the road.

restoring the women to life. Together there is balance and order, setting things right in the world, with the snake as a symbol of male reproductive power and Kunapipi and her daughter's symbols of the womb.

Dozens of stories are linked to Uluru and Kata Tjuta as sacred sites, which were both prominent landmarks along the dream tracks. These song lines were left by the spirits of the ancestors as they traveled across the land filling the Aboriginal people with a textbook of tribal lore and law. Something akin to the power of ley lines, or the Asian belief in the energetic power of chi'i and feng shui, these tracks give power to the landscape. Continued ritual at these sacred places by women or Aboriginal holy men, called *karadjs*, maintain the power to access ancient dreaming spirits. Aboriginal people believe performing ritual constantly restores and renews the potency of the land. Keeping the traditions of the Dreamtime alive further aids in making sure this mythology is never forgotten. Aboriginal people who are born near a sacred place often believe they become the incarnation of the ancestor beings of the place. When this occurs the person bears the great responsibility of becoming a guardian of that land.

Some Aboriginal stories name this area as the emergence spot of the ancestors onto land. Ancestor deities associated with the place are Wanambi, a snake that lives at Mount Olga, the highest peak in Kata Tjuta, rising to an elevation of 1,500 feet (457 m). The eastern side of the Olgas is home of the Mice Women with their two large rocks nearby said to be food piles, a metaphor for fertility. Two pinnacles, Malu, the kangaroo man, and Mulumura, the lizard woman, are thought to be siblings. Uluru also marks the site of a great battle between the Kuniya or python people with the Liru, a tribe of carpet snakes. It is believed this strife and ensuing massacre marked the end of the Dreamtime and the creation period.

It becomes clear sacred places like Uluru and Kata Tjuta are intricately connected within the spirituality of both men and women's business. Taking this paradigm of women's business connected to gender-embodied land, add in the belief that everything associated with the Dreaming, women's business and men's business is sacred and it becomes quite clear the Aboriginal people live on their land within an intricate web of spirituality, though in recent times some have lost touch with this rich heritage and fallen into despair. It adds more depth and dimension to how and why the land, creatures, the above and below, man and women, are all interconnected and sacred in a symbiotic relationship. It explains why environmental concerns are paramount to many of these people and additionally, why particular places associated with men's or women's business are kept secret and maintained by the tribes connected to particular sites.

Uluru was first seen by Europeans in 1872. In 1985 it was returned to

▲ Uluru is located in the red center of the Australian continent.

its rightful owners, the Aboriginal tribe called the Anangu, who lease the site back to the government on a 99-year contract, and offer tours and accurate information to visitors on indigenous culture. Often visitors can glimpse the many cave paintings around the base of Uluru.

The Olgas, or Kata Tjuta, are also known as "many heads" by the Aboriginal people. The Olgas rise about 20 miles (32 km) west of Uluru and is comprised of a range of about 36 red domes that rise out of the landscape, with the largest taller than Uluru standing about 656 feet (200 m) in height. The Olgas spread out over an 11-square-mile (28-sq.-km) area.

All manner of transportation are available to visit these stunning landscapes, from walking tours to camel rides. Sites associated with "women's business" are fenced off and access is with permission only, including the cave at Uluru known to be sacred to women. Inquiring about permission to climb either the Olgas or Uluru would be recommended as often times this rock climbing is disturbing and considered disrespectful, though permission to climb Uluru is often allowed.

Getting to Uluru and The Olgas

Located almost exactly in the center of the Australian continent, Uluru and the Olgas are a long way from the habitable coastline. Further isolated by desert on all four sides, travelers must be prepared for a sometimes harsh outback experience. Roads in remote areas are not suitable for conventional cars, and the lack of food, water, and gasoline can make travel hazardous even in four-wheel drive vehicles. Most travelers visiting this area opt to take a bus tour from the southern Australian cities. Alice Springs in the Northern Territory is the nearest major settlement to Uluru, some 300 miles (480 km) away. It is about a 45 minute climb to the summit of the rock on the east side.

Southern Australia

Hindmarsh Island

Murray Mouth, Goolwa, Hindmarsh Island, and "women's business" are discussed extensively in *Ngarrindjeri Wurruwarrin: A World That Is, Was and Will Be* by Diane Bell. Public knowledge of this sacred site came to the fore in the same manner as most do — during a public struggle with government or developers who wanted to alter the land in some way. Here the battle was to keep a bridge from being built between Goolwa and Hindmarsh Island because it was a sacred gender-embodied land. According to Dr. Geoffrey Partington, the 1995 Royal Commission believed the women of the area considered this area sacred for the following three reasons: Women had a tradition of burying aborted fetuses here; the land (presumably the mouth of the river) was shaped like female sexual organs thus being related to their fertility; and Aboriginal women believed the building of the bridge would "interrupt the meeting of the waters," thereby inhibiting their reproductive abilities.

South of the larger cities of Adelaide and Victor Harbor, and east of Kangaroo Island, difficult to find Hindmarsh Island is sandwiched between three bodies of water: Encounter Bay; Lake Alexandrina; and Lake Albert. It has a rugged coastline surrounded by salt water, rich sources of fish, plant and animal life. It also contains back scrub country, sweet fresh water sources prized by the Aboriginal people, all of which help sustain the many clans inhabiting the area. This is some of the richest and most fertile land in all of Southern Australia which is primarily dry, flat, and dusty. Steeped in the landscape is the women's Dreaming. To disturb the natural environment is to disturb the natural rhythms of the women themselves. Once on Hindmarsh Island visitors can follow walking trails, bird watch, and lookouts provide views to the mouth of the Murray River and nearby Lake Alexandrina.

Women's business is transmitted from the Dreaming. Diane Bell, feminist anthropologist, who spent quite some time with the Ngarrindjeri women near Hindmarsh Island in South Australia defines women's business as an imprecise term that refers to women's ritual, ceremonies, beliefs, practices, traditions, and knowledge as it relates to the land, themselves, their ancestors, women's rights and their responsibilities. Women's business encompasses everything involved with their responsibilities as wives, mothers, and stewards of the land. It might include organizing efforts to keep land safe from development or pollution. It certainly includes birth, death, menarche, and caring for families. It also includes ritualized circumcision of young men as a means of rebirth within "men's business." It informs about women's bodies and their reproductive lives. It also illustrates how women are connected to the "gendered embodied landscape."

Women speak of being so intimately connected to the land that should some defacement or disturbance happen to the land which they are responsible for or connected to, they actually feel the trauma in their bodies. There is an account of a woman warning against sticking wire into a sacred site associated with women's business because it would hurt the land and be felt by the women who used the sacred land. Another local Aboriginal woman commented that she believed their life spans were shortened because of the suffering they experienced in connection with their land that had not been properly respected.

In her study of the women of Ngarrindjeri at Hindmarsh Island in South Australia, anthropologist Diane Bell speaks of the importance of the *putari,* or midwife. A skilled and coveted position in which an apprenticeship must be served, the putari is often the only assistance for women in the outback. Schooled in the aspects of women's bodies, the putari is in charge in matters concerning birth, menstruation, and contraception. She can "read the signs" and knows herbal and folk remedies from bush medicine such as cobwebs to the stopping of bleeding. Women gather with the putari to enact rituals, sing songs, paint themselves with red ochre and grease. Red ochre is a symbol of life, blood, and the sacred, because it is the putari who affects the spiritual life of mothers and their children.

The putari is with the mother when she gives birth, preferably on the land, which begins the intimate relationship between a person and the land. She is also the one who assists the mother to "call their babies forth" to ensure a safe and speedy delivery. Bell further explains that in a culture such as this with an oral tradition, the spoken word is life, therefore, this act of calling to the child is believed to start the child's connection with their social world.

▲ The landscape of Hindmarsh Island is deeply intertwined with "women's business."

Getting to Hindmarsh Island

The gateway to Southern Australia is the city of Adelaide where visitors can find an airport, train, and bus station. To reach Hindmarsh Island, visitors first must find Goolwa, located just north of Victor Harbor, both of which are on the Fleurieu Peninsula. From Goolwa, the only way to Hindmarsh Island is by a ferry near the wharf. Basic hotels and camping accommodations can be obtained in Goowa or on Hindmarsh Island. Places of interest in Goolwa are the River Murray Interpretive Center, the Goolwa National Trust Museum, and other historic sites. Specific directions to the places of women's business cannot be provided as these are closely guarded secrets, however visitors are advised to look at the natural landscape.

Goddess Focus
The Putari, Miwi and Sacred Stones

A *putari*, or midwife, is often the only assistance a woman may receive with childbirth in the outback. According to feminist anthropologist, Diane Bell, she is believed to have a strong *miwi*, or spiritual wisdom, intuition, and soul substance as she facilitates the transfer of miwi between mother and child at birth when she cuts and handles the umbilical cord. Though sometimes circumstances may dictate otherwise, when a child is born, it is usually the putari who performs the art of cutting the umbilical cord. The cord has significant sacred meaning because it is believed the miwi of a person passes through the umbilical cord at birth, leaving spiritual wisdom from the mother to reside in the navel area of the child. The cord is a lifeline. Once it drops away, the miwi is within the child. It helps them later in life to discern truth, sacred places, and is considered the life force. It has been suggested the putari was probably involved in rituals surrounding birth, miwi, and umbilical cords, including usage of sacred stones. These particular stones collected from the landscape were painted with concentric circles (navel stones), and stone cairns were built over sites where the afterbirth was buried.

▲ A midwife was often the only help to a woman during childbirth.

Western Australia

Kapululangu Women's Center

Kapululangu is one of most isolated places of women's business in Australia, situated on the periphery of the Great Sandy Desert within the Wirrimanu and Balgo communities. It is *tjilimi*, or a traditional woman's camp, and home to several tribes known jointly as the Kutjungka. In 1999, the Law Women of Wirrimanu formed Kapululangu to assist them in enjoying, maintaining, and reviving their religious and cultural knowledge. It was also formed to help women fulfill their obligations to the ancestral lands. They attempt to teach younger generations of their cultural heritage and record knowledge for future generations.

Many of the elders of Wirrimanu were teenagers when the first Catholic missionaries moved into the area, yet they managed to continue to live their traditional lifestyle in the bush, thus keeping their culture alive. They are caretakers of Australia's sacred Women's Law, or *Yawulyu,* and considered custodians of their tribes' most enduring and time-honored ways of life. Elders spend their days taking care of spiritual obligations and ceremonies. The camp also serves as a refuge for younger women. It is a ceremonial ground for the keeping of ritual objects, a safe-house for abused women, and a general overall haven. Here women can get assistance in gathering bush food or medicine, network with other women so they do not feel isolated or alone, improve their standards of living, learn to become advocates for women's issues, and obtain financial resources. The arts and crafts center encourages the continuation of the women's talent for painting images from their Dreaming, or *Tjukurrpa*, which has become known the world over.

▲ As Australian Aboriginals become more accustomed to the Modern Age, so do those seekers of ancient wisdom who wish to highlight the native people's culture and mythology.

Sustaining the center is difficult, as the elders are aging, with the two oldest near 90 and 100 years of age. There is grave concern that their traditions will be lost and not passed on to younger generations. Some of the elders like Ngunytja Napanangka Mosquito speak: "We want people to learn about our culture. We got a lot of stories ... secret ones too. Too long people not listening to women. Not listening to Aboriginal people." The elders of Kapululangu have much to impart to the indigenous and non-indigenous women of the world. They have done this by putting on concerts to raise money, providing information booths where their crafts are sold, running raffles and collecting donations. The women also hold discussion nights explaining women's business and the work of the center.

According to Chris Sitka, scholar and social activist, the Kapululangu women elders have told her that the actions of their ancestors' forms the landscape so much so that each feature of it is actually an ancestor, or perhaps part of an ancestor's body. She explains there are dreaming tracks of connected sites which are women's places. One of the most spectacular and best known of these is a Seven Sisters Dreaming track which begins in southern South Australia and winds through thousands of kilometers of the Western desert, passing through the Northern Territory and Western Australia, before it goes out to sea north of Broome.

In ancestral times, the legendary Seven Sisters traveled along this track stopping to make camp, digging up "bush tucker" or wild food with their digging sticks, lit fires, scooped water from rock holes, menstruated, evaded marauding male pursuers, had mishaps, and performed ceremonial dances. At every location where one of these events occurred, a sacred women's site now exists. Other female ancestors who play an important part of the Aboriginal Dreamtime include Bara and Walo, both sun deities; the Djanggawul Sisters, considered founder deities who oversee ritual ceremonies; Eingana or Eiganu, a creatrix in the form of a snake; Warramurrungdji, the Goddess of creation, the sea, children, flora and fauna, as well as languages. Kunapipi oversees initiations and puberty rituals while her daughters, the Wawalug sisters are fertility Goddesses, and Yalungur is involved within female sexuality.

Getting to Kapululangu Women's Center

Kapululangu is located on the edge of the Great Sandy Desert of the Kimberly region of Western Australia within the Wirrimanu/Balgo community near Halls Creek, south of Lake Argyle near the Northern Australia border. This author was asked to not further reveal the location of the center. Those interested in further information can write: Kapululangu Women's Law and Culture Center, PMB 308, Wirrimanu/Balgo, via Halls Creek, WA 6770.

POLYNESIA

Within a nature oriented belief system, the Polynesians worshipped two categories of deities. The *akua*, or nature elements, personified as dynamic and natural forces associated primarily with male deities. Those were Kane (supreme creator), Kanaloa (sea and death god), Ku (war and labor god), and Lono (rain and agriculture god). The second category were *aumakua*, the minor gods, goddesses, and ancestral deities who were associated with places, beings, and forces that helped protect mere mortals and relatives. They could shape-shift into many forms of plant sea or animal life, yet be recognized by relatives and assisted kin in times of need. According to scholars, aumakua could be gods and ancestors conjoined, providing guidance, fortitude, prophecy or inspiration. As any good mentor, they might oversee one's actions in the world and if necessary, rebuke mistakes or lapses in judgment. They came to people in dreams to intervene with the akua on behalf of the mortals. Both the akua and the aumakua could take possession of a person to further one's spiritual journey.

The best known aumakua was Pele, who spewed fiery molten lava from her volcanic womb. Other aumakua or nature goddesses of Polynesia are Poliahu, known as the Snow Goddess of Mauna Kea, a mountain on the island of Hawaii, associated with clarity of thought. As the cold and wet opposition to the fiery mountain volcanoes, Poliahu is Pele's legendary rival who could quench Lady Pele's flames. Sibling goddesses of Pele are Hi'iaka and Laka, both associated with hula, the sacred dance of the Polynesians. All three were considered not just family aumakua, but major deities to the Hawaiian people. Last but not least is Hina, a multifaceted goddess who comes to us in many legends, in many aspects, and through her we weave a common thread among the many islands of Polynesia, across the waters to New Zealand.

Hawaii

Mauna Kea

The cool, crisp, and cloud-covered mountain sanctuary of Mauna Kea is home to no less than three snow goddesses: Lilinoe, Waiau, and Poliahu. Mauna Kea, associated with clearness of mind and tranquility, is balanced by its counterpart Mauna Loa, associated with the feminine aspects of Nature. Both mountains tower nearly 14,000 feet (420 m) on the Big Island of Hawaii, and are easily the tallest peaks in the Pacific. Once again travelers can see a dramatic landscape associated with the Feminine Creatrix, embodied in a magnificent mountainous realm. Clinton Stuart quotes W. D. Westervelt, an early chronicler of Hawaiian legend, who described the snow goddesses best: "... queens of beauty, full of wit and wisdom, lovers of adventure and enemies of Pele ... Pele has stepped forth again and again, and has hurled eruptions of mighty force and great extent against the maidens of the snow-mantle, but the natives say that in this battle Pele has been and always will be defeated."

As for the three goddesses, each has individual characteristics. Lilinoe was said to have a cave dwelling on the slope of Mauna Kea where she ruled over the realm of dead fires and desolation. It was thought she could hold back eruptions by quenching the volcanic fires in thick layers of snow from the peaks of Mauna Kea. Stories of Waiau are somewhat obscure, but she seems to be associated with a crater lake where the ancient Hawaiians came to dig for a particular kind of rock that is the hardest on the island. Lake Waiau, which means "Swirling Water," is

▲ On a clear day Mauna Kea can be seen from Hilo.

found at an elevation of about 13,020 feet (3,970 m) and never runs dry, fed by a constant layer of melting frost below the summit. Another account translates Waiau's name to mean "water of sufficient depth to bathe." This general area that includes Lake Waiau is now part of the Mauna Kea Ice Age Natural Area Reserve. Like Haleakala on Maui, Mauna Kea was glaciated during the last Ice Age. It is thought the summit of Mauna Kea once supported a sheet of ice 500 feet (152 m) thick. Most prominent among the snow goddesses residing on her peak is Poliahu, the constant rival of Pele. It is said Poliahu's domain rests on the north side of the island, while Pele's realm is the southern region. The on-again, off-again battles between hot and fiery Pele and cold and wet Poliahu seem a metaphor for the constant struggle for balance and duality. Poliahu, sometimes referred to as a chieftainess, is often described as wearing her snowy white mantle. She has competed with both Pele and Hina as the top Hawaiian chieftainess for the attentions of young lovers. In stories where she floats away with Opele, it is understood this is a metaphor for going into a trance.

Ethnographers did their best to preserve the indigenous mythology, but often times their subjects or themselves were influenced by their own Western or Christian viewpoints, thus preventing an authentic history from being recorded. One such example seems to be the apparent biblical associations with Mauna Kea. According to the Reverend William Ellis who was collecting Hawaiian mythology on the islands around 1823, he was hearing stories reminiscent of the Great Flood of Noah. He recorded one Hawaiian creation myth that spoke of a great flood inundating the land, "overflowed by the sea, except for a small peak on the top of Mauna Kea, where two human beings were preserved from the destruction that overtook the rest, but they say they had never before heard of a ship, or of Noah." Only in the early Kumulipo chant can researchers glean accurate concepts of Hawaiian mythology without any "post-contact manipulation." Later accounts begin to be influenced by biblical stories such as the Garden of Eden, Cain and Able, the Exodus, and the role of the serpent in Christianity, as taught to the indigenous people by the missionaries.

Getting to Mauna Kea

The lofty peak of Mauna Kea can be reached via Route 200 or Saddle Road, which slices the island of Hawaii in half, dividing Mauna Loa and Mauna Kea. From the Kona side of the island, Saddle Road is six miles (10 km) south of Waimea along Route 190, about halfway between Waimea and Waikoloa Road. From Hilo, follow Waianuenue Avenue inland. Saddle Road (which is also called Kaumana Drive) forks off to the left after about a mile (1.6 km). An observation complex, skiing in the winter, hiking trails, the Ice Age Natural Area Reserve and Visitor's Center all await travelers at the summit. Hikers should remember in this high altitude it takes longer to become acclimated. Look closely for the small caves and ancient quarry at Lake Waiau.

Kilauea

Mount Kilauea, a "shield" volcano, with fiery molten magma constantly churning several miles beneath its summit is a fitting home for the tempestuous Pele. When volcanic pressure builds to a crucial point the volcano erupts and sends molten lava, called Pele's Hair, down its slopes. Tear-shaped lapili glass from fire fountains of lava that dry in the air are called Pele's Tears. Pele has destroyed

▲ If a pre-contact Hawaiian ever saw this view they no doubt would believe Pele was just out of sight mixing up a fiery broth.

over a hundred buildings in recent history, but simultaneously creates additional landmass from her eruptions, causing Hawaii to constantly grow in size. Creation and destruction, life and death, all traditional realms of the goddess are seen in dramatic fashion in the guise of Lady Pele at Kilauea.

Polynesians understood Pele's tempestuous nature and regularly placated her with chants, o'helo berries, gin, and dances. Reporter Jennifer S. Holland quotes contemporary Pele practitioner, Keola Hanoa who explains, "We don't see her work as destruction but as cleansing. She's a creator. When she comes through, she wipes the land clean and leaves us new fertile ground. We don't get mad. It is all hers to begin with." With the coming of Christianity, worship of the old gods and goddesses was discouraged. Chieftainess Kapiolani, who had converted to Christianity, renounced Pele in a public display meant to discourage her worship by the Polynesians. She ate Pele's sacred o'helo berries and threw rocks into the crater at Halema'uma'u, the rim of Pele's sacred fire pit on Mount Kilauea. In doing so, she tested her power and dared Pele to punish her. When nothing happened, Kapiolani cited Pele's inaction as the goddess' weakness, or even nonexistence, in the face of a new religion which was at odds against the old.

For many, Pele was never forgotten. When Mauna Loa erupted in the late 1800s, aging Princess Ruth Keelikolani walked to the edge of the lava flow bearing gifts for Pele. She sang the sacred chants of the priestesses. Within a day of offering the chants, gin, and silk cloth to Pele, her fiery flows subsided and the city of Hilo was spared. In 1955, when lava threatened the city of Kapoho, villagers believed they were successful in turning the tide after they too offered Pele tobacco, food, and flowers. The lava bypassed the village. Similar stories have been documented in the mid-1990s when volcanic eruptions threatened life and property.

Offerings were regularly made to Pele from the *heiau*, or sacrificial altar, where the observatory at Mount Kilauea now stands. Holland interviewed park ranger Faelyn Jardine who must regularly clean away the offerings. "You'll see everything from fake money to raw pig heads out here," and she suggests "preferred offerings are chants and prayers." It is said the early priestesses of Pele wore robes

▲ The molten lava is the result of creatrix Pele at work.

whose hems and sleeves had been singed in a fire and they carried digging sticks which represented the digging stick which Pele used to create the volcanic islands and craters of the Hawaiian Island chain. They knew the incantations to soothe her, offering pigs, songs, and dances of the hula. Holland quotes Keola Hanoa who believes her octogenarian mother, named Pele, is an earthly incarnation of the fiery Goddess. Hanoa says, "In a dream about fire, my grandmother was told to name her Pele ... She's linked to a higher power. Pele, our *tutu*, our grandparent, is everything: the steam, the lava, the land. And my mother was handpicked to represent her." Holland states the mortal Pele possesses a quiet and poised demeanor and describes the priestess' visit to the visitor center to bless a new painting of Pele, the Goddess. "Wearing big glasses, a long red dress and floral crown to match, she faces the deity's bold image on the wall and prays aloud in Hawaiian, a bit of song in her voice. Then, still chanting, she walks through the room flicking water from a bowl of floating ti leaves into each corner with her fingers. Later she says that she waited for a sign to tell her what to do." She cites the mortal Pele, "I got up this morning and it came to me, that I should prepare the salt water, that I would sprinkle it through the room. In my prayer I asked Pele to protect this park and all the workers, and I cleansed the room of evil spirits."

It seems apparent that Pele is alive and well in the hearts of the indigenous people of Hawaii. For visitors they too can see the simultaneous acts of creation and destruction brought on by Pele. From the lava-scorched earth which purifies and transforms what has come before, life springs anew. Both flora and fauna manage to thrive on the volcanic environs created by Pele. Holland suggests some plants and trees have magical origins, such as the beautiful lehua blossom (whose pointed red petals might remind some of Pele's fiery lava plumes), and the ohi'a tree being cursed lovers turned into flora by the jealous Pele. Volcanoes National Park with its varied terrain and creatures certainly reflects the power of Madame Pele, the omnipotent, sensual, passionate, dynamic, and sometimes angry Goddess who would stomp her foot and cause an earthquake. Visitors may still view her fiery lava as it flows down into the sea, meeting her sister Na maka o Kahai, Goddess of the Sea, since the beginning of time. Women who embrace Pele are learning to embrace their anger, passion, and tenacity. Like when Pele's hot lava meets Namaka o Kahi's cool waters, transforming fire into land, they understand that something must be destroyed or transformed in order for new life or a new cycle to come forth.

Getting to Kilauea National Park

South of Hilo, along Highway 11 is a turn-off that leads to the village of Volcano. Here is the entrance to the national park. A few miles past the gate is the Visitor's Center, where it is easy to survey the area and decide how to proceed. Across from the Visitor's Center are the viewing sites for the caldera, Halema'uma'u, Pele's home. From this rim hikers can take a trail down to the caldera floor to Halema'uma'u. Some visitors are lucky enough to be there after a recent eruption and are able to walk on the cooling lava. Be sure to wear shoes that can be thrown away because the soles will surely melt — and don't forget the gin or berries!

Rainbow Falls

The Hawaiian name for the falls, Wai'anuenue meaning "rainbow seen in water," shrouds the dwelling of Hina. According to W. D. Westervelt, as quoted by *Sacred Texts*, the cavern beneath and behind the spectacular 80-foot (24-m) tall Rainbow Falls at the basin of the Wailuku River, near the city of Hilo, is a prominent residence of Hina, goddess of the moon. Visitors can take stone steps down to the legendary home of Hina. The circular pool into which the waterfall empties is 100 feet (30 m) in diameter, and when conditions are right, the most beautiful rainbows form to please the eye and feed the soul.

On the land adjacent to the waterfall is the location where Hina first beat the tapa to make cloth for the Hawaiian people. So beautiful was the tapa cloth that Hawaiians compared it to clouds in heaven. The nearby large banyan or ono tree is said to have been created by Hina. It was here that she and her son Maui waged war with the sun so that the days might be longer in order for her tapa sheets to dry. Maui lived nearby on the lands of the north bank of the river. Above the cave dwelled the reptile, Kuna (or Tuna), who regularly annoyed and threatened Hina, but Hina felt perfectly safe and content as long as she was within her cave. It is in this general location that the battle between Kuna, Hina, and her son Maui fought using magic clubs and boiling water. Legends say Kuna was ultimately defeated by Maui with the aid of Hina and her women using powerful chants and incantations.

Legends concerning Hina vary from island to island, often contradicting legends from other locations in Polynesia. A good example is the Hervey Islands, where Tuna was a god of eels who loved and died for Hina. When Hina buried his head, coconuts sprang forth which she gave to her people. It has been suggested that the reptilian Kuna harkens back to the myths of dragons and crocodiles told by the ancient Polynesians, who some think may have originated near the River Ganges in India. In Samoan myth, the battling duo was an owl and serpent, both traditional Western symbols of Goddess. Of course, not to be overlooked is the dwelling place of Hina — a cave near life-giving waters, which is a traditional association with Hina throughout Polynesia. Indeed, there are many Hinas within Polynesian myth and it is

▲ Hina resides in a misty cave behind Rainbow Falls.

263

believed Hina of the moon and Hina the tapa beater originated from the Tahitian Moon Goddess Hina. In Hawaii, Hina also became the earthly manifestation of Pele, named Hina-i-ka-malama. She was a chieftainess on Maui who competed with the Snow Goddess Poliahu for the attentions of their mutual lover. Another Hina is associated with fire (Hina-a-ke-ahi), a similar attribute of Pele. As the mistress of the flame, she instructed her people to make fire as well as cook in underground imu ovens. Hawaiian scholar Martha Beckwith states, "Life through fertility of the female here on earth is the dominant conception of both fire and moon worship, and that of the unity of the race through descent from a divine ancestress is the social incentive for merging the two as different aspects of a single divinity." Beckwith believes Hina the Moon Goddess became conjoined and entered into Pele myths because of her popularity, making these two female deities primary among the Hawaiians.

Scholar John Charlot explains Pele's worship spread first among the common Hawaiians before it filtered into other strata of society, with each class adding their own flavor to her story. Much like the worship of Demeter in Greece, the devotion to Pele as a private family deity later evolved into more widespread worship among all classes of people. Eventually she was seen as a goddess who might overthrow the status quo with her fiery explosions. Charlot says she could defeat and rule gods. It was because of her very nature to challenge fundamental ideas and opposition that the Pele religion survived the invasion of foreign influence of missionaries that decimated the rest of Hawaiian culture.

The great Earth Mother Hina (Ina) is known throughout the Polynesian Triangle, from Hawaii to Easter Island, all the way southwest to New Zealand. *Sacred Texts,* quoting W. D. Westervelt, tell us much of her legends and attributes, both complex and varied, sometimes overlapping and conflicting, but never dull. Hina is a Goddess who sometimes lived in the moon, though stories of how she got there varies from island to island. She inspired the Polynesians to name their moon Mahina or Masina, a derivative of her name. With her tapa-beating, she taught the Polynesians to make cloth as fine as silk, and according to Gary Kubota of *The Star Bulletin*, she is said to have given birth to the island of Molokai. Finally, she is known for discovering salt-free water so that crops might be grown. Patricia Monaghan sums up Hina in comprehensive fashion calling her an all-inclusive archetype, associated with death and the underworld, the warrior queen of the Island of Women where no men were allowed so trees impregnated the women. She was known to have two faces, one in the front as humans do, and one at the back of her head. She was the first female on earth, yet other legends have her mother as the Goddess Mahuea who taught the Maori about fire.

Getting to Rainbow Falls

From downtown Hilo head west on Waianuenue Avenue to the edge of town, pass Hilo High School and follow the signs to Wailuku River State Park where Rainbow Falls is located. The falls are best seen in the morning sunlight for photography, or stay the whole day and enjoy a picnic at the scenic overlook.

Kauai
Ke'e Beach

Several natural and human-made sites near Ke'e Beach are sacred to Goddess in her various manifestations. Wet caves located on the northern side of Kauai are believed by Polynesians to have been created by Pele with her digging stick as she moved across the island chain from the northwest searching for a home impervious to her sea sister Na-maka-o-kaha'i's attempts to inundate them. Once the sea goddess flooded a place, Pele moved on to the next island, eventually coming to the great Mount Kilauea. Kilauea was definitely too steep for her sister's flood waters to breech, so there Pele made her eternal home. Several structures in relatively close proximity on Ke'e Beach sites are remnants associated with the oldest traditions of hula and chant, or the *kahiko*. Ke'e Beach is home to the sacred dance of the Polynesians, as well as potent legends of Pele and both her sisters, Laka and Hi'iaka. Considered one of the most important sites in all of the Hawaiian Islands, here is where Hi'iaka, as the first *haumana hula* or student of hula, began the rich tradition of hula dance that embodies the heritage, oral traditions, and culture of the Hawaiians.

The first structure within the Ke'e *heiau* complex is near the parking lot and is called Lohi'au's House. Lohi'au was a young man whom both Pele and Hi'iaka fell in love with. After a series of unfortunate incidents provoked by Pele's jealousy, including the torching of the ohi'a forest, Lohi'au died and subsequently returned to life and lived happily ever after with Hi'iaka in Kauai. Along the shoreline where the trail to Ke Ahu a Laka turns uphill is a boulder named Kilioe. Some locals believe this was Lohi'au's sister, (remember — *aumakua* can take on many forms) and according to tradition, Hawaiians used to make small holes in the boulder to hold the umbilical cords, or *piko* of their newborns. In doing so, they hoped to garner a long life, prosperity, and a deeper connection with the Great Mother for their children. Hikers will soon pass the structure called Ka 'Ulu o Pa'oa, which might have been a place of sacrifice or a fishing shrine at some point in time. Next is the hula platform called Ke Ahu a Laka (the altar of Laka) or Ka'Ulu o Laka (inspiration of Laka). This place is sacred to Laka, sister of Pele. The altar is thought to be the cliff behind the topmost platform. Temporary structures called *halau hula* were built for use of dancers engaged in the strenuous and demanding study of the *kahiko*. Their teacher, or *kumu hula* would have put the students through rigorous regimes as they learned the sacred art of dance and chant which was the vehicle through which the Hawaiians preserved and taught all that they knew of their heritage and culture.

The Goddess Laka is the daughter of Haumea, the great Creatrix. Attributes of Laka, who ruled the domain of forests and vegetation, are believed to be domestication, taming wild spirits, gentleness, and attraction. According to the *Ka'Imi Na'auao O Hawai'i Nei*, these qualities were what a student of the *kahiko* would require in order to successfully become an instrument of the sacred arts. A student must learn to develop and master their untamed soul, mind, and body, which was the personification of Laka in her wild uncultivated forest domain. As students perfected their art, they would simultaneously go on a metaphoric journey from the chaos of the forest to the

▲ Wet caves are believed to have been created by Pele with her digging stick.

▲ The ritual area at Ke'e Beach features many well-preserved walls, platforms and heiaus.

sacred and disciplined cosmos of the *halua* hula. Martha Beckwith describes Laka as an "active form of reproductive energy," a desire which the hula student, who was required to be celibate, must have under control until after graduation.

In an interesting intersection of myth and science, reporter Jennifer S. Holland quotes volcanologist Don Swanson of the U. S. Geological Survey who states, "there are instances where it's clear that what's described in chant and song is a metaphor for what really happened." Holland quoting Swanson points to the legend of Pele having torched the ohi'a forest of her sister Hi'iaka, forcing her to dig for the body of her lover and suggests, "this act echoes the two largest volcanic events of Polynesian times: a 60-year Kilauea eruption in the 1400s in which vast tracts of forest burned, and its rock-flinging summit collapsed around 1500. Jennifer quotes Don who says, "Only in recent years have we scientists been figuring out the proper sequence of events, but it was all in the stories if we'd had the foresight to look there first."

Since the 1970s there has been a resurgence of the sacred hula art form of movement and voice. This resurgence insures not only oral traditions will live on in this unique style of chant and dance, but also their spirituality will endure, as well as the goddesses who are teachers, helpers and inspiration to the Hawaiian people. According to Roselle Bailey, Keahualaka, Laka's shrine, is the most celebrated of hula temples. It is also the shrine with the reputation for being one of the Hawaiian people's longest standing religious and cultural sites in continuous use. Pele's fiery personality served herself, her sister, and her people well according to John Charlot, scholar of Hawaiian lore. Had it not been for the challenging and determined nature of Pele and her devotees to stand up in opposition to the influence of missionaries and disruptive external forces, the hula and chants may have disappeared entirely.

Getting to Ke'e Beach

Ke'e Beach is located on the northwest side of the island of Kauai. Take the Kuhio Highway (Highway 56) through Haena State Park to the very end of the road where there is a parking lot at the beach. Here you can access Ke'e Beach and the trail to reach both above mentioned sites. From the west side of the parking lot there is a path along the ocean's edge. Follow the signs. The trailhead to the famous Kalalau Trail is also at the end of the road, but will not access Lohi'au's House or Ke Ahu a Laka.

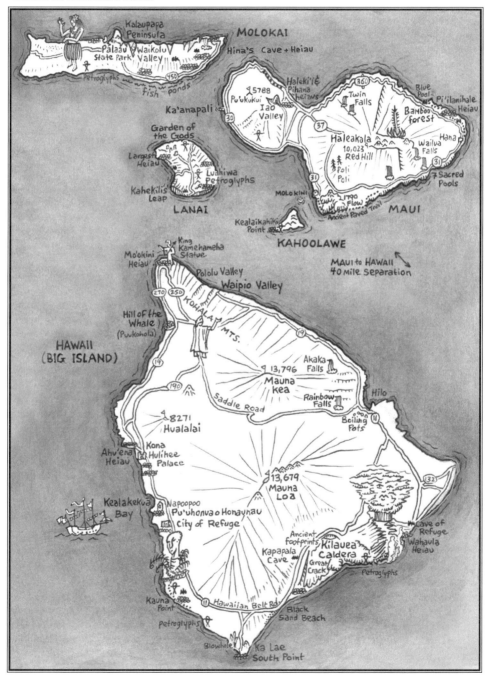

Maui

Ka'anapali Black Rock

While many of the sacred places of Hawaii are associated with human-made structures such as *maraes* and *heiaus* (usually dedicated to the male *akua,* or gods), most of the sites specific to Goddess are natural locations, such as Keka'a here on Ka'anapali Beach. Located beneath the Sheraton Maui for the last 40 years, the sacred black lava outcropping of Keka'a is believed by many to be the precise spot where Pele ignited her very first fire until thwarted by her sister of the sea, Na-maka-o-kaha'i. Hawaiians believe this is one of the most sacred places on Maui because it faces the setting sun, the direction associated with the end of one's life cycle, thus where departed souls would enter into the spirit world at their death. When the area was under construction to build the Sheraton, hundreds of bones were found that had to be reinterred, substantiating the site as a cemetery or holy site where the Polynesians believe the spirits of the departed still walk the land.

The infamous fiery and feisty Madame Pele, considered an *aumakua* of demi-goddess stature, is probably the best known female deity outside of the Hawaii Islands. Though prone to tantrums and impulsive actions, she is both a creator and destroyer. Daughter of the Earth Goddess, Haumea (sometimes called Hina), Pele is credited with creating the Hawaiian Islands when she arrived there by canoe with her sister, Hi'iaka, who Pele kept warm in an egg under her arm during their long journey across the ocean. Her most sacred place on the islands is the volcanic Kilauea Caldera on the Big Island of Hawaii. Polynesian stories have told of Pele's love affairs and legendary wrath when piqued might provoke firestorms of molten lava. Thus Pele is a goddess her people see as a powerful force of creation, transformation, and destruction that should be seriously attended to and given appropriate devotion, then and now.

Modern legends tell of Pele appearing in the form of an old woman alongside the roadway with her dog who mysteriously disappears from the backseat of the car after drivers have kindly picked them up. Other times she is young with flowing black hair. She is said to appear in the form of a woman before the eruption of volcanoes. Whatever her form, when an eruption occurs, Polynesians still beg her mercy and protection that their homes be spared destruction from her creeping, fiery magma. In recent history it has been told the homes of those making offerings to Pele have often been spared even when the abode was in the direct path of the lava flow. Mysteriously the fiery flow seemed to change direction sparing the inhabitants and their worldly possessions.

Professor Charlot explains that Pele's movement, while it saved many of the Hawaiian traditions, never really became fully immersed within Hawaiian culture. This is probably due to what he calls "Pele's counter society which demonstrated the power and self-sufficiency of women." Pele's determination, fiery nature and unwillingness to be subordinated naturally resulted in herself and her sisters forming a community of like-minded women. Their power was sourced from their intelligence, beauty, sexuality, and knowledge — quite an awesome combination! Within their stories they were the strong-willed, dominating characters, relegating men to less important, sometimes silly parts of their drama. According to Charlot, "The passion of the women for each other — both loving and hating, constructive and disruptive — are often the main motivations of the

▲ Black Rock is lower left, Ka'anapali beach is in the center, and Lahaina town can be seen in the upper right.

action. Those passions can be sexual, a clear reflection of the bisexuality (as well as heterosexuality and homosexuality) common in classical Hawaiian life."

Thus it would seem the attributes of Pele, Hi'iaka, and Laka would certainly seem attractive to women or men desiring self-empowerment or to break the bonds of repression. They might also be called upon in prayer by activists, lesbians and feminists seeking energetic support. Nothing is beyond the reach of Pele to achieve. As she told her sister Hi'iaka, "you will have no one to make your way troublesome." It should be noted that Hi'iaka was not quite as fiery as her sister, and was seen as much more gentle. Her powers were conferred upon her by Pele, who could revoke them at will. Pele and Hi'iaka became national figures, with countless newspaper articles detailing their stories establishing a Hawaiian identity and religious literature used by countless persons studying the varied subjects of hula, chants, prophecy, healing, sexuality — even the universe. Quite a legacy befitting this powerful Goddess!

Getting to Ka'anapali Black Rock

From Route 30, or the Honoapi'ilani Highway, turn off onto Ka'anapali Highway which will take drivers to the Sheraton Maui which sits atop Keka'a. Black Rock is about 5 miles (7 km) from Lahaina town. All beaches in Hawaii are public property so hotels like the Sheraton are required to provide beach access trails. A path leading to Ka'anapali Beach is just beyond the hotel. The three sides of Black Rock are popular with underwater enthusiasts observing the abundant sea life along the reef.

Molokai

Hina's Cave & Sacred Heiau

The Great Earth Mother Hina is believed to have given birth to the island of Molokai, making the entire island sacred and a "child" for the Goddess of the

▲ The Penis of Nanahoa is where barren women went to become fertile.

Moon. Once called *Pule-oo*, or Powerful Prayer, it was considered a sanctuary and refuge. It is an island of *heiaus*, wildlife sanctuaries, beaches, breathtaking waterfalls, sea cliffs, jungles, and human-made fishponds. Many small one room churches are scattered across the island. On a trek between Kalaupapa and Mao'ula Falls hikers can find the Peko and Kauleonanahoa stones, both symbols of the Hawaiian's ongoing connection with their earth-based-nature religion.

A tradition still followed on the island which speaks to the deep connection of the people to the Earth Mother is their rite of bringing the umbilical cord of newborns to a famous *piko* or *peko* stone near Kalaupapa. Here, just as at Ke'e Beach on Kauai, a mother will leave her baby's cord in the crevice of a rock in belief that this will garner the grace of the great Earth Mother for her child. According to Mary Kawena Pukui, expert on Hawaiian culture, there were actually three varieties of piko: One was a symbolic umbilical cord that connected the crown of one's head with the ancestor gods or aumakua. Another was the umbilical cord, which linked the infant with the mother and descendants. Third was the piko of the genitals which was representative of reproductive powers. While many Hawaiians placed the piko in stones such as this one on Molokai, they also placed them in places that symbolized good intentions for their loved ones, such as in the case of a woman who placed the piko in waters that flowed to the sea so that her grandchildren might travel across those waters, or the women who were thought to have placed pikos within the boat of Captain Cook, whom they regarded as a god, and would surely take their child to fantastic and wonderful places. Fertility is still a matter of importance between Polynesians and their Earth Mother. Women wishing to conceive bring offerings and sleep near the 6-foot (1.8-m) phallic Kauleonanahoa stone, (literally translated Penis of Nanahoa) believed to impart fertility upon them.

Hina-lau-ae was believed to have a cave considered the root or *kumu* of the island, located on the coast in the southeastern section of the island east of Kaluaaha. Hawaiian custom is to approach this sacred place with reverence and appropriate behavior. It is probably no coincidence that not far away is one of the oldest sacred altars on Molokai, the Ili' ili'opae Heiau. The *heiau* dates back to 1100 and 1300 CE, is 22 feet (7 m) high, 87 feet (27 m) wide, and 286 feet (87 m) long. Powerful *kahunas* practiced here and trained students in the sacred arts of their religion. The power of the Molokai kahunas was renowned as the strongest in the islands. Scholar Martha Beckwith states these heiau were built under the direction of the local chief who would direct the men of his district to line up and pass the stones from hand to hand until the heiau was built. It was important to construct the heiau quickly because the mortal workers of day became the nocturnal *Menehune*, or little people, of a mythical nature at night.

Getting to Hina's Cave and Sacred Heiau

Kalaupapa is located on the northern side of Molokai beyond Kiowea. Go north from Kaunakakai on Route 460 and turn onto Route 470 before reaching the village of Kaulapu'u. Beyond the parking lot walk about a quarter mile through the trees until reaching the Kalaupapa Lookout. There is a great view here, but one must continue another quarter mile (.4 km) to reach the Kauleonanahoa stone which is located in a ironwood grove. Special permission is needed from the descendents of the old Leper Colony of Klaupapa to visit the piko stone.

To reach Ili'ili'opae, located on the southeast side of the island, drive on Highway 450 east, toward Kamalo. Go three miles (4.8 km) past Kamalo and to reach the Ualapu'e Fish Pond. A mile and a half (2.41 km) further, begin looking for a gate on the roadway which leads to the Ili'ili'opae Heiau. This area is often open to visitors, but it is on private land. Owners of the property will take visitors by wagon to the site. All-inclusive day trip tours of Molokai are available on Maui, including boat transportation to and from the island.

Oahu

Pearl Harbor

Kapi'olani Community College tells of three other female *aumakua* deities, Kaihuopala'ai, Kanekua'ana and Ka'ahupahau, connecting them to the sacred locks of Pearl Harbor in Oahu. Kaihoupala'ai, a fish goddess, is daughter of Hina'aimalama, goddess of the undersea, and she is associated with fertility and nature. She is believed to have once resided in the sacred West Lock of Pearl Harbor. In keeping with the Polynesian spiritual cosmology where deities can change into plants or useful animals and fish, Kaihuopala'ai changed into a fish pond near Kapapaapuhi where *'anae,* or mullet, are raised and she is associated with the fall mullet migration. In this form, she provided nourishment and sustenance for her people. Kanekura'ana, is a *mo'o* or water lizard, and guardian goddess of fishponds. She is important to the people as a source of abundant fish and is believed to have brought pearl oysters, shrimp, and anchovies to these sacred waters. The *pipi*, or pearl oysters (where Pearl Harbor got its name), were said to be an abundant source of food until an old widow related to Kanekura'ana was cheated and robbed when harvesting the oysters at the lock. Ka'ahupahau, guardian and ancestral shark goddess protected and helped fishermen in the waters off Oahu and lived in an undersea cave in the West Lock. She guarded the entrance to Pearl Harbor from man-eating sharks, turning into a net to

▲ The Gardens of Waimea exhibits several original heiaus.

catch dangerous sharks before they entered her sacred waters and threatened her people. One legend states that she forbade any shark to eat a human in her waters. Another credits her wrath for the crash of a dry dock built by the U.S. Navy over her home in the locks. After building for four years (1909-1913), during which time construction was plagued with mishaps, the Navy finally completed the dock only to have it collapse into the sea. Legend says the skeleton of a large shark was actually found in the founda-

▲ Two images of Hina demonstrating the abilities she imparted to women.

tions. Ultimately the dock was replaced with a floating dry dock, but taking no further chances, a local priest or *kahuna,* was employed to appropriately bless the dock and make the prescribed chants and offerings to honor Ka'ahupahau. Since then, no further mishaps have befallen the dock. In Polynesian belief, building this structure on her sacred territory surely would have been an insult to Ka'ahupahau and they would have known not to tempt fate thereby angering their benefactress and protectress without appropriate "right of way" granted by the shark goddess.

Stepping away from Hawaiian mythology for a moment, it is necessary to consider the herstorical significance of the Fish Goddess. At first glance, the idea of a Fish Goddess may seem far-fetched — unless one relies on the creatures of the waters for sustenance! The Inuit goddess Sedna of the Sea, and imagery of mermaids may come to mind. Citing excavations along the Danube River at Lepenski Vir in northern Yugoslavia, Marija Gimbutas suggests the Fish Goddess was a "primeval creator or mythical ancestress" and her "power was renewal of life." Apparently some of the statuary from the archaeological site depicted the feminine gender with breasts, egg, fish, and female attributes. Gimbutas cites these shrines at Lepinski Vir as having "a rectangle altar built of stones, with an entrance in the shape of the Goddess' open legs. At the end of the altar stood one to two sculptures representing the Fish Goddess, a round or egg-shaped stone engraved with labyrinthine/uterine designs or a sacrificial container." She theorized the dead were buried in these triangular structures dating from the middle 7th and early 6th millennium BCE. Hence, at death they returned to the Mother to be reborn. In the language of Goddess, the fish became synonymous with the uterus or womb of the Divine Creatrix. This is suggested in the imagery of a Boeotian vase dated 700-678 BCE which shows Artemis with a fish drawn at her womb area. It comes as no surprise that both Artemis and the Fish Goddess were considered the Mistress of Life and Death. The image of goddess as fish was important iconography of the Neolithic and Copper Ages. Some imagery depicted the Fish Goddess as a net-like design and Gimbutas believed symbols of a fish, net, or life-giving uterine moisture became conceptually inter-change-able. Fish Goddess imagery was also found on Minoan art and at excavations in Malta. Gimbutas also suggests a linguistic link to support the close relationship between the womb, uterus, and fish. She states a connection between the Greek *delphis* or dolphins, and *delphys* or womb. Perhaps humankind's intuitive love for this beloved creature reflects a primal connection to the Mother. Interestingly, within Christian iconography Jesus Christ became associated with the symbol of the fish.

Generally speaking, the Hawaiian shark aumakua became much like a family pet who expects to be fed daily in exchange for driving fish into the family fishing nets. They kept predators at bay should a family member fall into the waters from a capsized boat, and they can act as a fetcher to kill an enemy, though after the arrival of Christianity, this practice was deemed inappropriate. Bodies of dead family members are dedicated to these ancestral sharks which can morph into other forms such as birds, fish, humans or lizards. Pele's brother was a shark and the Pele family routinely offered corpses to these shark gods in the traditional *kaku'ai* ceremony of transfiguration. The bones would be wrapped in yellow tapa before being offered to the sharks, likewise, when bones were offered to Pele at her volcano, the bones of the deceased would be wrapped in red or black tapa. The Hawaiians believed the shark gods held the bones, or *iwi*, the key of immortality to the dead person, under a fin until the remains transformed into a shark. Within a few days a kahuna or relative would be able to recognize the transfigured relative by the markings on the cheeks or sides of the newest little shark.

Getting to Pearl Harbor

West of Honolulu on Kamehameha Highway (Highway 99) you will find Pearl Harbor. This is a natural harbor with entrances to two inner locks, east and west. Daily harbor tours are available of the area, especially to the memorial of the U.S.S. Arizona, sunk by the Japanese at the beginning of World War II.

NEW ZEALAND

New Zealand, or *Aotearoa* as it is sometimes called by indigenous peoples, is home to the Maori, or the *Tangata Whenua*, "people of the land." The Maori consider themselves guardians, or *kaitiaki,* of the Earth and they have a strong identification with Papatuanuku, the Earth Mother. They consider all the Earth sacred and it is through the land that they are unified, sustained, and identify themselves as a people. One rite which verifies this strong connection to the soil is when a child is born. Its afterbirth, or *whenua,* is buried in a sacred place of Papatuanuku so that a strong spiritual bond is made between the newborn and Goddess.

To paraphrase New Zealand scholar Kathryn Rountree, the Maori religion is one of ancestral spirits and elemental goddesses and gods. There is Mahuika (or Mahuea), goddess of fire, or aspects of Hine associated with death, darkness and dawn, but there is a dearth of information available to non-indigenous people which connects Goddess to particular sites in Aotearoa. One does not find the same kind of sites connected to Goddess as can be found in Asia, Europe or the Americas. One begins to recognize a different kind of paradigm emerging in the spirituality here that carries over from Australia.

All tribes have a particular sacred mountain and lake or river within their ancestral territory. Rountree explains that when the Maori introduce themselves, they traditionally include the name of their sacred mountain or river, further demonstrating how people's personal identity is interwoven with the sacred landscape. These major sacred mountains and rivers are reasonably well-known in New Zealand, e.g., the Waikato River is sacred to the Waikato tribe, the Whanganui River is sacred to the Whanganui tribe, and Lake Rotorua is sacred to the Arawa tribe. There may be a tree or small pond which embodies the spirit of an ancestor, possibly considered sacred or powerful within a family. Sites might be used by

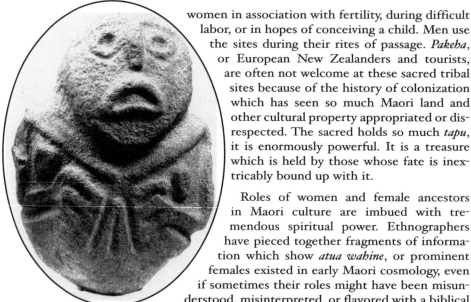

women in association with fertility, during difficult labor, or in hopes of conceiving a child. Men use the sites during their rites of passage. *Pakeha*, or European New Zealanders and tourists, are often not welcome at these sacred tribal sites because of the history of colonization which has seen so much Maori land and other cultural property appropriated or disrespected. The sacred holds so much *tapu*, it is enormously powerful. It is a treasure which is held by those whose fate is inextricably bound up with it.

Roles of women and female ancestors in Maori culture are imbued with tremendous spiritual power. Ethnographers have pieced together fragments of information which show *atua wahine*, or prominent females existed in early Maori cosmology, even if sometimes their roles might have been misunderstood, misinterpreted, or flavored with a biblical or Victorian slant. One example is Hine, Goddess of Death, who was called the Goddess of Hades, a place without a context within Maori spirituality. According to Shahrukh Husain, one myth has Hine-

▲ This stone carved Fish Goddess was revered for providing abundance from the sea and renewal of life.

nui-te-po with a vagina of teeth made of flint edges that generated sparks and lightning which killed Maui when he attempted to climb inside her in the form of a lizard. Some say men who set out on a journey or quest must seek the assistance of women to accomplish their task. In everyday life this is seen in the tradition that women must stay away when meeting houses are built, yet they are needed to remove some of the sacred potency within and this tapu can only be removed by a high ranking woman or *ruahine*. In myth it is reflected in the story of the hero Maui who brings fire to humankind stored in the fingernails of Mahuika, the mother of Hina (or Hine). Merlin Stone suggests Hina and Mahuika seem to be senior to Maui in myths, suggesting he may have actually been a later addition to the original beliefs about Goddess. More research is being done to uncover the clues of the atua wahine and she is reemerging into Maori culture. According to Maori scholar Aroha Yates-Smith, the consequence of these revelations may serve to positively affect Maori social, cultural, political, and environmental lives, with people beginning to realize the interconnection between Goddess, humankind, and the Universe.

Cape Reinga

In the northernmost tip of New Zealand is Cape Reinga, a mythical gateway to the Otherworld. This place is sacred to the Maori because it is where the spirits of the recently deceased leave this world for that of Hawaiiki, thus, it is a place where the name of Hine-nui-te-po would be invoked in Hina's aspect as Goddess of Death and Darkness. Legend has it that the departed will travel to Cape Reinga and quench their thirst in the underworld stream called Re-Wai-O-Raio-Po. At a promontory near the northernmost tip of the cape, the departed slides down into the sea, swims over to Three Kings Island and begins a trek to Hawaiiki, the Polynesian version of heaven.

As with so many Goddesses, their nature is that of duality; life and death, creation and destruction, above and below, dark and light. Hina embraces these dual attributes of life and death and as such, represents wholeness. Reflecting many deities whose whole manifestation is too all-encompassing to comprehend, Hina too has been divided into dozens of aspects throughout Oceania, all being variations of the one Goddess. Here at Cape Reinga she is particularly the Hina who fled to the Underworld when she was seduced by her father Tane and through his incestuous act, the Maori tribes believe death was brought to humankind because before this transgression humans were immortal. Though Tane tried to convince Hina to retreat from the Underworld and return to the Above, she refused, and there she waits for her children upon their passing.

She lives within every Maori *wharenui*, or meeting house, where spiritual ceremony is conducted. Within the walls is a *tangihanga* where the dead are mourned, thus a central figure to the *wharenui* is, again, Hine-nui-te-po, Goddess of Death and Darkness. When a family's loved one departs, it is to Hine, the Great Mother, in this her aspect of Death, one must return. According to the Journal of the Polynesian Society, she might be invoked in traditional rituals to restore a dead person to life. She has been associated with Papa, the female principle, who stated to her consort, Rangi, "Our offspring shall return to me in death, and I will conceal them." It was understood that Hina would protect her children in the spirit world, rather than be the cause of their death, becoming the caretaker of their souls. Both Papa and Hine were considered powerful atua wahine and beloved by generations of Maori. Hina's aspect as Hineteiwaiwa, Goddess of crafts and childbirth, also resides in the wharenui. In this aspect she is believed to hold the *mauri* of the *ruahine*, or spreads forth the ceremonial mat.

But that is not the extent of who she is. She is also the Hina of life. Born to Mahuea behind the waterfall of a hidden cave, Hina grew up and passed the knowledge of fire to humankind. She taught them to create fire and use it for cooking in the imu oven and for warmth. She is Goddess of agriculture and brought the salt-less water to the people so food would grow. She is Hina Turama who created the stars, and Hina'ea the Goddess of the sun, healing, and domestic life. She is Hina who birthed the sea and fish. She is Hina of fate, magic, arts, crafts, and tat-

tooing. She is Hina who went to live in the moon when she tired of her lazy husband. From there she smiles down and oversees the realms of behavior, menstruation, fertility, conception, weather, rebirth, communication, and cycles. When she is the dark moon, she is Goddess of Death. When she is the full moon, she is the potent mature woman. When she is the waxing moon she is the Creatrix full of potential, and when she is the waning moon, she is old woman, wise in her years, who

▲ Cape Reinga is a mythical "leaping off point" for recently deceased souls to enter the spiritual world.

▲ Another version of the Fish Goddess, as seen on pottery.

knows what must be let go and transformed. She might be associated with many such goddesses: Isis, Selene, Artemis and the Virgin Mary who have associations with the crescent moon. She is a mother who can move between the realms of heaven, earth, and the underworld, creating humankind and their culture. Still the protectress of the Tongan fire walkers, Hina and her legends have spanned across the many islands where she is believed to have traveled by canoe.

Today the trend in Maori culture mirrors that in other parts of the world where women are seeking to reclaim their rich female heritage that has been marginalized or omitted from historical records, thereby seeking a restoration of their self-esteem, personal empowerment, and an equality between genders. Christianity, Victorian influence, and two hundred years of colonization all took their toll on the authentic herstory of atua wahines and their role within Maori cosmology. Here in New Zealand, as in other parts of the world, as the female deities became insignificant, so did the women within society. Professor Aroha Yates-Smith states, "There was a strong presence of the feminine at the embryonic stage of Maori society." Their imagery is preserved in stone and wood artifacts. What survived in Maori stories, songs, incantations and anecdotes points to sexuality, childbirth and death being the domain of Goddess. In a modern context, Yates-Smith explains roles of today's women reflects the "generative function previously carried out by Papa, Hineteiwaiwa and Hinekorako." Other high-ranking female roles, or *ruahine*, were taken over by doctors and clergy.

Progress is being made, with women beginning to once again reclaim and embrace their ancient culture. Yates-Smith cites as example the tradition of returning the placenta of newborns to Papatuanuku. Women are reviving the ancient healing techniques and using them to complement Western medicine. Women are acting politically to regain tribal land, and sharing knowledge about the feminine is becoming more of a top priority. Another arena in which knowledge of the feminine is being spread is within film and performing arts, with the recently released and well-received independent film *Whalerider*, a successful example. As a result of this resurgence, men in Maori society are beginning to come around, and the environment is benefiting from a new attitude toward nature, but New Zealand is the same as other parts of the world, where indigenous values are in conflict with capitalism and corporate greed.

Getting to Cape Reinga

From Awanui, about 6 miles (10 km) north of Kaitaia, where Highway 1 and Highway 10 meet, it is about 65 miles (105 km) further along the Aupouri Peninsula to reach Cape Reinga, the northernmost tip of the island. Access is also possible from Ninety Mile Beach.

Tahiti

Ra'iatea

The island Ra'iatea was long considered the spiritual heart of the Society Islands. From here Hina, in her aspect as Hina fa'auru va'a (Hina-the-canoe-pilot), left with Ru (the Transplanter) by canoe and discovered many of the other islands including Hawaii. After their discoveries, other voyagers followed in their aftermath and culture was born on the islands of Oceania, thus Hina and Ru were the mother and father of the islands, representing the complementary nature of both genders. While this is legend, it has a foundation in science as archaeological evidence has since been discovered connecting the islands.

According to the Polynesian Voyaging Society quoting Teuira Henry, the canoe station of Hina and Ru was on the sacred peninsula called Motu-tapu and the passage from which their journey began was called Te-ava-o-Hina (the passage of Hina). Their sacred waterway, (now called the Te Ava Mao Pass) and canoe station was near the most sacred spot on Ra'iatea, the Taputapuatea Marae, located in the south east region of the island, near Opoa. Ancient navigators were aided by fires on the marae as they made their way through the sacred passage and out into the world beyond, as far as New Zealand. Hina is said to have made and spread her tapa here and embarked in her canoe on her first journey to the moon. Hina brought the first banyan tree into existence here. Some legends have the first man created in Tahiti for Hina's pleasure. She is revered to this day by Tahitian fire walkers.

From Taputapuatea other marae were founded using sacred stones borrowed from the structure of this international marae. Descendants and men from Taputapuatea later came to be invested and ordained king of their lands. Considered the largest and best preserved marae in the region, it stands 141 feet (43 m) long, 24 feet (7.3 m) wide, and is 9.8 feet (3 m) high. In front of the marae is a rectangular shaped courtyard made of black volcanic rock. A reproduction of the original image of Oro, god of war, now stands in the center of the marae. From that first venture into the world at the beginning of creation with Hina and Ru, came a lineage of 30 generations of kings in Ra'iatea and the various settlements throughout the South Pacific region were born.

▲ The Polynesian canoe carried seeds, animals, people, and culture over the wide expanse of the Pacific.

According to ethnographer Martha Beckwith, Tahiti was first settled by commoners who farmed the land. From this class arose warriors who intermarried with the elite and royal family, who then forced into service the commoners whenever a human sacrifice was required. Dotted across the island are two styles of marae: inland were the first platform style being built by the earlier commoners, followed by the wall style marae along the coast which was introduced later. The Taputapuatea site falls into the latter category.

The act of building a canoe was a spiritual experience for the community which involved not only humankind, but the willing participation of the deities. Rituals were conducted when a tree was cut, shaped, and brought down from the forest. Offerings were made to the forest deity for the gift of the tree. In Tahiti is has been said that following a wind, the tree would come down the mountain of its own accord, with the men who felled it inside the tree/canoe, until it reached the bottom of the mountain. Here the men would step from the canoe, which was light and easy to carry. This seems to be an example of what Beckwith describes as Polynesian legends reflecting the people's dependence on the cooperation of deity, which controlled resources. Just like with the completion of other sacred structures, canoes were an equally important community project that prompted a dedication ceremony, followed by village feasting and offerings.

Getting to Ra'iatea

Located on the southeastern side of the island, south of Faaroa Bay, continue beyond Opoa, 19.8 miles (32 km) from Uturoa where there is found the famous marae. International flights are plentiful to Tahiti. Once there rental cars or taxi are good options to visit the site.

GAIA ALERT
SOUTH PACIFIC

The Greenhouse Effect, the warming of the Earth due to fossil fuel emissions and the clearing of forests, is the greatest threat to Oceania. The Greenhouse Effect is causing polar ice caps and mountain glaciers to melt, causing seawater levels to rise, and at the current rate, within 100 years many coastlines may be destroyed. Saltwater will mingle with groundwater, making growth of food impossible in affected areas, causing shortages and higher prices. Warmer temperatures seem to have increased the number of annual hurricanes causing loss of life and property. Coral is being destroyed by pollution and non-sustainable fishing practices reducing fish stock, thereby affecting the economy of the islands. Industrialized countries are turning a blind eye to the problem, often denying the severity and complexity of the problem as we slide down a slippery slope from which a return may be impossible.

▲ Coral reefs and the aquatic life that depend on their health are all becoming increasingly threatened.

SOUTH AMERICA

AND WEST INDIES

The last of the Inka, who have lived in isolation for the last 500 years, have managed to preserve — relatively intact — the teachings of the way of the feminine, of the Earth, of power, of direct experience, of wisdom and knowledge.
—Alberto Villoldo, Ph.D. *and medical anthropologist*

I N SOUTH AMERICA, and especially the islands of the West Indies, there exists a delicious stew of Goddess spirituality. While today most of this region is predominately Roman Catholic, some Christian practitioners worship Goddess in the form of the Madonna. Other diverse spiritual ingredients of South America and the West Indies include Hinduism, shamanism, and versions of Yoruban spirituality which include dashes of Santeria, Voodoo, and Candomble, replete with trance worship. From the mystical splendor of Machu Picchu and the increasingly vulnerable Amazon rainforest, to the beaches of Salvador, and the cathedrals of Bolivia, the "feminine face of God" is being renewed and revered today in a delectable buffet. But that might not always have been the case.

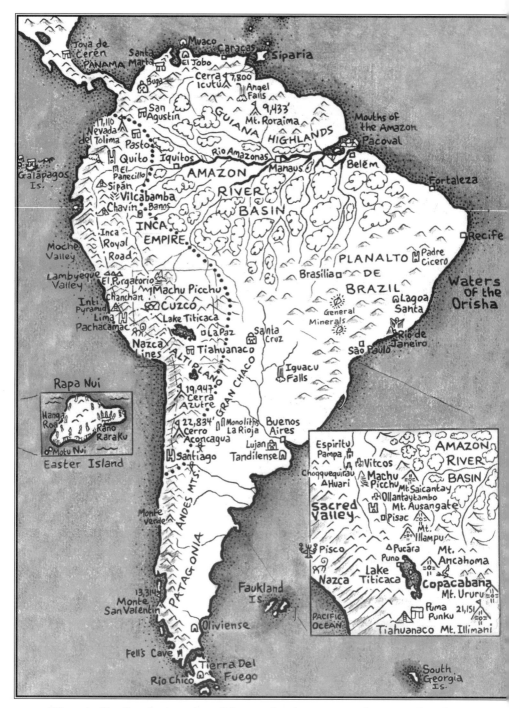

Historically, South America did not develop as a cohesive cultural unit. Some parts of the continent developed sophisticated ceremonial centers using advanced technology, while others remained locked in the Stone Age. Geography and the control of water in religious and functional ways were major factors in shaping the diverse cultural beliefs of the people. Yet certain common themes do seem to prevail. Religious beliefs and deities are associated with Nature as people tried to explain the world around them. Their rituals were celebrated on a fixed calendar that cited celestial movements to aid in agriculture. Human and animal sacrifice were employed, as was cannibalism particularly among Amazonian tribes who ate human flesh either to perpetuate the power of the dead person, or to gain their power and inflict revenge upon the tribe of the deceased. Ancestor reverence, recognition of sacred places in the natural landscape, and the use of hallucinogenic drugs for ritual purposes were also employed. One final pervasive belief that is important for our purposes is the belief in a male creator god. Whether called Viracocha, Pachacamac, Bochica, or Inti, the sole creator was passed on through oral traditions as male. That being said, there seems to have been earlier female dominance of the Earth among certain groups which are evident in myths that show male gods calling for a role reversal. Evident also are minor Goddesses or ones in which they are secondary to male gods, which might reflect the diminishing role of Goddess here as in other places worldwide that experienced an influx of dominating male deities. These myths hint at former female dominance, perhaps suggesting the worship of an earlier female Creatrix deity. These feminine deities may have been subverted, with only the primeval Inca Earth Goddess Pacha Mama remaining potent in the minds of the people. Considering there was no writing system, and history was passed down by knot makers, or *quipu camayoqs* tying bundles of string to aid their memory, certainly herstory might have been lost had a shift in gender equality occurred.

Still another component of this stew, according to Alberto Villoldo, is the exotic flavor of the shaman. In this world of the Inca are pathways to medicine teachings, knowledge and power based on our relationship to Pacha Mama or Mother Earth, and traditions of working and healing with light. Yaje Woman was said to have provided the rainforest tribes with hallucinatory plants which they used to commune with the other realms to gain knowledge and guidance. Adding still more spice are some lesser known Goddesses. Bachue was the large breasted Chiba Earth Goddess who emerged from a sacred lake and helped populate the world. When her job was done, she transformed herself into a serpent and returned to the sacred lake. She was associated with fertility and was a protectress of crops. Kasogonaga is particularly interesting as she was a sky Goddess who brought rain to the Earth. Along with the beneficent waters, she brought the red anteater and the giant beetle as the creators of First Man and First Woman. Urpay Huachac was the female Creatrix of fish who transformed herself into a dove to avoid the evil clutches of a sexual predator. Si, an androgynous Moon Goddess of the Moche and Chimu people was considered the supreme deity over humans, deities, and natural forces. Her early origins seem to be an armored war deity of unknown gender.

Devotees of all these spiritualities combine traditions and belief in Goddess from the earliest up to the modern times, with overlapping versions of religious expression in between. Whether one has the taste buds of a purist or turns up the heat with a more syncretized faith, Goddess, Nature, Mother Earth is a powerful influence on the psyche of millions in this part of the world as seen by the delectable assortment of worship and practitioners all at the table of the Divine Feminine.

BOLIVIA

B olivian native peoples developed an emergence story along common themes similar to other Andean creation myths. Humankind emerged from underwater or underground places like Lake Titicaca and near Cuzco. Goddess advocates would be very tempted to borrow that cosmology citing the emergence, or reemergence of the Divine Feminine within contemporary South America. Embracing the female deities from primeval times, up to and through the Spanish conquest, until today, brings a rich diversity of varying spiritual beliefs, each with their own name for the Divine Female. Some called her Pacha Mama, la Virgen, Kali, Aparecida, Mary, Oshun, and Yemaya (Iemanja). Others revered her in the Black and Brown Madonnas, called by many names in many aspects, which are the dark colored depictions of the Madonna or Goddess brought to this land by dark skinned persons and those of African descent. Historian Lucia Chiavola Birnbaum believes she is dark because she often reflects the people who revere her, people of negated cultures or subordinate classes. She is dark because of her connection to the dark Earth and regeneration, not because of soot from candle flames. To others her dark metaphor represents the veil behind which Goddess was forced to exist during days of repression and persecution. These images of the Black and Brown Madonnas hold sway over many worshippers, no matter the color of their skin. Coming full circle, the primeval Pacha Mama is often looked upon today as the Virgin Mary.

Virgin of Copacabana

While Black Madonnas are more often found in Spain, France, or regions where many people are of African descent, here on the Bolivian side of the shores of Lake Titicaca within the Cathedral of the Virgin de Candelaria resides a Black Madonna. Also known as the Virgin of Copacabana and the Queen of Bolivia, she is the country's matron saint and many miracles are attributed to her by devotees. Carved by Tito Yupanqui, a descendant of an Incan emperor, the statue of the Virgin took eight months to complete, but once she was installed in the cathedral in 1583, it is said miracles began to happen. Today devotees still believe this Black Madonna has magical powers to provide what they pray for and Catholics perform a kind of sympathetic magic to that end. Devotees come to the cathedral with small images or pictures of their needs and pray for success in obtaining their desires. In fact, vendors outside the church sell tiny replicas of cars, houses, and other assorted items the devoted can buy and take with them into the cathedral to represent their need to petition the Virgin.

▲ Copacabana is situated in a picturesque valley.

Another little known feature of the cathedral is a side entrance reminiscent of a cave where one enters a very long dimly lit room. Here petitioners write the object of their desire on the walls. Further along the hall is a room where there is an image of the Madonna where the faithful can light candles in Her honor and further petition the Virgin that a prayer be answered.

The Virgin stands on a large elaborate mechanical altar so that she faces the main chapel on weekends and is spun around to face a smaller chapel during the week. A silver ship at the bottom of the altar represents the moon and the gold on the altar represents the power of the sun, keen reminders of earlier times when Inti the Sun God, and Mama Quilla the Moon Goddess, were together worshipped by people of the area.

According to Willow LaMonte, one phenomena of the various Brown or Black Madonnas is that they are frequently attributed to various forms of resistance or non-compliance, depending on each Madonna's own legend. In keeping with this behavior of these Madonnas in general, the Copacabana Madonna is no exception. She is never moved nor leaves the cathedral. Legend has it that bad luck would befall the city and its inhabitants should she depart her domain.

A final interesting feature of this cathedral is the weekend *car cha'lla* or blessing. Vehicles are decorated with flowers, ribbons, flags, and assorted paraphernalia that the owner thinks will beautify the car, truck or bus. The vehicles line up and wait their turn to come to the church to ask that the vehicle and driver be blessed and receive protection from the Holy Mother. Cathedral priests come out and sprinkle holy water on the vehicle interior and under the hood. While this might

▲ Towering mountains and llamas dot the landscape around Copacabana.

suggest an air of fancy or folk magic, be assured, this is taken very seriously by the Bolivians who flock to the cathedral from all over the area in faith that their Virgin, a Black Madonna, will provide protection and all they may need.

Getting to the Cathedral of Copacabana

About 49 miles (79 km) from Huatajata, two bus companies run from LaPaz to Copacabana with daily departures. Tour companies provide sightseeing excursions from La Paz or Puno. If going by car from La Paz, follow El Alto Highway northwest to the Straits of Tiquina, then ferry or hydrofoil across the straits between San Pablo and San Pedro. It's about a two hour trip depending on traffic. While in the area, be sure to check out the Isla Del Sol, or Island of the Sun on sacred Lake Titicaca, believed to be the place where the Incan civilization was founded by Manco Capac and his sister/wife, Mama Ocllo as they emerged from the lake guided by Inti, the Sun God. Some hydro foils stop at Isla de la Luna, Island of the Moon enroute to Isla del Sol. Here one finds unrestored ruins of an ancient convent called Ajilla Wasi, House of the Chosen Women, associated with the Mama Cunas and acllas who were devoted to the Moon Goddess and Inti.

Goddess Focus
Fiesta del Espiritu: Pacha Mama Festival

According to *Lonely Planet*, miners of the city of Potosi in Bolivia consider Pacha Mama the mother of all Bolivians. In her honor, during the last three Saturdays of June and the first Saturday of August, they hold the Fiesta del Espiritu which includes as one of its celebratory rituals, the sacrificing of a llama. After a llama has been procured, the miners and their families drink alcohol and chew coca leaves. Next, the miners tie the feet of the llama and feed it alcohol and coca leaves. At high noon, an hour auspicious in many faiths, the llama offers its life to Pacha Mama so the miners might have good luck and safety in the coming year. Blood from the llama is sprinkled at the openings of the caves and tunnels in which the miners work in their belief this will effectively bless the space. The llama meat is then prepared by the women and served at the community feast which is followed by music, dancing and all manner of celebration. The head, feet and stomach of the llama are returned to Pacha Mama, buried in her dark soil.

BRAZIL

Water played a significant role in religious belief as indicated by Asima Si who was believed by her devotees to reside in the Amazon River. The Andean Mama Cocha lived in the sea, and Elizi, was the Voodoo Goddess of the waterfalls of Saut D'Eau in Haiti. Powerful women were not absent from the landscape as the Iamuricuma Women of the Brazilian river region of Xingu were known to be Amazon-like warriors who could transform themselves into spirits or capture those who looked upon them. Anyone thinking of Medusa turning her enemies to stone? It is believed these women were the inspiration for the river of the region being named Amazon as those who came upon these women believed they had discovered the Greek warrior women of the same name.

Sacred Waters of the Orisha

In modern times the people of Bahai, Salvador continue to pray at altars devoted to the African deities Yemaya, Oya, and Oshun. Practitioners build their altars in homes, in private niches, or in sacred spots they find naturally appearing on the beach. Devotees make offerings to these African Goddesses in rivers, oceans, and in the Salvador Sea. Fishermen pray for protection and abundance from Yemaya, Oya, and Oshun. Statues of African Goddesses can be found in stores throughout Brazil. Worship continues in Catholic basilicas and Candomble churches called *terreiros*, such as Casa Branca, Salvador's oldest. Watered-down theater performances of ancient rituals can be attended by tourists, although those with open minds and hearts are not turned away from the real thing. To her devotees, Yemaya (known as Agwe in Haiti) is the foundation and structure to most devotees' community life. She is both universal and intimate, a Creatrix who hears her followers' prayers and provides. Yemaya, a female *orisha,* or deity of the African Yorubans, holds court in her waters off the coast of Bahai. Originating from Nigeria and Benin, Yemaya is considered by her devotees as the offspring of Heaven and Earth. She is said to rule the sea waters, which cover three-quarters of the planet. She is considered a maternal force of creation and the mother of many other orishas, including the West African Goddesses

Oshun and Oya. Though venerated throughout the year in Brazil, Yemaya has her big celebration on February 2nd in Salvador and on December 31st in Rio de Janeiro. The Salvadoran Sea, called the Bay of All Saints, as well as beaches to the east of the city of Salvador, namely Itapoa, Rio Vermelho, Barra, and Pituba, are sacred to worshippers of every race, color and cultural origin. All are welcome to make offerings or become attuned with the "Queen of the Waters," or Goddess *Mae e Rainha das Aguas*, as she is called in the Portuguese tongue.

Whether in Salvador, Rio or other cities known for Yemaya worship, her celebration on feast days are similar in many ways. Macumba and Candomble practitioners dressed in blue and white process along the beaches at night with candles to illuminate their way. People from all walks of life and religions join together in the spirit of the occasion, casting into the sea offerings of money, food, flowers, rice, perfume, and lipstick, to honor this Goddess of the waters. Boats laden with presents are pushed toward the murky depths to curry favor

or thank Yemaya, just Egyptian Goddess Isis on traditions of long some devotees associ- Egyptian Isis, both continent of Africa. day, cities are trans- public carnivals open venerate this deity. ing, singing, drumming in the name of Yemaya, out the night until to Chiavola Birnbaum, laughter of the Goddess the dominate religion."

▲ Orisha and Yemaya.

as devotees of the do today based ago. Appropriately, ate Yemaya with originating on the On Yemaya's feast formed into grand to all wishing to Fireworks, danc- and celebrating, all continues through- dawn. According "Carnival is the at the pieties of Whether a Neo-

Pagan or New Age devotee of Yemaya (also Iemanja or Ymoya), or a traditional believer in the more ancient West African Yoruban spirituality which predates Christianity and Islam, this Goddess has long been deeply imbedded in the minds and hearts of her followers. Today we find veneration for her in syncretized versions of Yoruban spirituality in South America and the West Indies in the practice of Macumba, Santeria, Candomble, Voodoo, or Umbanda. Yemaya, along with her daughters Oshun and Oya, have their beginnings in the earliest days of West Africa before they migrated to the New World with victims of the slave trade. According to Luisah Teish, these three goddesses are aspects of nature which have an active and receptive consciousness. They are not an archetype or psychological state of mind.

During the days of European colonialism, slaves were forced to practice their Yoruban religion in secret. A combination of ancestor worship and the veneration of nature deities, or *orishas*, their spirituality was practiced in the guise of Catholicism so it could survive and avoid persecution. Major aspects and gods of their faith became associated with particular Catholic saints and the connections survive to the present day. Some have Yemaya associated with Saint Anne and Our Lady of the Immaculate Conception. Today, worship of Oshun and Yemaya are rightly very much out in the open as indicated by the aforementioned celebrations in Brazil. Bands compose and sing songs in their name, such as the group River Ocean with their song "Love and Happiness" with lyrics celebrating the powers of Yemaya and Oshun. Images of these Goddesses appear in some Catholic churches such as in the Igreja e Convento de Sao Francisco in Salvador. Makeshift altars in their honor can be found on many streets.

Just as devotees of Goddess cross ethnic and cultural lines as they are being drawn to or feeling called by the Indian Kali, Chinese Kwan Yin or the Egyptian Isis, some are drawn to the African-Brazilian Yemaya and Oshun, with little or no association with African roots. However, those with a Yoruban heritage honor both the nature goddesses and deified ancestors and it should be qualified that those with an African heritage connect with these deified ancestors on a deeper, blood kin level. Yemaya, Oya, and Oshun are part of who and what they are.

Getting to the Sacred Waters of the Orisha

Bahai is a state in Brazil located in the northeast part of the country where the Atlantic Ocean touches its western boundary. Salvador is the capital of Bahai where many of the most beautiful beaches in the world can be found. International and domestic flights are plentiful into Salvador. Once there, just get in a taxi and head for the beach! Good choices are the beaches of Itapoa, Abaete Lagoon, Jaguaribe Beach, Pitau, Praia do Farol near the Farol Flat Hotel, Rio Vermelho, Barra, or Corsario. Or hop on a schooner and visit one of the many adjacent islands within All Saint's Bay. Goddess is particularly fond of the ruins near Forte da Gamboa. From the bus station in the town of Valencia walk or take a taxi to the dock where a ferry sails for Gamboa on the island of Tinhare. Ferries take five hours, speed boats only two, but the ferry enables the traveler to see exotic flora of mangrove islands along the way.

Our Lady Aparecida Basilica

It is the contention of many devoted to Goddess that most cathedrals dedicated to Mary, Sophia, or Black and Brown Madonnas are in the realm where the Divine Creatrix shares a home with Catholic deities. The Brazilian sanctuary of the Black Madonna *Aparecida*, whose name means "appeared" in Portuguese, is one such example. Many believe that some Black Madonnas originate from the Indian Kali, Artemis Ephesia, or the Egyptian Isis, so it is no wonder Aparecida shares aspects with some of her counterparts. She is the protectress of travelers and benefactress of fisherman.

Her origin began in 1717 when several fisherman went out with their nets to catch fish for a community celebration near the Port of Itaguagnu. It was not the best fishing season so their nets kept coming up empty until they prayed to Our Lady of the Immaculate Conception (who is associated with the African Goddess Yemaya, known as 'Mother of Fish" in Brazil). In one last effort to catch any fish, the nets were cast and what came up from the depths was a statue of Our Lady of the Immaculate Conception. The fisherman took this as a sign to continue fishing and suddenly they were visited by an apparition of Aparecida, appearing in this her first miracle, along with nets so full of fish their boat almost capsized. Aparecida provided sustenance, a value commonly attributed to the powers of Black Madonnas. While no one knows how the statue

▲ Our Lady of Aparecida is featured on a Mexican postage stamp.

discovered by the fisherman ended up in the river, it was established the sculptor was Frei Agostino de Jesus, a monk from Sao Paulo. The clay statue, just less than three feet (.91 m) tall, is dark brown and dressed in ornately embroidered cloth. She wears a crown of precious stones and sits in her niche in the new monumental 70,000 square-foot basilica on Pitas Hill which can hold 30,000 devotees at once; second only in size to Saint Peter's in Rome.

From those humble beginnings, Our Lady of Aparecida, whose feast day is October 12th, has grown to establish a following rivaled by Our Lady of Guadalupe in Mexico City. Statistics cite seven million pilgrims visit Aparecida on an annual basis. A radio program meant to help the local people, the Catholic-operated Radio Aparecida located near her sanctuary, went on the air in 1951. Programs are aired promoting citizenship, moral, cultural, religious, artistic, literary and scientific education for the Brazilian people. Recently the $70 million Aparecida Magic, Cultural, Religious and Recreational Park was built by entrepreneurs only a stone throw away from the basilica. Targeting pilgrims of Aparecida, this is Brazil's first religious theme park, though it is not officially connected with the Church. Obviously this representation of the Dark Madonna, (who is also venerated by devotees of the West African Goddess Oshun, or Oxum in Brazil), has developed wide-spread influence and become quite a phenomenon. According to Lucia Chiavola Birnbaum, values attributed to Black Madonnas are usually nurturance, justice and transformation. In keeping with tradition, devotees would probably agree, Aparecida has been a busy Mother.

Getting to Our Lady Aparecida Basilica

The basilica is located on the highway connecting Sao Paulo and Rio de Janeiro called the Via Dutra or BR 116. It is 110 miles (177.4 km) from Sao Paulo and 120 miles (193.5 km) from Rio de Janeiro. Public transportation is available to this popular destination.

Goddess Focus
Mercado de Brujos: Witches Markets

Today, Andean witches can be found at two famous markets selling herbal remedies, items for a *despacho*, medicine bundles and good luck talismans. Called the Mercados de Brujos in Chiclayo, Peru and the Mercado de Herchiceria in La Paz, Bolivia, *curanderos* or healers skilled in the arts of magic and herbal healing prescribe and sell folk remedies handed down by their ancestors to ailing neighbors and tourists alike. Here you might arrange to participate in an Andean *despacho*, a ceremony where *huchas*, or heavy energies such as pain, disappointment, or suffering can be cleansed from within. From the whimsical to the macabre, ingredients for all manner of powerful potions can be obtained here, including statues of deities, hallucinogenic drugs, and herbal concoctions.

Unfortunately the word "witch" is charged with many uneducated, fear-based perceptions and negative connotations. A witch, *Webster's* stereotypical and inaccurate definition aside, is not one who practices black magic with the aid of the devil. Witches as devil-worshippers are an anomaly of popular culture since witches do not even believe in the devil. The devil is a character within Christianity, (though he is actually traced back to Zoroastrism or Mazdaism) not found in various Celtic, Germanic and other European agrarian forms of ancient paganism from where witches find their roots.

287

▲ Witches were the "wise women" and midwives versed in use of medicinal herbs.

Today, as in days long ago, "witches" were the wise women or men of the village, and this word later came to mean something entirely foreign to reality. They were the midwives who brought new life into the world. They were the healers skilled in herbal remedies who were called upon when neighbors became sick. Witches were in touch with the seasons and nature, often the people living close to the Earth in more rural or country locales. They were persecuted because eventually the Church perceived them as threats against authority and the medical profession. Sometimes a person was labeled a witch because they just did not fit in with the status quo, or perhaps the accused was a headstrong widow whose land was coveted by another. A cottage industry sprang up in Medieval Europe and elsewhere bent on exterminating mid-wives and herbal healers. To practitioners of Wicca, this was the first Holocaust, especially the Inquisition trials. Remnants of these atrocities are on display in both Oudawater, Holland and Cartegena, Columbia, where one can still see the 17th century wooden scales meant to weigh witches. If the woman was deemed too light, they imagined she could fly and so would be deemed a witch and burned alive. Do not believe the Hollywood hype or the contemporary propaganda. Witches do not turn into succubi or ride brooms. Neither are they delusional and need to be saved.

PERU

One can find Catholic churches in Peru where practitioners enjoy a blend of traditional worship stirred with a healthy pinch of pre-Columbian paganism, or a mixture of Catholicism with African Yoruban religion. These ceremonies are openly practiced at the Igreja e Convento de Sao Francisco in Salvador, Brazil or the Iglesia de Nuestra Senora de Regla in Regla, Cuba. Shamans of Peru add to this culinary masterpiece by making offerings to Pacha Mama and performing sacred rituals to help their people come into a proper relationship with all life through communion with Goddess.

Machu Picchu

New Age devotees of Goddess who return from Machu Picchu, consider it a yin mountain, claiming to feel "the energy of the feminine" pervading the land. They talk of doing ritual in Pacha Mama's subterranean temples or caves, such as the one facing Mount Putucusi. Machu Picchu and its connection to Goddess might at first seem a bit intangible. More often, along with the Sacred Valley, this city crowning a sharp mountain peak is in a class of its own, a site steeped in Earth mysteries relating to geomancy, theosophy, astronomy, archaeology, and altered states of consciousness. Yet, here visitors are beginning to say they feel a feminine deity's presence as a tangible force, especially in cavernous places considered the womb of the Mother. They talk of mountain peaks or *apu* holding the spiritual force of the Mother, or feeling these emanations from Pacha Mama stones. At Machu Picchu visitors find the Allacuhasi Precinct of the Chosen Women where the daughters of nobles were taught to weave royal garments, and with these women the Inca rulers perpetuated their lineage. Within the Allacuhasi area there is a central ritual space with two basins in the floor for use as a reflective mirror to the sky. According to teacher and artist Lydia Ruyle, one open window of the precinct looks toward Machu Picchu, or older Mother Mountain, while the opposite window opens toward Huayna Picchu, or Young Mountain, the puma, and male mountain. Rooms surrounding the larger precinct were where the women were thought to live. This suggests the co-mingling of the prevalent male energies and the reawakened female energies of this holy place reflects a hopeful coming into balance for this temple in the clouds. No longer a place of seeming male domination, Pacha Mama again infuse the sacred landscape.

According to author Paul Devereaux, Machu Picchu is on a geological fault and such places have been associated with extreme magnetic anomalies which can be felt by those who are particularly psychic or sensitive to such subtle sensations. Granite, a radio-active rock found to emit enhanced gamma radiation has been known to enhance trance capabilities and some-times induce astral projection if one is in contact with or within such an enclosed structure. An example of such a stone at Machu Picchu is called the Pacha Mama stone. It measures about 20 feet (6 m) long by 10 feet (3 m) high. Shamans claim it emits vibrations that enhance visions. Machu Picchu and the surrounding sacred areas are viewed by some as three dimensional portals that lead to the sacred landscape of the mental/upper, surface/present, inner/lower worlds. Here, when practitioners are in sync with subtle energies, it is believed they can access other dimen-sions or their higher self. Some say it is

▲ Allachuhasi Precinct of the Chosen Women of Machu Picchu.

289

▲ The sight of Machu Picchu is not one to be forgotten.

a place best visited with an experienced shaman well-versed in the teachings of Pacha Mama and with a direct connection with Mother Nature herself.

Located in the Peruvian Andes, Machu Picchu has long been the realm of Pacha Mama, or Earth Mother, since the earliest times of the Inca. It is a place where the Moon Goddess, Mama Quilla (who ruled cyclic nature and the menstrual cycle) was also worshipped alongside Inti, the Sun God. In some places, she was considered more powerful than Inti because she influenced the tides and could be seen during daylight hours. The emperor's wife was called Qoya and considered her earthly embodiment. Women felt a particularly close affinity with the Moon Goddess and Pacha Mama, as both shared the power of procreation and provided sustenance. The month we call September was set aside for celebrating the goddesses of the region to give thanks and pray for abundance. Present day inhabitants still make offerings of bread, fruit and coca leaves to Pacha Mama to keep the crops growing and life giving waters flowing, just as their agriculturally dependent ancestors did.

Scholars found no writing systems among the thousands of languages and dialects that were used to communicate throughout the continent of South America. Instead a device of tied string bundles called *quipu* was used by quipu camayoqs to help aid their memory to recount, interpret, and recite history and matters of business. These knot keepers aided Spanish clergy in recording Inca culture and history. This limited scope of the history and culture of the region left modern scholars such as Hiram Bingham who discovered Machu Picchu in 1911 to sometimes employ educated guesswork about what he discovered. During Bingham's excavations a majority of graves were found on the site which was originally believed to be of women, thus Machu Picchu became known as a women's site. The amazing city is home to the *aclla*, virgins or "chosen women," as well as priestesses called Mama Cunas who worshipped the moon and sun. More recently this belief was challenged as additional research has been done on the skeletons from the burial site by Yale University's Peabody Museum. Reanalysis shows there were as many men buried at Machu Picchu as women, thus perhaps rewriting the history of Machu Picchu being a site of the Virgins of the Sun, as the aforementioned women were called by Spanish chroniclers. The new findings do not negate Machu Picchu as an important ceremonial or goddess site. The ongoing worship of Pacha Mama by locals and visitors alike continue to this day. It is not hard they say, for one to become attuned with the powerful spiritual energy of this *huraca*, or sacred place.

Getting to Machu Picchu

Visitors usually get to Machu Picchu from Cuzco where trains depart for the 3.5 hour trip several times a day. The first stop of the train is at Aguas Calientes, which is at the foot of the mountain. The train continues to Puente Ruinas where busses await travelers to take them up to the ruins. Some hearty trekkers hike the Inca Trail that begins at Kilometer 88 (54.5 miles) outside Cuzco for a walk that takes from three to five days, while others take the newly installed cable car.

GAIA ALERT

PERUVIAN GRAVE ROBBERS

Unlawful looting of graves and sacred sites by smugglers all over Peru is a multimillion dollar underground smuggling business. Insatiable private collectors within the international antiquities community deny museums and scholars of new findings. Unfortunately most items go unstudied and unknown straight into the unscrupulous collectors' own private gallery. These stolen artifacts could possibly unlock mysteries or change the face of history as we know it today. Educational campaigns, rewards for information regarding looters, and government crackdowns have made some progress in diminishing this lucrative trade, but it still remains a huge problem.

▲ A ritual cave inside the Temple of the Sun at Machu Picchu.

Sacred Valley

The landscape of Peru continues to hold more mysteries than answers. The Sacred Valley containing the sites of Ollantaytambo, Quenko, Sacsayhuman, and Cuzco is no exception. Some associate this country with inter-planetary and inter-dimensional travel, ancient mummies, Atlantis, and Lemuria. It is home to the famous Nazca Lines now believed to have a connection with movements of the constellations. Pre-Inca civilizations left sophisticated ceremonial centers of megalithic proportions which show highly developed skill and style such as those of the Chavin, north of Lima, at Chavin de Huantar, believed to have been a sacred site of Pacha Mama. Throughout the country, we are left to largely speculate about the cosmology of the earliest inhabitants and their intriguing deities, such as Lanzon of the Chavin, an anthropomorphic god with both man and feline characteristics. What seems certain is the people of the Andes and Amazon were both wholly fascinated by the animals and birds of the rainforest region, as well as the qualities and powers they possessed, to the point these animals influenced their mythology. Hybrid beings were often depicted: bird headed warriors, winged beings, and particularly felines with human characteristics as the jaguar was believed to possess power, knowledge, fire, and weapons. Some mythology cites the jaguar as being the first being to inhabit the world. Later however the jaguar became a spirit that should be controlled, and it was the shaman who was called upon to reign in the beast.

291

SACRED PLACES OF GODDESS

▲ Megalithic stonework and Indigenous culture sprinkle the Sacred Valley with intrigue and color.

The Sacred Valley was a constant battleground between the Inca and the Spanish. For almost a century priests tried to convert the indigenous people. With the help of the Inca nobility they attempted to put a stop to ancestor worship of mummies, worship of celestial bodies, and the veneration of spirits that resided in sacred places. As the clergy wrote in their Idolatrias records, for a time they believed they were making progress, only to discover their "converts" were in truth firmly clinging to their local customs and beliefs. The late 16th and early 17th century marked some fierce conflict between the missionaries and the indigenous commoners reminiscent of the European Inquisition. Eventually the strangers from across the great ocean prevailed and conquered then plundered the region of its gold and other riches. Visitors today find little gold, instead they encounter a realm of wonder, places believed to be located along lines of power or special consciousness woven within the landscape often referred to as *ceques* or "ley lines." One important city in the Sacred Valley is Cuzco, considered the center or navel of the world to the Inca, where Mama Oclla taught women to weave. Other major cities in the region are Ollantaytambo, Quenko and Sacsayhuman, all having significant feminine energies of the Earth, some collectively referred to as Pacha Mama, Mama Ocllo, Mama Kyla and Mama Cocha.

From the Incan perspective, there were thousands of *huacas,* or sacred sites, in the form of springs, rocks, trees, hills, and caves. It has been determined these huacas were linked to ceques, or alignments, radiating forward consciousness or energy. In the Sacred Valley, we find many cities and shrines thought to have been built along the ceques. Worshippers in these areas believe offerings had to be made to the deities and deified ancestors of power to maintain a good relationship with them, thus insuring harmony, health, and prosperity for the people who shared this domain with the gods.

On a more mystical or esoteric level it has been theorized that by using the ceques, the Andeans as part of the cosmos, complemented and worked in harmony with nature, bringing into balance the three worlds of body, mind, and spirit. The goal was transcendence, evolution, and attaining enlightenment. Jose

Vallenas, professor and scholar of Andean culture explains. Mother Earth teaches devotees to attain this state through theosophical initiation with Her elements of water, air, earth, and water to reach awareness, perfect understanding and oneness with the Creator, which is reflected in the monuments in the Andes. The very stones themselves hold the esoteric knowledge and understanding of the cosmos. Initiates in these theories believe that an energy vortex of the Akashic Records, the source of all knowledge, had until recently been pointed to the masculine mountains of the Himalayas. With the dawning of time some acknowledge as the current Age of Aquarius there has been a shift of the vortex to the Andes, the place of feminine power, that will eventually bring about a time of balance and harmony in our world. Perhaps the resurgence of people doing ritual to honor the Earth energies of Pacha Mama in recent years have given this region a jumpstart toward this important state of being.

Special Sites in the Sacred Valley — Ollantaytambo

A fortress once sacred to the ancient Inca, Ollantaytambo is composed of seven granite monoliths not native to the area, implying great physical feats of transportation and building with stones of such magnitude akin to building the pyramids in Egypt. Considered a place with the most feminine energy on Earth, it was very sacred to the Incas. Located on the north end of the Sacred Valley, it consists of plazas, sacred niches, and shrines and is still in a good state of preservation.

Quenko

Thought by some to be a women's initiation site, Quenko gives the feeling of rebirth as one enters the structure through a vulva-like opening where visitors descend down through a doorway before emerging slightly up into the site. Dedicated to Pacha Mama, the site is made of massive stone limestone and includes a circular amphitheater, water channels, and a subterranean room. Drawings in the stone show images of animals such as the llama, condor, and an 18-foot (5.5-m) stone block depicting the image of a puma.

Sacsayhuman

A mystical sanctuary of incredible architectural skill believed to have been a military complex, Sacsayhuman nonetheless emits a strong feminine energy. It is here mystics and theosophy scholars such as Jose Altamirano Vallenas believe the esoteric cosmology of the aforementioned Andean culture is depicted as a part of the "spiritual center of the Andes." Some of the massive stones weigh as much as 125 tons (1133 kg) and were somehow transported here to build the site, taking thousands of laborers decades to complete. Many interior walls are gone, having been used to build other sanctuaries over time, but the Inca Throne remains. Here on the esplanade at the winter solstice, thousands gather to celebrate the *Inti Raymi*, or Festival of the Sun.

Cuzco

Cuzco was one of the most revered places of the Inca along with the Isle of the Sun on Lake Titicaca and Pachacamac. In the early times of Cuzco, the Inca ancestors, Manco Papac and Mama Huaco stood at the outskirts of the

▲ The stonework surrounding Cuzco is unrivaled in South America. It features some of the largest hewn stones in the world. Evidence suggests the largest cut stones are also the oldest.

city before entering and offered to Pacha Mama a llama for her blessing. Once a city of gold, the Spanish looted the beautiful city of Cuzco, seizing treasures of the Inca and melting them into bullion. Considered the Incan center of the universe, the city is a doorway to the Sacred Valley and some believe it is astronomically aligned with the Milky Way. Here you find the most important Inca place of worship, the Temple of the Sun, called today Iglesia Santo Domingo, or El Templo del Coricancha. This church has incorporated some of the stone from the original Incan temple which was believed to have been covered in gold with emerald and turquoise jewels. On one wall of the Temple of the Sun was a gold disc representing the sun and on another a silver disc, representing the moon.

The navel or center of the universe was called the Capac Usnu and stood in the center of the Coricancha, or golden enclosure, which was described as being a stone dias and seat with a vertical pillar of Usnu. The seat was considered the throne of the Incan emperor, or Sapa Inca, the Son of the Sun. As he was the earthly incarnation of the Sun God Inti, so too was his wife, called the Qoya, the earthly incarnation of the Moon Goddess, Quilla. From this throne the Sapa Inca was believed to control and maintain the forces of the universe. Here he received dignitaries, reigned over processions, rituals, and made libations to the gods. The pillar of Usnu was also thought to be citing point for astronomical observances such as the setting of the Pleiades and observing the Milky Way. Here was the center of the Inca universe and certainly the center of religious life. From here ceques are thought to radiate out from the capital to the outlying provinces.

There were several other temples and structures within the sacred compound of the Temple of the Sun or Coricancha, including the areas where the Mama Cunas, or priestesses of the sun and moon performed their duties. In what is today known as the Convento y Museo de Santa Catalina, were housed the priestesses and virgin *acllas*, taken into the sacred precinct as early as eight years of age. Here in the cloistered *acllahuasi* it is believed the Mama Cunas taught the acllas religion, weaving, and how to prepare *chicha*, a fermented corn drink used in sacred rituals or used for offerings. It has been said the acllas were also the keepers of the sacred flame of the Sun God Inti. The actual status of these women is not clear. Some say they were no more than concubines of the Inca emperor whom he gifted to important dignitaries for political aims. Some scholars suggest the roles of such women to the north in Central America diminished over time to mere servants in a temple which supported a large textile industry. These scholars believe the women lived a celibate life in cloister and performed chores such as making clothing for the clergy. With an emphasis on war and less interest in fertility, the role of women and Goddess became overshadowed.

Other temples within the Coricancha housed the six state gods, of which the Moon Goddess, Quilla, was one, where it is believed her image was depicted in silver. Eclipses of the moon were thought of as a dangerous time to the Inca who believed a serpent was trying to devour Quilla. During these celestial events, all gathered within the confines of the sacred precinct and made a cacophony of noise to scare away the dreaded serpent. There was an area set aside for the ancestor mummies which were taken out at specific times of the year and carried in procession. These mummies were dressed, offered food and drink, and remained a part of celebrations. The mummified bodies of former Qoyas were included in this group. There was also a sacred space for the captured *huacas*, or sacred objects of conquered regions. Craftsmen filled the sacred gardens with their creations in the forms of the animals they found fascinating: the butterfly, jaguar, llama. Recent archaeological study has revealed a series of tunnels linking the Temple of the Sun with the Convent of Santa Catalina. Archaeologists believe the tunnels spread out even farther into a series of galleries, chambers, fountains, and mausoleums under Cuzco. According to radar imaging, the connecting tunnels radiate out to Saqsayhuaman and beyond to other sites in the area but tourists are not allowed inside. They are reported to be in perfect astronomical alignment, further suggesting the ancients constructed their important sacred sites according to alignments with the sun, moon, and constellations. In an interesting account Warren Smith cites the founder of Theosophy, Madame Helene H. P. Blavatsky, learned about these tunnels during a visit in 1848. She described finding curious hieroglyphics on the surface of an enormous volcanic rock when the sun touched the structure in just the right way. These signs disclosed the location of the entrance of these underground tunnels that she believed started in Cuzco and ran underground to Lima before turning southward toward Bolivia. Custodians of the secrets of this underground network told Blavatsky of a treasure chamber within the tunnels but she kept the information a secret believing it impossible to secure the necessary cooperation from the Peruvian and Bolivian governments.

Getting to the Sacred Valley

Fly into Cuzco or come by tour. Driving and train are not recommended. It's easy to get a taxi or tour from Cuzco to the archaeological sites in the Sacred Valley. You can walk or take a bus from Cuzco to Sacsayhuman. Quenko is 4 miles (6.4 km) from Sacsayhuman. Ollantaytambo is farther northwest, about 36 miles (58 km) from Pisac, which is 18 miles (29 km) northeast of Cuzco. The ancient city of Cuzco, located in the Sacred Valley high in the Andes, rises 11,444 feet (3,490 m) above sea level and is an hour flight from Lima, the southern capital of the Inca empire. Modern Cuzco is a bustling city with an airport, a train station and many roads leading to the ancient capital, now a modern tourist hub.

GAIA ALERT

RAINFOREST DECIMATION

Even before the conquests of the Spanish, areas in Central and South America, including Peru and its inhabitants have been under siege and plundered of its cultural and natural resources. Despite the rich heritage of the indigenous peoples, the 16th century was a time when many in Spain and Portugal debated whether New World natives possessed a soul since their lineage as "sons of Adam and Eve" was brought into question. As time wore on, it became just as much a political and economic question as a religious one since soulless natives could easily be enslaved without fear of conscience and possible divine retribution. This perceived right gave the conquerors the freedom to seize and plunder the native lands as well, stripping it down for their own use.

Today the story of plundering resources is largely the same as the previous exploitation of peoples. We see multinational corporations exploring the region for oil and gas, pharmaceutical companies harvesting promising herbs indiscriminately, and old-growth trees that scrub the air of carbon dioxide and transform it into life-sustaining oxygen being cut down to clear land thereby causing erosion. Indigenous people and their cultures are displaced, often without any or fair compensation. Acid rain from burning petroleum in oil fields destroys ancient architecture and surrounding forests. The cost of modernization and providing a growing world with resources is extremely high.

While some progress is being made, the Amazon is home to over half of all the plant and animal species on the planet. As it quickly slips away, so does our hope to discover the treasures the rainforest might contain to cure our ailing planet; so we are all in peril. The challenge remains. How does the planet obtain the resources it needs without destroying the habitat in which the resources are found?

As travelers, keep in mind the concept of ecotourism: Look but do not touch. Walk lightly and leave only footprints. Think globally and act locally. Never buy souvenirs made from endangered species. Stay on the path. Never buy or threaten endangered species, alive or dead. We can all make a difference.

▲ The rainforest of South America holds the genetic key to many undiscovered disease cures.

Goddess Focus
Matrilocal Kuna Yala

Known the world over for their dedication to conservation, the Kuna people continue to live in thatched roof huts on the San Blas Archipelago of the Republic of Panama and still worship the Great Mother Goddess called Nan Dummad. Fiercely independent, the Kuna have little written language of their own, using instead pictograms, and cling to their religious beliefs that have helped them sustain the pristine state of their environment. Religious ceremony include female puberty rituals called *inna* which consist of several days of lavish celebration including chanting, dancing, feasting, and drinking, as well as an overall belief in sharing within the community. An indigenous democratic and autonomous people, they maintain a tradition of inheritance passing through the female lineage called a matrilocal society. When a man marries he enters his mother-in law's home and works with his father-in-law. Families are happy to have daughters because in this cultural system she will bring additional assistance to the family when she marries.

Scholars who have studied the area say jobs for men and women are clearly defined according to gender. Women and girls collect water, make clothes for the female family members, wash, cook, and clean the house. Their attire is much more colorful than males and includes gold nose rings, beaded bands for the arms and legs. You might even see some women with colorful vertical lines painted on their foreheads. Blouses feature the *moula*, a reverse appliqué embroidery technique which often depicts fish, birds, and abstract designs. Important happenings within the tribe are often documented in the designs of the moula which are made by the women and

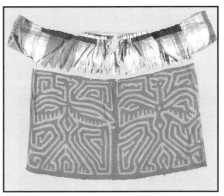

▲ The ritual clothing of the matrilineal Kuna Yala.

sold to earn money. It is by selling these coveted moulas the family earns much of its income. Men and boys make money selling coconuts they have gathered. They are involved with growing food, fishing, and chopping firewood. They also make clothes for male family members who have a traditional Western style of dress. Men are also known to do basket weaving and carving. Men are generally associated with verbal arts and women with visual arts.

The Kuna have begun to suffer from modernization and influences of the Western world, but are resisting outside forces to keep their culture intact and preserve the marine life, vegetation, and mammals on their island paradise, thus retaining their close veneration of the Great Mother.

"The Earth is Great Mother, they say.

Everything is born from her, they say.

Everything is born in her, they say.

Everything that is born of Mother will end in Mother."

— *Cacique Carlos Lopez, High Chief of Kuna Yala*

Haiti

Saut D'Eau Waterfalls

In Haiti, the Goddess of love and lust combines with the Virgin Mary who became impregnated without sin, thus reconciling the sexual and non-sexual aspects of the Divine Feminine. Catholicism and the West African Yoruban religion combine for a Voodoo flavor in Ville Bonheur where in 1847, the Virgin Mary was believed by the devoted to have appeared on a palm tree near the beautiful 100-foot (30-m) tall Saut D'Eau falls. Like Santeria, Macumba or Candomble, Voodoo was the African slaves' solution to having to hide their religion during the days of slavery and colonialism. It simply merged with Catholicism in the sense their *orishas,* or deities, took on the names and faces of Catholic saints. Running parallel, followers of the two religions, called *Voudouissants*, venerate Ezili, also called Erzulie Freda Dahomey, Goddess of love, lust, and sexuality, as a form of the Virgin Mary. Obviously Voodoo practitioners have ignored the Virgin Mother's traditional personae, being disassociated from sexuality, though some might say they have incorporated the missing piece of Mary's personae in her association with Ezili. Important as Mecca is to Muslims, Voudouissants are required to make a pilgrimage to Saut D'Eau at least once in their lifetime, on July 16th, the feast day of Ezili. To the Voudouissant, Ezili is an intermediary or *loa* who intervenes in the lives of humans, appearing to or completely possessing them. Not unlike her African "sister," the Egyptian Goddess Hathor, or the Greek Aphrodite, devotees call upon Ezili for affairs of the heart, for intervention with relationships, or marital bliss. She certainly would be a loa of women as the Goddess' domain is the home and all that is associated with family, sexuality, and marriage. While there seems to be no rigid rules about such things, and as aspects of Goddesses tend to sometimes mingle, there seems a strong case for overlap between Ezili and Voodoo loa, Erzulie Danto or Dantor. Erzulie Danto is also believed to oversee the realm of motherhood and menstruation, with her Catholic counterpart being Saint Barbara or the Black Madonna, Our Lady of Czestochowa in Poland.

Dancing and drumming are important components of a Voodoo ceremony. It is during the dancing that the loa is invoked and worshipped and might choose to possess or temporarily inhabit the body of the practitioner. Through association with the loa, ancestors, or nature deities, practitioners believe they receive guidance, blessings, and spiritual development. The Voudouissant's spirituality is a holistic religion of balance that unites body, soul, spirit, mind, and the senses. Remember, while anyone can participate in Voodoo, for Voudouissant, this spirituality is connected to

▲ Goddess lives at the Saut D'Eau Waterfalls.

their ancestral roots. It is not just a mere practice, it is in their blood and DNA and a part of who and what they are. Due to the sensationalism and distortion of Hollywood and some competing religious authorities, Voodoo has erroneously been associated with cannibalism, "walking-dead" or zombies, Satanism, and the practice of sticking pins in Voodoo dolls to smite one's enemies.

The popularity of the July pilgrimage to honor Ezili at Saut D'Eau has taken on somewhat of a commercial and carnival component, along with the spiritual, as voyeurs and practitioners alike converge at the waterfalls for the day's activities. Ville Bonheur, the small town near the waterfalls, has the feeling of a carnival or street fair atmosphere with musicians performing alongside pilgrims in song and prayer asking for offerings. But for the initiated, this is a religious experience. At Saut D'Eau, worshippers ritually bathe and allow their clothing to float down the river in a gesture of cleansing, transformation, and rebirth, or if one is of the Catholic persuasion, this is a symbol of releasing one's sins. Here they can connect with the energy and consciousness of Ezili and receive the guidance and help they seek.

Getting to the Saut D'Eau Waterfalls

International flights are available into Port-au-Prince, the capital of Haiti. From there, arrange private transportation or rent a car to the waterfalls. To get there follow Route 3, 60 miles (96.7 km) north of Port au Prince. Once at the town, you will have to walk the last four miles (6.2 km) to the sacred waterfalls. Political tensions ebb and flow. Haiti is a poor and unpredictable country so be sure to check with the U.S. Embassy before booking flights or accommodations.

Goddess Focus
Taino Creatrix Goddess

The Taino, indigenous people of the Caribbean, worshipped a "Mother of the Waters" before the influx of European, Catholic, or African influence. Central to Taino cosmology was Atabey, a female creative force, or *zemi,* important in the realms of fertility and fresh water. Successful farmers, the Taino lived in close harmony with the land using environmentally sustainable techniques for planting and harvesting. They had food in abundance and thrived on a diet of fruit, yucca, beans, peanuts, and corn. They also dried fish and hunted game birds along with small mammals and lizards. According to Gerald Singer, although the population levels of the Taino were on most islands similar to the population levels of today, the Taino had no problem feeding all their people, nor did they resort to the degradation of their environment to achieve short term goals. However, in today's "modern and advanced" culture, many Caribbean islands are presently experiencing devastating environmental problems as well as difficulty in providing enough food for all their inhabitants.

▲ The Black Madonna.

Trinidad

Siparia

Just hours away from the U.S. mainland, Goddess devotees can experience a taste of India transported to the West in uninhibited zeal! The Catholic La Divina Pastora, or The Divine Shepherdess of Christians is also called Siparee Mai, Mother of Siparia, by Hindu devotees. This Black Madonna of Siparia, a small town in southern Trinidad, has brought together people and religions from East and West under one temple spire. With a history of miracles under her crown, Mai may be small in stature, but compensates for her size in an amazing ability to garner devoted followers of both the Hindu, Buddhist, and Catholic faiths in the spirit of utmost inclusivity. Visitors to the church will find devotees have even incorporated devotion of the famous yogini Sai Baba in their practice alongside *murtis* or images of Jesus Christ. To the Trinidadians, this merging of faiths is not complicated. The simplest way to look at this may be the message to humanity for the new millennium. Goddess is working in concert with God, Mother and Father as One, to help everyone along with their lives.

According to Keith E. McNeal, since the 1890s, Siparee has been identified as Mother Kali and her earlier 20th century devotions in Siparia are said to have included the ceremonial services of male transvestite "Kali dancers" who would dance with newborn babies on the front steps of the church to bless them during the auspicious Siparia pilgrimage time. Though the statue belongs to the Roman Catholic Church and those devotees perform their rituals to her as the Virgin Mary, Hindus share her on other auspicious holy days such as Holy Thursday through Good Friday when thousands converge to pay homage to Siparee Mai or Kali Ma. Devotion includes *aarti* (the offering of lit flame) and *charawe* (touching her arms and feet then transferring her power to themselves with a touch to their foreheads). During this time offerings are made at their *puja* or ritual to Ma of olive oil, rice, candles, money or flowers. The candles are sold by the church to help parish finances and the olive oil is handed out to pilgrims who use it as a panacea for their ills throughout the year. Some temples of Kali in Trinidad still engage in the practice of sacrificing animals such as chickens and goats to the deity, who they revere as not only Kali, but also Lakshmi who is popular with both the Buddhists and Jains of India.

▲ Kali battles evil forces in Trinidad.

Another interesting aspect of this Kali worship seems phenomenologically similar to that of the Voodoo practitioner who may be possessed by the *loa*, though the ecstatic trance possession is actually imported from India, arriving here sometime in the mid 19th century. McNeal informs us that ecstatic manifestations of Mother Kali and several other related deities through the performances of possession-medium are also central to contemporary Trinidadian Kali worship. Both the live sacrifice and spirit possession practices feed into "mainstream" public opinion, which erroneously attributes Kali *puja* as demonic or dealing in *obeah,* or black magic.

300

Though these practices of possession and animal sacrifice may seem primitive, unorthodox, or taboo to someone outside this faith, or may even be looked upon with suspicion and fear by the uninformed, devotees of Kali are simply continuing a tradition handed down over the centuries. It should be noted that in most cases when animal sacrifice is employed, the animal is not wasted, but shared in a community feast and considered holy or blessed for having sacrificed its life to its Creatrix. Some temples in Trinidad and India no longer practice live animal sacrifice, such as the case of the Kali Mandir in California. In most cases Kali devotees usually do not ritually sacrifice animals, but are in fact strict vegetarians.

The Goddess at Siparia is sometimes called *jaladhija*, or waterborne, the Divine Shepherdess, also believed by followers to have emerged from the oceans, not unlike the Greek Aphrodite. Whether called Kali, Lakshmi, Mary, Venus or Durga, Mother is adored here by all those who worship at this temple on a regular basis. This adaptability and inter-identification of devis is extremely important as pilgrims the world over begin to recognize the common threads between She of Ten Thousand Names.

This Trinidad temple, like others, has been greatly influenced by the devotion of Kali in India and Guyana, South America, where 80 to 100 temples, or *koeloos*, practice daily and weekly devotions. This clearly points to the resurgence of dedication to Goddess beyond the United States and Europe and shows that worship is not limited to the spiritualities of Neo-Pagans, Wiccans and New Agers. Worship of Kali is growing by leaps and bounds within a Hindu context. Here Mother has been described as dark-skinned with black hair and pink cheeks. Her clothing is blue and often her statue is seen adorned with flowers or jewelry placed there by dedicatees. Celebrations include drumming and singing in many languages by practitioners of varied backgrounds from hymns of "Jesus Loves Me" to Indian mantras. To the faithful of Goddess spirituality, this temple is clearly representative of the ever-growing ecumenical power of the Mother to bridge oceans, cultures, and faiths.

Getting to Siparia

The Siparee Mai statue is located in the main Catholic Church in the town of Siparia in southern Trinidad. From San Fernando, the second largest city in Trinidad, proceed south on Erin Road for about seven miles (11.2 km) until you reach the town of Penal. From here proceed southwest on San Fernando Road for about five miles (8 km) to reach Siparia.

Goddess Focus
Sacred Trance Possession

The resurgence of Kali worship utilizing ecstatic expressions of drumming, dance, oracles, mysticism and body possession are on the rise in South America, Trinidad, Sri Lanka, and India. One such account of *uruvarutal*, or sacred trance possession, from scholar Patricia Lawrence, in the words of the possessed, or the deity-dancer, as they are called is as follows: "She enters the body by moving from the ground into the tip of the big toes and the Sakti (shakti) then rises, coming into the hips. First the legs will tremble, and the knees will shake, trembling like flowers on a tree. Then the pujari tucks cooling margosa leaves at the waist and place cilampu (heavy brass anklets or bracelets, which are sacralized) on

▲ Shaman could chant and dance until they became one with the natural world or divine source.

the wrists. After that, the pujari rubs sacred ash and turmeric powder on the center of our forehead while reciting mantras and the Sakti rises to the throat. There is a feeling of heat (vekkatayirukkum). Then we sit before the entrance to the inner sanctum that Sakti will be here between the hips. When I am dancing, Sakti is giving some words that she is expressing out (veliye sollutu). This is the moment of expressing oracles. Through my body. Through my tongue." Lawrence further explains the oracle or deity dancer usually does not remember what transpired during the possession. They often feel hot, they tremble, and shiver and experience overwhelming and uncontrollable emotion, or *avecam*. They do not speak in their own voice during trance and when they become possessed, the deity speaking may change identity, called "changing face."

MEXICO

You alone bestow intoxicating flowers, precious flowers. You
are the singer. Within the house of springtime, you make the
people happy.
*—Aztec Poet King Nezahualcoyotl for the Aztec Goddess
Xochiquetzal, 1450 CE As quoted from The Heart of the
Goddess, by Hallie Inglehart Austen*

MANY OF MEXICO'S SACRED SITES are the last vestiges of
a rich heritage of ancient civilizations spanning a long
period of time. Some of these indigenous inhabitants
include the Olmec, Toltec, Maya, and Aztec. Some contend that before
the Olmec, certain African cultures may have influenced the history of
the land. Much later, with the arrival of the Spanish, a new European
element was added to the mix. Unfortunately these plundering conquerors, in their crusader zeal to bring the Christian faith to the polytheistic
natives, burned indigenous literature that could have provided scholars
with the necessary tools to unravel pre-Columbian history. These were
a sophisticated people with an advanced grasp on mathematics, astrology, and architecture. They excelled in their understanding of time and
deciphering the mysteries of the cosmos. Some sites have been associated with alchemy and initiation rites, while others were associated with
blood or human sacrifices. Evidence of brutality, especially toward fallen
enemies, is everywhere to be found and yet Goddess and the influence
of the feminine maintained a presence. In fact, the Toltec, ancestors of
the Aztec, may have been a matrilineal people.

The "mother culture" of Mesoamerica is thought to be the Olmec civilization which developed a high culture with the primary deity having "shape-shifter" attributes. Early creation myths have the deity as androgynous or conjoined as male and female. We have discovered tantalizing clues about Goddess, women, and religion in Mesoamerica. Two such mysteries demanding more examination are an artifact found in the archaeological site of Monte Alban that depicts what seems to be the remnant of a jaguar cult of priestesses, and not too far away at Huijazoo, a tomb was uncovered which suggests the resting place of such a personage.

Scholars Linda Schele and David Freidel mention Lady Beastie, First Mother of the ancient Maya who "existed before the present creation," therefore it was believed "she carried into the new world the cumulative power of the previous existence." Through her divine right to the throne was manifested. She was said to be have been born December 7th, 3121 BCE, and operated in the lives of her people through her "spirit counterpart, the moon." According to Schele and Freidel, Lady Beastie was considered the mother of the gods and in the Maya view of the cosmos, therefore she was the Creatrix. Her consort, First Father, called G1, or G-one-prime by scholars, was the father of their children, thought to be born in this creation. We also know the Maya were devoted to Ix Chel, Goddess of the moon, childbirth, weaving, and healing. Artist and author Buffie Johnson suggests the Aztec, seen as a patriarchal society, still embraced the feminine in the symbol of

▲ Although Mary is the most common female deity of Mexico today, many preceded her.

the serpent, or Snake Woman, also called Terrible Mother, who ruled alongside the King. They saw duality in the serpent as both "a dark creature and a bringer of light and wisdom." While connotations of dark and light are open to interpretation, in this context, we might interpret the Aztecs as seeing deities capable of both positive and negative influence. The Aztec Goddess, Coatlique, "Lady of the Serpent Skirt," a Creatrix deity of the Aztec, was later associated with Tonantzin. In more recent history, we view the joining of cultures. The feminine, in the guise of the Christian Virgin of Guadalupe, unites at Tepeyac with the Aztec Tonantzin. The Spanish built the cathedrals to the Virgin Mother and through the Madonna the face of Goddess lives most openly today.

Today in Mexico the patriarchal form of Christianity dominates, even though there is a strong devotion to Mary, the Mother of Jesus and Our Lady of Guadalupe. Yet Aztec deities still live alongside the newer faces of the Goddess. According to Mary Devine, Nuestra Senora De Zapopan Del Camino (Our Lady of the Road) in Guadalajara is a new incarnation of the Aztec Xochiquetzal, "Blossom Plume" or "Lady of the Flowers." Devotees recognize her as a pleasure giving aspect of Tonantzin. In the maternal landscape of the mountains such as the Sierra Madre known as "Mother Mountain," the descendants of these ancient cultures have not forgotten the Goddesses of old. Whether viewed as an esoteric concept, an archetype, or divinity above, the Divine Creatrix is perceived as the Mother Goddess and many still invoke her ancient names.

Basilica of Guadalupe

Here on the ancient hill of Tepeyac (tep-eh-yak), a site that had long been an Aztec Shrine to Tonantzin, a generic name for the Earth Mother, Goddess once again proved the significance of her epitaph, "She Who Appears." Mother of the Gods gifted the Aztec Indian named Juan Diego with her apparition in 1531. In this vision, the Madonna told Juan, in his native language of Nahuatl, that she wanted a temple built on that spot and he should tell the local bishop of their meeting. Of course, when Juan went to the bishop he was not taken seriously. Only when Juan came bearing proof of The Lady who had continued to appear to Juan over several days did the bishop take notice. The evidence he brought was fresh flowers picked from a rocky, frigid place in the mountain where none could grow. The image of the Virgin of Guadalupe miraculously appeared on Juan's *tilma,* or shawl where he had carried the flowers. A basilica was eventually built to Tonantzin/Guadalupe. This very tilma is today prominently displayed behind glass above the altar. Pilgrims honor her as they ride past on moving walkways assisting the constant flow of visitors that arrive daily. After all these centuries, the colors on the tilma have not lost their vibrancy. Scientific testing on the cloth has gone on for hundreds of years, with one test done by NASA scientists in 1981 concluding that the pigments were from uncertain origins.

Here on Tepeyac time, spiritualities and cultures blend. The Aztec Coatlique is transformed or at least united with the Virgin of Guadalupe. Coatlique, also associated with Tonantzin (pronounced to nan tzeen), is considered the Earth Goddess of the vast heavenly cosmos and the underworld. She is birth and death. She is fertility and reciprocity. It has been claimed she birthed the Aztec pantheon, often called "flower covered Earth in spring." She represents the importance of transformation, residing on the threshold of change, since things

305

must change or die to
lee kuay) is also remi-
and symbolism, with
skirt of snakes. Some
the human race. She
mouth from which four
can be seen. Jones and
spurts of blood that
trude from the sides of
of the male and female
and Omecihuatl, the
Down her back are 13
the 13 Lords of Day,
and 13 Aztec heavens
the gods that reign
mordial darkness,
hands and feet, with
her neck. Known as

▲ Coatlique is a Goddess
who used to reign
supreme on Tepeyak ...

be reborn. Coatlique (kwat
niscent of Kali in aspect
her necklace of skulls and
say the snakes represent
has scales on her head and
fangs and a forked tongue
Molyneaux state the two
form snake heads and pro-
her torso are representative
principals, Ometecuhtli
Lord and Lady of Dualities.
tresses which correspond to
13 months of the calendar
or levels of cosmology and
therein. She is of the pri-
chthonic, with her talon
snakes springing forth from
"Lady of the Serpent Skirt"

she is also connected to female wisdom and infinity. She is associated with agriculture, the rainy season and thereby sustenance of her people.

Merlin Stone rings in on the homeland of Aztec Coatlicue, namely Aztlan, and relates its location possibly reaching somewhere from between the area north of Mexico City into the Southwestern United States of Colorado or New Mexico. She cites linguistic similarities between the Aztec and Native American Hopi tribes, which might offer a glimpse into enriching the essence of Coatlicue to contemporary readers. First, Coatlicue was said to live on a mountain surrounded by water. Considering Coatlicue's association with the Lord and Lady of Dualities, Ometecuhtli and Omecihuatl, Ometepi Island in Lake Nicaragua suggest a potential location of her abode from a linguistic view. *Ome* means two in Aztec and is related to the duality of the aforementioned cosmology principles. *Oma* means cloud and *omic* means high up in Hopi. When taking these three linguistic roots combined, it suggests to the scholars a possible connection between Coatlicue's serpent imagery with the prevailing cloud and fire motifs of the region. One can almost see Coatlicue wearing her serpent skirt, high atop her volcanic cloud covered mountain sanctuaries overlooking the domain of human-kind below alongside her consort, the cloud serpent, Mixcoatl, god of hunting. According to John Mini, a dimension of Coaltique is known in Aztec as Tlaliyolo, or Earth Heart when she is associated with caves where shamanistic ritual is often done deep in the womb of the Mother. Her statue can be found standing in the National Museum of Anthropology in Mexico City. Two other goddesses associated with the site are Cihuacoatl (see hwa kwat all) and Chalchiuhtlicue (chal chee ootlee kuay).

John Mini, in *The Aztec Virgin*, gives an esoteric context for Goddess Guadalupe's apparition legend which is translated from the Aztec language Nahuatl, in which many words and nuances cannot adequately be translated into Spanish. Some of these concepts associated with Tonantzin actually represented Omecihuatl, the feminine aspect of Ometeotl, a supreme being beyond our ability to describe. This being, who is the Heavenly Hermaphrodite of masculine and feminine energies thrive in dynamic balance. Remember the aforementioned Olmecs' androgynous creator god/goddess?

Mini suggests the Guadalupe/Tonantzin the time is right for us the Sixth Sun, the Sun ships. This epiphany is est potential, bringing flowering of human- connection between of the Sixth Sun and many believe is upon described by some as with the emergence ing an era when all ultimate Creatrix.

▲ ... now the Virgin of Guadalupe retains the top position.

apparition of Ometeotl/ is heralding the news that to enter the Solar Age of of Flowers and relation- about achieving our high- visions into reality, or the ity. Perhaps there is some the prophecy of the birth the Age of Aquarius which us. The Aquarius Age is an age of enlightenment, of the Sixth Sun announc- of humanity becomes the

The New Basilica shrine in Mexico, was the new basilica, is of Guadalupe, the holiest opened in 1987. Behind a museum as well as two older churches that used to hold the holy relic. Also on the grounds are other chapels, fountains and streams that mark particular spots associated with the story of the apparition. A cave with ancient relief carvings was once located here, but has since mysteriously disappeared. Scholars have determined this cave really existed from images drawn within the Codex Teotznantzin, containing some of the few remaining writings from the pre-Columbian civilization. Today, various fenced off areas designated for church officials only give rise to the suspicion that this cave still remains in one of these restricted places. The feast day of the Virgin of Guadalupe is December 12th when a grand festival is held in Her honor and millions converge on the site.

Getting to Basilica of Guadalupe

Located north of Mexico City, the huge basilica is located on the Calzada de Guadalupe, formerly an Aztec causeway. If traveling by car from Mexico City, take Paseo de la Reforma Norte until it forks into Calzada de Guadalupe, which leads directly to the shrine. By subway, use the #3 Metro line from downtown to Deportivo 18 de Marzo. Change to Line #6 toward Martin Carrera, getting off at the La Villa-Basilica stop. One of the best museums in Mexico, 100,000 square feet (30,480 sq. m) in size, the *Museo Nacional de Anthropoligia* (National Museum of Anthropology) has in addition to the statue of Coaltcue, reconstructed temples, fantastic displays and rebuilt ancient tombs. The museum is located at Paseo de la Reforma at Calle Gandhi, Section 1 of Bosque de Chapultepec (Chapultepec Park).

Sanctuary of Coyolxauhqui

In downtown Mexico City Goddess is wearing bells! Located in the Zocalo district, (also known as Cathedral Square), this archaeological site in the middle of modern Mexico City was once the Aztec capital of Tenochtitlan (tey noch teet lahn). After wandering for many years, it was here the Aztec saw the signs their gods told them to watch for — an island where an eagle would be perched on a cactus holding a serpent in its mouth. About 1325 CE the Aztec began to build one of the greatest empires on earth in this very area on the "hill of the serpent" or

▲ Xiucoatl, turquoise fire serpent who penetrated Coyolxauhqui's chest.

Coatepee, honoring the war and storm gods. In 1978, this site was accidentally discovered while workers were repairing a gas line. This is an important site of Goddess because while excavating here a 22-ton (1,996-kg) circular stone disk was found showing the dismembered Aztec Moon Goddess Coyolxauhqui, the daughter of the Goddess Coatlique, known as golden bells, for the ornamentation of bells on her cheeks and cap.

There are multiple conflicting and controversial meanings attached to the stone disc. Karl Taube explains the dismembered Moon Goddess as a symbol of an Aztec social conduct believing that human sacrifice was necessary for the continuity of the world. Adelle Getty suggests the disk depicts a metaphor for the "ascension to power of the masculine over the feminine." Other goddess advocates, noting the fact this artifact was found unscathed when all other images representing the male war or sun gods had vanished through the ages, contend this artifact is a metaphor for the rising of the feminine. Though Coyolxauhqui (coy ol shau kee) is depicted decapitated, she is in motion, suggesting a vibrant energy of renewal, integrity and strength. Her snake-like tourniquet could be a metaphor for the healing power of a loving community or a caring friend. Jones and Molyneaux say her decapitation plays out the Aztec myth that as the moon sets, the sun rises and drives away darkness and as such these celestial movements further symbolize the duality of the brother/sun, sister/moon struggle (or balance?) between day and night, light and dark, and good and evil. The huge disc, found at the bottom of the steps of the Great Temple pyramid (1428 CE) marked for the world the exact place the temple was built, making this four block archaeological site where the Aztec cult developed. Taube explains this was the hub of the Aztec universe and no other Mesoamerican site pertains so directly to indigenous mythology.

According to legend, it is here that the goddess Coatlicue, Cosmic Mother who birthed the 400 Southerners, the Milky Way and the stars of heaven, conceived the war god Huitzilopochtli (weet zi lohpoash tlee). Interestingly, Coatlicue became impregnated with a feather ball and thereby avoided sin, suggestive of the Virgin Mary motif. As Coatlicue was about to give birth, her daughter, the Moon Goddess, schemed to kill her own mother hoping the sun god would never see the light of day. Much to her chagrin, Coatlicue's son, the war and sun god, was born fully grown, wearing battle armor. In the end, the moon goddess, Coyolxauhqui, was slain rather than her brother, and her head thrown into the heavens where it became the moon.

The sun god sliced Coyolxauhqui into 14 pieces, perhaps representing a mythological time between the waxing and waning moon. Coyolxauhqui resembles her mother with serpents and skulls engraved on her body. Mini describes her as the warrior Goddess known as "She with Bells On Her Face," suggesting she represents the essence of those who have been defeated and the spirit of the enemy. He cites Coyolxauhqui as the cycle of destruction, having the power to intoxicate, enrapture, unbridle passions, and drive people mad. Consequently this made her a dangerous Goddess, always working mischief and mayhem, even to the point of destroying the Earth. Ultimately, she becomes the metaphor for self doubt, the voice speaking within each individual telling of hopelessness and futility in achieving even the moderate goals. Scandal, rumor, and doubt are her fellow-conspirators, tapping into vital positive energy and distracting the seeker from true purpose and enlightenment, crushing all at once, any potential for self-empowerment. Thus, Coyolxauhqui would represent the darker aspect of the duality of Goddess, and her mother, Coatlicue, the light. She might also in her many pieces be representative of the multi-faceted nature of human character.

Another stone monument was found here showing the Xiuhcoatl serpent penetrating Coyolxauhqui's chest. Taube suggests this is the mythic origin of heart sacrifices, but one cannot help but wonder if in keeping with the more esoteric interpretations of Mini that this piercing of the heart is metaphor for cutting away self doubt and obstacles blocking our full potential. The disk of Coyolxauhqui, along with 3,000 other artifacts unearthed from the site, are all located in the Museo del Templo Mayor, adjacent to the archaeological site.

Getting to the Sanctuary of Coyolxauhqui

Templo Mayor is located in what is called the Zocola or Plaza of the Constitution, an area of downtown Mexico City, at Seminario 8, at Republica de Guatemala. Entrance to the plaza is near the Metropolitan Cathedral. Call six weeks ahead to arrange an English language tour by museum staff if needed.

GAIA ALERT
WORKING TOWARD BETTER HEALTH

Mexico City, like many modern cities, is choking with smog from traffic clouding the skies and industrial pollution from refineries affecting both air and water. Without a doubt, atmospheric pollution here is one of the most severe cases in the world. Mexico City is a case study for MIT and the Harvard School of Public Health as they work toward resolution of the problems. While there have been strides in reducing lead, carbon monoxide, and sulfur dioxide poisoning, the altitude of Mexico City is an ideal environment for the accumulation of two other pollutants, ozone and small particles, both of which effect the lungs.

▲ Aztec healer gathering and preparing herbs and roots.

Sanctuary of Xochiquetzal

Xochiquetzal, Goddess of spring, pleasure, beauty, and sexuality blossoms at her sacred site! A Goddess of love, who encouraged sexual liberation, Hallie Iglehart Austen quotes scholar Merlin Stone who says, "when a woman felt the pleasures of her body, it brought special joy to Xochiquetzal." The first wife of Tlaloc (tlah loc) the rain god, she is often depicted as plumes of feathers and is called precious flower or richly plumed flower. An archetype for the Great Mother, Xochiquetzal (sho chee kets all) is said to have given birth to the people of the world and she embodies the lush flowering Earth. Her essence is the fecundity of people and plants, a Goddess of physical love who bestows the blessing of children upon women. It has been suggested that Goddess was worshipped here with many priestesses devoting themselves to Xochiquetzal who was associated with flowers and music, elements which help transcend the mundane. Austen recalls ancient rituals honoring Xochiquetzal where devotees dressed as hummingbirds and butterflies and danced around an image of the Goddess. Jones and Molyneaux cite Xochiquetzal as being "patroness of the *anianime* or *maqui*, the female courtesans and companions of Aztec warriors, sculptors, painters, weavers, and silversmiths."

Like many of the chthonic Goddesses, she is womb and tomb, associated with bringing life into the world, and likewise known within the realm of the dead. With flowers such as the traditional marigold in hand devotees would invoke her blessings at festivals reminiscent of our contemporary Day of the Dead celebrations when the ancestors and those beings of the underworld are remembered and honored.

For a momentary digression, Jones and Molyneaux cite some surreal Aztec sacrificial ceremonies that seem to suggest perhaps interesting twists on the annual dying/rising god rites. In the first ceremony of the Toxcatl festival, Xochiquetzal is one of four Aztec Goddesses that were impersonated by mortal virgins who were made to wed a chosen warrior who was the personification of the god Tezcatlipoca. Their union lasted for just a year when the mortal female or earthly incarnation of Xochiquetzal was sacrificed. Not the squeamish types, in ultimate bizarre fashion, a priest would then remove the woman's skin and wear it while he sat at a loom. As he sat there pretending to weave, craftsmen devoted to Xochiquetzal would dance around him and confess their sins to an idol of Xochiquetzal. They would then draw blood from their tongues as an offering and atone for their sins in a ritual bath. In another idea for the next Hollywood gore-fest, Jones and Molyneaux cite the ghastly Tlacaliliztli sacrificial rite where captives of war are mounted and shot with arrows and their deaths dedicated to the Goddesses Chicomecoatl and Teteoinnan to insure a good harvest. While this all seems quite gruesome by contemporary standards, readers are reminded to keep ancient contexts of sacrifice that insure the fertility of the land in mind. Some scholars also believe women were once revered in early Mesoamerican society and this shift toward a lack of reverence for the female developed as society became more focused on warfare.

▲ Xochiquetzal's attributes might be said to reflect Aphrodite.

Called "Place of the Flowers," Xochitecatl has been associated with the Olmecs and described in early writings as a hill with a mound on its summit and volcanoes in the background. In 1969 German archaeologist, Bodo Spranz found female figurines at the base of the Platform of Volcanoes. One of these has been identified as the Goddess Tlazolteotl (tla zol tay oh tal) whose image we sometimes find in a "giving birth" stance thought by some to be depicting the birth of Xochiquetzal. Then in 1978, two anthropomorphic sculptures were found on the hill. The large one represents a female figure with drooping breasts and hands placed over the abdomen, probably a representation of pregnancy. The second was a male figure. Tlazolteotl is another Goddess of love related to Coatlique and Cihualoatl. Like Xochiquetzal, she is considered to oversee the realm of carnal pleasures, desire, and fertility. She is venerated along with the Goddess of Corn (Chicomecoatl) and the oldest of the old Earth Goddess (Teteoinnan) at the Ochpanitztli festival. Often in codices she is seen wearing a band of cotton and holding spindles or bobbins on her headdress while other times she can be seen wearing the skin of sacrificial victim. Jones and Molyneaux suggest it may "represent new birth from the womb."

One of Tlazolteotl's manifestations is the Goddess Tlaelquani, called the "eater of excrement" which refers to her ability to purify inappropriate behavior for which she was a catalyst. Tlaelquani is sometimes depicted with a black mouth to indicate she has just ingested an unclean sexual act, sin, or deviant behavior. As such she may be considered a sort of savior or purification Goddess. Jones and Molyneaux state she was the patroness of young women forcefully recruited from within the citizenry of Tenochtitlan to serve the military in the capacity of satisfying the "fanaticism" of the soldiers. They indicate the women were kept within their own compound where they honored Tlaelquani until called upon for a "festival" of licentiousness. When the women had fulfilled their purpose, they were sacrificed. Current day goddess advocates, not taking Tlaelquani's epithet so literally, might call upon her to instead devour gossip, mean spirited or insidious behavior.

The Instituto Nacional de Antropologia e Historia describes Xochitecatl as a ceremonial center consisting of two plazas. The Pyramid of the Flowers, the Building of the Serpent, and the Platform of Volcanoes are in the main Plaza while the Building of the Spiral is located in the second plaza. In the Pyramid of the Flowers 30 burials of infants, and one adult, have been found. Beads or balls of green stone had been placed inside the mouth of some of the infants, perhaps to accompany them into the next world. Above the access staircase leading to the upper part of the building, offerings of more than 2,000 female clay figures had been deposited, as well as 15 stone zoomorphic and anthropomorphic sculptures. The figures represented women from childhood to old age. There were babies, elaborately dressed women, pregnant women, mothers with hollow bellies showing their babies in elaborate costumes, and mothers holding their children in their arms, over their legs, or tied to their backs with fabric bands.

Also at this site was found a representation of the Goddess Xochitl (zo chee tel). Legend says she turns into a serpent; the sculpture revealed a fleshless human face with the body of a rattlesnake believed to be Xochitl. Inside the building is a sculpture of a serpent with its jaws open from which springs out a human face. This was how divine beings were depicted in Aztec codices as coming forth or being birthed from one world into this one. Mini further describes Xochitl, whose name means flower, as representing purification, perfection, truth, completion, and bringing visions into reality. He states as a flower is associated with sexual organs, she is love and the search for union, or more universally, the flowering of humanity. In Guadalajara at the Nuestra Senora de Zapopan Del Camino or Our Lady of the Road, Xochiquetzal is worshipped as the pleasure giving aspect of Tonantzin. Xochiquetzal has been associated with other goddesses of love such as Lakshmi and Aphrodite and embodies the joys of the senses and the ripeness of springtime with all its promise of delight.

Getting to the Sanctuary of Xochiquetzal

Located in southern Tlaxcala, these two sites (Cacaxtla and Xochitecatl) are 71 miles (113 km) southeast of Mexico City and about 40 minutes away from Basilica of Our Lady of Octolan. Take Mexico City-Puebla toll road, Highway 150. At the San Martin Texmelucan exit off Highway 150 follow the signs 8 miles (12.5 km) east to the sites. This is actually a double site with museums at both, but the Xochitecatl museum houses most of the female figurines. Xochitecatl is the older of the two sites and is described above. It may have been the ritual center for the Cacaxtla elite. Be sure to see the Temple of Venus and the Red Temple within the Cacaxtla ruins. Allow about three hours for both sites.

Chalcatzingo

Stone relief carvings at Chalcatzingo continue the theme of Goddess being "womb and tomb," and the cave, like her body, the place of that transformation. Chalcatzingo (chahl caht zeen goe) was an important religious and trading settlement dating back to the Olmec culture. Situated in an impressive natural setting at the base of twin peaked mountains called Cerro de la Cantera, this sacred site perpetuates the type of landscape often chosen as sacred to Goddess. Chalcatzingo translated from Nahuatl means "venerated place of sacred water" or "place of precious jades," is sacred to Chalchiutlicue, the Goddess of Water. It is comprised of public terraces, central plazas, and ceremonial structures, with some of its most important features carved into the rock face of Mother mountain. These stone carvings, dating from about 700 and 500 BCE, are believed to have been made at the peak of the culture before the site declined in the face of other growing communities such as Cuicuilco and Teotihuacán.

Important in a Goddess context is the image of a person seated inside a cave between the open jaws of a monster, symbology for the transformation of being birthed from one cosmos into another. The person wears a headpiece adorned with quetzales and raindrops. Around the figure are images of clouds, raindrops, stylized corn plants and concentric circles which are symbols for water and jade. Some scholars believe this to be an image of Chalchiuhtlicue, Goddess of the Living Waters, emerging from her cave. According to Patricia Monaghan, Chalchiuhtlicue sent a flood to punish humans for their bad deeds but provided a bridge so that the good folks might emerge into the Fifth World of Aztec cosmology, where we reside today. This is

▲ The mountains of Chalcatzingo appear to be breasts on the landscape.

very reminiscent of the stories of Noah and the Ark, as well as Native American emergence mythology. She cites this rainbow reappears on occasion, while other myths say the good were saved not by way of the bridge, but by being transformed into fish so that they might swim away and survive the flood. Chalchiuhtlicue rules the domain of waters, both benevolent and malevolent. Monaghan describes her beautiful watery imagery as "wearing a jade necklace, turquoise earrings, a crown of iridescent blue feathers, and a skirt trimmed with water lilies."

Chalchiuhtlicue was known as "Lady of the Jade Skirt" and "the deep flowing waters of life." Jade, associated with many aspects of water in Aztec cosmology, was seen as a feminine and a life-giving resource. She comes from the waters of the Gulf of Mexico thought to be sacred to her and some say the rain god Tlaloc is her consort. She is a water Goddess associated with lakes and streams and Jones and Molyneaux state she is often portrayed as a river beside which a cactus tree stands. Interestingly, Martha Ann and Dorothy Myers Imel associate her with the period of time between 12:33 AM and 1:38 AM and cite her as the patroness of those dependent on the waters for earning a living.

The Instituto Nacional de Antropologia e Historia describes another relief, called the "mural of fertility," with symbols certainly related to Mother Earth. Depicted are a small square, a small channel, 14 cavities, a coiled serpent, pumpkin vine leaves, flowers and fruit, an unidentified figure, and another pumpkin vine. Also visible are a four-legged animal licking a cloud with rain, a saurian with cloud and raindrops, and a serpent or feline crouched down, also with a cloud diagonally across and more raindrops.

Getting to Chalcatzingo

Chalcatzingo is located south of Mexico City, east of Cuernavaca and Cuautla in the state of Morelos on kilometer 93 (58 miles) of Federal Highway 160. The site is five kilometers east of the town of Jonacatepec. The road is well marked but runs into a rough track just before the ruins are reached. There is no public transportation to the site so the best recommendation is to take a taxi from the village of Jonacatepec.

Cuicuilco

Ancient wisdom of time, transformation, and gender meld into oneness at Cuicuilco, the oldest ceremonial site in the Central Highlands. Meaning "place of frogs" (which are associated with female genitalia) or "place of singing and dancing," Cuicuilco is a land filled with bituminous lava rock which emanates measurable electro-magnetic energy. Visitors have described a feeling of tranquility, wholeness, well-being, and a connectedness with the earth. Approximately when Teotihuacán was emerging, Cuicuilco (kwee kweel coe), was abandoned (100-300 CE) due to the eruption of the nearby volcano, Xitle.

One of the unique features of this site was discovered when it was excavated in 1922 from beneath over 30 feet (9 m) of lava. Excavations revealed the "pyramid" was built in a conical or circular shape and not actually a pyramid as we would expect from the normal usage of the term. Author J. Kelly describes Cuicuilco as a "conical mound faced by a river boulder and basalt slab veneer." It is about 370 feet (110 m) high and the diameter measures 60 feet (20 m) at the base. He believed it to be much higher originally. The inhabitants here developed a

▲ Huehueteotl appears to be a wise elder awaiting an initiate's question.

complex religious practice and sophisticated ritual system that included making offerings of ceramic artifacts in their funerary practices.

Important for our purposes here is one particular deity artifact discovered at Cuicuilco. Called Huehueteotl (way way tay o tel) Xiuhtecuhtli (zeuhtl tay coot li) or "Old One of Fire," the deity found on one of the oldest known ceramic pieces from the area seems to be androgynous, combining the masculine and feminine, and concepts of time and fire. Huehueteotl, toothless and wrinkled, looks like a seated ancient one, with sagging breasts and bearded face, bending over an urn. To the inhabitants of the period, time was deity and deity was time. Gods could be male or female, terrestrial or celestial, beneficial or harmful, and provide energy for life or death. They could shape-shift into animals and move throughout the cosmos. While somewhat of an enigma, some scholars associate him as being the husband or consort of Spider Woman, supreme deity of Teotihuacán.

Huehueteotl might perhaps be a manifestation of the all-encompassing androgynous Ometeotl, a primitive, bisexual, creator deity that embodied the male (Ometecuhtli) and female (Omecihuatl) principles. The sons of Ometecuhtli and Omecihuatl were the cardinal direction of north, south, east, and west. Ometeotl was the source of all existence, including the gods and goddesses, and was too abstract for the average worshipper to comprehend. Ometeotl embodied the duality of opposites: light and dark, action and inaction, order and chaos, movement and stillness, silence and sound, male and female. Ometeotl lived in the realm of Omeyocan, outside of time and space. Also on this site is a cave-like kiva with ochre markings that evoked the mysteries of the Goddess. Red ochre is commonly associated with blood, and the kiva often denotes the menstrual hut. Scholars speculate the site might have been associated with purification, rebirth, and menstruation rites. Many figurines have been found there belonging to the style known as "pretty women" with large hips and thighs. Visitors comment they feel a sacred presence of the Mother here. This site is a major attraction at the spring equinox.

Getting to Cuicuilco

Cuicuilco is located in the suburbs of Mexico City, about 12 miles (18 km) to the south. It can be reached via Insurgentes Sur Avenue or by the Periferico Highway. The closest city to the circular pyramid/temple is Tlalpan, just 10 miles (16 km) south of Mexico City. The site is found at the south end of Insurgentes Sur Avenue, not far past Ciudad Universitaria. The Metro can be taken, but does not take travelers all the way to the site. Visitors should get off at the Cuidad stop and look for a taxi or bus marked Cuicuilco. A small museum is on the grounds. Generally mainstream tours will not take sacred site seekers to this location and it would be better to hire a taxi or go along on an escorted tour. The ruins of Cuicuilco B are located in the Villa Olimpica, which is across the Insurgentes Sur Avenue.

GAIA ALERT

ARCHAEOPOLITICS

Opposition to construction of a commercial and residential center on the Cuicuilco archaeological site has locals at odds with developers and politicians. Demonstrations raged against investors and government agencies that had modified land use designations to allow permits for construction. Another problem, urban sprawl, has prevented the site from being fully excavated and its significance understood. Archaeopolitics and the vulnerability of such sites are often at odds with the interest of capitalistic ventures, tourism, and modernization as represented here and in many other sites around the globe.

▲ Coyolxauhqui was known as "She With Bells on Her face," as can be seen here.

Cuicuilco is just one example of a sacred site in danger of destruction by developers. This problem is occurring with more frequency throughout the world. At the time of this writing there was talk of a Wal-Mart being planned in the shadow of the great Pyramid of the Sun at the sacred site of Teotihuacán.

Teotihuacán

Newly developed scholarship places Spider Woman, Creatrix of the Universe, as the supreme deity of Teotihuacán, (teh-oh-tee-wa-can). Built about the time of the birth of Christ, Teotihuacán actually received this name after the decline of Aztec civilization. A place of many shrines, temples, platforms, and dwellings, two of the primary monuments here are Pyramid of the Moon and Pyramid of the Sun, located along the Avenue of the Dead. Built by an unknown, yet highly advanced people, this city was obviously powerful and the nexus of great religious activities. It displays skilled urban planning on a monumental scale. Evidence suggests Teotihuacán controlled great trading networks extending throughout Mesoamerica as well as knowledge in a variety of disciplines, including urban planning, architecture, irrigation, astrology, and geomancy. Inhabitants believed here the sun, moon, and universe were first created and, according to many, this site later gave birth to the Fifth Sun, the present cosmic age. Once eight square miles (12.9 sq. km) in size and inhabited by over 250,000 people, the Aztec adopted the site into their religious system of belief. And even more important for our purposes, authors Jones and Molyneaux cite the imagery on the Tepantitla Palace murals, once believed to be that of Tlaloc, the rain god, are in actuality those of Spider Woman, the major female deity of this religious metropolis. They contend a fresh look at her imagery, depicting a mouth with fangs and palps of a spider, revealed the Creatrix Goddess. It is hard not to let Spider Grandmother of the Native Americans to the north spring to mind! Teotihuacán, meaning Place of the Gods, might soon require an adjustment in name change. Besides Spider Woman, Jones and Molyneaux cite a nameless Moon Goddess was also venerated here. There are other murals and images of other Goddesses at Teotihuacán that might even point to a prehistoric existence of Goddess. Scholars such as Esther Pasztory describe huge stone statues found here identified as Chalchiuhtlicue. In 1997, a new cache of female figures were found which invite further research of scholars.

▲ A depiction of Spider Woman from Teotihuacán.

The Pyramid of the Sun is built over an actual cave with four chambers that point to the four cardinal directions, important aspects within Aztec cosmology. (Within Mesoamerican cosmology, the four cardinal directions were the sons of the Olmec creator deity, the androgynous Ometeotl and caves were considered doorways to other realms). The pyramid was built so that it is oriented to the Pleiades constellation and equinoxes. The oldest monument on the site, its base is larger than that of the Cheops pyramid in Egypt, and it stands over 200 feet (60.9 m) in height. To the east of the Pyramid of the Sun stands the Tepantitla palace murals and the sacred precinct. Here depicted on the walls is the creation myth of Spider Woman. Jones and Molyneaux describe the imagery which includes a sacred mountain with springs flowing from the base and Spider Woman, central to the mural, is surrounded by her human children engaged in joyous pursuits such as singing, dancing, and playing. Sprinkled throughout the happy tableaux are flourishing trees, flowers, and butterflies.

Studying the murals of Teotihuacán (which possibly date as early as 650-700 CE), led some scholars to suggest that the masked Goddess within a storm god mural found at the Tepantitla complex may very well be the tribal goddess of the site. Now scholars are more certain she is Spider Woman. Other murals have images believed to depict her hands or heart. While no particular Goddess was definitively named, a masked shape-shifter Goddess known from ceramic pieces of a funeral censor is also associated with the site. At Tepantitla there is an image which depicts water, stars, and planets gushing from her womb.

The Pyramid of the Moon, 126 feet (38.4 m) high, once contained a well within the substructure. It is believed these underground womb-like places were sacred places of fertility to the early builders suggesting that rituals and shamanic initiation very likely occurred here. Near the Pyramid of the Moon is the Jaguar Palace with its motifs of serpents and plumed jaguars with shells running down their backs. Jones and Molyneaux describe either water or blood coming from the mouths of the jaguars and human hands grasp felines which are caught in a net. Jaguars and ocelots were important figures within the art and religion of the Mesoamericans. As a symbol of strength, courage and fierceness, they were associated

Pyramids of the Sun + Moon   Teotihuacán, MEXICO

▲ Teotihuacán is only partly excavated by archaeologists. At its peak the city was a thriving metropolis.

with many of the deities of the region. Jaguar gods, thought to possibly be Olmec in origin, represented the supernatural world and were sometimes associated with vision quests, nocturnal journeys and seen devouring the sun each night. Images of jaguars are prevalent on the Palace of the Jaguars and Pyramid of the Moon.

Also near the Pyramid of the Moon is the Palace of Quetzalpapalotl, or plumed butterfly. Jones and Molyneaux describe the motif of this place of worship or priestly quarters as being adorned with serpent heads, rippling water, abstract half-eyes, plumed butterflies, seashells and obsidian discs still inset within symbols. Precious stones might have long ago been set within all these designs. An earlier palace is beneath the platform which was called the palace of plumed shells. The murals on the walls included brightly colored green parrots with yellow beaks from which streams of water flow. There is an altar there decorated with red circles on a white background. These pyramids are very clearly ancient sacred sites honoring water, earth, sun, stars, and moon. They also honor God and Goddess of the peoples of the land as both they and their religion changed and shifted over time.

Getting to Teotihuacán

The site is located about an hour's drive northeast of downtown Mexico City via Highway 85 toward Pachuca, then turn onto the Teotihuacán Highway, a toll road. Public transportation is available every 20 minutes from the Central de Autobuses del Norte or Indios Verdes Metro station. Escorted tours often combine this site with that of Our Lady of Guadalupe. Be sure not to miss the elaborate museum on site. It is located south of the Pyramid of the Sun with a stone relief of Goddess at the entrance. South of the ruins is a hotel for overnight accommodations.

Goddess Focus
Women Play Ulama: Ballgame of the Ancients

The game of *Ulama* was played on ball courts found throughout archaeological sites in Central America. Originally thought to be a game for men only, artifacts attest to participation of women in Ulama. The Maya ballgame was traditionally associated with the losers being decapitated, their death bringing honor. The blood of the losing team was thought to feed the corn god, thus connecting the ballgame with sacrifice, fertility, and rebirth. Artifacts dating from 1200-900 showing women in ballgame attire have been found all over Mesoamerica supporting the concept of all women teams as well as mixed teams.

▲ A depiction of the popular ball game being played in prehistoric Mesoamerica.

While small groups of men still play Ulama, the tradition of women players is being continued by modern women who play a version of the ancient game called ulama de antebrazo, where the ball is lighter than the traditional nine pound rubber ball. Modern players can only hit the ball with their forearms rather than with their hips as was done by their ancient counterparts. Academic advocates continue to urge the Ministry of Education to have this ancient ball game recognized and protected by UNESCO in an effort to preserve this endangered cultural heritage.

Tlaxcala

Tlaxcala, which means tortilla, is home to a healing Madonna and apparition site of a Goddess named Senora de Octolan. The Lady's legend dates back to 1541 when a stream of healing waters appeared that cured village inhabitants afflicted with plague. As is the case with most of these miraculous appearances, some lucky person (sometimes several) is chosen to see the Divine, then that person has the task of convincing others of what they saw. In this case, the Virgin chose Juan Diego Bernardino as her emissary. Through him Our Lady of Octolan and the healing waters of the village became known to local inhabitants and the Franciscan monks of the nearby monastery. According to the Monks of Adoration, on February 27th, 1541 Juan was led by Our Lady of Octolan to a fountain of water from a spring that had not appeared before. The monk says Our Lady spoke to Juan saying, "My heart always desires to help those who are suffering. My heart cannot bear to see so much pain and anguish among people without healing them. Drink as much water as you desire." Besides curing the village with her sacred water, another legend surrounding the Lady of Octolan relates how Franciscan monks were called out to a forest apparently on fire, yet the flames did not damage any of the trees. As is the case with so many Black Madonna statues which are found in trees, here a certain octolan pine tree caught the attention of the monks because inside the tree they discovered a wooden image of the Virgin which is housed in the present-day church.

The first chapel was expanded by many over the years between 1670 and the late 1700s. Juan Escobar laid the foundations for a larger church, expanding on the simple chapel that first honored Our Lady. He also added a dome and other sections of the structure. Later the chaplains Francisco Fernandez Silva, Manuel Loayzaga, and Manuel Ponce de Leon all continued the expansion which included altars, a chapel of the well, the "Fortress of the Queen," pulpit, tabernacles, nave, and the outer facade. Most of the decorations are of a regional baroque style and date to the 18th century, though the church underwent some changes in the 19th century.

Located atop a hill, the church houses many niches and altars dedicated to feminine personages such as Our Lady of Guadalupe, Mary Magdalene, and the Virgin Mary as the Lady of Octolan. The original statue from the aforementioned miracle can be found in the famous Niche of the Virgin made of glass and silver at the main altar in the part of the church referred to as the sanctuary. She is almost 5 feet (1.48 m) tall and sculpted from a single piece of native pine tree. Paintings in the church nave tell the story of the image of Our Lady of Octolan. An octagon-shaped chapel depicts the life of the Virgin Mary. Columns within the church are decorated with angels and flowering fruit. Looking up at the dome, one sees a dove, symbolic of the Holy Spirit, or for our purposes, Sophia. The Chapel of Saint Lorenzo is significant within the shrine because it is believed that the miraculous statue was brought here when it first appeared. Within are paintings associated with those in the nave which tell a part

▲ Our Lady of Octolan appears to the faithful.

of the story of the miracle. There is a chapel for the Virgin of Guadalupe which holds her statue. The arched shell-like portal of the church entrance is flanked by two towers and depicts symbols of the Immaculate Conception. Once inside visitors cast their eyes upon an image of the Virgin which stands before a star-shaped window. According to Victor Jimenez, the interior of the church reflects "ascension, light, happiness, and movement, as though its creator had sought to communicate these ideas, through architecture, to the image of the Virgin, located not in a niche, but in the hollow of the great starry window of the choir that opens up in the center of the facade." Other features of the church include a Pieta, the famous image of Mary holding the dying Jesus upon her lap, as well as Saint Anne, Saint Elizabeth, and Anne the Prophetess.

Getting to Tlaxcala

Located about an hour, or 75 miles (120 km) southeast of Mexico City, the Sanctuary of Nuestra Senora de Octolan is 1/2 mile (.31 km) west of Tlaxcala. Take Juarez Avenue from downtown Tlaxcala toward Santa Ana Chiautempan. Turn right at Citalpopoca Street which leads to Octolan Park. Here you will find the sanctuary. Alternate route is from Puebla. Once at the Tiahuicole fountain, make a right turn toward Chiautempan. About 1 mile (1.6 km) directional signs indicating the sanctuary will show the way. Admission is free. Visitors should remember a container to collect sacred water. The archaeological sites of Cacaxtla and Xochiquetzal are about 40 minutes, or 12 miles (19 km) away.

Goddess Focus
Our Daily Bread: Diet and Behavior

Meaning no disrespect to those who might choose a vegetarian diet or pay homage to an agricultural deity, science weighs in on how diet may adversely affect behavior. Case in point, Aztecs may have been aggressive and practiced human sacrifice because of their intensive diet of maize! Those were the findings at a symposium on diet and health in Florence, Italy. It was presented that maize is a cereal lacking in tryptophan, which is the precursor of serotonin, an important neurotransmitter. Diets lacking serotonin and its precursors can result in adverse behavioral consequences. It was cited that Aztecs lacking adequate herbivorous animals as a protein source appear to have suffered from a serotonin deficiency. The majority of their food provided inadequate amounts of tryptophan and lysine. Symptoms of this deficiency are the inability to identify with the suffering of others, cannibalism, warfare, and religious fanaticism.

Another snapshot from the past shows mold may have also been a factor affecting behavior in another famous case. Ergotism, a mold shown to induce food poisoning, may have been a catalyst for the Salem Witch Trials of 1692. Ergot, a chemical with effects similar to LSD, is produced by the fungus *claviceps purpurea*, which is believed to have infected the rye crops in Salem, Massachusetts. It could have been responsible for the hallucinations, seizures, mental disturbances, miscarriages and deaths in small children — all of which could have been mistaken for witchcraft or satanic influences. Mold infected crops causing epidemics and mass hysteria can be dated as far back as the 14th century.

Xcarat

The Xcaret eco-archaeological park was created a few years ago to promote respect and enjoyment of nature and the cultural heritage of the Maya world. For those interested in Goddess, the park is a fun place to experience the essence of Ix Chel and Chalchiuhtlicue in a living, participatory, and natural environment. Xcaret, meaning "small inlet" was one of the most important Maya spiritual and ceremonial centers for more than a century. Goddess devotees who visit Xcaret will immediately be overwhelmed with all there is to do and see, which immerses the visitor in a communion with the spirit of Goddess — at an adult amusement park! Set in the steamy and lush tropical landscape just outside Cancun, Xcaret offers visitors a unique opportunity to feel *within Mother Nature's embrace,* like nowhere else. Set on the blue-green waters, filled with butterflies, felines, and colorful birds, Xcaret is a contemporary sanctuary of Goddess.

Starting with the naturally occurring underground rivers for which this region of Mexico is famous, (which quickly brings to mind Chalchiuhtlicue and "her watery jade skirt"), at Xcaret visitors can don a life jacket and flippers and immerse themselves in these cold, swift, and clear waters. The experience is almost one of rebirth. The cold water, compared to the heat of the temperature outside, causes swimmers to quickly catch their breath, in a sort of mini-death, only to gasp back life a few seconds later, feeling truly alive from the experience. The clear waters of the underground rivers are magical. One floats in this womb-like waterway for 1,600 feet (488 m), sometimes completely underground.

The animals kept at Xcaret certainly reflect the Mother, especially the large feline cats on Jaguar Island where there are adult and young pumas and jaguars for all to see. There are the exquisite butterflies in the Butterfly Pavilion. This pavilion is one of the largest in the world and unique for its self-sufficient butterfly reproduction. It is truly awe inspiring to sit amongst these beautiful and delicate creatures whose life is so fragile and transforms so quickly, a symbol of rebirth of the Mother. As an ecological park, Xcaret is providing breeding and care programs for the animals they house here, including the rare turtles and manatee. The park raises awareness of environmental concerns threatening both the animals and the environment in participatory programs such as careful swimming with the dolphins. There is a bat cave, wild bird aviary, reef aquarium, and native bee exhibit — all creatures of the Mistress of the Animals, known to embody her

▲ Swimming through Xcaret caves is reminiscent of passing through the body of Goddess.

▲ Xcaret features an authentic Mayan village.

very essence. One can also enjoy the mushroom and orchid farm or the tropical jungle path, all sources of her beauty and fertile bounty.

Maya culture comes alive among the actual archaeological ruins on site in a recreated Maya village, and especially during the nighttime activities. When the lights go down at Xcaret, and the activities of the day close with the setting sun, the ancient rituals of the Maya come to life. At dusk everyone gathers on the terraced seating for spectators to await viewing of Ulama, the actual ancient Maya ballgame. Under the watchful eye of Ix Chel, the Moon Goddess, the evening ceremony begins with a calling for the blessing of the elements of the four corners: air, fire, water, and earth, also associated with Ometeotl, the deity who embodies the duality of male and female. The ballgame then begins and spectators are instantly transported back in time, seeing players in native dress of the era, play an ancient game few ever have before witnessed.

At the conclusion of the ball game, spectators walk from the park along a particular route through a modern recreation of an ancient Maya village. The route takes them by various Maya rituals being performed to haunting music by individuals dressed in vivid and glorious costume. It is truly a unique experience and a rare glimpse at what life may have been like during the worship of the Goddesses in ancient Mexico. Sometimes the night activities include touring the underground rivers lit by only candlelight. This journey to the past is a fantastic experience.

The park has other activities not particularly related to Goddess, though are a continuing celebration of life that is the Divine Feminine within nature. There are opportunities to scuba dive, ride horses, see cultural performances and equestrian shows, and much more. There is a museum which displays detailed models of all the archaeological sites on the Yucatan peninsula. There are restaurants, locker rentals, a drug store, and all the modern conveniences of home. One is reminded of the words of the Popol Vuh, a sacred book of the Maya-Quiche, "Here is the story of the beginning, when there was not one bird, not one fish, not one mountain." Xcaret feels like a paradise, an Eden, a place far from mundane life, a pristine place of nature, from which all life may have been born.

Getting to Xcaret

Xcaret is located 35 miles (55 km) south of the International Cancun Airport between Xel-IIa and Cancun. All the hotels offer tours to Xcaret which include transportation to and from the ecological park and this method of reaching the park is advisable rather than private taxi. Packages can be purchased that include lunches, or visitors can purchase what they eat separately. This is an all-day activity, with some visitors purchasing a two-day package. To do everything in one day is impossible. Some enjoy the water attractions on one day, while they tour the non-water park activities the following day.

Chichén Itzá

While Quetzalcoatl (ketz all kwat all), usually comes to mind when thoughts turn to Chichén Itzá, (chee-chen-eet-sa), Goddess advocates believe it was a sacred metropolis and home of many Goddesses. Veneration of Coatlicue, supreme Aztec Earth Goddess, mother of the god of war and the Moon Goddess, was performed here as her image on the roof of the Temple of the Jaguars suggests. On this temple supported by serpentine columns, she bears her fangs and forked tongue for the world to see. The Aztec Goddess of carnal love and desire, Tlazolteotl, is shown in relief outside the Temple of the Plumed Serpent where she is depicted as the Great Birthing Mother, with her legs akimbo. She calls to mind the young women who venerated her counterpart Tlaequani who were pressed into service to assuage the lust of Aztec warriors. Artist and teacher Lydia Ruyle, believes the site to be linked to Michtlancachihuatl, or Mother Earth, who is represented on the four corners of the Venus Temple where she is shown birthing the divine energies as Venus, a constellation important to Maya cosmology. The stone relief is from about 1400 CE.

Finally, Ix Chel's husband, Itzamna, thought to be a manifestation of the Mayan Kukulkan or Aztec Quetzalcoatl, certainly would reside at the site with his consort. Quetzalcoatl, a patron of priests, being both human and divine, is associated with Venus, long known as a star of Goddess and a planet which the Aztec aligned many of their important religious buildings and observatories. Born of Ometeotl, he played a part in the creation myth alongside the Goddess Cihuacoatl. From "the place of the miraculous birth" she took fish bones which embodied the essence of humankind and ground them into powder and placed

▲ The "Observatory" is one of the most mysterious buildings at Chichén Itzá.

▲ Quetzalcoatl was instrumental in creation myths with goddess Cihuacoatl.

them into a clay pot. Added to the flour-like powder was the blood of deities (or some say Quetzalcoatl's penis). From this mixture of blood and powder the genders were molded and were sent out to inhabit the world. Cihuacoatl, was a serpent woman associated with birth, dying, and mother aspects. According to co-authors David Jones and Brian Molyneaux, she was considered the "passive principle in Aztec religious pluralism," and she became the surrogate mother of the god Quetzalcoatl after his mother died in childbirth, thus she came to be known as the patroness of women who died giving birth. They cite her name as that which was given to companions of Aztec kings.

Chichén Itzá is probably most famous for its central pyramid-shaped monument called El Castillo, the castle, or Temple of Kukulkan. Down each of the four sides of the pyramid is carved a plumed serpent representing Kukulkan, which appears to be moving when the sun hits it precisely right on spring and fall equinoxes. Kukulkan, who also corresponds to the Aztec god Quetzalcoatl or Green Serpent, is an interesting figure that is often seen as male, but has feminine characteristics of the Goddess, namely serpent and bird aspects. The snake that sheds its skin, and the bird with its feathers are symbols of rebirth, and transcendence — aspects usually attributed to Goddesses, leaving some scholars to think this figure either appropriated the role of the Goddess or might have been more of an androgynous being such as the aforementioned Ometeotl, having both masculine and feminine attributes. Quetzalcoatl/Kukulkan or plumed serpent in nahuatl, was known by other names in various regions of Mesoamerica. He is generally considered a benevolent agriculture god who brought the people corn. He ruled over science, arts, crafts and sometimes manifested as the wind god.

The site of Chichén Itzá is about 4.5 square miles (7.25 sq. km) in size and only about 40 of the several hundred buildings on the site have been excavated. Exhibiting a Maya/Toltec architectural influence. Archaeological evidence has been interpreted by some scholars as suggesting Chichén Itzá had for a time a matrilineal culture where property was passed along the line of the mother, affording women more freedom and a better quality of life. A site of religion and commerce, Chichén Itzá had many temples, ball courts, palaces, observatories and pyramids that served the needs of the people. The infamous sacred *cenote*, or well, with its life-giving waters was a place of sacrifice and ceremony indicated by the remains and artifacts that have been brought up from the abyss. Cenotes were also seen by the Maya as the home or doorway to godly realms. Recently underwater archaeologists diving in cenotes off the Yucatan have confirmed from bodies recovered that not all those who met their end in the watery depths were women, nor were they all sacrifices. While some bodies were just thrown in, others were deposited more carefully and covered with offerings. In both cases however, these "offerings" were probably an attempt by the Maya to placate the gods and keep the balance of nature and society intact. In times of turmoil or upheaval blood rituals involving body piercing might be performed. Blood from the piercing would be gathered on fabric or some indigenous textile and burned as offerings to the gods to end the chaos, warfare, blight or whatever force seemed to be inhibiting order and harmony.

Maya researcher Adalberto Rivera suggests the major purpose of Chichén Itzá was more esoteric. In temple relief carvings he sees corroboration for this site being used as a place of initiation where one could overcome their lower chakra nature, severing attachment to the material world and learning the female aspect of existence. Rivera theorizes the victors of the infamous ulama ball games did not actually die a physical death but were selected to metaphorically slay their egos (vices) through initiation rites that brought their virtues to light (birth).

Getting to Chichén Itzá

Chichén Itzá is located 72 miles (116 km) from Merida on Route 180. Most tours originate from Cancun for full day trips, or visitors can avail themselves of simple and clean hotels in the area in order to stay overnight and have a closer look at the many temples. Some day trips afford visitors the opportunity to also visit Tulum, a small archaeological site right along the Yucatan coastline with ethereal views of the blue-green waters that certainly remind us of Chalchiutlicue, Goddess of Water and her precious jade skirt. Murals on the walls of Tulum suggest, like Cozumel, this might have been a sanctuary of Ix Chel where women came for childbirth. Visitors should specifically look for Temple #45 and the Temple of the Frescoes where there is an image of Ix Chel. Unless travelers are on a tour oriented to Goddess related subjects, mainstream tour guide will rarely mention any of the female deities.

Cozumel

The entire island of Cozumel is an altar to Ix Chel, renowned as a sanctuary for healing, particularly for women in need of divine assistance with all matters of childbirth. Some women arrived here seeking to become pregnant, while others came to give birth. Meaning "Place of the Swallows," Cozumel (koh zoo mell) was a pilgrimage site for people living on the mainland and the priestesses of the island were known for their gifts of prophecy. According to Antoinette May, a priest or priestess would be stationed inside an idol and transmit messages to the people from the gods. This was much the same technique ancients in other cultures around the world communicated between their deity and their congregation.

San Gervasio is the main Maya and Toltec ruin on the island with a shrine dedicated to the Goddess. Inhabited from about 300-1500 BCE it is located in the forest. It is easy to reach and there is a small snack bar on site. Cozumel is just one of the many places in Mexico sacred to Ix Chel (ez shell) who is often depicted as a maiden, mother and toothless crone. She is known as a Goddess of the Moon, and associated with the rabbit, also a lunar creature. Another of her symbols was the jar which represents to some the womb and to other devotees the waters vital for irrigation of crops. She can be beneficent bestowing life-giving rains or the angry crone who can empty her vials of wrath in the form of rainstorms and floods upon humankind. She is sometimes said to be the wife of Kinich Ahau, the sun god, or one of his manifestations, including Itzamna, a creator god. Related to her Aztec counterparts Coatlique and Coyolxauhqui she shares in their attributes, therefore like Coyolxauhqui, she is a force of transformation which comes with giving birth. Like the fragmented Coyolxauhqui, synonymous with our complex, multi-faceted psyches and lives, she brings balance into our life. Like Coatlique, she rules over the domain of life and death. She shares lunar and warrioress aspects. She can be depicted as a warrioress standing guard with a spear and shield and surrounded by motifs of destruction.

She is a healing deity who ruled the domains of medicine and was a Goddess of the curative waters. As a Goddess who watched over women in childbirth, it is said a statue of Ix Chel would be put under the bed of women for easy deliveries. It was to Ix Chel they prayed to become pregnant. No doubt she was called upon by many working as midwives in this time. Anyone who has ever been sick knows there is a striking difference between the assistance given by women. In their empathy they are usually moved to reach out and give the balm of their caring nature as well as the prescribed pill or treatment. When one considers the female, or the mother as caregiver, is it any wonder so many Goddesses are called upon as healer deities? With a touch or a hug they connect with their patient and respond to their needs. Scientific studies have shown women do not just recognize a condition, they also share the emotion of the patient, consequently they are superior healers, integrating both rational thought as well as feelings. Ix Chel, like other healing goddesses, is surpassed by none in providing the proverbial chicken soup for our bruised bodies and psyches.

Cozumel was described in the Chilam Balam Chronicles as a paradise to the Maya. An island of natural tunnels and honeycombed passageways, it later became a hideout for pirates. The community on Cozumel was unfortunately devastated by the Spaniard Cortez and his men in 1519. Today Cozumel is a haven for fishermen and divers.

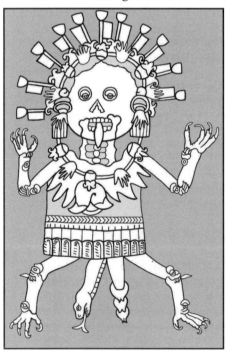

▲ The Aztec Death Goddess was present on Cozumel.

Getting to Cozumel

Travelers can fly directly into Cozumel or take a ferry from the mainland at Playa del Carmen. To reach San Gervasio from the main town of San Miguel, take Avenue Benita Juarez east to the San Gervasio access road. Turn left and follow the road for 4.5 miles (7 km) and follow the signs.

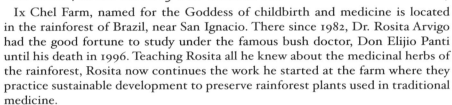

Goddess Focus
Ix Chel Farm: Saving our Resources

Ix Chel Farm, named for the Goddess of childbirth and medicine is located in the rainforest of Brazil, near San Ignacio. There since 1982, Dr. Rosita Arvigo had the good fortune to study under the famous bush doctor, Don Elijio Panti until his death in 1996. Teaching Rosita all he knew about the medicinal herbs of the rainforest, Rosita now continues the work he started at the farm where they practice sustainable development to preserve rainforest plants used in traditional medicine.

Dr. Arvigo works with medical doctors and medical organizations the world over trying to discover what secret cures the rainforest holds for diseases such as AIDS, cancer, diabetes, infertility, and hypoglycemia before deforestation makes it impossible. She offers seminars to doctors and has established the Panti Medicine Trail in honor of the late Dr. Panti, which teaches the medicinal uses of the herbs, trees and shrubs along this mile-long path above the banks of the Macal River. She is also trying to document many Maya cures for disease which she learns from local traditional healers before this important knowledge also disappears.

▲ A statue of Ix Chel
depicted weaving.

Isla de Mujeres

Another island sanctuary of Goddess Ix Chel, Isla de Mujeres, meaning "Island of Women," has a small but crumbling shrine where she was once venerated on its southern tip. Ix Chel must have permeated the everyday thoughts of her ancient people. A Goddess of magic, she was called upon to prophesy the future of the community. A Goddess of love and sexuality, she brought inspiration to average people as well as to artists and musicians alike. A Goddess of water, she was vital to farmers as they planted and harvested. One of the first domestic goddesses, she was with them as they ground corn, and made tortillas and tamales. She taught women how to weave and produce clothing for their families. Without a doubt, she is "Lady Rainbow," Goddess of renewal and creativity. She was invoked with her consort Itzamna during the month of Zip as the Moon Goddess of healing. She ruled the day called Caban, which meant earth. Associated with wild birds, she was sometimes depicted with eagle claws and crowned with feathers. It is not hard to imagine altars to Ix Chel in the homes of these people or in their fields.

▲ Ix Chel as the crone. Isla de Mujeres was her sacred island sanctuary.

In this lush natural habitat, the setting for her rituals at her shrine on Isla de Mujeres (iss-la day moo-hair-es), must have been spectacular. It is easy to vision the women in their festive and colorful clothing, adorned with shells and polished pieces of jade at their wrists and ankles, their neatly plaited hair, accented with flowers or feathers, coming across the waters in joyous prayer and song under the light of the full moon. Upon arriving, they danced, sang, and prayed to Ix Chel, as the *ciuapipiltin* or priestesses made offerings of incense, and special food or spices to the Goddess. On this island sanctuary, with faces raised upward toward Ix Chel the Moon Goddess, with the ocean breeze on their faces, her beneficent mist moistening their skin, her essence must have been powerfully tangible and transcendental as women became one with deity. The ambiance of the shrine urges the devoted to meditate by moonlight as they listen to the ebb and flow of her waters, lulling one into a light trance, so that they might more easily hear the Mother's voice and marvel at the beauty and splendor of her creativity.

At the site, a walkway from the ruin leads down to a natural arch. With the ocean on one side and the Bay of Women (Bahia Mujeres) on the other, it is quite a magnificent view. Isla de Mujeres is a small island about 5 miles (8 km) long that reminds most visitors of the shape of a fish. It is easy to walk most places or rent a moped or taxi. The island has become popular over the years as Cancun has grown by leaps and bounds. Snorkeling, fishing and diving are also major attractions.

Getting to Isla de Mujeres

Ferries and shuttle boats run to Isla de Mujeres from Cancun throughout the day. To find the Ix Chel shrine start at Avenide Rueda Medin and go southeast past Playa Lancheros into the El Grafon National Park. About 1/4 mi (1/2 km) farther along the road visitors will arrive at the shrine.

NORTH AMERICA

A goddess religion was ubiquitous throughout much of the world until the antecedents of today's religions — most of which still have a distinctly masculine orientation ... It seems obvious that a better understanding of a religious heritage preceding our own by so many thousands of years could offer us new insights into the nature of human experience.
—*Al Gore, former Vice President of the United States and author of* Earth in Balance, Ecology and the Human Spirit

NORTH AMERICA IS NOT ONLY HOME to Goddess-oriented sites of the indigenous and immigrant cultures, but also to a newer breed of devotees which have recently emerged within the United States and Canada. Here we find a home base for congregations within the ever-growing Goddess Movement. The associated sites also provide evidence to scholars that Goddess worship in the West is not only congruent with older traditions introduced in previous chapters from which they are derived, but are also living traditions. Worship is also being redefined and reconstructed so it is meaningful within a contemporary framework. New practitioners, by whatever label, have become Goddess advocates connected to an ancient heritage while liberating themselves from an autochthonic stance. With the merging of old and new, the lines between traditional worship of the past and emerging worship of the present become blurred. These Goddess sites of North America will provide evidence of the sacred where traditions of the old can stand comfortably alongside the traditions of the new. This is certainly a testament to indicate the unifying force of the Divine

Feminine across continents and cultures! Borrowing from the past, Goddess advocates reconstruct the present. Goddess is not simply a New Age creation — her origins and worship are very real and are being reawakened by many for whom the patriarchal religions no longer work. This reconstructed worship is carried on by a vast array of eclectic practitioners throughout the United States, and at many of the sacred sites listed in this chapter. They include groups which adhere to the Laws of Ma'at, an Egyptian Goddess, for their moral and religious code of justice and right living, equality of women, and the sacrality of Earth and Nature. In another example of a group borrowing from an ancient culture, men and women gather annually at a festival called Burning Man in the Black Rock Desert of Nevada. Some of these celebrants venerate Goddess before a Temple of Ishtar because they find absent a meaningful tradition within mainstream society and religion. At a temple in Laguna Beach, California, both the Hindu purist and the New Age Feminist venerate Kali shoulder to shoulder in sacred ritual, or *puja*. Groups with a Phoenician flavor honor the ancient Goddess Astarte with seasonal rites throughout the year while others, having a preference for the Egyptian pantheon, re-create in a modern context Egyptian and Greco-Roman rituals from antiquity.

The sacred sites of Goddess in the United States are a window into the worship of practitioners and the influence of Goddess that is congruent with its older cultural and spiritual origins. The sites also mark a turning point within society toward Goddess culture. In this chapter, unlike the others, readers are invited to explore not only the existing or traditional temples of the Divine Feminine, but readers will be challenged to see new temples of Goddess that they might not have recognized as such before and in the future to search out new ones of their own.

CANADA

Today, the Divine Feminine thrives in the heart, body, and mind of dedicates in Canada. She can be found in countless sacred places up in the Great White North, within a diverse array of cultural, social and spiritual traditions. While many Goddess sites embody some aspects of her various manifestations, one of the most important underlying principals of her female power is the catalyst, shakti, or activator of the life force. Simply put, without Goddess there is no God. Put in mundane terms, male power cannot act without first being "jump-started" by the feminine power. Ancient Goddess all, her many faces represent the Divine Feminine at sacred sites within the United States and the waters of North America.

Sedna's Watery Domain

Sedna, Woman of the Depth of the Sea, provides ecological balance from her sacred domed temple beneath the watery depths that surround the North American continent. Here in the land of the Midnight Sun, at alternating times of the year, inhabitants experience 24 hour periods of light followed six months later by 24 hours of darkness. The Inuits, or "the people," depended on this Creatrix for the animals of the waters. It is from these animals they sustain themselves as the sea creatures provide their food, clothing and other essentials for life such as weapons and tools to survive in this harsh environment.

▲ Two images of Sedna — Goddess of the Arctic underseas realm.

Sedna is known by many names in overlapping myths. She is called Nerrivik, Nuliajuk (Dear Wife), Nulirahak (Great Woman), or Siitna and in syncretized myths she is believed to have created the animals which live in the waters from the joints of her own fingers which were cruelly cut off, some say by her father, others say by villagers who rejected her. Consequently she and the animals and fish share DNA, thus whatever catastrophe befalls the animals and fish is also suffered by Sedna who has the power to apply justice and set things right. As each joint of her fingers was cut with an axe and fell into the murky depths, the creatures of the deep were born and in those depths Sedna lived among the creatures of the undersea. According to her legends, her beautiful domed house beneath the sea was guarded by seals that stand on their rear flippers and threaten to bite any trespassers, though fish, whales, seals, and sea birds may come and go as they will.

She finally gave up her human form to become Sedna, Goddess of the Sea and the Moon, controlling the fishes and other sea mammals for which her people depended on for food. She was believed by the Inuit to look like a mermaid with the head and torso of a woman and the tail of a fish. Some myths have her with one all-seeing eye in the middle of her forehead. She needed to be appeased for man to have a safe and successful hunt. As such she would have control over the fates of humankind. She is also associated with the domain of death which was believed to lie adjacent to her domed temple.

According to scholar Ake Hultkrantz, if pollution damaged the environment, if the flesh of sea and land creatures were cooked together, or if the Arctic wildlife was abused with unnecessary hunting and fishing, Sedna would punish the people for these taboos by calling back the animals and fish so food would be scarce. Effectively Sedna was the guardian of the creatures, the keeper of balance and Mistress of the Animals. In these many guises Sedna is reminiscent of the Eurasian Mother Goddess. In times of famine the shaman was called upon to journey down to the waters where Sedna lived and comb her unruly hair to attempt to soothe her anger, because remember, Sedna has no fingers. Hultkrantz explains the patriarchal view Sedna, explaining she is "the prototype of the woman who is ritually unclean" and is thus "still like her Paleolithic progenitor, the Goddess of Women." Hultkrantz parallels the finger-less Sedna who cannot comb her dirty hair with menstruating or childbearing Eskimo women who are not allowed to touch their hair because it is there her uncleanliness is concentrated.

331

The Inuit employed an animistic outlook toward their cosmology. Their shamans were healers and spiritual leaders often doing blessings and ritual mask dances to insure a good hunt or ward off bad luck or evil influences. The Inuit also had very specific rules and taboos about how animals could be hunted and handled, with utmost importance being to preserve harmony between man and animals. In Inuit villages the elder woman with the most influence or authority is sometimes still called Sedna. While most Inuit no longer follow the old ways, Sedna continues to be memorialized in Inuit carvings, coveted within artistic communities. In 1990, Vancouver sculptor George Pratt was commissioned by Canada's Royal Trust Bank to create a marble sculpture of Sedna for its Toronto Office. In the documentary, *Sedna, The Making of a Myth* by John Paskievich, a film about creation and cultural appropriation, the Goddess has been forever honored in film. Recently, scientists have named a star discovered in the cosmos beyond Pluto after Sedna.

Getting to Sedna's Watery Domain

Baffin Island off mainland Canada and the bodies of water surrounding Canada, Greenland, and Alaska, including the Pacific and Atlantic Oceans, Hudson Bay, the Labrador and Beaufort Seas are home to the Arctic Goddess, Sedna, who lives in the murky depths of the life-giving waters. It would be necessary to travel with an organized tour group in the summer months to visit such places of the extreme north.

UNITED STATES

The United States has long been known as a melting pot where immigrants of all countries could find safe haven and religious freedom of expression. In its most ideal sense, it is a place where freedom reigns, diversity is embraced, and all religions are tolerated. That being said, it would be remiss not to point out it has not always been that way and the struggle for religious acceptance still continues. In the early and formative years of the United States there was not much religious tolerance, and all people were not afforded equal rights and protection. Non-Christians particularly suffered at the hands of missionaries and businessmen. Women suffered and died in early settlements for allegedly practicing witchcraft, forcing their mid-wife and herbal skills underground. Not long ago indigenous Native American cultures, honoring Mother Earth, Spider Grandmother, and Corn Goddess suffered greatly in this land of the free. Decimated by European diseases, with their lands often stolen from them and their cultures oppressed almost to the point of genocide, the Native Americans were often forcefully converted to Christianity and confined to reservations under penalty of death. These people, many of whom were matrilineal, lived close to nature, were in sync with the natural landscapes in which they lived, revered the creatures whom they shared the Earth with, and were almost eradicated from the face of the planet. Fortunately today, hundreds of years after their oppression, some tribes are beginning to restore their vitality. Their culture, once demonized and misunderstood, is finally being recognized as one which has much to teach humankind. African slaves stolen from their home continent were also pressured to give up their traditional beliefs and had Christianity thrust upon them. Yet, the African tenacity to cling to their religious heritage has left the United States with a syncretized Yoruban faith that includes a face of Goddess. Consequently, there is now more worship of Yoruban deities in the New World than within the Old.

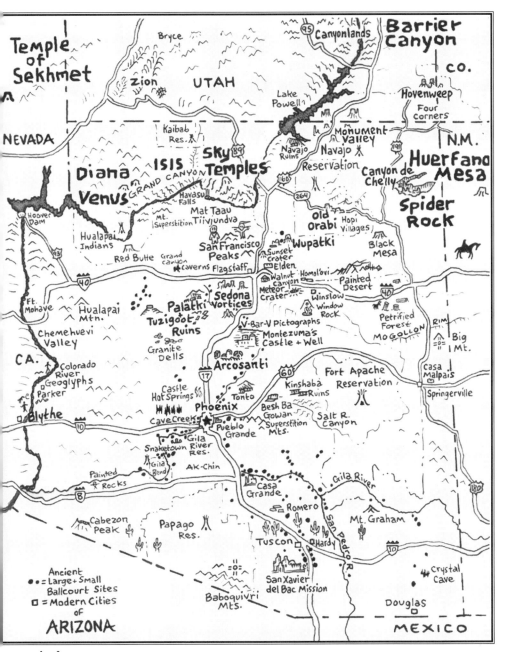

Arizona
Grand Canyon

Look the world over and you will find special mountains, plateaus, mounds, and mesas — all the high places — associated with the sacred. Humans have long held these to be the exalted domain of the gods, as places to reach for the heavens and thus to become closer to the divine. Humans have simulated their own mountains, such as the Great Pyramids in Egypt and the ziggurats in Mesopotamia,

▲ A view of the Colorado River as it cuts through the Grand Canyon.

to achieve monumental heights and be one with the Creatrix. Combine this instinct and desire with the grandeur of natural places, which is the domain and creation of Mother Earth, and the Grand Canyon naturally lends itself to becoming recognized as a contemporary sacred landscape.

The Grand Canyon is graced with no less than three mountain peaks named after famous Goddesses. Located throughout the Canyon are a triad of "rock temple" peaks already named in honor of the divinities Isis, Diana, and Venus. Not only are the particular contours of canyon, river, and peaks sometimes associated as the "Body of Goddess" but with a new perspective and vision these natural places are not only sacred but representative of the gifts of Mother Nature who can challenge, inspire, humble or teach. Like Diana, it is a lush, thriving place of independent eco-systems and wild creatures. Like Venus, it is sheer beauty, inspiration and creative force. Like Isis, the canyons are an ancient repository of magic, knowledge, and sustenance. The broad and flat pinnacle of Isis' sky temple soars to an elevation of 7,012 feet (2,138 m) and is topped with Coconino Sandstone, dated to be approximately 260 million years old. From this lofty natural temple one can look down upon the Colorado River, a waterway that figures prominently in the tribal myths of the Hopi, Ute, Navajo, Hualapai, and Havasupai.

The Hopi recognized the majesty of this sacred place and deemed it as the location of their ancestors' emergence from the underworld into the next life. Dating back two billion to 250 million years ago, this primeval Body of Goddess has held within its embrace a natural paradise of flora, fauna, waterfalls and a diversity of terrain. Visitors find five ecological zones and the splendor of the Colorado River, a source of life-giving waters, awaiting them. The river and sacred peaks are wondrously grasped between the North and South Rims of the Canyon. Here Mother Nature, by any of her names, lives in rugged splendor and devotees may visit and drink in the marvel of her creation. Here they can feel a communion with the Divine Creatrix who can nourish the soul.

The Native Americans instinctively knew this was a special place and chose to live within the canyon's embrace. One such tribe was the Havasupai, thought to be descendants of the Hokan, who migrated onto the North American continent some 30,000 years ago. Called Co'onin by the Hopi, the Havasupai were also known as the "People of the Blue Green Water." The Havasupai are thought to revere natural elements and the Wigeleeva, two pillar-like rock formations within Havasu Canyon, which they call God and Goddess, are thought to protect the people and insure good harvests. Some myths say if these pillars fall, so does civilization. These red pillars are approximately 10 feet (3 m) in diameter and 40 feet (12 m) tall. Havasupai named the Grand Canyon *Wikatata*, or Rough Rim, and their village and themselves as *Supai*. Their scattered ruins suggest inhabitation long before the Spanish passed through in the 16th century during their futile attempt to find the Seven Golden Cities of Cibola. The treasure the Spanish found, though not quite the riches they were looking for, no doubt enriched them as it has the lives of all who explore this very special place.

▲ Near Isis Peak in the Grand Canyon it is rumored an Egyptian tomb was discovered in 1909, then quickly silenced.

Satisfying the curiosity of those who seek Out Of Place Artifacts (OOPAs), author David Hatcher Childress reports there is published evidence from a front page article carried by the Phoenix Gazette dated April 5, 1909 that an excavation within a rock-cut vault of the Canyon uncovered an Egyptian tomb! The headlines read, "Mysteries of immense rich cavern being brought to light. Remarkable finds indicate ancient people migrated from Orient." The article went on to cite discoveries from within the long passageway which led to numerous rooms and caverns including a shrine which held a seated deity holding a lotus flower, vases, urns, copper cups, broken swords, and mummies. Hieroglyphics were evident on walls and the article mentions the Smithsonian hoped to soon be able to decipher the text, yet the Smithsonian, allegedly the sponsor of the dig, today claims no knowledge of any such discovery. According to G. E. Kinkaid, the explorer who helped find these chambers, they were "nearly inaccessible" and "the entrance is 1,486 feet down a sheer canyon wall." The caverns showed signs of habitation and was large enough to accommodate thousands of people which certainly must remind readers of the numerous Native American dwellings carved into cliff sides which dot the southwestern United States. Undaunted by the Smithsonian's denial of knowledge of this excavation, historian and linguist Carl Hart did some investigating and found that many of the areas within the Canyon are named for Egyptian and Hindu divinities. They are the Tower of Ra, Isis Temple, Osiris Temple, Manu Temple, and the Shiva Temple. Yet these locations were kept off-limits — only tantalizing the imagination even more! At first blush, this story seems incredible, but when one considers early hunters from Asia made it to North American via the Bering Land Bridge tens of thousands of years ago, is this so far fetched? We learn more everyday about just how mobile ancient people actually were. Perhaps one day the vaults of the Smithsonian, as well as those of the Vatican, might be opened for all the world to see and such mysteries might be revealed to the public.

This author would like to leave readers with another suggestion of how the Grand Canyon (and soon to be introduced Canyon de Chelly) might actually have some connections associated with Egypt, the Goddess Isis, and our infinite galaxy. Researcher Gary David reminds us of the hermetic maxim attributed to the Egyptian God Thoth — "As above, so below" — in his forthcoming book, *The Orion Zone: Ancient Star Cities of the American Southwest*. Here he explains how the ancient Anasazi people mirrored the location of their villages (which included the Grand Canyon and Canyon de Chelly among others) with the constellation Orion, much like Robert Bauval and Adrian Gilbert suggests the Giza Plateau of Egypt is linked to Sirius and Orion, and John Grigsby sees a relationship between Angkor in Cambodia and the constellation Draco. It is widely accepted that there is significant importance in many schools of thought between Orion and Sirius, with Sirius being closely associated with Isis. Scholar Murry Hope states "Isis appears to draw the power from Sirius (or is she herself Sirius?), from which star our solar system was seeded, and transmits it via the agency of Orion to the children of our own sun." She goes on to make associations between Sirius and its satellite star, Sirius B, or Digitaria, called by the Dogon and Bambara tribes the two stars of knowledge or the seat of all learning, with "the Eye Star and the Eye of Ra which was passed between the Egyptian deities Hathor, Bast and Sekhmet." In conclusion, Hope suggests galactic significance to the scientific, practical, esoteric and abstract "Veil of Isis" as being "involved with the Creatrix aspect of the feminine principle," as indicated long ago by the famous ancient Isis devotee, Lucius Apuleius, as he became initiated into the mysteries of Isis. Believe it, or not? Just remember not too long ago we thought the world was flat. What is certain is each new scientific discovery opens our minds to the vast possibilities which previously seemed unimaginable.

Getting to the Grand Canyon

The South Rim entrance is a four-hour drive or about 200 miles (320 km) north of Phoenix, via I-17 and Highway 180. Get a map from the Grand Canyon National Parks Visitor Center before you go, or when you arrive. Isis Peak is most easily seen from the South Rim near the Grand Canyon Village area. Within the Havasupai Indian Reservation, located west of the South Rim of the Grand Canyon, visitors can view the largest falls of Havasu Canyon, called "Mother of Waters" by the Havasupai. The reservation is not a part of the National Park Service. For information check out the website for the park at www.nps.gov/grca. Overnight accommodations can be obtained within the Grand Canyon or within Supai Village of Havasu Canyon.

Spider Rock

Grandmother Spider, Goddess of the indigenous Hopi, lives in her sacred place atop Spider Rock in Canyon de Chelly (pronounced da SHAY). Here many Native American tribes found habitation for thousands of years under her watchful eye. It is a canyon situated exactly within the four sacred mountains of the Navajo homeland called the "Sacred Mothers." The Anasazi, Hopi and Navajo all lived here because like a good Mother, the canyon provided them with water and a naturally defensible shelter. The terrain of Canyon de Chelly is filled with ancient cliff and plateau dwellings, as well as sacred petroglyphs. (It has even been suggested by researcher Gary David that some of the carvings on the Arizona landscape reflect those of Egyptians.) The Navajo is occupied by holy beings their Creatrix Goddess, called Spider Woman. cosmology the mountains were some of their major their tribal social structure spective with tribes being is transferred down mater- the husband moves into his

▲ Spider Woman in her human form communing with the insect world.

the Masons, Mayans, and and Hopi believe this area and ancestors, including Grandmother Spider, also Within Native American were considered female, as female deities. Likewise reflected their matristic per- matrilineal, where property nal lines and after marriage, wife's home.

Rising from the bottom Grandmother Spider's lofty of Canyon de Chelly is perch atop Spider Rock, an 800-foot (296-m) spire-shaped sandstone monument geologists believe began to form 230 million years ago. This huge pillar is prominent on the landscape, protruding upward as if it were an imprint of the finger of a giantess left behind as she molded and shaped the canyon. The *Dine,* or Navajo, revere Spider Woman as one of their most important Creator deities who spins her web and manifests the interconnectedness of life. According to David Leeming and Jake Page in *Mythology of Native North America,* she is seen as a midwife goddess, who helps birth new beginnings and as such is considered an emergence creation deity of physical or spiritual rebirth. She comes from the underground, or womb of the Earth, where she oversees this domain of magic and darkness. When called upon she comes forth to aid her people. Spider Woman protects them and helps

to establish their culture. Throughout many of their legends she brings them fire, bows, arrows, language, wisdom, and corn. She guides them and teaches them pot making, ceremonies, and rituals. One legends even says she took the thoughts of her husband Tawa, the sun god, and molded them into clay and thus the creatures of their world were born once Tawa and Spider Woman sang to them the magic song of life. As the mistress of spinning, ancient Americans believed Spider Woman first taught the art of weaving. Navajo women today still continue their rich heritage of being talented weavers and support their families making woven items which they in turn sell. Navajo children are chided into behaving by being told that if they misbehave, Spider Woman will take them with her atop her lofty spire. Spider Grandmother is thought to have created the moon and is associated with agriculture which sustains her people, thus she lives on as an important element in the hearts and minds of her people.

▲ Spider Rock, home of Spider Woman, is prominent in Canyon de Chelly.

Mother Earth is found everywhere within Native American cultures, and not just within agricultural tribes who use cultural constructs based on matrilineal descent. She usually presides over the realms that humans nance as well as being a birth to tribe, her manifestation she is represented by an ear Animals she may be thought ture, and as Mother Earth, on which tribes live. Scholars the Native American Earth where she was worshipped migrated onto the North the Ice Age. These 25,000 Ice Age revered a female accentuate her body parts Myths of Polynesia and influenced some western Interestingly, some of these going down into the under- cent of the Greek myths Later in post-Columbian is known to merge with female deities such as Our

▲ Spider Grandmother weaves the web of life.

need for continued suste- and death deity. From tribe can vary. As Corn Goddess of corn, as Mistress of the to embody a particular crea- she is the natural landscape believe the predecessor of Mother hails from Siberia by Paleolithic peoples who American continent during hunting cultures of the deity whose sacred figurines associated with procreation. Indonesia may have also Native American cultures. myths involve the Goddess world and are very reminis- of Persephone and Demeter. times, the Mother Goddess Christian personages and Lady of Guadalupe.

Paraphrasing scholar Ake Hultkrantz who cites three traits associated with the Goddess of Native American cultures: She is a patroness of women, associated with qualities of womanhood, and probably a guardian, inventor, or agent of agriculture. She is a birth Goddess who may merge with or usurp a male deity which may account for the appearance of bisexual gods. And finally, as a fertility Goddess she is associated with germinating powers beneath the Earth, thus linking her to the realm of the dead.

According to authors Anne Baring and Andrew Harvey, native traditions "initiate us into the three laws of sacred feminine reality: the Law of Unity, the Law of Rhythm, and the Law of the Love of the Dance. These three "laws" oppose to our fragmented, exploitative, self-obsessed forms of knowing and living an entirely different, far richer, and saner vision of what it is to be human and divine, and alive in nature." They further explain that when you become acquainted with the myths, songs, and rituals of any tribal people it becomes clear in these traditions that "all living things are related to everything else, in a web of extraordinary delicacy that stretches over the whole universe. All things are in this web and part of it, and everything done to one of the parts of the web is done to all of the others."

Getting to Spider Rock

The Canyon de Chelly Visitor Center is three miles (4.8 km) east from Highway 191 near the town of Chilne in northeastern Arizona. Spider Rock is 16 miles (25.8 km) from the Visitor Center at the end of South Rim Drive. Visitors must contact the National Parks Service for more information on camping and hiking in the canyon.

Goddess Focus
Kivas and Hogans: Body of Goddess

Just as the Goddess is being re-birthed in our time, emergence has been an important theme among Native Americans in the Southwest, which is reflected in the symbolism of their choice of dwellings and ceremonial structures. The underground *kiva* for instance, used for sacred ceremonies, is considered representative of Mother Earth as her maternal cave. According to Native American cosmology to enter the kiva is to return to the Mother. Authors Leeming and Page suggest the ladder used in a kiva is the "umbilical cord" that leads to the *sipapuni* or *sipapu*, the small hole in the floor which is the symbolic womb. This is also a link between the upper and sacred worlds. As part of ceremonies it is thought as one emerges from the darkness of the kiva, or womb, one experiences a spiritual or physical rebirth. Interestingly, some scholars see similarities between the various features of the kiva and the beehive architecture of Neolithic cultures including family shrines and roof ladders.

The *hogan*, representing the womb of the Mother, was the dwelling place of the Navajo, still having important ritual significance today. In myth, the first hogan was made of poles from Mountain Woman, Corn Woman, and Water Woman. The roof of the hogan is associated with Father Sky and the floor is Mother Earth. The round female hogan is associated with Huerfano Mesa, where Changing Woman is said to have come into puberty. The hogan itself is associated with the mountain and by that association is connected to the idea of "*shima*" or protection and sustenance aspects of motherhood. There are even gender related hogans

▲ The rounded shape of Navajo hogans resemble the womb.

with the female hogan being the larger in size with eight sides. The male hogan is used for a sweat house, is smaller, and has a forked top and is associated with Gobernador Knob where Changing Woman was believed to be first found.

The Navajo and other tribes might be called the first environmentalists of North America as they continue to live a life of harmony with the land. It is no surprise to learn that solar hogans are going up on reservations thanks to the efforts of those associated with the University of Colorado's College of Environmental Design and the Colorado Office of Energy Conservation.

California

Isis Oasis Sanctuary

The Isis Oasis Sanctuary is a rallying point for Goddess advocates who gather and hold worship services, conferences, and ritual performances within this Northern California compound. If one can believe in the divine hand of Goddess, then the Isis Oasis is a perfect example of such intervention. Open since 1978, Isis Oasis is a retreat center and the site of a modern temple dedicated to the

Egyptian Goddess Isis. The founder and owner of Isis Oasis is Loreon Vigne, artist, writer, and Archpriestess in the Temple of Isis and the Fellowship of Isis, an international organization.

Loreon believes Goddess bestowed her grace upon her as she moved into her first residence. Located with the backyard facing Isis Street, only one block long, her residence in San Francisco provided the means for Loreon to expand her successful pottery business. Before long however, her magical Isis Street residence was no longer large enough, and restrictions prohibited her exotic felines within city limits, so Loreon began looking for a new home. She inquired about property that had been previously used by the Bahai faith, complete with dining hall, theater, lodge, pool, prune plum vineyard and numerous unique living quarters. The owner of the property turned out to live across the street from her purple house on Isis Street, so she called her neighbor to express interest. At first, the property was beyond her financial reach. Within a short time however, the price was drastically reduced, and Vigne was able to purchase the property and its buildings. Loreon likes to recall that during this magical time she was reading *Moon Magic*, authored by the late Dionne Fortune, considered a powerful and influential teacher and Priestess in England during her time.

Unsure what she would do with her new property, she deliberated moving her ceramic factory from San Francisco to Geyserville until she met a student of Dionne Fortune who advised her to build a temple on the property. Coupled with an inspirational line in another Dionne Fortune book, and Loreon was inspired to sell her factory and begin the Isis Oasis Sanctuary. She commissioned an ornate Egyptian-style temple to Isis on the property complete with directional altars, a central altar to Isis, colorful murals depicting deities on the walls, with a stained glass window and skylight. The temple, which is open at all times, is perfect for quiet meditation or prayer.

▲ The facade of the Isis Temple at the Isis Oasis.

Historically, the worship of Isis, a mother Goddess, popular in ancient Egypt and the Greco-Roman world greatly rivaled that of Christianity. She was a favorite of the commoner and the elite persons alike. Her popularity was such competition to the fledgling Christian faith at the time that iconography featuring her seated on a throne suckling her son Horus, was co-opted by the Christians as a symbol for Mary and Jesus. Isis can be recognized by the symbolic throne on her head, which likely represents her sovereignty bestowed upon kings and pharaohs. In Greece and Rome she could be recognized by the Isis knot fashioned on clothing which identified her and her clergy. Part of her popularity was due to her accessibility and empathy as devotees felt she knew their pain, suffering, and longing. Isis enjoys a great revival in our modern day world as more and more men and women of many cultures discover her and find she hears their prayers. Mistress of Magic, She of Ten Thousand Names, "She who held the fates of men in Her hands" are just some of the titles and attributes associated with Isis. To be embraced in the golden wings of Isis would insure that your needs would be met with the greatest sympathy and gentleness. Practitioners who visit Isis Oasis share that sentiment today.

Located in the heart of wine country in a little town called Geyserville is where the sanctuary is located. Upon arrival, visitors come upon an obelisk marking the entrance and immediately find themselves at the entrance to the Temple of Isis, a small but lovely and ornate meditation building which houses the altar and image of the Goddess Isis and the four elements of earth, air, fire, and water. The entire retreat center has recently been renovated and the nearby dining pavilion boasts newly outfitted glass tables, each with a thatched umbrella and lotus decoration. This open and airy dining area affords visitors a glimpse across the beautifully manicured lawn toward a waterfall and butterfly garden. The pillar of this lovely natural setting is a 500 year-old douglas fir tree where many have gotten married or conducted their ordination ceremonies.

Within the freshly renovated lodge, no detail has been spared to afford visitors a magical experience. Some of the rooms are dedicated to particular Egyptian Goddesses with the decor beautifully and accurately representing each unique aspect. Rooms are dedicated to Bast, Sekhmet, Nepthys, Selket, Neith, Seshet, Hathor, Nuit, Mut, Wadjet, and Maat. The lounge in the lodge is decorated in an African safari motif. Another unique building within the sacred compound is the Tower dedicated to the great female Pharaoh Hatshepsut. Rooms in the large house are named in honor of queenly personages such as Queen Nefertari, Ankhsenamon, Ti, and Cleopatra. The vegetation around the sanctuary is lush and in keeping with ancient Egyptian traditions, animals and birds are kept within the compound. Felines such as servals, bobcats, and ocelots, find a home as do rare and unusual birds housed in the aviaries and pens.

The theater is a beautiful redwood structure with stained glass doors and chandeliers with a capacity for 100 persons. It holds a magnificent altar to the Goddess Isis, as well as other amazing artifacts including a replica of King Tut's throne. Beneath the theater is the Osiris Tomb Room used for rituals including re-birthing ceremonies. Open to all races, genders, and creeds, the Isis temple is guided by the 42 Laws of Maat encouraging a life of service, compassion, and truth. Isis Oasis is a nonprofit church recognized by the State of California and the federal government. It is attempting to give those with a fascination for the ancient Egyptian culture a place to worship as well as provide a home for alternative forms of belief which might not feel connected to patriarchal mainstream religions. The staff provides massage therapy, tarot, past life and astrology readings by appointment. The temple offers weekly temple services and educational opportunities making this sacred site of Goddess part of a modern living tradition embracing and reflecting Goddess in her multitude of aspects in a spirit of love, healing, and abundance.

Getting to Isis Oasis Sanctuary

Located 75 miles north of the Golden Gate Bridge, Isis Oasis Sanctuary is an hour and half drive north of San Francisco, off Highway 101, just north of Healdsburg. Take the Geyserville Avenue exit and follow the signs to Isis Oasis Sanctuary in Geyserville, CA at 20889 Geyserville Avenue. You can visit the website at www.isisoasis.org.

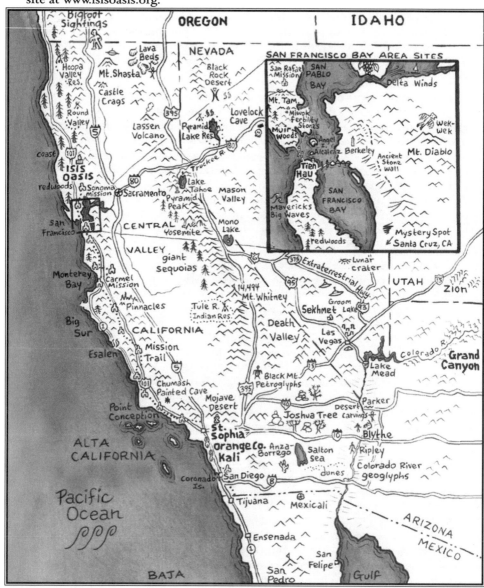

Goddess Temple of Orange County

The yearning among devotees for a brick and mortar place of worship was finally fulfilled as the Goddess Temple of Orange County opened its doors on the weekend of a fortuitous full moon, in March, 2004. The temple is open to women of all faiths who want to explore recapturing the Feminine Divine within themselves as well as discovering the Goddess within the world at large. Founded in 2002, the temple is no longer in someone's home or backyard, or beneath a grove of trees, nor does it move from locale to locale each season, renting space as other groups have been forced to do. Temple of the Goddess is permanently located in an industrial park and open during the week for women to visit and meditate, with services held every Sunday, including Healing Prayer Circles open to men and women on Wednesday nights. If there was even a glimmer of doubt that there was a need for such a temple, those doubts were soon swept away in the rising excitement, support, and growing attendance at the temple.

Decorated in the soft and feminine hues of pale pink, green and gold, the temple space is energetically alive, warm, and inviting. As one walks into the low light of the temple space, the focal point is the large golden altar in the north, or rear wall, with its lifesize Greco-Roman statue of Hebe, Goddess of Renewal, holding her cup aloft. Below her are altars with candles and white leather cushions on which visitors may kneel to pray or meditate. In the center of the room surrounded by chairs is a circular altar used for Sunday services. This altar changes every Sunday depending upon the topic of the guest priestess for that service.

Along the east and west walls leading up to the main altar, framed in draped gossamer gold fabric are three blessing altars. Each altar is dedicated to a different Goddess and set of qualities: Hygeia, Diana, Oshun, Lakshmi, Athena, and Kwan Yin are all represented. In the rear of the church are altar niches holding statuary and depictions of many other goddesses including Isis, Bast, the Cretan Snake Goddess, Guadalupe, Artemis, and the Black Madonnas. A recent addition to the temple space is a lovely and private meditation grotto. A temple for women of all faiths dedicated to restoring the Sacred Feminine in modern day spirituality, the temple is inclusive of all religions and forms of spirituality.

Liturgy and temple layout is a deliberate blend of many traditions from the worlds' major religions. Liturgy and altars were created with the specific intent to help individual woman from every tradition find at least one thing in the temple to which she can relate, that she can recognize as familiar, to help her feel she belongs there, to help her feel "safe," and to represent and honor as many women's cultures around the world as possible. Instead of creating services designed according to any specific traditions, the decision was made to create a fresh ceremony that is comfortable and satisfying to a very wide range of women. The focus is always of course on the Sacred Feminine and women are constantly finding new ways of honoring Goddess that is respectful to all these wonderful traditions in a general way. These are the concepts which hold this diverse group so closely together.

The temple is ripe with affirmations, positive thinking, and encourages love of Goddess and self. Some forms of prayers follow the Church of Religious Science's five principles for efficacious prayer: recognition of the Divine, unification with the Divine, the affirmation or prayer itself, an expression of gratitude, then release. A typical, very simple prayer might be: "Divine Goddess, of whom we are each an emanation, we send loving energy to the world from our hearts

▲ Goddess Hebe is prominent at the central altar at the Goddess Temple of Orange County.

now. We thank you for the many gifts you bring to our lives. Blessed Be. Ashe!" Other sources which inspire liturgy and prayer come from paths such as Dianic, Pagan, Wiccan, New Thought/Theosophy, traditions of indigenous peoples and metaphysics in the tradition of Ageless Wisdom.

Absent any dogma, especially one designed by the patriarchy, a blessing bestowed upon the temple on its opening day comes close to being a reflection of the core beliefs embodied within Goddess Spirituality: From within a large jeweled egg, the symbol of the womb, of potential, birth, and new beginnings, a woman reached within and drew out the following blessings for the temple and its congregation: "From the green element of Earth, may this womb of the Mother be blessed with abundant monetary support, and volunteer contributions of time and energy. From the blue element of water may love, respect, reciprocity and gratitude run deep within this well of Goddess. From the red element of fire, may strength, courage, justice, and integrity shine bright from this hearth of the Sacred Feminine. From the white element of air, may the beating wings of She of Ten Thousand Names help manifest creativity, progressive thinking, clear and concise communication with this abode of the Divine Feminine. From the heart, Goddess is All Things, and All Things Are Goddess. May those within this temple strive to integrate the spiritual and mundane dimensions of life within this temple. May this sanctuary for women be alive with the wisdom, compassion, and acceptance that is Goddess. May this temple be a beacon of Goddess radiating the beauty, inclusiveness, and power of her spirituality."

The Goddess Temple of Orange County is directed by Reverend Ava Park, notable for her semi-annual Gallery of the Goddess art shows which introduced many to rituals pertaining to the Divine Feminine. Ava also founded a well known animal advocacy group, Orange County People for Animals, hosted "Visionaries," a long-running radio show, and was named Citizen of the Year in 1998 by Orange County Weekly. A ritual priestess and minister, Ava leads the women's congregation in Sunday services, healing circles, seasonal rituals, and special ritual events. The temple and its mission statement set a distinct tone most welcoming to the multitudes for the future. It mirrors the all-embracing beauty, love, and inclusion of Goddess. One feels the work here is from the heart, reaching out, and encouraging everyone to feel a part of this wonderful love of the Divine Feminine, to know herein they have a like-minded community of support. The Goddess Temple of Orange County, under the leadership of Reverend Park, is encouraging more people to feel a part of this empowering and nurturing spirituality.

Getting to the Goddess Temple of Orange County

Located south of Los Angeles in the city of Irvine, the temple is housed in an industrial park at 17905 Skypark Circle, #A. From the 405 Freeway, exit on Mac Arthur and go north on MacArthur past two streets, Main and Sky Park East, to Red Hill. Take a left on Red Hill and it is one street to Sky Park North/Mitchel. Take a left on Sky Park North and look for the address. The temple is open to women for services on Sunday mornings and open to both genders for prayer circles on Wednesday evenings. The temple moved nearby to a larger space due to the overwhelming growth of the congregation. It is recommended to call ahead for scheduled services and special events, or check the website at www.goddesstempleoforangecounty.com.

Kali Mandir Temple

The Kali Mandir had its modest beginning as a "living room temple" when it was founded in 1993 by Elizabeth Usha Harding, author of *Kali: The Black Goddess of Dakshineswar*. Now, over ten years later, Kali Mandir is a thriving traditional temple in the process of purchasing property in the beautiful oceanside community of Laguna Beach, California, (Some say the state is named for the legendary and dark-skinned Amazonian Queen Califa, who some scholars believe is associated with Kali.) This temple is dedicated to the Divine Mother Kali in the more benign mother/child aspects. It has no presiding guru. Worshippers, both Indian and Western numbering in the thousands, attend services or *pujas* during the year with priests from the Dakshineswar Kali Temple in Calcutta brought to California to perform authentic pujas on an annual basis. Devotion is modeled after the Calcutta temple, with local devotees of India giving their stamp of approval to the Kali Mandir, which follows the spiritual tradition of Sri Ramakrisna.

Kali, a Hindu Triple Goddess from India, is an aspect of the Goddess whose worship has been unbroken for the longest

▲ Durga astride a lion in the Kali Mandir Temple.

▲ Kali resides inside the main altar of the temple devoted to her in Laguna Beach, California.

period of time, dating back thousands of years to her earlier manifestation as Nirriti, an aspect of the divine feminine venerated in the subcontinent as early as the middle of the second millennium BCE and directly related to an even more ancient earth deity. She is Goddess of preservation, transformation, creation, and destruction. She is thought to rejuvenate lives and remove obstacles in a person's life path. Her devotees believe that by facing one's fears an individual seeker may attain a sense of freedom which leads to a state of bliss. To use a Western illustration, in her triple aspects of virgin, mother, and crone, Kali can be depicted as either benevolent or fierce. As the virgin, she is white, as the mother she is red, but as the destroyer or crone, she is black, the latter color that absorbs all others. Often she will be black with a red tongue and palms, with white nails, eyes, and teeth.

Kali is a complex Goddess with many postures depicting several different aspects. She is often portrayed as black with a red outstretched tongue and many arms holding weapons. Sometimes she is standing atop or in sexual union with the god Shiva, her consort, to represent that power, or *shakti*, the feminine force, which comes from her and without her, there is no action in the universe. She is the primal creative principle. It is said that she sprang from the forehead of the Goddess Durga to obliterate demonic forces which the gods themselves could not overcome, therefore it is she who holds the key to restoring balance and peace. In her earliest form she may have been represented by a mound or a dark-colored rock and in some places still is today. An all encompassing Goddess, Kali is worshipped by men and women from all stations in life.

There are many temples of Kali the world over, yet here in California we see a new model for Goddess worship being born. This temple represents the blending of ancient disciplines from the East with newer expressions of Kali being birthed in the West. Under this roof is a home for both the Bengali purist and the woman seeking Kali as a model for personal empowerment. An ancient worship of the East is embraced and expanded on with a new Western understanding of Kali, and vice versa. At Kali Mandir, both groups, old and new, embrace Kali, standing shoulder to shoulder, merged harmoniously in their love of Goddess. Suggestions for offerings to Kali at her temples are fruit, natural scents, and perfume free of chemicals, candy or sweets free of animal products, a red scarf, red flowers, particularly hibiscus, which have not smelled by the giver. Kali Ma gets the first sniff!

Getting to the Kali Mandir Temple

The temple of Kali is located in Laguna Canyon on 1/2 acre (.20 ha) of land in a rural area sacred to the indigenous American Indians about an hour south of the Los Angeles International Airport. Take the 405 Freeway from the airport south to the 133 Freeway which turns into Laguna Canyon Road. The exact address of the temple cannot be provided. To get permission to visit the temple or updates on events, contact the caretakers at www.kalimandir.org. Interested visitors should always call, write, or email ahead as a courtesy to the staff. Mailing address is: Kali Mandir, Post Office Box 4700, Laguna Beach, CA 92652. Their phone number and email is on the website.

Saint Sophia Greek Orthodox Cathedral

Saint Sophia's Greek Orthodox Cathedral provides advocates a sacred site that links the Divine Feminine from biblical times, namely Sophia, or the Holy Spirit, with contemporary Goddess devotion. It also provides a sacred place where

the female image of Mary dominates the altar in magnificent proportion, though within Orthodox Christianity Mary, the mother of Jesus, is not recognized as Goddess, but rather like a saint, or *Theotokos*, the Bearer of God. The cathedral is named for the Hagia Sophia (or Aya Sophia) built in Istanbul, Turkey in the 6th century CE. Both places of worship venerate Sophia, which means "Wisdom." Gnostic texts of the Nag Hammadi scriptures discovered in 1945 in Egypt, written around the 2nd or 3rd centuries CE, clearly show Sophia written from a female voice when the ancient Mediterranean world was moving away from matristic forms of religious expression toward a more uniform patriarchal spirituality. The voice in the texts is believed to perhaps be the Goddess Isis beseeching her children not to forget her. The ancient writer Aelius Aristides from the 2nd century CE refers to Wisdom as "the mediatrix between Sarapis and men" — which is also an association with Isis. Below is an excerpt translated from these Gnostic texts called "Thunder, Perfect Mind."

"For I am the first and the last. I am the honored one and the scorned one. I am the whore and the holy one. I am the wife and the virgin. I am the mother and the daughter. I am the

▲ The altar at the Saint Sophia Greek Orthodox Cathedral near downtown Los Angeles.

members of my mother. I am the barren one and many are her sons. I am she whose wedding is great, and I have not taken a husband. I am the midwife and she who does not bear. I am the solace of my labor pains. I am the bride and the bridegroom, and it is my husband who begot me. I am the mother of my father and the sitter of my husband, and he is my offspring ... Give heed to me. I am the one who is disgraced and the great one."

The influence of Sophia was still a powerful force in the early church as many brought their strong adherence to feminine forms of the deity right along with them. Only gradually (over many centuries) did the church unify enough to enforce certain proscriptions that discouraged the primary focus on the feminine attributes of God among various sects, especially in Egypt and Syria.

Saint Sophia in California is a perfect example of a sacred site which has been reclaimed and shared by devotees of Goddess spirituality. Many visit this church in quiet contemplation and recognize it as a House of Goddess. This association is an easy fit for many. To quote religion scholar James Rietveld, "the confluence of Goddess streams pours into the Christian vessel. Whether Christians recognize it or not, the feminine is very much part of early Christianity, in the very Greek the New Testament is written in, and many forms of Eastern Christianity still retain a high regard for the feminine aspects of God. Sophia is always in feminine case in Greek. She is often equated with the Third Person of the Trinity, or the Holy Spirit. In the form of the Holy Spirit, the female *is* God."

To the Goddess advocate, Sophia, the Holy Spirit or Female Wisdom, continues a legacy of the Divine Feminine through the personages of Mary, the mother of Jesus, Mary Magdalene, and the Black Madonna, who by association are embodied within this California cathedral. Other reflections of a lost heritage of the matrifocal divinity reveal themselves within the cathedral of Saint Sophia in both language and iconography. The term *khouria* is the name given to the Greek Orthodox priest's wife, which when translated means priestess or mother. On the altar is the gold-leaf bishop's throne depicted with lions on either side strongly reminiscent of the artifact of the Anatolian Mother Goddess on her throne found in Catal Hüyük, and later imagery of the Goddess Cybele. A breathtaking painting of the Madonna with her embracing and outstretched arms, along with her child Jesus, is above the altar. When looked upon through the lens of an advocate one can see in this mural more veiled images of Goddess. While certainly Mary is Goddess, the Christ child is sometimes synonymous with the son-lovers of the Divine Feminine. This magnificent church with its crystal chandeliers, soaring ceilings, stained glass windows and dazzling beauty, are certainly ambiance befitting a sacred site of Goddess. It seems simply a matter of the ebb and flow of change that today Goddess advocates reclaim and share this Christian sacred site, viewing it as sacred to the Goddess, since many pagan sites in earlier times were claimed and built over by Christians, often, ironically, incorporating aspects of Goddess worship and imagery.

Getting to Saint Sophia Greek Orthodox Church

Saint Sophia's Greek Orthodox Cathedral is located near the southeast corner of Pico Boulevard and Normandie Avenue at 1324 South Normandie Avenue near downtown Los Angeles. Take the Normandie exit off the Santa Monica 10 Freeway and simply drive north two blocks to Pico Boulevard. The church is on the right.

Tien Hau Temple

The Chinese Goddess, Tien Hau, associated by some with Kwan Yin and Isis, has her sacred abode on the third floor in one of Chinatown's uniquely styled, colorful wooden buildings, home of the longest operating Taoist sect in the United States. Tien Hau, called Holy Mother of Heaven and Goddess of Sea, was once a mortal heroine, believed to be born around 960 CE on Meichow (Meizhou) Island in the Fujian Province of China. Temple literature and the temple caretaker claim this sacred site was founded in San Francisco in 1852 to honor Tien Hau. Devotees brought the decor directly from China over 150 years ago as the Chinese began to settle in this new land. Those devoted to her built this temple to give thanks for their safe journey across the seas to their new home. Tien Hau (also spelled Tin How) was the protector of seafarers, fishermen, merchants, and travelers, but women had particularly strong faith in Tien Hau and called upon her in times of need or distress. Also called Ma Zhu, Tian Hou Niang (Heavenly Empress), Tian Fei (Queen of Heaven), Tian Shang Sheng Mu (Divine Mother of Heaven), she is one of the deities most venerated by the Chinese for her gifts of courage, kindness, and humanitarianism.

According to legend, Tien Hau, the only daughter in a family with four sons, began her spiritual journey at the tender age of 11 only to have her great power over the seas revealed to her eight years later. Falling into a trance state when her brothers and father were overdue from a fishing trip, Tien Hau had a vision they had been caught in a storm and were in danger of drowning. It is believed, while in this state, she was able to fly through the heavens and pull them from the waters and place them safely in their boat. Unfortunately due to her mother's ministrations to pull Tien Hau from her seeming fainted condition, Tien Hau "awakened" before she could help her fourth brother. When she revived, she was grief stricken at his death in the raging sea.

From that time forward, word of her power to save those at risk at sea spread throughout the land and when she was in her "trance state" her mother no longer called her back before she finished her tasks. She was endowed with powers to cure, and exorcise evil, as well as summon wind and rain to help her people. Though partial to those in the maritime professions, She spent her life helping those in need and crusading against evil until she died prematurely at the age of about 28. On the day of her death legend says a rainbow appeared where she rose to the sky

▲ The Tien Hau Temple in the heart of San Francisco's Chinatown is the home of a Chinese Goddess.

and celestial music was heard from the heavens. Her body was preserved and is treasured in a temple on Meichow Island. Fisherman still claim they see her image clad in red clothing watching over them during rough seas.

When visiting Tien Hau's temple in San Francisco, it is appropriate to bring an offering such as fresh fruit or incense sticks which can be purchased at the temple. A statue depicting Tien Hau is located to the rear of the temple, resplendently decorated with red light bulbs, golden lanterns, and an ornate golden Chinese decor. Approach Tin Hau in reverence. Kneel on the red velvet pillows before her altar and speak to her. Another female deity of the temple is Madam Golden Lotus, and in keeping with the Taoist ideals of the balance of yin and yang, the masculine and feminine aspects of life, there are also Chinese gods residing in the temple. Visitors to the temple may bring their own deity statue and ask the residing caretaker or minister to endow the devotional icon with aspects of the

▲ The statue of Tien Hau on the main altar is accompanied by many other mythical figures from the Far East.

Goddess. It will be necessary to leave the statue overnight when clergy will perform a ritual to invite the deity's power and spirit to reside within the statue. This step should be taken with all due contemplation as those devoted to Tien Hau (or a related Goddess deity such as Kwan Yin) believe it comes with a responsibility. Once the statue embodies the Goddess, the devotee is instructed to place the image in a place of reverence and to attend to her daily by leaving fresh water or offerings such as a flower, incense, or prayer. Of course a donation is customary for this service provided by the temple. This practice is common in the Hindu faith, and ancient Egyptians also believed deities resided in the statuary of home altars and temples alike.

Devotion to Tien Hau represents a centuries-old tradition that is still alive today. In Asia, Tien Hau has over 100 million followers who worship her at over 1,500 temples. After the devastating tsunami in Thailand the day after Christmas in 2004, a statue of Tien Hau (also called Grandmother Ruby) was brought to the island of Phuket from Fujian for ghost clearing rites. Tien Hau will purify the place where thousands lost their lives making it once again an auspicious place to visit. Her most important temple is on Meichow (Meizhou) Island where it is believed she ascended into the heavens a Goddess. Celebrations in Asia in honor of Tien Hau include boat processions upon the water with fishermen decorating their boats with offerings and symbols of their devotion. Processions on land include pilgrimages to her temples and celebrations featuring competing dance teams dressed as golden dragons, colorful lions, and unicorns. Devotees all give thanks to her for keeping them safe and bringing them good luck. Here at Tien Hau's San Francisco temple in Chinatown, practitioners whose culture and spirituality are deeply rooted in the East welcome newcomers of the West just discovering the rich tableau and inter-connection of Goddesses such as Tien Hau or Kwan Yin.

Getting to the Tien Hau Temple

The Tien Hau Temple is located at 125 Waverly Place, one block west of Grant Street, which is the gateway to San Francisco's Chinatown. The temple, also called Tin How, is at the top of a clean and well-lit third floor walk-up. Temple hours are approximately 10 am — 4 PM daily. Chinatown is most easily reached on foot or by bus. This is a very congested part of San Francisco and driving is not the best mode of transportation. Chinatown is a also a wonderful place to purchase afford-able and good quality Goddess statuary, particularly of Kwan Yin.

Louisiana

Vieux Carre

The essence of the Goddess, as a celebration of life, holds sway in New Orleans within the core of the people. Life here moves at a slower pace and New Orleanians see no reason to catch up. It is a city proud of its diverse cultural and ethnic heritage, where people look for just about any excuse to indulge in the pleasures of food, drink, and partying. There is a sense of life being a bit more in-sync with the natural rhythms and life's simple pleasures. Despite the influ-ence of the Catholic Church, the lifestyle in New Orleans is hardly dogmatic or puritanical. In the Big Easy, as the city is often called, the spirit of the Feminine is also reflected in the Old World charm of the architecture in the Vieux Carre, in celebrations such as Mardi Gras with its pagan roots dating back to the rituals of the Lupercalia, Cybele and Attis, and in the worship of the Virgin Mary, Our Lady of Guadalupe, and various goddesses in the Yoruban pantheon.

Goddess lives in the steamy heat of the city whose motto is "let the good times roll," and where Stella's raw sexuality in the story *A Streetcar Named Desire* exploded onto the screen. Goddess is alive in the women who gather at Our Lady of Guadalupe Church on the fringe of the Vieux Carre (or French Quarter) to say their rosary and pray the novena for their families. Her spirit lives in the flora and fauna of the dense bayous, the groves of oak trees with their Spanish moss, and in the luscious and heady scent of the exquisite flowers of the magnolia tree. It might even be said she lives in the strength and determination at the core of the Southern Woman who might sit ladylike in her finery on the verandah sipping a Mint Julep one day and be found pulling up crab traps in her old blue jeans the next.

Goddess lives in the rituals of the Catholic Church which assimilated what it could not stamp out. She is an embodiment of life's earthy pleasures, and nowhere in the United States does she manifest her robust essence with such fun and flair as in her many faces that peak from behind her carnival masque in the Vieux Carre of New Orleans. Author Samuel Kinser cites carnival origins starting in an urban and country reaction to strict Lenten rules and a groundswell of interest in a variety of social and agricultural practices in pre-Christian Celtic, Germanic, Slavic, and Roman sun, wind, and water worship. On the other hand, Henri Schindler, a local author in New Orleans and an expert on Mardi Gras, believes the carnival season in New Orleans has its origins in spring rites of the Greek and Latin world, namely the two celebrations of the Lupercalia and those of the Goddess Cybele and her consort Attis. The ecstatic festival of the Lupercalia, held on February 15th, was associated with Romulus and Remus, said to be the founders of Rome, who had been suckled by a She Wolf (a metaphor for Mother Nature) when they were infants. During the Roman festival dogs and goats were sacrificed in a cave at the foot of Palatine Hill and the meat consumed. Some of the animal's skin was turned into whips, and its blood used to ritually paint the priests and two youths who were then wiped with wool dipped in milk, the nourishing fluid from the Mother. During the celebration priests chased naked men and women around the Palatine Hill of Rome and through the streets of other towns where the celebration was held, lashing out at them with whips, with the intention, according to Schindler, of forgiving them of their sins. We are reminded of self-flagellation as a penance for sin.

Other sources say women sought out the priests, thinking their touch from the bloody thong would cure them of barrenness in a form of fertility magic. Schindler states the sacramental strips of the whip were called Februa, so it might be a good time to mention Mardi Gras, like Lupercalia, is usually held in February! When there were not enough priests to perform the rituals, laypersons took over the duties and flayed themselves until they felt purified. It is no coincidence Mardi Gras, or Fat Tuesday, is the culmination of the carnival season, followed the next day by Ash Wednesday and the beginning of 40 days of Lent, when Catholics fast and pray and ask forgiveness of their sins. Lent then ends with the celebration of Easter, which marks the resurrection of Jesus, who died and arose for the sins of humankind. It was at Lupercalia, that Antony, the consul at Lupercus, offered a royal diadem to Caesar in 44 BCE. The festival of Lupercalia survived until at least 494 CE when the Bishop of Rome banned the rite and absorbed it into the Feast of Purification for the Virgin.

The Church was not happy with these celebrations, but they could not quash the traditions. In the 5th century some control was managed when they adapted the celebration and veiled it in Christian significance, renaming it *Carnelevamen*, a "consolation of the flesh," which came to be called carnival. In 600 CE, Pope Gregory officially set the often fluctuating date for Easter (which celebrates the resurrection of Christ) at the first Sunday following the Vernal Equinox. Thus the Christian celebration of Easter, would for all time overlay the spring rites of Cybele and Attis, Ishtar and Tammuz, and the Druids. Also it must be remembered that this time was set aside for the more ancient Goddess Aostara rituals. Eventually the ancient rituals to appease the gods and ask their forgiveness on a seasonal basis gave way to daily services on altars often without personal interaction by the masses. As Shindler puts it, mirth became taboo.

Long story short, carnival came to New Orleans with the French. New Orleans was founded in 1718 and the first Mardi Gras parade was held in 1837. The parade and masqued ball was a theatre-like performance meant for entertaining the members of the carnival club and was usually based on a particular theme drawn from mythology or history. The very first theme in North America portrayed Demon Actors from Milton's *Paradise Lost* with Persephone, the Fates, Furies, Gorgons, and Isis all making their acting debut in the New World. Parade themes such as Egyptian Theology have produced floats representing ideas of temples, tombs, palaces, pleasure, sacred animals, and resurrection. Since then, masked groups, called "krewes," wearing very androgynous looking costumes, have looked to the Feminine for inspiration as their organizations have taken the names of Pandora, Aphrodite, Diana, Isis, Rhea, Diana, Ishtar, Juno, Hestia, Nemesis, Hebe, Hera, Helena, Oshun, and Cleopatra. Obviously one of the carnival krewes of Mardi Gras did their homework because the Krewe of Babylon has as its Captain, King Sargon, the namesake of Ishtar's royal father.

▲ A statue of Mary in the grotto of Our Lady of Guadalupe Church.

Oddly enough, New Orleans may even have some Egyptian connections — and we certainly know Egypt influenced Greece and Rome! According to scholar, R. E. Witt, "the carnival of medieval and modern times is the obvious successor of the Navigium Isidis," an ancient festival that began in Egypt, but in time with the spread of Isis' worship, began to be practiced throughout the Greco-Roman world. In this festival, which included cross dressing, processions, and all manner of hilarity, music, and revelry, a ship laden with gifts being offered to the Goddess Isis was launched upon the waters in exchange for her blessings for anyone dependent on the waters and sailing season. It should be noted in the fishing villages south of New Orleans an annual Blessing of the Fleets is performed by Christian clergy for safety and abundance of the fisherman and their ships. This is an obvious remnant of the Isidis Navigium festival of ancient times. Witt also cites the Christian Feast of Lights or Epiphany with roots in the rituals of the priests of Isis. Interestingly, the Feast of the Epiphany, on January 6th is also known as Kings Day in New Orleans and it is the kick-off of the carnival season in "the city that care forgot." Beginning on Kings Day, New Orleanians begin a series of King Cake parties. Within the cake is a plastic doll. The person getting the piece of cake with the doll hidden inside is obligated to host the next party, thus the party season continues up until Mardi Gras. Neo-Pagans have taken to the idea of reclaiming the tradition of the King Cake and associating it with the ancient custom of cakes, bread, or the preparation thereof, as being sacred to the Goddess. And in one last association between Goddess and January 6th, a date with so much special meaning in New Orleans, Witt cites that within Gnosticism, this is the date Aeon/Horus was born to the Goddess Isis.

Like her sister cities of New York and Miami, the Goddess is also within the New Orleans View Carre in the guise of the worship of the Yoruban goddesses

353

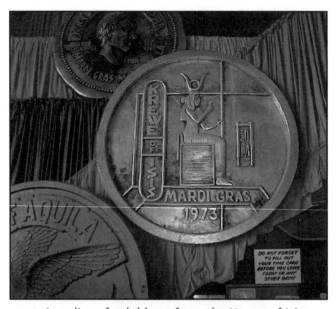

▲ A replica of a dubloon from the Krewe of Isis, which still parades today.

of Voodoo spirituality. Religion scholars who track such things cite the Yoruban deities being worshipped more in the New World than in the Old whence they came. While some believe shops selling Voodoo dolls are just for the tourists (some are!), there is a thriving community here that seriously worships the Goddesses Yemaya, Oshun, and Oya. The Voodoo Temple run by Priestess Miriam on North Rampart Street, along the fringe of the Vieux Carre is one such example of authentic spirituality. With New Orleans and the Vieux Carre located along the crescent of the Mississippi River, the aforementioned River Goddesses are right at home and their serious practitioners make an attempt to dispel misconceptions and teach those interested in their faith. There is an annual Voodoo Fest in New Orleans where visitors can get up close and personal with the reality of Voodoo in New 'Awlins where practitioners are involved in a hybrid version of syncretized Christian and Yoruban traditions. There is also a Neo-Pagan community actively involved in Goddess Spirituality, while others venerate the Feminine Divine in the guise of the Virgin and Our Lady of Guadalupe, the latter having a church honoring her on the outskirts of the Vieux Carre.

When coming to New Orleans during Mardi Gras, the most expensive time to visit for airfare and hotels, remember the parades begin about seven days prior to Fat Tuesday, culminating with Rex and Comos, the oldest clubs hitting the streets on Mardi Gras day and night. The larger, more elaborate parades are the weekend prior to Fat Tuesday. Scoring an invitation to a masqued ball is quite difficult unless you have some local connections. And remember, when that dubloon comes your way from the masqued rider on that float, let it drop to the ground, step on it, and when the crush of the crowd eases off, then bend over and pick it up! And remember to yell, "Throw Me Somethin' Mister." Mardi Gras is not about waving to the pretty girls sitting on the back of convertibles. It is about how much loot you can grab, then going to Bourbon Street, having a drink and eating a good meal. Sacred pleasures! Just do not forget your mask!

Getting to the Vieux Carre

The Vieux Carre, or French Quarter, the most free-spirited ten-square block area of New Orleans is located about 40 minutes from the New Orleans airport. Cars can be rented at the airport, but it is advisable to take a taxi to the Vieux Carre and walk through the Quarter, which is more of a pedestrian area. Parking is an expensive nuisance. Bring a reliable guide book with you. Do not rely on the carriage drivers or haunted tour guides to inform about the city unless pure entertainment is the goal. Priestess Miriam's Voodoo Temple is on North Rampart Street across from Armstrong Park, while the International Shrine of Our Lady of Guadalupe and Saint Jude is down the street at 411 North Rampart Street. The Summer of 2005 delivered multiple hurricanes to the shores of Louisiana. New Orleans was particularly devastated by Hurricane Katrina. In an attempt to understand such tragedy, goddess advocates cling to the knowledge that from death comes rebirth and transformation. As visitors travel to New Orleans today they will no doubt observe the essence of Goddess remaining, along with a celebration of life still prevalent among the people.

Nevada

Sekhmet Temple

The Sekhmet Temple of Nevada stands today because the lion-headed Egyptian Goddess answered one woman's prayer for fertility. Some consider it a miracle that through the grace of the Divine Feminine a woman in the mid 20th century brought forth multiple lives from her once seemingly barren womb. It is an actual event that in 1965, following years of unsuccessful attempts to become pregnant, this woman happened upon a statue dedicated to Sekhmet on a trip to Egypt. Having faith in Sekhmet's potential powers to bestow life from lifelessness, she made a vow that if she became a mother she would bestow upon Sekhmet a temple. Within days of making that promise Genevieve Vaughan conceived. She now has three daughters.

In 1992, the Sekhmet Temple was built on Western Shoshone Indian territory in the Mojave Desert. Vaughan and others devoted to Sekhmet feel the sacredness of this temple may heal the devastated land ravished by nuclear testing and war games dating from the 1950s until the present day. The building is described as "ecologically appropriate," made of straw-bale, using all non-toxic materials with a whitewashed stucco exterior with arched doorways on each of the four sides of the structure which represent the four elements of air, fire, water, and earth. Atop an opened circular roof are tubular copper spheres hollowed out to contain crystals from Taos, New Mexico. Within the temple, in the middle of the floor, is a fire pit used for ritual.

To one side is a life-size black seated statue of Sekhmet. The statue has the face of a lioness and the body of a woman. Across from Sekhmet is the Madre del Mondo, a goddess who represents Mother Earth. She has the features of a Native American woman and holds the Earth on her lap as a mother would hold her child. The statue of Madre del Mondo was created to honor and represent the Native American indigenous peoples and their deep connection to the land. Both statues were created by the late Marsha Gomez, an artist from Texas. In small niches and on altars throughout the temple are other images of goddesses from many traditions, but Sekhmet herself is the focal point.

Sekhmet's story is the perfect example of one that must be rethought and redefined. She is probably best known as a destroyer or warrior goddess. According to ancient texts, Sekhmet was close to destroying humanity, when she was tricked into drinking a sleeping potion which stopped the bloodshed. Many Egyptians feared Sekhmet, preferring the feline deity Bast. While Bast was also perceived as a sun goddess, unlike Sekhmet's association with raging flames, Bast represented the

▲ The Temple of Sekhmet in Nevada is ecologically appropriate.

warm nurturing aspects of the sun. This archaic version of Sekhmet's rampage does imply she is impulsive, deadly, and heartless. Quite the contrary according to devotees. Keeping in mind history is written by the conquerors, and myths can become distorted over time, consider a different face of Sekhmet. She is an entity of power and strength that enables manifestation and transformation. Sekhmet protects, heals, and seeks out justice. To those who revere her, Sekhmet is the best ally and powerhouse to have in one's corner.

Devotion to Sekhmet has experienced a resurgence among women as they empower themselves to seek equality and their rightful place in the world. For these women, Sekhmet is a destroyer and creatrix who helps one learn strength and purpose in the face of adversity and aids transformation which can be a very healing growth process. Not unlike the lioness that provides nourishment and protection for her young, Sekhmet is a powerful feline who can bear claws and teeth should something or someone try to hurt one of her own. But she employs discernment and is not a ruthless, wanton killer as her ancient myth implies. Instead, Sekhmet teaches anger as an appropriate response to boundaries being violated and reminds devotees that often something might need to be destroyed for something more appropriate to grow. A mother and a healer, she is the ultimate protectress who embodies beauty, capability and power in check. To fear Sekhmet is to fear one's own personal power as a man or woman.

According to the former temple caregiver, Patricia Pearlman, the sun disk atop Sekhmet's head is representative of fertility and the promise that with each new dawn comes hope and the spark of life. She explains the Goddess Isis embodies the caring, nurturing and mother aspect of Sekhmet who will kiss one's painful wound. Bast is an aspect of Sekhmet that is playful and is the teacher of children. Bast is Sekhmet's soft underbelly, usually hidden behind Sekhmet's stern face. Conjoined, their aspects are similar to a mother who scolds her child for wrongdoing, yet smiles inwardly to herself.

The Sekhmet temple has a guest house with overnight accommodations for women only, while the temple is open to both genders. Public ceremonies are held throughout the year and are open to families and children. The temple caregiver can perform weddings, funerals and rites of passage ceremonies such as cronings and menarche celebrations which are for women only. Sekhmet's feast days are January 7th and at high noon on October 31st every year.

Getting to the Temple of Sekhmet

To locate the temple coming from Las Vegas, drive north on Highway 95 toward Reno. About 45 miles (72.7 km) outside of Las Vegas, drive through the town Indian Springs. About 3 miles (4.8 km) past Indian Springs, on the left side of the road tall trees will be visible in the desert landscape. This is it. Just follow the small signs stating "Cactus Springs." There will be a turnoff to cross the highway on the left which leads to a dirt road. Signs show the way to the temple, which is visible about 1/2 mile (.8 km) off the road. For a schedule of events go to www.sekhmettemple.com or write the temple caregiver at P.O. Box 946, Indian Springs, NV 89018.

GAIA ALERT
ACTIVISM IN THE DESERT

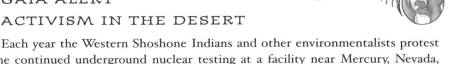

Each year the Western Shoshone Indians and other environmentalists protest the continued underground nuclear testing at a facility near Mercury, Nevada, only 15 miles (24 km) from the Sekhmet Temple. Under pressure and scrutiny this nuclear testing has diminished somewhat lately. In another ecological battle, a silent victory was recently won over the Bureau of Land Management (BLM) which approved mining very close to the temple. After many appeals and an outcry from the public, which included a letter and email campaign from devotees around the country, the sand and gravel company's permit to mine the land expired. Devotees of Sekhmet believe their prayers and protests helped stall the efforts of the mining company.

Finally, in an ironic twist of fate, former temple caregiver Patricia Pearlman was named an Honorary Steward of the BLM for her efforts in protecting the land and animals around Cactus Springs. Patricia diligently fought against gun clubs and "black powder people" re-enacting the backwoods culture of the 1820s who used an area near Cactus Springs for dumping, partying, and camping. Mesquite trees, the habitat for an endangered species of bird, were being cut down for firewood. Car batteries were dumped in the fresh spring located on the land resulting in the poisoning of wildlife dependent on the spring water. After trying to keep the area clean with the help of other members of the temple, and appealing to the BLM for years, the decision was finally made to erect a cable fence around five acres (2 ha) of the area. This prevents anyone from driving into the area and greatly restricts damage to the habitat and creatures of the land.

▲ An art installation of the earth on a catapult at the Burning Man festival.

New Mexico
Huerfano Mesa

In keeping with the recurring theme of the Earth landscape as the body of Goddess, Huerfano Mesa, (or Dzil Na'oodili) is known as "the lungs" of Changing Woman. Located within Navajo Country (or Holy People Encircling Mountain) Huerfano Mesa is where, according to legend, Changing Woman came into puberty, gave birth, and constructed the first *hogan* home for the Navajo people. Changing Woman, called Asdzaa Nadleehe in *Dine'*, represents the ideal Mother, and is one of the most powerful and important Navajo deities. Girls are taught to emulate this Goddess who is believed to have given birth of the original six Navajo clans by donating the skin from various parts of her upper body. She gave the Navajo the first hogan along with their most important ceremonies, such as the Blessingway Ceremony and the Kinaald, a girl's puberty ceremony.

Changing Woman is attributed with providing sheep, corn, and regulating the rainfall. To the Navajo, corn is the giver, sustainer, and producer of life. Corn is also a symbol of fertility and motherhood. Through Changing Woman gift of corn the Navajo had all they needed for livelihood. Changing Woman gift of corn danced on the four directions and from each point she brought gifts to her people. From her dance on the east came forth rain, from the north animals and maize, from the south appeared fabrics and jewels, and from the west came plant life. Author Rissetto citing scholar Gary Witherspoon explains the domain of Changing Woman as "an active reality," helping to maintain the social and economic livelihood of her people. She is the changing seasons, with the ability to restore herself as the land and life continue to cycle. Within Changing Woman's mythology, she descends from the heavens four times a year, each time wearing different clothes. During these times she is known by different names. Some of these are Abalone Woman, Turquoise Woman, White Shell Woman, and Salt Woman. These four representations of Changing Woman are thought to correspond to the changing seasons.

▲ Changing Woman has always presided in the spiritual realms around Huerfano Mesa.

Changing Woman is also associated with time, immortality, creation, life, death, and magic. She has the ability to manifest in the form of a young, mature, or old woman, and thus can constantly renew herself, reminiscent of some Greek Goddesses who represent the maiden, mother, and crone phases of a woman's life. According to Patricia Monaghan, "The Apache call the Earth Goddess Changing Woman because she never grew old. When her age began to show, she simply walked toward the east until she saw her form coming toward herself. She kept walking until her young self merged with her aging self and then, renewed, returned to her home."

According to some legends, Changing Woman was found by First Man atop Gobernador's Knob in the form of a small piece of turquoise. He brought her home to be cared for by First Woman who fed her pollen and dew. After various rituals, she took the form of a human woman. When Changing Woman reached puberty, some stories say she dressed in white and ran four times in the direction of the sun. So also do young girls during their puberty rituals. This Kinaalda ritual is the time when Changing Woman teaches young woman about their first menstruation. During the four days of ritual the young woman embodies Changing Woman who infuses the girl with her wisdom. At the conclusion of the ritual each girl is thought to be transformed into a woman with the ideal attributes to be a caring and capable member of the tribe. Touch seems to be particularly significant within the ceremonies and seems to mark a moment of transformation. During the Kinaalda there comes a point in the ceremony when an elder woman massages the initiate and it is thought at that moment the young woman becomes the earthly incarnation of Changing Woman. Likewise, in Changing Woman's own story, it is said when she was massaged by the Holy People in just the right fashion, she became pregnant and the skin from her body formed the Navajo people. In some stories (because the mythologies vary and overlap) Changing Woman had as her husband the Sun. Some stories say she birthed two sons, Monster Slayer and Child Born of Water, who grew up to be heroes of the people protecting them from monsters.

According to Raymond Friday Locke of the University of Virginia it is through Changing Woman's gift of corn and sheep, which the Navajo consider *shim,* the economics of the Navajo matrilineal tradition is maintained. Women own the hogan, children, sheep, money derived from weaving, and any personal family possessions. Men own what is given to them by their own clan or family but do not own what belongs to their wives. Women and their children stay a part of the mother's clan. This tradition gives women an important place in social and economic areas of society. Rissetto cites Witherspoon regarding the bond between child and mother being a primary one, with the strongest clan familial bonds. The father's relationship to his children is more secondary. He is "at best, a helpful friend, a good teacher, and a strong disciplinarian; at worst, he is a potential enemy, an undependable friend, or an unreliable ally." Though the social and economic aspects of the tribe are matrilineal, there is male dominance within the politics and religion of the tribes. To quote Professor Laura Tohe, herself a Navajo, "there is no word for feminism in the Navajo language." As girls grow up to emulate Changing Woman, they are self-reliant and self-sufficient, therefore Changing Woman is an excellent role model for Native American women, and in fact, for all women. Other names for Changing Woman are White Painted Woman and *Estsan Atlehi,* which means "Mother of All."

Getting to Huerfano Mesa

The large mesa, or flat topped mountain, is in the flatlands of northwestern New Mexico in the Four Corners area, about 25 miles (40.3 km) south of Bloomfield, NM. The road up the mesa starts a mile (.62 km) from Huerfano Trading Post and 3 miles (4.8 km) southwest of Blanco Trading Post, 2 miles (3.22 km) from Highway 44 connecting Bloomfield and Cuba, NM. Travel services are available in Bloomfield. The Bureau of Land Management can be contacted for maps.

GAIA ALERT

AMERICAN INDIAN SACRED SITES AT RISK

That was the headline of a press release from U. S. Representative Nick Rahall, Ranking Democrat from the House Committee on Resources. In an effort to curb the destruction of Indian sacred sites on federal lands due to development,

▲ The Bighorn Medicine Wheel in Wyoming has lost many of its stones to illegal souvenir collectors.

Rahall introduced the "Native American Sacred Lands Act" to provide Indian tribes the legal standing to halt proposed mining, timbering and other activities which would desecrate sites they hold sacred for religious purposes.

The press release went on to say that despite several laws being in place aimed to protect the religious freedom of Native Americans and the historic and cultural value of their lands, there is currently no legal mechanism to guarantee protection of sacred lands from energy development and other potentially harmful activities. This bill would enact into law a 1996 executive order designed to protect sacred lands, ensuring access and ceremonial use of sacred lands and mandating that all federal land management agencies will prevent significant damage to sacred land. It would also give Indian tribes the ability to petition the government to place federal lands off-limits when they believe proposed action would cause significant damage to their sacred land.

A recent attempt to provide legislation protecting sacred sites of Native Americans have been squashed by the Republican majority in the House of Representatives prompting U. S. Representative Rahall to state on the House floor, "Let their voices be heard above the roar of mining operations which threaten to sweep away sites that are sacred to them. Let their voices be heard above the din of drilling rigs which seek to desecrate their places of religious worship. Let their voices be heard above the babble of corporate greed which would sacrifice their lands and waters on the altar of profit and wealth. Most Americans understand a reverence for the great Sistine Chapel or the United States Capitol. Too often non-Indians have difficulty giving the same reverence we give to our sacred places to a mountain, valley, stream or rock formation."

New York

Lady Liberty

Whether holding her torch at the gateway to freedom or wrapped in her pink slip of activism, Lady Liberty is the political Goddess of the oppressed. Towering over the water gateway to New York City for more than a century, the Statue of Liberty is the first object millions of immigrants saw as they came to this new land, the "melting pot" of the world, seeking freedom and opportunity. But this is not where Lady Liberty was born. In a sense, she too immigrated to the United States. Lady Liberty, or *Libertas*, has her origins in ancient Rome where as an embodiment of freedom, she was deified with other virtues the Romans felt should be upheld as reverent. According to teacher and scholar Selena Fox, the Romans deified Freedom along with Hope, Justice, Piety, and Courage, virtues they believed warranted divine status. In Rome, the Goddess of Freedom was closely associated with Feronia, an agricultural and fire Goddess among the Etruscans, Sabine, and the freed peoples of Italy. Other times she might have been associated with the Roman god Jupiter. Libertas took the form of a Goddess in 238 BCE when her temple on Aventine Hill in Rome was dedicated.

Since Libertas' birth more than 2,000 years ago she has been the symbol or rallying point for many in their quest for independence, freedom, and social justice. For some it is not always enough to simply pray. Often there is more to be done to secure peace and justice. Throughout history, people came together within the embrace of her imagery to fight for a living wage, decent working conditions, personal freedoms, adequate funding for social reform, honest representation in government, or to seek fairness and justice. In these worthy causes it is common for her symbols and virtues to be invoked. Fox reports that in Rome, when a slave was freed, this life passage was marked with a ritual using symbols associated with Libertas, namely a cap, or *pilleus* and a rod, or *vindicta*. Lady Liberty was a symbol during the Revolutionary War between the United States and Great Britain and her image was adopted by the French Republic during its own revolution. After all, she was a gift from France to the United States. Dedicated in 1886, suffragettes circled Lady Libertas in boats demanding over megaphones that women be given the right to vote. In 1984, the United Nations designated the statue a World Heritage Site. Then in 1989, demonstrators in Beijing, China raised a 33-foot (10-m) styrofoam image in Tiananmen Square as they rallied for democracy in their own country.

The Statue of Liberty, one of the sacred sites in North America which personifies the Goddess as political, has been called upon in increasing fashion by citizens and politicians within the United States as liberties and freedoms seem threatened. In 1993, former Vice President Al Gore positively cited in his book detailing environmental concerns the Goddess and her worship as an example of "the fount of all life and who radiated harmony among all living things." The Divine Feminine continued to be called upon in various ways to lend her powerful image toward democracy and freedom. In an unprecedented act, the personified virtues of Goddess and Libertas conjoined were referred to by United States Democratic Congressman Dennis Kucinich in his formal announcement speech for the office of the Presidency of the United States given in Cleveland, Ohio in October of 2003. Kucinich stated: "I am running for President of the United States to enable the goddess of peace to encircle within her reach all the children of this country and all the children of the world. And we would protect our children from poverty and war, to hold them in the light of grace, and to hold them in the power of peace. I am running for President of the United States to challenge this system which traps so many Americans, children, and adults, in fear, in violence and poverty and makes us pay for wars we don't want and causes us to sacrifice our children's future."

▲ Lady Libertas, political goddess, represents freedom.

France gifted Lady Libertas to New York City in honor of America's 100th birthday. A smaller version of Libertas, or Marianne as her image was called by the French, rests today on an island in the Seine River near Paris. Symbols on the American statue include a crown of solar rays, each representing the seven continents and seven seas, and a torch representing freedom. Beneath her feet are broken chains representing the overcoming of enslavement. She holds a tablet inscribed with her Feast Day, July 4th, commemorating the signing of the Declaration of Independence, and she wears a flowing robe as she did in her earliest representations in Rome.

The Goddess of Freedom, like the Great Mother Goddess, opens her arms to humanity's children. Here in her embrace she offers rest if one is weary, locates warmth when one is cold, or finds strength when one is oppressed. Libertas at her sacred site in New York Harbor represents guidance, inspiration, protection, comfort and above all, liberation in all its forms — social, religious, and political. She embodies many of the attributes of the Divine Feminine and she is invoked by dedicates when there is oppression or tyranny to thwart and when a call for activism, courage, and justice is warranted.

Getting to the Statue of Liberty

View the Statue of Liberty on Liberty Island as you take a free ride on the Staten Island Ferry across New York Harbor. Board the Staten Island Ferry from the Staten Island Ferry Terminal just outside the South Ferry Subway Station on lines 1 and 9. Other options are tours or ferries to the island for a fee which enable you to walk up the 354 steps to the crown of Lady Liberty.

Goddess Focus
Dominator vs. Partnership Societies

Ethics of Goddess spirituality often incorporate the Golden Rule as a moral compass. It states, "Do unto others as you would have others do unto you." A second valuable axiom is The Threefold Law, "What you do comes back to you threefold." Another ethical principle is the Wiccan Rede, which gives permission to do as one wills provided it harms no one. Building on these codes for correct living, many advocates support the work of The Center for Partnership Studies and its founders, David Loye and Riane Eisler who are working to perpetuate

▲ Famous statues of Manship depict the Three Fates, on loan at Rockefeller Plaza.

a Partnership Society. Eisler, a noted author, scholar, futurist, and activist, promotes education toward a Partnership, rather than a Dominator model, for society. She cites key concepts that distinguish the difference between the two societal continuums: Dominator models operate using fear and aggression toward those considered unlike them, while the Partnership model encourages trust and reciprocity, sincerely embracing the diversity among people within other groups. Dominator models often bestow freedom for a selected few who are set above and apart. Generally those within Dominator models of society look down upon people and cultures deemed "other," judging them inferior and without any true value. In Dominator societies violence is a method used to hold onto control. This force can come in many forms, including rape, child and spousal abuse, taking away personal, civil, and religious rights, and war. In contrast, Partnership societies would link primary principles of the organization and work toward methods that "celebrate life-giving and life-enhancing activities." Fear and hatred are not perpetuated in a healthy Partnership society, but in Dominator models these emotions are stoked to keep people apart, thus promoting distrust and division among cultures and peoples. Femininity is neither valued nor honored in Dominator societies. Partnership societies seek to resolve conflict in a manner that is beneficial to all parties concerned, while Dominator models build hierarchies and empires through subjugation and power over methods.

Some practitioners within Goddess spirituality view the contemporary teachings of this "partnership paradigm" as a reflection of the earlier peaceful and harmonious Neolithic societies travelers have visited on this sacred sites sojourn. More information can be obtained about Partnership ideals in Riane Eisler's book, *The Partnership Way* or by going to the website for the Center for Partnership Studies listed in the Resources section at the back of this book.

South Carolina

Brookgreen Gardens

From ancient rock art to manicured meditation gardens, art within natural settings have long been associated with Mother Earth. Such renderings enlist the Brookgreen Gardens as a newly emerging sacred site which embodies Goddess spirituality reawakening today. Of particular interest are the metal sculptures by Paul Howard Manship (1885-1966) which have been described as "reflections of his passion for ancient art and mythology combined with modern form." Brookgreen Gardens, the oldest and largest public sculpture garden in America with over 550 works of displayed art on 300 acres (122 ha), is an enchanting combination of art and natural habitats. Hundred year old live oak trees, tranquil ponds, dogwood, magnolia and palmetto trees draped in Spanish moss are the setting for these beautiful images of Goddess and related themes. Manship's works related to Goddess spirituality are titled Time and Fates of Man, Maiden, Diana, Cycle of Life, and Evening. Manship, like the masters of old, was an accomplished artist. He studied at the American

▲ Richard Miller's "Wind on Water" seems to defy gravity.

▲ A statue of Diana in the Brookgreen Gardens depicts the Goddess as strong and regal.

Academy at Rome, and with famous sculptors of his day, before receiving prestigious recognition and awards.

Time and Fates of Man, the three Greek Fates, is clearly representative in the Triple Goddess, or the Maiden, Mother, Crone as Creator, Preserver, and Destroyer, in the context of past, present, and future. The Fates, named Clotho (maiden/the spinner), Lachesis (mother/the measurer), and Atropo (crone/the cutter of life's thread) are anchored in the Tree of Life. It is the Fates that weave one's destiny. Other features of the piece represent the four elements of water, earth, fire, and air. Maiden was designed to accompany the companion male sculpture, Youth. Together they represent humankind, the balance of female and male, yin and yang, the life force. Maiden might also be viewed independent and representative of the many Virgin Goddesses discussed throughout the book, such as Persephone and Athena.

Diana, a Roman Goddess, is depicted in her form as the Huntress with her bow and surrounded by her beasts. Her companion sculpture depicts Actaeon, the unfortunate hunter transformed into a stag by Diana when he accidentally came upon her bathing in a pool. Diana was quite a force in ancient times. When high ranking clergy tried to be rid of her, the people revolted. Eventually many of her temples were turned into churches as people transferred their devotion to Mary as the female intercessor, or face of God. Diana is also associated with Artemis and the Mistress of Animals from Asia Minor.

Cycle of Life is Manship's interpretation of mythology and astrological symbolism. Captured within the bronze sculpture are images of the four elements, a sundial, the zodiac, and hours of the day, all motifs reflective of both earth and time, certainly two components always associated with Goddess. Within the sphere a family of three is encircled much as the Goddess embraces her human children. This trio is reminiscent of the holy trinities Isis, Osiris, and Horus, or Parvati, Shiva, and Karttikeya.

To many there is no distinction between our spiritual and secular lives, both being interwoven like a beautiful tapestry. In keeping with the Creatrix deities such as Spider Grandmother, who are thought to weave and spin the heritage of their people, imagine if we all walked through each day with a higher awareness that each decision, deed, or word was sacred, or that each person, place, or thing was a part of the great interdependence and sacred web of life. What a different world humanity would together weave! With that thought in mind, places such as Brookgreen Gardens could be a conduit for those seeking to plug into the sacred. Here within the natural splendor, one can nourish the soul and feel connected to the cosmic threads of that larger tapestry of life — to Goddess as Mother Nature personified in art.

Getting to Brookgreen Gardens

Located on Highway 17 South between Murrells Inlet and Pawleys Island, on the South Carolina coast, the garden is about a 20-mile (32-km) drive from Myrtle Beach and 25 miles (40 km) from Georgetown. Check the website at www.brookgreengardens.com for further information.

Tennessee

The Nashville Parthenon

From her American Parthenon, the Goddess Athena's colossal statue towers over the cultural life of the people of Nashville, bringing the ancient imagery of the Divine Female into the public arena. Going unnoticed are the quiet offerings occasionally left at her feet by Goddess advocates honoring her. Before Nashville became known for country music, it was considered the Athens of the West as educators here tried to perpetuate the ideals of Classical Greece. Centrally located in urban Centennial Park is the city's art museum, the Nashville Parthenon, and inside stands an exact replica of the statue of the Goddess Athena that dominated the Parthenon in Athens, Greece. Built in 1895 for its centennial exposition, this modern replica stands almost 42 feet (13 m) high and is covered in gold leaf. The Parthenon in which Athena is housed is also a full scale replica of the original, with pediment reliefs copied from the originals housed in the British Museum in London.

Athena was the primary Greek warrior Goddess, instrumental in the Battle of Troy, who was birthed from the forehead of Zeus, the latter association leaving most scholars baffled. Even scholars such as Walter Burkert are a bit perplexed as he expounds on the birth of Athena, or more properly, Athenaia. "The birth myth is as popular as it is puzzling. It is scarcely to be derived from nature metaphor — birth from the mountain peak — and even less from allegory, whereby wisdom comes from the head. For the early Greeks, it is, if anything, the breath, the diaphragm which is the seat of right thinking. Individual motifs have Near Eastern parallels, such as the swallowing and birth from an unusual part of the body in the Kumarbi myth; the Egyptian Thoth, the god of wisdom, is born from the head of Seth." Scholars such as Nilssun cite her association to Mycenae where a temple in her honor stood. Authors Anne Baring and Jules Cashford relate Athena to even older divinities such as the Neolithic Bird

▲ A giant statue of Athena dominates the interior of the Nashville Parthenon.

▲ The Nashville Parthenon is an almost exact replica of the original Athens Parthenon in Greece.

Goddess, as well as the more classical representation of Pallas Athenaie, Goddess of heroes, armed maiden, protectress of a city.

Athena was sometimes referred to as a maiden or "Virgin Goddess" which actually had nothing to do with chastity or denial of sexuality, but more to do with being independent, not owned or controlled by man, a person unto herself. Burkert further describes Athena in association with Medusa: "The emblem and armor of Athena is the aegis; whenever she raises up the aegis, her enemies are overtaken by panic and soon are lost. The aegis, as its name tells, is a goat-skin; a special goat sacrifice forms a part of the Athena cult in Athens. Myth recounts how this goat was a monster, a Gorgo, which Athena herself killed and skinned; pictorial art turned the animal head into a Gorgon head and bordered the aegis with snakes while the Iliad poet speaks more circumspectly of golden tassels."

Baring and Cashford suggest another association with Medusa, the Gorgon, with her hair of snakes that could turn men who looked upon her to stone. They speculate this imagery might provide a clue to her association with wisdom in the form of discernment or contemplation before taking action. While the decapitation of Medusa to some may represent the death or silencing of the matriarchy, they seem to hypothesize that by having Medusa on her breastplate Athena makes a statement that it is by reflection we face and master an object or obstacle. They explain this in the metaphoric myth of Perseus; Athena gives him a mirror in which to reflect the gaze of the Gorgon back onto herself, protecting him from certain death. One must remember, that myths often take on multiple layers of meaning and interpretation, even changing over time, but for devotees of Athena, her essence or wisdom may be the idea of using forethought before taking action and refrain from impulsive or reflexive action. Athena herself takes on multiple meaning as she represents a shift in the perception of Goddess from the time of pre-Classical Greece to the time of the Olympian pantheon.

Though the Nashville Parthenon might not immediately be thought of as a sacred site in the traditional sense, consider this place and the archetype of Athena in this modern-day temple a monument representative of the reclaiming of Goddess and Her virtues for our culture and society. Here in a museum, a repository of culture, knowledge and artistry, the Goddess, standing in all her majesty, is surrounded by the beauty of the past and present, a fitting metaphor for the Divine Feminine. Visitors to the Parthenon seeing Athena in her splendor revived here, should enjoy a moment of quiet contemplation and personal reflection.

Getting to the Nashville Parthenon

From the Nashville International Airport, as you exit the parking lot take the I-40 west toward Nashville until you can merge with the I-24 west. Stay in the right lane and go about 1.7 miles (2.7 km) on the I-40/I-24. Stay on the I-40 (which is also the I-24 here) when it splits from I-24 and go a little less than 2 miles (3.22 km) to the Broadway exit. At the top of the ramp, go to the second light. Turn left onto Broadway. Less than half a mile (.8 km) down, Broadway and West End Avenue split. Continue on West End Avenue and go one mile (1.61 km) farther to Centennial Park on the right. Follow signs to the Parthenon parking lot.

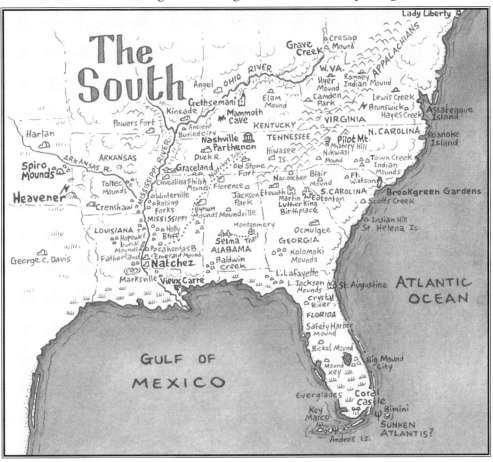

Utah

Canyonlands

An Archaic Creatrix Goddess births the trees and animals from her lofty rock cliff perch within the extraordinary landscape of Barrier Canyon. Is it religion? Is it art? Is it language? Art, creation myths, and expressions of spirituality are as varied as world cultures with these three subjects exemplified in Canyonlands National Park by one interesting rock art image which depicts the act of creation in intriguing fashion. Located in the remote Maze section of Horseshoe/Barrier Canyon, in southeast Utah between Green River and Hanksville, miles off the highway, is a pictograph dating perhaps to 1500-3000 BCE. The artists might have been the Fremont or Anasazi Native Americans, though others have dated the work to more ancient people.

SACRED PLACES OF GODDESS

▲ A pictograph of one of the most ancient Goddess images in North America.

Rock art is hard to interpret, though most feel it is a shaman's attempt to communicate with the world of deity, animals, spirit guides, or ancestors. Some believe rock art could have been part of initiation rites or healing ceremonies. Others view rock art as a language. This particular image is part of a mural with other large images called the Harvest Scene or the Bird Panel.

Goddess is represented here in a six-foot (1.8-m) tall rather ambiguous form. She is birthing trees, birds, and animals from her hands. This image is interpreted by some as Mother Nature birthing the world because it is from woman life is born. Look up at her towering image in this powerful place steeped in vast, quiet solitude, and the sacredness can hardly be denied. Here in Canyonlands National Park the visitor finds a powerful and untouched landscape of pinnacles, spires, rock cliffs, sand dunes and the occasional ruined pueblo or granary. The park is vast and the unusual contours of the land a visual feast. This part of Utah was believed to be home to prehistoric Native Americans thought to be hunter-gatherers who emerged into agriculture when the weather permitted.

It is thought the shaman made the pictograph images using ground hematite which creates a dark rusty red pigment, along with white lines and dots. The pigment could have been applied by hand or with brushes made of yucca fibers. These ancient artists were also known to apply pigments by blowing it onto the rock through reed tubes. These ethereal, other worldly, anthropomorphic images take on an almost alien appearance. They have large eyes, broad shoulders, trapezoidal bodies adorned with jewelry, clothing, and decorative headdresses. It is thought the images were created when the tribes gathered for religious ceremonies. What scholars know about these people is limited. They eventually learned to irrigate fields, make pottery, baskets, unique moccasins, and homes constructed of mud, stone, and wood. If the climate required them to be mobile, their shelters were rock alcoves and caves. Above all, it is believed they survived in this harsh landscape by their adaptability. They disappeared from the area about 1250 CE, and like the Anasazi, scholars are unsure of the reason. Some speculate they may have moved elsewhere or have been absorbed into neighboring tribes.

Getting to Canyonlands

Canyonlands National Park in southeast Utah is most easily reached from Highway 211 north of Monticello or Highway 313 north of Moab, which are the only paved access routes into the park. Fortunately, the extreme remoteness and rugged nature of the region has naturally discouraged many visitors and in doing so, has helped preserve the site. The image has even been taken off many maps to further protect this ancient and sacred art. In keeping with this intention, we will leave the exact location of this image a bit vague, though it is important to acknowledge her existence. For those who might visit and intend to honor the sacrality of the land, be aware overnight backcountry trips require a permit and it is a federal offense to deface archaeological sites. Those who venture in should be prepared and experienced. Those who do not have experience driving four-wheel drive vehicles over uneven terrain should not go. Those who cannot change a tire or have experience hiking and camping should reconsider. Visitors who do go must be prepared with food, water, and maps. It is always a good idea to check in with the Ranger Station and advise the authorities of your plans.

Goddess Focus
The Sacred Landscape: Yoni Stones

Found in many parts of California and throughout the world, "yoni stones" are natural clefts in rocks that display a strong resemblance to the female yoni or vulva. Throughout history, such places have long been sacred to many cultures as they represent among other things, the power of rebirth or a symbol of the life-force. To some it was the very vulva of the Earth Mother or a sacred place of the Divine Feminine. David Whitley, author of *A Guide to Rock Art Sites in Southern California and Southern Nevada* explains that to the shaman these places are gateways to the supernatural or signify the union or intercourse between the shaman and spirits on the other side. These sites were often places of initiation or puberty ceremonies for girls.

These natural formations are symbolic entrances to the womb, or in the case of death, the tomb. Some such sites have been worshipped as symbols of deities or the very deity herself. They are often considered sites of feminine power, sexual potency, fertility or openings to Mother Earth. While yoni stones appear naturally in rocks, crevices, craters and hills, often the yoni has been purposely carved or built into structures, such as the Sheila-na-Gigs. The yoni, long an enigma of

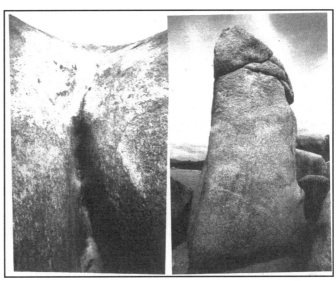

▲ Natural rock formations of the yoni and phallic.

power, magic, mystery, and allure, has been the subject of artistic and religious significance from the beginning of time. Just as women's sexuality and sexual pleasure have been denied since worship of Goddess has been repressed, so has the image of the yoni. Worshipped in some cultures, taboo in others, the image of the yoni reemerges as a powerful symbol of Goddess spirituality being reclaimed by women today. The yoni has in recent years seen a rebirth as monologues are written in her honor. The famous artist, Georgia O'Keefe, seems to use the yoni in all its symbolic glory as the focal point of much of her work.

Wisconsin

Circle Sanctuary Nature Preserve

For more than two decades the Circle Sanctuary Nature Preserve has been a sacred site of the Divine Feminine where Nature Religion practice overlaps with that of Goddess spirituality. Beginning in 1983, the preserve became a holy place of the Goddess within Nature and five years later it was officially zoned sacred land. For all this time Circle Sanctuary has been a place where like-minded folks could gather and share their love of the outdoors, the wild animals, and the Divine. According to one of the founders, Selena Fox, the nature preserve attracts many practitioners within and beyond the Wiccan and Neo-Pagan communities who come to enjoy the 200 acres (81 ha) of prairies, forests, and wetland ecosystems, and the many varieties of songbirds and other precious wildlife that lives there.

Visitors to the sanctuary will find many indoor and outdoor shrines located throughout the preserve as well as a Wiccan church and a pagan resource center. Circle's Temple Room includes a shrine to Lady Liberty, with her roots reaching back to the Roman pantheons of antiquity. Visitors can experience many outdoor shrines dedicated to gods and goddesses from all traditions along Ritual Ridge and Shrine Walk. They will find shrines to the Egyptian Goddess Bast as the Universal Feline Spirit, to Mother Earth, and the Shrine of the Great Mother. Those in need may visit the Healing Goddess Shrine. One of the newest ritual sites is the Animal Shrine honoring many creatures of the earth, including canines, deer, frogs, and birds. Most recently, work has been going on with Kwan Yin and her many attributes from a multi-cultural perspective.

▲ The Circle Sanctuary Nature Preserve features ritual areas among beautiful scenery. An especially potent time to visit is in the autumn.

Spirit Rock is an ancient Native American vision quest location used by people of many cultures as a place for communing with nature and receiving spiritual guidance. The congregation and visitors use the Temple Room and other outdoor circles for regularly scheduled events. These include interfaith and multicultural healing rituals, including Earth Day celebrations. There is a stream on the property in a willow grove by a sacred spring named for Brigid, the Celtic Goddess of healing and inspiration. Trees have long been perceived as sacred to Goddess and her devotees continue the practice of older traditions. They place prayers or ribbons on grove trees much as the Irish and Scottish place prayer strips on *clootie* trees and practitioners the world over place prayer flags on sacred trees when in need of divine intervention.

The founders of Circle Sanctuary have ministered to the community of nearby Madison for over three decades through media appearances, interfaith work, educational efforts, and spiritual counseling. They are most known on a national and international basis through their magazine, Circle Magazine, found in bookstores the world over. Circle Sanctuary is also the sponsor of the annual Pagan Spirit Gathering in Ohio, which attracts folks from all over the United States and beyond. Closer to home, events, festivals, and educational and spiritual opportunities are attended by people on pilgrimage from all parts of the world as well as locals who come regularly to Circle Sanctuary in the living tradition of Goddess Spirituality. In development on the premises is a large archival library of materials on paganism, Wicca, and Nature as a religion. Protecting the Earth, viewed by the devotees here, as Gaia, Our Mother, and sustaining natural places, are high priority issues. The practitioners and ministers of Circle Sanctuary Nature Preserve, with their many conservation, preservation, spiritual, and educational programs, are doing their part and walking their talk to honor and help preserve Mother Earth.

Getting to Circle Sanctuary Nature Preserve

Circle Sanctuary, located just north of the village of Barneveld, and about 13 miles (21 km) west of Mount Horeb in southwestern Wisconsin is not available for drop-in visitors. Interested parties are asked to call or email first or attend one of the many monthly events at the sanctuary throughout the year. Email circle@circlesanctuary.org, or you can also check out their website at www.circle-sanctuary.org.

CONCLUSION

Goddess will continue to emerge onto the world stage of
tomorrow with the help of all people of all races and religions as they come to understand the immense beauty,
power, and love of the Divine Feminine for all her children.
—*Contemporary Priestess of Isis*

T
O SOME, THIS MAY ALL COME as quite a surprise because until
now, particularly in the West, Goddess may have lived in the minds
of contemporary people as this one-dimensional, ill-tempered or
unsavory female caricature from Classical Greek mythology, certainly not taken
very seriously as a role model to shape societal or religious mores. Her image may
have been mingled and misrepresented with the stereotypical "blonde bombshell"
image perpetuated by Hollywood in the past. Non-scholars may have only learned
of the role of Goddess in recent years, if at all. Those who have not had the advan-
tages of classes in Women's Studies or Comparative Religions, usually including
Goddess Spirituality within their curriculums may only have an awareness of the
major three patriarchal religions of the world; Christianity, Judaism, and Islam.
Many mistakenly believe no religion existed before these three. Goddess as a matrifocal archetype and divinity may have only just been born in the minds of many
despite her long herstory. Yes, this all may come as a big surprise, particularly to
those in the United States, so cut off and isolated from her most ancient sites, and
so wrapped within the embrace of their Judeo-Christian beliefs. Still if one looks
deeply enough, or back into history a bit, both Christianity and Judaism have origins and rituals that once included Goddess, leaving today's temples and churches
saddled with the very remnants of the feminine these patriarchal religions tried so
hard to leave behind.

SACRED PLACES OF GODDESS

Goddess advocates are beginning to come together in their need for permanent and public temple spaces on local street corners and more groups are seeking out options toward that goal. However, in the meantime, absent an abundance of these gathering places, Goddess advocates of both genders meet in public places and living rooms to share discourse about all aspects of their emerging spirituality much like their ancestors who birthed early patriarchal religions once did. People paint murals on their walls at home depicting Goddess and her imagery. They have her altars representing her multi-cultural aspects in a designated sacred place in their abodes much like Catholics have always done with the image of the Virgin Mary. And the Virgin Mary sits upon these altars right alongside images of Isis, Kali, Benten, Kwan Yin, and Oshun. Taking another cue from their ancient predecessors, these modern practitioners turn their gardens into sanctuaries where rituals or meditation are performed. While brick and mortar structures designated for the sole purpose of Goddess veneration are still not found in abundance, more and more grassroots groups have devotees setting aside rooms in their homes as designated temple space; sanctified places where meetings, social gatherings, worship services, and important life-passage ceremonies are conducted. Many comfortably embrace a male face divinity, by whatever name he is called in their culture, alongside Goddess. Religion, or more accurately spirituality, has begun to take on an eclectic component, bridging cultures and philosophies, effectively perpetuating harmony, balance, inclusivity and tolerance among peoples.

▲ Metro station art in Paris, France.

Just as these sacred places are found within mainstream life, so are solitary individuals and groups of Goddess advocates facilitating their operation. Through their voices and efforts within the world in which they live, Goddess virtues are extolled and rallied round by practitioners from all walks of life including the environmentalist, social activist, reformer, and humanitarian. Consequently a Goddess Consciousness is emerging loud and strong. Political Goddess Lady Liberty has recently lent her image to activists who dressed her in a pink slip, a metaphor for firing sitting President George W. Bush for his administration's policies that some feel threaten freedom and liberty. Politicians mention Goddess as the embodiment of peace and prosperity in their platforms. Not only are documentaries about Goddess and the role of women in religion being made, but due to the public's voracious appetite for this subject matter, contracts are being negotiated in Hollywood with top name producers to develop Goddess-oriented films. Goddess-centered publications are on the rise. Unitarian Universalist Churches teach classes on the Queen of Heaven. Mimicking older times, processions that include advocates of Goddess spirituality march down public streets in full ritual regalia, carrying palanquins bearing images of the Divine Feminine. Practitioners herald the coming of a female messiah referred to as the "daughter." City-wide celebrations embody the spirit of Goddess. Goddess iconography is a recurring theme in art within public spaces and the subject of murals on multi-storey buildings. Scientists are naming a new planet after the Inuit Goddess, Sedna, and a plateau on the planet Venus is being called Ishtar for the Babylonian Goddess long associated with that planet.

CONCLUSION

The essence of the Divine Female lives in the core being of those men and women who insist females should reclaim their rightful and equal place within male-dominated patriarchal religious hierarchies. The imagery of the vulva, once a life-affirming symbol of the female and sacred sexuality, is once again being celebrated as overwhelmingly successful stage productions crisscross the country. These monologues depict the bliss and abuse of women within contemporary society, and by association the Sacred Female, through the lens of their vaginas. Goddess is celebrated at conventions held throughout the world devoted to discourse on her spirituality. Practitioners adorn their bodies with jewelry, clothing, and permanent tattoos that mark their devotion. Goddess embodied in the season is celebrated at dances, festivals, fairs, and balls. Devotees keep archives of their classes, communications, and publications. Digital and video footage is retained of special events and rituals. Some advocates have even gone a step farther, keeping libraries, lest one day books might again be burned or kept hidden in the vaults of institutions that have in the past oppressed competitive or alternative views. At the conclusion of this book, readers may never look at their surroundings in quite the same way again. Places, events, images, and people will take on a fresh new spiritual context.

For many, this tour book may be their first close look at sacred sites of these cultures at home and abroad. For others, it may be their first snapshot of Goddess within these holy places. Certainly other books have covered some of these locations, but few have done so through the lens of Goddess spirituality. Then again, for some, this may be a first look at the Divine Feminine in any context and her influence and prevalence throughout history may come as a complete surprise.

Goddess advocates yearn for an infusion of female ideals in the hope of establishing a new paradigm for social, religious, and cultural change. These adherents wish for the good of all because the pendulum has swung too far in the direction of a patriarchal, power over, "survival of the fittest" culture. Men and women turn to the Divine Female hungry for virtues that encourage a restoration of balance in the world, and they find her tenaciously thriving because humankind cannot exist without the Sacred Feminine. Without her they are not whole. To some Goddess is an archetype or possible pattern within our psyche; to others, she is a powerful force in the heavens who can alter our fate. No matter how one chooses to view Goddess and the spirituality being relearned and reconstructed around her many faces, she is being reborn today. To quote Marija Gimbutas on the return of the Divine Female, "The Goddess gradually retreated into the depths of forests or onto mountaintops, where she remains to this day in beliefs and fairy stories. Human alienation from the vital roots of earthly life ensued, the results of which are clear in our contemporary society. But the cycles never stop turning, and now we find the Goddess reemerging from the forests and mountains, bringing us hope for the future, returning us to our most ancient human roots."

People are beginning to look beyond Greek philosophy or patriarchal theology to find divinity and mold society. To quote religion scholar, Karen Jo Torjesen, "Women's sexuality as symbol or metaphor represents birth, the fragility and vulnerability of life, mortality and contingency — the opposite of male rationality and control." Practitioners believe denial of these female aspects has led society astray and down roads of destruction from which humankind may never fully recover. They think long ago the values of humankind might have been more in balance, with society living more in-sync with nature and a bit closer to universal truths than human-made dogmas. For so many, conventional religion no longer works. People are returning to ancient ways, reestablishing or continuing living traditions, and in some cases they are redefining this spirituality in a modern context — with travel to these sacred sites opening doors to herstory that have been closed far too long.

ACKNOWLEDGMENTS

As one of the many women who are childless by choice, choosing instead to birth and nourish ideas and projects rather than biological progeny, I considered the development of this book as a metaphor for birthing a child. Sitting down to reflect on whose assistance most nourished the growth of this offspring, I was reminded of the work of two notable women, Senator Hillary Rodham Clinton, and scholar Karen Jo Torjesen. Relevant to the process of writing this book was Torjesen's statement, "all scholarship is collaborative — ideas are tested and reworked in dialogues with colleagues ... and during conversations with friends." So was Clinton's premise in the title of her book *It Takes a Village* to raise a child. It took the effort, experience, and ideas of several beloved friends and devoted people to develop this book from conception to delivery onto bookshelves. Once the book was conceived, a blessing in itself, sustenance and support came

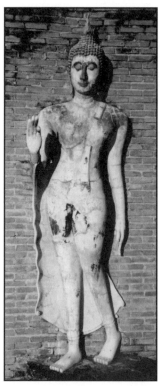

from many male and female "mid-wives," and sometimes in the most serendipitous ways, but I am most profoundly grateful to three generous men. Their patience, assistance, and nurturance greatly aided the "birth of this child."

First and foremost, I sincerely thank Roy, my husband and partner of 20-something years. He is the yang to my yin, my travel companion, computer guy, and photographer. He counts heads on tours to make sure no one is left behind before the bus pulls off. He kept the hearth fires burning and meals on the table during the long gestation period of this book. Roy, your love, sacrifice, and support were invaluable and never forgotten. Next is the brilliant James Rietveld, a graduate of Claremont University's School of Religion. He is a good friend and religion scholar who aided me as an editor and research assistant. He was my Lamaze coach as each chapter burst forth into the world. James, I humbly thank you for your dedication and belief in the project and extend my appreciation to you for sharing your vast wealth of knowledge. Finally, my publisher and editor, Brad Olsen, who helped me through the labor pains of a first book with ease, faith, courage, and an open mind. Brad, thanks for a skillful delivery and for insuring the "child had all its fingers and toes" in perfect order.

Another mid-wife who offered her valuable time and extraordinary editing assistance was Jeanne Leiter and I thank her for her patience and commitment. Keeping

▲ This Buddhist Goddess from Sukhothai, Thailand did not make the 108 list.

me together was no easy task! Special thanks also goes to Cary Egerton and Willow LaMonte for their own special contributions, support, and guidance.

Trying to choose which 108 sites of Goddess from the tens of thousands around the world was no easy task, and I am grateful for the collective wisdom of former tour participants, travel companions, intrepid solo travelers, and scholars whom I polled to determine which sites might make the final cut. To others who offered photographs, inspiration, assistance and guidance, I thank you too from the bottom of my heart. May you all receive three-fold abundance for your generous giving. They are Lydia Ruyle, Jeanne Davis Kimball, Vicki Noble, Marguerite Rigoglioso, Chandra Alexandre, Miri Hunter Haruach, Peggy Grove, Chris Sitka, Cecilia Corcoran, Sandi Sariel Spencer, Laura Chamberlain, Dianne Jenette, Selena Fox, Patricia Pearlman, Loreon Vigne, Matt Levy, Debora Whitehouse, Xia, Michelle Hart, Kathryn Rountree, Sabina Magliocco, Larry Lorusso, Leslie Delano, Kristy Coleman, Lucia Chiavola Birnbaum, Catherine Wright, Deborah Rose, Aron Crowell, Allyson Rickard, Jennifer Reif, Dan Hooker, Phil Bouterie, Henri Schindler, Jane Harrison, Kathleen Zundell, Ava Park, Hemi Whaanga, John Charlot, Shell Peczynski, Mark Maxam, Ed Taylor, Carol Nowlan, Gary Layda, Marlene Ehrenberg, Suzanne Coutanceau, and Lady Olivia Robertson. Special thanks to the National Park Service, Belili Productions, Metro Government of Nashville, and the Catal Hüyük Research Project. My apologies to anyone whom I might have failed to mention.

Special thanks also goes to our tour guides. The Japan Crew made our journey to the land of Amaterasu a true joy. Before we left home Gojiro Norikawa was our Japanese "ambassador" and translator. Levanah Shell Bdolak, Yuri Ohno, and Ikari were our awesome guides once we arrived. Our experience was certainly enriched by your helpfulness. Mr. Tadashi Sato and Singapore Airlines are credited with enabling Roy and I to have our absolute best experience flying to Asia. Singapore Airlines will forever be our airline of choice!

Honorable mention also goes to Claremont Graduate University's School of Religion, The Getty Museum, and the Classics Department of the University of California at Los Angeles (UCLA). I immensely enjoyed the lectures sponsored by these institutions and thank them for making continuing education available to the general public who wishes to enrich their lives through these informal venues.

Finally, I'd like to thank all the volunteer Stars of Sothis of the Isis Ancient Cultures and Religion Society for an assortment of assistance, but particularly Olwen, Mike, Marsha, Joanne and Charles, for keeping the energy flowing when I would go into "the cave" to write and research. Many of the Goddesses in this text might easily have chapters written about them and we thank those scholars such as Walter Burkert, Patricia Monaghan, Barbara Walker, David Kinsley, Miriam Robbins Dexter, Anne Baring and Jules Cashford for their dedication to bring to readers an understanding of the thousands of Goddesses around the world.

You are all the true embodiment of partnership and Goddess.

Karen Tate

Venice Beach, California

GLOSSARY OF GODDESS

Al-Lat (*Arabian*) Her name means Goddess; she is one of the "helping cranes" within the *Koran* as mentioned in the Satanic Verses. Her symbol is the moon, believed by some to be on the flag of Islam. Muhammad's tribe venerated her. She is the feminine version of Allah. She was further associated with contracts and fidelity.

Al-Uzza (*Arabian*) Mighty One, Goddess of the Ka'ba stone of pre-Islamic Mecca. Worshippers circumambulated the Ka'ba stone of Al-Uzza seven times, just at contemporary Muslims do today during the Hajj. Along with Menat and Al-Lat, she was the third of the Arabian trinity of Goddesses. Her star symbol is depicted on the flag of Islam, along with the moon or crescent of Al-Lat.

Amaterasu (*Japanese*) Represented by a mirror or the rising sun on the Japanese flag, the Shinto Sun Goddess is believed to rule over all Japanese deities. Considered the unseen spirit of the Universe, she guided her people toward creating their civilization and way of life.

Aphrodite (*Greek/Anatolian*) Goddess of love and beauty had her earliest roots in the eastern Mediterranean region where she began as a much more complex Creatrix deity or Universal Mother Goddess on par with Ishtar, Kali, Isis, and Cybele. She was later associated with ritual prostitution. The Romans renamed her Venus.

Apsaras (*Indian/Cambodian*) The well-endowed and sensual dancing females who are sometimes described as celestial water nymphs, they also may be depictions of even more ancient River Goddesses of the Vedic culture.

Artemis (*Greek/Anatolian*) Mother Goddess, Virgin Goddess, Mother of the Animals, beloved by the Amazons, the complex Artemis is best known by her image which depicts her polos headdress and multiple breasts, though she was once worshipped in the guise of a meteorite or tree. Known for her magical powers, her temple in Ephesus became one of the Seven Wonders of the Ancient World. The Romans renamed her Diana.

Asherah (*Canaanite*) Mentioned often in the Old Testament, she was worshipped by the common people and elite of Jerusalem despite the protests of patriarchal Hebrews. Often depicted as a tree, whose image may still be hiding in plain sight on Jewish altars in the form of the menorah. Sometimes, like Ishtar, she is depicted naked, riding a lion, with lilies in her hands. (Also called Ashtoreth)

Astarte (*Phoenician/Semitic*) Associated with Ishtar, Asherah, she was Goddess of love and war, a creatrix and destroyer. A forerunner of the Virgin Mary, called Queen of Heaven, Astarte was associated with Venus, the Morning Star, who bestowed sovereignty upon kings.

Athena (*Greek*) Goddess of heroes, wisdom, and war, noted to be born from the head of Zeus. With Athena rational thought became more important than traits attributed to the feminine. She was thought to have Minoan or Mycenaean origins with her early realm being that of a household deity. The Romans renamed her Minerva.

Auset (*Egyptian*) See Isis.

Baalat (*Phoenician*) Combines the aspects of Hathor, Aphrodite, and Astarte where she is the Lady of Byblos. Chief deity of the Phoenicians and the female equivalent of Baal, sometimes called "wise old lady of the trees." She is often showed well endowed and naked, or worshipped in the form of a stone.

Bast (*Egyptian*) Depicted as a woman with the head of a cat or lioness, she was associated with pleasure, music, childbirth, and the sun. Her sacred animal was the feline with many being mummified and buried in the cat cemeteries of her great temple in Bubastis. Associated with Isis, Diana, and Sekhmet. Also called Bastet.

Baubo (*Greek*) The raucous and bawdy nature of Baubo brought a smile to the face of Demeter and there was once again fertility in the land. Her counterpart is the Japanese Uzume who assisted Amaterasu in exactly the same variety of restoration myth.

Benten (*Japanese*) The only female divinity among the seven Japanese gods of good luck, she is the patroness of musicians and geishas, who brings wealth to the devoted. Associated with the Hindu Sarasvati, she also oversees speech, and learning. Sometimes assumes the form of a snake.

Black Madonna (*Western European*) These depictions of the Virgin Mary are shown with her hands and face black or dark brown, and thought to represent her pagan roots connected with the Goddess and Earth. The darkness is also a metaphor for the Goddess which "hides behind her veil." Black Madonnas are often the focus of pilgrimages. Some have been identified as earlier Goddesses under the top coat of paint.

Brigid (*Celtic*) Christian saint and Goddess of fire, healing, sacred waters, poetry and smith craft. Her roots probably date back to pre-Celtic or Neolithic times. Pronounced "breed," in Ireland, she is called Brigantia in England, Brigandu in France, and Bride in Scotland.

Chalchiuhtlicue (*Aztec*) Water Goddess, known as "Lady of the Jade Skirt," considered a life-giving deity associated with lakes, rivers and bodies of water.

Changing Woman (*Navajo/Apache*) Symbol of fertility and motherhood among the Native Americans. She gives her people a code to live by through her myths and is a role model for womanhood. Creatrix deity associated with magic, immortality, and time.

Cihuacoatl (*Aztec*) Serpent woman associated with birth, dying, and mother aspects. Surrogate mother of Quetzalcoatl, who becomes the patroness of women who have had children die in childbirth, or women who have died while giving birth.

Coatlicue (*Aztec*) Associated with Our Lady of Guadalupe and Tonan or Tonantzin, this preeminent Aztec deity of life and death is depicted wearing a skirt of serpents and a necklace of skulls. Known as "Lady of the Serpent Skirt," she is reminiscent of Kali.

Coyolxauhqui (*Aztec*) Moon Goddess, daughter of Coatlicue, often depicted with bells on her cheeks and cap, serpents and skulls on her body. According to myth she is sliced into 14 pieces, representative to some of the time between waxing or waning moon, and the multi-faceted nature of our psyches.

Cybele (*Phrygia/Anatolia*) First worshipped as a meteorite that fell from the heavens; the Great Mother Goddess was the embodiment of Earth herself. Later associated with Artemis. Her consort was her grandson/lover, Attis. Often shown depicted with lions, she was often referred to as "Mother Mountain," and became famous in Rome for her wild rituals and clergy who sometimes castrated themselves in ecstatic frenzy.

Demeter (*Greek*) Personified the fertility of Earth, with her daughter, Persephone, they combine with Hekate, to embody the trinity of Maiden, Mother, and Crone, also a metaphor for the on-going rebirth of the seasons. Earth Mother associated with Gaia. The Romans renamed her Ceres.

Dewi Danu (*Balinese*) Goddess of the Lake at Mount Batur in Bali. Provides water for the cultivation of rice, thus she provides abundance and fertility for her people.

Dewi Sri (*Balinese*) Rice Goddess of Bali feeds her people, providing sustenance, good fortune, and life.

Diana (*Roman*) Though often associated with Artemis, Diana has a different personality. She is more accurately represented associated with the sky, nature, childbirth, and wild creatures. A virgin Goddess, she is called upon by contemporary women seeking independence and personal empowerment.

Durga (*Indian*) Hindu Goddess of life, death, love, justice, usually seen shown astride a lion. She is one of the most powerful Goddesses, a manifestation of the all encompassing Devi. Like Kali, her offspring, she is prayed to by the oppressed seeking liberation.

Ezili (*Haitian*) Yoruban loa or intermediary considered Goddess of love, lust, and sexuality. An aspect of Oshun, and form of the Virgin Mary.

Ganga (*Indian*) Hindu Goddess of the waters who provided her people with abundance from her life-giving waters. She is believed to be sourced in the Milky Way and streams down onto Earth in the Ganges River of India.

Guadalupe (*Mexican*) Some consider her the Virgin Mary, others Tonan or Tonantzin; she is the apparition which appeared in Mexico City and hears the cries of the Mexican people.

Hathor (*Egyptian*) Often depicted as a cow or a woman wearing a headdress of horns surrounding a solar disc. She is the Goddess of love, beauty, pleasure, sexuality, marriage, whose aspects were later assumed by Isis. Other depictions show her as a sycamore tree or a lioness. Associated with the sun, Ra, and Horus, she is a multi-faceted Goddess, reminiscent of Aphrodite, whose worship continued on for over three thousand years.

Hekate (*Greek*) Goddess of the heavens, earth and sea, regeneration, life and death. Embodies warrioress and midwife aspects. Later she becomes more associated with the underworld, waning moon, and crossroads of life. She can be depicted with three faces, or in the guise of a dog, horse, and serpent.

Hera (*Greek*) Primordial creatrix who annually bathed in the River Imbrasus renewing her virginity, thus her ritual is a metaphor for the eternal cycle of life and the growing seasons. A female of independence and dignity until the Olympian myths turned her into Zeus' petulant wife. She represents the three phases of womanhood: maiden, mother, and crone. The Romans renamed her Juno.

Hina (*Polynesian*) Complex female deity with many aspects, usually associated with the moon, life, death, and fire. She is a primary female principle, said to have helped populate the world and to have taught her people to cook in underground ovens.

Inari (*Japanese*) Rice Goddess associated with the fox. Shrines often have fox statuary throughout, sometimes wearing red bibs, with keys to the storehouse within their jaws. Some say the Rice Goddess took the form of the fox, or the fox was her emissary.

Inanna (*Sumerian*) Queen of Heaven, also associated with the Ishtar. Her city of Uruk in Iraq dates back 6,000 years and may have been the first city in the world. Keeper of the Divine Law, she dispensed justice and kept the forces of the world in balance. Goddess of birth and death, she was beloved by the famous priestess Enheduanna.

Ishtar (*Semitic Akkadian*) Contemporary of Isis, Innana, and Cybele, she was omnipotent in all phases of life: fecundity, love, sexuality, life, death, beauty, war, wisdom. Early images show her depicted as a staff atop a granary, or naked wearing a conical hat, with a pronounced pubic triangle. Her titles and symbols later are associated with Mary, mother of Jesus. Like many Goddesses, her son-lover was the vegetation god. Related to Astarte and Asherah.

Isis (*Egyptian*) She of Ten Thousand Names, wife of Osiris, mother of Horus, the Goddess thought by some to have given fledgling Christianity the most competition in early times. An accessible Goddess, thought by her devotees to be able to relate to their mortal suffering, she was beloved by the common and elite alike. Her worship, which offered devotees eternal salvation, spread outside Egypt, through the Mediterranean and Europe, moving as far north as England. Today she is still worshipped around the world. Also know as Auset.

Ix Chel (*Mayan*) Moon Goddess who ruled the domains of medicine, weaving, childbirth, and curative waters. Often depicted holding a fan, cup, or basket, she is associated with Coatlicue and Coyolxauhqui and shares their attributes.

Izanami (*Japanese*) Mother of Amaterasu. Together with Izanagi, her husband, they created the islands of Japan with all the natural splendors that fill the lands. Underworld Queen of Death.

Juno (*Roman*) Mother of Mars, patroness of women, reproduction, phases of childbirth, and marriage, later assimilated with Hera. Juno, Minerva and Jupiter comprised the Capitoline triad that ruled Rome with temples throughout the Roman Empire. Sometimes called Regina, or "The Queen," she was associated with time and the menstrual cycle.

Kali (*Indian*) Hindu Goddess of life, death, and rebirth, often depicted with black skin, extended red tongue, necklace of skulls, and many arms all holding weapons within her hands. Considered the Mother of Time she is shown standing upon her consort. She is the catalyst of the Shakti, the female force, which "jump starts" all energy. Probably one of the most misunderstood Goddesses, she frees her devotees of fear. She is the offspring of Parvati/Durga.

Kannon (*Japanese*) See Kwan Yin.

Kumari (*Nepalese*) "The Living Goddess," a supreme Tantric Goddess worshipped by the Hindus as Durga and by the Buddhists as Vajradevi. This Virgin Goddess validates the kingship of the king of Nepal in contemporary times. She represents exoteric and esoteric dualism.

Kwan Yin (*Chinese*) Most beloved Chinese Buddhist bodhisattva, or Buddha in the making, throughout China and Japan. She pours out mercy and compassion to the world from the bottle which she holds. She hears the cries of the tormented. Rather than transcend to the heavens, she decided to stay behind and assist humankind. To some she is the male bodhisattva, Avalokita, and Tibetan Goddess Tara combined. Also called Kuan Yin, Kannon or Guan Yin.

Laka (*Polynesian*) Goddess of the forest and uncultivated areas, reminiscent of Diana. Patroness of hula dancers.

Lakshmi (*Indian*) Hindu Goddess with very few temples, though her image is depicted everywhere from home calendars to bank buildings as she is the poster girl for abundance and prosperity. Cows are sacred to Lakshmi and sometimes are called by her name. She is considered a symbol of spiritual enlightenment and associated with time. Possibly a pre-Vedic Goddess, associated with rice harvests and cultivation.

Libertas (*Roman*) Lady Liberty or Libertas originated in Rome, however her effigy has been co-opted as a political symbol of freedom from oppression in contemporary times.

Magna Mater (*Roman*) Mother Goddess, or Great Mother, generic term used throughout Roman empire.

Mary (*Judeo-Christian*) The Mother of Jesus, daughter of Saint Anne, thought by some to be kin of the tribe that worshipped the Queen of Heaven, within the lineage of queen mothers honoring Asherah, became the repository for the hope and desire of humankind to maintain the Divine Feminine within their religion. As such, she has assimilated many of the titles and aspects first belonging to Goddess, represents to many the Divine Feminine.

Mary Magdalene (*Judeo-Christian*) One of the apostles, possibly Jesus' wife and partner, some say the mother of his child, Mary Magdalene represents that which the Christian Church suppressed: sexuality, leadership by women, the Divine Feminine. As such, she too is elevated and worshipped by Goddess advocates as the embodiment of Goddess.

Menat (*Arabian*) Together with Al Lat and Al Uzza, she forms the triad of Arabian Goddesses. Moon Goddess, considered by some to be the ruler of fate and time. Together they form the trinity of maiden (Al-Uzza), Mother (Al-Lat) and Crone (Manat). Like her sisters, she was worshipped in the form of a stone.

Nagas (*Indian*) Holders of mystic knowledge, protectors of the source of life, often depicted in the form of a snake are a more unusual representation of the Divine Feminine. Thought to inhabit watery places and associated with the Vedic Goddess Kadru.

Nirriti (*Indian*) One of the earliest Hindu deities, she may have been associated with the pre-Aryan Jara who has been described as youthful and monstress, a discrepancy which may be related to the reconciliation between pre-Aryan and Vedic traditions. Nirrti later becomes associated with Kali, Yami, and Earth itself.

Omecihuatl (*Aztec*) Feminine aspect of Ometeotl, the supreme being having both male and female aspects. Also associated with Tonantzin.

Oshun (*African*) Yoruban River Goddess of love, beauty, and fertility who mated with her consort Shango to have human children. Originating in Nigeria, her worship moved to the West Indies, the United States, Central and South America. She is depicted with golden bracelets, a mirror, and combing her hair. She becomes associated with the Virgin Mary.

Pacha Mama (*Incan*) Earth Mother who presided over agriculture.

Parvati (*Indian*) Hindu Goddess known as Uma and Shakti, she embodies the benevolent or virgin aspect of Kali. Wife of Shiva, mother of Ganesha, she is the patroness of women and her union with Shiva represents the union of man and woman in ecstasy and sexual bliss.

Pele (*Polynesian*) Fire Goddess, independent and strong-willed, is credited with saving the spiritual and cultural heritage of the Hawaiian people from post-contact destruction. By the very nature of Pele's worship, with its challenging and assertive qualities, the Christian missionaries could not obliterate it from the lifestyle of devotees as hula, songs, and chants, vital to the core Hawaiian life remained intact. Today offerings are still made to Pele at her volcano and she is believed to manifest in the form of an old woman who can be seen walking the dark highways with her dog.

Persephone (*Greek*) Daughter of Demeter, she personifies the maiden and Spring, though for part of the year she resides in the Underworld with her consort Hades. She is part of the Greek trinity with Demeter and Hecate.

Poliahu (*Polynesian*) Snow Goddess of Mauna Kea in Hawaii, often depicted wearing her white mantle of snow. Pele's rivals for young male lovers, their battles are seen as a metaphor for the struggle for balance and the duality between the forces in Nature and the cosmos.

Sarasvati (*Indian*) Hindu Goddess called Mother of the Vedas. Considered a wisdom Goddess, who bestows bounty and fertility, she is a patroness of the arts, music, speech, intellect, science, learning and inspiration. She can be seen depicted with rosary-like prayer beads, water pot, lute, and book.

Sedna (*Inuit*) Woman of the Depths of the Sea, is believed to have created all the sea creatures from the digits of her fingers. She protects the creatures of the waters and brings her wrath upon humankind who upset the balance of the environment.

Sekhmet (*Egyptian*) Lion-headed woman, associated with the sun and its life sustaining powers of strength. Warrioress, healer, mother, she is personified as a lioness who protects her young from those who would hurt them. Often misunderstood, she is not a blood-crazed, wanton killer, but a powerful avenger and protector. Liberator and symbol of personal empowerment and self esteem.

Sheila-na-Gig (*Celtic*) Carvings on cathedrals, churches and monasteries which are representative of the fecundity of earth, and the reproductive and protective powers of the Earth Mother. Carvings depict hag-like females in a reclining position, legs akimbo, with yonis exposed. Contemporary women have adopted the imagery as symbols of personal liberation.

Snake Goddess (*Minoan*) Weaver of the web of life, Mistress of the Animals, creatrix and destroyer Goddess of regeneration, represents the dualism of life.

Sophia (*Gnostic Christian*) Goddess of Wisdom, written in the female voice in Gnostic texts of the Nag Hammadi scriptures, she is both Creatrix and Redeemer. To the Goddess advocate, Sophia, the Holy Spirit and Female Wisdom continues the legacy of the Divine Feminine, sometimes through the personages of Mary, mother of Jesus, Mary Magdalene and the Black Madonnas within Christianity, Gnosticism, and Judaism.

Spider Grandmother (*Navajo/Hopi*) Also called Spider Woman, a creatrix and weaver who spins her web and weaves the interconnections of life for her people. Goddess of emergence, or rebirth, she comes from the underworld of magic and darkness and aids her people. From the thoughts of her husband, she molded into clay the creatures of the world and sang them to life.

Spider Woman (*Aztec*) Creatrix of the Universe newly discovered at Teotihuacán.

Tanit (*Punic/Phoenician*) Heavenly Goddess, or Dea Caelestis was associated with the sky, motherhood, death, rebirth, resurrection, shamanic rites, healing, the underworld, and fertility. Astarte evolved into the personage of Tanit, who was represented by her symbol: triangle on the tip of which rests a horizontal bar, itself surmounted by a circle or disc. Tanit evolved into Juno Caelestis.

Tien Hau (*Chinese*) Taoist Goddess, sometimes associated with Kwan Yin, called Holy Mother of Heaven and Goddess of the Sea, once a mortal heroine, venerated for her gifts of courage, kindness, and humanitarianism. She spent her life helping those in need and crusading against evil.

Uzume (*Japanese*) Shaman Goddess who lured Amaterasu from her cave with bawdy antics, much as Baubo does with Demeter, thus fertility is restored to the land.

Venus See Aphrodite.

Xochiquetzal (*Aztec*) Goddess of spring, pleasure, beauty and sexuality, who embodies sexual liberation, she might be considered an Aztec version of Aphrodite. She symbolizes the flowering and fecundity of Earth and its people and has been said to have given birth to the people of the world. Chthonic Goddess, from womb to tomb. Marigolds are her favorite flower.

Yemaya (*African*) Yoruban Goddess or female orisha originates from Nigeria and Benin, Africa. She is the maternal force of creation and rules over the waters of the world. Mother of Oya and Oshun, sometimes associated with Saint Anne and Our Lady of the Immaculate Conception. (Also called Ymoya or Iemanja)

Author's Favorite Museums

Goddess' iconography, spirituality, and sacred places dominated the herstorical natural and cultural landscape around the world in centuries past. Though she is not as fully emerged within the world as she once was, Goddess still reigns supreme behind the protective precincts of her contemporary temples — the museums. Here the literal and armchair traveler can find the artifacts that connect the dots of herstory enabling a deeper clarity and vision of a time past. Spending time in these fabulous museums and at sacred sites can open a visitor to untold enrichment and aid in experiencing Goddess within specific cultures. Seeing the imagery and artifacts has a profound impact on the psyche. Visitors can visualize how cultures without language used emblems or symbols to express themselves and otherworldly ideas. Often the artifacts and iconography in museums were the very glue which held communities together and gave cohesion to their society. Anthropologists believe symbols and iconography within cultures are actually indispensable to the survival of individuals and that society as a whole. That idea is equally relevant today as in times past. During the extensive travels of the author which has made this book possible, both within the United States and abroad, a handful of museums stand out as personal favorites.

Beginning in the United States, two museums earn the privilege of making the list of personal favorites. On the east coast of the United States, the **Metropolitan Museum of Art** in New York City takes the top spot. With its vast collection of Goddess artifacts, including rarely seen Sekhmet statues, along with the reconstructed Egyptian Temple of Dendur on display, it squeaks by the smaller and more intimate Cloisters on the Hudson River as a favorite. Closer to home, on the west coast of the United States, the museum not to be missed is the **Rosicrucian Egyptian Museum and Planetarium** in San Jose, California. This museum has one of the largest collections of Egyptian artifacts west of the Rockies, including a replica rock tomb beneath the museum, and a new wing dedicated to Sekhmet, which includes her larger than life seated statue where devotees have left offerings at her feet. Certainly worth mentioning is the lovely recurring Egyptian motif which adorns all the buildings within the complex, including a replica of a small temple on the grounds which transports the visitor back in time.

Moving "across the pond" the stellar museums not to be missed in Western Europe are the **British Museum** in London and the **Louvre** in Paris. No surprises here. These museums hardly need any introduction. Travelers can lose themselves for days within the cavernous halls and labyrinthine corridors finding Goddesses of all cultures and time periods. Also in Paris, of special interest is the **Cluny Museum.** Located in a Gothic style church-museum, the Cluny houses the sensational Lady and the Unicorn tapestries and other medieval artifacts. Moving a bit south toward the boot of Italy, the **Vatican Museum** takes top priority in Rome where there is the most unique Egyptian collection of artifacts — not to mention the other treasures the Vatican has come to possess over the centuries! *Museo Archeologico Nazionale* or **National Archaeological Museum of Naples** also scores a big hit. Here are the artifacts from the Temple of Isis in Pompeii and the most gorgeous black Artemis of Ephesus anyone could ever want to see. Speaking of **Pompeii**, though technically an archaeological site, it is a literal window into the past, a museum/city in situ, and not to be missed! Leaving the European continent, continuing across the beautiful blue waters of the Mediterranean Sea, the **Heraklion Archaeological Museum** in Crete, in this author's opinion, is heads above the National Archaeological Museum in Athens. Home of the Snake Goddess, with its plethora of double axes, it will be exceedingly more interesting to Goddess advocates.

Leap-frogging onto the continent of Africa, travelers find themselves in Alexandria, once the city of the famed Library where the greatest minds of the ancient world shared ideas. Here one does not want to miss the quaint **Greco-Roman Museum of Alexandria** which houses a fine collection spanning seven centuries. Moving still farther south, we come to the **Egyptian Museum of Cairo** which has on display anything and everything Egyptian. From the smallest beaded necklace to the ornate golden sarcophagus of King Tut, it all awaits the intrepid traveler!

Hitching a ride on a cruise ship headed north toward Turkey, or Anatolia as it was called in those days of yesteryear, a favorite museum that is a must see is the *Anadolu Medeniyetleri Muzesi*, or the **Museum of Anatolian Civilizations** in Ankara. Here on display is a replica of a home/shrine from Catal Hüyük and some of the loveliest Neolithic artifacts. A particularly famous statue is the Anatolian Mother Goddess seated on her lion throne. This museum also gets a thumbs up for its availability of unique and hard-to-find statuary travelers might purchase for their own collections.

Last, but hardly least, we travel to the Far East. The **National Archaeological Museum of Tokyo** is the last stop on this whirlwind museum express. Unique to this museum is the large collection of Buddhist art, but even more unique is the Neolithic Joman statuary hardly seen anywhere else.

Suggested Reading List

It is always fun to have a great paperback on long journeys, particularly if the book is related to the country you are visiting or the focus of your trip. Here is a wide variety of fiction and non-fiction books for adults, young and old, guaranteed to double the pleasure of any goddess-oriented destination. A brief description of each book and its setting is provided for easier selection. Do not forget to peruse the bibliography by continent for more great reading ideas!

Fiction Reading List

The Mists of Avalon (Marion Zimmer Bradley): England, Middle Ages – Priestesses in Arthurian Legends

Sea Priestess (Dion Fortune): England – Modern woman walks an ancient path

Moon Magic (Dion Fortune): England – Magical duo investigates esoteric mysteries

Pandora (Anne Rice): Italy – Priestess of Goddess in Pompeii with vampire overtones

The Red Tent (Anita Diamant): Middle East – Women's society in Biblical times

The DaVinci Code (Dan Brown): Europe – Modern thriller uncovers Divine Feminine

Daughter of God (Lewis Perdue): Europe – Uncovering clues to the female messiah

Throne of Isis (Judith Tarr): Egypt – Cleopatra themes

The Eight (Katherine Neville): France/North Africa – Modern day, French Revolution flashbacks, esoteric

The Fifth Sacred Thing (Starhawk): Futuristic, 21st century California – spirituality and politics

Amazon (Barbara Walker): Woman warrior from the past time travels to the present

The Moon Under Her Feet (Clysta Kinstler): Middle East – Mary Magdalene theme

Aphrodite's Riddle (Jennifer Reif): Greece – Priestess of Aphrodite in ancient times

The Red-Haired Girl from the Bog (Patricia Monaghan): Ireland – experiential account of author

The Snake, the Crocodile, and the Dog (Elizabeth Peters) Egypt – one of multi-book series

Non-Fiction Reading List

When God Was A Woman (Merlin Stone): Multi-cultural, herstory of Goddess spirituality

The Chalice & the Blade (Riane Eisler): Multi-cultural, herstory of Goddess spirituality

The Templar Revelations (Lynn Picknett & Clive Prince): Multi-cultural, multi-themed, and controversial

Holy Blood, Holy Grail (Michael Baigent, Richard Leigh, Henry Lincoln): Multi-cultural, multi-themed

Daughter of the Goddess, The Sacred Priestess (Naomi Ozaniec): Middle East, Mediterranean Areas

Sacred Places Around the World: 108 Destinations (Brad Olsen): A comprehensive guide to all sacred sites on earth

The Once and Future Goddess (Elinor W. Gadon): Multi-cultural, herstory of Goddess spirituality

The Mysteries of Demeter (Jennifer Reif): Demeter worship reconstructed

The Mysteries of Isis (deTraci Regula): Egypt, concise account of Isis worship for novice

Isis Magic (M. Isadora Forrest): Egypt, more on worship of Isis and becoming a priestess

Women Who Run With the Wolves (Clarissa Pinkola Estes): Multi-cultural, archetypes

When Women Were Priests (Karen Jo Torjesen): Multi-cultural, uncovering roles of women leaders

The Dark Archetype, Exploring the Shadow Side of the Divine (Denise Dumars and Lori Nyx): Multi-cultural

The Woman With the Alabaster Jar (Margaret Starbird): Europe/Middle East – Mary Magdalene themes

The Search for Om Sety (Jonathan Cott): Egypt – Modern day priestess of Egyptian pantheon

Sacred Places North America: 108 Destinations (Brad Olsen): A comprehensive guide to sacred sites in North America

AUTHOR RECOMMENDED RESOURCES

Environmental, Social, and Animal Rights Organizations

Center for Partnership Studies

Post Office Box 51936
Pacific Grove, CA 93950-1936
831/626-1004
www.partnershipway.org

Dedicated to a better future by educating adults and children on the value of partnership. Areas of interest include teaching about equitable and peaceful gender relations, improving childhood relations, and working toward economic measures and systems of reward that encourage empathy and creativity, giving real value to caring for self, others, and nature. A final cornerstone is the reexamining of beliefs, myths and stories that promote partnership and the discarding of those that do not.

Greenpeace International

Ottho Heldringstraat 5
1066 AZ Amsterdam
The Netherlands
Phone: +31 20 5148150
www.greenpeace.org/international_en/contact

International arm of Greenpeace, with a presence in 40 countries across Europe, the Americas, Asia and the Pacific. Working to stop climate change, protect ancient forests, save the oceans, stop whaling, saying no to genetic engineering, stopping nuclear threats, eliminating toxic chemicals and encouraging sustainable trade.

Greenpeace USA

702 H Street NW
Suite 300
Washington, DC 20001
800/326-0959
www.greenpeaceusa.org

Founded in 1971, Greenpeace USA is the leading independent campaigning organization that uses non-violent direct action and creative communication to expose global environmental problems and to promote solutions that are essential to a green and peaceful future.

Heifer International

Post Office Box 8058
Little Rock, AR 72203

800/422-0474
www.heifer.org

Works in partnership with indigenous people around the globe respecting their culture, boosting their viability, in particular the status of women, by donating farm animals and trees. Heifer's mission is to work with communities to end hunger and poverty and to care for the Earth.

The Isis Ancient Cultures & Religion Society (IACRS)
2554 Lincoln Boulevard, Box 678
Venice, CA 90291
310/450-6661

Open to men and women this organization is dedicated to raising awareness of universal truths, ancient wisdom and cultures, and Goddess through educational, social, spiritual, artistic and cultural events. IACRS works in partnership with individuals and groups to re-create ancient festivals and rituals in a modern context. Social and cultural activism related to the rights and well being of animals, women, and the environment.

Nature Conservancy Network
4245 North Fairfax Drive, Suite 100
Arlington, VA 22203-1606
800/628-6860
www.nature.org

Established since 1951, with worldwide offices, this group works to preserve the plants, animals and natural communities that represent the diversity of life on Earth by protecting the lands and waters they need to survive.

Natural Resources Defense Council
40 West 20th Street
New York, NY 10011
212/727-2700
www.nrdc.org

Nation's most effective environmental action organization, using law, science, and the support of more than one million members and online activists to protect the planet's wildlife and wild places and to ensure a safe and healthy environment for all life things.

Publications & Education

California Institute of Integral Studies
1453 Mission Street
San Francisco, CA 94103
415/575-6100
www.ciis.edu

CIIS is an accredited institution of higher learning that strives to embody spirit, intellect, and wisdom in service to individuals, communities, and the Earth. Honoring the spiritual dimension of intellectual life, CIIS prepares students to work in the areas of psychology, religion, philosophy, and the humanities by fostering rigorous scholarship and supportive community. The logo of CIIS is the sri yantra, a device for spiritual advancement, and a symbol of the Mother of the Universe.

Claremont Graduate University

The School of Religion
831 N. Dartmouth Avenue
Claremont, CA 91711
909/621-8085
religion@cgu.edu

Claremont offers a wealth of programs, events, and lectures which are open to the public.

Circle Network News Magazine

Post Office Box 219
Mt. Horeb, WI 53572
608/924-5964
circle@circlesanctuary.org

A Nature Spirituality quarterly publication which provides articles, news, rituals, and other information pertaining to Wiccan traditions, Shamanism, Goddess spirituality, Ecofeminist, Animism, and other forms of contemporary Paganism. Affiliated with Circle Sanctuary which sponsors events and rituals throughout the year.

Ecotheology: The Journal of Religion, Nature and the Environment

Department of Theology and Religious Studies
University College
Chester, Parkgate
CH1 4BJ
United Kingdom

Focus of magazine is on the nexus of interrelationships between religion and nature, particularly in the light of environmental and ecological concerns. Articles are from various theological perspectives and religious traditions.

The Getty Museum

Visitor Services
1200 Getty Center Drive
Suite #1000
Los Angeles, CA 90049
310/440-7300
visitorservices@getty.edu

Exhibits and lecture series sponsored by the Getty are valuable assets to continuing education.

Goddess Alive!

Whitewaves
Boscaswell Village
Pendeen, Penzance,
Cornwall TR19 7EP England
www.goddessalive.co.uk

Goddess oriented publication focused on groups, events, publications in Europe.

Goddessing International News Journal

Post Office Box 269
Valrico, FL 33595

This biannual international news journal is published by Willow LaMonte who has her finger on the pulse of the most current and cutting-edge Goddess oriented tours, scholarship, art, and events in the world of the Divine Female. Information is available by going to artist Sid Reger's website, www.goddessmandala.com or writing the publisher at the above address.

Institute of Archaeomythology
www.archaeomythology.org

Archaeomythology is an interdisciplinary approach to scholarship, formulated by archaeologist Marija Gimbutas that expands the basis for interpretation of prehistoric cultural material with an emphasis on ideology and symbolism. International organization of scholars dedicated to fostering an archaeomythology approach to cultural research. I of A promotes dialogue among specialists from diverse fields by sponsoring international conferences and symposia, by publishing collected papers and monographs, and by promoting creative collaboration within an atmosphere of mutual support.

Journal of Mediterranean Archaeology
Department of Classical Studies
University of Michigan
2160 Angell Hall
435 South State Street
Ann Arbor, MI 48109

Dealing with the multicultural world of Mediterranean archaeology. The magazine encourages reader contributions dealing with contemporary approaches to gender, agency, identity and landscape.

Max Dashu
Suppressed Histories Archives
www.suppressedhistories.net

Live visual presentations on Goddess studies and global women's history, including *Icons of the Matrix; Woman Shaman; Priestesses; Goddess Cosmologies*, and more. Catalog, articles, book excerpts and reviews.

The Pomegranate: The International Journal of Pagan Studies
Pomegranate Magazine
Colorado State University – Pueblo
2200 Bonforte Boulevard
Pueblo, CO 81001

Peer reviewed journal of pagan studies providing a forum for papers, essays, and symposia on both ancient and contemporary pagan religious practices.

ReVision, A Journal of Consciousness and Transformation
c/o Heldref Publications
1319 Eighteenth Street, N.W.
Washington, D.C. 20036

ReVision is dedicated to the future of humanity and the Earth, emphasizing the transformative dimensions of current and traditional thought and practice. Journal advances inquiry and reflection on fields of philosophy, religion, psychology, social theory, science and the arts. Articles explore new models of interdisciplinary, multicultural, dialogical, and socially engaged inquiry, as well as ancient ways of knowing.

Sacred History Society Magazine

Post Office Box 2260
Chino Hills, CA 91709
www.sacredhistory.org
www.sacredhistorymagazine.com

The Sacred History Society focuses on the history of Christianity, especially examining its context and general makeup as it relates with other religious traditions, and does so within the kaleidoscope of various approaches — whether religious, historical, theological, archaeological, philosophical or through the arts. Engages the popular audience with the very best scholars, creating a place open to all points of view.

Temple of the Goddess

P.O. Box 660021
Arcadia, CA 91066
818-771-5778
Templeofthegoddess.org

The purpose of Temple of the Goddess is to bring the Divine Feminine back into Western consciousness. Without the equal balance of female with the male principle, we as an individual, a society, and an Earth Village will not survive. TOG celebrates Sabbats, creates ritual theater, ordains ministers, educates while exploring the connection between spirit, art, and healing.

UCLA – University of California at Los Angeles

Classics Department & Women's Studies
P. O. Box 951417
Los Angeles, CA 90095
310/825-4171

Both the Classics and Women's Studies Departments at UCLA continue to work with the community to provide quality continuing education in the form of informal lectures and presentations for students and the general public.

Utne Magazine

1624 Harmon Place
Minneapolis, MN 55403
612/338-5040
www.utne.com/magazine

A different read on life, Utne Magazine reprints the best articles from over 2,000 alternative media sources bringing you the latest ideas and trends emerging in our culture. Provocative writing from diverse perspectives, insightful analysis of art and media, with useful down-to-earth news and resources.

Travel Related

A Special Journey Travel

2554 Lincoln Boulevard, Box 678
Venice, CA 90291
specialjourn@earthlink.net
www.karentate.com

Specialist in Goddess oriented tours for men and women since 1995. Limited to small groups interested in scholarship, ecotourism, and the herstorical perspective of international destinations, including ritual and workshops at destinations. Tour guide and educational services available.

GATE: Global Awareness Through Experience
912 Market Street
La Crosse, WI 54601-8800

Offers a rich tradition of alternate tourism built on people-to-people experiences. Learn from the poor as well as from people who are making a difference in developing countries. Write GATE for information about upcoming Cultural Immersion Programs.

Glastonbury Goddess Conference
www.goddessconference.com
Annual summer Goddess conference in Glastonbury, England.

Pantheacon Annual Conference
c/o Ancient Ways Store
4075 Telegraph Avenue
Oakland, CA 94609
pantheacon@ancientways.com

An annual conference for pagans and nature religion ideas that includes rituals, music, workshops, and vendors.

Reformed Congregation of the Goddess – International
Gatherings for Priestesses and Goddess Women
Post Office Box 6677
Madison, WI 53716
www.rcgi.org
rcgi@chorus.net

Annual May and October events welcome women only to enjoy a weekend filled with meaningful rituals, workshops, ordinations and fun. Located in beautiful Wisconsin Dells, Wisconsin, travelers enjoy women's spiritual community in wooded setting. Hot meals, cabins, showers, vendors, flush toilets! Established in 1990. Women's tours to sacred sites are periodically organized.

Singapore Airlines
800/742-3333

In this author's opinion, *the best airline* ever experienced, even when flying economy class! Service and amenities were excellent and more elbow room than one usually finds in coach.

Solas Bhride
14 Dara Park
County Kildare
Kildare, Ireland

Contact the Solas Bhride regarding Brigid's Flame and Celtic spirituality in the spirit of Brigid of Kildare.

Womongathering
Post Office Box 559
Franklinville, NJ 08322

An intense spiritual quest for the obliterated knowledge of what it means to be "whole," nurtured by a Universal Feminine Principle as embodied in the ancient Goddess of Ten Thousand Names. Annual festival is for womyn and gyrls only and includes rituals, drumming, workshops, crafts, and marketplace. Open to women and girls of all ages, colors and sexual preferences.

BIBLIOGRAPHY

Author's Karma Statement & Introduction

ABC News, *Jesus, Mary and DaVinci*, televised Monday, November 3, 2003

Baring, Anne, **Cashford**, Jules, *The Myth of the Goddess: Evolution of an Image*, London, UK, Penguin Books, 1993

Campbell, Joseph, **Moyers**, Bill, *The Power of Myth*, Edited by Sue Flowers, New York, Doubleday, 1988

Devereux, Paul, *Secrets of Ancient and Sacred Places, The World's Mysterious Heritage*, London, UK, Brockhampton Press, 1992

Gimbutas, Marija, *The Language of the Goddess*, New York, NY, Harper Collins Publishers, 1991

Hodder, Ian, "Towards a Reflexive Excavation Methodology," Avenel, NJ, *Antiquity*, 1997, Vol. 71, #273

Husain, Shahrukh, *The Goddess, Living Wisdom*, London, UK, Time-Life Books, 1997

Eisler, Riane, *The Chalice and the Blade*, San Francisco, Harper Collins, 1987

Read, Donna, **Starhawk**, *Signs Out of Time, The Life & Work of Marija Gimbutas*, Belili Productions, 2003 (video)

Rountree, Kathryn, *Goddess Pilgrimages and the Politics of Performance*, a lecture given to the Social Anthropology Department of the School of Social and Cultural Studies at Massey University in Auckland, New Zealand.

Stone, Merlin, *When God Was A Woman*, New York, Barnes and Noble Publishers, 1976

Torjesen, Karen Jo, *When Women Were Priests*, San Francisco, Harper Collins, 1995
www.thebluespace.com
www.vedicheritage.org
www.mailerindia.com

Europe

ABC News, *Jesus, Mary and DaVinci*, televised Monday, November 3, 2003

Baring, Anne, **Cashford**, Jules, *The Myth of the Goddess: Evolution of an Image*, London, UK, Penguin Books, 1993

Bayhan, Suzan, *Priene, Miletus Didyma*, Istanbul, Keskin, 2002

Bean, George, *Turkey Beyond the Maeander*, London, Ernest Benn Limited, 1971

Burkert, Walter, *Greek Religion,* Stuttgart, Germany, Verlag W. Kohlhammer, 1977. English translation by Basil Blackwell Publishers and Harvard University Press, 1985

Cichon, Joan, "Archaeomythology Conference: Deepening the Disciplines," *Goddessing Regenerated*, Valrico, FL, 1999, Issue #10

Claridge, Amanda, Editor, *The Oxford Archaeological Guide to Rome*, Oxford, England, Oxford University Press, 1998

Condit, Tom, Editor, "Bru na Boinne ... Newgrange, Knowth, Dowth and the River Boyne," *Archaeology Ireland*, County Wicklow, Supplement to Volume 11 #3

Dexter, Miriam Robbins, *Born of the Foam: Goddesses of River and Sea in the "Kingship in Heaven" Myth*, Antioch University

De Boer, Jelle Zeilinga and **Hale**, John, R., "The Oracle of Delphi – Was She Really Stoned?," *Archaeology Odyssey*, Washington, DC, November/December 2002

Dexter, Miriam Robbins, *Whence the Goddesses, A Source Book, The Athene Series*, Elmsford, NY, Pergamon Press, 1990

Dumars, Denise and **Nyx**, Lori, *The Dark Archetype, Exploring the Shadow Side of the Divine*, Franklin Lakes, NJ, New Page Books, 2003

Eiteljorg, Harrison, "Antiquity's High Holy Place, The Athenian Acropolis," *Archaeology Odyssey*, Washington, DC, November/December 2004

Facaros, Dana and **Pauls**, Michael, *Rome*, London, Cadogan Books, 1997

Sacred Places of Goddess

Facaros, Dana and **Pauls**, Michael, *Western Turkey*, London, Cadogan Books, 1995

Fisher, Liz, "Review of The Ancient British Goddess: Goddess Myths, Legends, Sacred Sites and Present Revelations by Kathy Jones of Ariadne Publications, 2001" Valrico, FL, *Goddessing Regenerated*, Issue #16

Gadon, Elinor, *The Once & Future Goddess, A Symbol for Our Time*, New York, Harper San Francisco, 1989

Gage, Eleni N., Editor, *Let's Go Budget Guide to Greece and Turkey*, New York, St. Martin's Press/Harvard Student Agencies, Inc., 1995

Gimbutas, Marija, *The Language of the Goddess*, New York, NY, Harper Collins Publishers, 1991

Grant, Michael, *A Guide to the Ancient World*, New York, Barnes & Noble Books, 1986

Hodder, Ian, *Women and Men at Catal Hoyuk*, Scientific American, New York, NY, Vol. 15, Number 1

Malone, Caroline, **Bonanno**, Anthony, **Gouder**, Tancred, **Stoddart**, Simon, **Trump**, David, *The Death Cults of Prehistoric Malta*, Scientific American, New York, NY, Vol. 15, Number 1

Monaghan, Patricia, *The New Book of Goddesses & Heroines*, St. Paul, MN, Llewellyn Publishing, 2000

Muhly, James, D., "Excavating Minoan Sites," *Archaeology Odyssey*, Washington, DC, March/April 2004

Olsen, Brad, *Sacred Places Around the World: 108 Destinations*, San Francisco, CA, Consortium of Collective Consciousness, 2004

O'Kelly, Claire, *Concise Guide to Newgrange*, Cork, Ireland, Claire O'Kelly Publisher, 1996

Portugal News, "Fatima to Become Interfaith Shrine," 11/1/03

Portugal News, "Traditional Catholics Attack Fatima Interfaith Congress," 9/20/03

Portugal News, "Vatican Denies Fatima Will Become Interfaith Shrine," 11/29/03

Richardson, L., *A New Topographical Dictionary of Ancient Rome*, London, John Hopkins University Press, 1992

Rietveld, James, *The Image of Artemis Ephesia: Magical Goddess and Amulet on the Via Sacra*. Preliminary PhD diss., School of Religion, Claremont Graduate University, 2004

Rietveld, James, *Olympian and Chthonic Gods* Working paper, Greco-Roman Religion, School of Religion, Claremont Graduate University, 2003

Rietveld, James, *Eleusis* Working paper, Greco Roman Religion, School of Religion, Claremont Graduate University, 2003

Reif, Jennifer, *Mysteries of Demeter, Rebirth of the Pagan Way*, York Beach, ME, Samuel Weiser, Inc., 1999

Rigoglioso, Marguerite, *The "Other" Eleusis: Mysticism and Misogyny in the Navel of Sicily*, Oakland, CA, Dissertation Soon to be Published, 2001

Rufus, Anneli S. and **Lawson**, Kristan, *Goddess Sites: Europe*, San Francisco, Harper Collins, 1991

Scanlon, Thomas, R., "Games for Girls," *Archaeology*, Archaeological Institute of America, New York, NY, July/August, 1996

Starbird, Margaret, *The Woman with the Alabaster Jar, Mary Magdalene and the Holy Grail*, Santa Fe, NM, Bear & Co., 1993

Streep, Peg, *Sanctuaries of the Goddess, The Sacred Landscapes and Objects*, Boston, Bulfinch Press/Little, Brown and Company, 1994

Stone, Merlin, *When God Was A Woman*, New York, Barnes and Noble Publishers, 1976

Torjesen, Karen Jo, *When Women Were Priests*, San Francisco, Harper Collins, 1995

Veen, Veronica, *Female Images of Malta, Goddess, Giantess Farmeress*, Haarlem, Holland, Inanna, 1994

Walker, Barbara, *The Woman's Dictionary of Symbols and Sacred Objects*, San Francisco, Harper & Row, 1988

Walker, Barbara, *The Women's Encyclopedia of Myths and Secrets*, Edison, NJ, Castle Books, 1996

Wilson, Colin, *The Atlas of Holy Places & Sacred Sites*, New York, NY, DK Publishing, 1996

Witt, R. E., *Isis in the Ancient World*, Baltimore and London, The Johns Hopkins University Press, 1971
www.pio.gov.cy/cyprus_today
www.belili.org

Africa

Ackerman, Susan, "The Queen Mother and the Cult in the Ancient Near East," *Women and Goddess Traditions in Antiquity and Today*, Edited by Karen King, Minneapolis, MN, Augsburg Fortress, 1997

Ancient Life, "Origins of a Housecat, Woman's Best Friend," *Archaeology Odyssey*, Washington, DC. March/April 2004

Baring, Anne, **Cashford**, Jules, *The Myth of the Goddess: Evolution of an Image*, London, UK, Penguin Books, 1993

Birnbaum, Lucia Chiavola, *Dark Mother, African Origins and Godmothers*, Lincoln, NB, Author's Choice Press, 2001

Boone, Sylvia Ardyn, *Radiance from the Waters*, Yale University Press, 1986

Burkert, Walter, *Greek Religion,* Stuttgart, Germany, Verlag W. Kohlhammer, 1977. English translation by Basil Blackwell Publishers and Harvard University Press, 1985

Clark, Rosemary, *The Sacred Traditions in Ancient Egypt*, St. Paul, MN, Llewellyn Worldwide, 2000

Cockburn, Anthony, "Yemen United," *National Geographic*, Vol. 197, #4, April 2000

Constantine, Storm and **Coquio**, Eloise, *Bast and Sekhmet, Eyes of Ra*, London, England, Robert Hale, 1999

Cott, Jonathan, *The Search for Omm Sety, Reincarnation and Eternal Love*, Garden City, NY, Doubleday & Company, Inc. 1987

Field Notes, *Archaeology Odyssey*, Vol. 7 #5, September/October 2004

Frankenfurter, David, *Religion in Roman Egypt: Assimilation and Resistance*, Princeton, NJ: Princeton University Press, 1998

Hart, George, *A Dictionary of Egyptian Gods & Goddesses*, London, England, Routledge & Kegan Paul, Inc. 1986

Haruach, Ph.D, Miri Hunter, *You Acting Womanish: The Queen of Sheba as an Ancestral Grandmother,* - a research paper

Hassan, Fekri, "The Earliest Goddesses of Egypt," *Ancient Goddesses*, edited by Lucy Goodison and Christine Morris, London, England, British Museum Press, 1998

Husain, Shahrukh, *The Goddess, Living Wisdom*, London, UK, Time-Life Books, 1997

Leach, Maria, Editor, *Funk & Wagnalls Standard Dictionary of Folklore, Mythology and Legend*, New York, NY, Harper Collins Publishers, 1972

Hornblower, Simon and Spawforth, Anthony, Editors, *The Oxford Classical Dictionary*, 3rd ed., Oxford, England, Oxford University Press, 1996

Malek, Maromir, *The Cat in Ancient Egypt*, Philadelphia, University of Pennsylvania Press, 1993

Masters, Robert, *The Goddess Sekhmet, The Way of the Five Bodies*, Warwick, NY, Amity House, 1988

McCarthy, Terry and **Dorfman**, Andrea, "Nowhere to Roam," *National Geographic*, Vol. 164, #8

Monaghan, Patricia, *The New Book of Goddesses & Heroines*, St. Paul, MN, Llewellyn Publishing, 2000

Murphy, Joseph M., "Oshun the Dancer," *The Book of the Goddess, Past and Present,* edited by Carl Olson, New York, NY, Crossroad Publishing Co., 1990

Noble, Vicki, *The Double Goddess, Women Sharing Power*, Rochester, VT, Bear and Company, 2003

Noble, Vicki, *Artemis and the Amazons*, Berkeley, CA - a research paper

Potter, Charles Francis, *Funk & Wagnalls Standard Dictionary of Folklore, Mythology and Legend*, Edited by Maria Leach, New York, NY, Harper Collins Publishers, 1972

Rogerson, Barnaby, **Baring**, Rose, *Tunisia*, London, England, Cadogan Guides, 1992

Schindler, Henri, *Mardi Gras New Orleans*, New York, NY, Flammarion, 1997

Sjoo, Monica, "Goddess 3000 & Other Travels," Valrico, FL, *Goddessing Regenerated Magazine*, Issue #17, 2003

Teubal, Savina, J., "The Rise and Fall of Female Reproductive Control as Seen through Images of Women," *Women and Goddess Traditions in Antiquity and Today*, Edited by Karen King, Minneapolis, MN, Augsburg Fortress, 1997

Walker, Barbara, *The Women's Encyclopedia of Myths and Secrets*, Edison, NJ, Castle Books, 1996

West Africa, Victoria, Australia, Lonely Planet Publications, 1999

Witt, R. E., *Isis in the Ancient World*, Baltimore and London, The Johns Hopkins University Press, 1971

http://news.nationalgeographic.com
www.awf.org
http://news.bbc.co.uk
www.worldtrek.org
www.amaranthine.freeserve.co.uk
www.trekshare.com

The Middle East

Ackerman, Susan, "The Queen Mother and the Cult in the Ancient Near East," *Women and Goddess Traditions in Antiquity and Today*, Edited by Karen King, Minneapolis, MN, Augsburg Fortress, 1997

Andrae, Tor, *Mohammed: The Man and His Faith*, New York, Harper, 1960

Aulama, Mohsen, M., *Jerash, A Unique Example of a Roman City*, Amman, Jordan, Al-Alaulama & Barhoumeh Publishers, 1995

Bahat, Dan, *The Illustrated Atlas of Jerusalem*, New York, Simon & Schuster, 1990

Baring, Anne, **Cashford**, Jules, *The Myth of the Goddess: Evolution of an Image*, London, UK, Penguin Books, 1993

Birnbaum, Lucia Chiavola, *Dark Mother, African Origins and Godmothers*, Lincoln, NB, Author's Choice Press, 2001

Brooks, Dorian, "Building a Living Democracy - Vandana Shiva: Ecofeminist and Force of Nature," *Goddessing Regenerated Magazine*, Valrico, FL, Issue #18, 2003

Burkert, Walter, *Greek Religion,* Stuttgart, Germany, Verlag W. Kohlhammer, 1977. English translation by Basil Blackwell Publishers and Harvard University Press, 1985

Butcher, Kevin, *Roman Syria and the Near East*, Los Angeles, CA, Getty Publications, 2003

Camphausen, Rufus, C., *The Yoni, Sacred Symbol of Female Creative Power*, Rochester, VT, Inner Traditions International, 1996

Caubet, Annie, **Pouyssegur**, Patrick, *The Origins of Civilization, The Ancient Near East*, Paris, France, Editions Pierre Terrail, 1997

Dexter, Miriam Robbins, *Whence the Goddesses, A Source Book, The Athene Series*, Elmsford, NY, Pergamon Press, 1990

Eisenberg, Ph.D., Jerome M., "Archaeological News From Philadelphia to the AIA Conference," *Minerva*, London, England, Volume 13 #1, May/June 2002

Field Notes, Archaeology Odyssey, Vol. 7 #5, September/October 2004

Gadon, Elinor, *The Once & Future Goddess, A Symbol for Our Time*, New York, Harper San Francisco, 1989

Garfinkel, Yosef, "Neolithic Sha'ar Hagolan: Art, Cult, and Settlement in the Jordan Valley," *Minerva*, London, England, Volume 13 #4, July/August 2002

Getty, Adelle, *Goddess, Mother of Living Nature*, New York, NY, Thames & Hudson, 1990

Gimbutas, Marija, *The Language of the Goddess*, New York, NY, Harper Collins Publishers, 1991

Haag, Michael, *Syria & Lebanon*, London, England, Cadogan Books, 1995

Hoyland, Robert G. *Arabia and Arabs*, London: Routledge, 2001

Guillaume, Alfred, *The Traditions of Islam*, Oxford: Oxford University Press, 1924

Ibn-Hisham, *The Life of Muhammad*, translated by Alfred Guillaume, London: Oxford University Press, 1955

Johnson, Buffie, *Lady of the Beasts, The Goddess and Her Sacred Animals*, Rochester, VT, Inner Traditions International, 1994

Khoun, Rami, G., "A Jewel in Jordan: The Greco-Roman City of Jerash," *Archaeology*, January/February, 1985

Lancel, Serge, *Carthage: A History*, Oxford: Blackwell, 1995

Long, Asphodel, "Asherah – Goddess of the Grove, the Menorah and the Tree of Life," *Goddessing Regenerated*, Valrico, FL, Issue #9, 1998

Meador, Betty De Shong, *Inanna, Lady of Largest Heart, Poems of the Sumerian High Priestess Enheduanna*, Austin, TX, University of Texas Press, 2000

Millar, Fergus, *The Roman Near East: 31 BC-AD 337*, Cambridge, Harvard University Press, 1993

Monaghan, Patricia, *The New Book of Goddesses & Heroines*, St. Paul, MN, Llewellyn Publishing, 2000

Nakhai, Beth, *Mother & Child Images of the Middle East*, lecture at Claremont University, Spring 2004

Nehme', Laila, "The World of the Nabateans," *The Levant*, Edited by Olivier Binst, Cologne, Germany, Konemann, 1999

Noble, Vicki, *The Double Goddess, Women Sharing Power*, Rochester, VT, Bear and Company, 2003

Olsen, Brad, *Sacred Places: 101 Spiritual Sites Around the World*, San Francisco, CA, Consortium of Collective Consciousness, 2000

Peters, E. *Muhammad and the Origins of Islam*, Albany, State University of New York Press, 1994

Rietveld, James, *Great is Artemis of the Ephesians*, lecture held at home of Cary Egerton, Summer 2003

Silberman, Neil Asher and **Goren**, Yuval, "Faking Biblical History," Long Island City, NY, *Archaeology*, September/October 2003, Vol. 56, #5

Stern, Ephraim, "Pagan Yahwism: The Folk Religion of Ancient Israel," *Biblical Archaeology Review*, May June, 2001

Tate, Karen, "Otherworldly Petra ... Sandbox of the Divine," Mr. Horeb, WI, *Circle Magazine*, Fall, 2001

Teixidor, Javier, *The Pantheon of Palmyra*, Leiden: Brill, 1979

Teubal, Savina, J., "The Rise and Fall of Female Reproductive Control as Seen through Images of Women," *Women and Goddess Traditions in Antiquity and Today*, Edited by Karen King, Minneapolis, MN, Augsburg Fortress, 1997

Walker, Barbara, *The Women's Encyclopedia of Myths and Secrets*, Edison, NJ, Castle Books, 1996

Westenholz, Joan Goodnick, "Three Goddesses of the Ancient Near East 3000-1000 B.C.E.," *Ancient Goddesses,* Edited by Lucy Goodison and Christine Morris, London, England, British Museum Press, 1998

Zacharias, ancient writer
www.kibbutz.co.il

www. hum.huji.ac.il
www.news.nationalgeographic.com
www.sacredsites.com
www.wrmea.com
www.fathom.com
www.arch.cam.ac.uk

The Asian Sub-Continent

Bhattacharji, Sukumari, *The Indian Theogony*, Cambridge, MA, Cambridge University Press, 1970

Burkert, Walter, *Greek Religion,* Stuttgart, Germany, Verlag W. Kohlhammer, 1977. English translation by Basil Blackwell Publishers and Harvard University Press, 1985

Campbell, Joseph, **Moyers**, Bill, *The Power of Myth*, Edited by Sue Flowers, New York, NY, Doubleday, 1988

Camphausen, Rufus, C., *The Encyclopedia of Sacred Sexuality*, Rochester, VT, Inner Traditions International, 1999

Camphausen, Rufus, C., *The Yoni, Sacred Symbol of Female Creative Power*, Rochester, VT, Inner Traditions International, 1996

Chouinard, Patrick, "Earliest Written Script Surfaces in India," *Ancient America*, Colfax, WI, Wayne May, Publisher, Vol. 9, Issue 57

Dallapiccola, Anna, *Dictionary of Hindu Lore and Legend*, London, Thames and Hudson, Ltd, 2002

Dimmitt, Cornelia and **van Buitenen** J.A.B., *Classical Hindu Mythology: A Reader in the Sanskrit Puranas*, Philadelphia, Temple University Press, 1978

Dowman, Keith, *Power Places of Kathmandu, Hindu and Buddhist Holy Sites in the Sacred Valley of Nepal*, Rochester, VT, Inner Traditions International, 1995

Dumars, Denise and **Nyx**, Lori, *The Dark Archetype, Exploring the Shadow Side of the Divine*, Franklin Lakes, NJ, New Page Books, 2003

Gadon, Elinor, W., "The Devi in India: Traditions of Village Goddesses in Transition," *Goddessing Regenerated Magazine*, Valrico, FL, Issue #18, 2003

Gadon, Elinor, W., "Probing the Mysteries of the Hirapur Yoginis," *ReVision, A Journal of Consciousness and Transformation*, Washington, D.C., Volume 25 #1, Summer 2002

Ghose, Aruna, Managing Editor, *India Eyewitness Travel Guide*, London, Dorling Kindersley Ltd., 2002

Goodwin, William, *India, Modern Nations of the World*, San Diego, CA, Lucent Books, 1943

Gupta, Sanjukta, "The Domestication of a Goddess: Carana-tirtha Kalighat, the Mahapitha of Kali," *Encountering Kali in the Margins, At the Center, In the West,* edited by Rachel Fell McDermott and Jeffrey **Kripal**, J., Berkeley and Los Angeles, CA, University of California Press, 2003

Hamilton, Roy W., *The Art of Rice, Spirit and Sustenance in Asia*, Los Angeles, CA, University of CA, UCLA Fowler Museum of Cultural History, 2003

Harding, Elizabeth, U., *Kali, The Black Goddess of Dakshineswar*, York Beach, ME, Nicholas-Hayes, Inc, 1993

Huntington, John C. and **Bangdel**, Dina, *The Circle of Bliss, Buddhist Meditational Art*, Columbus, OH, Columbus Museum of Art and Serinda Publications, Inc, 2003

Humes, Patricia, "Wrestling with Kali: South Asian and British Constructions of the Dark Goddess"

Encountering Kali in the Margins, At the Center, In the West, edited by Rachel Fell **McDermott** and Jeffrey **Kripal**, J., Berkeley and Los Angeles, CA, University of California Press, 2003

Husain, Shahrukh, *The Goddess, Living Wisdom*, London, UK, Time-Life Books, 1997

Jacobson, Doranne Wilson, "Purdah: Life Behind the Veil," *National Geographic*, Washington, DC, National Geographic Society, Vol. 152, No. 2, August 1977

James, E. O., *The Cult of the Mother Goddess*, New York, Barnes & Noble, 1994

Johnson, Buffie, *Lady of the Beasts, The Goddess and Her Sacred Animals*, Rochester, VT, Inner Traditions International, 1994

Johnsen, Linda, *The Living Goddess*, St. Paul, MN, Yes International Publishers, 1954

Kinsley, David R., *Hindu Goddesses: Visions of the Divine Feminine in the Hindu Religious Tradition*, Berkeley and Los Angeles, CA, University of California Press, 1988

Kinsley, David R., "Kali," *Encountering Kali in the Margins, At the Center, In the West*, edited by Rachel Fell McDermott and Jeffrey J. Kripal, Berkeley and Los Angeles, CA, University of California Press, 2003

Klum, Mattias, "Asia's Last Lions," *National Geographic Magazine*, Vol. 199, No. 6, June 2001

Kripal, Jeffrey J. and **Fell McDermott**, Rachel, "Introducing Kali Studies," *Encountering Kali in the Margins, At the Center, In the West*, edited by Rachel Fell McDermott and Jeffrey J. Kripal, Berkeley and Los Angeles, CA, University of California Press, 2003

Lawrence, Patricia, "Kali in Context of Terror: The Tasks of a Goddess in Sri Lanka's Civil War" *Encountering Kali in the Margins, At the Center, In the West*, edited by Rachel Fell McDermott and Jeffrey **Kripal**, J., Berkeley and Los Angeles, CA, University of California Press, 2003

Levering, Miriam, "Stories of Enlightened Women in Ch'an and the Chinese Buddhist Female Bodhisattva/Goddess Tradition" *Women and Goddess Traditions in Antiquity and Today*, Edited by Karen King, Minneapolis, MN, Augsburg Fortress, 1997

Marton, Kati, "A Worldwise Gender Gap," *Newsweek Magazine*, May 10, 2004

McNeal, Keith E., "Doing the Mother's Caribbean Work: On Shakti and Society in Contemporary Trinidad," *Encountering Kali in the Margins, At the Center, In the West*, edited by Rachel Fell McDermott and Jeffrey J. Kripal, Berkeley and Los Angeles, CA, University of California Press, 2003

Moran, Kerr, *Nepal Handbook*, Third Edition, Emeryville, CA, Avalon Travel Publishing, 2000

Noble, Vicki, *The Double Goddess, Women Sharing Power*, Rochester, VT, Bear and Company, 2003

Ozaniec, Naomi, *Daughter of the Goddess, The Sacred Priestess*, London, Aquarian Press, 1993

Piggott, Stuart, *Ancient Europe: From the Beginnings of Agriculture to Classical Antiquity*, Chicago, Aldine Publishing Co., 1965

Potts, E. Daniel, *British Baptist Missionaries in India, 1793-1837: The History of Serampore and its Missions*, Cambridge, MA, Cambridge University Press, 1967

Thomas, Paul, *Christians and Christianity in India and Pakistan: A General Survey of the Progress of Christianity in India from Apostolic Times to the Present Day*, London, George Allen and Unwin, 1954

Urban, Hugh B., "India's Darkest Heart," *Encountering Kali in the Margins, At the Center, In the West*, edited by Rachel Fell McDermott and Jeffrey J. Kripal, Berkeley and Los Angeles, CA, University of California Press, 2003

Walker, Barbara, *The Women's Encyclopedia of Myths and Secrets*, Edison, NJ, Castle Books, 1996

Wilson, Colin, *The Atlas of Holy Places and Sacred Sites*, New York, DK Publishing Inc., 1996

www.buddhistview.com
www.templenet.com
www.amma.org
www.khandro.net/deities_Tara1.htm
www.geocities.com/zennum12_8/tara2.html
www.metmuseum.org
www.usao.edu
www.bardofavalon.com/indus/indusorigin.htm
http://members.aol.com/donnaclass/indialife.htm
http://primetours.com.pk
www.amritapuri.org
www.indiantravelportal.com
www.keralatourism.com
www.awakenedwoman.com
http://amnesty.org

SACRED PLACES OF GODDESS

East Asia

Ackerman, Jennifer, "Japan's Winter Wildlife," *National Geographic*, Vol. 203 # 1, January 2003

Bornoff, Nicholas, *Pink Samurai, Love Marriage and Sex in Contemporary Japan*, New York, NY, Pocket Books, Division of Simon and Schuster, 1991

Camphausen, Rufus, C., *The Encyclopedia of Sacred Sexuality*, Rochester, VT, Inner Traditions International, 1999

Camphausen, Rufus, C., *The Yoni, Sacred Symbol of Female Creative Power*, Rochester, VT, Inner Traditions International, 1996

Dahlby, Tracy, "Crossroads of Asia, South China Sea," *National Geographic*, Vol. #194, #6, December 1998

Dahlby, Tracy, "Living Dangerously - Indonesia," *National Geographic*, Vol. 199 # 3, March 2001

Dahlby, Tracy, "Tokyo Bay," *National Geographic*, Vol. 202 #4, October 2002

Dashu, Max, "Streams of Wisdom, Taoist & Hindu Wisdom Goddesses," *Goddessing Regenerated*, Issue #11, 1999

Davis-Kimball, Jeannine, *Warrior Women, An Archaeologist's Search for History's Hidden Heroines*, New York, NY, Warner Books, 2002

Fitzhugh, William W. and **Dubreuil**, Chisato O., Editors, *Ainu, Spirit of a Northern People*, Artic Studies Center, National Museum of Natural History, Smithsonian Institution, University of Washington Press, 1999

Freeman, Michael & **Warner**, Roger, *Angkor, The Hidden Glories*, Boston, MA, Houghton, Mifflin Co, 1990

Getty, Adele, *Goddess, Mother of Living Nature*, New York, NY, Thames & Hudson, 1990

Gimbutas, Marija, *The Civilization of the Goddess*, Marler, Joan, editor, NY, Harper San Francisco, 1991

Griffith, Clare, Editor, *Laos and Cambodia*, Insight Guides, APA Publications, a part of the Langenscheidt Publishing Group, Maspeth, NY, 2005

Hamilton, Roy W., *The Art of Rice, Spirit and Sustenance in Asia*, Los Angeles, CA, University of CA, UCLA Fowler Museum of Cultural History, 2003

Harris, Victor, Editor, *Shinto, The Sacred Art of Ancient Japan*, London, The British Museum Press, 2001

Husain, Shahrukh, *The Goddess*, Time-Life Books, Alexandria, VA 1997

Johnson, Buffie, *Lady and the Beasts, Goddess & Her Sacred Animals*, Rochester, VT, Inner Traditions International, 1994

King, Karen L., Editor, *Women and Goddess Traditions In Antiquity and Today*, Minneapolis, MN, Fortress Press, 1997

Mason, Antony, **Goulden**, Felicity, and **Overton**, Richard, *Bali*, United Kingdom, Cadogan Books, 1989

Leeming, David, *A Dictionary of Asian Mythology*, Oxford University Press, New York, NY, 2001

Love, Rebecca, "Women of the Motherland, A Year in China," Bellingham, WA, *The Beltane Papers*, Issue #5, 1994

Mannikka, Eleanor, *Angkor Wat: Time, Space and Kingship*, University of Hawaii Press, Honolulu, HI, 1996

Motomochi Nakamura, Kyoko, "The Significance of Amaterasu in Japanese Religious History," *The Book of Goddess, Past and Present*, Edited by Carl Olson, New York, Crossroad Publishing, 1990

Myers Imel, Martha Ann & Dorothy, *Goddesses in World Mythology, A Biographical Dictionary*, New York, NY, Oxford University Press, 1993

Niederer, Barbara, "Women in Chinese Script," *China for Women, Travel and Culture*, New York, The Feminist Press at the City University of New York, 1995

BIBLIOGRAPHY

Noble, Vickie, *Medea and the Shaman Women of the Silk Road*, 2003 - a research paper.

Olsen, Brad, *Sacred Places Around the World: 108 Destinations*, San Francisco, CA, Consortium of Collective Consciousness, 2004

Ono, Sokyo, *Shinto, The Kami Way*, Boston, MA, Tuttle Publishing, 1962

Polosmak, Natalya, "Mummy Unearthed From the Pastures of Heaven," *National Geographic*, Vol. 186, #4, October 1994

Ozaniec, Naomi, *Daughter of the Goddess, The Sacred Priestess*, London, Aquarian Press, 1993

Palmer, Betty, *Rough Guide to Cambodia*, Rough Guides, Ltd, 2002

Parry, Richard Lloyd, *Japan*, London, Cadogan Books, 1995

Rabinowitz, Alan, "Valley of Death," *National Geographic*, Vol. 205 #4, April 2004

Sargent, Denny, "Buddhist Paganism & the Goddess in Japan," *Green Egg Magazine*, Ukiah, CA, Church of All Worlds, Vol. 29,, #116, 1996

Smith, Patrick, "Inner Japan," *National Geographic*, Vol 186, #3, September 1994

Stone, Merlin, *Ancient Mirrors of Womanhood*, Vol. I, New York, New Sibylline Books, 1979

Sullivan, Lawrence E., *Nature and Rite in Shinto, Religions of Humanity*, Broomall, PA, Chelsea House Publishers, 2002

Walker, Barbara G., *The Woman's Dictionary of Symbols and Sacred Objects*, New York, NY, Harper & Row Publishers, 1988

Walker, George, *Angkor Empire,* Calcutta, India, Signet Press, 1955

World Wildlife Fund, Editorial Staff: "Sumatran Tiger on the Brink of Extinction," *Focus*, Issue May/June 2004, Vol. 26 #3
http://members.aol.com/bjw1106/marian8htm
www.pref.kyoto.jp/eco_message/message_e.html
www.pacificenvironment.org/articles/altaipipeline.htm
www.baliforyou.com/bali/bali_accommodation/kintamani.htm
www.circlesanctuary.org/articles/pantheon/kwanyin
www.holymtn.com/gods/kuanyin.htm
www.geocities.com/zennun12_8/kuan-yin.html
http://english.ctrip.com/Destinations/subguide.asp?guide=putuoshan
http://japanupdate.com/en/?id=4080
www.wsu.edu:8080/-dee/ANCJAPAN/WOMEN.HTM
www.onmarkproductions.com
www.isejingu.or.jp

Oceania

Beckwith, Martha, *Hawaiian Mythology*, University of Hawaii Press, Honolulu, HI, 1970

Barrere, Dorothy B., *Kumuhonua Legends, A Study of Late 19th Century Hawaiian Stories of Creation and Origins*, Pacific Anthropological Records #3, Department of Anthropology, Bernice P. Bishop Museum, Honolulu, HI, 1969

Bell, Diane, *Ngarrindjeri Wurruwarrin; a world that is, was, and will be*, N. Melbourne, Australia, Spinifex Press Pty Ltd, 1998

Bisignani, J. D, (Estate of), *Big Island of Hawaii*, 4th. Edition, Emeryville, CA, Avalon Travel Publishing/Moon Travel Handbooks, 2001

Charlot, John, "Pele and Hi'aka, The Hawaiian-Language Newspaper Series," *Anthropos* Vol 93, 1998

Duane, Kit, Managing Editor, *Hawai'i*, Fifth Edition, Fodor's Travel Publications, 2001

Gimbutas, Marija, *The Language of the Goddess*, San Francisco, Harper Collins, 1991

Gimbutas, Marija, *The Goddesses and Gods of Old Europe, Myths and Cult Images*, Berkeley, University of California Press, 1974

Harpur, James, *The Atlas of Sacred Places, Meeting Points of Heaven and Earth*, Henry Hold & Co., New York, NY, 1994

Hempstead, Andres and **King**, Jane, *Moon Handbooks: New Zealand*, 6th Edition, Emeryville, CA, Avalon Travel Publishing, 2002

Harvey, Andrew and **Baring**, Anne, *The Divine Feminine, Exploring the Feminine Face of God Throughout the World*, Berkeley, CA, Conari Press, 1996

Holland, Jennifer S., "American Landscapes, Red Hot Hawaii, Hawaii Volcanoes National Park," *National Geographic*, Vol. 206, #4, October 2004

Husain, Shahrukh, *The Goddess, Living Wisdom*, London, Time Life Books, 1997

Leeming, David & **Page**, Jake, *Goddess, Myths of the Female Divine*, New York, Oxford University Press, 1994

Littleton, C. Scott, General Editor, *Mythology, The Illustrated Anthology of World Myth and Storytelling*, Duncan Baird Publishers, London, 2002

Monaghan, Patricia, *The New Book of Goddesses & Heroines*, St. Paul, MN, Llewellyn Publications, 2000

Nilsen, Robert, *Moon Handbooks: Maui*, 6th Edition, Emeryville, CA, Avalon Travel Publishing/Moon Travel Handbooks, 2001

Pukui, Mary Kawena, **Haertig**, E.W., **Lee**, Catherine, *Nana I Ke Kumu*, Hui Hanai, Honolulu, HI, 1979

Roberts, Ainslie, **Melva**, Jean, *Dreamtime Heritage, Australian Aboriginal Myths in Paintings*, Melbourne, Rigby Limited, 1975

Scorzazie, Seph, *Gulaga, The Mother* - Government Heritage Writing Competition, Heritage Rave

Stanley, David, *South Pacific Handbook*, 7th edition, Emeryville, CA, Avalon Travel Publishing/Moon Travel Handbooks, 2000

Stone, Merlin, *Ancient Mirrors of Womanhood, Our Goddess & Heroine Heritage*, Volume I, New York, NY, New Sibylline Books, 1979

Stuart, Clinton, *Local Legends, Borrowed Gods, Ancient Myths of an Island World*, New York, Guest Informant, LIN Broadcasting Corporation, 1989

Yates-Smith, Aroha, "Reclaiming the Ancient Feminine in Maori Society", *Journal of Maori & Pacific Development*, February 2003

Yates-Smith, Aroha, *Maori Goddesses in Literature Part 1 & 2*, School of Maori & Pacific Development, University of Waikatato, New Zealand
    www.alternative-hawaii.com
    www.kaimi.org/articles.htm
    http://keith.martin.home.att.net
    http://globetrekkertv.co.uk/destination_guide
    www.pha.org.nz/conference 2003/marae.html
    http://academic.evergreen.edu
    www.sacredtexts.com
    www.pvs.hawaii.org
    www.cr.nps.gov/history/online_books/kona/history1h.htm
    http://apdl.kcc.hawaii.edu
    www.healingisland.net
    www.sitesaver.org
    http://ea.gov.au/parks/kakadu/artculture/art/nourlangie.html
    http://home.vicnet.net.au
    www.iratiwanti.org
    www.globaladventure.us/articles/maori.html
    www.ew.govt.nz/ourenvironment/land/maoriandtheland.htm
    www.ahc.gov.au
    www.samuelgriffith.org.au

South America & West Indies

Altamirano Vallenas, Jose F., Saqsaywaman, *The Most Powerful Temple of the Andean Culture - A Mystical Interpretation*, Cusco, Peru, Editorial Andina S. R. L., 1993

BIBLIOGRAPHY

Baquedano, Elizabeth, *Aztec, Inca and Maya, Eyewitness Books*, New York, Dorling Kindersley Ltd., 1993

Bloom, Pamela, *Brazil Up Close, The Sensuous & Adventurous Guide*, Edison, NJ, Hunter Publishing, Inc. 1997

Devereux, Paul, *Secrets of Ancient and Sacred Places, The World's Mysterious Heritage*, London, UK, Brockhampton Press, 1992

Devine, Mary, *Magic from Mexico*, St. Paul, MN, Llewellyn Publications, 1992

Insight Guides, Peru & South America, New York, Langenscheidt Publishers, Inc.

Jones, David M. and **Molyneaux**, Brian L., *Mythology of the American Nations*, London, Hermes House/Annes Publishing, 2004

Kahn, Abraham H., *Kali-Mai Puja in Guyana in Religion Vol. VII*, Spring 1977, London UK

LaMonte, Willow, "Lucia Chiavola Birnbaum Interview," Valrico, FL, *Goddessing Regenerated Magazine,* Issue 6, 1997

Lawrence, Patrice, *Kali in a Context of Terror, Encountering Kali*, Berkeley, University of CA Press, 2003

McNeal, Keith, E., "Doing the Mother's Caribbean Work: On Shakti and Society in Contemporary Trinidad," *Encountering Kali,* Berkeley, University of California Press, 2003

Monaghan, Patricia, *Goddesses & Heroines*, St. Paul, MN, Llewellyn Publishers, 2000

Moseley, Michael E., *The Incas and their Ancestors, The Archaeology of Peru*, New York, Thames & Hudson, 1992

Rigoglioso, Marguerite," Luisah Teish Interview," Valrico, FL, *Goddessing Regenerated Magazine*, Issue 7, 1997

Smith, Warren, "The Mystery of South America's Subterranean Tunnels," *Ancient American, Archaeology of the Americas Before Columbus*, Colfax, WI, Wayne N. May, Volume 8, Issue 53

Sullivan, Mark, editor, *Fodors South America*, New York, NY, Random House, 2002

Swaney, Deanna, *Bolivia*, Oakland, CA, Lonely Planet, Fourth Edition

Taube, Karl, *The Legendary Past, Aztec & Maya Myths*, Austin, TX, University of Texas Press/ British Museum Press, 1993

Wright, Ruth, M. & **Valencia Zegarra**, Alfredo, *The Machu Picchu Guidebook, A Self Guided Tour*, Boulder, CO, Johnson Books, 2001
www.thefourwinds.com

Mexico

Austen, Hallie Inglehart, *The Heart of the Goddess*, Berkeley, CA, Wingbow Press, 1990

Devereux, Paul, *Secrets of Ancient and Sacred Places, The World's Mysterious Heritage*, London, UK, Brockhampton Press, 1992

Corcoran, Cecilia, *The Goddess of Central Mexico: Contemporary Feminist Reflections*, Doctural Dissertation, 1998

Devine, Mary, *Magic from Mexico*, St. Paul, MN, Llewellyn Publications, 1992,

Fodor's Mexico 2002, New York, Random House, 2002

Getty, Adele, *Goddess, Mother of Living Nature*, London, UK, Thames & Hudson, 1990

Inglehart Austen, Hallie, *The Heart of the Goddess*, Berkeley, CA, Bookpeople/Wingbow Press, 1990

Imel, Martha Ann and **Imel**, Dorothy Myers, *Goddesses in World Mythology, A Biographical Dictionary*, New York, Oxford University Press, 1993

Jones, David M. and **Molyneaux**, Brian L., *Mythology of the American Nations*, London, Hermes House/Annes Publishing, 2004

Johnson, Buffie, *Lady of the Beasts, The Goddess & Her Animals*, Rochester, VT, Inner Traditions International, 1994

Kelly, J, *The Complete Visitor's Guide to Mesoamerican Ruins*, University of Oklahoma Press, 1982

Martin, Amy, *Sacred Sites as Natural Altars of Goddess*, Circle Magazine, Winter 2001

May, Antoinette, *The Yucatan, A Guide to the Land of Maya Mysteries*, San Carlos, CA, Wide World Publishing/Tetra, 1993

Mini, John, *The Aztec Virgin, The Secret Mystical Tradition of Our Lady of Guadalupe*, Sausalito, CA, Trans-Hyperborean Institute of Science, 2000

Monaghan, Patricia, *The New Book of Goddesses & Heroines*, St. Paul, MN, Llewellyn Publications, 2000

Morales, Demetrio Sodi, *The Maya World*, Mexico, Editorial Minutiae Mexicana, 2002

Pasztory, Esther, **Berrin**, Kathleen, Teotihucan, editors, *Art From The City of the Gods*, San Francisco, Thames & Hudson, 1993

Perring, Stefania, **Perring**, Dominic, *Then & Now, Wonders of the Ancient World Brought to Life*, New York, Prentiss Hall MacMillan, 1991

Popson, Colleen, "Extreme Sports," *Archaeology*, September/October 2003

Rough Guide to Central America, London, 2001

Rivera, Adalberto, *The Mysteries of Chichen Itza*, Universal Image Enterprise, 1995

Ruyle, Lydia, *Goddess Icons, Spirit Banners of the Divine Feminine*, Boulder, CO, Woven Word Press, 2002

Salvador, Mari Lyn, Editor, *The Art of Being Kuna, Layers of Meaning Among the Kuna of Panama*, Los Angeles, UCLA Fowler Museum of Cultural History, 1997

Schele, Linda and **Freidel**, David, "Lady Beastie: First Mother," *A Forest of Kings: The Untold Story of the Ancient Maya*, New York, William Morrow and Company, Inc, 1990

Taube, Karl, *The Legendary Past, Aztec & Maya Myths*, Austin, University of Texas Press, 1995

Vesilind, Priit, "Watery Graves of the Maya," *National Geographic*, Vol. 204, #4, October 2003
www.inah.gob.mx
www.mexicodesconocido.com.mx
www.monksofadoration.org

North America

Aristides, Aelius, *Sacred Tales*, words from 45.17 k - pages 139-140, 142

Arizona and New Mexico, AAA Tour Book, Heathrow, FL, AAA Publishing, 2000

Austen, Hallie Inglehart, *The Heart of the Goddess*, Berkeley, CA, Wingbow Press, 1990

Baring, Anne, **Cashford**, Jules, *The Myth of the Goddess: Evolution of an Image*, London, UK, Penguin Books, 1993

Baring, Anne, **Harvey**, Andrew, *The Divine Feminine, Exploring the Feminine Face of God Around the World*, Berkeley, CA, Conari Press, 1996

Barlow, Bernyce, *Sacred Sites of the West*, St. Paul, MN, Llewellyn Publications, 1996

Burkert, Walter, *Greek Religion,* Stuttgart, Germany, Verlag W. Kohlhammer, 1977. English translation by Basil Blackwell Publishers and Harvard University Press, 1985

Camphausen, Rufus, *The Yoni: Sacred Symbol of Female Creative Power*, Rochestester, VT, Inner Traditions International, 1996

David, Gary A., "Arizona's Mystery Mesa," *Ancient American*, Colfax, WI, Vol. 8, No. 49

David, Gary A., "As Above, So Below" in Ancient Arizona, Ancient American, Colfax, WI, Vol. 7, No. 46

Eisler, Riane, and **Loye**, David, *The Partnership Way, New Tools for Living and Learning*, Brandon, VT, Holistic Education Press, 1998

BIBLIOGRAPHY

Gadon, Elinor, *The Once & Future Goddess, A Symbol for Our Time*, New York, Harper San Francisco, 1989

Getty, Adelle, *Goddess, Mother of Living Nature*, London, UK, Thames and Hudson, 1990

Gill, Sam D., and **Sullivan**, Irene F., *Dictionary of Native American Mythology*, Santa Barbara, CA, ABC-CLio, Inc., 1992

Gore, Al, *Earth in the Balance, Ecology and the Human Spirit*, New York, A Plume Book/Penguin Books, USA, 1993

Hardy, Arthur, *Arthur Hardy's Mardi Gras in New Orleans*, Metairie, LA, Arthur Hardy Enterprises, 2001

Hope, Murry, *The Sirius Connection*, Shaftesbury, Dorset, Element, 1996

Hultkrantz, Ake, "The Religion of the Goddess in North America," *The Book of the Goddess Past and Present*, Edited by Carl Olson, New York, The Crossroad Publishing Company, 1990

Husain, Shahrukh, *The Goddess, Living Wisdom*, London, UK, Time-Life Books, 1997

Johnson, Buffie, *Lady of the Beasts, The Goddess and Her Sacred Animals*, Rochester, VT, Inner Traditions International, 1994

Kinser, Samuel, *Carnival American Style*, Chicago, University of Chicago Press, 1990

Lamonte, Willow, "Temple of Goddess Spirituality Dedicated to Sekhmet," Valrico, FL *Goddessing Regenerated*, Issue #16, 2003

Leeming, David, **Page**, Jake, *The Mythology of Native North America*, University of Oklahoma Press, 1998

Locke, Raymond Friday, *The Book of the Navajo*, Mankind, 1992

Monaghan, Patricia, *The New Book of Goddesses & Heroines*, St. Paul, MN, Llewellyn Publishing, 2000

Mookerjee, Ajit, *Kali The Feminine Force*, Rochester, VT, Inner Traditions International, 1988

Noble, David Grant, *Ancient Ruins of the Southwest: An Archaeological Guide*, Flagstaff, AZ, Northland Publishing, 1991

Olsen, Brad, *Sacred Places North America: 108 Destinations*, San Francisco, CA, Consortium of Collective Consciousness, 2002

Schindler, Henri, *Mardi Gras New Orleans*, New York, NY, Flammarion, 1997

Tohe, Laura, "There is No Word for Feminism in My Language," *Wicazo Sa Review, A Journal of Native American Studies*, University of Minnesota, Minneapolis, MN, Fall 2000

Walker, Barbara, *The Women's Encyclopedia of Myths and Secrets*, Edison, NJ, Castle Books, 1996

Whitley, David, *A Guide To Rock Art Sites: Southern California and Southern Nevada*, Missoula, MT, Mountain Press Publishing, 1996

Witherspoon, Gary, *Navajo Kinship and Marriage*, University of Chicago Press, 1975

Witherspoon, Gary, *Language and Art in the Navajo Universe*, University of Michigan Press, 1977

http://www.lapahie.com
http://xroads.virginia.edu
http://cytafex.com
www.circlesanctuary.org/circle/articles/pantheon/GoddessFreedom
www.cnn.com/2004/TECH/space/03/14/planet.discovery/index.html
www.kucinich.us

AUTHOR BIOGRAPHY

A prolific writer, published author, and tour organizer, Karen Tate blends her experiences of women-centered multiculturalism evident in archaeology, anthropology and mythology with her unique literary talents and travel experience throughout the world to pen *Sacred Places of Goddess: 108 Destinations*. Tate's published articles have appeared in both domestic and international publications since 1995. Sacred tours she has led and organized have itineraries that circle the globe.

An ordained minister, independent scholar of the Sacred Feminine, and graduate of The Women's Thealogical Institute, specializing in Goddess and Women's Spirituality, Karen's particular emphasis is on the roles of women and the study of ancient cultures in a modern context. It is no surprise then that she is the founder of the nonprofit educational, art, and cultural organization, The Isis Ancient Cultures & Religion Society. As an Adepta within the International Fellowship of Isis, the author also founded the Iseum of Isis Navigatum more than a decade ago to help raise awareness of Goddess and facilitate her rebirth in contemporary society. Tate's scholastic achievements and special interests help define her focus of building bridges between spiritual communities and promoting ideals of partnership, inclusivity, compassion and education. To accomplish these goals, she is instrumental in sponsoring informative programs, workshops, ritual performances and artistic and cultural events in and around Los Angeles. Karen resides in Venice, CA with her husband, Roy, her life partner for more than twenty years. They are the caretakers of the Isis Temple of Thanksgiving. She can be contacted through her website www.karentate.com

▲ The Isis Temple of Thanksgiving.

INDEX

A

Abdul-Baha, 21
Aboriginal culture 20, 245, 246–247, 258
Abu Simbel 72, 112
Abydos 120, 139
Acheulian Period 13
Ackerman, Susan 136, 150–151
Acropolis 47–50
Adonis 35, 36, 161, 162
Africa 43, 57, 111–140, 176, 177
Agamemnon 49
Ainu culture 226, 229, 231–232, 237
Akashic Records 293
al-Arabi, Ibn 163
Ali Shah, Ikbal 166
Allah 24, 102, 159, 165–167, 166, 167, 169
Altai region 215, 216, 219–221
Al Lat 155, 158, 159, 165, 166, 167, 168–170, 378
Al Uzza 142, 158, 165–168, 167, 378
Amaterasu 90, 223, 226, 227, 228, 229, 235–237, 238, 378
Amazonian tribes 281, 284
Amazon rainforest 279
Ammachi 16, 174, 189–191
Amritapuri Ashram 189–191
Anasazi culture 336, 367–368
Anati, Emmanuel 135
Angkor Wat 223
anime 209, 238
Annapurna 186, 196
Anubis 76
Aparecida 282
Aphrodiasis 92
Aphrodisia 36–37
Aphrodite 34–37, 63, 92, 98, 116, 130, 152, 161, 165, 211, 222, 301, 378
Aphrodite's Rock 34
Apollo 49, 55, 63, 68, 94, 106, 156
Apsaras 210, 211, 223, 378
Apuleius, Lucius 336
Argos 60, 61
Ariadne 44
Aristides, Aelius 347
Arizona 333–338
Arnhem Land 250–252
Artemis 33, 37, 41, 43, 53, 56, 61, 63, 64, 82, 91–92, 94–97, 103–106, 108, 109, 124, 126–128, 130, 156–158, 170, 217, 222, 272, 286, 364, 378
Artemis Temple 62, 95, 156–157
Arvigo, Rosita 327
Asakusa Kannon 240–242
Asherah 35, 90, 150, 151, 154, 378
Ashtoreth 35

Astarte 35, 37, 88, 114, 116, 126, 130, 136, 143, 149, 168, 330, 378
Atargatis 35
Athena 18, 47–50, 55, 56, 60, 149, 165, 170, 188, 365–366, 378
Athens 47, 50, 59, 62, 365
Atlantis 291
Attica 47–48, 57, 59
Attis 35, 78, 83, 127, 352
Australia 245–258
Avalon 40
axis mundi 17, 174, 186, 225
Axum 114, 129–130
Ayers Rock (Uluru) 252–254
Aztec culture 303, 304, 305–306, 313, 316, 320, 326
Aztlan 306

B

Baalat 160–162, 165, 169, 378
Babylon 143–145
Bailey, Roselle 266
Bali 223–225
Banerjee, S.C. 174
Banteay Srei 212
Baring and Cashford 37, 121, 143, 144, 146, 365–366
Baring and Harvey 338
Barrginj 250
Barrier Canyon 367–368
Basilica of Guadalupe 305–307
Bast 90, 122, 123–126, 336, 355, 370, 379
Bastet 118, 123–126
Batari Sri Dewi 224–225
Baubo 56, 57, 73, 74, 185, 236, 379
bears 215, 231–232
Beastie, Lady 304
Beckwith, Martha 264, 266, 270, 278
Bell, Diane 254, 255, 256
Bendis 107
Benten 223, 232–233, 241, 242, 243, 379
Bhattacharji, Sukumari 205–206
Bible 33, 46
Bighorn Medicine Wheel 360
Bingham, Hiram 290
Birnbaum, Lucia Chiavola 135, 282, 285, 287
Black Madonna 20, 41, 42, 91, 122, 282–283, 286, 298, 300, 319, 348, 379
Black Virgin 42, 101
Blavatsky, Helene H. P. 295
Bleeker, C. J. 119
Bochica 281
Bolen, Jean Shinoda 17
Bolivia 279, 282–284
Botticelli 34
Boyne River 71, 72–73
Brahman 188
Branchids 96
Brazil 284–287
Brier, Bob 120
Brigid 40, 64, 65, 66–69, 72,

73, 74, 371, 379
Brochtoroff Circle 88
Brookgreen Gardens 363–365
Brown, Dan 151
Bubastis 123–126
Buddhism 233, 234, 238, 240, 240–241, 244
Budge, Wallis 118
Burkert, Walter 48–49, 52, 57, 58, 64, 109, 126–127, 157, 365–366
Burning Man 330, 357
butterflies 321
Byblos 149, 160–162

C

California 339–351
Caligula 78, 84
Cambodia 210–212, 336
Cambrensis, Geraldus 67
Campbell, Joseph 11, 16, 42, 97–98, 190, 199, 201
Camphausen, Rufus 73, 165, 168, 174, 183–184
Canada 329, 330–332
Candomble 279, 285, 298
cannibalism 281
Canyonlands 367–369
Canyon de Chelly 336–338
Cape Reinga 274–276
Carnute 41
Castalian Spring 18, 55
Catal Hüyük 32, 53, 71, 92–94, 155, 348
Cathars 45, 89, 101
Catholicism 83–84, 90–91, 163, 288, 298, 351
Celtic culture 23, 66, 72, 73, 287
Ceres 81
Chalcatzingo 312–313
Chalchiuhtlicue 321, 379
Chalcolithic period 33
Chandler, Richard 95
Changing Woman 339, 358–359, 379
Charlot, John 264, 266, 268–269
Chartres 41–45, 69
Chausath Yogini Temple 198–200
cheetahs 139–140
chess 13–14
Chichén Itzá 323–325
Childress, David Hatcher 335
China 192, 213–215, 221, 222, 229
Chinese 14–15
Christianity 11, 14, 42–46, 66–68, 83, 89, 142, 149, 287, 303, 332
Chthonic Mother 47
Church of Santa Maria in Aracoli 82–83
Church of Santa Maria in Cosmedin 81
Cichon, Joan 74
Cihuacoatl 324, 379
Circle Sanctuary Nature Preserve 370–371

Clark, Rosemary 116, 125
Cleopatra 113–114, 126, 160, 168, 341
Clonegal Castle 64–66, 69
Coatlicue 323, 326, 379
Coatlicue 305–306, 308, 326
Cook, Roger 155
Constantine 162
Cott, Jonathan 119
Council at Ephesus 82, 104
Coyolxauhqui 326, 379
Cozumel 325–327
Crete 50–54, 222
Crusades 43
Cuicuilco 312, 313–315
cup of Christ 39
Cupid 36
Cuzco 282, 291, 292, 293–295
Cybele 35, 37, 43, 78, 83, 95, 103, 106, 126–128, 128, 130, 165, 217, 348, 352, 379
Cypress 33–37, 60, 165

D

Dagna 72, 73
Dakshineswar Temple 177–179, 345
Dallapiccola, Anna 194, 199, 206
Darling, Patrick 129
Dashu, Max 220
David, Gary 336, 337
Davis-Kimball, Jeannie 217, 218, 219, 221, 222
Dehejia, Vidya 199–200
Delos 63–64, 76, 156
Delphi 18, 44, 54–55, 58
Demeter 33, 52, 53, 55–59, 63, 65, 87, 93, 106, 108, 126, 206, 236, 264, 338, 380
Dendera 114–117
Devereaux, Paul 289
Devi 172, 175, 180, 189, 198, 202, 212
Dewi Danu 224–225, 380
Dewi Sri 196, 380
Dexter, Miriam Robbins 36, 48, 67, 74, 80, 107, 146
De Boer and Hale 54, 55
De Shong Meador, Betty 147–148
Diamant, Anita 183
Diana 67, 82, 130, 334, 364, 380
didgeridoo 246
Didyma 44, 94–97
Diego, Juan 305, 319
Dogon tribe 130
dolphins 321
Dordogne Valley 24
Dougga 136–138
Dowman, Keith 202
Druid culture 41–42, 68, 128
Dumuzi 35, 141
Durga 146, 175, 176, 183, 186, 199, 202, 206, 207, 212, 223, 346, 380

E

Earth Mother of Willendorf 20, 32

East Asia 209–244
Egypt 24, 77, 113–126, 193, 334, 335–336
Eileithyia 47
Eiteljorg, Harrison 50
Eleusian Mysteries 55, 57, 58
Eleusis 55–59
Eliade, Mircea 132
Enheduanna 145, 147–148
Enna 59
Ephesus 33, 46, 62, 63, 64, 92, 103–106
Eros 36
Eurasian Steppes 216–223
Europe 31–90, 172
Evans, Sir Arthur 51–54
Ezili 298, 299, 380

F

Far East 121
Fátima 89–91
Ferguson, Everett 57
Fisher, C. S. 156
Fisher, Liz 40
Fish Goddess 272, 274, 276
Fortuna 81
Fortune, Dionne 340
Fossey, Dian 134
Fox, Matthew 16
Fox, Selena 250, 360, 361, 370
France 41–45, 64, 121, 282, 352, 361
Frankfurter, David 104, 120–121
Frazer, Sir James 138
Fuchi 223, 229, 231–232
Fushimi Inari Taisha Shrine 233–235

G

Gabriel 44, 167
Gadon, Elinor 33, 44, 198–199
Gaelic culture 72
Gaia 15, 34, 49, 54, 371
Ganga 186, 187, 380
Ganges River 18–19, 172, 181, 186–188
Garfinkel, Yosef 153
Gauri 206
genital mutilation 134, 177, 195
genital worship 184–185
Getty, Adelle 243, 308
Ggantija 70, 85–89
giant pandas 215
Gimbutas, Marija 11, 16, 19, 31, 32, 36, 53, 67–68, 70, 71–72, 74, 86–87, 92, 97–98, 135, 143, 168, 207, 217, 228, 272, 375
Glastonbury 39–41
Glastonbury Goddess Conference 40
Gleason, Judith 112
Gnostic texts 41, 45, 99, 151, 347
Goddess Temple of Orange

County 343–345
Goode, Starr 74
Gore, Al 329, 361
gorillas 134–135
Gozo 85–89
Grand Canyon 333–336
Grandmother Ruby 350
Grandmother Spider 336–338, 384
Graves, Robert 67
grave robbers 291
Great Britain 38–41, 121
Greece 24, 46–63
Grigsby, John 336
Grimaldi figurine
Grove, Margaret 250–251
Guerra, Luciano 90
Guillaume, Alfred 166
Guinevere 40
Gupta, Sanjukta 180

H

Hades 56, 57, 59, 109
Hagar Qim 87
Hagia Sophia 98–102, 347
Haiti 284, 298–299
Hamilton, Roy 197, 224, 234
Hanoa, Keola 261, 262
Harappa 207–208
Hardian 58
Harding, Elizabeth Usha 178, 345
Harris, Victor 227
Hart, Carl 335
Haruach, Miri Hunter 114, 129, 130
Hase Dera Kannon Temple 229–231
Hassan, Fekri 114, 115
Hathor 52, 72, 90, 112, 114–117, 122, 123, 138, 151, 161, 206, 336, 380
Hatshepsut 114, 341
Havasupai culture 334, 336
Hawaii 259–273
Hebe 343, 344
Hekate 58, 61, 74, 99, 104, 106–109, 157, 380
Heket 107
Henry, Teuira 277
Hephaistos 34
Hera 33, 60–62, 63, 172, 380
Heraea games 61
Hermes 48
Herodotus 123, 125, 143, 151, 163, 169, 213, 217, 221
Hesiod 34, 100, 107
Hi'iaka 245, 259, 265, 266, 268, 269
Hina 245, 259, 263–264, 268, 269–271, 274, 275, 276, 277–278, 380
Hina's Cave & Heiau 269–271
Hindmarsh Island 254–256
Hindu culture 171–200, 279, 300–301, 335
Hine 273, 274
Hodder, Ian 16, 93–94, 98
Holland, Jennifer S. 261–262, 266

Holy Grail 40, 43, 45
Homer 34, 63
Hope, Murry 336
Hopi 336–337
Hopi culture 306, 334
Horus 33, 36, 43, 76, 83, 99, 114, 121, 123, 124, 206
Huehueteotl 314
Huerfano Mesa 339, 358–359
Hultkrantz, Ake 331, 338
Humes, Cynthia 182
Hurricane Katrina 355
Husain, Shahrukh 74, 274

I

Ice Maiden 219–220
Ida Ratu 223
Images 286
Inanna 141, 143, 145–147, 164, 198
Inanna/Ishtar 35, 143–144, 381
Inari 223, 231, 233, 233–235, 241, 242, 243, 381
Inca culture 279, 281, 292–295
India 14, 121, 140, 172–201, 209, 238, 243, 300
Indonesia 196, 209, 216, 223–225, 338
Indra 197
Indus Valley 172, 207–208, 211
Inquisition 16, 41, 44, 288, 292
Inti 281, 283, 290, 294, 295
Inuit culture 272, 330–332
Iraq 143–149
Ireland 64–73, 236
Ise Jingu 226–228, 236
Ise of Kyoto 235–237
Ishaq, Ibn 166
Isis 11, 23, 30, 33, 35, 36, 41, 43, 56, 63, 64–66, 76–78, 83–84, 90, 99, 103–104, 114, 116, 120–123, 124, 126, 130, 157, 158, 161, 203, 206, 214, 285, 286, 334, 336, 341–342, 347–348, 373, 381
Isis Oasis 339–342
Islam 142, 149, 165–166, 167, 169–170
Isla de Mujeres 327–328
Israel 149–155
Italy 74–84
Ix Chel 304, 321, 322, 325–326, 327–328, 381
Izanami 227, 228, 381

J

Jacobson, Doranne Wilson 204–205
jaguars 295, 317, 321
James, E. O. 131, 132
Japan 209, 216, 223, 226–244
Jara 206
Jardine, Faelyn 261
Jerash 156–158

Jerusalem 44, 149–153
Jesus Christ 33, 43, 45–46, 100, 144, 151, 190, 206, 272, 300
Jewish culture 100, 142, 150–151
Jimenez, Victor 319–320
Johnson, Buffie 194, 233, 304
Johnson, Linda 197
Joman Period 226, 227, 228–229, 231, 237
Jones, Kathy 39, 40
Jones and Molyneaux 306, 308, 310, 311, 313, 316–317, 324
Jordan 155–160
Joseph of Arimathea 40
Judaism 149
Jung, Carl 206
Juno 81, 82, 126, 150, 381
Jupiter 82, 83, 150, 162, 361
Justinian 33, 98, 102, 123

K

Ka'anapali Black Rock 268–269
Kaaba stone 126, 165–166, 169
Kabbalism 101, 143, 150, 154, 164
Kali 172, 176, 177, 178, 179–181, 182, 201, 203, 205, 223, 282, 286, 300–301, 330, 345–346, 381
Kalighat Temple 179–182
Kali Mandir Temple 178, 301, 345–347
Kamadeva 36
Kamakhya Temple 174–176
kami 234, 235, 236
Kangjiashimenzi Petroglyphs 218–219
Kannon 214, 223, 229–231, 233, 235, 239–240, 240–242, 242, 381
Kanyakumari Temple 183–184
Kapiolani 261
Kapululangu 257–258
Karnak 117–119
Karttikeya 364
Kashyapa 194
Kathmandu 202–204
Kawena Pukui, Mary 270
Ke'e Beach 264–266, 270
Keelikolani, Ruth 261
Kelly, J. 313
Kenoyer, J. Mark 207
Kilauea 260–263, 265, 266, 268
Kildare 66–70
Kindaichi, Kyosuke 232
King, Karen 45, 46
King Arthur 39, 40
King Nezahualcoyotl 303
King Sargon 145, 147
Kinkaid, G. E. 335
Kinser, Samuel 351–352
Kinsley, David 186, 206
kiva 44, 339
Klum, Mattias 197–198
Knights Templar 43–44, 45, 89, 101
Knock 64

Knossos 39, 50–54
Knowth and Dowth 39, 73
Kojiki 236
Kripal, Jeffrey 182
Krishna 179, 180, 190, 197, 212
Kubota, Gary 264
Kucinich, Dennis 361
Kukulkan 324
Kumari 52, 174, 183–184, 202, 202–204, 381
Kumari Temple 202–204
Kunapipi 245
Kuna people 297
Kurgan burial mounds 213, 217, 220, 221
Kwan Yin 65, 121, 202, 212, 213–215, 223, 233, 239, 242, 286, 349, 370, 381

L

labyrinth 40, 44, 52, 53, 79
Lady Liberty 79, 360–362, 370, 374, 382
Lady of Avalon 39
Lagina 107–109
Laka 245, 259, 265, 266, 269, 382
Lake Batur 224–225
Lake Pergusa 59–60, 64
Lake Titicaca 282, 293
Lakshmi 65, 196–197, 202, 203, 212, 223, 300, 382
LaMonte, Willow 283
Lancel, Sege 139
Lascaux 75
Lawrence, Patricia 201, 301–302
Lazarus 45
Lebanon 160–162
Leeming and Page 337, 339
Lemuria 291
leopards 139–140, 215, 219
Lepinski Vir 32, 272
Leptis Magna 126–129
Levering, Miriam 192–193
Levy, Gertrude 51
ley lines 17, 26, 92, 253
Libya 126–129
Lilinoe 259
Lillith 142, 143, 198
lingam 184, 369
lions 139–140, 197–198
llamas 283, 284, 293, 295
Locke, Raymond Friday 359
Long, Ashphodel 112
Lourdes 64, 69
Louvre 4, 74, 84, 155
Love, Rebecca 214–215
Loye and Eisler 362–363
Lucian 161
Lucian of Samosata 162
Lupercalia 352

M

Machu Picchu 279, 289–290
Macrinus 162
Madam Golden Lotus 350
Magdalene, Mary 16, 20, 41, 43, 44, 45–46, 101, 132, 151–152,

Magdalene, Mary (*continued*) 164, 319, 348, 382
Magna Mater 79, 95, 103, 382
Mahakali 202
Mahalakshmi Temple 196–197
Mahatmya, Devi 171
Mahuea 245
Mahuika 274
Maier, Franz George 38
Mallory and Mair 222
Malta 32, 44, 70, 74, 85–89
Mama Quilla 283
Manat 165, 166, 167, 168, 170
manatee 321
Manship, Paul Howard 362, 363–364
Manu 172
Maori culture 245, 273–274, 276
Mardi Gras 128, 352–353
Marier, Joan 98
Mars 77
Martin, Wood 69
Marton, Kati 176
Mary of the Maltese 85
Masks of God 98
Masters, Robert 117
matrifocal society 32, 50, 210, 297, 348, 373
Mauna Kea 259–260
May, Antoinette 325
Maya ballgame 318, 322, 325
Maya culture 303, 304, 321–322, 323–325
McCarthy and Dorfman 139
McNeal, Keith 177–178, 300
Mecca 19, 24, 126, 165–167, 169, 170, 226, 298
Medusa 130, 198, 284, 366
Mellaart, James 92, 93
Menat 115, 382
Mera 210, 223
Mercados de Brujos 287–288
mermaids 331
Mesoamerica 19, 304, 308, 310, 316, 317, 318, 324
Mesopotamia 74, 76, 334
Metis 48
Mexico 140, 303–328
Meyer, Marvin 58
Middle East 14, 35, 44, 57, 114, 121, 141–170
Millar, Fergus 162
Minerva 84, 126, 136, 138, 150
Mini, John 306–307
Minoan Crete 32, 39, 44, 47, 51–53, 92
Mithras 75
Mohammed 90, 102, 139, 150, 165, 166, 167–168
Mohenjo-daro 205, 207–208
Monaghan, Patricia 60–61,

62, 68, 108, 128, 132, 136–137, 162, 234, 264, 312–313, 358
Mongolia 209, 213, 216, 221
Monpazier figurine
Morinis 17
Moses 145, 150, 155
Mother Theresa 180
Mount Batur 224–225
Mount Fuji 17, 229, 231
Mount Gulaga 247–248
Mount Parnassus 54
Mount Vesuvius 75, 78
Mycenaean culture 38, 47, 92, 365
Myers Imel, M & D 233, 235, 243

N

Nagas 192–195, 202, 203, 382
Naga Temple of Mannarsala 192–195
Nag Hammadi Scrolls 111
Nakhai, Beth 154
Nanna 145, 147, 148
Nashville Parthenon 365–367
Navajo culture 336–338, 339, 358
Naville, E. 125
Nazca Lines 291
Neith 111
Nepal 140, 176, 177, 185, 192, 202–205
Neumann, Erich 37
Nevada 330
Newgrange 39, 44, 70–73, 85
New Orleans 128
New Zealand 273–277
Niederer, Barbara 244
Nigeria 130–134, 284
Nike 48, 49
Nile River 28
Nilus 166
Nirriti 205–206, 346, 382
Noble, Vicki 130, 200, 207, 222
Nu Kwa 214
Nyx, Lori 108, 201

O

O'Keefe, Georgia 369
Oba 112
Oceania 245–278
ocelots 317, 341
Oden, R. A. 137
Ohnuki-Tierney, E. 232
Olgas 252–254
Ollantaytambo 291, 292, 293, 295
Olmec culture 303, 304, 311–312
Ometeotl 314, 382
Omm Sety 119–120
oracle 54–55, 87, 94, 96, 201, 224, 301
orangutans 215, 216
Orion 336
Orisha 284–286, 298
Ortiz, Fernando 132
Oshun 112, 131, 282, 284–285, 287, 354, 382
Osiris 36, 76, 77, 121, 123, 124,

151, 159, 161, 206, 364
Otto, Walter F. 49
Our Lady of Aparecida 286–287
Our Lady of Guadalupe 287, 304, 305–307, 319, 338, 351, 353
Our Lady of Octolan 312, 319
Ovid 80, 127
Oya 284–285, 286, 354
Ozaniec, Naomi 115, 201, 238

P

Pachacamac 281, 293
Pacha Mama 281, 282, 284, 288, 289, 290, 291, 292, 383
paganism 23, 68, 84, 99, 109, 351, 371
Pakistan 205–208
Palace of Versailles 45
Palaepaphos 34–37
Palatine Hill 78–80, 127, 352
Palladium 80
Palmyra 168–170
Panama 297
Panathenais Festival 49
Pantheon 83
Papatuanuku 273
Park, Ava 344–345
Parthenon 47, 49
Partington, Geoffrey 254
Parvati 172, 175, 180, 196, 202, 205, 206, 212, 364
Paskievich, John 332
Paul, Diana 193
Pausanias 95, 103
Pearlman, Patricia 356, 357
Pearl Harbor 271–273
Pele 245, 259, 260, 260–262, 264, 265, 266, 268–270, 273, 383
Persephone 52, 55–56, 57, 58, 59, 87, 93, 109, 126, 206, 338, 383
Peru 19, 287, 288–296
Petra 155, 158–160
Philae 18, 120–123
Phrygian Matar 217
Phuket 350
Piazza del Collegio Romano 83–84
Pinkola, Clarissa 58
Plato 100–101
Pleiades 115
Plouton 47
Plutarch 55, 58, 111
Pneuma 100
Pokrovka cemeteries 217, 221–223
Poliahu 259–260, 264, 383
Polosmak, Natalya 219
Polynesia 258–278, 338
Polynesian culture 246, 258–259, 268–269
Pompeii 75–78
Pope John Paul II 89
Popol Vuh 322
Portugal 89–91, 296
Poseidon 47, 48
Po Ino Nogar 210, 211
Prasantarutasagaravati 209

INDEX

Price, Simon 57
Ptah 119
Ptolemy 76, 96, 104
Purgatorium 77
putari 255, 256
Pu Tuo Shan Island 213–215
Pythia 18, 54–55

Q

Quammen, David 139
Queen Noor 157
Queen of Sheba 114, 129–130, 150, 164
Queen Zenobia 160, 168, 170
Quenko 291, 292, 293, 295
Quetzalcoatl 323, 324
Quilla 294, 295

R

Ra 114, 115, 118, 124
Ra'iatea 277–278
Rabinowitz, Allan 139–140
Rahall, Nick 359–360
Rainbow Falls 263–264
Ramses 72, 119
Rasmani, Rani 177
Regula, deTraci 159
Reif, Jennifer 57, 58
Rennes le Chateau 46
Rhiannon 40
Rietveld, James 54, 57, 96, 103, 104, 105–106, 126, 127, 139, 154, 157, 179, 348
Rigoglioso, Marguerite 59–60
ritual prostitution 160, 162, 162–164, 184
Riveria, Adalberto 325
Robertson, Lady Olivia 64–66, 120
Roman culture 38, 72
Roman Forum 80–81
Rome 74, 78–85, 114, 127, 137, 361
Romer and Romer 106
Rountree, Kathryn 17, 23, 25, 273
Rudenko, Sergei 222
Rufus and Lawson 42, 58, 68, 81
Rushdie, Salman 165
Ruyle, Lydia 289, 323

S

sacred marriage 162–164
sacred prostitution 36, 74, 162–164
Sacred Valley 289, 291–295
Sacsayhuman 291, 292, 293, 295
Saint Anne 320
Saint Maximin 45–46
Saint Patrick 67–68
Saint Sophia's Cathedral 347–349
Salem Witch Trials 320
Salzman, Renee 127
Sanctuary of Coyolxauhqui 307–309

Sande Society 133–134
Sanju Sangendo 239–240
Sano, Toshiyuki 234
Santa Maria Maggiore 82
Santa Sabina 82
Santeria 279, 285, 298
San Nicola in Carcere 81
Sappho 37
Sarasvati 186, 187, 188, 212, 223, 232, 241, 383
Sati 175, 179
Saudi Arabia 129, 165–167
Saut D'Eau Falls 284, 298–299
Scanlon, Thomas 61
Schele and Freidel 304
Schindler, Henri 127–128
Scorzazie, Seph 248
Sedna 272, 330–332, 374, 383
Sekhmet 84, 90, 114, 117–119, 122, 124, 125, 198, 336, 355–356, 383
Sekhmet Temple of Nevada 355–357
Selene 108
Serapis 76, 84, 104
Severus, Alexander 84
Sha'ar Hagolan 153–155
Shakti 150, 164, 172, 176, 178, 183, 185, 198, 207, 301
shakti pitha 175, 179, 181, 185, 186, 196
shamaness 220, 221, 226, 232, 237–238
shamanism 222, 232, 238, 279, 288, 331–332, 369
Shan, Miao 214
Shaw, Miranda 200
Sheila-na-Gigs 66, 73–74, 81, 184, 369, 383
Shikibu, Murasaki 244
Shintoism 209, 227, 229, 232–233, 235–236, 238
Shiva 18, 150, 175, 179, 183, 185, 194, 199, 202, 206, 207, 212, 346, 364
Shiva, Vandana 188–189
Shoshone culture 355, 357
Siberia 215, 216
Sibyls 78
Sicily 59–60, 64, 85, 86
Siddi Lakshmi 18, 36
Sigebert 45
significance of 108 18–19
Silber, Cathy 244
Silk Road 213, 216, 218, 219, 223
Singer, Gerald 299
Sinicropi, Enrico 59
Siparia 300–301
Sirius 122, 130, 144, 336
Sita 197, 212
Sitka, Chris 258
Sjoo, Monica 137
Snake Goddess 47, 51–52, 54, 383
Sophia 43, 98–102, 347–348, 383
South America 279–296
Spain 282, 296
Spess, David 200

Spider Grandmother 332, 337, 364, 384
Spider Rock 336–338
Spider Woman 316–317, 337, 384
Spretnak, Charleen 58
sri yantra 19, 150
Starbird, Margaret 43–44, 45, 151
Statue of Liberty 16, 360–362
Stern, Ephraim 150
Stone, Merlin 37, 214, 274, 306, 310
Stonehenge 39, 68
Strabo 55, 60, 106
Streep, Peg 51, 70, 87
Stuart, Clinton 259
Stuart-Fox, David J. 225
Sudhanas 209
Sumeria 142
Swanson, Don 266
Syria 34, 168–170

T

Tabiti 217
Tahiti 277–278
Taino culture 299
Taj Mahal 72, 171, 172
Tammuz 35, 352
Tanit 63, 67, 88, 130, 136–138, 384
Tara 18, 176, 202
Taube, Karl 308, 309
Teish, Luisah 285
Teixidor, Javier 169, 170
temples of Angkor 210–212, 336
Temple Mount 149–153
Temple of Al Lat 168–170
Temple of Artemis 96, 99, 103–105
Temple of Baalat Gebal 160–162
Temple of Hera 60–63, 96
Temple of Isis 75–77, 138
Temple of Oshun 130–133
Teotihuacán 312, 313, 316–318
Tepeyac 304, 305
Terence and Plautus 78
Tertullian 13, 79
Teubal, Savina 152
Thebes 116
Theodosius 33, 34, 95, 96, 102
Theseus 44
Thevadas 210, 211
Thoth 30, 65, 336, 365
Thuggees of Kali 68, 182
Tiamat 149
Tiberius 84
Tien Hau 223, 349–351, 384
tigers 139–140, 215
Tlaloc 313
Tlaxcala 318–320
Tlazolteotl 323
Tohe, Laura 359
Toltec culture 303, 325
Tonantzin 304, 305
Torjesen, Karen Jo 101, 375, 376
Tower of Babel 143

Toyouke 226
Trinidad 300–301
Troy 80, 160, 365
tsunamis 350
Tunisia 135–138
Turcan, Robert 127
Turkey 92–109, 121
turtles 321

U

Ueno Park 242–243
Uga 233
Ukok Plateau 215, 219–221
Uluru (Ayers Rock) 252–254
Uma 205, 206, 212
United States 329, 332–372
Ur 147
Urban, Hugh 182
Uruk 145–147
Uzume 185, 237, 242, 384

V

Vac 188
Vallenas, Jose 292, 293
van der Leeuw, G. 119
Varnasi 19, 177, 186–188
Vatican 46, 74, 84, 90, 91, 101, 336
Vaughan, Genevieve 355
Vedas 186, 187–188, 200, 205, 206, 212
Veen, Veronica 85
Veil of the Virgin 42
Venus 77, 80, 114, 126, 136, 144, 162, 166, 170, 323, 334, 384
vesica piscis 40
Vesta 80–81
Vestal Virgins 80–81
Vieux Carre 351–355
Vigne, Loreon 340
Villoldo, Alberta 279, 281
Viracocha 281
Virgin Mary 20, 41, 44, 62, 82, 89–90, 99, 104, 111, 122, 132, 144, 151, 157, 206, 214, 226, 240, 282, 298, 308, 319, 348, 351, 374, 382
Virgin of Copacabana 282–283
Virgin of Guadalupe 305–307, 380
Virgo 44
Vishnu 175, 196, 197, 203, 212
Von Rudloff, Robert 108
Voodoo 279, 284, 285, 298, 299, 300, 354

W

Walker, Barbara 67, 68, 130, 136, 163, 190, 193, 243
Warramurrungdji 251, 258
Warren, Peter 53
Westervelt, W. D. 259, 263, 264
Whitley, David 369
Wicca 288, 301, 332, 344, 362, 370
Witches Market 287–288
Witherspoon, Gary 358, 359

Witt, R. E. 76, 99, 124, 125, 353
Woolley, Sir Leonard 147

X

Xaghara 87
Xcaret 321–323
Xena, Warrior Princess 34
Xochiquetzal 303, 304, 310–312, 320, 384
Xochitl 311–312

Y

Yami 206
Yates-Smith, Aroha 274, 276
Yemaya 112, 282, 284, 285, 286, 354, 384
yogini temples 171, 197, 199
yoni 40, 74, 166, 174, 175, 184–185, 237, 252, 369
yoni stones 17
Yoruban culture 112, 130–132, 284, 285, 288, 298, 332, 351
Yoruban spirituality 279, 286, 354

Z

Zenairai Benten 232–233
Zeus 33, 34, 47, 56, 60, 62, 63, 104, 156, 188, 365

WORLD STOMPERS
A GLOBAL TRAVEL MANIFESTO
FIFTH EDITION

When you are ready to leave your day job, load up your backpack and head out to distant lands for extended periods of time, Brad Olsen's "Travel Classic" will lend a helping hand. It will save you hundreds of dollars in travel expenses, prepare you for an extended journey, keep you safe & healthy on the road, find you a job overseas, and get you psyched to travel the world! For a good time, read the book Publishers Weekly called a "Quirky Chain Pleaser" and Library Journal recommended as "A great addition to your collection."

"Travel can be a nightmare when you find yourself in the wrong place at the wrong time. This subversive masterpiece of travel writing might just save your sanity the next time you go out there. Get it. It makes life fun!" —film director Oliver Stone

"A traveling guide for a new generation" —Last Gasp

"This brightly colored post-psychedelic cover conceals what may be more than you ever knew existed about (travel)." —Chicago Tribune

ISBN 1-888729-05-8   288 pages $17.95
Maps and illustrations by Brad Olsen

IN SEARCH OF ADVENTURE
A WILD TRAVEL ANTHOLOGY

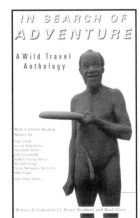

In Search of Adventure celebrates the wild side of contemporary travel writing. This epic collection of 100 traveler's tales applauds the roving prose of Tim Cahill, Marybeth Bond, Jeff Greenwald, Robert Young Pelton and Simon Winchester. Revealing, humorous, sometimes naughty stories by acclaimed authors. Written and compiled by Bruce Northam and Brad Olsen.

"Lovers of storytelling and anyone looking for summer vacation inspiration shouldn't miss this (book.)" —Guardian

ISBN 1-888729-03-1   465 pages $17.95
All CCC Publishing titles may be ordered from:
Independent Publishers Group (800) 888-4741

SACRED PLACES NORTH AMERICA
108 DESTINATIONS

Travel along with author, photographer, and cartographer Brad Olsen as he reveals the many spiritual sites that abound in North America. "Pilgrimage is one way we can find ourselves and this book will provide a guide," raved the Twin Cities Wellness paper. The venerable Midwest Book Review said: "Sacred Places North America is a revealing, useful, and enthusiastically recommended guide." Spirituality and Health noted: "In this handy and helpful resource, Brad Olsen demonstrates his respect for sacred places." And the Orlando Sentinel reviewed: "He offers information on each site, juxtaposing local folklore and Native American legend with scientific theories or physical evidence to provide context." Read the critically acclaimed North America guide to 108 Destinations. Want to visit wondrous, exotic, incredibly gorgeous locales and experience a sense of mystical transcendence? You don't need a plane ticket, a passport, or even a psychedelic drug. In fact, there's probably such a place within driving distance of your home" observed Fearless Books.

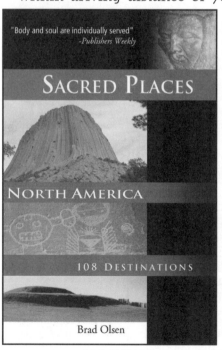

■ Who were the first Europeans in North America: the Vikings, Celts, or ancient Phoenicians?

■ Why did Native Americans revere certain mountains?

■ Where are the most frequent sightings of Bigfoot and UFOs?

■ Why does attendance at Graceland increase every year?

■ Where do people of the New Age movement convene to experience Earth energy?

■ How did certain prehistoric civilizations mark seasonal equinoxes and solstices?

108 B&W Photographs / 66 Maps and Graphics

ISBN 1-888729-09-0   304 pages   USA $17.95   Canada $26.95

Travel / Spirituality / History

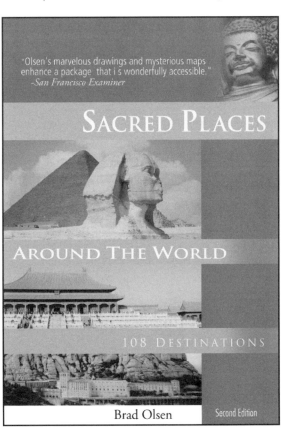

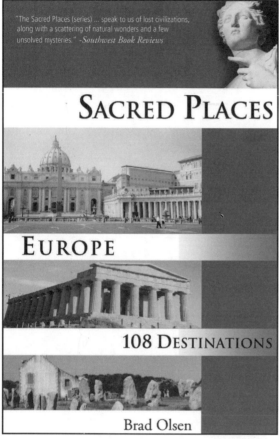